Sears, Roebuck Home Builder's Catalog

The Complete Illustrated 1910 Edition

Sears, Roebuck and Co.

Dover Publications, Inc., New York

Copyright © 1990 by Dover Publications, Inc.
All rights reserved under Pan American and International Copyright Conventions.

Published in Canada by General Publishing Company, Ltd., 30 Lesmill Road, Don Mills, Toronto, Ontario.
Published in the United Kingdom by Constable and Company, Ltd.

This Dover edition, first published in 1990, is an unabridged republication of *Our Special Catalog for Home Builders*, published by Sears, Roebuck and Co., Chicago, n.d. [1910]. A new Publisher's Note has been added.

Manufactured in the United States of America
Dover Publications, Inc., 31 East 2nd Street, Mineola, N.Y. 11501

Library of Congress Cataloging-in-Publication Data

Our special catalog for home builders.
    Sears, Roebuck home builder's catalog : the complete illustrated 1910 edition / Sears, Roebuck and Co.
        p.   cm.
    Reprint. Originally published: Our special catalog for home builders. Chicago : Sears, Roebuck, 1910.
    ISBN 0-486-26320-7
    1. Architecture, Domestic—United States—Designs and plans—Catalogs. 2. Sears, Roebuck and Company—Catalogs. I. Sears, Roebuck and Company. II. Title.
NA7205.087 1990
728'.0973—dc20   90-2752
                                         CIP

Publisher's Note

B Y 1910 SEARS, ROEBUCK was easily the biggest mail-order house in the world. The firm had thoroughly exploited the basic sources of mail-order success—principally, the economies of scale, the elimination of an expensive middleman in the form of the rural retailer (little of Sears's business would be urban till years later), and the enormous and continuing growth of the rail system, which made it possible to reach customers in the far corners of the country and to offer them a variety of goods formerly obtainable only in the cities. As a result, Sears was by then marketing over 100,000 items, through its general catalog and some seventy special catalogs such as this one.

These catalogs were read eagerly from cover to cover by many thousands of rural families with scant access to literature and limited sources of manufactured goods. A cardinal element in the firm's success had been the advertising prose of Richard W. Sears. Not for Sears, Roebuck the dry jargon of other manufacturers; the Sears descriptions were alive, colorful, friendly, informative, and exaggerated. Even though the movement toward "truth in advertising" was already under way and starting to dampen the notorious excesses of nineteenth-century promotional language, the lively imaginations of the copywriters Richard Sears had trained continued to impart an alluring aura to even the most negligible widget. The famous Sears guarantee and the ubiquitous customers' testimonials engendered confidence. And at the prices offered—virtually wholesale prices, as Mr. Sears never ceased to remind his public—few rural customers were going to seriously dispute claims that a given knob or hinge was the finest that had ever existed.

Not only quality but also style was enthusiastically promoted to the rural consumer. The home builder is informed that "nearly every house now being built uses cresting" on its roof ridge (p. 69), that "no new house is really complete without one of our fine Cabinet Grand Grilles" (p. 84), that "every modern building today . . . uses maple or oak flooring" (p. 77), and so on. With such enticements, could anyone have spent ten minutes with this catalog and not begun itching to build himself a house, or at least a new wing, regardless of whether he needed one?

Various aesthetic styles jostle each other in these pages. The closely related "craftsman" and "Mission" styles, popularized in the influential journal *The Craftsman* since 1901, show up in many categories. "Colonial" style is said (p. 87) to be enjoying a renaissance. Art Nouveau stained glass from Sears is claimed to be in use "in all modern houses where a high class window is desired" (p. 47). And Victorian filigree, too ambient to even need a descriptive label here, abounds. It may surprise some readers today to see how many ornamental features were mass-produced millwork rather than the work of actual craftsmen—grilles, brackets, stained glass, complete fireplaces, and so on.

The illustrations are mostly woodcuts, but many halftone wash drawings, the precursors of photographs in such catalogues, are also used, particularly where wood grains are depicted. Though extreme economy is evident—for example, in the use of nearly unreadable 5-point type on many pages and the almost total lack of white space—the eight pages of color provide a handsome garnish.

Anyone contemplating restoring a house from the early decades of the century will find this volume a rich resource of unimpeachable authority. So instructive is the text that a neophyte may still learn much about house construction from it. And as an evocation of an era of exuberant growth and prosperity, it will provide the amateur historian with a vital complement to sources devoted to other aspects of American life.

GENERAL INDEX

To Everything in Our Catalog for Home Builders

CONSULT THIS INDEX FOR ANYTHING YOU HAVE DIFFICULTY IN FINDING.

OUR METHODS GUARANTEE BOTH MONEY SAVING AND BETTER QUALITY

If you have bought other supplies such as wearing apparel, household hardware and other necessities from us, you of course know that we are furnishing the best standard of merchandise at lower prices than they can be bought for anywhere else, saving you in some cases 25 per cent, in others 35 per cent and in others 50 per cent or even more. We have applied the same principles of merchandising to building material of all kinds, and it is simply because it is applied on such a large scale that the savings we offer seem so striking. They are only the natural result of a method that spells economy from start to finish.

Our direct from factory to consumer method. We ship direct from one of the largest and most finely equipped mill work and building material factories in this country; we own and control saw mills that manufacture our lumber. Our mills being centrally located, enable us to make prompt shipments with very low freight charges. The latest improved high grade machinery is installed in these plants and the most skilled workmen are employed. We thus have absolute control of quality. To supply the demand, we keep on hand at all times immense finished stocks of all these goods and can make shipment more promptly than any other factory of its kind in the country. **Our goods are bright, new, fresh and clean, handled only once,** and they cannot be compared with the ordinary building material that has been handled several times and usually arrives in a soiled or otherwise unsatisfactory condition.

We also manufacture our own roofing, plumbing goods and paints. We control the outputs of large plants manufacturing builders' hardware, gas and electric light fixtures, heating plants and concrete block machinery and molds. These goods are shipped direct from factories or from our Chicago store, as indicated in the descriptions of the merchandise. These direct factory connections give us complete control of quality. The goods are manufactured according to our own specifications. This is the reason why we can guarantee to furnish you a better average quality throughout than you can readily obtain on the market.

Consider our factory connections as above explained, how they enable us to control quality, and you have the complete answer to any question that may arise in your mind as to the quality of our goods. You can therefore see that our low prices are not due to any sacrifice of quality but simply due to the natural results of an economical system of business, where every item of unnecessary expense is removed and **you get the full benefit.**

To carpenters, contractors and builders: We specially solicit your trade; we are supplying many of the largest carpenters, contractors and builders in the country, which is substantial proof that our prices are lower than can be secured elsewhere and that our goods are satisfactory. You can increase your percentage of profit considerably and save your customers a great deal of money besides if you let us furnish you all your building material. We suggest that you offer prospective customers estimates based on the prices you find in this book and we know that you will make a distinctly favorable impression, because we are sure they will find it impossible to duplicate your offer through any other source, for we do not know of any other system that contains the elements of money saving for consumers that ours does. Just take the time to look through this catalog, compare the prices on a number of items with the prices you are asked to pay elsewhere and you can quickly convince yourself that we are stating nothing but the plain facts.

Grading of our mill work. We guarantee our mill work to be strictly up to or better than the official grades adopted by the Sash, Door and Blind Manufacturers' Association of the Northwest, which is a sufficient guarantee to protect customers who are skeptical about quality. We endeavor to improve our quality even beyond the qualifications laid down by this association. Few concerns can improve quality beyond the official grade of the association because they do not enjoy the wonderful facilities we have, for we are interested in some of the largest and best timber tracts in the United States, as well as the best equipped mills for manufacturing building material of every description in the world, controlling the quality of our stock from the time the tree is felled until it is a finished product.

OUR TERMS.

We require cash with each order, our terms being net cash without discount, no matter how large the order may be. Our prices represent the lowest factory cost and one profit. You will find these prices the lowest you can get, quality considered. We are shipping many carload orders every day at these prices. The best way to send money is in the form of an express or postoffice money order, a bank draft or your personal check.

Saved Nearly Half, Quality Considered.

Roselle Park, N. J.

Sears, Roebuck and Co., Chicago, Ill.

Gentlemen:—I enclose herewith photograph of my house, the same which I built according to the general layout of plan No. 114. The picture of the house as you will see is identical with that shown in your catalog, but with a few exceptions. The layout of the rooms and trimmings are also somewhat different from the original. Am very glad to say that on whatever I purchased from you for my house, which I think amounted to $800.00, the quality of the material was very satisfactory. I know that I could not have obtained the same material here for less than about twice the amount, considering quality. Comparing the cost of my last house, which I sold, with the present one, the latter cost me only about $500.00 more than the former, which contained only six rooms and bath, my new house containing nine rooms and bath, besides one or two other conveniences. Furthermore, my present house is much better built. In conclusion, would state that all transactions between you and me have been attended to promptly and fairly in every respect. I shall certainly favor you with as many orders as I can.

Your customer,
JOHN C. JOHNSON.

Suburban Home Builder Saves $1,000.00.

Washington, D. C.

Sears, Roebuck and Co., Chicago, Ill.

Gentlemen:—I am a builder of suburban residences. Two years ago I commenced using Sears, Roebuck and Co.'s material, mill work, hardware, mantels, furnaces, ranges, etc. I have used them in six houses and estimate the saving thereby to be fully **$1,000.00.** I expect to continue the use of Sears, Roebuck and Co.'s goods, which I would not do if they were not satisfactory.

Very respectfully,
CHAS. T. CALDWELL.

Quality Satisfies Him and Saved $1,000.00.

Cohoes, N. Y.

Sears, Roebuck and Co., Chicago, Ill.

Gentlemen:—I am sending you a photograph of the house built from material shipped by you and according to your plans. I am pleased to say that I am well satisfied with the quality of material and your prompt shipment. Your plans are a great help to anyone who wants to build after a close estimate. I can say that I saved **$1,000.00** on this property.

Very truly yours,
FRANK CHAMBERLAND.

Picture of Mr. Chamberland's house is shown in our free Book of Modern Homes, mentioned on page 5.

The Wizard Is a Perfect Concrete Block Machine.

334 Euclid Ave., Lynn, Mass.

Sears, Roebuck and Co., Chicago, Ill.

Dear Sirs:—I cannot help but write you and gladly give you my opinion of the Wizard Concrete Building Block Machine. The Wizard machine is a perfect concrete block making machine, far superior in speed to any other machine I have or have seen. It is of good, durable and well finished construction, and the simplicity with which it works is an object in itself and it is 50 per cent cheaper than any other first class machine bought by anyone that makes concrete blocks in my vicinity. I shall be only too pleased to show and demonstrate the merits of the Wizard Concrete Block Machine to anybody in my neighborhood who is interested.

Yours truly,
JOHN STEVENSON.

One Man Makes 175 Blocks in Nine-Hour Day.

505 Second St., N. W., Washington, D. C.
Plant: Hillbrook, D. C.

Sears, Roebuck and Co., Chicago, Ill.

Dear Sirs:—My experience with the Wizard Concrete Block Machine has been very successful. Can say it is the fastest working machine I have ever handled. One of my men has made 175 blocks in a nine-hour day, doing all the work himself, such as mixing the material, moving and curing the blocks. In my opinion and from what I have seen of the Wizard Block Machine, comparing it with other makes, I can say it is the best machine made for concrete block purposes, and I will never hesitate in recommending your Wizard machine as the best in the market.

Yours truly,
B. BONNABEL.
Manufacturer of Concrete Building Blocks.

Much Pleased With Material and Saved 25 Per Cent.

Altoona, Penn.

Sears, Roebuck and Co., Chicago, Ill.

Gentlemen:—Under separate cover am mailing you a picture of our house built from your plan No. 115, the material for which, with the exception of the rough lumber, was bought from your firm. I was much pleased with all the material and would also state that we saved fully 25 per cent on the present local prices in buying from your firm.

Yours truly,
E. N. HARRAR.

Picture of Mr. Harrar's house is shown in our free Book of Modern Homes, mentioned on page 5.

Wouldn't Take $500.00 for His Hot Air Furnace.

31 Park St., Cortland, N. Y.

Sears, Roebuck and Co., Chicago, Ill.

Dear Sirs:—I ordered one Acme Tropic Furnace with all registers, pipe, elbows and fittings complete for heating my house. You had agreed to furnish everything, excepting lumber for the cold air box, for the sum of $60.29, guaranteeing the furnace to heat my house to 70 degrees in the coldest weather, providing I would install the furnace according to the plans furnished by you. I installed it and all piping fitted together perfectly. I started a fire and an abundance of heat came from each and every register. The fire did not go out during the winter and the best and most grand thing of all is that the thermometer in the northwest corner of our front room stood at 71 to 73 degrees during the cold wave of the week beginning January 2d, with a strong northwest wind and the thermometer registering 16 below zero. I am a locomotive fireman on the Lehigh Valley Railroad and was firing a passenger train at the time I installed this heating plant and I did all the work alone during spare hours. Thus you may see everything fitted nicely. The whole plant, including freight, cartage, etc., cost me $68.00, including the lumber, etc., for the cold air box. Parties here wanted $135.00 to heat these same rooms. I saved **$67.00.** I dare say I would have received a poorer article from those asking double the money. If unable to get another like it, $500.00 would not take this one out. Best wishes for Sears, Roebuck and Co.

Very sincerely,
A. G. BROWN.

Saved $500.00, Besides Getting Better Material.

York, Neb.

Sears, Roebuck and Co., Chicago, Ill.

Gentlemen:—We were more than satisfied with everything we received as we failed to find even one piece of poor material in the entire bill. This home will stand the closest inspection. Scores of people who have come to see the so called "Sears, Roebuck house" have been favorably impressed with the plan and material which they found while carefully looking over the building, and many of them are now ordering mill work from you who previously hesitated to do so. We have saved fully **$500.00** on this building besides having better material than we could possibly have gotten at our home town. We were greatly surprised, too, at the manner and promptness in which our order was handled, as we received most of the material within nine days from the time we mailed our order, the distance being nearly 700 miles.

Very truly yours,
J. P. BERCK.

ABSOLUTELY NO RISK IN ANY TRANSACTION WITH US

WE GUARANTEE SAFE DELIVERY

We guarantee safe delivery of all our building material. We will replace broken glass on condition that you send us the paid freight expense bill with a notation thereon signed by the freight agent stating the condition of doors or windows on arrival at station, so that we may use this statement in making claim against the railroad company for damages; or if you can buy the glass from your local dealer you may do so, sending us receipted bill, together with freight receipt with the agent's notation thereon, and we will promptly return the cost of the glass. Always get the agent's notation on the paid expense bill if any goods arrive in a damaged condition and we will promptly adjust the matter to your entire satisfaction. You assume no risk whatever.

FREIGHT CHARGES AMOUNT TO VERY LITTLE

Do not allow the freight charges to cause you any concern, for they amount to very little indeed as compared with the great saving we make for you on building material. No matter where you live, we can save you money on your purchase. Remember, that no matter from whom you buy building material, you are always obliged to pay freight charges. Delivered prices on building material bought elsewhere always include the freight, and when freight charges are added to our net prices you will find that the total amounts to a great deal less than the delivered prices quoted elsewhere on the same grade of goods. Our factories and other shipping points are centrally located, securing for you the lowest possible freight rates.

OUR CAREFUL METHODS OF PACKING

The illustration of crates and bundles on page 160 gives you an idea of the great care we exercise in packing and shipping building material. We realize that no matter how good the quality may be or how low our prices may be the transaction will not be satisfactory to you if the goods do not arrive at their destination in perfect order. We have made an exceedingly careful study of the best materials and methods for packing mill work and other building material. All glass is amply protected by a good grade of ½-inch lumber; all finished doors are protected with heavy building paper. We positively guarantee every shipment to arrive at destination in first class order. In fact, they will be found to be much cleaner and much more satisfactory than goods purchased elsewhere, which are usually handled many times before reaching you. Our goods come straight to you from the factories with only one handling.

OUR GUARANTEE

The purpose of this guarantee is to safeguard your interests, to remove all risk in buying from us, to insure you against any possible disappointment. Each and every article in this catalog is therefore offered with the understanding and agreement that it must satisfy you perfectly, that it will give the service you have a right to expect, that it represents full value for the money you pay. If there is the slightest dissatisfaction for any reason whatsoever you may return the purchase to us at our expense and we will exchange it for exactly what you want, or will, if you prefer, return your money and any transportation charges you paid on the shipment.

Our Heating Plant Conquers Terrific Winds and Severe Cold.

R. R. No. 1, Ypsilanti, Mich.

Sears, Roebuck and Co., Chicago, Ill.

Dear Sirs:—I take great pleasure in telling you that the one thing in our home which stands ahead of everything else in the satisfaction and comfort it gives us is the hot water heating plant which I purchased of you. We have a large twelve-room house always open from attic to cellar and we are situated in the country where we have absolutely no shelter from the winds, which are something terrific here. We have had a gale blowing here when the temperature was at zero and that means harder to heat a house than at 20 degrees below in still weather. There was never a time when we could not keep the temperature at 70 degrees where our thermometer hung by the side of the north window and away from a radiator. This point was the coldest part of the house. The house was all open and we very seldom had the radiators open in four of the six rooms upstairs, as the heat from below kept them more than comfortable. Another point as to fuel. We have lived in a number of houses with different heating systems. None of these houses was as large as this, but it took from $80.00 to $100.00 worth of fuel and we were never as comfortable as here. I never could burn gas coke in any other furnace with success. Here I burn nothing but gas coke and in this furnace it equals hard coal, ton for ton, in my estimation. Furnace never went out all winter with coke as fuel. The coke costs only half as much as hard coal. Last winter I would check the furnace at night and the temperature was never below 60 degrees in the morning. I can raise the temperature of the water in the whole system from 100 degrees to over 200 degrees in less than two hours on the coldest days. There has never been a time when we did not have plenty of reserve heat on the coldest days. In cold weather I warm the water for my stock to drink by drawing off hot water from the bottom of my furnace. This is great convenience. It is putting it mildly when I say that we are more than pleased with the furnace. I installed the whole plant alone, from the putting in of the radiators to starting the system, without any help except what I got from the set of tools I got of you. I did not have a single leak when I started the plant and never since. I never did any pipe fitting myself before, but have watched it done. Another point in which it beats any furnace I ever saw, I can clean every part of that furnace in just three minutes without disturbing the system in any way, and when I say clean it, I mean thoroughly. I can do this cleaning with a white shirt on and never get a speck of dirt on me. We would be lost completely without that heating system. You may use this or refer to me. I worked off and on for ten days installing the plant. I could not put in long hours, as I had routine work to do.

O. BUTTON.

Local Firms Said, "We Cannot Compete with Those Prices," and We Furnished Him Superior Material.

Capleville, Tenn.

Sears, Roebuck and Co., Chicago, Ill.

Dear Sirs:—I am now living in my new home built after your house plan No. 102. All of the material entering into the construction of this house was bought of you except the rough lumber, brick, etc. I sent to you rather than to our home town (Memphis, Tenn.), because I found out that it would be money saved to order of you. It is impossible to say how much I saved, because upon many items, such as doors and windows, I could not get our local firm to bid at all after they saw your figures. They said, "We cannot compete with these prices." However, judging from some of the material on which I did get bids, I judge that I saved at least **$200.00** by ordering of you. I am much pleased at the superior kind of material furnished. My order received prompt attention and the shipments were made with great dispatch and reached us at once in the best of order. When anything was damaged in transit you replaced it with good material without delay. It is with pleasure that I write this to you, since we are so well pleased with all transactions had with your house.

Yours truly,
DR. F. M. MALONE.

Hot Air Furnace Heats the House Just Fine.

Huron, S. Dak.

Sears, Roebuck and Co., Chicago, Ill.

Dear Sirs:—I have received my furnace which was shipped from your foundry. I received it in good condition. Everything came through in fine shape. There was not one piece broken or lost. I have it up and am very much pleased with it in every way. It heats the house just fine. I shall remain as ever, Your customer,

MRS. ETTA WETHERILL.

Heats Nine-Room House to 70 in Zero Weather.

Box 157, Derry, Penn.

Sears, Roebuck and Co., Chicago, Ill.

Dear Sirs:—The hot water heating plant purchased from you is giving perfect satisfaction to me in every form. It keeps a nine-room house to 70 degrees in zero weather when the heater registers about 185 degrees. It also does not require any more fuel than it would take for a stove that would heat only one or two rooms and requires my attention only twice daily. I would recommend your heaters to any one requiring a plant at small cost and very little fuel and labor, as I can run my heater with coke at a cost of $16.80 per season.

HARRY L. HEACOX.

Will Use Our Mantels in the Future.

R. F. D. No. 6, Marshall, Texas.

Sears, Roebuck and Co., Chicago, Ill.

Gentlemen:—I have been more than pleased with the mantel I ordered from you. I expect to give you all of my orders in future for same goods. Also mill work which I ordered from you is perfectly satisfactory. I only regret that I didn't order my paint from you for my own residence. I am a contracting builder and any time I have a job that demands mantels, etc., you can expect my order. I am a "Sears, Roebuck man."

Yours truly,
W. B. KEASLER.

Makes More Blocks on the Wizard Than on Any Other Machine He Ever Saw.

Montowese, Conn.

Sears, Roebuck and Co., Chicago, Ill.

Gentlemen:—I received the Wizard Concrete Building Block Machine in perfect order and have given it a trial. It has proven perfectly satisfactory in all respects and I can produce more blocks on this machine than on any other I have ever seen.

Yours very truly,
LEROY BROCKETT.

The Wizard Is a Wonder, the Best Machine He Ever Saw, Simple in Construction and Easy to Operate.

Congress Heights, Washington, D. C.
Randall Lane.

Sears, Roebuck and Co., Chicago, Ill.

Gentlemen:—I received the Wizard Concrete Block Machine on November 19th, and wish to thank you for the kind consideration on your part in sending me the Wizard machine instead of the X-L-ALL which I ordered of you, thus showing the interest you take in pleasing your customers. The machine is a wonder. There is not room in my letter to state all the good points about this machine. I did not have one line of instructions to go by or know how to work it, but the machine is so simple in construction it could fairly talk, and we went right to work making blocks and have made several hundred. The machine is worked by myself and son-in-law and we can now make a block every two minutes. The rock face is a work of art and the most perfect design of cut stone I ever saw produced on any block in use around this section of the country (and there are a great many). This machine is far superior to any machine I have seen, some of which they are asking $125.00 for. I have recommended your machine to several friends who live in other suburban cities around Washington and you will, no doubt, receive some orders for a Wizard before long. Thanking you again for your kindness in sending me the Wizard machine, I remain,

Yours respectfully,
JOHN W. BROWN.

Our Steam Heating Plant Enables Him to Keep His House at 72 to 80 Degrees When the Temperature Outside Is 35 Degrees to 49 Degrees Below Zero.

Northfield, Vt.

Sears, Roebuck and Co., Chicago, Ill.

Gentlemen:—We have six months of winter here that we have to keep fire, and some of it from zero to 35 to 49 degrees below, and I can keep my house from 72 to 80 degrees all the time. I can fix the fire at night at 9 o'clock, and if I want to I can fix the dampers so that it will keep up to 70 degrees all night, but that is a little too warm to sleep in. I cannot say enough about the heating plant. I am very well pleased with it. There is no noise or hammering in the pipes. The only way you know there is any steam coming is to put your hand on the radiators. Now I heat the whole house—ten rooms and hall—with the same amount of coal I used in two stoves, and I can have every room warm enough to sit in in any kind of weather we have here, anywhere from 72 to 80 degrees; that is hot enough. All last winter when it was anywhere from 10 to 30 degrees below zero, it was 72 degrees in the house. The plant cost me somewhere about $200.00. My local plumber asked me $380.00, so you can see how much I saved. Anyone can come and see the plant any time. I would be glad to have them. Now you can pick out as much of this to publish as you wish. I presume all of it would not look well, but I have got it pretty well advertised in this town just the same. ELMER E. BILISS.

No. 102

FOR $861.00 we will furnish all the material to build this ten-room house. This price includes mill work, lumber, building paper, eaves troughs, hardware and painting material. By allowing a fair price for labor this house can be built for $1,995.00.

No. 131

FOR $1,420.00 we will furnish all the material to build this thirteen-room two-family house. This price includes mill work, lumber, building paper, eaves troughs, mantels, hardware, and painting material. By allowing a fair price for labor this house can be built for $3,157.00.

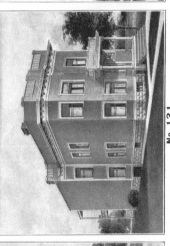

No. 123

FOR $1,073.00 we will furnish all the material to build this ten-room house. This price includes mill work, lumber, building paper, eaves troughs, mantels, hardware and painting material. By allowing a fair price for labor this house can be built for $2,578.00.

No. 111

FOR $879.00 we will furnish all the material to build this nine-room house. This price includes mill work, lumber, building paper, eaves troughs, hardware and painting material. By allowing a fair price for labor this house can be built for $2,130.00.

No. 103

FOR $532.00 we will furnish all the material to build this six-room house. This price includes mill work, lumber, building paper, eaves troughs, hardware and painting material. By allowing a fair price for labor this house can be built for $1,278.00.

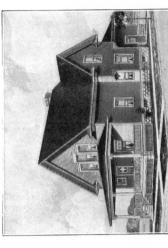

No. 34

FOR $873.00 we will furnish all the material to build this eight-room house. This price includes mill work, lumber, building paper, eaves troughs, hardware and painting material. By allowing a fair price for labor this house can be built for $1,790.00.

No. 52

FOR $744.00 we will furnish all the material to build this nine-room concrete block house. This price includes mill work, lumber, hardware and painting material. By allowing a fair price for labor this house can be built for $1,998.00.

OUR $100.00 BUILDING PLANS COST YOU NOTHING

AS EXPLAINED ON THE OPPOSITE PAGE.

IN OUR BOOK OF MODERN HOMES we illustrate eighty different styles of houses adapted for city dwellings, suburban homes, country and farm houses, ranging in cost for building from $500.00 to $5,000.00. A few of these are illustrated on this and the opposite page.

OUR PLANS are the work of the best known licensed architects specially engaged by us for this service. They fully investigated the requirements of home builders everywhere in the United States and have embodied in our plans the very latest ideas of the best posted contractors and builders in this country, giving us a variety of houses specially adapted for city, town or farm homes. Ideas and suggestions impossible for you to secure elsewhere at any price.

OUR BUILDING PLANS, specifications and bill of materials, which cost you nothing, as explained on opposite page, include the following:

1—A complete set of working drawings, blue prints, with all details and dimensions plainly marked, drawn to the scale of ¼ inch to the foot, a most convenient scale. They are so complete that any mechanic can understand and follow them easily.
FRONT ELEVATION, showing the front view of the house.
RIGHT SIDE ELEVATION, showing the right side view of the house.
LEFT ELEVATION, showing the left side view of the house.
REAR ELEVATION, giving a back view of the house.
FOUNDATION PLANS, giving information with reference to excavation, foundation, etc.
FIRST FLOOR PLANS, with sizes of rooms, partitions, doorways, windows, etc., given in detail.
SECOND FLOOR PLANS (if a two-story structure) giving size of rooms, partitions, location of windows, doors, etc., in detail.

DETAILED DRAWINGS OF MATERIALS, showing stair finish, balusters, style of window trimmings, hardware, porch finish, cornice finish, and all the material necessary to give style and character to the structure inside and out.
2—Complete specifications of material and labor required, outlining all the conditions under which a contract may be let, enabling you to protect your interests perfectly if house is to be built by contract.
3—Complete bill of materials, explaining the cost, quantity and dimensions of timbers required, also the quantity and kind of exterior finishing lumber, porch work, roofing, flooring, window and door frames, doors and windows, inside finishing lumber including all molding, stairwork, etc., building hardware, such as door locks, hinges, cupboard catches, drawer pulls, sash locks, gutters and eaves troughs, glass, paints, varnishes and fillers for outside and inside painting.

COMPARE THE COST ESTIMATES of the houses illustrated on this and the opposite site page with the cost of houses erected in your neighborhood during the past five years. Our plans and building material prices enable you to save fully one-third or more.

OUR PLANS AND SPECIFICATIONS CALL FOR THE HIGHEST GRADE MATERIALS AND LABOR.

We specify the best grade of mill work, dimension lumber, hardware and paint, as well as the highest grade workmanship throughout. Our estimates, therefore, provide them by giving you exact figures on every item. We send you as typewritten bill of materials with double blue print and specifications. We guarantee our prices on lumber, mill work, such as windows, doors, interior trim, flooring, siding, hardware, paint, mantels, plumbing and heating. On these we save you nearly one-half. Write and get our Book of Modern Homes at once.

First Floor Plan for No. 102 Modern Home shown above

KITCHEN 10'X14'-0"
PANTRY
PANTRY
LIVING ROOM 11'-0"X16'-0"
HALL 7'-6"X19'-6"
DINING ROOM 11'-3"X14'-6"
PARLOR 11'-0"X14'-0"
GRILLE
PORCH
PORCH

Second Floor Plan for No. 102 Modern Home shown above

CHAMBER 11'-0"X12'-6"
CHAMBER 11'-0"X13'-0"
TOILET OR STORE ROOM 7'-6"X9'-0"
HALL 7'-6"X10'-6"
CHAMBER 11'-0"X11'-6"
CHAMBER 11'-6"X14'-0"
CLOSET

4

SEARS, ROEBUCK AND CO., CHICAGO, ILLINOIS.

No. 124

FOR $838.00 we will furnish all the material to build this nine-room house. This price includes mill work, lumber, building paper, eaves troughs, mantel, hardware and painting material. By allowing a fair price for labor this house can be built for $1,960.00.

No. 129

FOR $1,426.00 we will furnish all the material to build this twelve-room house. This price includes mill work, lumber, building paper, eaves troughs, hardware and painting material. By allowing a fair price for labor this house can be built for $3,336.00.

No. 126

FOR $609.00 we will furnish all the material to build this six-room bungalow. This price includes mill work, lumber, building paper, eaves troughs, mantel, hardware and painting material. By allowing a fair price for labor this bungalow can be built for $1,466.00.

No. 118

FOR $1,298.00 we will furnish all the material to build this nine-room house. This price includes mill work, lumber, building paper, eaves troughs, mantel, hardware and painting material. By allowing a fair price for labor this house can be built for $2,782.00.

First Floor Plan for the $2,782.00 House shown above.

Second Floor Plan for the $2,782.00 House shown above.

No. 125

FOR $546.00 we will furnish all the material to build this eight-room bungalow. This price includes mill work, lumber, building paper, eaves troughs, hardware and painting material. By allowing a fair price for labor this bungalow can be built for $947.00.

No. 115

FOR $403.00 we will furnish all the material to build this six-room house. This price includes mill work, lumber, building paper, eaves troughs, hardware and painting material. By allowing a fair price for labor this house can be built for $703.00.

No. 24

FOR $659.00 we will furnish all the material to build this eight-room house. This price includes mill work, lumber, building paper, eaves troughs, hardware and painting material. By allowing a fair price for labor this house can be built for $1,497.00.

FREE — THIS BEAUTIFULLY ILLUSTRATED — BOOK OF EIGHTY MODERN HOMES — AND POSTPAID

THIS HANDSOME BOOK illustrates over eighty modern styles of dwellings adapted for farm homes, country and city residences, cottages, roomy houses, flat buildings and bungalows.

Just write and say, "Send me free your Book of Modern Homes," and this complete book with order blank and full information about our building plans, as described on page 4, will go to you at once free and postpaid.

HOW OUR $100.00 PLANS COST YOU NOTHING. When you get our Book of Modern Homes, observe the illustrations of the finished houses and of the floor plans, read our descriptions and pick out the house that suits you best. Then write us telling us the number of the house for which you wish to get plans and enclose $1.00 with your request, merely as a temporary deposit, and we will immediately send a complete set of plans, blue prints, specifications and bill of materials, as described on page 4, and at the same time we will send you a certificate for your $1.00 which we will apply as cash on any order for $10.00 worth or more of mill work for building material which you may send us. Thus the plans cost you nothing. We are obliged to ask for the nominal sum of $1.00 merely to protect ourselves against requests for plans from those who are not interested in building, such as curiosity seekers or youths who have no intention to use our plans for the purpose intended.

EACH HOUSE IN THIS BOOK is shown by a beautiful halftone illustration of a finished house, with first and second floor plans in reduced size, with number of rooms, sizes, etc., plainly marked, and our accurate estimate of cost printed with each illustration. Remember, our cost estimates are not guesswork. They are positively accurate. We prove them by giving you a typewritten bill of materials, specifying every item of building material. We tell you to a dollar what the house will cost when complete ready for occupancy. The plans are so carefully drawn that you can make a big saving in your methods of building alone, and as we save you nearly one-half on lumber, mill work and building material as shown in this catalog, we enable you, for example, to build the average $3,000.00 house for about $2,000.00.

DON'T FAIL TO WRITE AND GET THIS BOOK OF MODERN HOMES AT ONCE

WHEN YOU GET OUR COMPLETE SET OF PLANS and specifications, and examine them carefully, note the style and quality of the material we specify, the splendid quality of the mill work, its beautiful designs. Note the class of hardware specified, note everything we specify, all of which we furnish; then compare the quality with what you can secure elsewhere. Compare our prices with the prices you are obliged to pay elsewhere. As a favor to us, make this comparison carefully, because we know you will then find our prices so much lower than all others, and our qualities so much better, that you will have no hesitation in giving us your entire order for building material.

DON'T BREAK GROUND OR SIGN A BUILDING CONTRACT before you get a copy of our Book of Modern Homes. We can positively save you one-third or more in the cost of your home. You will get better results out of our building plans, you pay other architects $100.00 or more for.

WHETHER YOU ARE A CONTRACTOR AND BUILDER OR INTEND TO BUILD YOUR OWN HOME, YOU POSITIVELY CANNOT AFFORD TO BE WITHOUT THIS BOOK OF MODERN HOMES. WRITE FOR IT TODAY.

BOOK OF MODERN HOMES AND BUILDING PLANS

SEARS, ROEBUCK & CO. CHICAGO

OAK AND BIRCH VENEERED FRONT DOORS

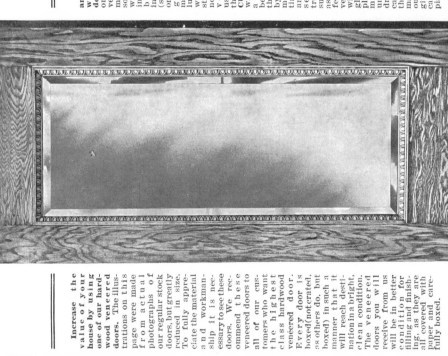

Increase the value of your house by using one of our hardwood veneered doors. The illustrations on this page were made from actual photographs of our regular stock doors, but greatly reduced in size. To fully appreciate the material and workmanship it is necessary to see these doors. We recommend these veneered doors to all of our customers who want the highest class hardwood veneered door. Every door is boxed (not crated, as others do, but boxed) in such a manner that it will reach destination in a bright, clean condition. The veneered doors you will receive from us will be in better condition for filling and finishing, as they are all covered with paper and carefully boxed.

Why we guarantee our hardwood veneered doors. The inside or core of our veneered doors is made of seasoned soft pine strips, which are made into a solid piece by our special interlocking joint (see illustration on page 12), and glued, which makes an absolutely solid core which is light, strong and will not warp. The veneers we use are made by the "ROTARY CUT PROCESS," which gives them a much more beautiful grain than can be had by any other method of cutting. Our veneers are all carefully selected and treated and only such pieces used as will take a perfect finish. This veneer is applied with the very best glue, and held in place under enormous pressure until thoroughly dry. The same care is exercised throughout in the manufacture of our doors as is given the finest cabinet work and piano cases.

MARS, Furnished Only in Oak, 1¾ Inches Thick

SIZES Width Ft.	In.	Height Ft.	In.	VENEERED OAK No. 63B60 Glazed Bevel Plate	Approximate Shipping Weight, Pounds
2	8	6	8	$10.40	105
2	10	6	10	10.80	106
3	0	7	0	11.40	112
3	0	7	0	12.80	120

BEAUTY, Furnished in Oak and Birch, 1¾ Inches Thick

SIZES Width Ft.	In.	Height Ft.	In.	VENEERED OAK No. 63B92 Glazed Bevel Plate	VENEERED OAK No. 63B93 Glazed *Colon Design	VENEERED BIRCH No. 63B96 Glazed Bevel Plate	VENEERED BIRCH No. 63B97 Glazed *Colon Design	Approximate Shipping Weight, Pounds Glazed Bevel Plate	Approximate Shipping Weight, Pounds Glazed *Colon Design
2	8	6	8	$10.25	$6.75	$ 9.45	$5.90	105	99
2	10	6	10	10.90	7.45	10.60	6.20	106	100
3	0	7	0	12.10	7.80	11.05	6.50	108	103
3	0	7	0	12.70	7.90	11.50	6.75	115	110
							6.80	115	115

VENUS, Furnished Only in Oak, 1¾ Inches Thick

SIZES Width Ft.	In.	Height Ft.	In.	VENEERED OAK No. 63B62 Glazed Bevel Plate	Approximate Shipping Weight, Pounds
2	8	6	8	$11.50	105
2	10	6	10	11.90	106
3	0	7	0	12.55	112
3	0	7	0	13.95	120

*COLON DESIGN OF GLASS (CATALOG Nos. 63B93 AND 63B97) IS ILLUSTRATED IN COLON DOOR ON PAGE 7.

SEARS, ROEBUCK AND CO., CHICAGO, ILLINOIS.

OAK AND BIRCH VENEERED FRONT DOORS

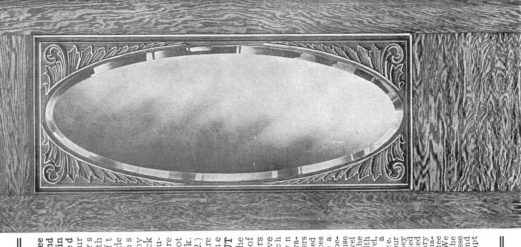

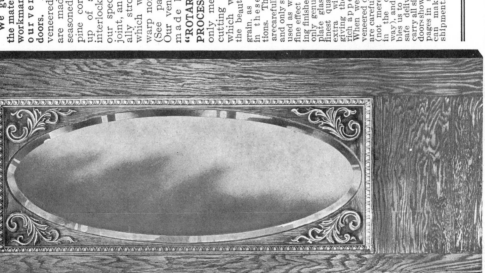

The doors shown on this and the preceding page are designs most generally used and are correct from an architectural standpoint. You can select from these doors suitable designs for the highest priced residence or for a home of moderate cost. There is nothing that adds more to the appearance of a home than one of our hardwood veneered doors. We manufacture them in very large quantities, which greatly reduces our cost, hence a very low selling price.

We guarantee the material and workmanship in our veneered doors. All our veneered doors are made with seasoned soft pine core made up of strips interlocked by our special lock joint, an unusually strong core which will not warp nor check. (See page 12.) Our veneers are made by the "ROTARY" CUT PROCESS, the only method of cutting veneers which will give the beautiful rich grain, as shown in these illustrations. The veneers are carefully selected and only such pieces used as will give a fine effect after being finished. We use only genuine bevel plate glass of the finest quality with extra wide bevel, giving the door a rich appearance. When we ship our veneered doors they are carefully crated (not merely boxed in the customary way), and this enables us to guarantee safe delivery. We carry all sizes of the doors shown on these pages in stock and can make prompt shipment.

COLON, Furnished Only in Oak, 1¾ Inches Thick

SIZES				VENEERED OAK	Approximate
Width		Height		No. 63B64	Shipping
Ft.	In.	Ft.	In.	Glazed, as Illustrated	Weight, Pounds
2	8	6	8	$8.00	105
2	10	7	0	8.65	112
3	0	7	0	9.20	120

SUPERBA, Furnished in Oak and Birch, 1¾ Inches Thick

SIZES				VENEERED OAK		VENEERED BIRCH		
Width		Height		No. 63B94 Glazed *Colon Design	No. 63B95 Glazed as Illustrated. Bevel Plate	No. 63B98 Glazed *Colon Design	No. 63B99 Glazed as Illustrated. Bevel Plate	Glazed Sand Blast, Approximate Shipping Weight. Lbs.	Glazed Bevel Plate, Approximate Shipping Weight. Lbs.

Width Ft.	In.	Height Ft.	In.	No. 63B94 Glazed *Colon Design	No. 63B95 Glazed as Illustrated. Bevel Plate	No. 63B98 Glazed *Colon Design	No. 63B99 Glazed as Illustrated. Bevel Plate	Glazed Sand Blast Approximate Shipping Weight. Lbs.	Glazed Bevel Plate Approximate Shipping Weight. Lbs.
2	8	6	8	$10.30	$14.15	$9.55	$13.40	100	105
2	10	7	0	11.05	15.00	10.35	14.65	103	108
3	0	7	0	11.45	16.50	10.40	15.65	115	115

PANAMA, Furnished Only in Oak, 1¾ Inches Thick

SIZES				VENEERED OAK	Approximate
Width		Height		No. 63B66	Shipping
Ft.	In.	Ft.	In.	Glazed Bevel Plate	Weight, Pounds
2	8	6	8	$11.90	105
2	10	7	0	13.55	112
3	0	7	0	14.75	120

*COLON DESIGN OF GLASS, CATALOG Nos. 63B94 AND 63B98, IS EXACTLY SAME LACE DESIGN AS SHOWN IN COLON DOOR ON THIS PAGE.

BIRCH VENEERED FRONT DOORS

Wisconsin Birch possesses more possibilities for staining and finishing than any other kind of wood. The heart of a birch log is reddish brown and the outside portion or sap is white, and when selected for color the all heart is known as red birch and the all sap as white birch. Our birch veneers contain both the red and white shades, which give a variegated color effect which is very rich. Wisconsin birch properly stained perfectly imitates mahogany, cherry, black walnut, butternut and other woods.

We give the most liberal guarantee on veneered doors. All our veneered doors have soft wood cores, made of thoroughly kiln dried soft pine strips locked together by our special lock joint (see illustration on page 12), which absolutely prevents any warping or checking. It has been demonstrated for a great many years that veneered work is far superior to any other method of construction. Our birch veneers are all made by the "ROTARY CUT PROCESS" which gives them an unusually beautiful grain, in fact, a grain which cannot be duplicated by any other method of cutting veneers. Our hardwood doors are all carefully sanded before shipping. All carvings or ornaments are genuine solid wood carvings.

TORONTO DOORS are glazed with leaded art glass, in colors, or bevel plate glass.

QUEBEC DOORS are glazed with best grade double strength glass, sand blast design, like illustration, or bevel plate glass.

HAMILTON DOORS are glazed with leaded crystal sheet glass (see illustration), or with bevel plate glass.

TORONTO, Furnished in Birch, 1¾ Inches Thick

SIZES Width Ft. In.	Height Ft. In.	No. 63B80 Glazed Bevel Plate	No. 63B81 Glazed as Illustrated	Approximate Shipping Wt., Pounds
2 8	6 8	$ 8.90	$7.95	89
2 10	6 10	9.90	8.75	91
2 10	7 0	10.15	9.25	95
3 0	7 0	10.65	9.75	98

QUEBEC, Furnished in Birch, 1¾ Inches Thick

SIZES Width Ft. In.	Height Ft. In.	No. 63B85 Glazed as Illustrated	No. 63B84 Glazed Bevel Plate	Approximate Shipping Wt., Pounds
2 8	6 8	$5.70	$ 8.85	89
2 10	6 10	6.25	9.85	91
2 10	7 0	6.50	10.10	95
3 0	7 0	6.70	10.75	98

HAMILTON, Furnished in Birch, 1¾ Inches Thick

SIZES Width Ft. In.	Height Ft. In.	No. 63B88 Glazed Bevel Plate	No. 63B89 Glazed Leaded Glass as Illustrated	Approximate Shipping Wt., Pounds
2 8	6 8	$6.75	$5.70	89
2 10	6 10	7.80	6.45	91
2 10	7 0	9.05	6.70	95
3 0	7 0		6.95	98

SEARS, ROEBUCK AND CO., CHICAGO, ILLINOIS.

OAK VENEERED FRONT DOORS

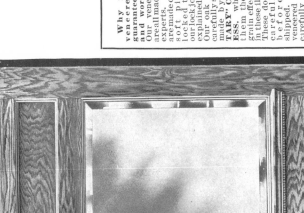

These designs are suitable for the highest class residence or the home of moderate cost and will match any kind of an interior. Doors are furnished in stock sizes only as listed. Whether you are putting up a new building or remodeling, you can greatly improve the building by using our hardwood veneered doors. Our enormous sales enable us to sell more veneered doors than any other retail concern, hence our low prices.

DIANA DOORS are glazed with bevel plate glass or with sand blast design, like that shown in the Quebec Door on page 8.

PHOEBE DOORS are glazed with bevel plate glass or with leaded crystal sheet glass, like that shown in the Hamilton Door on opposite page.

Why not buy veneered doors of guaranteed material and workmanship? Our veneered doors are all made by veneer experts. The cores are made of kiln dried soft pine strips, locked together by our lock joint, as fully explained on page 12. Our oak veneers are carefully selected and made by the ROTARY CUT PROCESS, which gives them the beautiful grain effect, as shown in these illustrations. These doors are all carefully sanded before being shipped. All of our veneered doors are carefully boxed (not merely crated), which insures their reaching destination in good condition. We guarantee safe delivery.

CIRCE DOORS are glazed with bevel plate glass or with leaded art glass, like that shown in the Toronto Door on page 8.

DIANA, Furnished in Oak, 1¾ Inches Thick

SIZES Width Ft.	In.	Height Ft.	In.	No. 63B86 Glazed Bevel Plate	No. 63B87 © Glazed Quebec Design	Approximate Shipping Weight, Pounds
2	8	6	8	$9.35	$6.45	89
2	10	6	10	10.40	7.15	91
2	10	7	0	10.95	7.50	95
3	0	7	0	11.30	7.75	98

© Quebec design glass shown on page 8.   Catalog No. 63B85.

PHOEBE, Furnished in Oak, 1¾ Inches Thick

SIZES Width Ft.	In.	Height Ft.	In.	No. 63B90 Glazed Bevel Plate	No. 63B91 ♦ Glazed Hamilton Design	Approximate Shipping Weight, Pounds
2	8	6	8	$7.45	$6.50	89
2	10	6	10	8.45	7.30	91
2	10	7	0	8.80	7.75	95
3	0	7	0	9.90	7.95	98

♦ Hamilton design glass shown on page 8.   Catalog No. 63B89.

CIRCE, Furnished in Oak, 1¾ Inches Thick

SIZES Width Ft.	In.	Height Ft.	In.	No. 63B82 Glazed Bevel Plate	No. 63B83 ★ Glazed Toronto Design	Approximate Shipping Weight, Pounds
2	8	6	8	$9.55	$8.70	89
2	10	6	10	10.70	9.25	94
2	10	7	0	11.00	10.25	98
3	0	7	0	11.45	10.60	103

★ Toronto design glass shown on page 8.   Catalog No. 63B81.

THESE DOORS ARE MADE WITH ROTARY CUT OAK VENEERS.

The veneer used in the building of Craftsman doors is cut by the "ROTARY" CUT PROCESS from select oak logs. The core or foundation of our doors is built up of pine strips glued and interlocked, making a warrproof foundation for the door. The core is then planed down until it has a perfectly true surface on both sides, after which the face veneers are applied and glued with the very best waterproof glue obtainable and subjected to hydraulic pressure for some time. A good veneered door is superior in every way to the old style solid oak door, as it will neither warp, shrink nor check. The solid oak door invariably checks and owing to its great weight is liable to pull apart at the joints. The veneered door is lighter in weight and is made with tight, true joints.

A STYLE THAT HAS COME TO STAY.

On these two pages we illustrate six doors of the new Craftsman style. You could not use three more handsome designs for outside doors than Craftsman M, O and R. Doors of this style are being used for the bungalow, Craftsman cottage and Mission style of residence. Any of the doors on these two pages will give your home an air of simplicity and elegance. When you choose doors like these, substantially made by the best cabinet makers, perfect in design, you create a lasting and pleasing impression. They not only look well, but hang true, so that opening and shutting these doors is a real pleasure. They greatly enhance the value of your home, whether it be a bungalow, Craftsman cottage or Mission residence. Even the average house will have a style and dignity that would be lacking without these doors.

When "Craftsman R" Door is glazed with leaded glass, the wood bars are taken out and the door is glazed with the same design as shown in the "Craftsman O" Door.

CRAFTSMAN M
Veneered Oak, 1¾ Inches Thick.

No. 63B1204 Glazed Clear Double Strength Glass	Sizes of Craftsman M Doors Width Ft. In.	Height Ft. In.
$6.35	2 8	6 8
6.60	2 8	7 0
7.30	3 0	7 0

CRAFTSMAN O
Veneered Oak, 1¾ Inches Thick.

No. 63B1205 Glazed Bevel Plate Glass	Approximate Shipping Weight, Pounds	No. 63B1206 Glazed Leaded Glass	Sizes of Craftsman O Doors Width Ft. In.	Height Ft. In.	No. 63B1207 Glazed Bevel P'ate Glass
$10.10	82	$ 9.75	2 8	6 8	$10.00
10.65	90	10.05	2 8	7 0	10.55
11.35	97	11.20	3 0	7 0	11.25

CRAFTSMAN R
Veneered Oak, 1¾ Inches Thick.

No. 63B1208 Glazed Leaded Glass	Approximate Shipping Weight, Pounds	Sizes of Craftsman R Doors Width Ft. In.	Height Ft. In.	No. 63B1209 Glazed Bevel Plate Glass
$ 9.80	82	2 8	6 8	$10.05
10.10	90	2 8	7 0	11.30
11.25	97	3 0	7 0	

SPECIAL HIGH CLASS TRIM, INCLUDING CASING, BASE, ETC., FOR CRAFTSMAN DOORS SHOWN ON PAGES 60 AND 61.

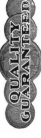

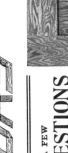

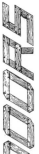

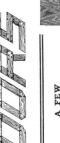

QUALITY GUARANTEED

CRAFTSMAN DOORS

QUALITY GUARANTEED

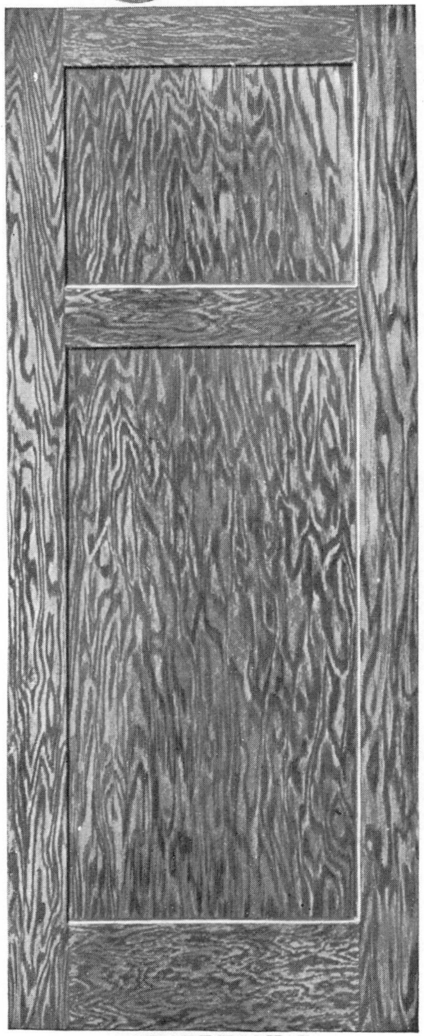

CRAFTSMAN G

CRAFTSMAN

ITS MEANING

The meaning of the term "Craftsman" as applied to architecture and furniture is something that has been turned out by a master workman. It is very similar in design to the Mission style, with which everyone is familiar. Of late years, after the bungalow, Craftsman cottage and Mission dwellings became so popular, doors similar in design to those illustrated on this page have been used exclusively. The illustrations on this page will give you some idea of the beautiful grain effects of these inside doors. The large panels shown on our Craftsman G door are one continuous piece, there being no joints or no butting of veneers, as a veneer made by the **"rotary" cut process** may be of almost any width up to 8 feet. We show a variety in the different arrangements of panels from which you may select, and at the prices we quote we put these doors within the reach of anyone.

Furnished only in plain red oak.

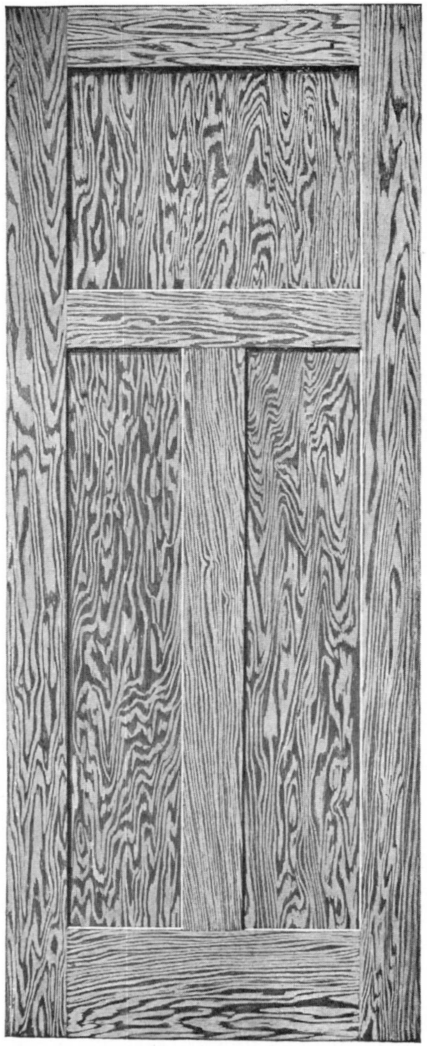

CRAFTSMAN H

A FEW

SUGGESTIONS

IN REGARD TO HARDWOOD DOORS

Never hang your door in a damp, freshly plastered building. Plaster contains large quantities of water, and until the moisture has thoroughly dried out of the walls the house is not fit for occupancy; neither is it in the right condition to receive hardwood doors or any other fine woodwork that would be affected by climatic conditions. All wood is porous, and the more thoroughly seasoned it is the more readily it will absorb moisture. When an unfinished hardwood door is placed in a damp room it quickly absorbs the moisture in the air and generally expands, or swells; when it returns to its normal condition, or becomes dry, the door is warped or twisted out of shape, particularly if it is a solid oak door. A hardwood door should not be hung where it will be exposed to the weather, that is, where it will not have the protection of a porch. To obtain the best results, give the door at least one coat of filler immediately upon receiving it; as it reaches you in the white or unfinished and is susceptible to moisture. The door will also take a more beautiful finish if this precaution is taken.

Furnished only in plain red oak.

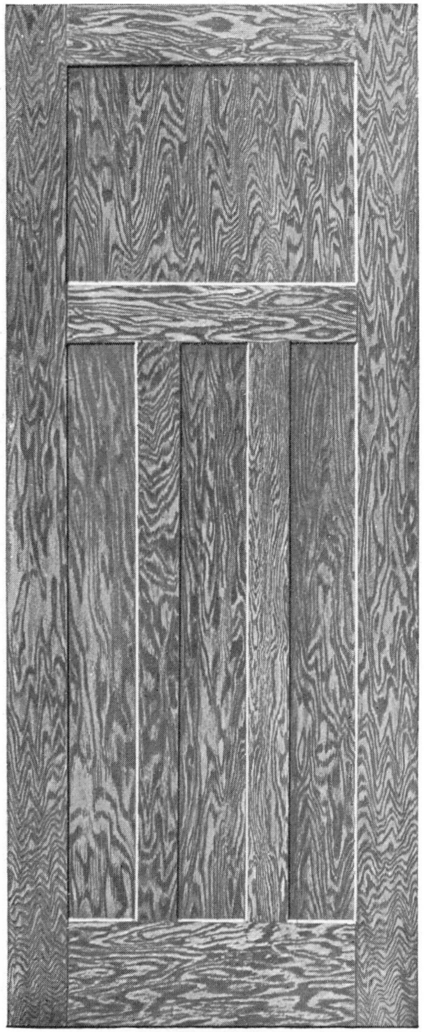

CRAFTSMAN I

No. 63B1211 1⅜ Inches Thick	Sizes of Craftsman G Doors				No. 63B1212 1¾ Inches Thick	Approximate Shipping Weight		No. 63B1213 1⅜ Inches Thick	Sizes of Craftsman H Doors				No. 63B1214 1¾ Inches Thick	Approximate Shipping Weight		No. 63B1215 1⅜ Inches Thick	Sizes of Craftsman I Doors				No. 63B1216 1¾ Inches Thick
	Width Ft.	Width In.	Height Ft.	Height In.		1⅜ In. Thick	1¾ In. Thick		Width Ft.	Width In.	Height Ft.	Height In.		1⅜ In. Thick	1¾ In. Thick		Width Ft.	Width In.	Height Ft.	Height In.	
$4.85	2	8	6	8	$5.40	75 lbs.	80 lbs.	$4.90	2	8	6	8	$5.45	75 lbs.	80 lbs.	$4.95	2	8	6	8	$5.50
5.55	2	8	7	0	6.15	83 lbs.	88 lbs.	5.60	2	8	7	0	6.20	83 lbs.	88 lbs.	5.65	2	8	7	0	6.25
5.90	3	0	7	0	6.50	89 lbs.	95 lbs.	5.95	3	0	7	0	6.55	89 lbs.	95 lbs.	6.00	3	0	7	0	6.60

SPECIAL HIGH CLASS TRIM, INCLUDING CASING, BASE, ETC., FOR CRAFTSMAN DOORS, SHOWN ON PAGES 60 AND 61.

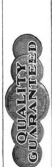

VENEERED HARDWOOD PANEL DOORS

Why Our Veneered Doors are Superior to All Other Kinds of Hardwood Doors.

The most beautiful and expensive pieces of cabinet and panel work are made by veneer process. It has been demonstrated by long years of actual service that for interior work, veneered work is far superior in every way to the old time way of using thick, solid wood. The very finest piano cases are, without exception, veneered. Any solid piece of wood of the thickness, width and length necessary to make veneered doors would warp and check or split when thoroughly dried and would present a very unsightly appearance when made up into a door, piece of carved work or piano case. In order to overcome this warping and checking tendency it is necessary to make the core or inside out of soft, thoroughly kiln dried and selected pine, and to get the best results the core is made of narrow strips held together by our self locking joint (see illustration) and also glued and held in place by enormous presses until dry. This makes the core a solid piece which will not warp or check. In order to get highly figured veneers it is necessary to cut them a certain way or method which is known as the "ROTARY" CUT PROCESS. It is not possible to get the beautifully figured effect in any veneer unless it is cut in this way. It would be impossible to get any piece of solid wood which would have the beautiful figure which is shown in the rotary cut veneers. A hardwood door 2 inches thick when made solid would be extremely heavy and unhandsome. In fact, it would be so heavy that it would be liable to pull open at the joints. This objection is entirely overcome by the veneering process. In order to get the best results, however, and to make it possible for us to guarantee our doors it is necessary to have skilled workmen who are thoroughly experienced in veneer construction, and also suitable and modern machinery for making the cores and applying the veneers, etc. By purchasing your veneered doors from us you get them direct from our factory where we make a specialty of veneered work. It is only natural that with our experienced veneer workmen and specially constructed veneer machinery we can make the most reliable veneered doors. As soon as you receive your veneered door we recommend that you paint the top and bottom edges so that the cores cannot absorb any moisture. The lumber from which these doors are made was especially treated in dry kilns and the lumber was entirely dry when the door was shipped. It is, therefore, much safer to paint the top and bottom edges so that the door will not absorb any moisture. It is also advisable to give the entire door at least one coat of filler as soon as received, as the veneers will take a much better finish when treated in this way.

PACKING. Our veneered doors are not merely crated, but are covered with tough paper and carefully boxed with strong boards, insuring safe arrival at destination. We guarantee safe delivery on all of our doors.

QUALITY GUARANTEED

WILCOX

SIZES Width Ft. In.	Height Ft. In.	Thickness Inches	No. 63B6252 Veneered Plain Red Oak	No. 63B6253 Veneered Wisconsin Birch
2 0	6 6	1⅜	$3.57	$2.78
2 6	6 6	1⅜	3.59	3.06
2 4	6 6	1⅜	3.73	3.13
2 6	6 6	1⅜	3.64	3.10
2 8	6 8	1⅜	3.74	3.18
2 8	6 8	1⅜	3.75	3.19
2 10	6 10	1⅜	3.60	3.71
2 6	7 0	1⅜	4.39	3.57
2 8	7 0	1⅜	4.40	3.59
2 10	7 0	1⅜	4.45	3.67
2 10	7 0	1⅜	4.60	3.78
3 0	7 0	1⅜	4.67	3.92
3 0	6 8	1¾	4.24	3.67
3 0	6 10	1¾	5.08	4.19
2 4	6 7	1¾	4.91	4.05
2 6	7 0	1¾	4.92	4.09
2 8	7 0	1¾	4.94	4.17
2 10	7 0	1¾	5.13	4.27
3 0	7 0	1¾		4.41

WOODLAWN

SIZES Width Ft. In.	Height Ft. In.	Thickness Inches	No. 63B6250 Veneered Plain Red Oak	No. 63B6251 Veneered Wisconsin Birch
2 0	6 6	1⅜	$3.15	$2.50
2 0	6 6	1⅜	3.19	2.78
2 4	6 6	1⅜	3.33	2.86
2 6	6 6	1⅜	3.34	2.82
2 6	6 8	1⅜		2.89
2 8	6 8	1⅜	3.35	2.90
2 10	6 10	1⅜	4.03	3.42
2 6	7 0	1⅜	4.05	3.28
2 8	7 0	1⅜	4.06	3.32
2 10	7 0	1⅜	4.15	3.40
2 10	7 0	1⅜		3.50
3 0	6 8	1⅜	4.26	3.64
3 0	6 10	1¾	4.70	3.40
3 0	7 0	1¾	4.52	3.92
2 6	7 0	1¾	4.53	3.80
2 8	7 0	1¾	4.55	3.89
2 10	7 0	1¾	4.75	3.99
3 0	7 0	1¾		4.12

WOODLAWN

FOR SINGLE SLIDING DOOR TO MATCH SEE PAGE 33.

WILCOX

$16 85 FOR MASSIVE FRONT COMPLETE

THIS FRAME GLAZED WITH PLAIN DOUBLE STRENGTH GLASS

The above is an example of the extremely low prices we can make on the highest grades of doors, frames, side lights and everything in the building material line. The above price includes the following items:

One Door, size 2 ft. 8 in. by 6 ft. 8 in., 1¾ in. thick, like illustration, Nona pine, plain glass....$3.85
Two Side Lights, 1 ft. 2 in. by 6 ft. 8 in., like illustration, Nona pine, plain glass, at $1.40.........2.80
One Transom, 16 inches high, Nona pine, plain glass...2.50
One Triple Frame for above, like illustration..7.70

All above glazed with plain double strength glass............................TOTAL....$16.85
If you want the above door, side lights and transom glazed with fine bevel plate glass, price will be. 28.40

If You Will Notice the more expensive residences and buildings you will find a large percentage of them have at least one entrance with a nice front door and side lights. An entrance of this kind immediately marks any building as a high grade structure on account of the high price usually charged for an entrance of this kind. Until recently only builders who were expending considerable money could afford to put in a front of this kind. The low prices we quote will enable builders of moderate means to use these magnificent entrances.

This is a Strictly First Class Frame and suitable for the very best buildings. The oak and pine lumber we use in these frames is the same high grade material we use in our hardwood and Nona pine doors, which is the highest grade of lumber ever used for this purpose. This frame will match our best doors in both material and workmanship. If it were not for the fact that we carry hundreds of carloads of lumber on hand at our factory and ship the finished frame direct to you, it would be impossible for us to furnish a frame so well made and from such high grades of lumber at these low prices.

The Design and Proportion of This Frame is entirely correct from an architectural stand-point. This design was proportioned and drawn up by our architect and a great deal of care has been given to the detailed construction and the proportions of the different members of this frame. Our object is to give our customers the very best frame possible and to make the price as low as possible and figure on furnishing only first class workmanship and material.

This Frame is Made in Six Different Sizes to fit our various sizes of front doors. The side lights are all made 1 foot 2 inches wide (glass size 10 inches wide) and of the same height as the door. We cannot make this frame in sizes larger than shown in the table below without greatly increasing the cost, but if it is necessary to have a larger front we can furnish it and the price will be much higher, as all of the material will have to be made specially to order.

This Frame Will Be Shipped Knocked Down, that is, in bundles, carefully crated, but the parts will all be cut to size so that they will fit together readily, and all you will have to do will be to nail the different members together, which will be a very easy and short job. We ship the frame knocked down for the reason that it will reach you in much better condition and will take a much lower freight rate than if shipped in any other manner.

The Prices Below are for the Frame Only. Price does not include the door, side lights or transom. Doors and side lights of every description are illustrated, described and priced in this catalog.

BOTH OUR NONA PINE AND OAK FRAMES HAVE A HEAVY OAK SILL.

WHEN ORDERING BE SURE TO GIVE FOLLOWING SIZES: Width, thickness and height of front door; width and height of side lights, and height of transom.

Size of Door	Size of Side Lights	Height of Transom	Clear Soft Pine. Price for Frame Only. Catalog No. 63B712O	Clear Oak. Price for Frame Only. Catalog No. 63B7226
3 ft. by 7 ft. or smaller	1 ft. 2 in. by 7 ft.	16 inches or less	$7.70	$11.85

Any of Our Stock Front Doors and Side Lights Can Be Used in This Frame.

Select the front door and side lights you want from our stock designs in this catalog and to their prices add the price on this page for frame and transom. Transoms will be made 16 inches high and 1⅛ inches thick and will be furnished for $2.50 each double strength glass and $7.00 if glazed bevel plate.

In the Accompanying Detail the members which are shaded dark represent the parts furnished with this frame. The sections of the detail which are merely an outline in white represent the studding, the sheathing, etc., which are a part of the building and are merely shown to suggest the proper way in which to fit this frame in the building.

QUALITY GUARANTEED

DOOR 2¾X5⅝

1⅞X4½

2X4

DETAIL SECTIONAL DRAWING.

Strictly "A" Grade or No. 1 Quality Doors With Wide Stiles

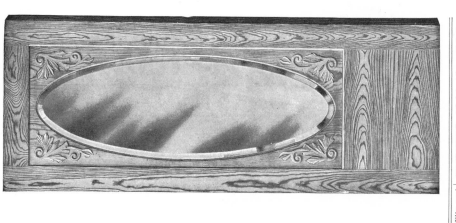

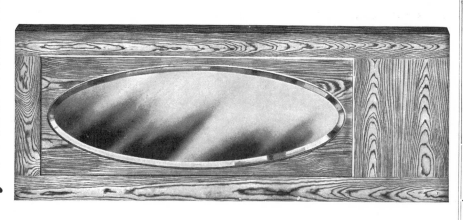

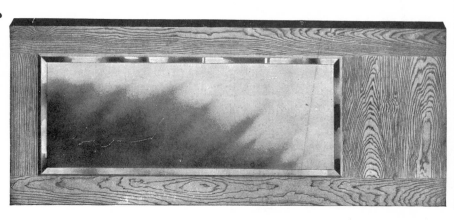

DUBLIN, 1⅜ inches thick	Sizes of Dublin and Majestic Doors			
No. 63B331 Glazed Bevel Plate	Width		Height	
	Ft.	In.	Ft.	In.
$7.90	2	6	6	6
8.65	2	8	6	8
9.85	2	10	6	10
9.55	2	0	7	0
10.90	3	0	7	0

MAJESTIC, 1⅜ inches thick		Approximate Shipping Weight of All Doors on This Page, Pounds
No. 63B111 Glazed Bevel Plate	No. 63B101 Glazed "A" Quality D. S. Glass	
$ 8.20	$3.70	90
8.95	3.90	93
10.15	4.45	95
9.85	4.50	95
11.15	4.75	100

VILLA, 1⅜ inches thick	Sizes of Villa and Jenkins Doors				JENKINS, 1⅜ inches thick
No. 63B919 Glazed Bevel Plate	Width		Height		No. 63B949 Glazed Bevel Plate
	Ft.	In.	Ft.	In.	
$ 8.55	2	6	6	6	$ 9.40
9.25	2	8	6	8	10.10
10.35	2	10	6	10	11.20
10.25	2	0	7	0	11.90
11.30	3	0	7	0	12.15

NOTE—We furnish any door on this page 1¾ inches thick for $1.00 extra to the prices shown above. When ordering be sure to write the word "Special" after the catalog number.

WOOD—"A" grade *Nona white soft pine, thoroughly seasoned.

STILES—Extra wide.

WORKMANSHIP—The best. All doors sanded and polished ready for oil finish. Strong and durable; will not warp or check under ordinary conditions.

GLAZING Dublin, Majestic } Bevel plate } The Majestic Door also furnished Villa, Jenkins { glass } with "A" quality double strength glass.

PACKING—Covered with tough paper and substantially crated. GUARANTEED to arrive at destination in perfect condition.

We furnish only such sizes as are listed above. When ordering give catalog number, quantity, size and price.

*White soft Western spruce pine, superior to Northern white pine.

Strictly "A" Grade or No. 1 Quality Doors With Wide Stiles

ELIPSE, 1⅜ in. thick

No. 63B910 Glazed Bevel Plate
$7.75
8.10
9.00
9.50
9.75

JULIEN, 1⅜ inches thick

No. 63B999 Glazed as Illustrated	No.63B909 Glazed Clear D. S. Glass
$5.40	$5.35
5.65	5.55
6.10	6.05
6.25	6.20
6.55	6.50

Sizes of Elipse and Julien Doors

Width Ft. In.		Height Ft. In.	
2	6	6	6
2	8	6	8
2	10	6	10
3	0	7	0

Approximate Shipping Weight, Pounds

If Glazed D. S. Glass	If Glazed Bevel Plate or Leaded Art
67	90
71	93
74	95
75	95
78	100

VICTORIA, 1⅜ inches thick

No. 63B222 Glazed as Illustrated, Leaded Art	No. 63B202 Glazed Clear D. S. Glass
$5.40	$3.40
6.00	3.60
6.90	4.15
6.85	4.45
7.40	

LOUISE, 1⅜ inches thick

No. 63B555 Glazed as Illustrated	No. 63B505 Glazed Clear D. S. Glass
$3.25	$3.15
3.45	3.25
4.05	3.85
4.10	3.90
4.20	4.10

Sizes of Victoria and Louise Doors

Width Ft. In.		Height Ft. In.	
2	6	6	6
2	8	6	8
2	10	6	10
2	10	7	0
3	0	7	0

NOTE—We will furnish any of the doors on this page 1¾ inches thick at $1.00 extra in addition to the above prices. When ordering be sure to write the word "Special" after the catalog number.

WOOD—"A" grade *Nona white soft pine, thoroughly seasoned.

STILES—Extra wide.

PANELS—Heavy raised.

WORKMANSHIP—The best. All doors sanded and polished ready for oil finish. Strong and durable; will not warp or check under ordinary conditions.

*White soft Western spruce pine, superior to Northern white pine.

Elipse—Bevel plate glass.

Julien } Sand blast designs

Louise }

Victoria—Leaded art glass.

The Julien, Victoria and Louise Doors can also be furnished with "A" quality double strength glass.

GLAZING—

PACKING—Covered with tough paper and substantially crated.

GUARANTEED to arrive at destination in perfect condition.

We furnish only such sizes as are listed above. When ordering give catalog number, quantity, size and price.

QUALITY GUARANTEED

Strictly "A" Grade or No. 1 Quality Doors With Wide Stiles

ELDRIDGE, 1⅜ in. thick				BLAINE, 1⅜ in. thick				Sizes of Eldridge and Blaine Doors						Approximate Shipping Weight of All Doors on This Page, Pounds	ST. CLAIR, 1⅜ in. thick				Sizes of St. Clair and Hendricks Doors						HENDRICKS, 1⅜ in. thick			
								Width		Height									Width		Height								
								Ft.	In.	Ft.	In.								Ft.	In.	Ft.	In.							
No. 63B306 Glazed as Illustrated		Glazed Clear D. S. Glass		No. 63B302 Glazed as Illustrated		Glazed Clear D. S. Glass									No. 63B950 Glazed as Illustrated		Glazed Clear D. S. Glass								No. 63B403 Glazed as Illustrated		Glazed Clear D. S. Glass	
$2.95		$2.85		$3.50		$3.50		2	6	6	6			58	$3.65		$3.50		2	6	6	6			$3.55,		$3.25	
3.10		3.00		3.75		3.65		2	8	6	8			62	3.80		3.65		2	8	6	8			3.80		3.50	
3.50		3.40		4.15		4.10		2	10	6	10			65	4.20		4.10		2	10	6	10			4.25		3.90	
3.60		3.50		4.40		4.15		2	8	7	0			67	4.55		4.20		2	8	7	0			4.30		3.95	
3.85		3.75				4.40		3	0	7	0			70			4.40		3	0	7	0			4.55		4.35	

NOTE—We will furnish any of the doors on this page 1¾ inches thick at $1.00 extra in addition to the above prices. When ordering be sure to write the word "Special" after the catalog number.

WOOD—"A" grade *Nona white soft pine, thoroughly seasoned.
STILES—Extra wide.
PANELS—Heavy raised panels.
ORNAMENTS—Hand carved of solid wood.
WORKMANSHIP—The best. All doors sanded and polished ready for oil finish. Strong and durable; will not warp or check under ordinary conditions.
*White soft Western spruce pine, superior to Northern white pine.

Eldridge } Sand blast designs
Blaine } like illustrations
St. Clair } above.
Hendricks }

GLAZED— The Eldridge, St. Clair and Hendricks Doors can also be furnished with "A" quality double strength glass.

PACKING—Covered with tough paper and substantially crated.
GUARANTEED to arrive at destination in perfect condition.
When ordering give catalog number, quantity, size and price. We furnish only such sizes as are listed above.

Strictly "A" Grade or No. 1 Quality Doors With Wide Stiles

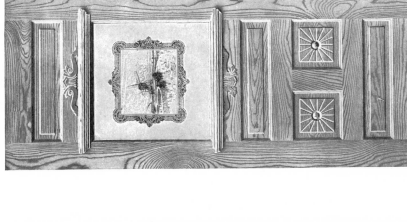

CLEVELAND, 1⅜ in. thick		Sizes of Cleveland and Grant Doors				GRANT, 1⅜ in. thick	Approximate Shipping Weight of All Doors on This Page, Pounds
No. 63B970 Glazed as Illustrated	No. 63B980 Glazed Clear D. S. Glass	Width Ft.	In.	Height Ft.	In.	No. 63B406 Glazed as Illustrated	
$3.75	$3.60	2	6	6	6	$3.35	58
3.90	3.75	2	8	6	8	3.50	62
4.35	4.20	2	10	6	10	3.90	65
4.45	4.30	3	0	7	0	4.00	67
4.70	4.55					4.25	70

GARFIELD, 1⅜ in. thick		Sizes of Garfield and Lincoln Doors				LINCOLN, 1⅜ in. thick
No. 63B504 Glazed as Illustrated	No. 63B524 Glazed Clear D. S. Glass	Width Ft.	In.	Height Ft.	In.	No. 63B605 Glazed as Illustrated
$3.45	$3.30	2	6	6	6	$3.30
3.60	3.45	2	8	6	8	3.45
4.00	3.85	2	10	6	10	4.05
4.35	4.15	3	0	7	0	4.30

NOTE—We furnish any door shown on this page 1¾ inches thick for $1.00 extra to the prices shown above. When ordering be sure to write the word "Special" after the catalog number.

WOOD—"A" grade *Nona white soft pine, thoroughly seasoned.
STILES—Extra wide.
PANELS—Heavy raised.
WORKMANSHIP—The best. All doors sanded and polished ready for oil finish. Strong and durable; will not warp or check under ordinary conditions.
*White soft Western spruce pine, superior to Northern white pine.

GLAZED— Cleveland, Grant, Garfield, Lincoln } Sand blast designs. The Cleveland and Garfield Doors can also be furnished with "A" quality double strength glass.
PACKING—Covered with tough paper and substantially crated.
GUARANTEED to arrive at destination in perfect condition.
We furnish only such sizes as are listed above. When ordering give catalog number, quantity, size and price.

QUALITY GUARANTEED

Strictly "A" Grade or No. 1 Quality Doors With Wide Stiles

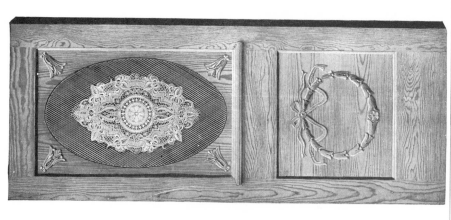

Sizes of Harrison and Jackson Doors

Width Ft.	In.	Height Ft.	In.
2	6	6	6
2	8	6	8
2	10	6	10
3	0	7	0

HARRISON, 1⅜ in. thick

No. 63 B 870 Glazed as Illustrated	No. 63 B 880 Glazed Clear D. S. Glass
$2.95	$2.85
3.15	3.00
3.55	3.40
3.85	3.75

JACKSON, 1⅜ in. thick

No. 63 B 890 Glazed as Illustrated	No. 63 B 900 Glazed Clear D. S. Glass
$5.20	$5.05
5.40	5.20
5.85	5.60
6.10	5.95

Approximate Shipping Weight of all Doors on this Page, Pounds

58
62
65
67
70

McKINLEY, 1⅜ inches thick

No. 63 B 704 Glazed as Illustrated	No. 63 B 724 Glazed Clear D. S. Glass
$3.45	$3.30
3.65	3.45
4.00	3.85
4.35	4.05

Sizes of McKinley and Payne Doors

Width Ft.	In.	Height Ft.	In.
2	6	6	6
2	8	6	8
2	10	6	10
3	0	7	0

PAYNE, 1⅜ inches thick

No. 63 B 144 Glazed Bevel Plate	No. 63 B 145 Glazed Clear D. S. Glass
$5.00	$2.85
6.30	2.95
7.15	3.45
7.85	3.65

NOTE—We will furnish any of the doors on this page 1¾ inches thick at $1.00 extra in addition to the above prices.

When ordering be sure to write the word "Special" after the catalog number.

All doors on this page can also be furnished with "A" quality double strength glass.

GLAZING—
Harrison ⎫ Sand blast designs
Jackson ⎬ like illustrations
McKinley ⎭ above.
Payne—Bevel Plate.

PACKING—Covered with tough paper and substantially crated.
GUARANTEED to arrive at destination in perfect condition.
When ordering give catalog number, quantity, size and price. We furnish only such sizes as are listed above.

WOOD—"A" grade* Nona white soft pine, thoroughly seasoned.
STILES—Extra wide.
PANELS—Heavy raised.
ORNAMENTS—Hand carved of solid wood.
WORKMANSHIP—The best. All doors sanded and polished ready for oil finish. Strong and durable; will not warp or check under ordinary conditions.
*White soft Western spruce pine, superior to Northern white pine.

Strictly "A" Grade or No. 1 Quality Doors With Wide Stiles

JEFFERSON, 1⅜ in. thick No. 63B602 Glazed as Illustrated	Sizes of Jefferson and Scott Doors Width Ft. In.	Height Ft. In.	SCOTT, 1⅜ in. thick No. 63B408 Glazed as Illustrated	No. 63B428 Glazed Clear D. S. Glass	Approximate Shipping Weight of all Doors on this Page, Pounds	ADAMS, 1⅜ inches thick No. 63B604 Glazed as Illustrated	No. 63B624 Glazed Clear D. S. Glass	Sizes of Adams and Buchanan Doors Width Ft. In.	Height Ft. In.	BUCHANAN, 1⅜ in. thick No. 63B807 Glazed as Illustrated
$3.40	2 6	6 6	$3.50	$3.35	58	$3.20	$3.05	2 6	6 6	$3.10
3.45	2 8	6 8	3.65	3.50	62	3.35	3.20	2 8	6 8	3.25
3.95	2 10	6 10	4.10	3.95	65	3.75	3.60	2 10	6 10	3.70
4.00	2 8	7 0	4.15	4.00	67	3.85	3.70	2 8	7 0	3.75
4.25	3 0	7 0	4.50	4.35	70	4.10	3.95	3 0	7 0	4.00

NOTE—We furnish any of the doors shown on this page 1¾ inches thick at $1.00 extra in addition to the above prices. When ordering be sure to write the word "Special" after the catalog number.

WOOD—"A" grade *Nona white soft pine, thoroughly seasoned.

STILES—Extra wide.

PANELS—Heavy raised.

WORKMANSHIP—The best. All doors sanded and polished ready for oil finish. Strong and durable; will not warp or check under ordinary conditions.

*White soft Western spruce pine, superior to Northern white pine.

GLAZING— Jefferson / Scott / Adams / Buchanan — Sand blast designs. The Scott and Adams Doors can also be furnished with "A" quality double strength glass.

PACKING—Covered with tough paper and substantially crated.

GUARANTEED to arrive at destination in perfect condition.

We furnish only such sizes as are listed above. When ordering give catalog number, quantity, size and price.

QUALITY GUARANTEED

Strictly "A" Grade or No. 1 Quality Doors With Wide Stiles

POLK, 1⅜ in. thick No. 63B402 Glazed as Illustrated	Sizes of Polk and Van Buren Doors				VAN BUREN, 1⅜ in. thick No. 63B705 Glazed as Illustrated	Approximate Shipping Weight of All Doors on This Page, Pounds
	Width Ft.	In.	Height Ft.	In.		
$3.45	2	6	6	6	$3.35	58
3.55	2	8	6	8	3.50	62
4.05	2	10	6	10	4.00	65
4.10	2	8	7	0	4.05	67
4.35	3	0	7	0	4.25	70

TAYLOR, 1⅜ in. thick		Sizes of Taylor and Cass Doors				CASS, 1⅜ in. thick No. 63B308 Glazed as Illustrated
No. 63B506 Glazed as Illustrated	No. 63B566 Glazed Bevel Plate	Width Ft.	In.	Height Ft.	In.	
$3.40	$4.85	2	6	6	6	$3.45
3.55	5.20	2	8	6	8	3.65
3.95	5.90	2	10	6	10	4.10
4.05	5.95	2	8	7	0	4.15
4.25	7.30	3	0	7	0	4.40

NOTE—We furnish any of the doors shown on this page 1¾ inches thick at $1.00 extra in addition to the above prices. When ordering be sure to write the word "Special" after the catalog number.

WOOD—"A" grade *Nona white soft pine, thoroughly seasoned.

STILES—Extra wide.

PANELS—Heavy raised.

WORKMANSHIP—The best. All doors sanded and polished ready for oil finish. Strong and durable; will not warp or check under ordinary conditions.

*White soft Western spruce pine, superior to Northern white pine.

GLAZING— Polk / Van Buren / Taylor / Cass — Glazed as Illustrated, with sand blast designs. { Taylor Door is also furnished glazed with bevel plate glass.

PACKING—Covered with tough paper and substantially crated.

GUARANTEED to arrive at destination in perfect condition.

We furnish only such sizes as are listed above. When ordering give catalog number, quantity, size and price.

QUALITY GUARANTEED

Strictly "A" Grade or No. 1 Quality Doors With Wide Stiles

FREMONT, 1⅜ inches thick	Sizes of Fremont and Empire Doors			
No. 63B301 Glazed as Illustrated	Width Ft.	In.	Height Ft.	In.
$3.50	2	6	6	6
3.75	2	8	6	8
4.25	2	10	6	10
4.35	2	8	7	0
4.55	3	0	7	0

EMPIRE, 1⅜ inches thick		Approximate Shipping Weight of All Doors on This Page, Pounds.	
No. 63B333 Glazed as Illustrated, with Bevel Plate	No. 63B303 Glazed Clear D. S. Glass	Glazed Plate Glass	Glazed Other Glass
$7.05	$3.65	63	58
7.65	3.85	66	62
8.75	4.30	70	65
8.30	4.40	74	67
9.30	4.75	76	70

WINDSOR, 1⅜ inches thick	
No. 63B444 Glazed as Illustrated, with Leaded Crystal Sheet Glass	No. 63B404 Glazed Clear D. S. Glass
$4.10	$3.30
4.35	3.45
4.90	3.90
5.00	3.95
5.35	4.25

METROPOLE, 1⅜ inches thick		Sizes of Windsor and Metropole Doors			
No. 63B777 Glazed as Illustrated	No. 63B707 Glazed "A" Quality D. S. Glass	Width Ft.	In.	Height Ft.	In.
$3.00	$2.90	2	6	6	6
3.25	3.10	2	8	6	8
3.60	3.55	2	10	6	10
3.70	3.60	2	8	7	0
3.95	3.90	3	0	7	0

The Empire, Windsor and Metropole Doors can also be furnished with "A" quality double strength glass.

GLAZING— Fremont, Metropole } Sand blast designs. Empire - Bevel plate glass. Windsor - Leaded crystal sheet glass.

PACKING—Covered with tough paper and substantially crated.
GUARANTEED to arrive at destination in perfect condition.
We furnish only such sizes as are listed above. When ordering give catalog number, quantity, size and price.

NOTE—We will, if desired, furnish any of the doors shown on this page 1¾ inches thick at $1.00 extra in addition to the above prices. When ordering be sure to write the word "Special" after the catalog number.
WOOD—"A" grade *Nona white soft pine, thoroughly seasoned.
STILES—Extra wide.
PANELS—Heavy raised.
WORKMANSHIP—The best. All doors sanded and polished ready for oil finish. Strong and durable; will not warp or check under ordinary conditions.
*White soft Western spruce pine, superior to Northern white pine.

Strictly "A" Grade or No. 1 Quality Doors With Wide Stiles

HANCOCK, 1⅜ inches thick	
No.63B905 Glazed as Illustrated	No.63B925 Glazed Clear D. S. Glass
$3.20	$3.05
3.35	3.20
3.85	3.70
3.90	3.75
4.10	3.95

Sizes of Hancock and Madison Doors			
Width		Height	
Ft.	In.	Ft.	In.
2	6	6	6
2	8	6	8
2	10	6	10
2	0	7	0

MADISON, 1⅜ in. thick	
No.63B307 Glazed as Illustrated	No.63B327 Glazed Clear D. S. Glass
$2.95	$2.80
3.15	3.00
3.60	3.45
3.65	3.40
3.90	3.75

Approximate Shipping Weight of All Doors on This Page, Pounds
58
62
65
67
70

MONROE, 1⅜ inches thick	
No. 63B850 Glazed as Illustrated	No. 63B860 Glazed Clear D. S. Glass
$2.95	$2.85
3.15	3.00
3.55	3.40
3.65	3.40
3.85	3.75

Sizes of Monroe and Clay Doors			
Width		Height	
Ft.	In.	Ft.	In.
2	6	6	6
2	8	6	8
2	10	6	10
2	0	7	0

CLAY, 1⅜ inches thick
No. 63B407 Glazed as Illustrated
$2.95
3.15
3.60
3.65
3.95

NOTE—We furnish any of the doors shown on this page 1¾ inches thick at $1.00 extra in addition to the above prices. When ordering be sure to write the word "Special" after the catalog number.

WOOD—"A" grade *Nona white soft pine, thoroughly seasoned.
STILES—Extra wide.
PANELS—Heavy raised.
WORKMANSHIP—The best. All doors sanded and polished ready for oil finish. Strong and durable; will not warp or check under ordinary conditions.

The Hancock, Madison and Monroe Doors can also be furnished with "A" quality double strength glass.

GLAZING: Hancock } Sand blast designs.
Madison
Monroe
Clay..... Chipped glass.
PACKING—Covered with tough paper and substantially crated.
GUARANTEED to arrive at destination in perfect condition.
We furnish only such sizes as are listed above. When ordering give catalog number, quantity, size and price.

*White soft Western spruce pine, superior to Northern white pine.

QUALITY GUARANTEED

SEARS, ROEBUCK AND CO., CHICAGO, ILLINOIS.

"B" GRADE OR No. 2 QUALITY SASH DOORS

DU PAGE
1¾ Inches Thick

Sizes of Du Page and Metropole Doors				No. 63B797 Glazed as Illustrated	No. 63B787 Glazed Clear D.S. Glass
Width Ft.	In.	Height Ft.	In.		
2	6	6	6	$2.68	$2.48
2	8	6	8	2.86	2.68
2	10	6	10	3.30	3.15
2	8	7	0	3.30	3.15
3	0	7	0	3.60	3.45

If you do not intend using an oil finish or varnish on your front doors, you will find our "B" grade sash doors entirely satisfactory. The only difference between our "B" grade and our regular No. 1 grade is, the "B" doors contain a few defects, such as small sound knots, small sap stains, etc., which are not allowed in our No. 1 "A" quality doors, but if painted make a thoroughly reliable and satisfactory door. These doors also have wide stiles, but the workmanship and material are not quite so good as our No. 1 "A" quality doors.

METROPOLE
1⅜ Inches Thick

Approximate Shipping Weight of all Doors on this page, Pounds	No. 63B777½ Glazed as Illustrated	No. 63B707½ Glazed Clear D.S. Glass
58	$2.72	$2.61
62	2.90	2.80
65	3.30	3.25
67	3.35	3.35
70	3.65	3.60

DESPLAINES
1⅜ Inches Thick

Sizes of Des Plaines and Fox Doors				No. 63B995 Glazed as Illustrated	No. 63B985 Glazed Clear D.S. Glass
Width Ft.	In.	Height Ft.	In.		
2	6	6	6	$3.00	$2.85
2	8	6	8	3.10	2.95
2	10	6	10	3.55	3.45
3	0	7	0	3.60	3.50
				3.75	3.60

FOX
1⅜ Inches Thick

No. 63B895 Glazed as Illustrated	No. 63B875 Glazed Clear D.S. Glass
$2.80	$2.73
2.90	2.80
3.45	3.35
3.50	3.45

Our DuPage, Metropole, Desplaines and Fox Doors are glazed, as illustrated above, with neat sand blast designs. These four doors can also be furnished in "A" quality double strength glass. The doors are carefully crated and we guarantee them to arrive at destination in perfect condition. We furnish only such sizes as are listed above. When ordering give catalog number, quantity, size and price. Doors shown on this page can be furnished 1¾ inches thick for $1.00 extra.

LOW GRADE PAINTED AND GRAINED SASH DOORS

Grained to Imitate Oak.

Grained to Imitate Oak.

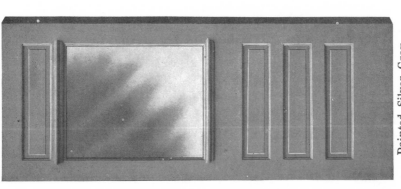

Painted Silver Gray.

Painted Silver Gray.

RHINE 1⅜ Inches Thick No. 63B6700 Glazed Clear S.S. Glass	Sizes of Rhine and Amazon Doors				AMAZON 1⅜ Inches Thick No. 63B6704 Glazed Clear S.S. Glass	Approximate Shipping Weight of All Doors on This Page, Pounds
	Width Ft.	Width In.	Height Ft.	Height In.		
$1.92	2	6	6	6	$1.99	58
2.01	2	8	6	8	2.10	62
2.24	2	10	6	10	2.33	65
2.27	2	0	7	0	2.35	67
2.31	3				2.50	70

NILE 1⅜ Inches Thick No. 63B6626 Glazed Clear S.S. Glass	Sizes of Nile and Hudson Doors				HUDSON 1⅜ Inches Thick No. 63B6624 Glazed Clear S.S. Glass
	Width Ft.	Width In.	Height Ft.	Height In.	
$2.05	2	6	6	6	$2.13
2.14	2	8	6	8	2.22
2.37	2	10	6	10	2.46
2.45	2	0	7	0	2.48
2.55	3				2.54

STANDARD GRADE PAINTED AND GRAINED SASH DOORS

The four doors shown on this page are the same grade of painted and grained doors as are being furnished by some of the leading retail dealers, wholesale dealers and jobbers throughout the country as nice grade of doors.

They are in reality made of No. 4 or "D" quality stock, containing large knots and defects. These knots and defects are not covered with the same care we exercise in painting and graining our HIGH GRADE doors, but if you just want a cheap door and are not particular about the appearance, these doors will answer your purpose.

Even in these low grade doors we aim to turn out a better door than is being furnished by most dealers, but we do not represent the doors to our customers as being good painted and grained doors.

If you want a really fine painted and grained sash door and one that you need never feel ashamed of, then refer to our line of HIGH GRADE painted and grained sash doors on pages 25 and 26.

QUALITY GUARANTEED

AS REPRESENTED.

FANCY PAINTED HIGH GRADE SASH DOORS WITH WIDE STILES

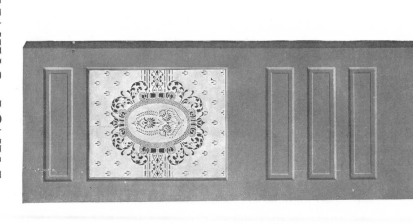

POTTAWATOMIE HIGH GRADE 1⅜ Inches Thick		Sizes of Pottawatomie and Pawnee Doors				PAWNEE HIGH GRADE 1⅜ Inches Thick		Approximate Shipping Weight of All Doors on this Page, Pounds
No. 63B6699 Glazed as Illustrated	No. 63B6698 Glazed Clear D.S. Glass	Width Ft.	In.	Height Ft.	In.	No. 63B6697 Glazed as Illustrated	No. 63B6696 Glazed Clear D.S. Glass	
$2.38	$2.29	2	6	6	6	$2.52	$2.38	58
2.51	2.41	2	8	6	8	2.65	2.50	62
2.76	2.68	2	10	6	8	2.90	2.78	65
2.81	2.71	2	8	7	0	2.95	2.81	67
2.87	2.76	3	0	7	0	3.01	2.87	70

CHOCTAW HIGH GRADE 1⅜ Inches Thick		Sizes of Choctaw and Iroquois Doors				IROQUOIS HIGH GRADE 1⅜ Inches Thick	
No. 63B6691 Glazed as Illustrated	No. 63B6690 Glazed Clear D.S. Glass	Width Ft.	In.	Height Ft.	In.	No. 63B6689 Glazed as Illustrated	No. 63B6688 Glazed Clear D.S. Glass
$2.37	$2.29	2	6	6	6	$2.56	$2.39
2.50	2.41	2	8	6	8	2.68	2.51
2.75	2.68	2	10	6	10	2.94	2.79
2.80	2.71	2	8	7	0	2.97	2.82
2.86	2.76	3	0	7	0	3.03	2.88

QUALITY GUARANTEED

WE SELL THE BEST PAINTED DOORS. The doors illustrated on this page are **heavily coated with two coats of silver gray paint applied with a brush by hand.** Before applying the first coat all knots are shellaced and other imperfections puttied. Being low priced doors they are sold in very large quantities for use in low priced residences.

THE DOOR UNFINISHED. Doors which are painted or grained are made from kiln dried stock and very durably constructed but, like other painted doors, are made from a much lower grade of material than used in our Nona Soft Pine "A" and "B" quality doors and as a result contain knots and other imperfections which are covered with shellac and putty before applying the two coats of paint. These defects in no way detract from the durability of the door. We therefore cannot guarantee our painted doors to be perfect as far

as the woodwork is concerned but we do guarantee to sell a better painted door than is usually produced by any other concern. If you are looking for a door without imperfections we would refer you to our large line of No. 1 Nona Soft Pine Doors, illustrated and described on all pages from 14 to 22, inclusive, or "B" Grade Nona Pine Doors, page 23.

GLAZING. All doors on this page are glazed with fancy design glass which is made by the sand blast process on double strength glass. The glass is embedded in putty and held in place by glass stops thus reducing the chance of breakage which so often happens by the slamming of a door. Contractors and builders claim that our painted and grained doors are just as good as "A" quality doors for painted work, as after the door is in position no one would ever know that it was not strictly "A" quality.

FANCY GRAINED HIGH GRADE SASH DOORS WITH WIDE STILES

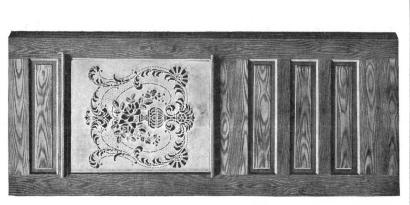

MOHAWK
HIGH GRADE
1⅜ Inches Thick

No. 63B6630 Glazed as Illustrated	No. 63B6631 Glazed Clear D. S. Glass
$2.53	$2.45
2.70	2.60
2.95	2.88
2.99	2.90
3.05	2.96

Sizes of Mohawk and Penobscot Doors

Width Ft. In.	Height Ft. In.
2 6	6 6
2 8	6 8
2 10	6 10
2 8	7 0
3 0	7 0

PENOBSCOT
HIGH GRADE
1⅜ Inches Thick

No. 63B6632 Glazed as Illustrated	No. 63B6633 Glazed Clear D. S. Glass
$2.63	$2.54
2.80	2.70
3.05	2.97
3.09	3.01
3.14	3.06

Approximate Shipping Weight of All Doors on This Page, Pounds

58
62
65
67
70

OJIBWAY
HIGH GRADE
1⅜ Inches Thick

No. 63B6634 Glazed as Illustrated	No. 63B6635 Glazed Clear D. S. Glass
$2.55	$2.49
2.73	2.63
2.98	2.91
3.02	2.93
3.98	2.99

Sizes of Ojibway and Sioux Doors

Width Ft. In.	Height Ft. In.
2 6	6 6
2 8	6 8
2 10	6 10
2 8	7 0
3 0	7 0

SIOUX
HIGH GRADE
1⅜ Inches Thick

No. 63B6638 Glazed as Illustrated	No. 63B6639 Glazed Clear D. S. Glass
$2.69	$2.54
2.88	2.70
3.13	2.97
3.18	3.01
3.24	3.06

WE SELL THE BEST GRAINED DOORS MADE. Compare our grained doors with those offered by other mill work concerns and judge for yourself which is the better quality. On page 35 we illustrate some of the finest styles of our grained doors which are reproduced from photographs of our regular line of doors. On page 34 we show and quote prices on the Standard Grade grained door, the illustration being reproduced from a photograph of the door made by one of the largest mill work concerns of this country. If you are interested in a good grained door, by all means refer to pages 34 and 35 which fully explain the differences in the qualities of grained doors.

THE WAY WE GRAIN. To produce the best we spare no expense in giving everything, including the paint and grain, the most expert and careful attention. Unlike other so called grained doors, we give the door two coats of paint and then carefully apply our graining, which is done by expert grainers, closely imitating the grain of an oak door. To bring out all details and, to produce a lasting luster we apply a heavy coat of varnish, giving it a finish unequaled by any other concern.

THE DOOR UNFINISHED. Doors which are grained and painted are made from kiln dried stock and very durably constructed, but like all other grained doors, are made from a much lower grade of material than used in our Nona Soft Pine Doors, and as a result, contain knots and other imperfections which are covered up by shellac and putty, but when finished in no way detract from the durability of the door. We therefore cannot guarantee our grained doors to be perfect as far as the woodwork is concerned but we do guarantee to sell you a better painted and grained door than is usually produced by any other concern.

GLAZING. All doors on this page are glazed with fancy designed glass made by the sand blast process on double strength glass. The glass is embedded in putty and held in place by glass stops.

HIGH GRADE PAINTED AND GRAINED SASH DOORS

DELTA, 1⅜ Inches Thick	
No. 63B6762 Painted and Glazed Clear Glass	No. 63B6764 Grained and Glazed Clear Glass
$2.03	$2.22
2.14	2.35

Sizes of Delta and Alpha Doors			
Width Ft.	In.	Height Ft.	In.
2	6	6	6
2	8	6	8

ALPHA, 1⅜ Inches Thick	
No. 63B6766 Painted and Glazed Chip as Illustrated	No. 63B6767 Grained and Glazed Chip as Illustrated
$2.44	$2.64
2.63	2.82

Approximate Shipping Weight of All Doors on This Page, Pounds
58
62

BETA, 1⅜ Inches Thick	
No. 63B6754 Painted and Glazed Clear S. S. Glass	No. 63B6756 Grained and Glazed Clear S. S. Glass
$2.11	$2.30
2.18	2.37

Sizes of Beta and Omega Doors			
Width Ft.	In.	Height Ft.	In.
2	6	6	6
2	8	6	8

OMEGA, 1⅜ Inches Thick	
No. 63B6770 Painted and Glazed as Illustrated	No. 63B6771 Grained and Glazed as Illustrated
$2.30	$2.50
2.43	2.63

UNIVERSAL DESIGNS OF PAINTED AND GRAINED SASH DOORS.

They are constructed of the same stock and are of the same general description as the high grade painted and grained doors described on the two preceding pages, except glass is puttied instead of being fastened with bead stops. We have these doors in only the two sizes listed and cannot furnish other sizes. The Delta Door is glazed with single strength glass, which is plenty strong enough for this size glass. Alpha Door is glazed with double strength chip glass. Beta Door glazed with clear single strength glass. Our Omega Door is glazed with designed glass, made by the sand blast process on double strength glass. Most dealers use single strength glass on doors of this design. Our aim is, that goods purchased from Sears, Roebuck and Co. shall be better, grade for grade, than can be procured from regular dealers, and at the same time lower in price.

PAINTED STORM DOORS

GRAINED STORM DOORS

QUALITY GUARANTEED

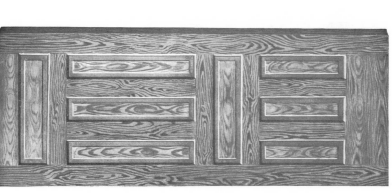

ZERO, 1⅛ Inches Thick	SIZES				JACK FROST, 1⅛ Inches Thick		Approximate Shipping Weight of All Doors on This Page, Pounds
No. 63B6806	Width		Height		No. 63B6800 Glazed D. S. Glass	No. 63B6802 Glazed Chipped or Frosted Glass	
	Ft.	In.	Ft.	In.			
$1.45	2	6¾	6	7	$2.18	$2.36	58
1.49	2	8¾	6	9	2.30	2.50	62
1.67	2	10¾	6	11	2.54	2.76	65
1.72	2	8¾	7	1	2.64	2.90	67
1.73	3	0¾	7	1			70

Storm Doors, such as we illustrate on this page, will more than save their cost during the first cold season, as they are great fuel savers. No house is complete without them. If you are building a house be sure to buy your storm doors when you place your order for the other items in mill work, as it costs little to fit them while the carpenter is still on the job. **The prices we name for these doors are very low, in fact,** they cost you but a trifle more than the ordinary batten doors.

Our Zero and Jack Frost Doors, as illustrated above, are **manufactured from kiln dried white pine** having sound knots and other imperfections, but have no defects which will affect their durability or appearance. The painted doors are attractively hand painted with two coats of silver gray paint after the knots are shellaced and the defects puttied. Our Jack Frost Door is glazed with clear "A" quality double strength glass or chipped glass. These doors are only sold in sizes as specified above.

BLIZZARD, 1⅛ Inches Thick	MEDICINE HAT, 1⅛ Inches Thick		SIZES			
No. 63B6807	No. 63B6801 Glazed D. S. Glass	No. 63B6803 Glazed Chipped or Frosted Glass	Width		Height	
			Ft.	In.	Ft.	In.
$1.65	$2.37	$2.56	2	6¾	6	7
1.69	2.50	2.70	2	8¾	6	9
1.87	2.70	2.96	2	10¾	6	11
1.92	2.74	2.99	2	8¾	7	1
1.93	2.83	3.10	3	0¾	7	1

Our Blizzard and Medicine Hat Grained Doors, illustrated above, are **manufactured from kiln dried white pine stock,** having some sound knots and other imperfections, but have no defects that affect their durability or appearance. These doors are highest grade grained doors, being attractively grained, as shown in the illustration above. Like all our grained doors, they are painted with two heavy coats of paint after all knots are shellaced and defects puttied, and then varnished, bringing out all details of the grain, making a good imitation of red oak.

Our Medicine Hat Door, as illustrated above, is glazed with clear "A" quality double strength glass. We furnish these doors only in the sizes specified above.

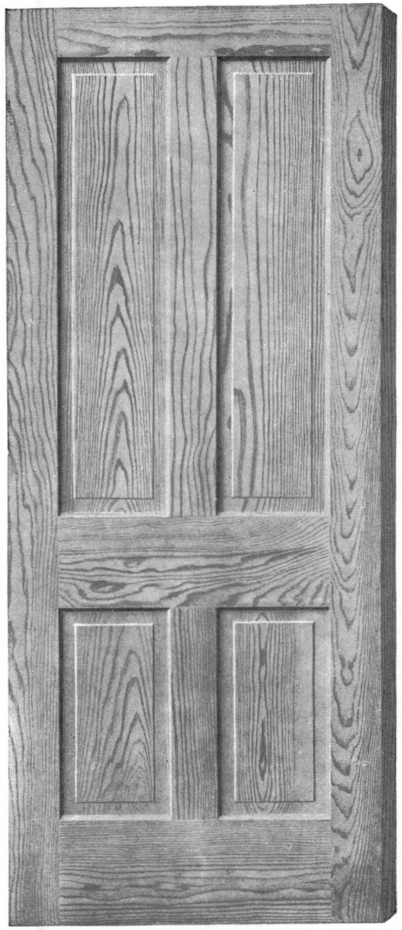

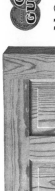

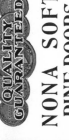

FOUR-PANEL

QUALITY GUARANTEED

NONA SOFT PINE DOORS

No. 1 QUALITY "A" GRADE

ABOUT NONA SOFT PINE.

Nona soft pine is white, soft and easily worked. Doors made from this stock have no equal for strength and durability, for they will not check, warp nor shrink under the most severe conditions. The grain does not rise up and they are free from pitch and sap; perfectly adapted for either oil finish or paint.

Of special importance to you is the fact that the lumber used in our doors is first left in piles until it is thoroughly air dried and is then put through dry kilns and at no time is the drying process rushed. Lumber which is hurried into hot dry kilns when it is green or wet is literally cooked in the rush to get it sufficiently dry to make into doors. When treated in this way it is almost sure to crack and check and much of the natural beauty of the grain is absolutely destroyed. Our drying process is the natural process and there is a science in properly drying lumber which few people appreciate.

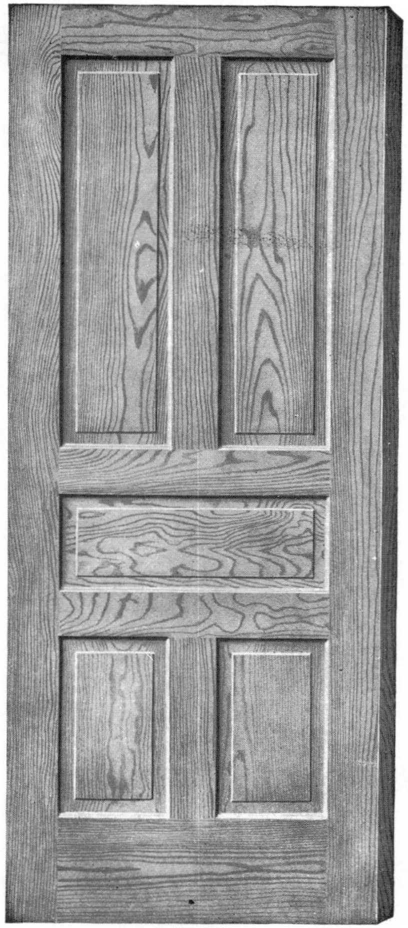

FIVE-PANEL

QUALITY GUARANTEED

NONA SOFT PINE DOORS

No. 1 QUALITY "A" GRADE

All our panel doors are O. G. sticking bevel raised panels, two sides, as per illustration, except the ⅞-inch doors which are raised panel one side only.

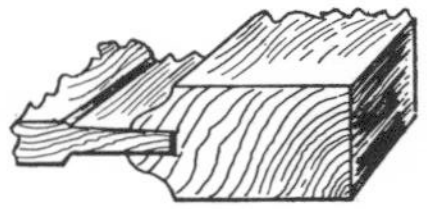

The low prices charged for these high grade doors are made possible by our plan of shipping direct to you from our factory. There is only one cost of handling and shipping and our small percentage of profit added to the actual factory cost and the freight costs you no more. Compare these prices with those you have paid or been asked in the past, ask your local dealer today if he will furnish you strictly "A" grade No. 1 quality doors at these prices. These are lower prices than quoted by any concern selling direct to the consumer.

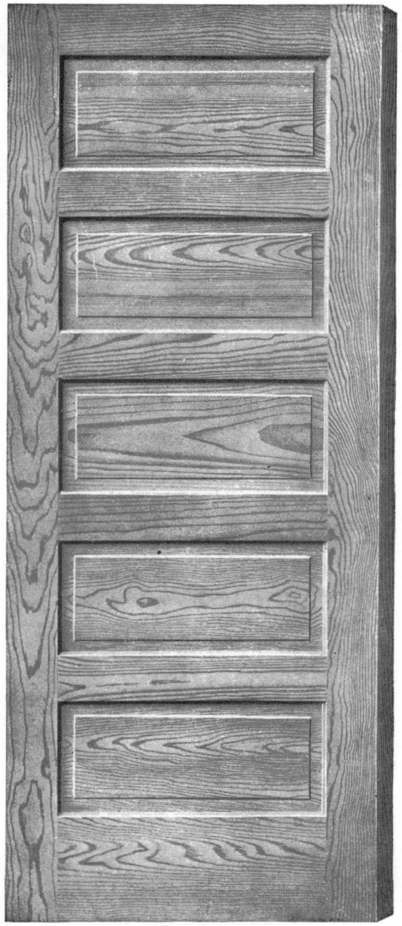

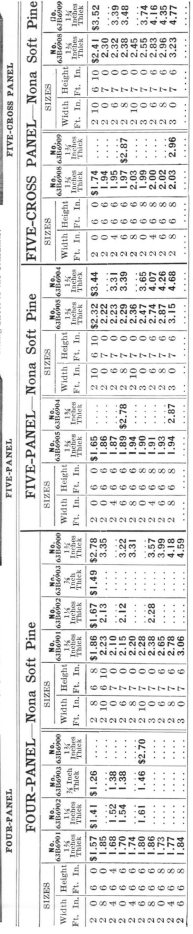

FIVE-CROSS PANEL

FOUR-PANEL—Nona Soft Pine

Width Ft.	Width In.	Height Ft.	Height In.	No. 63B6901 1⅜ Inches Thick	No. 63B6902 1⅛ Inches Thick	No. 63B6903 ⅞ Inch Thick	No. 63B6900 1¾ Inches Thick
2	0	6	0	$1.57	$1.41	$1.26	....
2	8	6	0	1.85	....	....	....
2	4	6	4	1.68	1.52	1.38	....
2	0	6	6	1.70	1.54	1.38	....
2	4	6	6	1.74	....	....	....
2	6	6	6	1.80	1.61	1.46	$2.70
2	8	6	6	1.86	....	....	....
2	0	6	8	1.73	....	....	....
2	4	6	8	1.77	....	....	....
2	6	6	8	1.84	....	....	....

Width Ft.	Width In.	Height Ft.	Height In.	No. 63B6901 1⅜ Inches Thick	No. 63B6902 1⅛ Inches Thick	No. 63B6903 ⅞ Inch Thick	No. 63B6900 1¾ Inches Thick
2	8	6	8	$1.86	$1.67	$1.49	$2.78
2	10	6	10	2.23	2.13	....	3.35
2	0	7	0	2.10	....	....	....
2	6	7	0	2.15	2.12	....	3.22
2	8	7	0	2.20	....	....	3.31
2	10	7	0	2.28	....	....	....
3	0	7	0	2.38	2.28	....	3.57
2	6	7	6	2.65	....	....	3.99
2	8	7	6	2.78	....	....	4.18
3	0	7	6	3.06	....	....	4.59

FIVE-PANEL—Nona Soft Pine

Width Ft.	Width In.	Height Ft.	Height In.	No. 63B6905 1⅜ Inches Thick	No. 63B6904 1¾ Inches Thick
2	0	6	0	$1.65	....
2	0	6	6	1.86	....
2	4	6	6	1.87	....
2	6	6	6	1.89	$2.78
2	8	6	6	1.94	....
2	0	6	8	1.90	....
2	4	6	8	1.91	....
2	6	6	8	1.93	....
2	8	6	8	1.94	2.87

Width Ft.	Width In.	Height Ft.	Height In.	No. 63B6905 1⅜ Inches Thick	No. 63B6904 1¾ Inches Thick
2	10	6	10	$2.32	$3.44
2	0	7	0	2.22	....
2	6	7	0	2.23	3.31
2	8	7	0	2.29	3.39
2	10	7	0	2.36	....
3	0	7	0	2.47	3.65
2	6	7	6	2.74	4.07
2	8	7	6	2.87	4.26
3	0	7	6	3.15	4.68

FIVE-CROSS PANEL—Nona Soft Pine

Width Ft.	Width In.	Height Ft.	Height In.	No. 63B6908 1⅜ Inches Thick	No. 63B6909 1¾ Inches Thick
2	0	6	0	$1.74	....
2	0	6	6	1.94	....
2	4	6	6	1.95	....
2	6	6	6	1.97	$2.87
2	8	6	6	2.03	....
2	0	6	8	1.99	....
2	4	6	8	2.00	....
2	6	6	8	2.02	....
2	8	6	8	2.03	2.96

Width Ft.	Width In.	Height Ft.	Height In.	No. 63B6908 1⅜ Inches Thick	No. 63B6909 1¾ Inches Thick
2	10	6	10	$2.41	$3.52
2	0	7	0	2.30	....
2	6	7	0	2.32	3.39
2	8	7	0	2.38	3.48
2	10	7	0	2.45	....
3	0	7	0	2.55	3.74
2	6	7	6	2.83	4.16
2	8	7	6	2.96	4.35
3	0	7	6	3.23	4.77

QUALITY GUARANTEED

OUR MILL WORK PLEASES HIS CUSTOMERS AND MADE A SAVING OF 20 TO 50 PER CENT.

Box 71, Zanesville, Ind.
Sears, Roebuck and Co.,
Chicago, Ill.

Gentlemen:—Yours received and in reply will say that the mill work ordered from you was all right and in good shape and pleased my customers in every instance at a saving of from 20 to 50 per cent.
Yours truly,
U. G. SMUTS.

OUR GUARANTEE

We guarantee these doors to contain less defects than the regular "A" grade or No. 1 quality door graded according to the grading rules adopted by the Wholesale Sash, Door and Blind Manufacturers' Association of the Northwest, which are the grading rules generally used by large manufacturers. We can make this guarantee for the reason that our Nona pine is unusually free from defects and that we use good grades of short leaf yellow pine for panels. If you find these doors are not as we claim, return them and we will return your money and also pay freight charges both ways.

ALL DOORS ON THIS PAGE

NONA PINE
STILES AND RAILS
WITH
SHORT LEAF YELLOW PINE PANELS

STRICTLY "A" GRADE No. 1 QUALITY.

ALL O. G. STICKING. HEAVY RAISED PANELS BOTH SIDES.

Made Especially for Oil Finish or Stain but Perfectly Adapted to Paint or Enamel.

The Nona pine used in the stiles and rails of these doors is fully described on page 29. Only the high grades of short leaf yellow pine are used in the panels. These doors will be shipped direct to you from our factory and you will receive bright, clean, fresh stock.

Our plan of shipping direct to you from the factory has cut out all extra expense and we are now offering you higher grade doors at lower prices than any other concern in the business. Compare our new reduced prices with those quoted by any other concern, compare them with what you have paid in the past. Remember our guarantee and decide for yourself if you can afford to buy your mill work elsewhere.

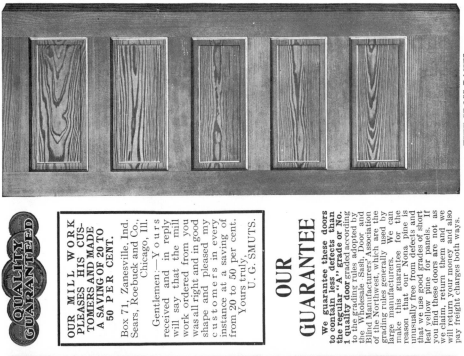

FIVE-CROSS PANEL

FIVE-PANEL

FOUR-PANEL

FIVE-CROSS PANEL—Yellow Pine Panels

Width Ft. In.	Height Ft. In.	No. 63B6852 1⅜ Inches Thick	No. 63B6847 1¾ Inches Thick
2 0	6 0	$1.80	....
2 6	6 6	2.00	....
2 4	6 6	2.01	$2.97
2 6	6 6	2.04	....
2 8	6 6	2.10	....
2 0	6 8	2.06	....
2 4	6 8	2.07	....
2 6	6 8	2.09	....
2 8	6 8	2.10	3.06
2 10	6 10	$2.49	$3.65
2 6	7 0	2.39	3.51
2 6	7 0	2.40	3.60
2 8	7 0	2.46	....
2 10	7 0	2.54	....
3 0	7 6	2.64	3.87
2 6	7 6	2.93	4.31
2 8	7 6	3.06	4.50
3 0	7	3.35	4.94

FIVE-PANEL—Yellow Pine Panels

Width Ft. In.	Height Ft. In.	No. 63B6851 1⅜ Inches Thick	No. 63B6846 1¾ Inches Thick
2 0	6 0	$1.71	....
2 6	6 6	1.92	....
2 4	6 6	1.93	....
2 6	6 6	1.95	$2.88
2 8	6 6	2.01	....
2 10	6 8	1.97	....
3 0	6 8	1.98	....
2 4	6 8	2.00	....
2 6	6 8	2.01	2.97
2 10	6 10	$2.40	$3.56
2 6	7 0	2.30	....
2 8	7 0	2.31	3.42
2 8	7 0	2.37	3.51
2 10	7 0	2.45	....
3 0	7 6	2.55	3.78
2 6	7 6	2.84	4.22
2 8	7 6	2.97	4.41
3 0	7 6	3.26	4.85

FOUR-PANEL—Yellow Pine Panels

Width Ft. In.	Height Ft. In.	No. 63B6850 1⅜ Inches Thick	No. 63B6845 1¾ Inches Thick
2 0	6 0	$1.62	....
2 6	6 6	1.86	....
2 4	6 6	1.74	....
2 6	6 6	1.76	....
2 4	6 6	1.80	$2.79
2 6	6 6	1.86	....
3 0	7 0	1.92	....
2 6	7 0	1.79	....
2 8	7 0	1.83	....
3 0	7 6	1.91	....

FOUR-PANEL

Solid Short Leaf Yellow Pine Doors

O. G. STICKING. RAISED PANELS TWO SIDES.

Short leaf yellow pine is **softer, contains less pitch,** has a more beautiful grain and is in every way superior to other kinds of yellow pine for the manufacture of doors. We use particular care in selecting and drying our lumber, as fully explained on page 29. These doors are **very carefully machined** and **all surfaces,** even including the bevel raise on the panels, are sanded by the best sanding or smoothing machines made.

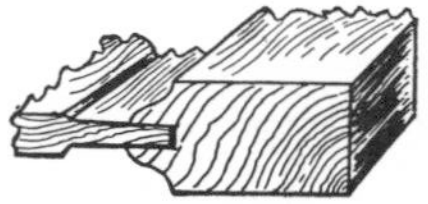

This illustration shows sticking and raise at panels.

FIVE-PANEL

Solid Short Leaf Yellow Pine Doors

We make two grades of yellow pine doors, No. I quality or "A" grade, and No. 2 quality or "B" grade. Our No. 1 quality doors have few defects and we **absolutely guarantee them to be better,** higher graded doors and to contain **less defects** than the doors graded by the regular published grading rules for yellow pine doors used by most manufacturers. Our No. 2 quality "B" grade doors contain defects not allowed in the No. 1 quality door, but no defects are permitted that will affect the lasting qualities in any way. We claim we can now furnish the best yellow pine doors on the market at the lowest prices direct to the consumer.

The prices on this page are the lowest quoted by any concern for doors of the same high quality. Compare them with any of the prices you now have and see if your local dealer can furnish the same high grade door for anywhere near the same price.

Remember our guarantee: They are better, grade for grade, than the regular commercial doors.

FIVE-CROSS PANEL

FOUR-PANEL—Solid Yellow Pine

Width Ft. In.	H'ght Ft. In.	1⅜ Inches Thick No. 63B6860 No. 1 Quality	1⅜ Inches Thick No. 63B6875 No. 2 Quality	1⅛ Inches Thick No. 63B6874 No. 1 Quality	1⅛ Inches Thick No. 63B6876 No. 2 Quality	No. 63B6877 ⅞ Inch Thick No. 2 Quality
2 0	6 0	$1.57	$1.31	$1.41	$1.17	$0.75
2 6	6 0	1.80	1.51	1.62	1.36	....
2 4	6 4	1.68	1.42	....	1.28	....
2 0	6 6	1.70	1.43	1.54	1.30	....
2 4	6 6	1.74	....	....	....	....
2 6	6 6	1.80	1.51	1.62	1.36	1.23
2 0	6 8	1.73	1.44	....	....	....
2 4	6 8	1.77	....	....	....	....
2 6	6 8	1.84	1.54	1.65	1.39	....

Width Ft. In.	H'ght Ft. In.	1⅜ Inches Thick No. 63B6860 No. 1 Quality	1⅜ Inches Thick No. 63B6875 No. 2 Quality	1⅛ Inches Thick No. 63B6874 No. 1 Quality	1⅛ Inches Thick No. 63B6876 No. 2 Quality	No. 63B6877 ⅞ Inch Thick No. 2 Quality
2 8	6 8	$1.86	$1.55	$1.67	$1.40	$1.27
2 10	6 10	2.23	1.88	2.13	1.78	....
2 0	7 0	2.10	1.77	....	....	....
2 6	7 0	2.15	1.80	2.12	1.77	....
2 8	7 0	2.20	1.85	....	....	....
3 0	7 0	2.38	2.00	2.28	1.89	....
2 6	7 6	2.65	....	....	....	....
2 8	7 6	2.78	....	....	....	....
3 0	7 6	3.06	....	....	....	....

FIVE-PANEL—Solid Yellow Pine

Width Ft. In.	H'ght Ft. In.	1⅜ Inches Thick No. 63B6862 No. 1 Quality	1⅜ Inches Thick No. 63B6878 No. 2 Quality
2 0	6 0	$1.65	$1.39
2 0	6 6	1.86	1.57
2 6	6 6	1.89	1.59
2 0	6 8	1.90	1.61
2 4	6 8	1.91	....
2 6	6 8	1.93	1.62
2 8	6 8	1.94	1.63
....	....	....	....

Width Ft. In.	H'ght Ft. In.	1⅜ Inches Thick No. 63B6862 No. 1 Quality	1⅜ Inches Thick No. 63B6878 No. 2 Quality
2 10	6 10	$2.32	$1.96
2 0	7 0	2.22	....
2 6	7 0	2.23	1.88
2 8	7 0	2.30	1.93
3 0	7 0	2.47	2.08
2 6	7 6	2.74	....
2 8	7 6	2.87	....
3 0	7 6	3.15	....

FIVE-CROSS PANEL—Solid Yellow Pine

Width Ft. In.	H'ght Ft. In.	1⅜ Inches Thick No. 63B6864 No. 1 Quality	1⅜ Inches Thick No. 63B6882 No. 2 Quality
2 0	6 0	$1.74	$1.47
2 0	6 6	1.94	1.65
2 6	6 6	1.97	1.67
2 0	6 8	1.99	1.69
2 4	6 8	2.00	....
2 6	6 8	2.02	1.70
2 8	6 8	2.03	1.71
....	....	....	....

Width Ft. In.	H'ght Ft. In.	1⅜ Inches Thick No. 63B6864 No. 1 Quality	1⅜ Inches Thick No. 63B6882 No. 2 Quality
2 10	6 10	$2.41	$2.04
2 0	7 0	2.31	....
2 6	7 0	2.32	1.96
2 8	7 0	2 40	2.01
3 0	7 0	2.55	2.16
2 6	7 6	2.83	....
2 8	7 6	2.96	....
3 0	7 6	3.23	....

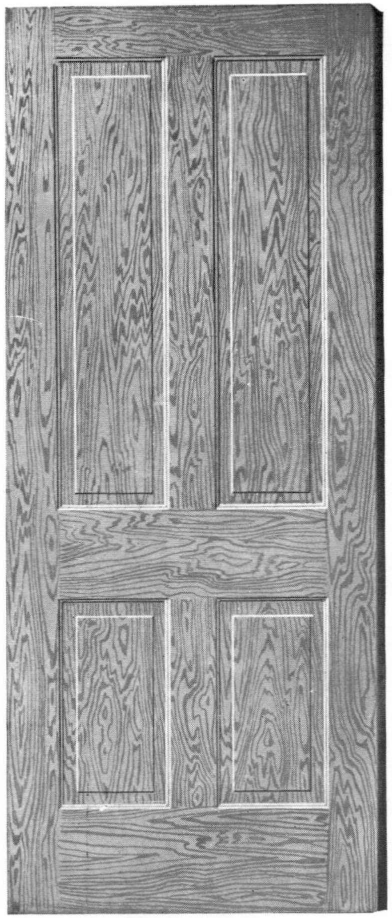

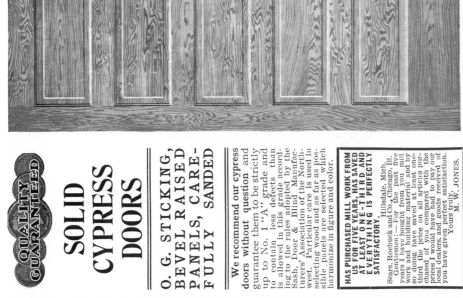

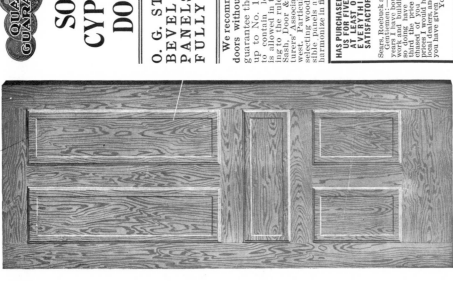

FOUR-PANEL

QUALITY GUARANTEED

SOLID CYPRESS DOORS

O. G. STICKING, BEVEL RAISED PANELS, CAREFULLY SANDED

We carry in stock a large assortment of high grade cypress doors. The cypress lumber which we use is put in lumber piles until it is thoroughly air dried and is then passed through our dry kilns and treated until it is in perfect condition for the manufacture of doors. Cypress is noted for its beautiful grain and its durability. This wood is not susceptible to climatic conditions and is a wood which is used to a great extent in the parts of the country where it is damp, such as along the seashore, many parts of the South and along the Great Lakes. Cypress takes a beautiful finish and can be stained or finished natural.

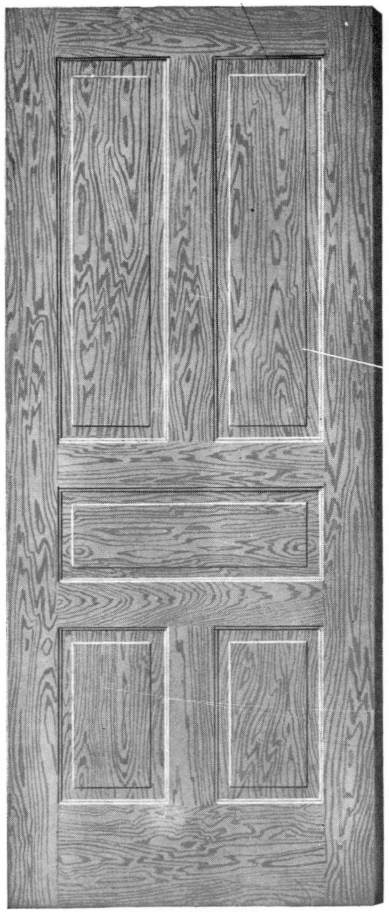

FIVE-PANEL

QUALITY GUARANTEED

SOLID CYPRESS DOORS

O. G. STICKING, BEVEL RAISED PANELS, CAREFULLY SANDED

We recommend our cypress doors without question and guarantee them to be strictly up to No. 1 "A" grade and to contain less defects than is allowed in this grade according to the rules adopted by the Sash, Door & Blind Manufacturers' Association of the Northwest. Particular care is used in selecting wood and as far as possible panels are selected which harmonize in figure and color.

HAS PURCHASED MILL WORK FROM US FOR FIVE YEARS, HAS SAVED AT LEAST ONE-THIRD AND EVERYTHING IS PERFECTLY SATISFACTORY.

Hillsdale, Mich.

Sears, Roebuck and Co., Chicago, Ill.

Gentlemen:—For the past five years I have bought from you mill work and building material and by so doing have saved at least one-third the price on all articles purchased of you compared with the prices I would have had to pay our local dealers, and goods received of you have given perfect satisfaction.

Yours truly,
M. W. JONES.

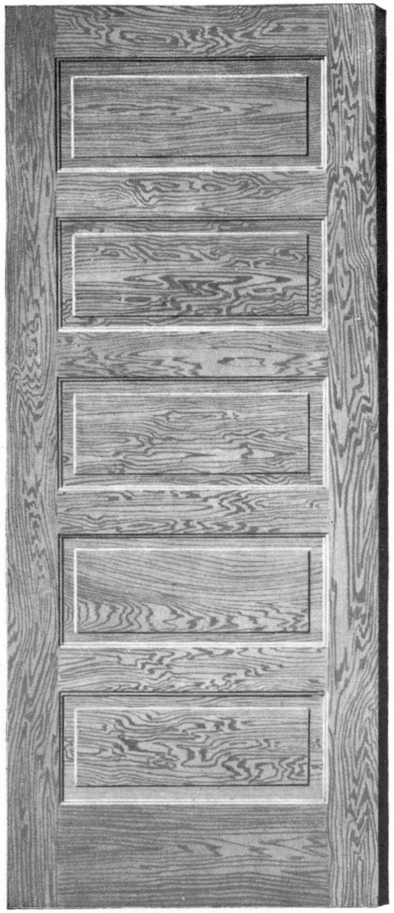

FIVE-CROSS PANEL

FOUR-PANEL—Solid Cypress

Width Ft.	Width In.	Height Ft.	Height In.	No. 63B6815 1⅜ Inches Thick	No. 63B6816 1¾ Inches Thick	Width Ft.	Width In.	Height Ft.	Height In.	No. 63B6815 1⅜ Inches Thick	No. 63B6816 1¾ Inches Thick
2	0	6	0	$1.65	....	2	8	6	8	$1.97	$2.93
2	6	6	0	1.89	....	2	10	6	10	2.35	3.52
2	4	6	4	1.77	....	2	0	7	0	2.21	....
2	0	6	6	1.78	....	2	6	7	0	2.26	3.39
2	4	6	6	1.83	....	2	8	7	0	2.32	3.48
2	6	6	6	1.87	$2.84	2	10	7	0	2.39	....
2	8	6	6	1.95	....	3	0	7	0	2.50	3.75
2	0	6	8	1.81	....	2	6	7	6	2.79	4.19
2	4	6	8	1.86	....	2	8	7	6	2.93	4.39
2	6	6	8	1.94	....	3	0	7	6	3.22	4.83

FIVE-PANEL—Solid Cypress

Width Ft.	Width In.	Height Ft.	Height In.	No. 63B6817 1⅜ Inches Thick	No. 63B6818 1¾ Inches Thick	Width Ft.	Width In.	Height Ft.	Height In.	No. 63B6817 1⅜ Inches Thick	No. 63B6818 1¾ Inches Thick
2	0	6	0	$1.75	....	2	10	6	10	$2.44	$3.61
2	0	6	6	1.85	....	2	0	7	0	2.33	....
2	4	6	6	1.95	....	2	6	7	0	2.35	3.48
2	6	6	6	1.97	$2.93	2	8	7	0	2.52	3.57
2	8	6	6	2.04	....	2	10	7	0	2.55	....
2	0	6	8	2.00	....	3	0	7	0	2.69	3.84
2	4	6	8	2.01	....	2	6	7	6	2.88	4.29
2	6	6	8	2.07	....	2	8	7	6	3.02	4.48
2	8	6	8	2.08	3.02	3	0	7	6	3.31	4.93
....		....		....	....	....		....		....	....

FIVE-CROSS PANEL—Solid Cypress

Width Ft.	Width In.	Height Ft.	Height In.	No. 63B6819 1⅜ Inches Thick	No. 63B6820 1¾ Inches Thick	Width Ft.	Width In.	Height Ft.	Height In.	No. 63B6819 1⅜ Inches Thick	No. 63B6820 1¾ Inches Thick
2	0	6	0	$1.85	....	2	10	6	10	$2.53	$3.71
2	0	6	6	1.97	....	2	0	7	0	2.52	....
2	4	6	6	2.07	....	2	6	7	0	2.54	3.56
2	6	6	6	2.08	$3.02	2	8	7	0	2.63	3.66
2	8	6	6	2.18	....	2	10	7	0	2.65	....
2	0	6	8	2.13	....	3	0	7	0	2.80	3.93
2	4	6	8	2.14	....	2	6	7	6	2.97	4.38
2	6	6	8	2.17	....	2	8	7	6	3.11	4.58
2	8	6	8	2.19	3.11	3	0	7	6	3.40	5.02
....		....		....	....	....		....		...	....

Cupboard Doors

Many people like to have cupboards built in their houses, as they are very convenient. We carry cupboard doors in stock in sizes listed below. 1¼ inches thick, made from the best quality of pine or plain red oak.

NOT RABBETED. RAISED PANELS.

SIZES			Thick-ness Inches	No. 63B6975 Nona Pine Price, Each	No. 63B6995 Plain Red Oak Price, Each
Width Ft. In.	Height Ft. In.				
1 6	2 6		1¼	56c	$0.69
1 6	4 0		1¼	63c	.75
1 8	4 0		1¼	87c	1.11
			1⅜	97c	1.18

Single Sliding Door

MATCHES FIVE-CROSS PANEL DOORS.

5 FEET WIDE BY 7 FEET HIGH, 1¾ INCHES THICK. HEAVY RAISED PANELS. ALL SURFACES CAREFULLY SANDED.

No. 63B6972 Solid Nona Soft Pine. Price, each..$7.10
No. 63B6973 Nona Pine Stiles and Rails, solid yellow pine panels. Price, each..............7.50

Woodlawn Single Sliding Door

MATCHES WOODLAWN VENEERED DOORS, PAGE 12.

5 FEET WIDE BY 7 FEET HIGH, 1¾ INCHES THICK. TWELVE FLAT PANELS. ALL SURFACES CAREFULLY SANDED.

No. 63B6974 Veneered Plain Red Oak.
Price, each........................$10.60
No. 63B6976 Veneered Birch (not selected for color). Price, each........................10.15

Side Lights for Doors.

Side lights are used in many sections of the country, as they give considerable light in a large hall which otherwise might be comparatively dark. We carry these in stock in "A" quality Nona soft pine, in the sizes listed below. One panel; top glazed; either "A" quality double strengthglass, or bevel plate glass, at prices as shown below. Thickness, 1⅜ inches.

SIZES			Glazed Double Strength Glass. Price, each	No. 63B6979	No. 63B6980 Glazed Bevel Plate Glass, Price, each
Width Ft. In.	Height Ft. In.				
1 2	6 6		$1.35		$2.89
1 2	6 8		1.40		3.03
1 2	7 0		1.52		3.25

China Closet Sash

The up to date builder is now putting china closets into his residences. They add considerably to the looks of a dining room or kitchen. We carry the sash in stock, made of Nona soft pine or plain red oak. 1⅛ inches thick and glazed in sizes listed below. Glazed with either plain or leaded glass.

SIZES			NONA SOFT PINE		PLAIN RED OAK	
			No. 63B6983 Glazed Double Strength Glass, Price, Each	No. 63B6985 Glazed Leaded Crystal Glass, Price, Each	No. 63B6986 Glazed Double Strength Glass, Price, Each	No. 63B6987 Glazed Leaded Crystal Glass, Price, Each
Width Ft. In.	Height Ft.					
1 6	4		$0.99	$1.85	$1.46	$1.61
1 8	4		1.12	2.15	2.35	2.66

GRAINED DOORS—STANDARD GRADE

ON this and the following pages we illustrate and describe grained doors in various sizes, furnished in two grades, our High Grade, the finest grained door made, shown on the next page, and the Standard Grade, which we illustrate on this page, the kind furnished by all dealers, but a door which in no way compares with our High Grade Door. Do not order until you have carefully read all we say about these two different grades, as every word will interest you.

Our Standard Grade Grained Doors

The Kind for Which Other Manufacturers and Dealers Ask as Much as We Do for Our High Grade Doors on Opposite Page.

Standard Grade Grained Doors, which we illustrate on this page, represent doors which were photographed from the actual goods furnished by some of the leading mill work concerns who advertise same as "good" grained doors at a low price.

Compare the two illustrations on this page with the illustrations of our High Grade Grained Doors shown on next page. Note how poorly the Standard Doors are grained compared with those illustrated on the next page.

THE REASON: Standard Grained Doors are made of No. 4 or "D" quality stock and contain large knots and imperfections of the worst kind. Mind you, these defects in the Standard Doors are not even puttied with sufficient care to cover these glaring defects. The graining consists of a mixture of cheap paint and shellac applied over a thin coat of primer, and when completed appears as though the work had been done with a broom instead of graining tools. Some concerns apply the coat of primer by simply dipping the door in a tank of paint, which, of course, leaves the paint in streaks and patches. Even in our low grade Standard Door we aim to give you a better grained door than those offered by other concerns, but recommend that you pay a little more and get a real grained door, one which will be in keeping with the best interior finish.

If you want the finest quality grained door made, one which will add to the beauty of your home, we recommend that you order our High Grade Grained Door, which is illustrated and described on the next page.

We guarantee quick and safe delivery to you and your order will be filled as soon as we receive it, and the goods will reach you securely crated and in perfect condition. The freight charges amount to very little, especially when compared with the immense price saving we make for you. Compare our prices with those of other manufacturers and dealers, and you will readily see what a big saving we can make you, especially so in this catalog, as our prices are lower than ever this year. We do not guarantee these Standard Grained Doors, but assure you they are the equal of doors sold by other dealers and manufacturers at much higher prices and advertised by them as "good" grained doors. Nevertheless, if you want a cheap door, Standard Grained Doors are a better quality at our price than you can procure anywhere else, and are the same grade for which others ask a higher price.

STANDARD GRADE FOUR-PANEL GRAINED DOORS

SIZES		No. 63B6890 1⅜ inches thick	No. 63B6891 1¾ inches thick	No. 63B6892 ⅞ inch thick
Width Ft. In.	Height Ft. In.			
2 0	6 6	$1.19	$1.12	$1.04
2 6	6 6	1.30	1.21	1.12
2 8	6 8	1.36	1.25	.....
2 10	6 10	1.53	.....	.....
2 8	7 0	1.56	.....	.....
2 8	7 0	1.57	.....	.....
3 0	7 0	1.58	.....	.....

STANDARD GRADE FIVE-PANEL GRAINED DOORS

SIZES		No. 63B6893 1⅜ inches thick	No. 63B6894 1¾ inches thick
Width Ft. In.	Height Ft. In.		
2 0	6 6	$1.25	$1.17
2 6	6 6	1.36	1.27
2 8	6 8	1.43	1.31
2 10	6 10	1.60	.....
2 8	7 0	1.64	.....
2 8	7 0	1.65	.....
3 0	7 0	1.66	.....

OUR HIGH GRADE GRAINED DOORS

The Finest Grained Doors on the Market Regardless of Price

IT PAYS TO BUY THE BEST.

Our High Grade Grained Doors illustrated on this page are in a class by themselves, and after comparison with the illustrations of the doors shown on the preceding page, you will not hesitate in ordering our High Grade Doors. These illustrations are exact reproductions taken from photographs of our High Grade Grained Doors. They are grained doors of quality, unlike any others.

Why our High Grade Doors are superior to all others. We select from the grades usually used for painting or graining purposes the best in the lot. We carefully shellac all knots and putty any defects. We then apply two coats of pure linseed oil paint which is permitted to become thoroughly dry.

How we grain our High Grade Grained Doors. Next we apply one heavy coat of graining color, of the best quality, imitating red oak. **Here is where the real graining takes place.** We employ only skilled grainers on our High Grade Grained Doors, and as a result our doors while only costing a few cents more than our Standard grades (grades like others sell) are in reality worth a great deal more. After this coat becomes thoroughly dry the doors are coated with a coat of good varnish, which gives luster to the finish, bringing out the grain clear and bright, and adds to the wearing qualities of the door. In the **Standard Grade,** shown on the preceding page, the extra coat of varnish is omitted and a small percentage of varnish is included in the graining coat, which gives a very unsatisfactory finish.

Consider the extra cost of making grained doors in this manner and then note how little more you pay for the highest class grained door compared with the prices asked for poor, unsightly grained doors.

We could quote lower prices on these doors by slighting the painting **and graining,** but we strictly adhere to our high standard of quality, furnishing you only the best workmanship on our doors. No dealer or manufacturer can quote you lower prices on doors of this quality, but if lower prices are offered you they are on doors of the same or similar quality listed on the preceding page, and we would be pleased to have you prove this statement to your satisfaction by ordering the doors you need at the lower prices quoted you; then order the same lot from us and when they reach you compare them side by side, and if in your opinion ours are not better in quality of wood, varnish, finish, appearance, etc., return them to us at our expense and we will return both the price and transportation charges you have paid.

HIGH GRADE FOUR-PANEL GRAINED DOORS

SIZES		No. 63B6940 1⅜ inches thick	No. 63B6941 1¾ inches thick	No. 63B6945 ⅞ inch thick
Width Ft. In.	Height Ft. In.			
2 0	6 0	$1.42	$1.33	$1.25
2 6	6 6	1.53	1.43	1.33
2 8	6 8	1.54	1.48	1.38
2 8	6 10	1.60	1.66	....
2 10	7 0	1.79	....	....
2 8	7 0	1.83	....	....
2 8	7 0	1.84	....	....
3 0	7 0	1.85	1.71	....

HIGH GRADE FIVE-PANEL GRAINED DOORS

SIZES		No. 63B6946 1⅜ inches thick	No. 63B6949 1¾ inches thick
Width Ft. In.	Height Ft. In.		
2 0	6 0	$1.48	$1.39
2 6	6 6	1.60	1.50
2 8	6 8	1.67	1.55
2 10	6 10	1.86	1.72
2 8	7 0	1.90	....
2 8	7 0	1.91	....
3 0	7 0	1.92	1.78

FOUR AND FIVE=PANEL PAINTED DOORS

COMPARE OUR PRICES
WITH THE PRICES YOU HAVE PAID FOR PAINTED DOORS

WE SAVE YOU MONEY
ON PAINTED DOORS AND GIVE YOU THE BEST

Do not buy a cheap grade of Painted Doors when a good grade can be had at our extremely low price.

We furnish Painted Doors in two qualities, our Special High Grade Door which is by far the best door on the market, and our Standard Grade Door which is exactly the same quality as is furnished by other dealers.

About our Special High Grade Doors. Realizing that the trade in general appreciate a good quality painted door, we have decided to have especially made a door which is far superior to any other door made or offered by any other concern; in fact, better than it would be possible for you to have made by a high priced painter. Painted and grained doors are made from "D" stock or No. 4 grade, which contains large sound knots and other defects, which will not seriously affect the durability of the door. We select from our "D" quality stock the best and use great care in covering all knots with shellac, putty all defects in a careful manner and give them two heavy coats of the best quality silver gray paint which **entirely conceals all defects**, producing a door second to none. This is the kind you get when you order our Special High Grade Painted Doors.

Our Standard Grade Painted Doors are exactly the same in every respect as those sold by the average dealer. They are made from second choice "D" quality stock, after selecting the best for our High Grade Doors (see page 34), and are covered with two coats of low grade gray paint and in no way compare with our Special High Grade Painted Doors, but we guarantee that they are equally as good as painted doors furnished by other concerns. We recommend that you specify our High Grade Doors, as we know you will find them worth 25 per cent more than the Standard Grade and they will cost you but a trifle more.

OUR HIGH GRADE FIVE-PANEL PAINTED DOORS

STANDARD FOUR AND FIVE-PANEL PAINTED DOORS
See Description Above.
WE DO NOT GUARANTEE OUR STANDARD GRADE PAINTED DOORS

	FOUR-PANEL PAINTED DOORS			FIVE-PANEL PAINTED DOORS

SIZES				No. 63B6926	No. 63B6927	No. 63B6928	No. 63B6929
Width		Height		1⅜ inches thick	1¾ inches thick	⅞ inch thick	1⅜ inches thick
Ft.	In.	Ft.	In.				
2	0	6	6	$1.07	$1.00	$0.92	$1.14
2	6	6	6	1.19	1.09	1.00	1.24
2	8	6	8	1.24	1.14	....	1.31
2	10	6	10	1.41	....	....	....

OUR SPECIAL HIGH GRADE PAINTED DOORS

OUR HIGH GRADE FOUR-PANEL PAINTED DOORS

SIZES				No. 63B6933	No. 63B6934	No. 63B6935
Width		Height		1⅜ inches thick	1¾ inches thick	⅞ inch thick
Ft.	In.	Ft.	In.			
2	0	6	0	$1.25	$1.16	$1.06
2	6	6	6	1.36	....	....
2	6	6	6	1.37	1.26	1.16
2	8	6	8	1.43	1.31	1.21
2	10	6	10	1.62	1.49	....
2	6	7	0	1.65	....	....
2	8	7	0	1.66	....	....
3	0	7	0	1.67	1.54	....

FIVE-PANEL PAINTED DOORS

SIZES				No. 63B6936	No. 63B6937
Width		Height		1⅜ inches thick	1¾ inches thick
Ft.	In.	Ft.	In.		
2	0	6	0	$1.31	$1.22
2	6	6	6	1.43	1.33
2	8	6	8	1.50	1.38
2	10	6	10	1.69	1.55
2	6	7	0	1.73	....
2	8	7	0	1.74	....
3	0	7	0	1.75	....

Colonial or Queen Anne Windows and Gable Sash

SUITABLE FOR ANY STYLE OF BUILDINGS.

BEAUTIFY YOUR HOME by using some of our Colonial or Queen Anne Windows. These designs are now being specified by the best architects in this country. You can always depend upon the quality of windows we furnish. We aim to produce the best quality of open sash, and we glaze with the best quality of glass and the highest grades of putty.

AT THE VERY LOW PRICES WE QUOTE for these fancy windows, which heretofore have been so exceedingly high in price, anyone with moderate means can well afford to beautify his home by adding a few of these artistic windows.

THE WINDOWS ON THIS PAGE are made specially to your order, therefore you must allow one week's time to enable us to furnish you a first class job.

SASH 1⅜ INCHES THICK, CHECK RAIL.

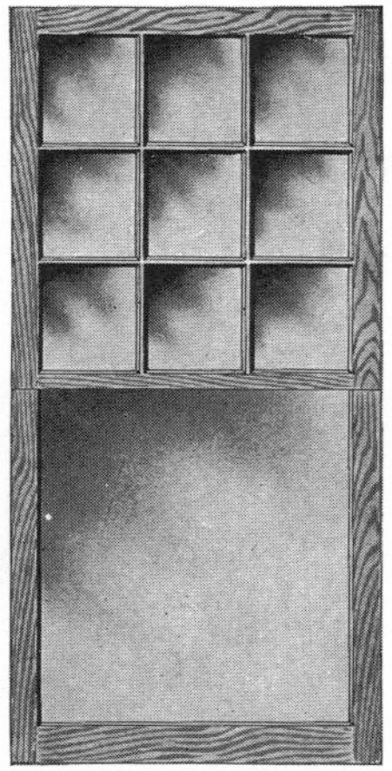

TOP AND BOTTOM SASH GLAZED WITH HIGH GRADE CLEAR PLAIN GLASS.

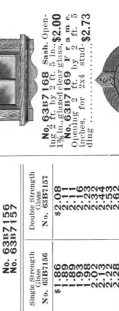

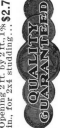

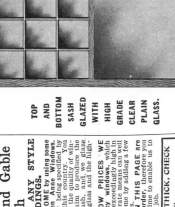

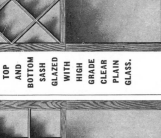

No. 63B7160
No. 63B7161

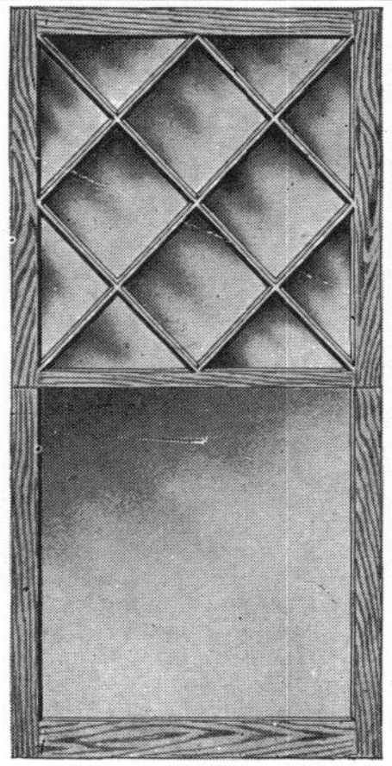

TOP AND BOTTOM SASH GLAZED WITH HIGH GRADE CLEAR PLAIN GLASS.

No. 63B7152
No. 63B7153

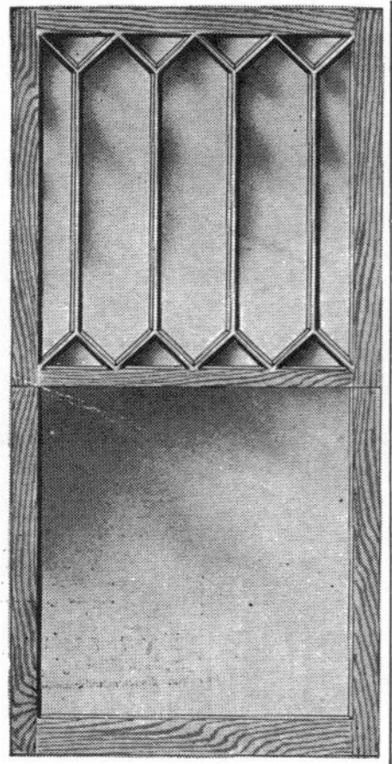

TOP AND BOTTOM SASH GLAZED WITH HIGH GRADE CLEAR PLAIN GLASS.

No. 63B7154
No. 63B7155

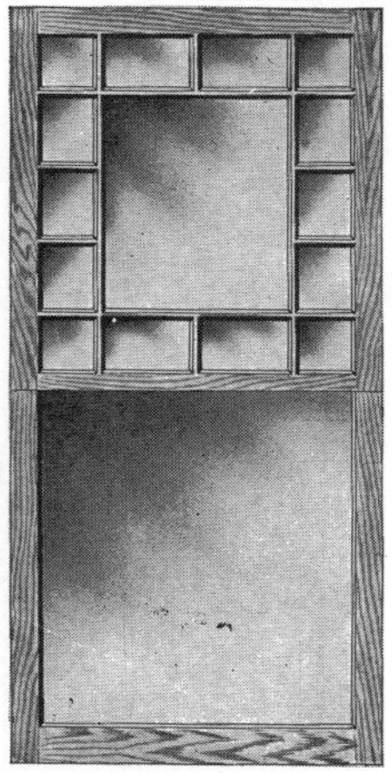

TOP SASH, CENTER GLAZED WITH HIGH GRADE CLEAR GLASS. BORDER IN ASSORTED COLORS. BOTTOM SASH, CLEAR PLAIN GLASS.

No. 63B7156
No. 63B7157

Size of Glass in Lower Sash	Size of Sash Opening Width Ft. In. x Height Ft. In.	Single Strength Glass No. 63B7160	Double Strength Glass No. 63B7161	Single Strength Glass No. 63B7152	Double Strength Glass No. 63B7153	Single Strength Glass No. 63B7154	Double Strength Glass No. 63B7155	Single Strength Glass No. 63B7156	Double Strength Glass No. 63B7157
20x20	2 0⅛ x 3 10	$1.26	$1.48	$1.76	$1.98	$1.76	$1.98	$1.86	$2.08
20x22	2 0⅛ x 4 2	1.29	1.51	1.79	2.01	1.79	2.01	1.89	2.11
20x24	2 0⅛ x 4 6	1.29	1.51	1.79	2.01	1.79	2.01	1.89	2.11
20x26	2 0⅛ x 4 10	1.33	1.56	1.83	2.06	1.83	2.06	1.93	2.16
20x28	2 0⅛ x 5 2	1.38	1.63	1.88	2.13	1.88	2.13	1.98	2.23
20x30	2 0⅛ x 5 6	1.42	1.72	1.92	2.22	1.92	2.22	2.02	2.32
20x32	2 0⅛ x 5 10	1.53	1.84	2.03	2.34	2.03	2.34	2.13	2.44
20x34	2 0⅛ x 6 2	1.62	1.93	2.12	2.43	2.12	2.43	2.22	2.53
20x36	2 0⅛ x 6 6	1.68	2.02	2.18	2.52	2.18	2.52	2.28	2.62
22x20	2 2⅛ x 3 10	1.28	1.54	1.78	2.04	1.78	2.04	1.88	2.14
22x22	2 2⅛ x 4 2	1.34	1.56	1.84	2.06	1.84	2.06	1.94	2.16
22x24	2 2⅛ x 4 6	1.34	1.58	1.84	2.08	1.84	2.08	1.94	2.18
22x26	2 2⅛ x 4 10	1.37	1.63	1.87	2.13	1.87	2.13	1.97	2.23
22x28	2 2⅛ x 5 2	1.42	1.70	1.92	2.20	1.92	2.20	2.02	2.30
22x30	2 2⅛ x 5 6	1.51	1.83	2.01	2.33	2.01	2.33	2.11	2.43
22x32	2 2⅛ x 5 10	1.60	1.94	2.10	2.44	2.10	2.44	2.20	2.54
22x34	2 2⅛ x 6 2	1.74	2.09	2.24	2.59	2.24	2.59	2.34	2.69
22x36	2 2⅛ x 6 6	1.77	2.22	2.27	2.72	2.27	2.72	2.37	2.82
24x20	2 4⅛ x 3 10	1.35	1.64	1.85	2.14	1.85	2.14	1.95	2.24
24x22	2 4⅛ x 4 2	1.37	1.67	1.87	2.17	1.87	2.17	1.97	2.27
24x24	2 4⅛ x 4 6	1.39	1.68	1.89	2.18	1.89	2.18	1.99	2.28
24x26	2 4⅛ x 4 10	1.43	1.70	1.93	2.20	1.93	2.20	2.03	2.30
24x28	2 4⅛ x 5 2	1.51	1.82	2.01	2.32	2.01	2.32	2.11	2.42
24x30	2 4⅛ x 5 6	1.57	1.95	2.07	2.45	2.07	2.45	2.17	2.55
24x32	2 4⅛ x 5 10	1.65	1.98	2.15	2.48	2.15	2.48	2.25	2.58
24x34	2 4⅛ x 6 2	1.75	2.12	2.25	2.62	2.25	2.62	2.35	2.72
24x36	2 4⅛ x 6 6	1.77	2.13	2.27	2.63	2.27	2.63	2.37	2.73
26x24	2 6⅛ x 4 6	1.48	1.85	1.98	2.35	2.56	2.93	2.08	2.45
26x26	2 6⅛ x 4 10	1.55	1.89	2.05	2.39	2.63	2.97	2.15	2.49
26x28	2 6⅛ x 5 2	1.67	2.03	2.17	2.53	2.75	3.11	2.27	2.63
26x30	2 6⅛ x 5 6	1.71	2.09	2.21	2.59	2.79	3.17	2.31	2.69
26x32	2 6⅛ x 5 10	1.74	2.11	2.24	2.61	2.82	3.19	2.34	2.71
26x34	2 6⅛ x 6 2	1.97	2.40	2.47	2.90	3.05	3.48	2.57	3.00
26x36	2 6⅛ x 6 6	1.98	2.42	2.48	2.92	3.06	3.50	2.58	3.02
28x24	2 8⅛ x 4 6	1.60	1.99	2.10	2.49	2.68	3.07	2.20	2.59
28x26	2 8⅛ x 4 10	1.69	2.05	2.19	2.55	2.77	3.13	2.29	2.65
28x28	2 8⅛ x 5 2	1.72	2.10	2.22	2.60	2.80	3.18	2.32	2.70
28x30	2 8⅛ x 5 6	1.74	2.13	2.24	2.63	2.82	3.21	2.34	2.73
28x32	2 8⅛ x 5 10	1.96	2.37	2.46	2.87	3.04	3.45	2.56	2.97
28x34	2 8⅛ x 6 2	2.03	2.49	2.53	2.99	3.11	3.57	2.63	3.09
28x36	2 8⅛ x 6 6	2.12	2.61	2.62	3.11	3.20	3.69	2.72	3.21
28x40	2 8⅛ x 7 2	2.39	2.77	2.89	3.27	3.47	3.85	2.99	3.37
30x24	2 10⅛ x 4 6	1.68	2.15	2.18	2.65	2.76	3.23	2.28	2.75
30x26	2 10⅛ x 4 10	1.81	2.29	2.31	2.79	2.89	3.37	2.41	2.89
30x28	2 10⅛ x 5 2	1.84	2.32	2.34	2.82	2.92	3.40	2.44	2.92
30x30	2 10⅛ x 5 6	2.04	2.58	2.54	3.08	3.12	3.66	2.64	3.18
30x32	2 10⅛ x 5 10	2.09	2.61	2.59	3.11	3.17	3.69	2.69	3.21
30x34	2 10⅛ x 6 2	2.12	2.63	2.62	3.13	3.20	3.71	2.72	3.23

Prices for windows on this page include both top and bottom sash glazed as illustrated.

For prices of window frames for these windows, see pages 54 to 56 inclusive.

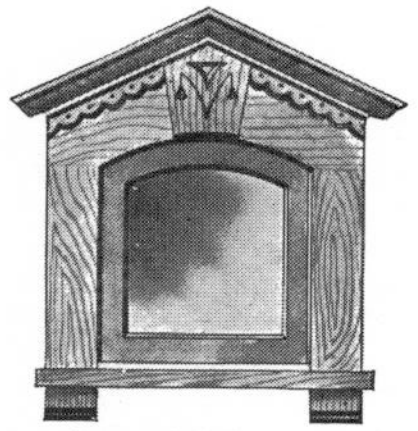

No. 63B7164 Sash. Opening 2 ft. by 2 ft. 5 in., 1⅜ in., glazed clear glass. **99c**

No. 63B7165 Frame. Opening 2 ft. by 2 ft. 5 inches, for 2x4 studding **$2.48**

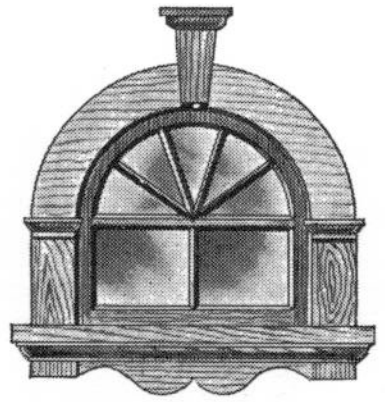

No. 63B7168 Sash. Opening 2 ft. by 2 ft. 5 in., 1⅜ in., glazed clear glass, **$2.00**

No. 63B7169 Frame. Opening 2 ft. by 2 ft. 5 inches, for 2x4 studding **$2.73**

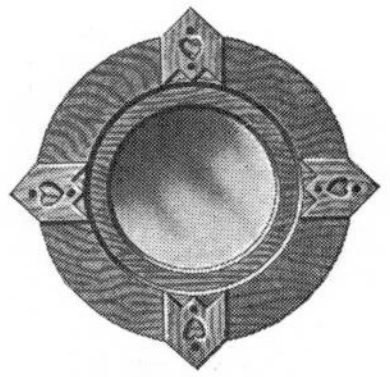

No. 63B7162 Sash. Opening 2 ft. by 2 ft., 1⅜ in., glazed clear glass.. **$2.35**

No. 63B7163 Frame. Opening 2 ft. by 2 ft., for 2x4 studding...... **$2.73**

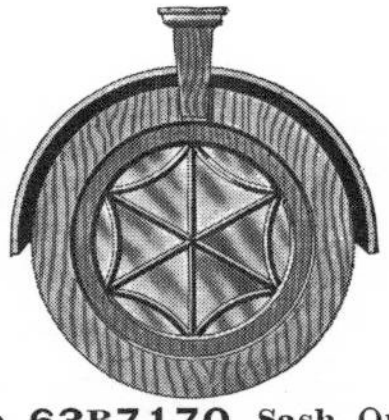

No. 63B7170 Sash. Opening 2 ft. by 2 ft., 1⅜ in., glazed clear glass.. **$4.35**

No. 63B7171 Frame. Opening 2 ft. by 2 ft., 1⅜ in., for 2x4 studding... **$2.75**

Prices on First Quality Windows, Frames, Storm Sash, Blinds, Etc.

NO CHANCE FOR MISTAKES. In the table below, the column of sizes under the heading "Sizes of Glass" shows the size of glass in inches in the window and all prices on the same line in the other columns refer to **Window Frames, Storm Sash** and **Blinds** to fit a window with that particular size of glass. For illustration, take a two-light window, glass size 24x28, price on a window glazed single strength is $1.05, price on a pulley window frame for this size window $1.73 and the size of the sash opening of this same window is 2 feet 4⅛ inches by 5 feet 2 inches. The price on a storm sash for this size window is $1.08 and for the blinds $1.11; weight of this window is 22 pounds, and the sash weight is 5½ pounds, which is found by d viding the entire weight of the window by four, and gives you the weight of each of the four weights required to balance the window. Blinds for two-light 12-inch and 14-inch widths are made in single piece.

FOR THE EXACT OPENING SIZE AND A MORE DETAILED DESCRIPTION REGARDING STORM SASH REFFER TO PAGE 41.

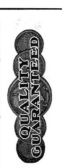

QUALITY GUARANTEED

OUR CATALOG SO SIMPLE TO ORDER FROM HE WOULD NOT TAKE $5.00 FOR IT.

Sears, Roebuck and Co., Chicago, Ill. Dansville, N. J.

Dear Sirs:—I want to thank you for the promptness with which you filled my order and the way you crated the goods. I never saw goods crated so well. I sent for sixteen windows and ten doors and one window was an extra large one, and everything came through in first class order. By giving you my order I saved about $13.00. The Mill Work Book you sent me gratis I would not take $5.00 for if I couldn't replace it. It was worth more than that to me in the saving of time. In making my window frames I went according to the book and never made the slightest mistake. I did not have to go at it the old way, but referred to the Mill Work Book and it was exactly correct. If my influence will do any good you will perhaps get more orders from Dansville, also get my orders in the future. If you want to use this as a testimonial as to your honesty and uprightness and fair and square dealing, you are at liberty to do so. Thanking you again, I am, Sincerely yours, G. W. VAN HOOSER.

P. S.—I think I already have an order for you for windows from a gentleman who is repairing a house. G. W. V H.

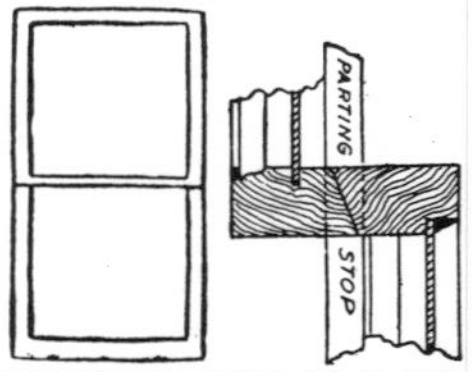

1⅜ INCH CHECK RAIL TWO-LIGHT WINDOWS

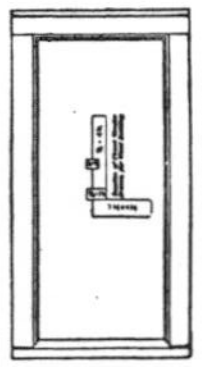

WINDOW FRAME INCLUDING PULLEYS

For other Frames, $1.00 and up, see page 53.

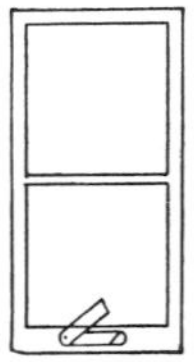

STORM SASH Ventilator 15 cents extra

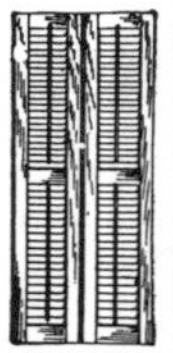

BLINDS 1 Inch Longer than Sash Opening

WEIGHT OF WINDOW AND SIZE OF SASH WEIGHTS REQUIRED

Four sash weights are necessary to hang each window. In the table below we give the size of each weight to be ordered, also the approximate weight of the entire window.

For Sash Weights see page 40.

SIZE OF GLASS	1⅜-Inch Thick Check Rail: Single Strength Glass No. 63B7186	Double Strength Glass No. 63B7187	Price, Per Frame Knocked Down No. 63B7955	For Details See Pages 54 and 55. Size of Sash Opening (Width Ft. In. x Height Ft. In.)	1⅛ Inches Thick, 1 Inch Wider, about 2 Inches Longer than Sash Opening: Single Strength Glass No. 63B7292	Double Strength Glass No. 63B7293	1⅛-Inch Thick Rolling Slats Price, Per Pair No. 63B7335	Approximate Wt. of Entire Window: Single Strength Glass Lbs.	Double Strength Glass Lbs.	Size of Each Sash Weight Required for Window Glazed: Single Strength Glass Lbs.	Double Strength Glass Lbs.
12x20	$0.65	......	$1.65	1 4⅛x3 10	$0.66	......	$0.68	12	..	3	...
12x24	.69	......	1.66	1 4⅛x4 6	.70	......	.69	12	..	3	...
12x26	.77	......	1.67	1 4⅛x4 10	.82	......	.71	13	..	3	...
12x28	.81	......	1.68	1 4⅛x5 2	.83	......	.73	14	..	3½	...
12x30	.83	......	1.85	1 4⅛x5 6	.86	......	.76	15	..	3½	...
12x32	.88	......	1.86	1 4⅛x5 10	.91	......	.80	15	..	[illegible]	...
14x20	.67	......	1.65	1 6⅛x3 10	67	......	.80	12	..	3	...
14x24	.69	......	1.67	1 6⅛x4 6	.71	......	.81	13	..	3	...
14x26	.78	......	1.68	1 6⅛x4 10	.83	......	.82	14	..	3½	...
14x28	.82	......	1 69	1 6⅛x5 2	.84	......	.86	15	..	3½	...
14x30	.83	......	1.85	1 6⅛x5 6	.87	......	.90	17	..	4	...
14x32	.88	......	1 86	1 6⅛x5 10	.93	......	.93	18	..	4½	...
16x20	.68	$0.82	1.67	1 8⅛x3 10	.68	$0.87	.90	14	15	3½	3½
16x22	.69	.85	1.68	1 8⅛x4 2	.71	.91	1.00	15	16	3½	4
16x24	.71	.92	1.69	1 8⅛x4 6	.72	.97	1.01	16	17	4	4
16x26	.79	1.05	1.70	1 8⅛x4 10	.84	1.12	1.09	16	17	4	4
16x28	.82	1.11	1 71	1 8⅛x5 2	.85	1.18	1.11	17	18	4	4½
16x30	.84	1.16	1.86	1 8⅛x5 6	.88	1.25	1.16	18	19	4½	4½
16x32	.91	1.23	1.87	1 8⅛x5 10	.94	1.32	1.20	19	21	4½	5
18x20	.72	.91	1.67	1 10⅛x3 10	.73	.95	.90	14	15	3½	3½
18x22	.77	1.00	1.68	1 10⅛x4 2	.80	1.06	1.00	15	16	3½	4
18x24	.80	1.05	1.69	1 10⅛x4 6	81	1.11	1.01	16	18	4	4½
18x26	.84	1.09	1.70	1 10⅛x4 10	.86	1.16	1.09	17	19	4	4½
18x28	.89	1.21	1.71	1 10⅛x5 2	.90	1.29	1.11	18	20	4½	5
18x30	.89	1.23	1.86	1 10⅛x5 6	.91	1.31	1.16	19	21	4½	5
18x32	.95	1.31	1.87	1 10⅛x5 10	.97	1.39	1.20	21	23	5	5½
20x20	.79	1.02	1.68	2 0⅛x3 10	.80	1.06	.90	16	17	4	4
20x22	.82	1.05	1.69	2 0⅛x4 2	.84	1.09	1.00	17	18	4	4½
20x24	.83	1.06	1.70	2 0⅛x4 6	.84	1.10	1.01	18	20	4½	5
20x26	.87	1.09	1.71	2 0⅛x4 10	.88	1.15	1.09	20	22	5	5½
20x28	.93	1.16	1.72	2 0⅛x5 2	.94	1.23	1.11	21	23	5	5½
20x30	.95	1.30	1.87	2 0⅛x5 6	1.00	1.31	1.16	22	25	5½	6
20x32	1.06	1.36	1.88	2 0⅛x5 10	1.10	1.45	1.20	24	27	6	6½
20x34	1.15	1.48	1.90	2 0⅛x6 2	1.19	1.55	1.49	25	28	6	7
20x36	1.21	1.58	1.91	2 0⅛x6 6	1.25	1.62	1.60	26	29	6½	7
22x20	.86	1.08	1 68	2 2⅛x3 10	.85	1.11	1.00	15	16	3½	4
22x22	.87	1.09	1.69	2 2⅛x4 2	.89	1.15	1.01	16	17	4	4
22x24	.88	1.12	1.70	2 2⅛x4 6	.89	1.16	1.02	18	20	4½	5
22x26	.90	1.14	1.71	2 2⅛x4 10	.92	1.23	1.10	19	21	4½	5
22x28	.97	1.23	1.72	2 2⅛x5 2	.99	1.30	1.11	20	22	5	5½
22x30	1.05	1.34	1.87	2 2⅛x5 6	1.09	1.44	1.16	21	24	5	6
22x32	1.12	1.46	1.88	2 2⅛x5 10	1.17	1.56	1.20	22	25	5½	6
22x34	1.25	1.61	1.90	2 2⅛x6 2	1.31	1.70	1.49	24	27	6	6½
22x36	1.27	1.73	1.91	2 2⅛x6 6	1.34	1.84	1.60	25	27	6	6½
24x20	.88	1.16	1.69	2 4⅛x3 10	.90	1.21	1.00	17	19	4	4½
24x22	.91	1.20	1.70	2 4⅛x4 2	.93	1.27	1.01	17	19	4	4½
24x24	.94	1.21	1.71	2 4⅛x4 6	.97	1.28	1.02	19	21	4½	5
24x26	.97	1.24	1.72	2 4⅛x4 10	.98	1.30	1.10	21	23	5	5½
24x28	1.06	1.35	1.73	2 4⅛x5 2	1.08	1.43	1.11	22	25	5½	6

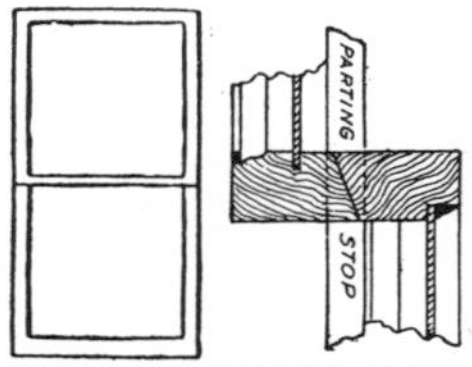

1⅜-INCH CHECK RAIL TWO-LIGHT WINDOWS

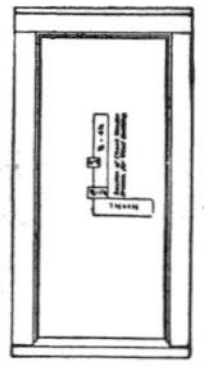

WINDOW FRAME INCLUDING PULLEYS

For other Frames, $1.00 and up, see page 53

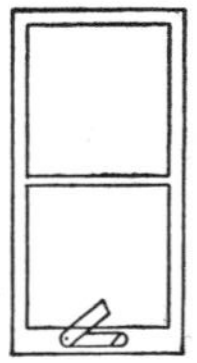

STORM SASH Ventilator 15 cents extra

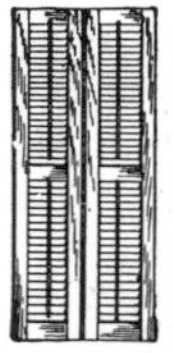

BLINDS 1 Inch Longer than Sash Opening

WEIGHT OF WINDOW AND SIZE OF SASH WEIGHTS REQUIRED

Four sash weights are necessary to hang each window. In the table below we give the size of each weight to be ordered, also the approximate weight of the entire window.

For Sash Weights see page 40.

SIZE OF GLASS	1⅜-Inch Thick Check Rail: Single Strength Glass No. 63B7186	Double Strength Glass No. 63B7187	Price, Per Frame Knocked Down No. 63B7955	For Details See Pages 54 and 55. Size of Sash Opening (Width Ft. In. x Height Ft. In.)	1⅛ Inches Thick, 1 Inch Wider, about 2 Inches Longer than Sash Opening: Single Strength Glass No. 63B7292	Double Strength Glass No. 63B7293	1⅛-Inch Thick Rolling Slats Price, Per Pair No. 63B7335	Approximate Wt. of Entire Window: Single Strength Glass Lbs.	Double Strength Glass Lbs.	Size of Each Sash Weight Required for Window Glazed: Single Strength Glass Lbs.	Double Strength Glass Lbs.
24x30	$1.12	$1.44	$1.89	2 4⅛x5 6	$1.16	$1.55	$1.16	23	26	5½	6½
24x32	1.19	1.49	1.90	2 4⅛x5 10	1.24	1.60	1.20	24	27	6	6½
24x34	1.29	1.63	1.91	2 4⅛x6 2	1.35	1.75	1.49	25	28	6	7
24x36	1.33	1.66	1 92	2 4⅛x6 6	1.36	1.76	1.60	27	31	6½	7½
26x24	1.01	1.35	1.72	2 6⅛x4 6	1.04	1.44	1.10	21	22	5	5½
26x26	1.10	1.42	1.73	2 6⅛x4 10	1.13	1.51	1.11	22	24	5½	6
26x28	1.19	1.50	1.74	2 6⅛x5 2	1.27	1.66	1.16	23	26	5½	6½
26x30	1.25	1.60	1.90	2 6⅛x5 6	1.31	1.72	1.23	25	28	6	7
26x32	1.28	1.63	1 91	2 6⅛x5 10	1.33	1.74	1.26	26	29	6½	7
26x34	1.50	1.90	1.92	2 6⅛x6 2	1.57	2.03	1.56	26	29	6½	7
26x36	1.51	1.91	1.93	2 6⅛x6 6	1.58	2.06	1.68	29	32	7	8
28x24	1.15	1.52	1.86	2 8⅛x4 6	1.16	1.60	1.10	22	24	5½	6
28x26	1.23	1.56	1 88	2 8⅛x4 10	1.28	1.68	1.11	24	26	6	6½
28x28	1.26	1.61	1.90	2 8⅛x5 2	1.31	1.72	1.16	25	28	6	7
28x30	1.27	1.64	1.92	2 8⅛x5 6	1.32	1.74	1.23	26	29	6½	7
28x32	1.47	1.87	1 93	2 8⅛x5 10	1.56	2.02	1.26	27	31	6½	7½
28x34	1.58	1.99	1.94	2 8⅛x6 2	1.66	2.15	1.56	28	32	7	8
28x36	1.63	2.10	1.95	2 8⅛x6 6	1.74	2.28	1.68	30	34	7½	8½
28x40	1.95	2.34	1.98	2 8⅛x7 2	2.01	2.41	1.93	33	37	8	9
30x24	1.24	1.66	1.88	2 10⅛x4 6	1.27	1.76	1.28	24	27	6	6½
30x26	1.35	1.79	1 90	2 10⅛x4 10	1.42	1.94	1.33	25	28	6	7
30x28	1.38	1.83	1.91	2 10⅛x5 2	1.43	1.95	1.43	27	30	6½	7½
30x30	1.55	2.08	1.93	2 10⅛x5 6	1.66	2.25	1.46	30	33	7½	8
30x32	1.62	2.11	1.94	2 10⅛x5 10	1.72	2.26	1.53	31	34	7½	8½
30x34	1.65	2.13	1.95	2 10⅛x6 2	1.74	2.28	1.61	32	35	8	8½
30x36	1.67	2.15	1.96	2 10⅛x6 6	1.75	2.29	1.71	33	37	8	9
30x40	2.08	2.63	1.99	2 10⅛x7 2	2.13	2.75	1.98	36	40	9	10
32x30	1.92	2.41	2.16	3 0⅛x5 6	2.01	2.60	......	31	34	7½	8½
32x32	......	2.44	2.18	3 0⅛x5 10	......	2.61	......	..	35	...	8½
32x34	......	2.45	2.19	3 0⅛x6 2	......	2.62	......	..	37	...	9
32x36	......	2.77	2.20	3 0⅛x6 6	......	2.97	......	..	38	...	9
32x40	......	3.19	2.30	3 0⅛x7 2	......	3.44	......	..	40	...	10
36x24	1.67	2.07	1.97	3 4⅛x4 6	1.78	2.23	......	27	32	6½	8
36x26	1.88	2.35	1.97	3 4⅛x4 10	2.00	2.51	......	28	34	7	8½
36x28	2.06	2.57	1.98	3 4⅛x5 2	2.17	2.76	......	30	35	7½	8½
36x30	2.07	2.60	2.20	3 4⅛x5 6	2.18	2.78	......	33	37	8	9
36x32	......	2.86	2.21	3 4⅛x5 10	......	3.09	......	..	38	...	9
36x36	......	3.11	2.23	3 4⅛x6 6	......	3.35	......	..	40	...	10
40x24	......	2.42	1.97	3 8⅛x4 6	......	2.59	......	..	35	...	8½
40x26	......	2.63	1.98	3 8⅛x4 10	......	2.83	......	..	36	...	9
40x28	......	2.66	1.99	3 8⅛x5 2	......	2.85	......	..	37	...	9
40x30	......	2.94	2.21	3 8⅛x5 6	......	3.16	......	..	39	...	10
40x32	......	3.14	2.22	3 8⅛x5 10	......	3.38	......	..	40	...	10
40x36	......	3.86	2.25	3 8⅛x6 6	......	4.15	......	..	42	...	10
44x30	......	3.41	2.24	4 0⅛x5 6	......	3.68	......	..	47	...	12
44x32	......	3.87	2.26	4 0⅛x5 10	......	4.18	......	..	48	...	12
44x36	......	3.94	2.28	4 0⅛x6 6	......	4.23	......	..	50	...	12
44x40	......	4.75	2,65	4 0⅛x7 2	......	5.12	......	..	52	...	13

IMPORTANT. The term "window" in these tables means two sashes (upper and lower) with glass. The prices shown in the columns headed catalog Nos. 63B7186 and 63B7187 include both the top and bottom sash, also the glass glazed and secured in the sash by putty and metal points.

Prices on First Quality Windows, Frames, Storm Sash, Blinds, Etc.—Continued.

NO CHANCE FOR MISTAKES. In the table below, the column of sizes under the heading "Size of Glass" shows the size of glass in inches in the window and all prices on the same line in the other columns refer to a window with glass of that size. For illustration, take a four-light window, glass size 10x20 price on a window glazed single strength is 73 cents, price on a pulley window frame for this size window is $1.68, and the size of the sash opening of this same window is 2 feet 1 inch by 3 feet 10 inches; the price on a storm sash for this size window is 74 cents and for the blinds 90 cents; weight of this window is 19 pounds, and weight of each sash weight is 4½ pounds, which is found by dividing the entire weight of the window by four.

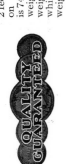

QUALITY GUARANTEED

SAVED $104.00 ON A MILL WORK ORDER OF $330.22.

Urbana, Ill.

Sears, Roebuck and Co., Chicago, Ill.

Dear Sirs:—Regarding the mill work will say the amount saved on Mr. Corson's bill was something over $100.00; about $104.00 as near as I can remember. That much against the best and more against others.

Yours very truly,
JOHN L. ALLMAN.

Note—Mr. Corson's order amounted to $330.22.

FOR THE EXACT OPENING SIZE AND A MORE DETAILED DESCRIPTION REGARDING STORM SASH, REFER TO PAGE 41.

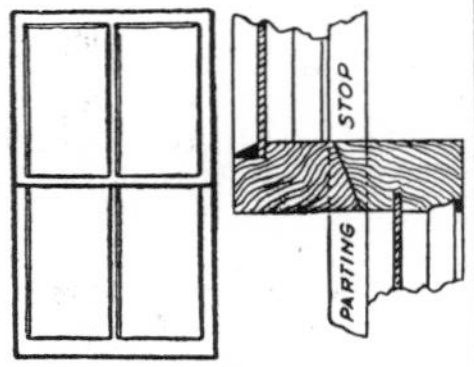

1⅜-INCH CHECK RAIL FOUR-LIGHT WINDOW

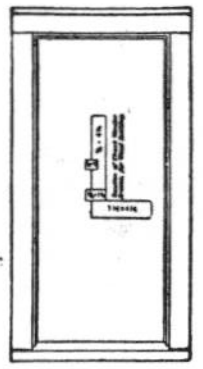

For other Frames, $1.00 and up, see page 53.

WINDOW FRAME INCLUDING PULLEYS

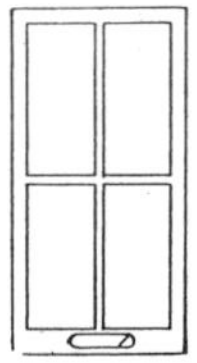

STORM SASH Ventilator 15 Cents Extra

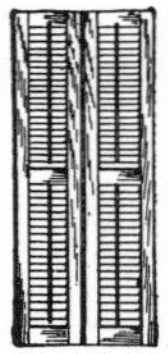

BLINDS 1 Inch Longer Than Sash Opening.

WEIGHT OF WINDOW AND SIZE OF SASH WEIGHTS REQUIRED

Four sash weights are necessary to hang each window. In the table below we give the size of each weight to be ordered, also the approximate weight of the entire window. For Sash Weights see page 40.

SIZE OF GLASS	1⅜-Inch Thick Check Rail: Single Strength Glass No. 63B7189	1⅜-Inch Thick Check Rail: Double Strength Glass No. 63B7190	Price, Per Frame Knocked Down No. 63B7955	For Details See Pages 54 and 55. Size of Sash Opening (Ft. In. Ft. In.)	1⅛ Inches Thick, 1 Inch Wider, About 2 Inches Longer than Sash Opening. Single Strength Glass No. 63B7295	Double Strength Glass No. 63B7296	1⅛-Inch Thick Rolling Slats Per Pair No. 63B7336	Approximate Wt. of Entire Window: Single Strength Glass Lbs.	Approximate Wt. of Entire Window: Double Strength Glass Lbs.	Size of Each Sash Weight Required for Window Glazed: Single Strength Glass Lbs.	Size of Each Sash Weight: Double Strength Glass Lbs.
10x20	$0.74	......	$1.68	2 1 x 3 10	$0.74	......	$0.90	19	..	4½	..
10x22	.79	......	1.69	2 1 x 4 2	.82	......	1.00	19	..	4½	..
10x24	.82	......	1.70	2 1 x 4 6	.83	......	1.01	21	..	5	..
10x26	.86	......	1.71	2 1 x 4 10	.89	......	1.10	21	..	5	..
10x28	.95	......	1.72	2 1 x 5 2	.96	......	1.11	22	..	5½	..
10x30	1.03	......	1.87	2 1 x 5 6	1.06	......	1.16	22	..	5½	..
10x32	1.15	......	1.88	2 1 x 5 10	1.18	......	1.20	23	..	5½	..
12x20	.81	......	1.69	2 5 x 3 10	.82	......	.90	19	..	4½	..
12x22	.89	......	1.70	2 5 x 4 2	.92	......	.96	19	..	4½	..
12x24	.94	......	1.71	2 5 x 4 6	.95	......	1.00	21	..	5	..
12x26	.99	......	1.72	2 5 x 4 10	1.00	......	1.10	21	..	5	..
12x28	1.05	......	1.73	2 5 x 5 2	1.06	......	1.11	22	..	5½	..
12x30	1.15	......	1.89	2 5 x 5 6	1.16	......	1.16	24	..	6	..
12x32	1.20	......	1.90	2 5 x 5 10	1.23	......	1.20	25	..	6	..
12x34	1.45	......	1.91	2 5 x 6 2	1.49	......	1.50	26	..	6½	..
12x36	1.47	......	1.92	2 5 x 6 6	1.49	......	1.60	27	..	6½	..
12x40	1.78	......	1.98	2 5 x 7 2	1.82	......	1.85	30	..	7½	..
14x20	.93	......	1.84	2 9 x 3 10	.96	......	1.10	22	..	5½	..
14x22	1.03	......	1.85	2 9 x 4 2	1.05	......	1.11	22	..	5½	..
14x24	1.05	......	1.86	2 9 x 4 6	1.05	......	1.12	23	..	5½	..
14x26	1.14	......	1.88	2 9 x 4 10	1.16	......	1.13	23	..	5½	..
14x28	1.20	......	1.90	2 9 x 5 2	1.21	......	1.16	24	..	6	..
14x30	1.28	......	1.92	2 9 x 5 6	1.31	......	1.23	26	..	6½	..
14x32	1.35	$1.92	1.93	2 9 x 5 10	1.39	$2.03	1.26	28	31	7	7½
14x36	1.63	2.29	1.95	2 9 x 6 6	1.66	2.32	1.68	30	33	7½	8
14x40	1.89	2.52	1.98	2 9 x 7 2	1.93	2.57	1.93	31	34	7½	8½
15x20	1.22	......	1.96	2 11 x 3 10	1.23	......	1.28	23	..	5½	..
15x24	1.25	1.54	1.97	2 11 x 4 6	1.25	1.58	1.29	24	27	6	6½
15x26	1.31	1.68	1.98	2 11 x 4 10	1.33	1.76	1.33	24	27	6	6½
15x28	1.37	1.83	1.99	2 11 x 5 2	1.39	1.92	1.43	25	30	6	7½
15x30	1.44	1.92	2.20	2 11 x 5 6	1.46	2.01	1.46	27	33	6½	8
15x32	1.50	2.04	2.21	2 11 x 5 10	1.54	2.15	1.53	29	34	7	8½

REPLACE THE OLD EIGHT-LIGHT AND TWELVE-LIGHT WINDOWS IN YOUR RESIDENCE WITH MODERN TWO-LIGHT OR FOUR-LIGHT WINDOWS.

We list below six sizes of two-light and four-light windows, which we carry in stock, to replace your old eight-light and twelve-light windows in the sizes most commonly used. These two and four-light windows will fit the old frames of the size mentioned. At a very low cost you can replace your old windows with the modern two-light and four-light design.

Two-Light Windows, 1⅜ inches thick.
Check rail made to fit old eight-light and twelve-light openings.

SIZE OF GLASS	Number of Lights	Outside Sash Measurement (Ft. In. Ft. In.)	Size of Old Window	Single Strength Glass No. 63B7201	Double Strength Glass No. 63B7202
21 x24	2	2 1 x4 6	8 lt. 10x12	$0.89	$1.13
21 x28	2	2 1 x5 2	8 lt. 10x14	.98	1.25
27½x24	2	2 7½x4 6	12 lt. 9x12	1.17	1.53
27½x28	2	2 7½x5 2	12 lt. 9x14	1.27	1.63

Four-Light Windows, 1⅜ inches thick.
Check rail made to fit old twelve-light openings.

SIZE OF GLASS	Number of Lights	Outside Sash Measurement (Ft. In. Ft. In.)	Size of Old Window	Single Strength Glass No. 63B7206
13½x24	4	2 7½x4 6	12 lt. 9x12	$1.07
13½x28	4	2 7½x5 2	12 lt. 9x14	1.20

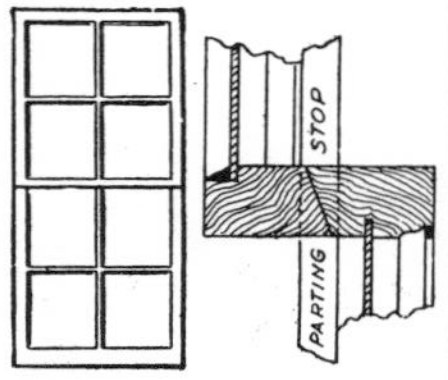

1⅜-INCH CHECK RAIL EIGHT-LIGHT WINDOW

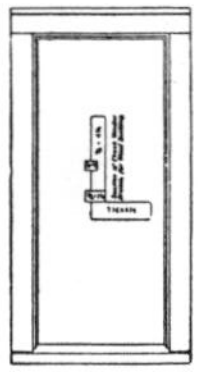

For other Frames, $1.00 and up, see page 53.

WINDOW FRAME INCLUDING PULLEYS

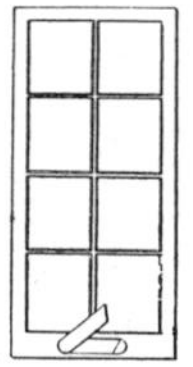

STORM SASH Ventilator 15 Cents Extra

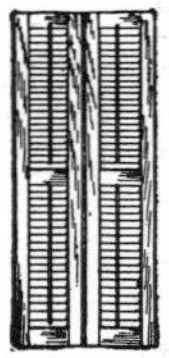

BLINDS 1 Inch Longer Than Sash Opening.

WEIGHT OF WINDOW AND SIZE OF SASH WEIGHTS REQUIRED

Four sash weights are necessary to hang each window. In the table below we give the size of each weight to be ordered, also the approximate weight of the entire window. For Sash Weights see page 40.

SIZE OF GLASS	1⅜-Inch Thick Check Rail: Single Strength Glass No. 63B7192	Price, Per Frame Knocked Down No. 63B7955	For Details See Pages 54 and 55. Size of Sash Opening (Ft. In. Ft. In.)	1⅛ Inches Thick, 1 Inch Wider, About 2 Inches Longer than Sash Opening. Single Strength Glass No. 63B7300	1⅛-Inch Thick Rolling Slats Per Pair No. 63B7337	Approximate Wt. of Entire Window: Single Strength Glass Lbs.	Size of Each Sash Weight Required for Window Glazed. Single Strength Glass, pounds
9x12	$0.80	$1.70	1 11 x 4 6	$0.80	$1.00	17	4
9x14	.88	1.72	1 11 x 5 2	.91	1.11	18	4½
10x12	.82	1.70	2 1 x 4 6	.83	1.00	18	4½
10x14	.91	1.72	2 1 x 5 2	.92	1.11	19	4½
10x16	1.05	1.88	2 1 x 5 10	1.08	1.20	22	5½
12x14	1.04	1.73	2 5 x 5 2	1.05	1.11	23	5½
12x16	1.15	1.90	2 5 x 5 10	1.16	1.20	24	6
12x18	1.28	1.92	2 5 x 6 6	1.32	1.60	27	6½
14x16	1.35	1.93	2 9 x 5 10	1.37	1.26	28	7
14x18	1.53	1.95	2 9 x 6 6	1.57	1.68	31	7½
14x20	1.68	1.98	2 9 x 7 2	1.72	1.93	35	8½

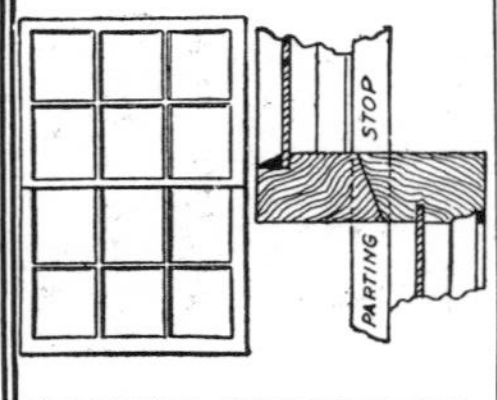

1⅜-INCH CHECK RAIL TWELVE-LIGHT WINDOW

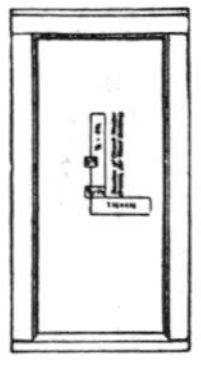

For other Frames, $1.00 and up, see page 53.

WINDOW FRAME INCLUDING PULLEYS

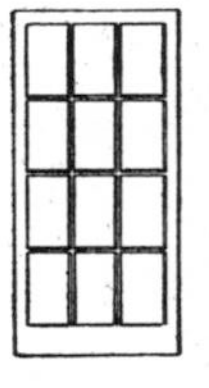

STORM SASH Ventilator 15 Cents Extra

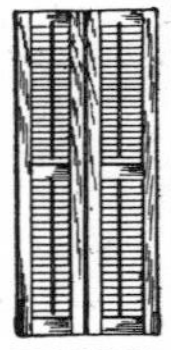

BLINDS 1 Inch Longer Than Sash Opening.

WEIGHT OF WINDOW AND SIZE OF SASH WEIGHTS REQUIRED

Four sash weights are necessary to hang each window. In the table below we give the size of each weight to be ordered, also the approximate weight of the entire window. For Sash Weights see page 40.

SIZE OF GLASS	1⅜-Inch Thick Check Rail: Single Strength Glass No. 63B7195	Price, Per Frame Knocked Down No. 63B7955	For Details See Pages 54 and 55. Size of Sash Opening (Ft. In. Ft. In.)	1⅛ Inches Thick, 1 Inch Wider, About 2 Inches Longer than Window. Single Strength Glass No. 63B7305	1⅛-Inch Thick Rolling Slats Per Pair No. 63B7338	Approximate Wt. of Entire Window: Single Strength Glass Lbs.	Size of Each Sash Weight Required for Window Glazed. Single Strength Glass, pounds
8x10	$0.84	$1.69	2 4½ x 3 10	$0.85	$0.90	19	4½
8x12	.96	1.71	2 4½ x 4 6	.99	1.00	20	5
9x12	1.02	1.86	2 7½ x 4 6	1.03	1.10	22	5½
9x14	1.18	1.90	2 7½ x 5 2	1.21	1.16	24	6
10x12	1.11	1.88	2 10½ x 4 6	1.12	1.28	23	5½
10x14	1.24	1.91	2 10½ x 5 2	1.25	1.43	26	6½
10x16	1.40	1.94	2 10½ x 5 10	1.44	1.53	29	7

IMPORTANT. The term "window" in these tables means two sashes (upper and lower) with glass. The prices shown in the columns headed catalog Nos. 63B7189, 63B7190, 63B7192, 63B7195, 63B7201, 63B7202 and 63B7206, include both the top and bottom sash and also the glass glazed and secured in the sash by putty and metal points.

Prices on First Quality Windows, Frames, Blinds, and Glazed Cellar Sash, Barn Sash, Etc.—Continued.

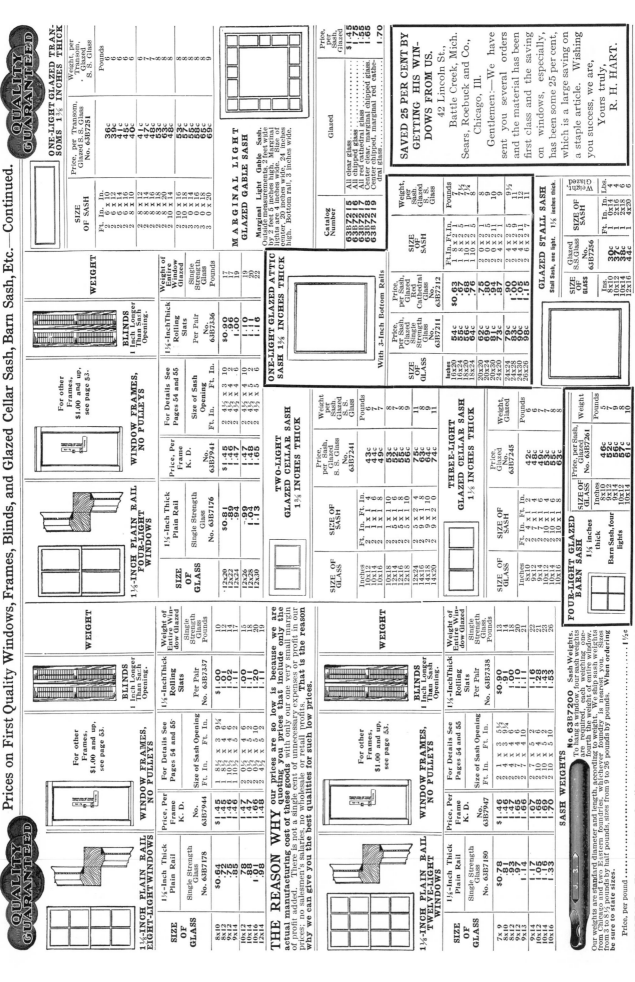

NOW IS THE TIME TO ORDER YOUR STORM SASH

DON'T WAIT UNTIL THE LAST MINUTE, when the snow flies and the wind whistles in around your windows, when it keeps you busy running up and down the cellar steps filling coal scuttles in order to keep warm.

In one season storm sash will more than pay for themselves through the saving in your fuel bill. They will last indefinitely and after the first season you will save one-half of what you generally paid for fuel bills. Think of the profit on your investment.

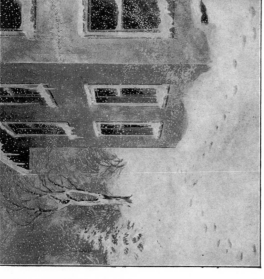

TWO-LIGHT STORM SASH.

Two-Light Storm Sash. 1⅛ inches thick. Carried in stock in the following sizes only. Ventilators, 15 cents each, extra. Prices do not include ventilators.

SIZE OF GLASS	Outside Measurement of Sash Width Ft. In.	Height Ft. In.	No. 63B7292 Price, Glazed Single Strength Glass	No. 63B7293 Price, Glazed Double Strength Glass
12x20	1 5	4 0	$0.66	....
12x24	1 5	4 8	.70	....
12x26	1 5	5 0	.82	....
12x28	1 5	5 8	.86	....
12x32	1 5	6 0	.91	....
14x20	1 7	4 0	.67	....
14x24	1 7	4 8	.80	....
14x28	1 7	5 4	.84	....
14x30	1 7	5 8	.87	....
14x32	1 7	6 0	.93	....
16x20	1 9	4 0	.68	$0.87
16x22	1 9	4 4	.72	.91
16x24	1 9	4 8	.82	.97
16x28	1 9	5 4	.85	1.12
16x30	1 9	5 8	.88	1.25
16x32	1 9	6 0	.94	1.32
18x20	1 11	4 0	.73	.95
18x22	1 11	4 4	.80	1.05
18x24	1 11	4 8	.86	1.16
18x26	1 11	5 0	.90	1.29
18x28	1 11	5 4	.91	1.30
18x30	1 11	5 8	.97	1.39
20x20	2 1	4 0	.80	1.06
20x22	2 1	4 4	.84	1.12
20x24	2 1	4 8	.88	1.23
20x28	2 1	5 4	.94	1.45
20x30	2 1	5 8	1.00	1.52
20x34	2 1	6 4	1.25	1.55
22x20	2 3	4 0	.85	1.15
22x24	2 3	4 8	.92	1.30
22x26	2 3	5 0	.99	1.30
22x30	2 3	5 8	1.17	1.44
22x34	2 3	6 4	1.34	1.70
22x36	2 3	6 8	....	1.84
24x20	2 5	4 0	.90	1.27
24x22	2 5	4 8	.93	1.28
24x24	2 5	5 0	.98	1.30
24x28	2 5	5 4	1.08	1.43

SIZE OF GLASS	Outside Measurement of Sash Width Ft. In.	Height Ft. In.	No. 63B7292 Price, Glazed Single Strength Glass	No. 63B7293 Price, Glazed Double Strength Glass
24x30	2 5	5 8	$1.16	$1.55
24x34	2 5	6 4	1.24	1.60
24x36	2 5	6 8	1.36	1.76
26x24	2 7	4 8	1.04	1.44
26x28	2 7	5 4	1.13	1.51
26x30	2 7	5 8	1.31	1.66
26x32	2 7	6 0	1.37	1.72
26x34	2 7	6 4	1.58	2.06
28x24	2 9	4 8	1.08	1.60
28x28	2 9	5 4	1.28	1.74
28x30	2 9	5 8	1.31	1.74
28x32	2 9	6 0	1.56	2.02
28x34	2 9	6 4	1.66	2.12
28x36	2 9	6 8	2.01	2.28
30x24	2 11	4 8	1.27	1.76
30x26	2 11	5 0	1.43	1.94
30x28	2 11	5 4	1.66	1.95
30x30	2 11	5 8	1.66	2.06
30x32	2 11	6 0	1.74	2.28
30x34	2 11	6 4	2.75	2.29
30x40	2 11	7 4	....	2.60
32x24	3 1	4 8	2.01	2.61
32x32	3 1	6 0	....	2.62
32x34	3 1	6 4	....	3.44
32x36	3 1	6 8	....	...
32x40	3 1	7 4	....	...
36x24	3 5	4 8	1.78	2.23
36x26	3 5	5 0	2.07	2.76
36x30	3 5	5 8	2.18	2.78
36x32	3 5	6 0	....	3.09
36x36	3 5	6 8	....	3.35
40x24	3 9	4 8	2.59	...
40x26	3 9	5 0	2.83	...
40x30	3 9	5 8	3.16	...
40x32	3 9	6 0	3.35	...
40x36	3 9	6 8	4.18	...
44x30	4 1	5 8	3.68	...
44x32	4 1	6 0	4.23	...
44x36	4 1	6 8	4.23	...
44x40	4 1	7 4	5.12	...

STORM SASH FOR COTTAGE WINDOWS.

Three-Light Storm Sash. 1⅛ inches thick. Carried in the following sizes only. Ventilators, 15 cents each, extra.

SIZE OF GLASS	No. 63B7294 Glazed Double Strength Glass	Outside Measurement of Sash Width Ft. In.	Height Ft. In.
40x14-40	$2.85	3 9	5 2
40x14-42	2.95	3 9	5 4
40x16-48	3.30	3 9	6 0
44x16-40	3.35	4 1	5 4
44x16-44	3.55	4 1	5 8
48x18-42	3.65	4 5	5 8
48-18-50	3.75	4 5	6 4

FOUR-LIGHT STORM SASH.

Four-Light Storm Sash. 1⅛ inches thick. Carried in stock in the following sizes only. Ventilators, 15 cents each, extra.

SIZE OF GLASS	No. 63B7295 Single Strength Glass	No. 63B7296 Double Strength Glass	Outside Measurement of Sash Width Ft. In.	Height Ft. In.
10x20	$0.74	....	2 2	4 0
10x22	.82	....	2 2	4 4
10x24	.83	....	2 2	4 8
10x28	.89	....	2 2	5 5
10x30	.96	....	2 2	5 8
10x32	1.18	....	2 2	6 0
12x20	.96	.82	2 6	4 0
12x22	1.05	.92	2 6	4 4
12x24	1.21	.95	2 6	4 8
12x26	1.23	1.06	2 6	5 0
12x28	1.49	1.23	2 6	5 4
12x30	1.82	1.49	2 6	6 0
12x36	....	1.82	2 6	7 4
14x20	.96	....	2 10	4 0
14x24	1.05	....	2 10	4 8
14x26	1.21	....	2 10	5 0
14x28	1.39	....	2 10	5 4
14x30	1.66	$2.03	2 10	6 0
14x40	.93	2.57	2 10	7 4
15x20	1.23	1.58	3 0	4 0
15x24	1.39	1.62	3 0	4 8
15x26	1.46	2.01	3 0	5 0
15x30	1.54	2.15	3 0	5 8
15x32	2.15	2.15	3 0	6 0
20x27	2.80	2.83	4 0	5 4
22x28	2.50	3.00	4 0	5 8
23x30	2.50	3.30	4 0	6 0

EIGHT-LIGHT STORM SASH.

Eight-Light Storm Sash. 1⅛ inches thick. Carried in stock in following sizes only. Prices do not include ventilators. Ventilators, 15 cents each, extra.

SIZE OF GLASS	No. 63B7300 Single Strength Glass	Outside Measurement of Sash Width Ft. In.	Height Ft. In.
9x12	$0.80	2 0	4 8
9x14	.91	2 0	5 4
10x12	.83	2 2	4 8
10x16	1.08	2 2	6 0
12x14	1.05	2 6	5 6
12x16	1.32	2 6	6 0
14x16	1.37	2 10	6 0
14x20	1.72	2 10	7 4

TWELVE-LIGHT STORM SASH.

Twelve-Light Storm Sash. 1⅛ inches thick. Carried in stock in the following sizes only. Ventilators, 15 cents each, extra.

SIZE OF GLASS	No. 63B7305 Single Strength Glass	Outside Measurement of Sash Width Ft. In.	Height Ft. In.
8x10	$0.85	2 5½	4 0
8x12	.99	2 5½	4 8
9x12	1.03	2 8½	4 8
9x14	1.21	2 8½	5 4
10x12	1.12	2 11½	4 8
10x14	1.25	2 11½	5 4
10x16	1.44	2 11½	6 6

THE BEST COTTAGE WINDOWS ON THE MARKET

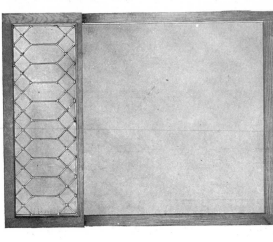

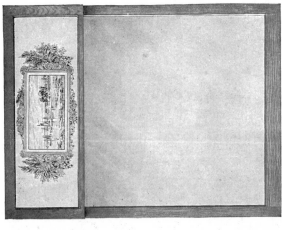

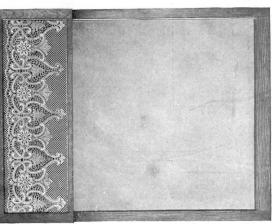

CRYSTAL

Illustration shows top glazed clear leaded crystal sheet. Bottom glazed clear double strength "A" quality glass.

The fancy cottage windows illustrated on this page have the bottom glazed with **"A" quality clear double strength glass.** The upper lights are selected to give our customers a variety to select from, and the designs are such as will harmonize with our front door glass designs. The sash is soft pine, 1⅜ inches thick, made in two pieces. **Odd sizes not listed take a much higher price.** We pack our windows with great care and guarantee safe delivery to destination.

BAYVIEW

Illustration shows top glazed sand blast landscape design, carefully executed on double strength glass. Bottom glazed clear double strength "A" quality glass.

GEM

Illustration shows both top and bottom glazed clear double strength "A" quality glass.

REX

Illustration shows top glazed Duchesse sand blast lace design on double strength glass. Bottom glazed clear double strength "A" quality glass.

If made in one piece add 45 cents extra to the price of the window wanted and write the word "Special" after the catalog number, stating "window is to be made in one piece." Any of the windows on this page can be **glazed with plain plate glass in bottom sash instead of double strength.** For price refer to the columns headed "Plate Glass", and add the amount opposite the proper size to the price of the window you have selected glazed double strength bottom and write the word "Plate" after the catalog number.

FANCY FRONT WINDOWS, CHECK RAIL 1⅜ Inches Thick

SIZE OPENING Width Ft. In.	Height Ft. In.	TOP GLASS Width, Inches	Height, Inches	BOTTOM GLASS Width, Inches	Height, Inches	CRYSTAL No. 63B7106 Glazed as Illustrated	BAYVIEW No. 63B7118 Glazed as Illustrated	PLATE GLASS Extra if Bottom Sash is Glazed with Plain Plate Glass
3 8	5 0	40	14	40	40	$3.73	$3.27	Add $6.95 extra
3 8	5 2	40	14	40	42	3.99	3.56	Add 7.05 extra
3 8	5 4	40	14	40	44	4.08	3.60	Add 7.45 extra
3 8	5 6	40	14	40	46	4.09	3.69	Add 7.75 extra
3 8	5 10	40	16	40	48	4.44	3.82	Add 8.15 extra
4 0	5 2	44	16	44	40	4.39	3.80	Add 7.45 extra
4 0	5 6	44	16	44	44	4.77	4.08	Add 8.10 extra
4 0	5 10	44	16	44	48	5.37	4.71	Add 8.40 extra
4 4	5 6	48	18	48	42	5.37	4.40	Add 8.50 extra
4 4	5 10	48	18	48	46	5.97	5.03	Add 8.90 extra
4 4	6 0	48	18	48	48	6.45	5.53	Add 9.00 extra
4 4	6 2	48	18	48	50	6.47	5.55	Add 9.45 extra
4 4	6 6	48	22	48	50	6.90	5.65	Add 9.45 extra

FANCY FRONT WINDOWS, CHECK RAIL 1⅜ Inches Thick

SIZE OPENING Width Ft. In.	Height Ft. In.	TOP GLASS Width, Inches	Height, Inches	BOTTOM GLASS Width, Inches	Height, Inches	REX No. 63B7136 Glazed as Illustrated	GEM No. 63B7142 Top and Bottom Sash Glazed D. S. Glass	PLATE GLASS Extra if Bottom Sash is Glazed with Plain Plate Glass
3 8	5 0	40	14	40	40	$3.25	$2.92	Add $6.95 extra
3 8	5 2	40	14	40	42	3.53	3.18	Add 7.05 extra
3 8	5 4	40	14	40	44	3.57	3.27	Add 7.45 extra
3 8	5 6	40	14	40	46	3.69	3.30	Add 7.75 extra
3 8	5 10	40	16	40	48	3.78	3.50	Add 8.15 extra
4 0	5 2	44	16	44	40	3.76	3.40	Add 7.45 extra
4 0	5 6	44	16	44	44	4.01	3.67	Add 8.10 extra
4 0	5 10	44	16	44	48	4.20	3.84	Add 8.40 extra
4 4	5 6	48	18	48	42	4.34	4.17	Add 8.50 extra
4 4	5 10	48	18	48	46	4.93	4.76	Add 9.00 extra
4 4	6 0	48	18	48	48	5.42	5.25	Add 9.00 extra
4 4	6 2	48	18	48	50	5.44	5.27	Add 9.45 extra
4 4	6 6	48	22	48	50	5.57	5.40	Add 9.45 extra

SEARS, ROEBUCK AND CO., CHICAGO, ILLINOIS.

Windows Like These Increase the Value and Beauty of Your Home

ART GLASS WINDOWS. The kind that will add beauty and value to your cottage, house or bungalow. **EVERY DESIGN A NEW ONE. All new** this season and specially low in price. Our aim in presenting these leaded glass windows in colors is to give our customers a better idea of the combination of colors. The really beautiful effects, however, can only be appreciated after the glass is in place, as natural light produces effects which cannot be duplicated by color printing.

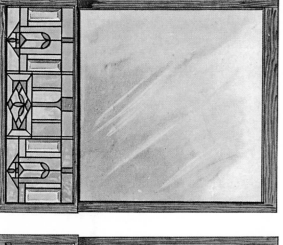

FLEUR DE LIS

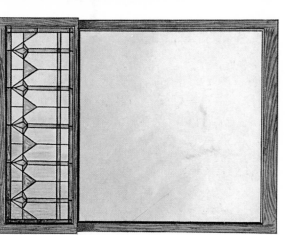

CRESCENT

ROMAN

VENICE

All windows on this page are illustrated in exact combination of colors we furnish, and can only be furnished in colors as shown. Bottom light is glazed with clear "A" quality double strength glass at the prices printed directly below name of window. The upper lights are carefully selected to produce pleasing and harmonious effects. These designs will harmonize with our front door glass designs. These cottage windows are made of Venetian colored glass securely held in place by leaded bars, which will not rust nor corrode. The wood frames are made of soft pine. We carefully pack these windows and guarantee safe delivery to destination, as explained in the first pages of this book. The bottom sash may be raised, or the upper sash lowered, if hung with sash weights. **If made in one piece add 45 cents net to price of window wanted and write the word "Special"** after the catalog number. Any of the windows on this page can be glazed with plain plate glass in bottom sash instead of double strength. For price refer to column headed "Plate Glass" and ADD the amount quoted opposite the proper size to the price of the window you have selected glazed double strength bottom, and write the word "Plate" after the catalog number.

FLEUR DE LIS	PLATE GLASS	CRESCENT	FANCY FRONT WINDOWS, CHECK RAIL 1⅜ Inches Thick								ROMAN	PLATE GLASS	VENICE
			SIZE OPENING		TOP GLASS		BOTTOM GLASS						
No. 63A6534 Glazed as Illustrated	Extra if Bottom Sash is Glazed with Plain Plate Glass	No. 63A7100 Glazed as Illustrated	Width, Ft. In.	Height, Ft. In.	Width, Inches	Height, Inches	Width, Inches	Height, Inches			No. 63A6535 Glazed as Illustrated	Extra if Bottom Sash is Glazed with Plain Plate Glass	No. 63A6536 Glazed as Illustrated
$4.35	Add $6.95 extra	$4.68	3 8	3 0	40	14	40	40			$5.44	Add $6.95 extra	$5.97
4.61	Add 7.05 extra	4.96	3 8	3 2	40	14	40	42			5.70	Add 7.05 extra	6.23
4.73	Add 7.75 extra	5.08	3 8	3 6	40	14	40	46			5.82	Add 7.75 extra	6.35
5.08	Add 8.15 extra	5.43	3 8	3 10	40	16	40	48			6.53	Add 8.15 extra	6.91
5.17	Add 7.45 extra	5.62	4 0	3 6	44	16	44	40			6.79	Add 7.45 extra	7.19
5.44	Add 8.10 extra	5.87	4 0	3 6	44	16	44	44			7.06	Add 8.10 extra	7.45
5.97	Add 8.40 extra	6.48	4 0	3 10	44	16	44	48			7.59	Add 8.40 extra	7.99
6.27	Add 8.50 extra	6.62	4 4	4 6	48	18	48	42			8.25	Add 8.50 extra	8.75
6.86	Add 8.90 extra	7.21	4 4	4 10	48	18	48	46			8.84	Add 8.90 extra	9.34
7.37	Add 9.45 extra	7.72	4 4	4 2	48	18	48	50			9.35	Add 9.45 extra	9.85

ALL SIZES OF THE ABOVE WINDOWS CARRIED IN STOCK AND CAN BE SHIPPED ON RECEIPT OF ORDER.

RICH ART GLASS FOR DOORS AND WINDOWS

ART GLASS DOORS AND WINDOWS add tone and refinement to the home. They increase its value far more than other trimmings or any kind of furnishings. A few dollars spent for a few designs will prove a splendid investment.

ON THE FOLLOWING PAGES we illustrate a large assortment of art glass designs suitable for windows, doors, transoms; in fact, for any purpose where an artistic colored window is wanted. We also list in this catalog all the materials for the interior trimming of this beautiful reception room: the panel work, the beam ceiling and staircase.

THE ABOVE PICTURE illustrates how much a high class leaded art glass window adds to the beauty of the interior of a home. The illustration in no way does justice to the beautiful light effects to be had by using our Venetian or L'Art Nouveau glass designs, as the richest effects are produced by the natural light passing through these beautiful color panes, giving a soft and mellow glow which adds to the comfort and the coziness of the home. The leaded art glass designs as viewed from the street also add much to the appearance of a house.

IF YOU WANT TO GET THE BIGGEST VALUES ever offered in leaded art glass designs, choose any of the patterns illustrated on this and the following pages, as our prices are about one-half the prices charged by the retail dealer.

PRICES FOR ART GLASS SHOWN ON THIS PAGE.

ART GLASS DESIGN, as shown in staircase window as illustrated above. The various pieces of cathedral glass shown in this beautiful window are securely held in place by copper plated bars.

No. 63A6498 Dutch Windmill Design. Price, per square foot......$4.50

THE ART GLASS DOOR DESIGN shown in the above picture is made of beautiful cathedral glass. All pieces of glass are securely held in place by copper plated bars.

No. 63A6499 Price, per square foot..............$1.85

Copper plated bars, while a trifle more expensive than leaded bars, are worth the difference in price as much is added to the beauty and strength of the window or door when constructed in this manner.

THE BEAUTY OF A FRONT DOOR DEPENDS UPON THE MANNER IN WHICH IT IS GLAZED

HALLS AND BED-ROOMS can be beautified and made to appear larger by using bevel plate glass mirror doors.

$9.06 FOR THIS BEAUTIFUL PANEL OAK DOOR

Furnished in Red Oak or Wisconsin Birch, with hand carvings. For full description see page 12. Venetian leaded art glass adds much to the appearance of a door. It excludes the view of an intruder and yet does not exclude the light. This door or any other door illustrated in this catalog can be glazed with this design or any other leaded design which is illustrated in colors on the following pages, at a slight difference in price.

LEADED ART GLASS IS MADE TO ORDER. Be sure to allow at least fifteen days, the time required to get a first class job.

LEADED ART GLASS DOORS
VENEERED OAK DOORS, 1¾ inches thick.

SIZES			Veneered Plain Red Oak	No. 63A6537
Width Ft. In.	Height Ft. In.		No. 63A86 Glazed Bevel Plate Glass	Leaded Art Glass as Illustrated
2 8	6 8		$ 9.35	$ 9.06
2 10	6 10		10.40	10.19
2 10	7 0		10.95	10.78
3 0	7 0		11.30	11.20

The prices printed on this page are for doors in the white. We do not fill, stain or varnish our mill work or interior trim.

EVERY SASH DOOR IN THIS CATALOG will prove to be rich and attractive if glazed with plate glass or one of the rich art glass designs shown on this and the following pages.

$25.00 MIRROR DOOR FOR $11.20

Furnished in Red Oak, Birch or Nona Pine. The illustration to the left shows our Mirror Door, made of birch stained to imitate mahogany. Very effective when used with white enamel trimming in bedrooms, also very effective when stained to imitate cherry, walnut or other woods.

$10.25 FOR THIS $20.00 BEVEL PLATE GLASS DOOR

Read the description and see detail of construction on page 12.

BEVEL PLATE GLASS DOORS
VENEERED DOORS, 1¾ inches thick.

SIZES		Unselected Birch	Red Oak
Width Ft. In.	Height Ft. In.	No. 63A96 Glazed Bevel Plate	No. 63A92 Glazed Bevel Plate
2 8	6 8	$ 9.45	$10.25
2 10	6 10	10.60	11.55
3 0	7 0	11.50	12.70

MIRROR DOORS See prices below.
All these doors are 1⅜ inches thick.

Catalog Number	Width Feet In.	Height Ft. In.	Kind of Wood	Price, Including Bevel Plate Mirror	Price, Including Plain Plate Mirror (not beveled)
63A6776	2	6 8	Nona Pine	$13.10	$11.20
63A6777	2	6 8	Birch	15.75	13.85
63A6778	2	6 8	Red Oak	16.50	14.60
63A6779	2	7 0	Nona Pine	14.00	12.05
63A6780	2	7 0	Birch	16.25	14.30
63A6781	2	7 0	Red Oak	16.95	14.95

HIGHEST CLASS ART GLASS FOR DOORS AND WINDOWS

RICH AND HANDSOME DESIGNS appropriate for dining room, front hall light, staircase light, interior and exterior door lights and windows.

THESE DESIGNS ARE HIGH CLASS in every sense of the word. They are made of carefully selected colored glass, as per illustrations, **bringing out strong and harmonious effects.** Such designs as these are sure to beautify your house when viewed from the street and add a tone of refinement and an added comfort and coziness to the interior, due to the beautiful effects produced by the light passing through these artistic color arrangements, such as are illustrated on this page. The various pieces of colored glass are firmly held in place by leaded metal bars made of non-corrosive metal and which will not rust or corrode when subjected to the weather.

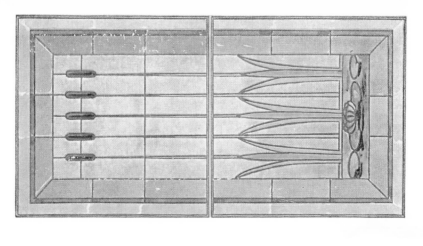

No. 63A6533 Price, per square foot............**$1.35**

No. 63A6532 Price, per square foot **$3.25**

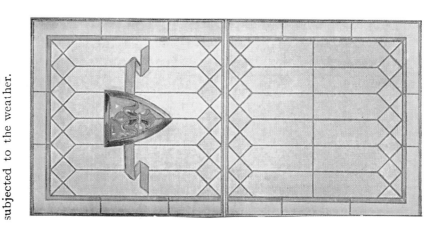

No. 63A6531 Price, per square foot..........**$1.15**

LEADED ART GLASS IS MADE TO ORDER. Be sure to allow fifteen days, the time required to get a first class job.

LATEST DESIGNS IN L'ART NOUVEAU LEADED GLASS

THESE ARE STRICTLY NEW AND UP TO DATE DESIGNS, expressly designed for us. Used in all modern houses where a high class window is desired. **ARTISTIC IN DESIGN.** New and novel creations in the art of leaded glass making. Made of selected colored glass (not stained glass), as per illustrations, producing artistic and harmonious effects. The various colors and kinds of colored glass are firmly held in place by leaded metal bars which are made of non-corrosive metal which will not rust or discolor.

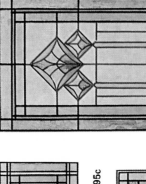

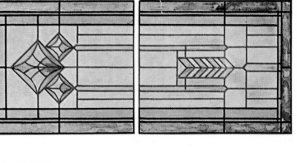

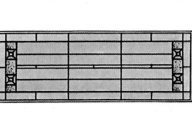

No. 63A6516 Price, per square foot............98c

No. 63A6520 Price, per square foot......$1.29

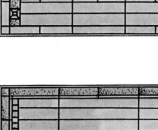

No. 63A6517 Price, per square foot, 95c

No. 63A6519 Price, per square foot .. 69c

No. 63A6518 Price, per square foot...68c

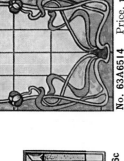

No. 63A6514 Price, per square foot.......$1.50

No. 63A6515 Price, per square foot............$1.23

No. 63A6509 Price, per square foot.. $1.65

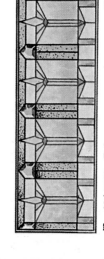

No. 63A6512 Price, per square foot.......96c

No. 63A6513 Price, per square foot............$1.25

No. 63A6511 Price, per square foot.. $1.15
*No. 63A6510 Price, per square foot.. $1.05

LEADED ART GLASS IS MADE TO ORDER. Be sure to allow at least fifteen days, the time required to get a first class job.

VENETIAN AND LEADED ART GLASS

STRICTLY NEW DESIGNS. Beautiful colors, exactly like illustrations. Show them to your architect or contractor, he knows the designs are correct and the prices are extremely low. You will appreciate them when you get them. Made of carefully selected colored glass and securely held in place by leaded bars made of non-corrosive metal and which will not rust or corrode when subjected to the weather.

THESE DESIGNS ARE SUITABLE FOR WINDOWS of every description, **door lights, transom lights, etc.** The very low prices we name for this high class material should enable anyone to beautify their home at a price little above what they would ordinarily pay for plain crystal glass.

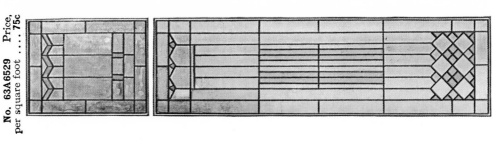

No. 63A6529 Price, per square foot **75c**

No. 63A6530 Price, per square foot .. **$1.14**

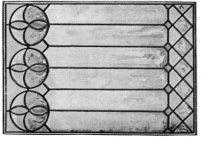

No. 63A6527 Price, per square foot **90c**

No. 63A6528 Price, per square foot **$1.26**

No. 63A6524 Price, per square foot **84c**

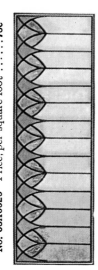

No. 63A6525 Price, per square foot **73c**

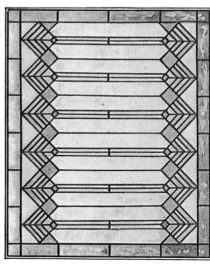

No. 63A6526 Price, per square foot **$1.45**

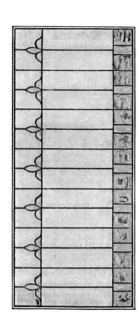

No. 63A6522 Price, per square foot.......**$1.33**

No. 63A6521 Price, per square foot **82c**

No. 63A6523 Price, per square foot..**83c**

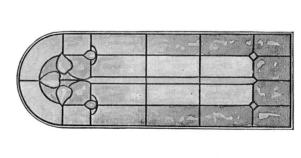

LEADED ART GLASS IS MADE TO ORDER. Be sure to allow at least fifteen days, the time required to get a first class job.

HIGH CLASS L'ART NOUVEAU AND VENETIAN GLASS

NEW CREATIONS, exceptionally new and attractive designs. **Make your selection.** They are all pretty and are excellent values, just about one-half regular prices, in many instances considerably less than half. While these patterns are inexpensive they will add wonderfully to the value of the house. These leaded glass windows, such as we show on this and the following pages, add tone and refinement when viewed from the exterior, while the soft and delicate colors add comfort and coziness to the interior, as well as enriching its beauty a hundredfold. We furnish in colors exactly like colored illustrations.

No. 63A8916 Price, per square foot.....80c

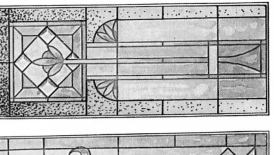

No. 63A6505 Price, per square foot...99c   No. 63A6506 Price, per square foot.....$1.30

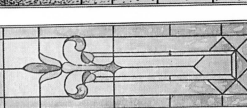

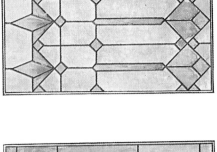

No. 63A6508 Price, per square foot.........95c

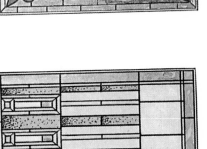

No. 63A8920 Price, per square foot.......$1.00

No. 63A6507 Price, per square foot.........89c

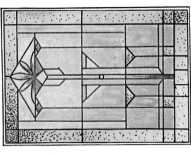

No. 63A6504 Price, per square foot.......$1.08

LEADED ART GLASS IS MADE TO ORDER. Be sure to allow at least fifteen days, the time required to get a first class job.

No. 63A8918 Price, per square foot.........$1.00

No. 63A6502 Price, per square foot.........90c

No. 63A6503 Price, per square foot.........$1.27

No. 63A6501 Price, per square foot.........82c

GAS AND ELECTRIC FIXTURES

On this page we show you in colors a few fixtures selected from our magnificent line of high grade gas and electric fixtures. Each is designed by an artist and represents the most perfect symmetry of design and perfection of color blending. Our stock is so complete that we can supply any type of fixture from the most inexpensive single light bracket to the richly embossed and handsomely carved chandeliers illustrated here. We can also furnish all chandeliers on this page in any number of lights, either gas, electric or combination. Every fixture on this page, as well as the balance of our fixture line, is fully described on pages 108 and 109.

The quality of our fixtures is uniformly the very best. Only the finest quality of solid brass of extra heavy gauge (weight) is used in their construction. The finish is rich satin brass (brush brass), buffed and polished by hand. No pains or expense have been spared to make the details of construction absolutely perfect. The connecting joints, sockets, etc., are thoroughly cemented. Each part fits perfectly and the embossing and workmanship are faultless. We guarantee the electric fixtures to be properly wired and insulated, and all gas fixtures to hold gas without leakage. They conform in every particular with the requirements of the Board of Insurance Underwriters. No better fixtures are made at any price.

Our prices are for the fixtures complete, as illustrated, and we urgently invite comparison with the prices of other dealers. The profit to retail dealers on this class of goods is generally excessive. By purchasing of us the retailer's profit is eliminated, which makes it possible for us to sell fixtures, grade for grade, at an astonishing reduction from the price charged by the retail dealer. In fact, we unqualifiedly state that similar articles cannot be purchased elsewhere at anywhere near our prices. Remember, our prices are for the fixtures absolutely complete, ready to hang, which includes complete electric wiring, Edison key sockets, brass shade rings, glass shades, gas pillars, lava tips and insulating joints where necessary. These parts add one-fourth to the value.

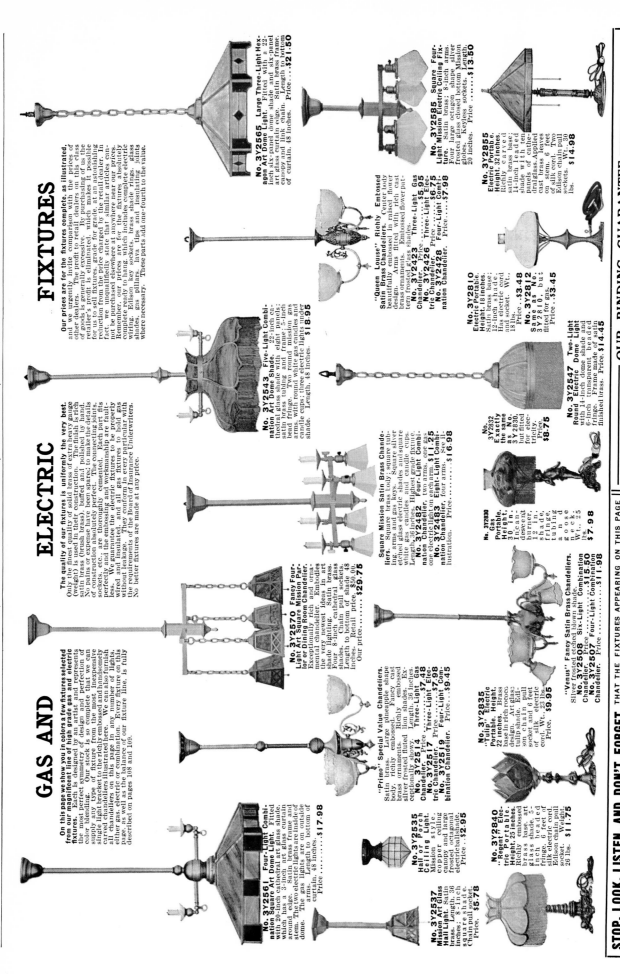

No. 3Y2561 Four-Light Combination Square Art Dome Light. Fitted with 20-inch cathedral glass shade which has a 3-inch art glass curtain around edge. Satin brass frame and stem. The two electric lights are on outside of dome. The gas lights are on inside of arms. Length to bottom of curtain, 48 inches. Price....$17.98

No. 3Y2537 Mission Art Glass Hall Light. Satin brass. Length, 36 inches; 8-inch square shade. Chain pull socket. Price....$5.78

No. 3Y2535 Mission Style Ceiling Light. Satin brass, copper ceiling canopy and large frosted octagonal glass shade. Price..$2.95

No. 3Y2840 "Regent" Electric Portable. Height, 25 inches. Richly embossed brass base, art glass shade, 5-inch beaded fringe. 6 feet of silk electric cord. Weight, 26 lbs. $11.75

"Primo" Special Value Chandeliers. Satin brass, richly embossed body, richly embossed brass ornaments. Four cast silver frosted fluted shades. Exceptionally showy. Length, 36 inches.
No. 3Y2514 Four-Light Gas Chandelier. Price....$7.48
No. 3Y2517 Three-Light Electric Chandelier. Price....$5.98
No. 3Y2519 Four-Light Combination Chandelier. Price....$9.45

No. 3Y2835 "Tulip" Electric Portable. Height, 22 inches. Brass base in rich rococo design. Art glass tulip shade. Edison chain pull socket and 6 feet of silk electric cord. Wt., 23 lbs. Price, $9.95

No. 3Y2570 Fancy Four-Light Art Square Mission Parlor or Dining Room Chandelier. Exceptionally rich and ornamental chandelier. Embodies the very newest ideas in art shade lighting. Satin brass. Four 8-inch cathedral glass shades. Chain pull sockets. Length to bottom of shade 48 inches. Retail price, $50.00. Our price......$29.75

"Venus" Fancy Satin Brass Chandeliers. Silver frosted etched blown shade.
No. 3Y2508 Six-Light Combination Chandelier. Price....$15.50
No. 3Y2507 Four-Light Combination Chandelier. Price....$11.98

No. 3Y2543 Five-Light Combination Art Dome Shade. 22-inch cathedral glass shade with eight panels; satin brass tubing and frame; 5-inch bead fringe. Two round mission gas arms, with round white gas candles and candle cups; three electric lights under shade. Length, 48 inches. $18.95

Square Mission Satin Brass Chandeliers. Square brass body; square tubing, arms and gas keys. Square silver etched glass electric shades and square white gas candles and candle cups. Length, 36 inches. Highest grade fixture.
No. 3Y2482 Four-Light Electric Chandelier, two arms, one gas one electric light on each arm. $11.25
No. 3Y2483 Eight-Light Combination Chandelier, four arms. See illustration. Price......$16.98

No. 312830 Gas Portable. Height, 30 inches. Incandescent burner, 12 in. shade, fringe, making a gooseneck. Wt., 25 lbs. $7.98

No. 3Y2830 Gas Portable. Height, 18 inches. Satin brass base. Has electric cord and socket. Wt., 18 lbs. Price...$3.48
No. 3Y2812 Same as No. 3Y2810, but fitted for gas. Price...$3.45

"Queen Louise" Richly Embossed Satin Brass Chandeliers. Center body beautifully embossed in raised flower design. Arms fitted with rich cast brass ornaments. Embossed flower pattern frosted glass shades.
No. 3Y2423 Three-Light Gas Chandelier. Price....$6.95
No. 3Y2426 Three-Light Electric Chandelier. Price...$6.75
No. 3Y2428 Four-Light Combination Chandelier. Price....$7.98

No. 3Y2810 Electric Portable. Height, 18 inches.

No. 3Y2547 Two-Light Round Electric Dome Light with 14-inch dome shade and 6-inch transparent beaded fringe. Frame made of satin finished brass. Price. $14.45

No. 3Y2832 Exactly the same as No. 3Y2830, but fitted for electricity. Price. $8.75

No. 3Y2565 Large Three-Light Hexagon Art Dome Light. Fitted with a 22-inch six-panel dome shade and six-panel art glass curtain edge. Satin brass frame, canopy and link chain. Length to bottom of curtain, 48 inches. Price....$21.50

No. 3Y2585 Square Four-Light Mission Electric Ceiling Fixture. Satin brass; 8-inch arms. Four large octagon shape silver frosted glass closed bottom Mission globes. Keyless sockets. Length, 20 inches. Price $13.50

No. 3Y2855 Electric Portable. Richly carved satin brass base; 14-inch leaded shade with ten panels of cathedral glass. Applied cast brass leaves on stem. 6 feet of silk cord. Two Edison chain pull sockets. Wt. 30 lbs. $14.98

LEADED BEVEL PLATE GLASS AND FANCY SHEET GLASS

THE LEADED BEVEL PLATE AND CRYSTAL GLASS shown on this page are standard designs and have proven to be quite popular. You will find the prices to be bargains when you consider the good workmanship and the high grade of materials used in the manufacture of this leaded glass. **IN ORDERING, ALWAYS SPECIFY WIDTH OF GLASS FIRST, LENGTH LAST. SPECIAL LEADED OR SHEET GLASS CANNOT BE RETURNED.**

FANCY SHEET GLASS

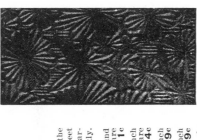

At prices quoted below, we furnish the best brands and designs of fancy sheet glass, cut to any size required. All carried in stock and can be shipped promptly.

No. 63B8875 Plain white ground double strength glass. Price, per square foot..........**11c**

No. 63B8880 Maze glass, ⅛ inch thick, plain white. Price, per square foot..........**14c**

No. 63B8885 Cathedral, ⅛ inch thick, wine. Price, per square foot. **9c**

No. 63B8890 Cathedral, ⅛ inch thick, green. Price, per square foot. **9c**

No. 63B8895 Cathedral, ⅛ inch thick, blue. Price, per square foot. **9c**

No. 63B8900 Ribbed glass, ⅛ inch thick, white, for skylights. Price, per square foot..........**9c**

No. 63B8870
Single Process Chipped Double Strength White Glass.
Price, per square foot. **12c**

ON ALL THE ABOVE FANCY SHEET GLASS ADD 25 CENTS (PER ORDER) FOR BOXING.

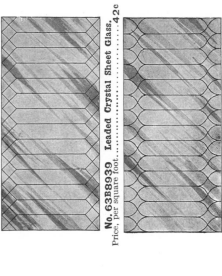

No. 63B8872
Double Strength Colonial or Florentine Glass.
Price, per square foot. **14c**

No. 63B8939 Leaded Crystal Sheet Glass..........**42c**
Price, per square foot.

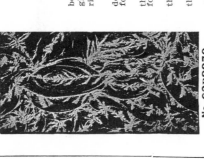

No. 63B8935.
Leaded Crystal Sheet Glass.
Price, per square foot...**42c**

No.63B8941 Leaded Crystal Sheet Glass..........**45c**
Price, per square foot.

Cannot be made less than 22 inches high.
No. 63B8925
Leaded Bevel Plate Glass.
Price, per square foot.**$1.85**

No. 63B8933
Leaded Bevel Plate Glass.
Price, per square foot.............**$1.45**

No. 63B8931
Leaded Bevel Plate Glass.
Price, per square foot.............**$1.35**

No. 63B8929
Leaded Bevel Plate Glass.
Price, per square foot..**$1.85**

Cannot be made less than 22 inches high.
No. 63B8927
Leaded Bevel Plate Glass.
Price, per square foot.**$1.80**

WHEN ORDERING ANY OF THE LEADED DESIGNS (NOT FANCY SHEET GLASS) GLAZED IN SASH, SEE RULE FOR ORDERING ON PAGE 46.

BIG PROFITS BY USING HOTBEDS

ONLY $1⁶⁸

Early Vegetables Bring High Prices

You can have from six weeks to two months earlier start with your **garden by using hotbeds.** Consider what this means to you. You will have vegetables or strawberries before anyone in your neighborhood, and what you are unable to use, your neighbors will be glad to take off your hands at your own price. Truck gardeners fully appreciate the advantages gained by the use of hotbeds. We carry the largest stock of hotbed sash in the country and therefore are able to quote and make the lowest possible prices and make prompt shipments no matter what the size of the order may be. We find after several years' experience that the hotbed sash 3 feet wide by 6 feet long with four or five rows of narrow glass is the most practical, because where the wider glass is used it requires broader bars, which have a tendency to throw a shadow over certain plants and in that way retard their growth, while the hotbed sash that we handle have narrow bars and do not obstruct the sunlight.

A SIMPLE WAY OF MAKING A HOTBED

For the benefit of those who have not used our hotbed sash we have illustrated on this page a sectional view of a hotbed.

LOCATION—The best location for a hotbed, if practical, is on the south side of your barn where the bed will be protected from the cold north and northwest winds and where it will get the full benefit of the sun's rays. This location will also be handy on account of being near the manure pile.

SIZE—A hotbed may vary in size according to the number of sash used. It is found that a hotbed that requires four or five sash and is from 12 to 15 feet long is the most practical. The pit should be about 2 feet deep and boarded up on the sides with common lumber, 2-inch stock being generally used. There should be about 4 or 5 inches slope to the length of the hotbed, the slope being toward the south. The surface of the hotbed should be about 5 inches from the sash at all points. This is important, for where the sash is higher at the upper end of the bed the plants will grow tall and spindling and where the sash is near to the hotbed the plants become short and bushy. After the pit has been dug take rich fresh manure containing plenty of straw and place it in the bottom of the pit, tamping it down firmly in layers to a depth of about 20 inches; and it is a good idea to put the sash on then, leaving it from three to five days before adding the soil. After the bed has been covered with soil to a depth of about 6 inches, leave it for from ten days to two weeks for the soil to become warm and the weed seed to germinate. The bed will then be about 4 inches from the glass and after settlement takes place there will be about 6 inches space between the sash and the bed. The hotbeds should be made about two weeks before the time to sow seed.

IMPORTANT—Every morning raise the sash a little for ventilation, being careful not to allow too much cold air into the hotbed. Close the sash at night in order to retain the heat.

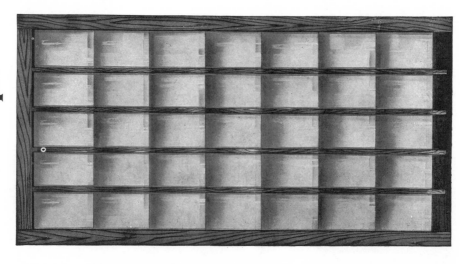

HOTBED SASH.

Hotbed Sash. 1⅜ inches thick. Size of opening, 3 feet by 6 feet.

No. 63B7271 Price, Glazed 4 rows 7-inch Glass	No. 63B7272 Price, Glazed 5 rows 6-inch Glass	Weight, Glazed, Pounds
$1.82	$1.68	29

QUALITY GUARANTEED

No. 2 QUALITY DOOR AND WINDOW FRAMES $1.00 AND UP

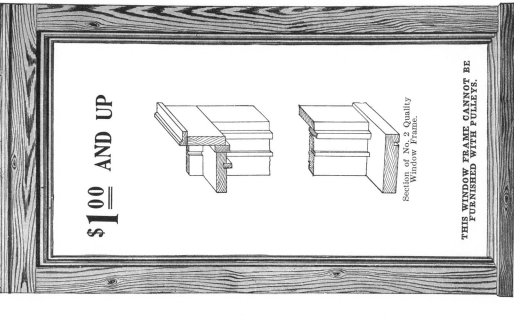

$1⁰⁰ AND UP

Section of No. 2 Quality Window Frame.

THIS WINDOW FRAME CANNOT BE FURNISHED WITH PULLEYS.

TO MEET THE DEMAND for a low priced window frame, we quote on this page door and window frames of No. 2 quality, one grade below our strictly first quality frames illustrated and described on pages 54 and 55. Our No. 2 window and door frames contain but few defects such as sound knots and sap stains and will compare in quality with the frame that is usually sold by most manufacturers as a No. 1 quality frame. We recommend our strictly No. 1 frames shown on page 54 and 55 in preference to our No. 2 frames shown on this page because our No. 1 frames are much better value for your money. They are perfectly clear, free from knots and sap and are frames that are far superior in every way to frames furnished by the average mill work concern.

SHIPPED TO YOU KNOCKED DOWN, in bundles, in that way eliminating all possible chance of breakage while in transit. These frames furnished only with 7/8-inch outside casing. Blinds 1⅛ inches thick can be used with the 7/8-inch casing, as the blind stop is rabbeted on these frames. The window frame listed to the right is furnished with only a single sill and does not have the sub sill as shown on the high grade frames listed on pages 54 and 55.

Door frames are furnished only in two sizes, 2 feet 8 inches by 6 feet 8 inches and 3 feet by 7 feet, from which they may be cut to fit any smaller size opening. **Window frames furnished in only four sizes,** from which they may be cut to fit any smaller size opening than openings listed.

DOUBLE OR TWIN FRAMES ARE TWICE THE PRICE OF ONE REGULAR FRAME. TRIPLE FRAMES ARE THREE TIMES THE PRICE OF ONE REGULAR FRAME.

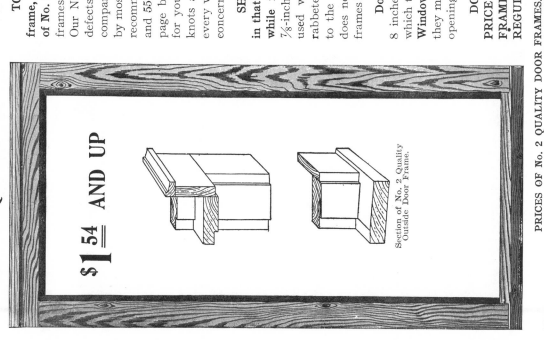

$1⁵⁴ AND UP

Section of No. 2 Quality Outside Door Frame.

AS REPRESENTED

QUALITY GUARANTEED

PRICES OF No. 2 QUALITY DOOR FRAMES.

No. 2 Quality Outside Door Frames. Knocked down and carefully bundled for shipment.	Size, 2 ft. 8 in. by 6 ft. 8 in. or smaller. Price	Size, 3 feet by 7 feet or smaller. Price	No. 2 Quality Outside Door Frames with Transom Head.	Size, 2 ft. 8 in. by 6 ft. 8 in. or smaller. Price	Size, 3 feet by 7 feet or smaller. Price
No.63B7967 Outside Casing, 7/8 in. thick	$1.54	$1.63	No.63B7968 Outside Casing, 7/8 in. thick	$2.01	$2.20

PRICES OF No. 2 QUALITY WINDOW FRAMES.

Size of Window to be Used		7/8-Inch Thick Outside Casing Without Pulleys No. 63B7823
Width	Height	
1 foot 8 inches	4 feet 6 inches or smaller	$1.00
2 feet 6 inches	5 feet 2 inches or smaller	1.03
2 feet 10 inches	6 feet 6 inches or smaller	1.25
2 feet 10 inches	7 feet 2 inches or smaller	1.33
3 feet 8 inches	6 feet 6 inches or smaller	1.40

QUALITY GUARANTEED

PLAIN DRIP CAP DOOR AND WINDOW FRAMES

QUALITY GUARANTEED

Good substantial frames made of practically clear lumber now within the reach of contractors and builders at reasonable prices. Heretofore it has been necessary for contractors and builders to pay very high prices for frames equal in grade to ours or else go to the trouble and expense of buying the lumber and making the frames on the job.

Made in lots of 1,000 by the latest improved machinery. For this reason we are able to make the most perfect frames at reasonably low prices. Cut to the exact size of the window or door for which they are intended and all that is necessary is to nail them together, which takes but a few moments. Door and window frames made for buildings with regular 2x4-inch studding. All frames are shipped in bundles so they will reach you in a clean and perfect condition. They take a much lower freight rate when shipped this way and there is no possible chance of breakage.

DETAILS AND EXACT MEASUREMENTS.

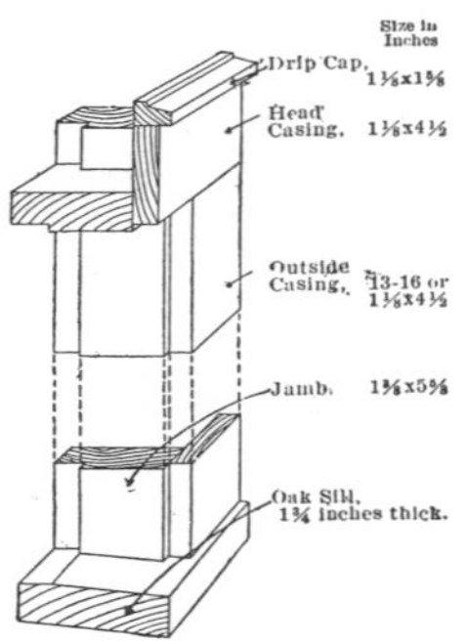

Size in Inches
Drip Cap, 1⅛x1⅝
Head Casing, 1⅛x4½
Outside Casing, 13-16 or 1⅛x4½
Jamb, 1⅜x5⅝
Oak Sill, 1¾ inches thick.

DOOR FRAMES.

Made with ⅞-inch or 1⅛-inch outside casing and made with or without transom head. Where jambs are wanted wider than 5⅝ inches add 25 cents for each additional inch or fraction thereof in the width of the jamb.

When ordering door frames be sure to give thickness of the door for which the frame is intended.

PRICES OF DRIP CAP DOOR FRAMES.

Catalog Number	Size of Outside Casing	Size, 2 ft. 8 in. by 6 ft. 8 in. or smaller. Price	Size, 3 ft. by 7 ft. or smaller. Price
No. 63B7942	⅞ inch	$1.80	$1.91
No. 63B7975	1⅛ inch	1.96	2.09
WITH TRANSOM HEAD.			
No. 63B7943	⅞ inch	$2.40	$2.51
No. 63B7976	1⅛ inch	2.56	2.69

PLAIN DRIP CAP OUTSIDE DOOR FRAMES.

When ordering frames with transom head be sure to give height of transom.

PRICES OF FRAMES FOR CHECK RAIL WINDOWS.

TWO LIGHTS.

Size of Glass	Size of Opening Ft.In. x Ft.In.	No. 63B7824 Price	No. 63B7948 Price
12x20	1 4⅛ x 3 10	$1.26	$1.40
12x24	1 4⅛ x 4 6	1.27	1.41
12x26	1 4⅛ x 4 10	1.28	1.42
12x28	1 4⅛ x 5 2	1.29	1.43
12x30	1 4⅛ x 5 6	1.41	1.60
12x32	1 4⅛ x 5 10	1.42	1.61
14x20	1 6⅛ x 3 10	1.26	1.40
14x24	1 6⅛ x 4 6	1.28	1.42
14x26	1 6⅛ x 4 10	1.29	1.43
14x28	1 6⅛ x 5 2	1.30	1.44
14x30	1 6⅛ x 5 6	1.41	1.60
14x32	1 6⅛ x 5 10	1.42	1.61
16x20	1 8⅛ x 3 10	1.28	1.42
16x22	1 8⅛ x 4 2	1.29	1.43
16x24	1 8⅛ x 4 6	1.30	1.44
16x26	1 8⅛ x 4 10	1.31	1.45
16x28	1 8⅛ x 5 2	1.32	1.46
16x30	1 8⅛ x 5 6	1.42	1.61
16x32	1 8⅛ x 5 10	1.43	1.62
18x20	1 10⅛ x 3 10	1.28	1.42
18x22	1 10⅛ x 4 2	1.29	1.43
18x24	1 10⅛ x 4 6	1.30	1.44
18x26	1 10⅛ x 4 10	1.31	1.45
18x28	1 10⅛ x 5 2	1.32	1.46
18x30	1 10⅛ x 5 6	1.42	1.61
18x32	1 10⅛ x 5 10	1.43	1.62
20x20	2 0⅛ x 3 10	1.29	1.43
20x22	2 0⅛ x 4 2	1.30	1.44
20x24	2 0⅛ x 4 6	1.31	1.45
20x26	2 0⅛ x 4 10	1.32	1.46
20x28	2 0⅛ x 5 2	1.33	1.47
20x30	2 0⅛ x 5 6	1.43	1.62
20x32	2 0⅛ x 5 10	1.44	1.63
20x34	2 0⅛ x 6 2	1.46	1.65
20x36	2 0⅛ x 6 6	1.47	1.66
22x20	2 2⅛ x 3 10	1.29	1.43
22x22	2 2⅛ x 4 2	1.30	1.44
22x24	2 2⅛ x 4 6	1.31	1.45
22x26	2 2⅛ x 4 10	1.32	1.46
22x28	2 2⅛ x 5 2	1.33	1.47
22x30	2 2⅛ x 5 6	1.43	1.62
22x32	2 2⅛ x 5 10	1.44	1.63
22x34	2 2⅛ x 6 2	1.46	1.65
22x36	2 2⅛ x 6 6	1.47	1.66
24x20	2 4⅛ x 3 10	1.30	1.44
24x22	2 4⅛ x 4 2	1.31	1.45
24x24	2 4⅛ x 4 6	1.32	1.46
24x26	2 4⅛ x 4 10	1.33	1.47
24x28	2 4⅛ x 5 2	1.34	1.48
24x30	2 4⅛ x 5 6	1.45	1.64
24x32	2 4⅛ x 5 10	1.46	1.65
24x34	2 4⅛ x 6 2	1.47	1.66
24x36	2 4⅛ x 6 6	1.48	1.67
26x24	2 6⅛ x 4 6	1.33	1.47
26x26	2 6⅛ x 4 10	1.34	1.48
26x28	2 6⅛ x 5 2	1.35	1.49
26x30	2 6⅛ x 5 6	1.46	1.65
26x32	2 6⅛ x 5 10	1.47	1.66
26x34	2 6⅛ x 6 2	1.48	1.67
26x36	2 6⅛ x 6 6	1.49	1.68
28x24	2 8⅛ x 4 6	1.42	1.61
28x26	2 8⅛ x 4 10	1.44	1.63
28x28	2 8⅛ x 5 2	1.46	1.65
28x30	2 8⅛ x 5 6	1.48	1.67
28x32	2 8⅛ x 5 10	1.49	1.68
28x34	2 8⅛ x 6 2	1.50	1.69
28x36	2 8⅛ x 6 6	1.51	1.70
28x40	2 8⅛ x 7 2	1.54	1.73
30x24	2 10⅛ x 4 6	1.44	1.63
30x26	2 10⅛ x 4 10	1.46	1.65
30x28	2 10⅛ x 5 2	1.47	1.66
30x30	2 10⅛ x 5 6	1.49	1.68
30x32	2 10⅛ x 5 10	1.50	1.69
30x34	2 10⅛ x 6 2	1.51	1.70

TWO LIGHTS—Continued.

Size of Glass	Size of Opening Ft.In. x Ft.In.	No. 63B7824 Price	No. 63B7948 Price
30x36	2 10⅛ x 6 6	$1.52	$1.71
30x40	2 10⅛ x 7 2	1.55	1.74
32x30	3 0⅛ x 5 6	1.67	1.91
32x32	3 0⅛ x 5 10	1.69	1.93
32x34	3 0⅛ x 6 2	1.70	1.94
32x36	3 0⅛ x 6 6	1.71	1.95
32x40	3 0⅛ x 7 2	1.81	2.05
36x24	3 4⅛ x 4 6	1.52	1.72
36x26	3 4⅛ x 4 10	1.52	1.72
36x28	3 4⅛ x 5 2	1.53	1.73
36x30	3 4⅛ x 5 6	1.71	1.95
36x32	3 4⅛ x 5 10	1.72	1.96
36x36	3 4⅛ x 6 6	1.74	1.98
40x24	3 8⅛ x 4 6	1.52	1.72
40x26	3 8⅛ x 4 10	1.53	1.73
40x28	3 8⅛ x 5 2	1.54	1.74
40x30	3 8⅛ x 5 6	1.72	1.96
40x32	3 8⅛ x 5 10	1.73	1.97
40x36	3 8⅛ x 6 6	1.76	2.00
44x30	4 0⅛ x 5 6	1.75	1.99
44x32	4 0⅛ x 5 10	1.77	2.01
44x36	4 0⅛ x 6 6	1.79	2.03
44x40	4 0⅛ x 7 2	2.16	2.40

FOUR LIGHTS.

Size of Glass	Size of Opening Ft.In. x Ft.In.	No. 63B7824 Price	No. 63B7948 Price
10x20	2 1 x 3 10	$1.29	$1.43
10x22	2 1 x 4 2	1.30	1.44
10x24	2 1 x 4 6	1.31	1.45
10x26	2 1 x 4 10	1.32	1.46
10x28	2 1 x 5 2	1.33	1.47
10x30	2 1 x 5 6	1.43	1.62
10x32	2 1 x 5 10	1.44	1.63
12x20	2 5 x 3 10	1.30	1.44
12x22	2 5 x 4 2	1.31	1.45
12x24	2 5 x 4 6	1.32	1.46
12x26	2 5 x 4 10	1.33	1.47
12x28	2 5 x 5 2	1.34	1.48
12x30	2 5 x 5 6	1.45	1.64
12x32	2 5 x 5 10	1.46	1.65
12x34	2 5 x 6 2	1.47	1.66
12x36	2 5 x 6 6	1.48	1.67
12x40	2 5 x 7 2	1.54	1.73
14x20	2 9 x 3 10	1.40	1.59
14x22	2 9 x 4 2	1.41	1.60
14x24	2 9 x 4 6	1.42	1.61
14x26	2 9 x 4 10	1.44	1.63
14x28	2 9 x 5 2	1.46	1.65
14x30	2 9 x 5 6	1.48	1.67
14x32	2 9 x 5 10	1.49	1.68
14x36	2 9 x 6 6	1.51	1.70
14x40	2 9 x 7 2	1.54	1.73
15x20	2 11 x 3 10	1.51	1.71
15x24	2 11 x 4 6	1.52	1.72
15x26	2 11 x 4 10	1.53	1.73
15x28	2 11 x 5 2	1.54	1.74
15x30	2 11 x 5 6	1.71	1.95
15x32	2 11 x 5 10	1.72	1.96

EIGHT LIGHTS.

Size of Glass	Size of Opening Ft.In. x Ft.In.	No. 63B7824 Price	No. 63B7948 Price
9x12	1 11 x 4 6	$1.31	$1.45
9x14	1 11 x 5 2	1.33	1.47
10x12	2 1 x 4 6	1.32	1.45
10x14	2 1 x 5 2	1.33	1.47
10x16	2 1 x 5 10	1.44	1.63
12x14	2 5 x 5 2	1.34	1.48
12x16	2 5 x 5 10	1.46	1.65
12x18	2 5 x 6 6	1.48	1.67
14x16	2 9 x 5 10	1.49	1.68
14x18	2 9 x 6 6	1.51	1.70
14x20	2 9 x 7 2	1.54	1.73

DETAILS AND EXACT MEASUREMENTS.

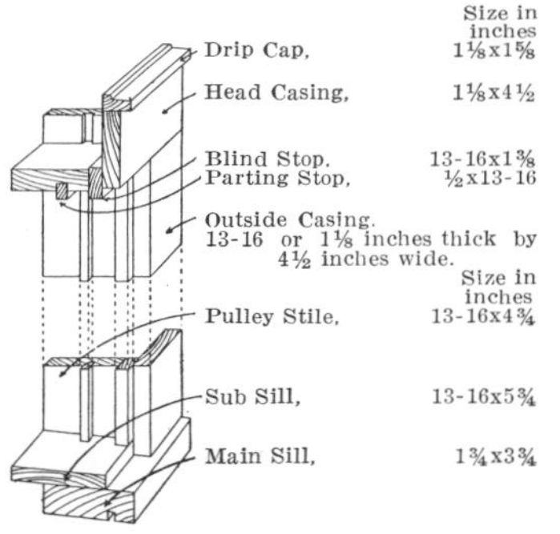

Size in inches
Drip Cap, 1⅛x1⅝
Head Casing, 1⅛x4½
Blind Stop, 13-16x1¾
Parting Stop, ½x13-16
Outside Casing, 13-16 or 1⅛ inches thick by 4½ inches wide.
Size in inches
Pulley Stile, 13-16x4¾
Sub Sill, 13-16x5¾
Main Sill, 1¾x3¾

WINDOW FRAMES.

Made with two-member sill, furnished with 1⅛-inch or ⅞-inch outside casing, made for buildings with regular 2x4-inch studding. Where jambs for window frames are wanted wider than listed, add 20 cents for each additional inch or fraction thereof in the width of the jamb. If window frames are wanted with pulleys and pockets add 25 cents to the price and write the word "Special" after the catalog number. (We use only the best grade of pulleys.)

Double or twin frames are twice the price of one regular frame. Triple frames are three times the price of one regular frame.

PLAIN DRIP CAP WINDOW FRAMES.

QUALITY GUARANTEED CROWN MOLD CAP DOOR AND WINDOW FRAMES QUALITY GUARANTEED

THE DOORS AND WINDOW FRAMES listed on this page are strictly first class frames made of practically clear lumber with three-member crown mold cap. All frames are shipped knocked down, securely packed, complete frame to the bundle. We cut to the exact size of the opening for which they are intended. All that is necessary after receiving these frames is to nail them together, which takes but a few moments' time. Made for buildings with regular 2x4-inch studding.

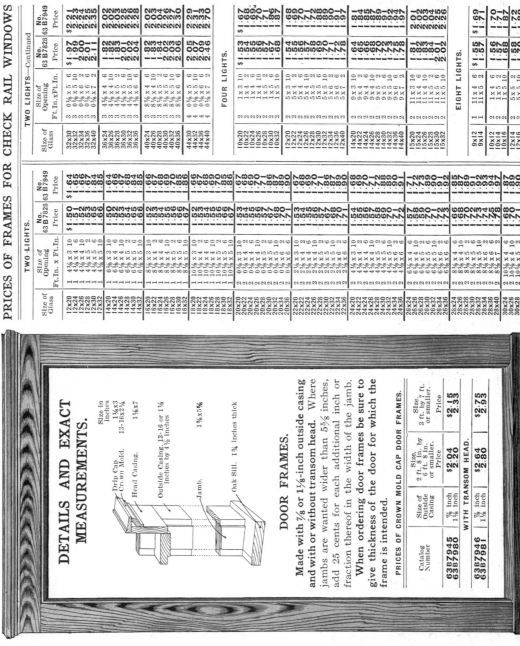

DETAILS AND EXACT MEASUREMENTS.

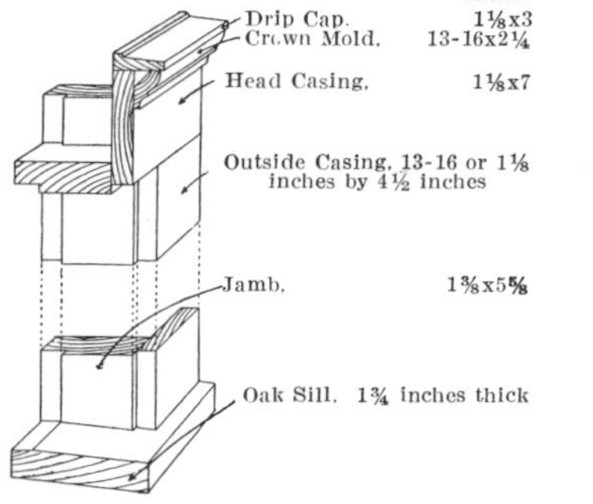
Size in inches
Drip Cap. 1⅛x3
Crown Mold. 13-16x2¼
Head Casing. 1⅛x7
Outside Casing, 13-16 or 1⅛ inches by 4½ inches
Jamb. 1⅜x5⅝
Oak Sill. 1¾ inches thick

DOOR FRAMES.

Made with ⅞ or 1⅛-inch outside casing and with or without transom head. Where jambs are wanted wider than 5⅝ inches, add 25 cents for each additional inch or fraction thereof in the width of the jamb.

When ordering door frames be sure to give thickness of the door for which the frame is intended.

PRICES OF CROWN MOLD CAP DOOR FRAMES.

Catalog Number	Size of Outside Casing	Size, 2 ft. 8 in. by 6 ft. 8 in. or smaller. Price	Size, 3 ft. by 7 ft. or smaller. Price
63B7945	⅞ inch	$2.04	$2.15
63B7980	1⅛ inch	2.20	2.33
WITH TRANSOM HEAD.			
63B7946	⅞ inch	$2.64	$2.75
63B7981	1⅛ inch	2.80	2.93

CROWN MOLD CAP OUTSIDE DOOR FRAMES.

When ordering frames with transom head be sure to give height of transom.

PRICES OF FRAMES FOR CHECK RAIL WINDOWS

TWO LIGHTS.

Size of Glass	Size of Opening Ft.In. x Ft.In.	No. 63B7828 Price	No. 63B7949 Price
12x20	1 4⅛ x 3 10	$1.50	$1.64
12x24	1 4⅛ x 4 6	1.51	1.65
12x26	1 4⅛ x 4 10	1.52	1.66
12x28	1 4⅛ x 5 2	1.53	1.67
12x30	1 4⅛ x 5 6	1.65	1.84
12x32	1 4⅛ x 5 10	1.66	1.85
14x20	1 6⅛ x 3 10	1.50	1.64
14x24	1 6⅛ x 4 6	1.52	1.66
14x26	1 6⅛ x 4 10	1.53	1.67
14x28	1 6⅛ x 5 2	1.54	1.68
14x30	1 6⅛ x 5 6	1.65	1.84
14x32	1 6⅛ x 5 10	1.66	1.85
16x20	1 8⅛ x 3 10	1.52	1.66
16x22	1 8⅛ x 4 2	1.53	1.67
16x24	1 8⅛ x 4 6	1.54	1.68
16x26	1 8⅛ x 4 10	1.55	1.69
16x28	1 8⅛ x 5 2	1.56	1.70
16x30	1 8⅛ x 5 6	1.66	1.85
16x32	1 8⅛ x 5 10	1.67	1.86
18x20	1 10⅛ x 3 10	1.52	1.66
18x22	1 10⅛ x 4 2	1.53	1.67
18x24	1 10⅛ x 4 6	1.54	1.68
18x26	1 10⅛ x 4 10	1.55	1.69
18x28	1 10⅛ x 5 2	1.56	1.70
18x30	1 10⅛ x 5 6	1.66	1.85
18x32	1 10⅛ x 5 10	1.67	1.86
20x20	2 0⅛ x 3 10	1.53	1.67
20x22	2 0⅛ x 4 2	1.54	1.68
20x24	2 0⅛ x 4 6	1.55	1.69
20x26	2 0⅛ x 4 10	1.56	1.70
20x28	2 0⅛ x 5 2	1.57	1.71
20x30	2 0⅛ x 5 6	1.67	1.86
20x32	2 0⅛ x 5 10	1.68	1.87
20x34	2 0⅛ x 6 2	1.70	1.89
20x36	2 0⅛ x 6 6	1.71	1.90
22x20	2 2⅛ x 3 10	1.53	1.67
22x22	2 2⅛ x 4 2	1.54	1.68
22x24	2 2⅛ x 4 6	1.55	1.69
22x26	2 2⅛ x 4 10	1.56	1.70
22x28	2 2⅛ x 5 2	1.57	1.71
22x30	2 2⅛ x 5 6	1.67	1.86
22x32	2 2⅛ x 5 10	1.68	1.87
22x34	2 2⅛ x 6 2	1.70	1.89
22x36	2 2⅛ x 6 6	1.71	1.90
24x20	2 4⅛ x 3 10	1.54	1.68
24x22	2 4⅛ x 4 2	1.55	1.69
24x24	2 4⅛ x 4 6	1.56	1.70
24x26	2 4⅛ x 4 10	1.57	1.71
24x28	2 4⅛ x 5 2	1.58	1.72
24x30	2 4⅛ x 5 6	1.69	1.88
24x32	2 4⅛ x 5 10	1.70	1.89
24x34	2 4⅛ x 6 2	1.71	1.90
24x36	2 4⅛ x 6 6	1.72	1.91
26x24	2 6⅛ x 4 6	1.57	1.71
26x26	2 6⅛ x 4 10	1.58	1.72
26x28	2 6⅛ x 5 2	1.59	1.73
26x30	2 6⅛ x 5 6	1.70	1.89
26x32	2 6⅛ x 5 10	1.71	1.90
26x34	2 6⅛ x 6 2	1.72	1.91
26x36	2 6⅛ x 6 6	1.73	1.92
28x24	2 8⅛ x 4 6	1.66	1.85
28x26	2 8⅛ x 4 10	1.68	1.87
28x28	2 8⅛ x 5 2	1.70	1.89
28x30	2 8⅛ x 5 6	1.72	1.91
28x32	2 8⅛ x 5 10	1.73	1.92
28x34	2 8⅛ x 6 2	1.74	1.93
28x36	2 8⅛ x 6 6	1.75	1.94
28x40	2 8⅛ x 7 2	1.78	1.97
30x24	2 10⅛ x 4 6	1.68	1.87
30x26	2 10⅛ x 4 10	1.70	1.89
30x28	2 10⅛ x 5 2	1.71	1.90
30x30	2 10⅛ x 5 6	1.73	1.92
30x32	2 10⅛ x 5 10	1.74	1.93
30x34	2 10⅛ x 6 2	1.75	1.94
30x36	2 10⅛ x 6 6	1.76	1.95
30x40	2 10⅛ x 7 2	1.79	1.99

TWO LIGHTS—Continued

Size of Glass	Size of Opening Ft.In.xFt.In.	No. 63B7828 Price	No. 63B7949 Price
32x30	3 0⅛ x 5 6	$1.97	$2.21
32x32	3 0⅛ x 5 10	1.99	2.23
32x34	3 0⅛ x 6 2	2.00	2.24
32x36	3 0⅛ x 6 6	2.01	2.25
32x40	3 0⅛ x 7 2	2.11	2.35
36x24	3 4⅛ x 4 6	1.82	2.02
36x26	3 4⅛ x 4 10	1.82	2.02
36x28	3 4⅛ x 5 2	1.83	2.03
36x30	3 4⅛ x 5 6	2.01	2.25
36x32	3 4⅛ x 5 10	2.02	2.26
36x36	3 4⅛ x 6 6	2.04	2.28
40x24	3 8⅛ x 4 6	1.82	2.02
40x26	3 8⅛ x 4 10	1.83	2.03
40x28	3 8⅛ x 5 2	1.84	2.04
40x30	3 8⅛ x 5 6	2.02	2.26
40x32	3 8⅛ x 5 10	2.03	2.27
40x36	3 8⅛ x 6 6	2.06	2.30
44x30	4 0⅛ x 5 6	2.05	2.29
44x32	4 0⅛ x 5 10	2.07	2.31
44x36	4 0⅛ x 6 6	2.09	2.33
44x40	4 0⅛ x 7 2	2.46	2.70

FOUR LIGHTS.

Size of Glass	Size of Opening Ft.In.xFt.In.	No. 63B7828 Price	No. 63B7949 Price
10x20	2 1 x 3 10	$1.53	$1.67
10x22	2 1 x 4 2	1.54	1.68
10x24	2 1 x 4 6	1.55	1.69
10x26	2 1 x 4 10	1.56	1.70
10x28	2 1 x 5 2	1.57	1.71
10x30	2 1 x 5 6	1.67	1.86
10x32	2 1 x 5 10	1.68	1.87
12x20	2 5 x 3 10	1.54	1.68
12x22	2 5 x 4 2	1.55	1.69
12x24	2 5 x 4 6	1.56	1.70
12x26	2 5 x 4 10	1.57	1.71
12x28	2 5 x 5 2	1.58	1.72
12x30	2 5 x 5 6	1.69	1.88
12x32	2 5 x 5 10	1.70	1.89
12x34	2 5 x 6 2	1.71	1.90
12x36	2 5 x 6 6	1.72	1.91
12x40	2 5 x 7 2	1.78	1.97
14x20	2 9 x 3 10	1.64	1.81
14x22	2 9 x 4 2	1.65	1.84
14x24	2 9 x 4 6	1.66	1.85
14x26	2 9 x 4 10	1.68	1.87
14x28	2 9 x 5 2	1.70	1.89
14x30	2 9 x 5 6	1.72	1.91
14x32	2 9 x 5 10	1.73	1.92
14x36	2 9 x 6 6	1.75	1.94
14x40	2 9 x 7 2	1.78	1.97
15x20	2 11 x 3 10	1.81	2.01
15x24	2 11 x 4 6	1.82	2.02
15x26	2 11 x 4 10	1.83	2.03
15x28	2 11 x 5 2	1.84	2.04
15x30	2 11 x 5 6	2.01	2.25
15x32	2 11 x 5 10	2.02	2.26

EIGHT LIGHTS.

Size of Glass	Size of Opening Ft.In.xFt.In.	No. 63B7828 Price	No. 63B7949 Price
9x12	1 11 x 4 6	$1.55	$1.69
9x14	1 11 x 5 2	1.57	1.71
10x12	2 1 x 4 6	1.56	1.70
10x14	2 1 x 5 2	1.57	1.71
10x16	2 1 x 5 10	1.68	1.87
12x14	2 5 x 5 2	1.58	1.72
12x16	2 5 x 5 10	1.70	1.89
12x18	2 5 x 6 6	1.72	1.91
14x16	2 9 x 5 10	1.73	1.92
14x18	2 9 x 6 6	1.75	1.94
14x20	2 9 x 7 2	1.78	1.97

DETAILS AND EXACT MEASUREMENTS.

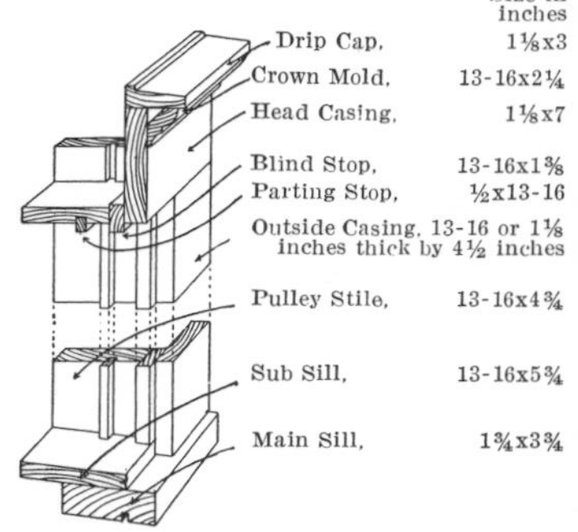
Size in inches
Drip Cap. 1⅛x3
Crown Mold. 13-16x2¼
Head Casing. 1⅛x7
Blind Stop. 13-16x1⅜
Parting Stop. ½x13-16
Outside Casing, 13-16 or 1⅛ inches thick by 4½ inches
Pulley Stile. 13-16x4¾
Sub Sill. 13-16x5¾
Main Sill. 1¾x3¾

WINDOW FRAMES.

Made with two-member sill, furnished with 1⅛ or ⅞-inch outside casing. Made for buildings with regular 2x4-inch studding. Where jambs for window frames are wanted wider than listed, add 20 cents to price of Catalog Nos 63B7828 and 63B7948 according to the width of outside casing wanted.

If window frames are wanted with pulleys and pockets, allow 25 cents extra and write the word "Special" after the catalog number.

Double or twin frames are twice the price of one regular frame. Triple frames are three times the price of one regular frame.

CROWN MOLD CAP WINDOW FRAMES.

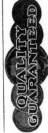

WINDOW AND SASH FRAMES

THE window frames quoted below are for check rail windows. They are furnished knocked down, carefully bundled for shipment. The frames are dadoed for sill but not for head jamb; this enables the carpenter to cut to fit smaller sizes. When ordering give size of glass and number of lights in window. Orders for single sash frames will be furnished at price of window frames of same size opening. **Pockets and pulleys are included.** If pulleys are not wanted deduct 24 cents and mark word "Special" after catalog number.

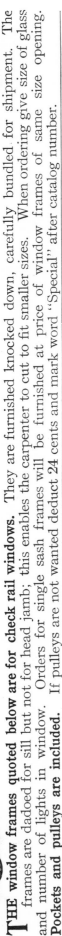

WINDOW FRAMES FOR STONE OR SOLID BRICK BUILDINGS.

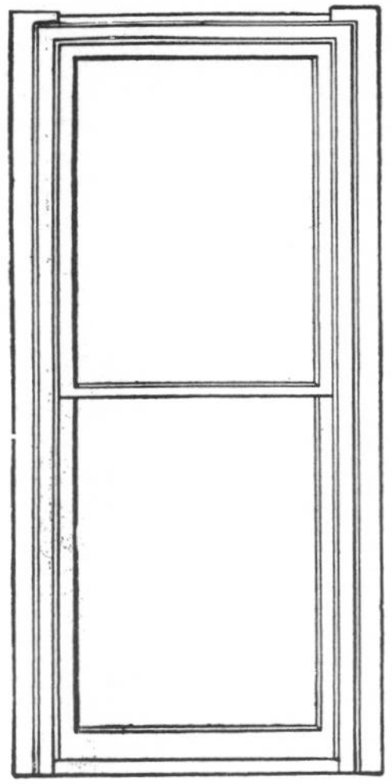

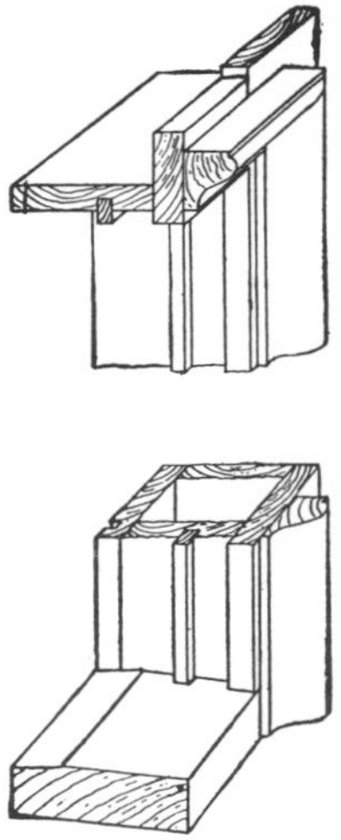

Section of Window Frame for Stone or Solid Brick Building.

SPECIFICATIONS FOR THE ABOVE FRAME.

Brick Mold .... Size, 1⅛x1⅝ inches
Blind Stop .... Size, ⅞x5 inches
Pulley Stile .... Size, ⅞x4½ inches
Parting Stop .... Size, ½x13/16 inches
Rabbeted Box Lining .... Size, ⅞x4½ inches
Back Box Lining .... Size, ⅞x4½ inches

The box linings are made from low grade lumber as they are entirely covered up; the balance is made from good sound stock allowing but few defects. A jamb lining is used with these frames when they are used in residences, which any carpenter can make and fit.

Window frames for stone or solid brick buildings. Knocked down and carefully bundled for shipment, as described above.

PRICES INCLUDE PULLEYS.

SIZE		Price, per Frame
Width	Height	No. 63B8027
2 feet 6 inches	5 feet 2 inches or smaller	$2.22
2 feet 10 inches	6 feet 6 inches or smaller	2.56
2 feet 10 inches	7 feet 2 inches or smaller	2.68
3 feet 8 inches	5 feet 2 inches or smaller	2.63
3 feet 8 inches	7 feet 2 inches or smaller	2.98
4 feet 4 inches	6 feet 6 inches or smaller	2.96

No. 63B8031 Mullion or Double Frames are double the price of regular frames of same window opening size.

No. 63B8032 Triple Frames are three times the price of regular frames of same window opening size.

WINDOW FRAMES FOR CONCRETE BLOCK BUILDINGS.

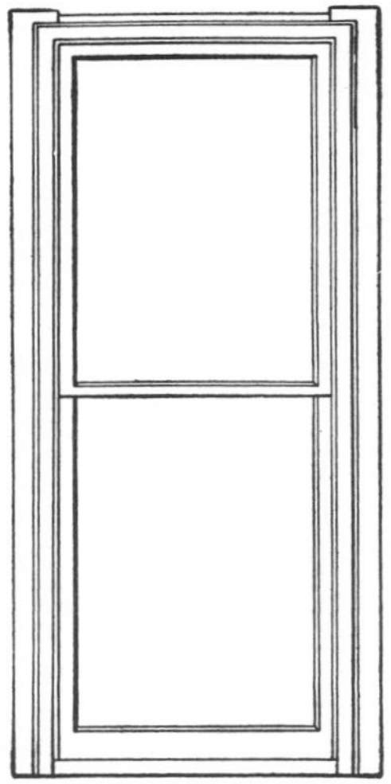

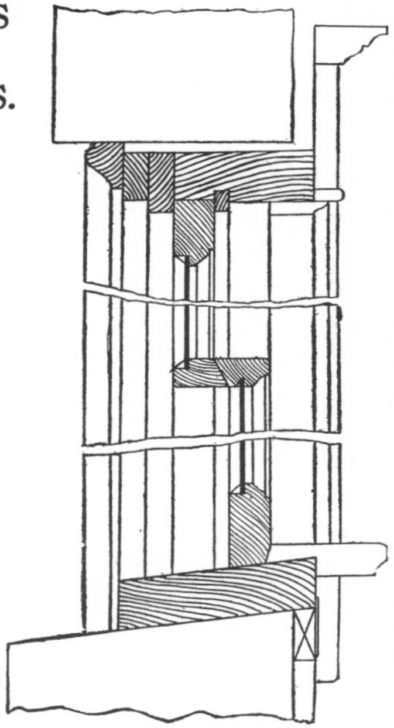

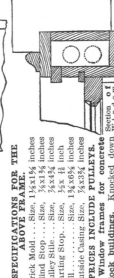

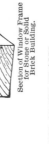

SPECIFICATIONS FOR THE ABOVE FRAME.

Brick Mold .... Size, 1⅛x1⅝ inches
Blind Stop .... Size, ⅞x1⅜ inches
Pulley Stile .... Size, ⅞x4¾ inches
Parting Stop ... Size, ½x13/16 inch
Sill .... Size, 1¾x6⅝ inches
Outside Casing . Size, ⅞x3¾ inches

PRICES INCLUDE PULLEYS.

Window frames for concrete block buildings. Knocked down and carefully bundled for shipment, as described above.

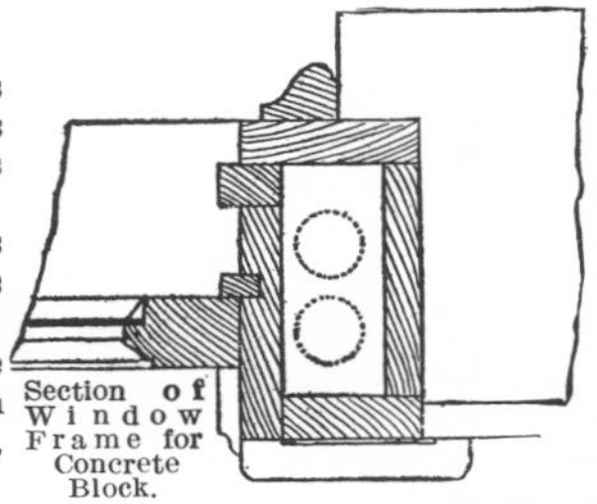

Section of Window Frame for Concrete Block.

SIZE		Price, per Frame
Width	Height	No. 63B8035
2 feet 6 inches	5 feet 2 inches or smaller	$2.42
2 feet 10 inches	6 feet 6 inches or smaller	2.75
2 feet 10 inches	7 feet 2 inches or smaller	2.88
3 feet 8 inches	5 feet 2 inches or smaller	2.88
3 feet 8 inches	7 feet 2 inches or smaller	3.26
4 feet 4 inches	6 feet 6 inches or smaller	3.28

No. 63B8048 Mullion or Double Frames are double the price of regular frames of same window opening size.

No. 63B8049 Triple Frames are three times the price of regular frames of same window opening size.

WINDOW FRAMES FOR BRICK VENEER BUILDINGS.

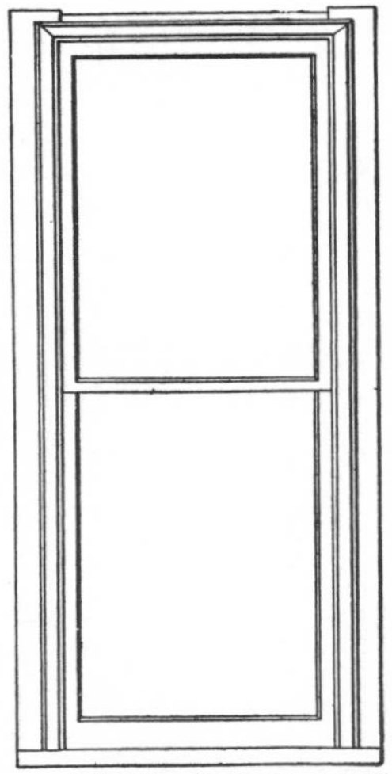

This frame has a 1⅛x1⅝-inch clear brick mold, ⅞x3¾-inch blind stop, ⅞x5⅝-inch jamb including blind stop, ½x13/16-inch parting stop, 1¾x7½-inch sill. The blind stop, while made of a sound grade, need not be as good as the balance, as it is practically all covered up; the rest of the frame is made from good sound material, allowing but few defects.

PRICES INCLUDE PULLEYS.

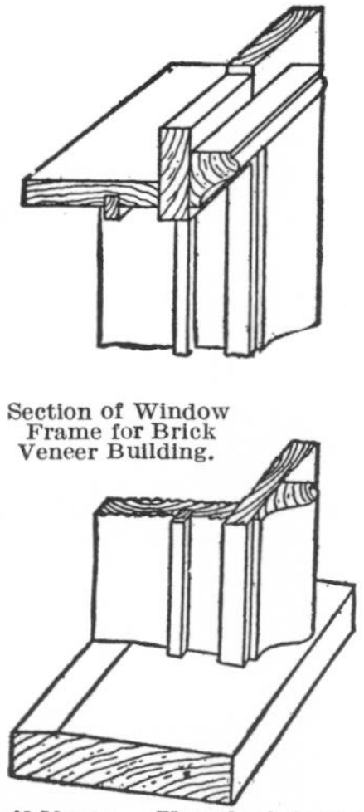

Section of Window Frame for Brick Veneer Building.

Window frames for brick veneer buildings. Knocked down and carefully bundled for shipment, as described above.

SIZE		Price, per Frame
Width	Height	No. 63B8040
2 feet 6 inches	5 feet 2 inches or smaller	$1.90
2 feet 10 inches	6 feet 6 inches or smaller	2.17
2 feet 10 inches	7 feet 2 inches or smaller	2.27
3 feet 8 inches	5 feet 2 inches or smaller	2.30
3 feet 8 inches	7 feet 2 inches or smaller	2.60
4 feet 4 inches	6 feet 6 inches or smaller	2.45

No. 63B8044 Mullion or Double Frames are double the price of regular frames of same window opening size.

No. 63B8045 Triple Frames are three times the price of regular frames of same window opening size.

PLANK CELLAR SASH FRAMES.

Our Plank Cellar Sash Frames are made with a 1¾x7½-in. jamb, 1⅛x1¾-in. clear brick mold. Knocked down, bundled, ready for shipment.

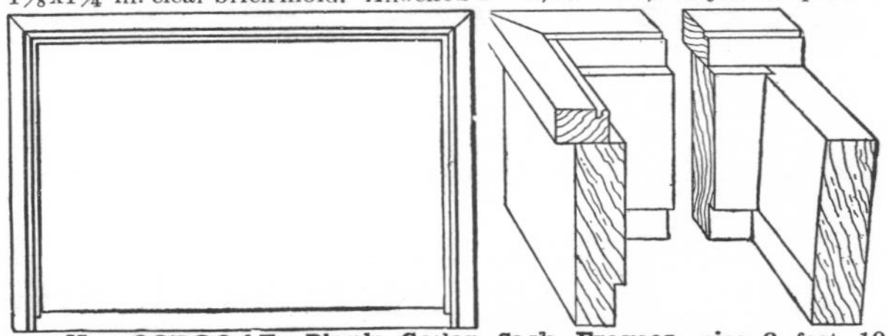

No. 63B8047 Plank Cellar Sash Frames, size 2 feet 10 inches by 2 feet or smaller opening size. Price 98c

DOOR FRAMES FOR STONE OR SOLID BRICK BUILDINGS

This frame has a 1⅛x1⅝-inch clear brick mold and 1⅜ x 5⅝-inch jamb, good, sound and practically clear, only occasional defects being allowable. No sill furnished with this frame.

No. 63B7988 Door Frame for stone or solid brick buildings, knocked down and carefully bundled for shipment, as stated above, for door 3 feet by 7 feet or smaller opening.
Price.....................$1.85

No. 63B7989 Door Frame, same as described above, except with transom head.
Price.....................$2.45

PROMPT SHIPMENT.

We can ship your order for door frames immediately upon receipt of your order.

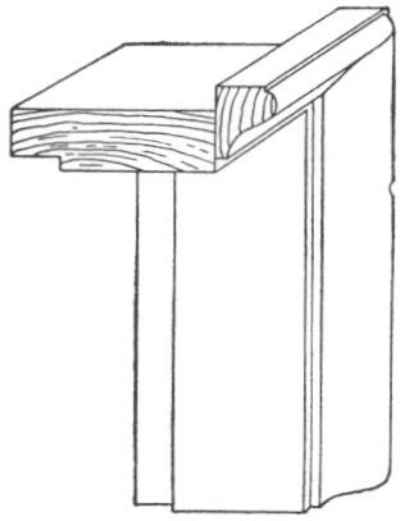

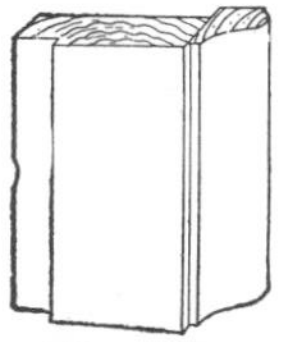

Section of Door Frame for Stone or Solid Brick Building.

DOOR FRAMES FOR CEMENT BLOCK OR BRICK VENEER BUILDINGS

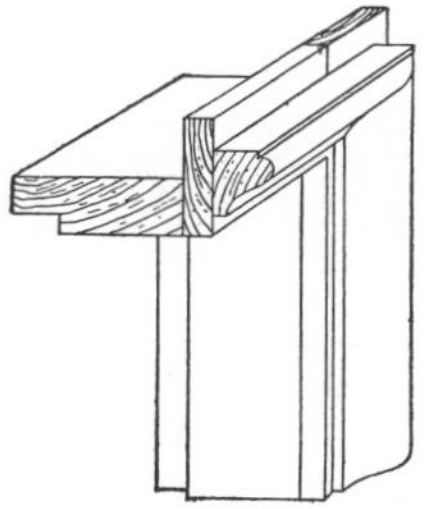

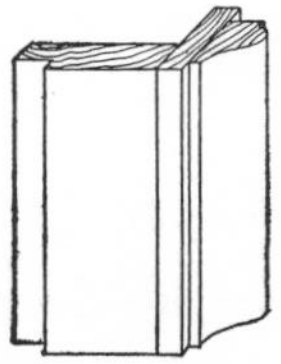

This frame has a 1⅛x1⅝-inch clear brick mold, a ⅞ x 3¾-inch casing or stop and 1⅜x5⅝-inch jamb, all good, sound stock, allowing only occasional defects. No sill furnished with this frame.

No. 63B7992 Door Frame for cement block or brick veneer buildings, knocked down and carefully bundled for shipment, as stated above, for door 3 feet by 7 feet or smaller opening.
Price.....................$2.03

No. 63B7993 Door Frame, same as described above, except with transom head.
Price.....................$2.63

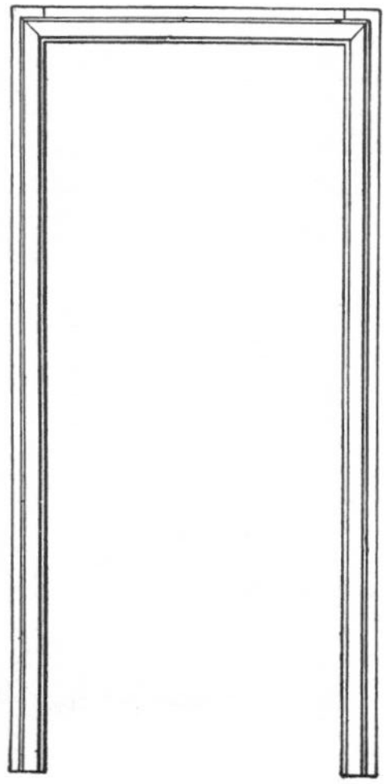

Section of Door Frame for Cement Block or Brick Veneer Building.

INSIDE DOOR JAMBS

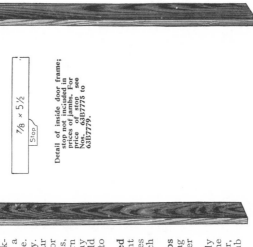

7/8 × 5½
Stop

Detail of inside door frame; stop not included in prices of jambs. For price of stop see Nos. 63B7775 to 63B7779.

Made of clear stock in the following woods: **Nona soft pine** (clear soft Western spruce pine), **yellow pine, plain red oak, Wisconsin birch and cypress.** Carpenters and contractors cannot afford to make door jambs when high grade jambs such as we list on this page can be had at such reasonable prices. Every piece of lumber going into the manufacture of these jambs is first cut to ⅞ inch by 5½ inches, there being absolute uniformity in thickness. The side jambs are dadoed with a machine made for this particular purpose. The head jamb fits into this dado perfectly. All jambs are surfaced and sanded with our heavy sanding machinery and are ready for finishing when received. In other words, where it takes us but a few minutes to turn out a perfect jamb, it would take you many times as long to make jambs which would not be anywhere near as perfect, owing to its all having to be done by hand.

When inside door jambs are wanted with transom head, be sure to give height of transom when ordering. The prices shown below do not include stops which should be ordered separately.

For single or double sliding door jambs allow twice the price of 8x7 foot opening jamb and mark the word "Special," after the catalog number.

Shipped knocked down, carefully bundled for shipment, ready to set up. The jamb is ⅞x5½ inches. If wanted wider, add 30 per cent to the price of the jamb for each inch or fraction thereof.

SIZE In. Ft.			No. 63B7950 Nona Soft Pine	No. 63B7951 Yellow Pine	No. 63B7952 Plain Red Oak	No. 63B7953 Wisconsin Birch	No. 63B7957 Cypress
Ft.	In.						
2	8	8x6 or smaller	$0.69	$0.56	$1.07	$1.02	$0.73
3	0	0x7 or smaller	.70	.57	1.10	1.05	.75
8	0	0x7 or smaller	.90	.70	1.40	1.35	1.00
9	0	0x9 or smaller	1.28	1.01	2.01	1.94	1.43

INSIDE DOOR JAMBS, WITH TRANSOM HEAD, WITH MOLDED TRANSOM BAR.

When ordering be sure to state height of transom.

SIZE In. Ft.			No. 63B7960 Nona Soft Pine	No. 63B7961 Yellow Pine	No. 63B7962 Plain Red Oak	No. 63B7963 Wisconsin Birch	No. 63B7965 Cypress
Ft.	In.						
2	8	8x6 or smaller	$1.20	$1.05	$1.65	$1.55	$1.25
3	0	0x7 or smaller	1.25	1.10	1.70	1.65	1.30

WINDOW GLASS AT CARLOAD PRICES

2½ CENTS A LIGHT AND UP

21 CENTS A LIGHT AND UP

DO NOT PAY FANCY RETAIL PRICES

QUALITY GUARANTEED

SAFE DELIVERY GUARANTEED

Our window glass is packed in strong boxes as carefully as possible by experienced packers and when we make delivery to the transportation company we get a receipt showing the glass is in good order. Be sure to examine your boxes before paying freight bill or removing from freight depot. If the box contains any broken glass it will rattle when the box is shaken. If the box rattles, have it opened in the presence of the agent and have him note on the expense bill that box rattled and state the number of lights broken. Send this noted expense bill to us and we will replace glass without expense to you or refund value of the broken glass. We positively will not replace glass broken in transit without the agent's notation on the bill which you get when you pay out the freight, but it will be a very easy and simple matter to examine your glass before you take it away from the depot, and if it contains any broken glass have the agent make notation as outlined above. We ship a great deal of glass and have very, very few complaints of breakage, and only in exceptional cases do we have to make claims and refunds for broken lights.

LOW FREIGHT RATES

Window glass in box lots takes a very low freight rate and the small amount of freight you pay will amount to nothing in comparison with the great saving we can make you on the cost of your glass. We have several different points from which we can make shipment of our glass in box lots and when we receive your order we will make shipment from the factory which is nearest you. For instance, we have an Indiana connection which we use in furnishing glass to our Eastern customers. We also ship glass from Eastern Iowa with mill work. When we receive your order we will be careful to make the freight as low as possible for you by shipping from the nearest glass factory.

GRADES

All window glass in box lots is graded at the glass factories by expert graders and the glass we furnish you will be just as it was graded by factory graders. In other words, you will absolutely receive the original factory grading. There is a practice among a large number of dealers to buy "B" glass and regrade and sell it as "A" grade, but we will give you the original factory grades which will insure your getting the very best glass. On account of defects any lights less than 14x40 inches can be used in "B" grade and, no doubt, be very satisfactory as the size of the light will not make the defects very noticeable. On all lights larger than 14x40 inches "A" grade will be furnished.

The window glass which we offer in this list is the same grade and quality which we use in glazing our windows. Double strength glass varies in thickness, but eight lights taken at random should measure 1 inch. If one should pick out eight of the thickest lights, they would be more than 1 inch thick. If you should select eight of the thinnest lights they would be less than 1 inch thick. Single strength glass selected at random will measure 1 inch thick.

BOXING CHARGED ON ORDERS AMOUNTING TO LESS THAN 75 CENTS.

On account of extra expense of handling and packing lights, we cannot accept an order for glass amounting to less than 75 cents at these prices. The cost of packing a single light is about the same as packing a whole box of glass. Anything less than a full box will be charged at single light price. We carry all this glass in stock in box lots and each box contains the number of lights shown in the table below and that portion of any order which necessitates repacking will be charged on the single light basis. For instance if you should want twelve lights 24x30 inches we would send you one full box containing ten lights at the box price and two extra lights at the single light price. Add 25 cents extra for boxing on all orders amounting to less than 75 cents.

Size in inches	Catalog Nos. 63B9005 Single Strength, per Light	63B9030 Double Strength, per Light	Number of Lights in Box	63B9041 Single Stre'gth, per Box	63B9052 Double Strength, per Box
20x22	$0.24	$0.36	16	$3.37	$4.95
20x24	.26	.38	15	3.37	4.95
20x26	.28	.41	14	3.37	4.95
20x28	.30	.44	13	3.37	4.95
20x30	.32	.48	11	3.48	5.08
20x32	.36	.53	11	3.48	5.08
20x34	.43	.60	10	3.68	5.20
20x36	.26	.38	15	3.37	4.95
22x22¸	.28	.41	14	3.37	4.95
22x26	.30	.44	13	3.37	4.95
22x28	.32	.48	11	3.48	5.08
22x30	.40	.53	11	3.48	5.08
22x32	.32	.48	12	3.37	4.95
24x24	.36	.53	11	3.48	5.08
24x28	.40	.58	10	3.48	5.08
24x30	.43	.60	10	3.68	5.20
24x32	.47	.67	9	3.68	5.20
24x34	.47	.67	9	3.68	5.20
24x36	.59	.81	9	3.68	5.60
24x38	.59	.92	8	4.09	5.08
24x40	.43	.60	8	3.68	5.60
26x26	.47	.67	8	3.68	5.20
26x30	.47	.67	9	3.68	5.20
26x32	.59	.81	9	3.48	5.60
26x34	.59	.81	8	4.09	5.60
26x36	.47	.67	8	3.68	5.08
28x28	.47	.67	9	4.09	5.20
28x30	.22	.32	18	3.37	4.95

Size in inches	Catalog Nos. 63B9005 Single Strength, per Light	63B9030 Double Strength, per Light	Number of Lights in Box	63B9041 Single Strength, per Box	63B9052 Double Strength, per Box
14x20	$0.13	...	26	$2.84	...
14x22	.14	...	24	2.98	...
14x24	.16	...	22	2.98	...
14x26	.17	...	20	2.98	...
14x28	.19	...	19	3.13	...
14x30	.21	...	17	3.13	...
14x32	.23	...	16	3.13	...
14x34	.24	...	15	3.13	...
14x36	.26	...	14	3.19	...
16x20	.28	$0.25	23	2.98	$4.55
16x22	.16	.25	21	2.98	4.55
16x24	.18	.28	19	2.98	4.55
16x26	.19	.34	17	3.37	4.95
16x28	.23	.36	16	3.37	4.95
16x30	.24	.38	15	3.37	4.95
16x32	.26	.41	14	3.37	4.95
16x34	.30	.44	13	3.37	5.08
16x36	.31	.45	13	3.48	5.08
16x44	.43	.60	10	3.68	5.20
18x20	.22	.26	20	2.98	4.55
18x22	.22	.32	18	2.98	5.20
18x24	.23	.34	17	3.37	4.95
18x26	.24	.36	16	3.37	4.95
18x28	.28	.41	14	3.37	4.95
18x30	.30	.44	13	3.37	4.95
18x32	.33	.48	12	3.48	5.08
18x34	.36	.53	11	3.48	5.60
18x36	.36	.53	11	3.48	5.60
18x48	.81	...	8	3.48	5.08
20x20	.22	.32	18	3.37	4.95

Size in inches	Catalog Nos. 63B9005 Single Strength, per Light	63B9030 Double Strength, per Light	Number of Lights in Box	63B9041 Single Strength, per Box	63B9052 Double Strength, per Box
7x 9	$0.02½	...	115	$2.71	...
8x10	.04	...	90	2.71	...
8x12	.04	...	75	2.71	...
8x14	.05	...	64	2.71	...
9x12	.05	...	67	2.71	...
9x14	.06	...	57	2.71	...
10x12	.05	...	60	2.71	...
10x14	.06	...	52	2.71	...
10x14	.06	...	45	2.84	...
10x16	.07	...	40	2.84	...
10x18	.08	...	36	2.84	...
10x20	.09	...	33	2.84	...
10x22	.10	...	30	2.84	...
10x24	.11	...	28	2.98	...
10x26	.12	...	26	2.98	...
10x30	.13	...	24	2.98	...
12x14	.08	...	43	2.84	...
12x16	.09	...	38	2.84	...
12x18	.10	...	34	2.84	...
12x20	.11	...	30	2.84	...
12x22	.12	...	27	2.84	...
12x24	.14	...	25	2.98	...
12x26	.15	...	23	2.98	...
12x28	.16	...	22	2.98	...
12x30	.18	...	20	3.13	...
12x32	.19	...	19	3.13	...
12x34	.20	...	18	3.13	...
12x36	.21	...	17	3.19	...
12x40	.24	...	15	3.19	...
14x16	.10	...	32	2.84	...
14x18	.11	...	29	2.84	...

lights from 100 lights, eight of the thinnest lights they would be less than 1 inch thick, twelve lights they would be less than 1 inch thick, also varies in thickness.

Size in inches	Catalog Nos. 63B9005 Single Strength, per Light	63B9030 Double Strength, Per Light	63B9052 Double Strength, per Box	63B9041 Single Strength, per Box	Number of Lights in Box
28x32	$0.59	$0.81	$4.95	$3.37	16
28x34	.59	.81	4.95	3.37	15
28x36	.67	.92	4.95	3.37	14
28x38	.67	.92	4.95	3.37	13
28x40	.59	.81	5.08	3.48	11
30x30	.59	.92	4.95	3.48	11
30x32	.67	.92	5.08	3.48	10
30x34	.67	.92	4.95	3.37	15
30x36	.67	.92	5.20	3.68	13
30x40		1.08	4.95	3.37	11
30x44		1.18	4.95	3.37	10
32x32	.67	.92	5.08	3.48	12
32x34		1.08	4.95	3.37	11
32x36		1.18	5.08	3.48	10
32x40		1.42	4.95	3.37	12
34x34		1.42	5.08	3.48	11
36x38		1.42	5.08	3.48	10
36x40		1.42	5.20	3.68	9
40x40		1.81	5.20	3.68	9
40x44		1.81	5.60	4.09	8
40x48		1.92	5.08	3.48	11
42x44		2.11	4.95	3.37	10
44x44		2.11	5.20	3.68	9
44x50		2.87	5.60	4.09	8
46x48		2.87	5.60	4.09	8
48x48		3.37	5.20	3.68	9
48x50		3.37			

Size in inches	Catalog Nos. 63B9005 Single Strength, per Light	63B9030 Double Strength, Per Light	Number of Lights in Box	63B9041 Single Strength, per Box	63B9052 Double Strength, per Box
28x32	$0.59	$0.81	8	$4.09	$5.60
28x34	.59	.81	8	4.09	5.60
28x36	.67	.92	7	4.09	5.60
28x38	.67	.92	7	4.09	5.60
28x40	.59	.81	8	4.09	5.60
30x30	.59	.92	7	4.09	5.60
30x32	.67	.92	7	4.09	5.60
30x34	.67	.92	7	4.09	5.60
30x36	.67	.92	7	4.09	5.60
30x40		1.08	6		5.60
30x44		1.18	6		6.15
32x32	.67	.92	7		5.60
32x34		1.08	6		6.15
32x36		1.18	6		6.15
32x40		1.42	5		6.15
34x34		1.42	5		6.28
36x38		1.42	4		6.28
36x40		1.42	4		6.68
40x40		1.81	4		6.08
40x44		1.81	4		7.36
40x48		1.92	4		7.36
42x44		2.11	4		7.48
44x44		2.11	3		7.48
44x50		2.87	3		7.48
46x48		2.87	3		8.80
48x48		3.37	3		8.80
48x50		3.37	3		

Highest Grades of Material for Beamed Ceilings, Wainscot and Plate Rail

WHICH ARE ESPECIALLY DESIGNED FOR STRICTLY UP TO DATE INTERIORS.

ORDER THIS MATERIAL FOR YOUR NEXT HOUSE

In place of bare ceilings and bare walls build an artistic beamed ceiling and a plaster panel wainscot. It will add beauty and refinement to your home which cannot be duplicated by the most expensive furnishings; in fact, a room finished with beamed ceiling and wainscoting, such as described on this page, is practically furnished. All that is required is a few pieces of ordinary furniture and the room presents the appearance and has a touch of refinement which can only be found in mansions of the highest order.

BEAMED CEILINGS WILL ADD HUNDREDS OF DOLLARS TO THE VALUE OF AN OLD HOUSE

The cost of remodeling is very small and, by the addition of a few dollars in the cost of material and labor, an out of date house can be transformed into an up to date interior. The materials we furnish are shipped knocked down in readiness to put in place and all that is required is the use of a square and a saw, and the job can be completed with very little labor. The services of an expert mechanic are not required.

$9.00 WILL PAY FOR ALL THE MATERIAL NECESSARY FOR THE CONSTRUCTION OF A CEILING OF A ROOM 12x12 FEET. THE SAME IDENTICAL BILL IS SOLD IN SOME LOCALITIES FOR TEN TIMES THIS AMOUNT.

THE ABOVE ILLUSTRATION SHOWS A MODERN DINING ROOM WITH BEAMED CEILING AND WAINSCOTING MADE FROM MATERIAL ILLUSTRATED AND DESCRIBED BELOW.

IN ORDERING BEAMED CEILINGS first decide whether narrow beams or wide beams are desired, bearing in mind that for a room 12 feet by 12 feet narrow beams No. 63B4010 or No. 63B4015 are preferable. For larger rooms than size 12 feet by 12 feet we recommend wide beams No. 63B4020 or No. 63B4025, or a combination of both, which can be alternated with a good effect.

FOR A DINING ROOM we recommend our plate rail and plaster panel wainscot. They will harmonize with either style of Beamed Ceiling. They give a very pleasing effect, as illustrated by the picture to the left.

IF IN DOUBT ABOUT THE QUANTITY OF MATERIAL YOU WILL REQUIRE for beamed ceilings, wainscot and plate rail, send us a rough sketch or diagram of the room you wish to finish with material shown on this page and we will tell you to the penny what the entire job will cost and guarantee to furnish you a grade of material which is equal, if not superior, to the kind that you would be able to get in your home town at many times the amount you would be obliged to pay us. Be sure to order by catalog number and state whether oak or pine finish is desired.

MEDIUM BEAM.

4½-Inch Drop.

6 Inches Wide.

No. 63B4010 **Yellow Pine.** Price, per lineal foot........8c
No. 63B4015 **Plain Oak.** Price, per lineal foot.........14c

LARGE BEAM.

4½-Inch Drop.

13 Inches Wide.

No. 63B4020 **Yellow Pine.** Price, per lineal foot........12c
No. 63B4025 **Plain Oak.** Price, per lineal foot.........21c

HALF BEAM.

No. 63B4060 **Yellow Pine.** Per lineal foot..........4½c
No. 63B4063 **Plain Oak.** Per lineal foot...........7c

WAINSCOTING.

Cap.

Stile.

Base.

No. 63B4030 **Cap,** complete, yellow pine. Per lineal foot........7c
No. 63B4031 **Cap,** complete, plain oak. Per lineal foot........11c
No. 63B4040 **Stile,** yellow pine. Per lineal foot..2¾c
No. 63B4043 **Stile,** plain oak. Per lineal foot....3½c
No. 63B4050 **Base,** yellow pine. Per lineal foot...6c
No. 63B4055 **Base,** plain oak. Per lineal foot......9c

CRAFTSMAN TRIM

CRAFTSMAN PLATE RAIL.

We illustrate below a neat and tasty design of Craftsman Plate Rail.

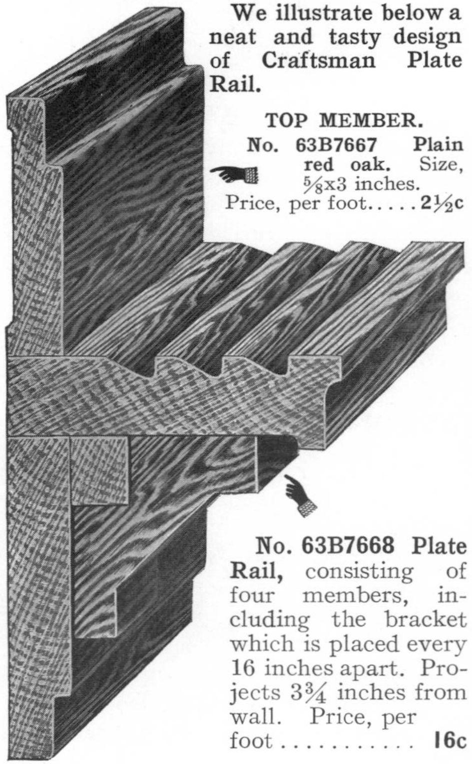

TOP MEMBER.

No. 63B7667 Plain red oak. Size, ⅝x3 inches. Price, per foot.....2½c

No. 63B7668 Plate Rail, consisting of four members, including the bracket which is placed every 16 inches apart. Projects 3¾ inches from wall. Price, per foot........... **16c**

CRAFTSMAN BASE BLOCK.

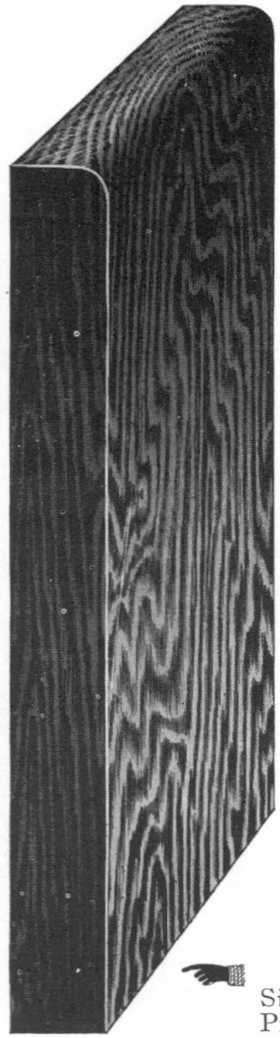

No. 63B7670 Oak. Size, 13-16x7½ inches. Price, each **6c**

We illustrate on this and the opposite page our **Craftsman trim,** consisting of base blocks, plate rail, casing, base, stair rail, in fact, practically everything for inside trim. This molding and trim is being specified by the leading architects throughout the country. You will notice by referring to these illustrations that there is practically no surface where the dust can accumulate, making these the cleanest of all moldings. When similar trim is specified by architects it has been necessary heretofore to have the moldings made up special to order, which brings the prices up to about three times the prices quoted on this page. This material is particularly adapted to match the Craftsman doors shown on pages 10 and 11.

CRAFTSMAN THREE-MEMBER BASE

Consisting of Base Mold, Base and Carpet Strip.

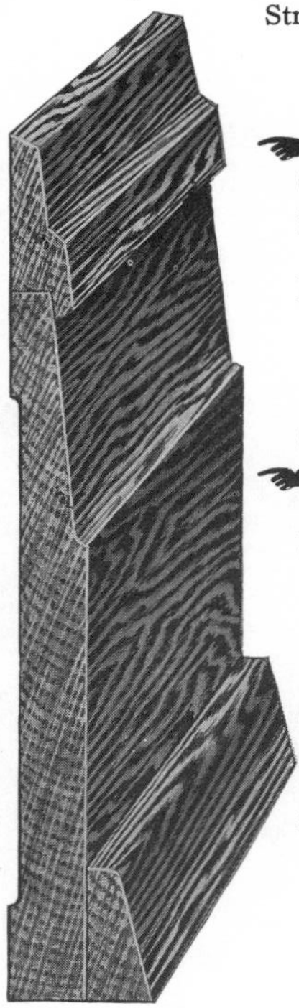

BASE MOLD.

No. 63B7673 Oak. Size, ½x1⅝ inches. Price, per 100 lineal feet....**$1.14**

BASE.

No. 63B7674 Oak. Size, ⅝x5¾ inches. Price, per 100 lineal feet....**$4.75**

CARPET STRIP.

No. 63B7675 Oak. Size, ½x1⅛ inches. Price, per 100 lineal feet..........**89c**

CRAFTSMAN BEDROOM BASE.

Consisting of Three Members.

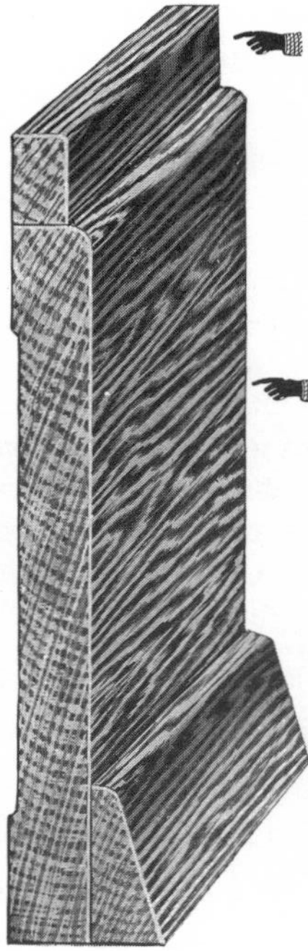

BASE MOLD.

No. 63B7681 Oak. Size, 7-16x¾ inch. Price per 100 lineal feet.............**82c**

No. 63B7682 Birch. Price per 100 lineal feet........**62c**

BASE.

No. 63B7683 Oak. Size, ⅝x5¾ inches. Price, per 100 lineal feet...........**$4.75**

No. 63B7684 Birch. Price, per 100 lineal feet......**$3.75**

CARPET STRIP.

No. 63B7686 Oak Size, ½x1⅛ inches. Price, per 100 lineal feet, **89c**

No. 63B7687 Birch. Price, per 100 lineal feet........**67c**

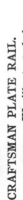

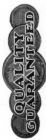

CRAFTSMAN CASING.

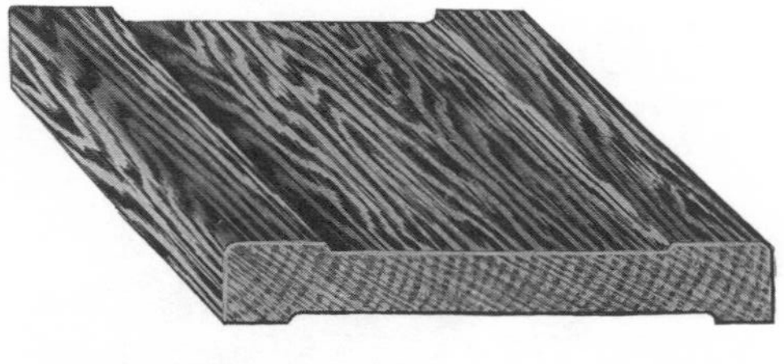

No. 63B7602 Oak. Size, 9-16x3¾ inches. Price, per 100 lineal feet...**$3.15**

CRAFTSMAN DOOR AND WINDOW STOP.

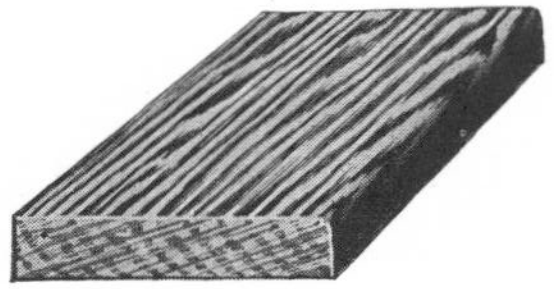

No. 63B7672 Oak. Size, ⅜x2 inches. Price, per 100 lineal feet.........**$1.20**

CRAFTSMAN PANEL STRIP.

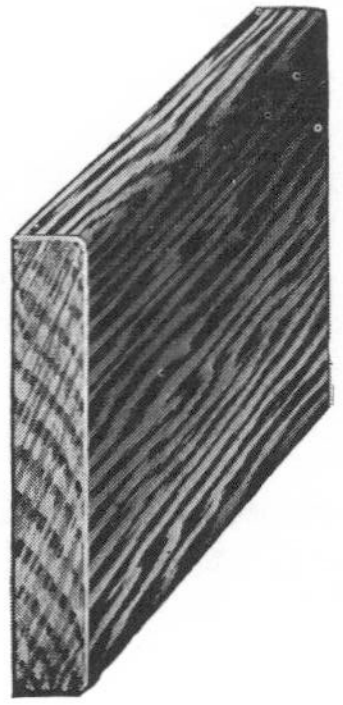

To be used **underneath each plate rail bracket** giving the wall a nice panel effect.

No. 63B7627 Oak. Size, ⅜x2¼ in. Price, per 100 lineal feet....**$1.73**

CRAFTSMAN PICTURE MOLD.

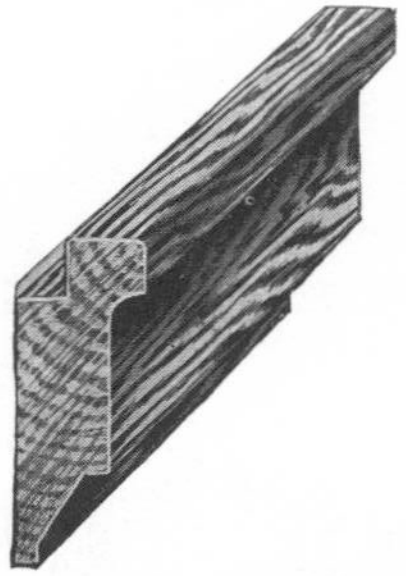

No. 63B7628 Oak. Size, ¾x1⅞ inches. Price, per 100 lineal feet........**$1.61**

QUALITY GUARANTEED

CRAFTSMAN TRIM

QUALITY GUARANTEED

Neat, Simple and Artistic. Will Lend an Air of Elegance to Any Home.

CRAFTSMAN CAP TRIM.

The illustration shows our beautiful Craftsman Cap Trim and the manner in which it is put up.

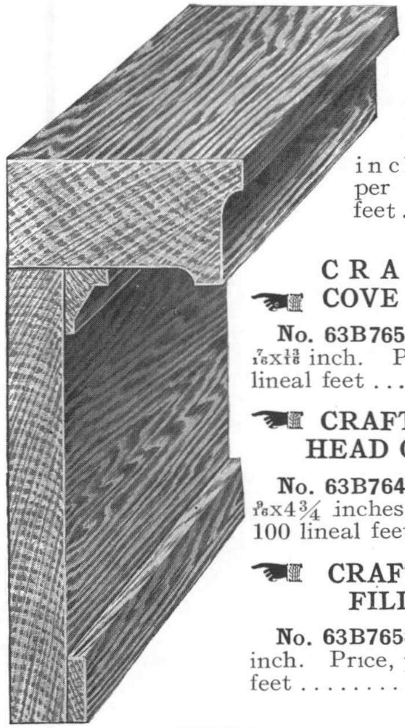

CRAFTSMAN CAP MOLD.

No. 63B7626 Oak. Size, $1\frac{3}{8}$x$2\frac{1}{2}$ inches. Price, per 100 lineal feet........**$4.50**

CRAFTSMAN COVE MOLDING.

No. 63B7655 Oak. Size, $\frac{7}{16}$x$\frac{13}{16}$ inch. Price, per 100 lineal feet............**71c**

CRAFTSMAN HEAD CASING.

No. 63B7642 Oak. Size, $\frac{3}{16}$x$4\frac{3}{4}$ inches. Price, per 100 lineal feet.......**$3.94**

CRAFTSMAN FILLET.

No. 63B7654 Size, $\frac{3}{16}$x$\frac{11}{16}$ inch. Price, per 100 lineal feet..................**71c**

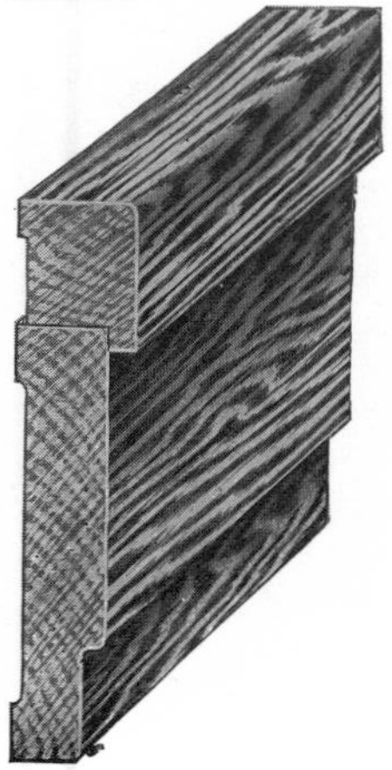

CRAFTSMAN CASING AND CAP.

Size, $\frac{3}{4}$x$3\frac{3}{4}$ inches; two-member.

No. 63B7666 Oak. Price, per 100 lineal feet..........**$3.25**

No. 63B7669 Birch. Price, per 100 lineal feet..........**$2.54**

These prices include both members.

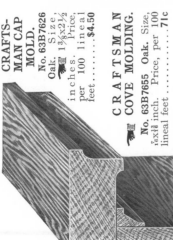

CRAFTSMAN WAINSCOT RAIL.

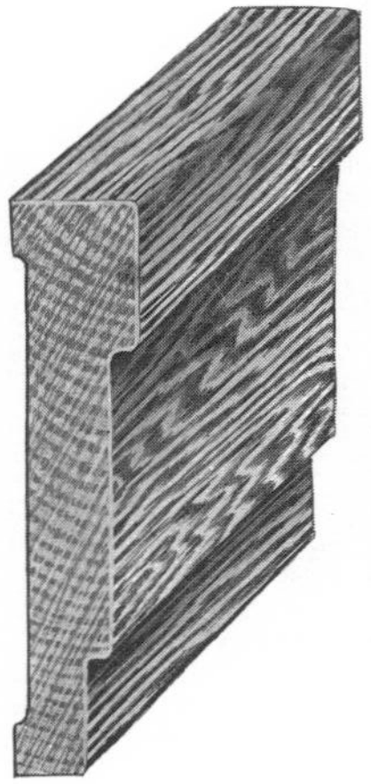

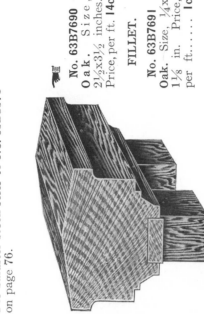

No. 63B7603 Oak. Size, $\frac{13}{16}$x$3\frac{3}{4}$ inches. Price, per 100 lineal feet, **$3.15**

CRAFTSMAN STAIR RAIL.

Rabbeted for $1\frac{1}{8}$-inch balusters. For baluster stock refer to No. 63B8371 on page 76.

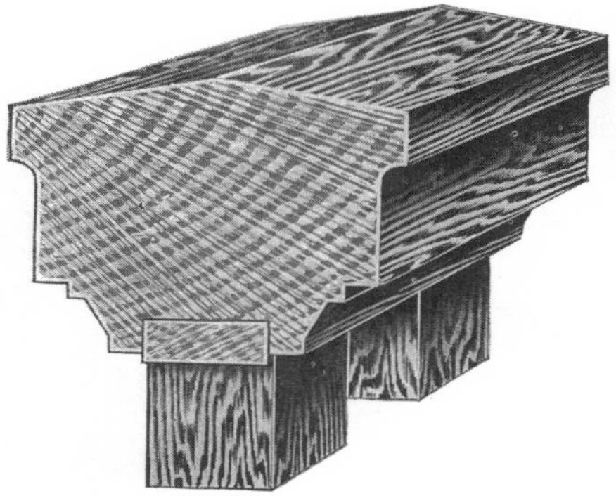

No. 63B7690 Oak. Size, $2\frac{1}{2}$x$3\frac{1}{2}$ inches. Price, per ft. **14c**

FILLET.

No. 63B7691 Oak. Size, $\frac{1}{4}$x$1\frac{1}{8}$ in. Price, per ft...... **1c**

CRAFTSMAN STOOL AND APRON.

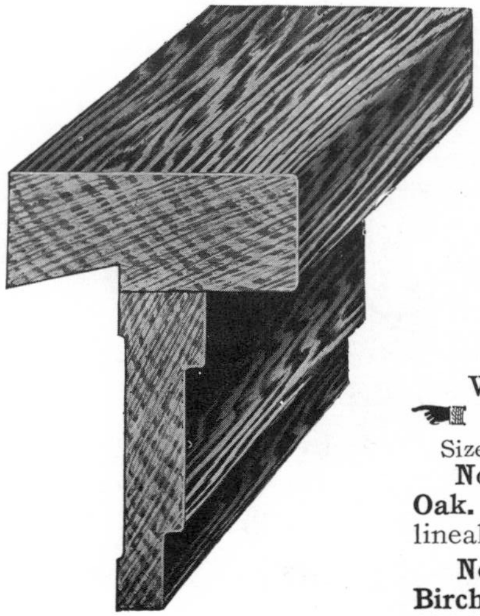

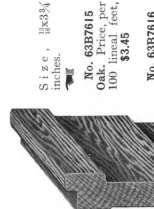

WINDOW STOOL.

Size, $1\frac{1}{8}$x$3\frac{3}{4}$ inches.

No. 63B7715 Oak. Price, per 100 lineal feet....**$4.52**

No. 63B7606 Birch. Price, per 100 lineal feet....**$3.91**

WINDOW APRON

Size, $\frac{13}{16}$x3 inches.

No. 63B7608 Oak. Price, per 100 lineal feet...**$2.44**

No. 63B7607 Birch. Price, per 100 lineal ft. .**$1.93**

CRAFTSMAN BEDROOM PICTURE MOLD.

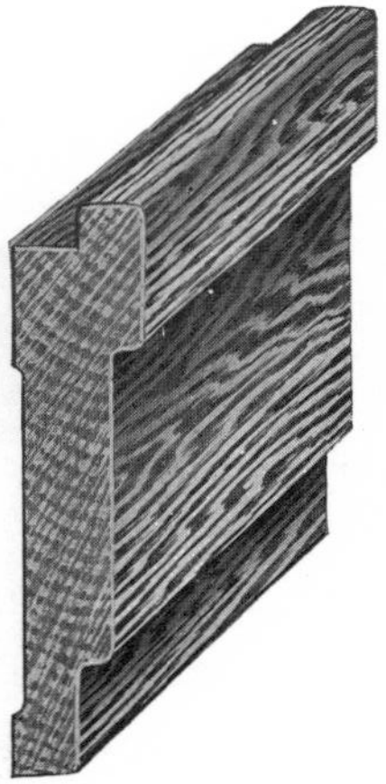

Size, $\frac{13}{16}$x$3\frac{3}{4}$ inches.

No. 63B7615 Oak. Price, per 100 lineal feet, **$3.45**

No. 63B7616 Birch. Price, per 100 lineal feet......**$2.49**

CRAFTSMAN NEWEL.

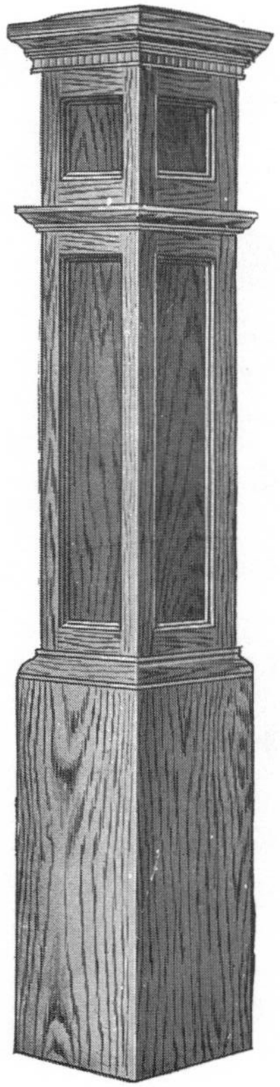

Base, 8 inches square. Height of post, 4 feet. Panels on four sides.

No. 63B7644 Oak. Price, each **$3.25**

HIGHEST GRADE OAK FOR INSIDE FINISH

Made from the finest selected red oak for oil finish. The base, base molding, casing and other moldings shown on this page are selected from the clear red oak and are suitable for the finest homes. Moldings are made in random lengths, from 6 to 16 feet, the majority of pieces being over 10 feet long. We charge 15 per cent extra for specified lengths.

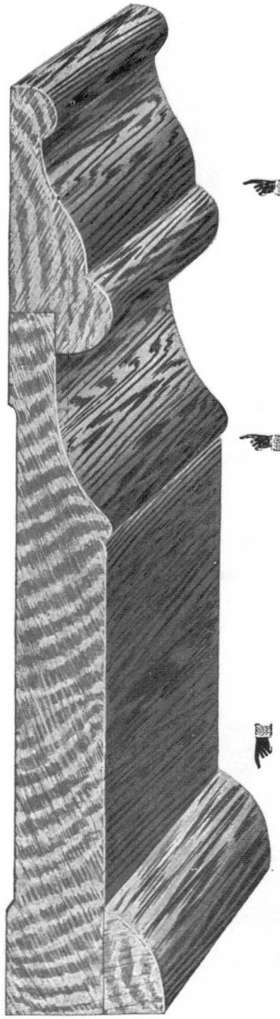

BASE MOLD.

Base Mold. Size, $\frac{13}{16}$x$2\frac{1}{4}$ inches.

No. 63B7502 Plain Red Oak. Price, per 100 lineal feet............**$1.88**

BASE.

Base. Size, $\frac{13}{16}$x$7\frac{1}{2}$ inches.

No. 63B7517 Plain Red Oak. Price, per 100 lineal feet in random lengths..............**$5.68**

CARPET STRIP.

Carpet Strip. Size, $\frac{1}{2}$x$\frac{7}{8}$ inch.

No. 63B7532 Plain Red Oak. Price, per 100 lineal feet..............**66c**

All our moldings are carefully packed and bundled face inside and guaranteed to arrive in perfect condition.

PILASTER CASING.

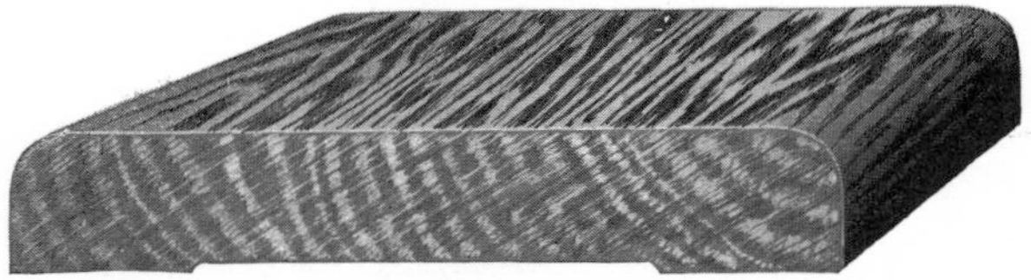

The illustration above shows a neat and tasty design of Pilaster Casing. Dust cannot collect on this style of casing. Carried in stock in sizes listed below:

Pilaster Casing. Price, per 100 lineal feet in random lengths:

	Chair Rail $\frac{13}{16}$x$3\frac{3}{4}$ in.	Casing $\frac{13}{16}$x$4\frac{1}{4}$ in.	Casing $\frac{13}{16}$x$4\frac{3}{4}$ in.
No. 63B7597 Plain Red Oak.	**$2.90**	**$3.25**	**$3.70**

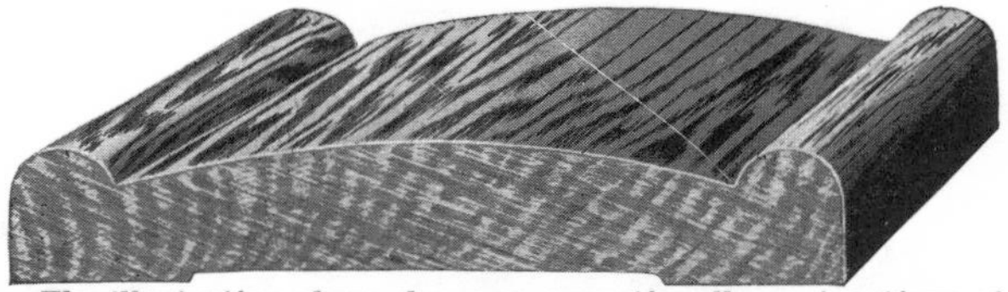

The illustration above shows an exceptionally neat pattern of Molded Pilaster Casing. Carried in stock in sizes listed below.

Pilaster Casing. Price, per 100 lineal feet, in random lengths:

	Size, $\frac{13}{16}$x$4\frac{1}{4}$ inches	Size, $\frac{13}{16}$x$4\frac{3}{4}$ inches
No. 63B7612 Plain Red Oak............	**$3.26**	**$3.74**

WINDOW STOOL.

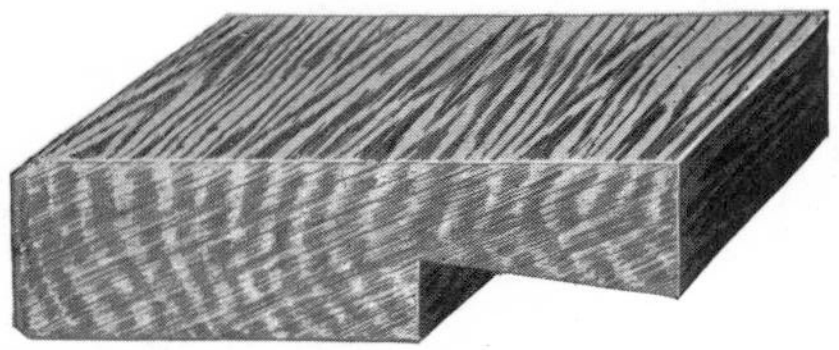

The illustration above shows the most popular design of Window Stool. Carried in stock.

Window Stool. Size, $1\frac{1}{8}$x$3\frac{3}{4}$ inches. Price, per 100 lineal feet in random lengths:

No. 63B7715 Plain Red Oak..........................**$4.52**

WINDOW APRON.

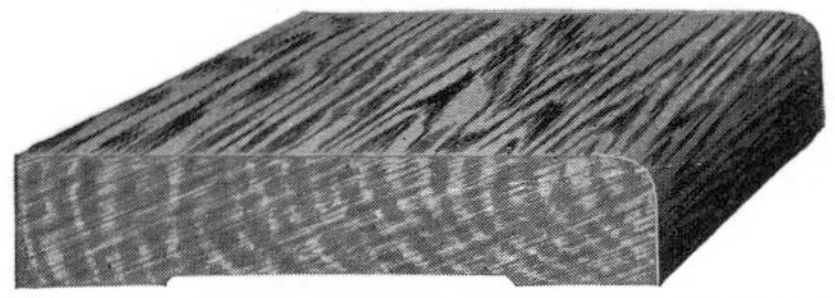

The illustration above shows a very neat design of Window Apron that is used under window stool to make a neat finish. Carried in stock.

Window Apron. Size, $\frac{13}{16}$x$3\frac{3}{4}$ inches. Price, per 100 lineal feet in random lengths.

No. 63B7722 Plain Red Oak..........................**$2.94**

QUARTER ROUND MOLDING.

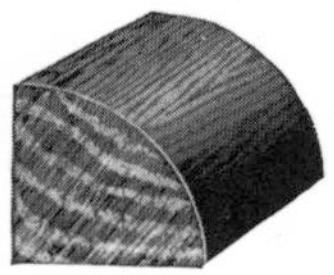

Used for base shoe or to cover joints in corners. Size, $\frac{7}{8}$x$\frac{7}{8}$ inch.

No. 63B7788 Plain Red Oak. Price, per 100 lineal feet...**66c**

COVE MOLDING.

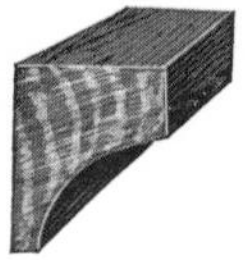

May be used the same as quarter round and is used under stair treads, steps, stools, etc. Size, $\frac{3}{4}$x$\frac{7}{8}$ inch.

No. 63B7819 Plain Red Oak.

Price, per 100 lineal feet.......................**66c**

PICTURE MOLDING.

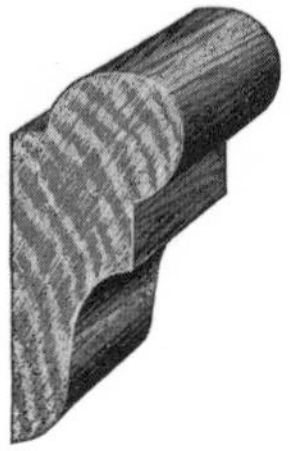

Picture Molding. Size, $\frac{13}{16}$x$1\frac{3}{4}$ inches. Improves the appearance of a room and saves driving nails into plaster when hanging pictures.

No. 63B7800 Plain Red Oak. Price, per 100 lineal feet....................................**$1.32**

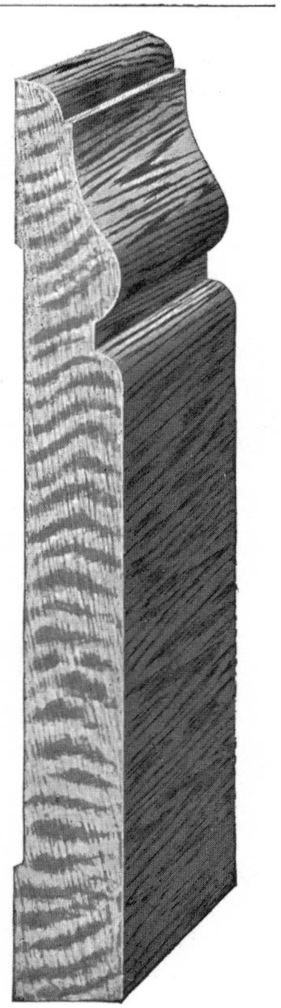

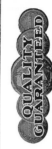

BASE.

Size, $\frac{13}{16}$x$7\frac{1}{4}$ inches.

No. 63B7548 Plain Red Oak. Price, per 100 lineal feet in random lengths............**$5.69**

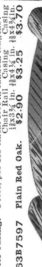

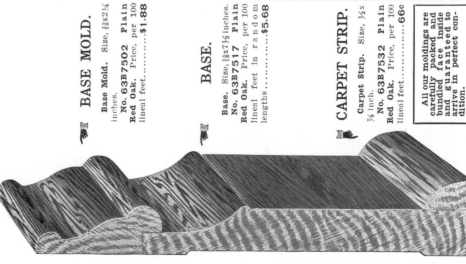

HIGH GRADE OAK AND YELLOW PINE INSIDE MOLDINGS

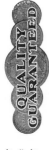

WE illustrate on this page two very neat designs in Door and Window Cap Trim. At the left is shown our Three-Member Cap Trim, consisting of cap mold, head casing and fillet. On the right hand side is a Four-Member Cap Trim, in which we use embossed molding and dust cap. **Molding is made in random lengths from 6 to 16 feet, the majority of pieces being over 10 feet long. We charge 15 per cent extra for specified lengths.**

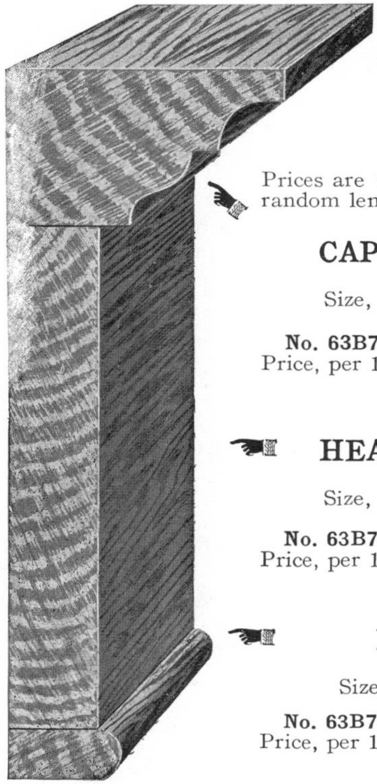

The illustration at the left shows a neat and tasty design for cap trim and the manner in which it is put up.

Prices are for 100 lineal feet in random lengths.

CAP MOLDING.

Size, $1\frac{3}{8}$x$2\frac{1}{2}$ inches.

No. 63B7622 Plain Red Oak. Price, per 100 feet $3.73

HEAD CASING.

Size, 13-16x$4\frac{1}{2}$ inches.

No. 63B7637 Plain Red Oak. Price, per 100 feet $3.43

FILLET.

Size, 7-16x1 inch.

No. 63B7648 Plain Red Oak. Price, per 100 feet 76c

SLIDING DOOR ASTRAGALS.

Furnished in Oak and Yellow Pine.

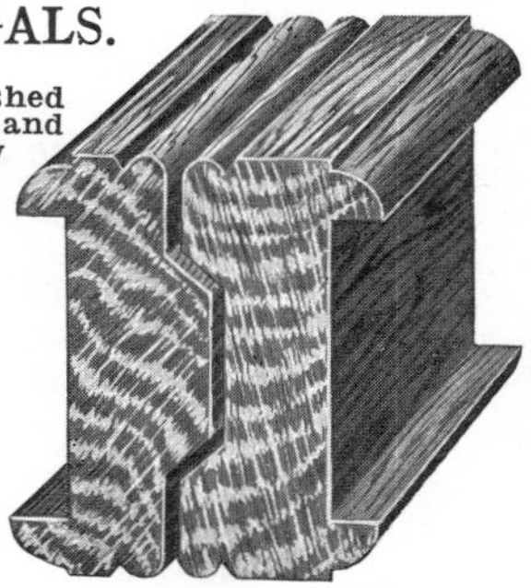

No. 63B7970 Yellow Pine. For $1\frac{3}{8}$-inch door, 8 feet high or less. Price, per pair 50c

No. 63B7972 Yellow Pine. For $1\frac{3}{4}$-inch door, 8 feet high or less. Price, per pair 55c

No. 63B7971 Oak. For $1\frac{3}{8}$-inch door, 8 feet high or less. Per pair, $1.00

No. 63B7973 Oak. For $1\frac{3}{4}$-inch door, 8 feet high or less. Per pair, $1.10

We illustrate above a reproduction of our Two-Member Oak Astragal used for inside sliding doors. Astragals of this kind add much to the general appearance of a room and are necessary to make a tight joint when the doors are closed. We carry these astragals in stock for both $1\frac{3}{8}$-inch and $1\frac{3}{4}$-inch doors. **When ordering be sure to state thickness of doors.**

FOLDING DOOR ASTRAGALS

Furnished in Oak and Yellow Pine.

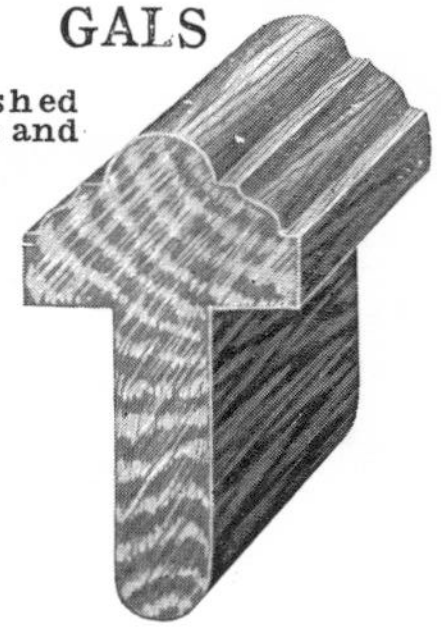

No. 63B7977 Yellow Pine. For $1\frac{3}{8}$-inch door, 8 feet high or less. Price, each..........................25c

No. 63B7979 Yellow Pine. For $1\frac{3}{4}$-inch door, 8 feet high or less. Price, each 30c

No. 63B7978 Oak. For $1\frac{3}{8}$-inch door, 8 feet high or less. Price, each 45c

No. 63B7982 Oak. For $1\frac{3}{4}$-inch door, 8 feet high or less. Price, each, 50c

This single "T" Astragal is used for double folding doors. It is nailed to the edge of one of the doors and forms a rabbet or shoulder against which the other door can swing. **When ordering this astragal be sure to specify thickness of the doors for which it is intended.**

DOOR AND WINDOW STOP.

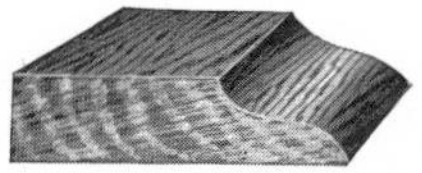

Door and Window Stop is carried in sizes as listed below. Prices are for 100 lineal feet in random lengths.

Size, inches	No. 63B7778 Plain Red Oak Per 100 lineal feet	Size, inches	No. 63B7778 Plain Red Oak Per 100 lineal feet
$\frac{3}{8}$x$1\frac{1}{8}$	$0.66	$\frac{1}{2}$x$1\frac{1}{8}$	$0.73
$\frac{3}{8}$x$1\frac{3}{8}$	.73	$\frac{1}{2}$x$1\frac{3}{8}$	.79
$\frac{3}{8}$x$1\frac{3}{4}$	.92	$\frac{1}{2}$x$1\frac{3}{4}$	1.06

BASE CORNERS.

BASE CORNERS, TURNED TOP. SAVES MITERING CORNERS OF BASE.

Crates contain fifty base corners.

No.	Quality.	Size, inches.	Price, each.	Price, per crate.
63B7905	Soft Pine.	$1\frac{3}{8}$x14	2c	$0.90
63B7906	Yellow Pine.	$1\frac{3}{8}$x14	2c	.90
63B7907	Plain Red Oak.	$1\frac{3}{8}$x14	3c	1.40
63B7908	Wisconsin Birch.	$1\frac{3}{8}$x14	$3\frac{1}{4}$c	1.50
63B7910	Cypress.	$1\frac{3}{8}$x14	$2\frac{1}{4}$c	1.05

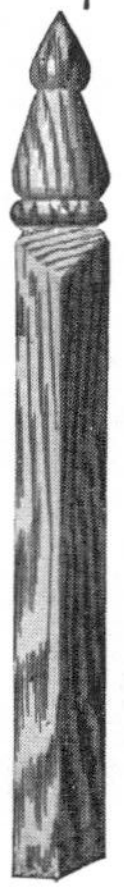

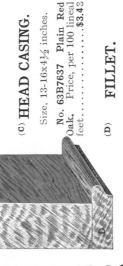

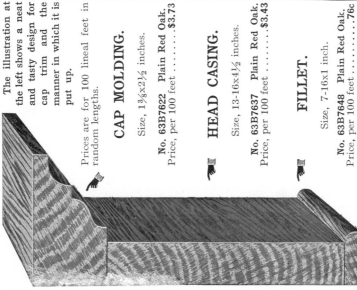

HAS FOUND OUR MATERIAL, WORKMANSHIP AND OUR TREATMENT OF HIM ALL HE COULD ASK.

Basco, Ill.

Sears, Roebuck and Co.,
Chicago, Ill.

Dear Sirs:—I have received several orders of mill work from you, and as to my dealings with you, am glad to say that I have found material and workmanship up to your professions, and the treatment as to shipment all I could ask. I am,

Yours very truly,
E. H. BRYANT.

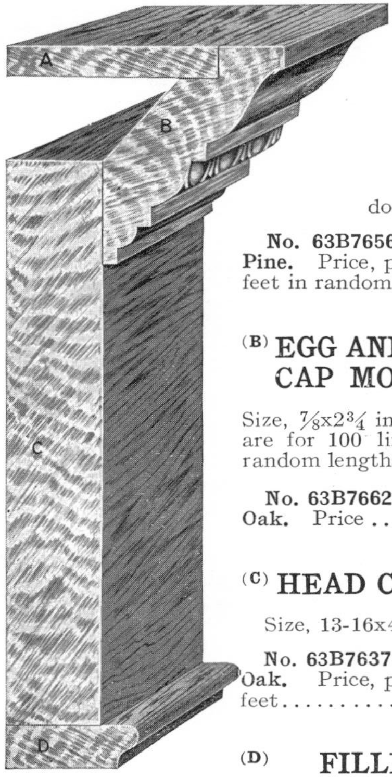

(A) DUST CAP.

Size, 5-16x$1\frac{3}{4}$ inches. Used with any cap mold, as it does not show.

No. 63B7656 Yellow Pine. Price, per 100 lineal feet in random lengths. 42c

(B) EGG AND DART CAP MOLDING.

Size, $\frac{7}{8}$x$2\frac{3}{4}$ inches. Prices are for 100 lineal feet in random lengths.

No. 63B7662 Plain Red Oak. Price $2.20

(C) HEAD CASING.

Size, 13-16x$4\frac{1}{2}$ inches.

No. 63B7637 Plain Red Oak. Price, per 100 lineal feet.................$3.43

(D) FILLET.

Size, 7-16x$1\frac{1}{8}$ inch.

No. 63B7652 Plain Red Oak. Price, per 100 lineal feet..................83c

THE ABOVE ILLUSTRATION shows a very tasty design of Four-Member Oak Cap Trim for Doors and Windows. It is not absolutely necessary that you use a dust cap with this cap trim, but it is generally considered advisable to do so.

QUALITY GUARANTEED

INTERIOR MOLDINGS IN YELLOW PINE, NONA WHITE SOFT PINE, CYPRESS, BIRCH AND SPECIAL SOFT WOOD

QUALITY GUARANTEED

On this and the following pages we illustrate, describe and name the lowest prices ever made on high grades of moldings. All of our moldings are clean and bright. All our moldings are run at a low speed, producing an excellent smooth finish.

Clear soft wood moldings are made of different woods such as spruce, poplar, etc., perfectly machined and are suitable for paint or enamel finish.

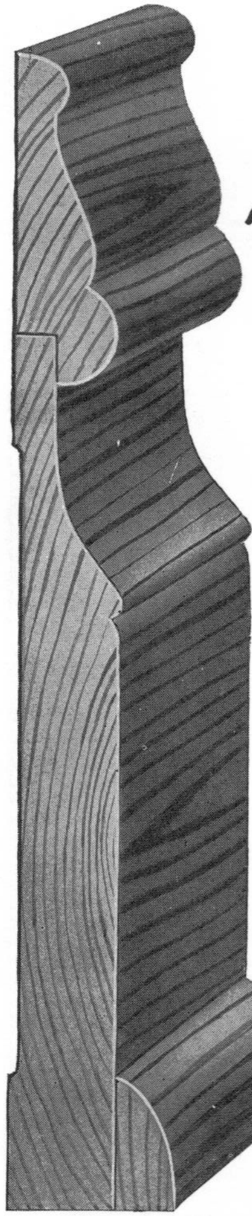

Base Molding. Size, $\frac{13}{16}$x$2\frac{1}{4}$ inches. Price, per 100 lineal feet in random lengths:

No. 63B7499 Clear Soft Wood, for paint $0.96

No. 63B7500 *Nona White Soft Pine.................1.17

No. 63B7501 Yellow Pine........ .96

No. 63B7503 Wisconsin Birch... 1.37

No. 63B7505 Cypress........... 1.18

Base. Size, $\frac{13}{16}$x$7\frac{1}{2}$ inches. Price, per 100 lineal feet in random lengths:

No. 63B7514 Clear Soft Wood, for paint $2.93

No. 63B7515 *Nona White Soft Pine 3.44

No. 63B7516 Yellow Pine........ 3.14

No. 63B7518 Wisconsin Birch.... 4.40

No. 63B7520 Cypress............ 3.42

Carpet Strip. Size, $\frac{1}{2}$x$\frac{7}{8}$ inches. Price, per 100 lineal feet in random lengths:

No. 63B7529 Clear Soft Wood, for paint...33c

No. 63B7530 *Nona White Soft Pine......39c

No. 63B7531 Yellow Pine..................31c

No. 63B7533 Wisconsin Birch..........48c

No. 63B7535 Cypress...................39c

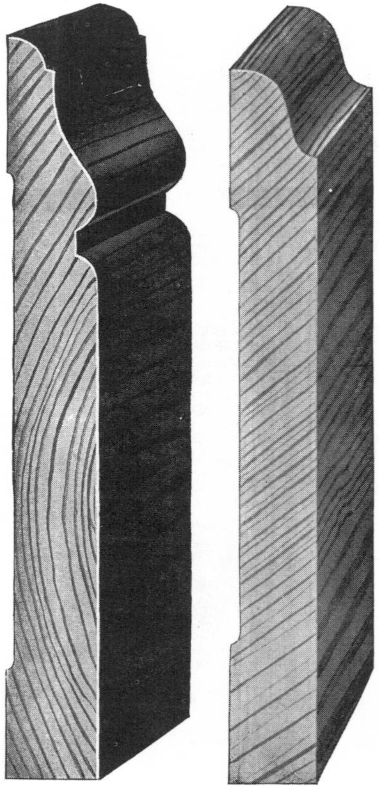

Why pay double these prices elsewhere?

We guarantee the quality.

"Your money back if you are not satisfied."

Base. Size, $\frac{13}{16}$x$7\frac{1}{4}$ inches. Price, per 100 lineal feet in random lengths:

No. 63B7545 *Nona White Soft Pine...........$3.32

No. 63B7546 Yellow Pine 3.04

No. 63B7547 Wisconsin Birch.......... 4.26

No. 63B7550 Cypress 3.39

O. G. Base. Size, $\frac{13}{16}$x$7\frac{1}{4}$ inches. Price, per 100 lineal feet in random lengths:

No. 63B7565 Clear Soft Wood, for paint $2.84

No. 63B7566 *Nona White Soft Pine............3.31

No. 63B7567 Yellow Pine.......................3.03

* Nona White Soft Pine is a soft Western spruce pine, easily worked and superior to Northern white pine.

Molding made in random lengths from 6 to 16 feet, the majority of pieces being over 10 feet long. We charge 15 per cent extra for specified lengths.

PILASTER CASINGS.

The illustration above shows a neat and tasty design of Pilaster Casing. Dust cannot collect on this style of casing. Carried in stock in woods and sizes listed below.

Pilaster Casing. Price, per 100 lineal feet in random lengths:

		Chair Rail $\frac{13}{16}$x$3\frac{3}{4}$ in.	Casing $\frac{13}{16}$x$4\frac{1}{4}$ in.	Casing $\frac{13}{16}$x$4\frac{3}{4}$ in.
No. 63B7594	Clear Soft Wood, for paint	$1.51	$1.71	$1.89
No. 63B7595	*Nona White Soft Pine	1.76	2.00	2.21
No. 63B7596	Yellow Pine	1.65	1.83	2.02
No. 63B7598	Wisconsin Birch	2.27	2.56	2.83
No. 63B7600	Cypress	1.81	2.01	2.22

The illustration above shows an exceptionally neat pattern of Molded Pilaster Casing. Carried in stock in woods and sizes listed below.

Pilaster Casing. Price, per 100 lineal feet in random lengths:

		Size, $\frac{13}{16}$x$4\frac{1}{4}$ inches	Size, $\frac{13}{16}$x$4\frac{3}{4}$ inches
No. 63B7609	Clear Soft Wood, for paint	$1.71	$1.89
No. 63B7610	*Nona White Soft Pine	2.01	2.22
No. 63B7611	Yellow Pine	1.84	2.03
No. 63B7613	Wisconsin Birch	2.56	2.83
No. 63B7614	Cypress	2.02	2.23

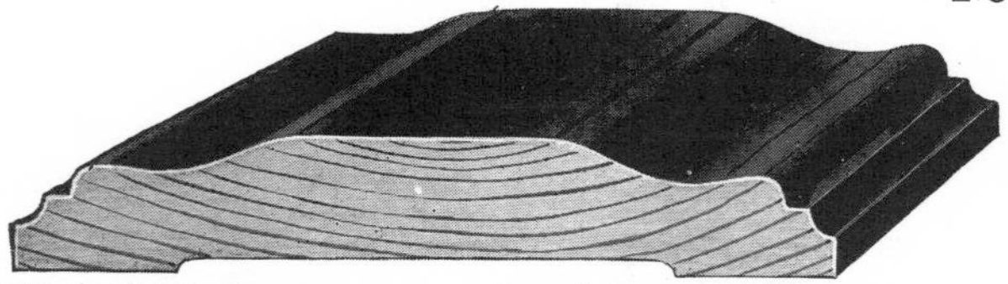

The illustration above shows a very neat and tasty design of Pilaster Casing. We do not recommend this design, as it does not pack well and bundles are liable to loosen in transit, thus soiling the casing. We furnish this design only $4\frac{3}{4}$ inches wide.

Pilaster Casing. Price, per 100 lineal feet in random lengths:

No. 63B8657 Yellow Pine Casing, $4\frac{3}{4}$ inches wide..............................$2.02

The illustration above shows a very popular design of Beaded Pilaster Casing. Carried in stock in woods and sizes listed below.

Pilaster Casing. Price, per 100 lineal feet in random lengths:

		Size, $\frac{13}{16}$x$4\frac{1}{4}$ inches	Size, $\frac{13}{16}$x$4\frac{3}{4}$ inches
No. 63B7584	Clear Soft Wood, for paint	$1.71	$1.89
No. 63B7585	*Nona White Soft Pine	2.02	2.23
No. 63B7586	Yellow Pine	1.85	2.04
No. 63B7589	Cypress	2.03	2.24

Interior Moldings in Yellow Pine, Nona White Pine, Birch, Cypress and Special Soft Woods

Why use the old style block trim for your doors and windows when cap trim can be had so cheap? It is up to date and costs but little more. All architects are now specifying cap trim for up to date buildings, both public and private. Our moldings are all made from thoroughly kiln dried stock with the latest improved machinery. Clear soft wood moldings are made of different woods such as spruce, poplar, etc., perfectly machined and are suitable for paint or enamel finish. For oak moldings refer to pages 62 and 63.

The illustration at the left shows a neat and tasty design for cap trim and the manner in which it is put up.

Prices are for 100 lineal feet in random lengths.

We carry this design in stock in woods listed below.

CAP MOLDING.

Size, 7⁄8x2¾ inches. Prices are for 100 lineal feet in random lengths.

No. 63B7661 Yellow Pine. Price, per 100 feet $1.80
No. 63B7663 Wisconsin Birch. Price, per 100 feet $2.45
No. 63B7665 Cypress. Price, per 100 feet $2.35

HEAD CASING.

Size, 13-16x4½ inches.

No. 63B7634 Clear Soft Wood, for paint. Price, per 100 feet .. $1.75
No. 63B7635 *Nona Soft Pine. Price, per 100 feet $2.10
No. 63B7636 Yellow Pine. Price, per 100 feet $1.93
No. 63B7638 Wisconsin Birch. Price, per 100 feet $2.70
No. 63B7640 Cypress. Price, per 100 feet $2.11

FILLET.

Size, 7-16x1 inch.

No. 63B7645 Clear Soft Wood, for paint. Price, per 100 feet .. 37c
No. 63B7646 *Nona Soft Pine. Price, per 100 feet 44c
No. 63B7647 Yellow Pine. Price, per 100 feet 36c
No. 63B7649 Wisconsin Birch. Price, per 100 feet 55c
No. 63B7651 Cypress. Price, per 100 feet 45c

DUST CAP.

Size, 5-16x1¾ inches. Can be used with any cap mold.

No. 63B7656 Yellow Pine. Price, per 100 lineal feet in random lengths ... 42c

WAINSCOTING CAP.

Wainscoting Cap. Size, 13-16x2¾ inches. Carried in stock in woods listed below. Covers wainscoting in kitchen, dining room and bathroom. May also be used for back band on casing.

No. 63B7809 Clear Soft Wood, for paint. Price, per 100 feet ... $1.15
No. 63B7810 *Nona Soft Pine. Price, per 100 feet $1.39
No. 63B7811 Yellow Pine. Price, per 100 feet $1.16
No. 63B7812 Cypress. Price, per 100 feet $1.40

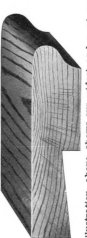

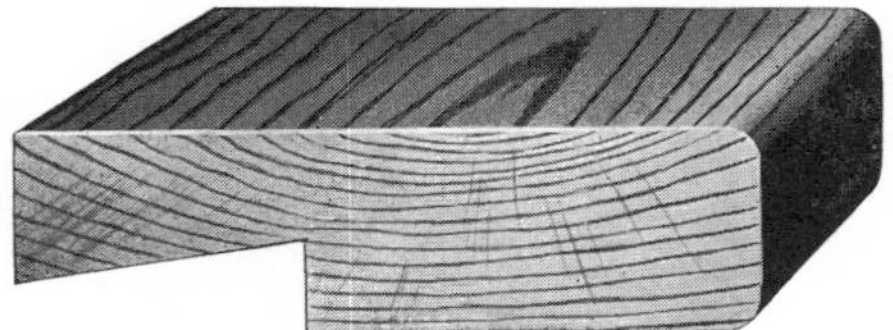

WINDOW STOOL.

A popular design of Window Stool that is easily shaped at ends and saves mitering. Carried in stock in woods listed below.

Window Stool. Size, 1⅛x3¾ inches. Price, per 100 lineal feet in random lengths.

No. 63B7711 Clear Soft Wood, for paint $2.31
No. 63B7712 *Nona Soft Pine. $2.77
No. 63B7713 Yellow Pine ... $2.54
No. 63B7606 Wisconsin Birch. $3.91
No. 63B7714 Cypress $2.78

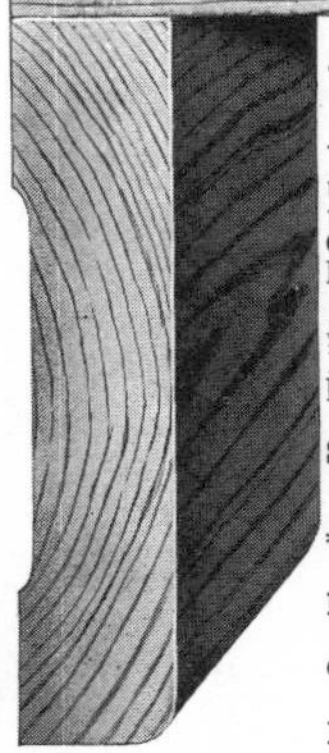

A neat design of Window Apron that is used under window stool to make a neat finish. Carried in stock in woods listed below.

Window Apron. Size, ⅛x3¾ inches. Price, per 100 lineal feet in random lengths.

No. 63B7719 Clear Soft Wood, for paint .. $1.42
No. 63B7720 ....
*Nona Soft Pine. $1.77
No. 63B7721 Yellow Pine $1.63
No. 63B7723 Wisconsin Birch. $2.10
No. 63B7725 Cypress. $1.78

The illustration above shows our widest and most popular design of Window Stool. Carried in stock in woods listed below.

Window Stool. Size, 1⅛x4¼ inches. Price, per 100 lineal feet in random lengths.

No. 63B7694 Clear Soft Wood, for paint $2.86
No. 63B7695 *Nona Soft Pine 3.13
No. 63B7696 Yellow Pine 2.87
No. 63B7697 Plain Red Oak 5.25
No. 63B7698 Wisconsin Birch 3.25
No. 63B7700 Cypress 3.14

The above illustration shows a popular design of O. G. Casing. Carried in stock in the woods listed below. Price, per 100 lineal feet in random lengths. Size, ⅞x4¼ inches.

No. 63B7559 Clear Soft Wood, for paint $1.71
No. 63B7560 *Nona Soft Pine 2.01
No. 63B7561 Yellow Pine 1.85
No. 63B7563 Cypress 2.04

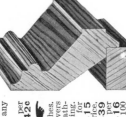

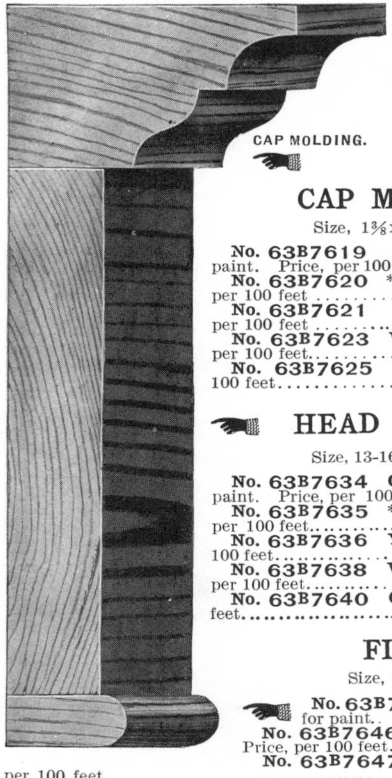

A neat and tasty design for cap trim and the manner in which it is put up. Carried in stock in woods listed below. Prices are for 100 lineal feet in random lengths.

CAP MOLDING.

CAP MOLDING.

Size, 1⅜x2½ inches.

No. 63B7619 Clear Soft Wood, for paint $1.97
No. 63B7620 *Nona Soft Pine. $2.29
No. 63B7621 Yellow Pine. $2.10
No. 63B7623 Wisconsin Birch. $2.73
No. 63B7625 Cypress. Price, per 100 feet ... $2.30

HEAD CASING.

Size, 13-16x4½ inches.

No. 63B7634 Clear Soft Wood, for paint. Price, per 100 feet ... $1.80
No. 63B7635 *Nona Soft Pine. $2.10
No. 63B7636 Yellow Pine. Price, per 100 feet ... $1.93
No. 63B7638 Wisconsin Birch. $2.70
No. 63B7640 Cypress. Price, per 100 feet ... $2.11

FILLET.

Size, 7-16x1 inch.

No. 63B7645 Clear Soft Wood, for paint. Price, per 100 feet ... 37c
No. 63B7646 *Nona Soft Pine. 44c
No. 63B7647 Yellow Pine. Price, per 100 feet ... 36c
No. 63B7649 Wisconsin Birch. Price, per 100 feet ... 55c
No. 63B7651 Cypress. Price, per 100 feet ... 45c

PICTURE MOLDING.

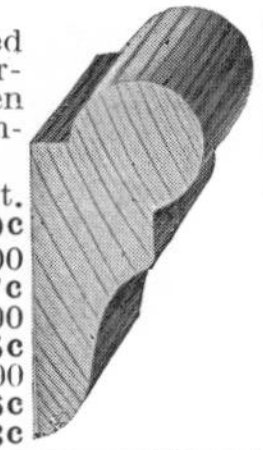

Picture Molding. Size, 13-16x1¾ inches. Carried in stock in the woods listed below. Improves the appearance of a room and saves driving nails in plaster when hanging pictures. Prices are for 100 lineal feet in random lengths.

No. 63B7797 Clear Soft Wood, for paint. Price, per 100 feet ... 59c
No. 63B7798 *Nona Soft Pine. Price, per 100 feet ... 77c
No. 63B7799 Yellow Pine. Price, per 100 feet ... 65c
No. 63B7801 Wisconsin Birch. Price, per 100 feet ... 96c
No. 63B7803 Cypress. Price, per 100 feet ... 78c

QUALITY GUARANTEED

* Nona soft Pine is soft Western Spruce Pine, easily worked and is superior to Northern White Pine.

HIGHEST GRADE INSIDE MOLDINGS AT LOW PRICES

SUITABLE FOR OIL FINISH, PAINT, STAIN OR ENAMEL.

Moldings and plate rail are made from either clear soft wood, Nona soft pine, yellow pine or Wisconsin birch. Refer to pages 60 to 65 for other inside trim.

Clear soft wood moldings are made of different woods such as spruce, poplar, etc., perfectly machined and are suitable for paint or enamel finish.

Molding made in random lengths from 6 to 16 feet, the majority of pieces being over 10 feet long. We will charge 15 per cent extra for specified lengths.

PLATE RAIL MOLDINGS.

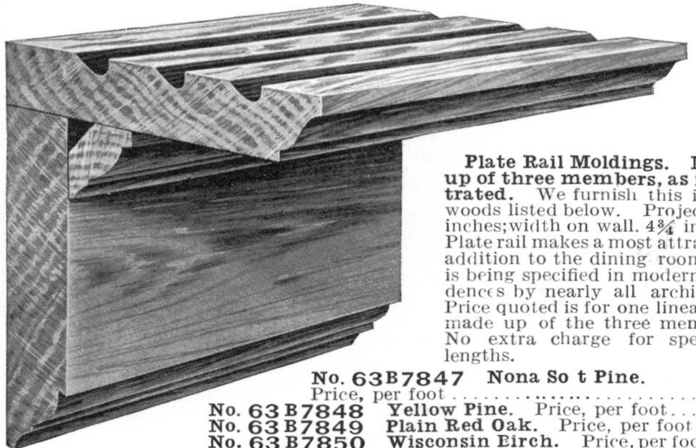

Plate Rail Moldings. Made up of three members, as illustrated. We furnish this in the woods listed below. Project 4¼ inches; width on wall, 4¾ inches. Plate rail makes a most attractive addition to the dining room and is being specified in modern residences by nearly all architects. Price quoted is for one lineal foot made up of the three members. No extra charge for specified lengths.

No. 63B7847 Nona so t Pine.
Price, per foot 7c
No. 63B7848 Yellow Pine. Price, per foot .. 5½c
No. 63B7849 Plain Red Oak. Price, per foot. 10c
No. 63B7850 Wisconsin Birch. Price, per foot. 9c
No. 63B7852 Cypress. Price, per foot.........8c

PLATE RAIL BRACKETS.

Illustrated below you will find plate rail brackets, used in connection with the plate rail illustrated and quoted above, under catalog Nos. 63B7847 to 63B7852 inclusive. Note how these brackets improve the appearance of the plate rail. The small inside brackets should be placed every 12 or 16 inches apart or over each stud. The large end brackets to be used between the door or window casing and the ends of the plate rail. Can be used on plate rail catalog Nos. 63B7854 and 63B7855; also Craftsman plate rail, catalog No. 63B7668 shown on page 58.

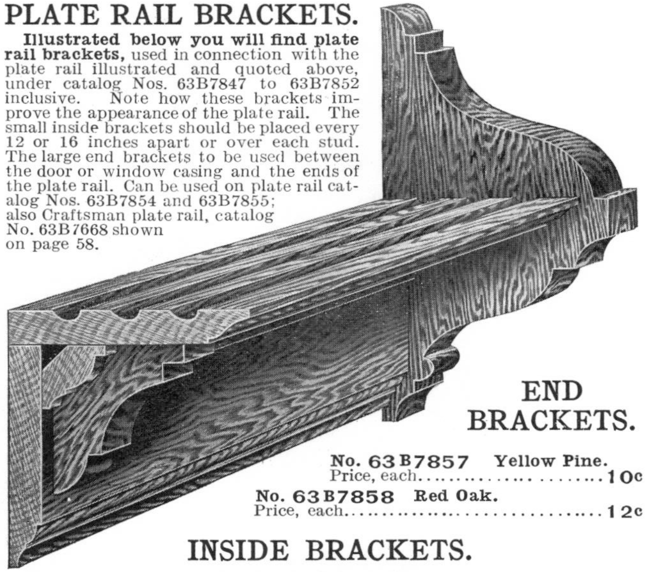

END BRACKETS.

No. 63B7857 Yellow Pine.
Price, each...................10c
No. 63B7858 Red Oak.
Price, each...................12c

INSIDE BRACKETS.

No. 63B7859 Yellow Pine, Price, each........5c
No. 63B7862 Red Oak. Price, each........6c

COVE MOLDINGS.

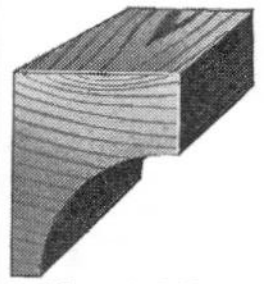

Cove Moldings are carried in stock in the woods and sizes listed below. May be used the same as quarter round, and is used under stair treads, steps, stools, etc. Prices are for 100 lineal feet in random lengths.

No. 63B7814 Clear Soft Wood. Size, ¾x⅞ inch. Price, per 100 lineal feet. 31c
No. 63B7816 Nona Soft Pine. Size, ¾x⅞ inch. Price, per 100 lineal feet. 39c
No. 63B7817 Yellow Pine. Size, ¾x⅞ inch. Price, per 100 lineal feet. 31c
No. 63B7820 Wisconsin Birch. Size, ¾x⅞ inch. Price, per 100 lineal feet. 48c
No. 63B7815 Clear Soft Wood. Size, ½x1⅛ inches. Price, per 100 lineal feet. 41c
No. 63B7816½ Nona Soft Pine. Size, ½x1⅛ inches. Price, per 100 lineal feet. 48c
No. 63B7817½ Yellow Pine. Size, ½x1⅛ inches. Price, per 100 lineal feet. 39c

QUARTER ROUND MOLDINGS.

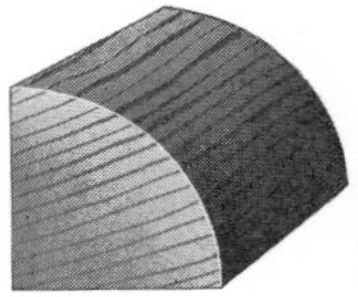

Used for Base Shoe or to Cover Joints in Corners. Quarter Round Molding is carried in stock in the woods and in sizes listed herewith. Sizes not priced are not carried in stock. Prices are for 100 lineal feet in random lengths.

SIZE	No. 63B7784 SOFT WOOD	No. 63B7786 YELLOW PINE	No. 63B7783 CYPRESS	No. 63B7789 WISCONSIN BIRCH
⅝x⅝ inches	23c	31c	39c	.....
¾x¾ inches	.....	31c	39c	.....
⅞x⅞ inches	.....	31c	39c	48c

DOOR AND WINDOW STOP.

Door and Window Stop is carried in stock in woods and sizes as listed below. Sizes not priced are not carried in stock. Prices are for 100 lineal feet in random lengths.

SIZE, inches	No. 63B7775 NONA SOFT PINE Per 100 lineal feet	No. 63B7776 YELLOW PINE Per 100 lineal feet	No. 63B7779 WISCONSIN PINE Per 100 lineal feet	No. 63B7790 CYPRESS Per 100 lineal feet
⅜x1¼	39c	31c	48c	40c
⅜x1⅜	42c	34c	53c	43c
⅜x1¾	54c	43c	66c	55c
½x2	62c	57c	.....	68c
½x1⅛	46c	34c	53c	43c
½x1¾	62c	40c	58c	47c
½x2	76c	50c	80c	63c

TWO-MEMBER PLATE RAIL.

No dining room is complete without plate rail. Artistic in design and simple and easy to put up. At these low prices no dining room should be without it.

No. 63B7854 Oak. Projects 3½ inches from wall.
Price, per foot 7c
No. 63B7855 Yellow Pine. Projects 3½ inches from wall.
Price, per foot 4c

4c PER LINEAL FOOT.

PARTITION MOLDS.

The illustrations below represent moldings which are used above and below partitions. The lower right hand member is set on the floor and the partition fits in the groove. The other is a cap, so to speak, and is set down over the top of the partition. In a great many places where a partition is made of ceiling or other suitable material it is very necessary in dividing off certain spaces, and by using this cap and base you can have a very attractive partition at a very small expense.

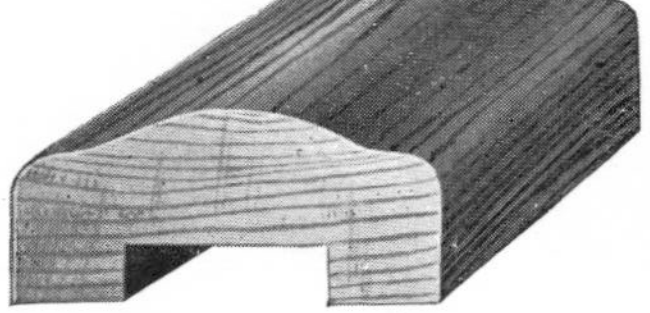

No. 63B7983 Yellow Pine.
Size, ¾x1¾ inches.
Price, per 100 lineal feet....70c

No. 63B7984 Yellow Pine.
Size, ⅞x2¼ inches.
Price, per 100 lineal feet....88c

EMBOSSED MOLDINGS

Our Embossed Molding is clean, clear and deep cut, and superior to others.

Catalog No.	Size, inches		Price, per 100 feet	Catalog No.	Size, inches		Price, per 100 feet
63B7860	3/8x1/2	Yellow Pine	$0.80	63B7861	3/8x1/2	Oak	$0.85
63B7865	3/8x5/8	Yellow Pine	.95	63B7866	3/8x5/8	Oak	1.20
63B7870	5/8x 1	Yellow Pine	1.15	63B7871	5/8x 1	Oak	1.30

We sell any quantity. Extra charge for specified lengths.

EMBOSSED PICTURE MOLDINGS.

Embossed Picture Molding gives a very handsome effect in a room at small cost. We sell any quantity. Price is for 100 lineal feet.

No. 63B7876 Yellow Pine. Size, 7/8x1 1/2 inches. Price, per 100 feet.......... **$1.40**
No. 63B7877 Oak. Size, 7/8x1 1/2 inches. Price, per 100 feet................ **1.75**

For Plain Picture Molding see pages 62 and 65.

HARDWOOD THRESHOLDS.

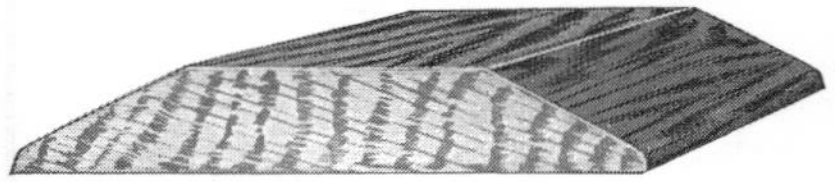

Should be used under every door.

No. 63B7890 Birch Thresholds. Size, 5/8x3 3/4 inches by 3 feet. Price, per bundle of ten, **39c**; each, **4c**

No. 63B7891 Oak Thresholds. Size, 5/8x3 3/4 inches by 3 feet. Price, per bundle of ten, **44c**; each..... **4 1/2c**

CORNER BEADS.

Corner Bead, round turned. Size, 1 3/8 inches by 4 feet. Protects plaster corners.

No. 63B7895 Nona Soft Pine. Price, each **8c**
No. 63B7896 Yellow Pine. Price, each **7c**
No. 63B7897 Plain Red Oak. Price, each **11c**
No. 63B7898 Wisconsin Birch. Price, each **11c**
No. 63B7900 Cypress. Price, each **9c**

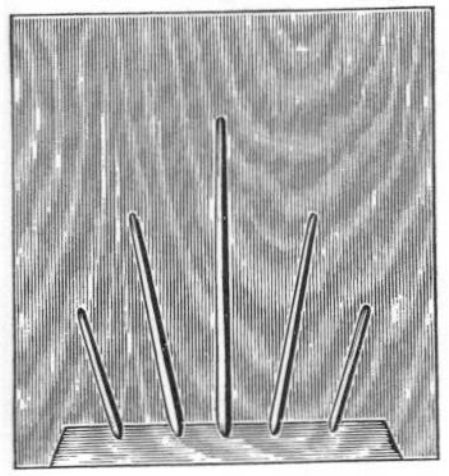

SINK TRIMMINGS.

Our Sink Trimmings are made of plain red oak thoroughly kiln dried.

DRIP BOARDS.

No. 63B7792 Oak Drip Boards. Grooved and beveled. Size, 7/8x22x24 inches. Nice clear, clean stock.
Price, each.......... **49c**

SINK LEGS.

No. 63B7793 Oak Sink Legs. Size, 1 3/4 x 1 3/4 x 30 inches. Smoothly turned and sandpapered.
Price, each.......... **11c**

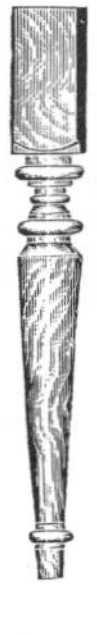

SINK APRONS.

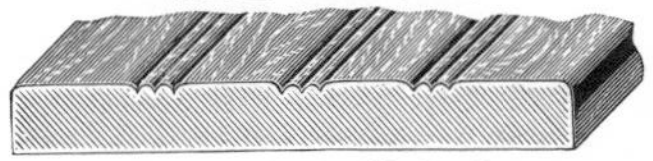

No. 63B7794 Oak Sink Aprons. Size, 7/8x7 inches. Price, per lineal foot... **5 1/4c**

SINK CAPPING.

No. 63B7795 Oak Sink Capping. Size, 7/8x3 inches. Price, per lineal foot .. **2 3/4c**

FROM A CONTRACTOR.

Fifield, Wis.

Sears, Roebuck and Co.,
Chicago, Ill.

Dear Sirs:—It is a great pleasure to say a few words about your mill work. I handle mill work as contractor and especially as paint contractor over twenty-five years and must say that your mill work is far above the mill work I ever handled. The nice smooth finish from the doors to the quarter round is unexcelled and even in the painted doors from other factories. I have used in my house painted doors received from you four years ago, but there is today not the slightest warp or shrinkage of any kind. Nobody will believe that these are the cheapest grade of doors and I have saved from 25 to 40 per cent compared with the average factory prices.

Yours very truly,
HERMAN BECKER.

SAVED $300.00 ON AN ORDER OF $850.00.

Massena, Iowa.

Sears, Roebuck and Co.,
Chicago, Ill.

Gentlemen:—I received the carload of mill work lumber within a few days from the time I ordered it. I was surprised to find it in such a fine shape, so well packed and crated, and nice bright new clean material. My carpenter said it was the best lot of finished lumber he ever looked at. On this order of $850.00 I have saved $300.00.

Very truly yours,
JOHN P. WATERS.

A PLEASED CUSTOMER.

Long Pine, Neb.

Sears, Roebuck and Co.,
Chicago, Ill.

Dear Sirs:—I was more than pleased with all mill work purchased of Sears, Roebuck and Co. I was building a residence for myself and as it is now completed, will not require any more mill work for the present but rest assured if I need any mill work at any future time you shall certainly receive my order.

Yours truly,
THOMAS C. WRIGHT.

QUALITY GUARANTEED

HEAD, BASE AND CORNER BLOCKS

CORNER BLOCKS.

Corner Blocks are carried in stock in woods and sizes listed below. The pattern permits any size to be trimmed down to smaller sizes if desired.

Be sure to state size wanted when ordering.

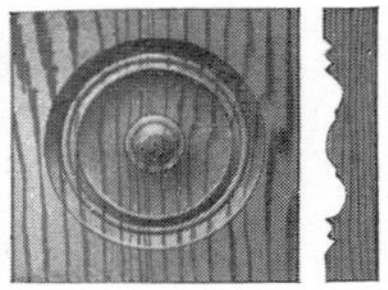

Catalog Number	Wood	Size, inches, 4 1/2x4 1/2x1 1/8 Price, each	Size, inches, 5x5x1 1/8 Price, each
63B7732	Nona Pine..	2c	2c
63B7733	Yellow Pine	2c	2c
63B7737	Cypress....	2 1/4c	2 1/4c

HEAD BLOCKS.

Head Blocks are carried in stock in woods and sizes listed below. The pattern permits any size to be trimmed down to smaller sizes if desired. **Be sure to state size wanted when ordering.**

Catalog Number	Wood	Size, inches, 4 1/2x10x1 1/8 Price, each	Size, inches, 5x10x1 1/8 Price, each
63B7742	Nona Pine..	4c	4c
63B7743	Yellow Pine	4c	4c
63B7747	Cypress.....	4 1/2c	4 1/2c

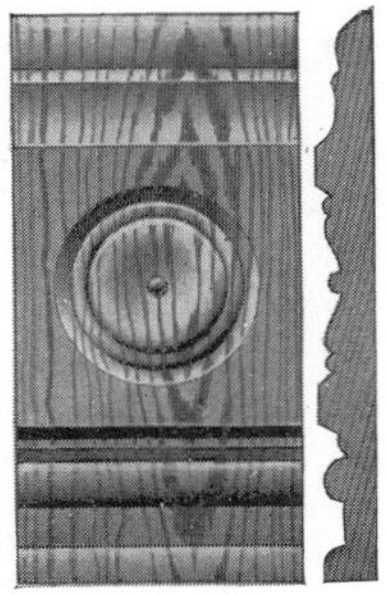

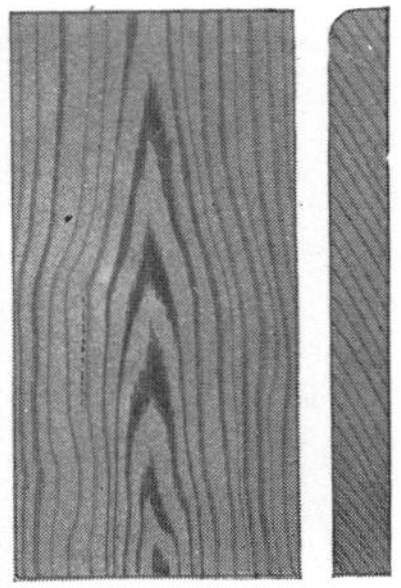

BASE BLOCKS.

Base Blocks are carried in stock in the woods and sizes listed below. This design can be trimmed down to smaller intermediate sizes if desired. **Be sure to state size wanted when ordering.**

Catalog Number	Wood	Size, inches, 4 1/2 x 10x 1 1/8 Price, each	Size, inches, 5 x 10 x 1 1/8 Price, each
63B7753	Nona Pine..	4c	4c
63B7754	Yellow Pine	4c	4c
63B7755	Oak.........	5 1/2c	5 1/2c
63B7756	Birch.......	5 1/2c	5 1/2c
63B7758	Cypress	4 1/2c	4 1/2c

BASE BLOCKS.

Base Blocks are carried in stock in woods and sizes listed below. Be sure to state size wanted when ordering.

Catalog Number	Wood	Size, inches, 4 1/2 x 10 x 1 1/8 Price, each	Size, inches, 5 x 10 x 1 1/8 Price, each
63B7763	Nona Pine..	4c	4c
63B7764	Yellow Pine	4c	4c
63B7760	Cypress....	5c	5c

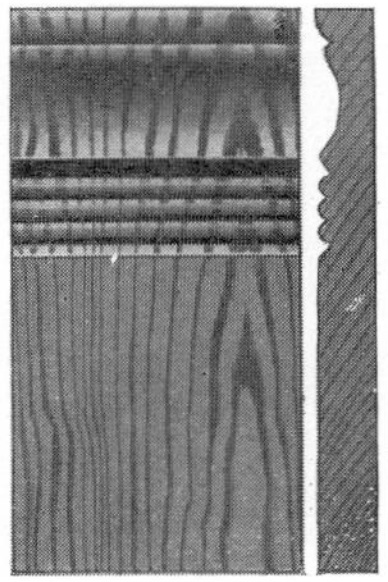

WE SELL BLOCKS IN ANY QUANTITY AT THE PRICES LISTED.

SOFT WOOD MOLDINGS FOR OUTSIDE USE

We illustrate on this page a full line of moldings for outside use. These moldings are selected from the most suitable of soft woods for painting, such as spruce, fir, poplar, etc. We guarantee these moldings, as well as all the rest of the material in this book, to reach you in a nice, clean, new condition, as all our moldings and other mill work are made from the best kiln dried stock. Moldings cut to order or special lengths will be charged 15 per cent additional to the price quoted and we in every case charge for the even foot, as our molding comes in 6, 8, 10, 12, 14 and 16-foot lengths.

CROWN MOLDINGS.

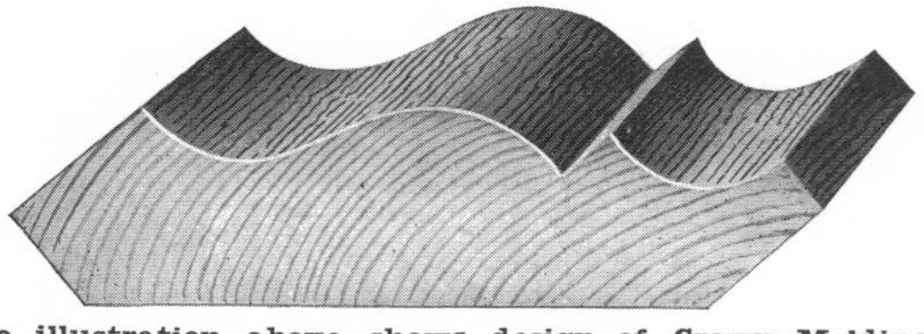

The illustration above shows design of Crown Molding we carry in stock, in sizes listed below. Prices are for 100 lineal feet in random lengths.

Size, inches	$\frac{13}{16}$x2¾	$\frac{13}{16}$x3¼	$\frac{13}{16}$x3¾	$\frac{13}{16}$x4¼	$\frac{13}{16}$x4¾
No. 63B7919 Clear Soft Wood, for paint	$1.05	$1.23	$1.40	$1.58	$1.75

BED MOLDING.

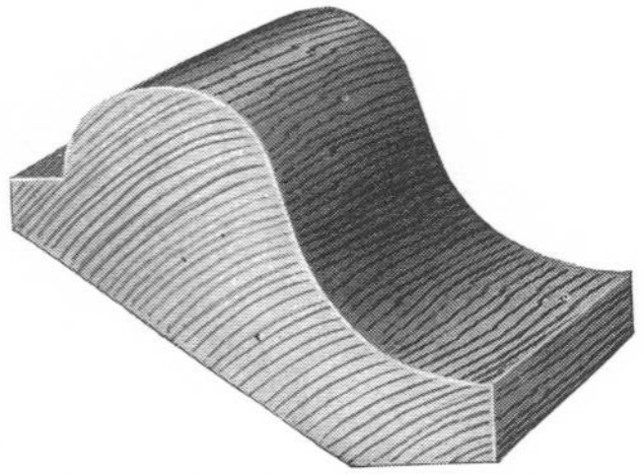

The illustration here shows design of Bed Molding we carry in stock in sizes listed below.

No. 63B7926 Clear Soft Wood. Size, $\frac{13}{16}$x2 inches. Price, per 100 lineal feet **79c**

No. 63B7927 Clear Soft Wood. Size, $\frac{13}{16}$x2¼ inches. Price, per 100 lineal feet.. **88c**

No. 63B7928 Clear Soft Wood. Size, $\frac{13}{16}$x2¾ inches. Price, per 100 lineal feet, **$1.05**

DRIP CAP FOR WINDOW AND OUTSIDE DOOR FRAMES.

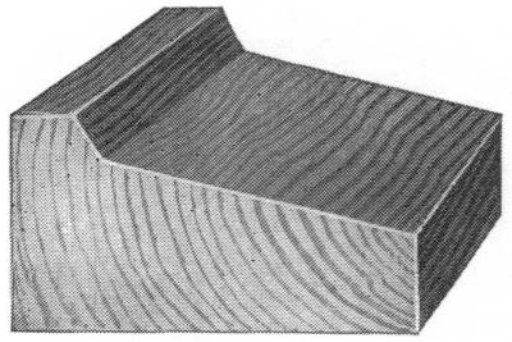

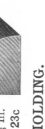

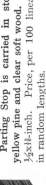

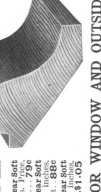

Drip Cap is carried in stock in sizes listed below. Prices are for 100 lineal feet in random lengths. We sell any quantity.

No. 63B7930 Clear Soft Wood, for paint. Size, 1⅛x1⅝ inches. Price, per 100 feet........... **$1.14**

No. 63B7931 Clear Soft Wood, for paint. Size, 1⅛x2 inches. Price, per 100 feet.......... **$1.43**

No. 63B7932 Clear Soft Wood, for paint. Size, 1⅛x2½ inches. Price, per 100 feet **$1.73**

No. 63B7933 Clear Soft Wood for paint. Size, 1⅛x3 inches. Price, per 100 feet **$2.05**

COVE MOLDINGS.

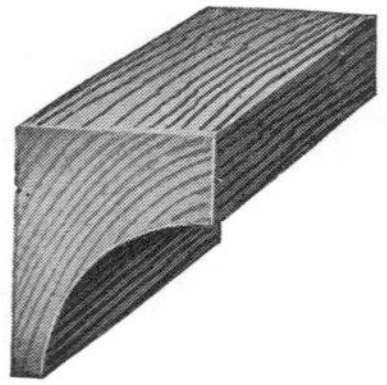

Cove Molding is carried in stock in the sizes listed below. May be used the same as quarter round, and is used under stair treads, steps, stools, etc. Prices are for 100 lineal feet in random lengths.

No. 63B7814 Clear Soft Wood. Size, ¾x⅞ inch. Price, per 100 lineal feet.... **31c**

No. 63B7815 Clear Soft Wood. Size, $\frac{13}{16}$x1⅛ inches. Price, per 100 lineal feet.. **41c**

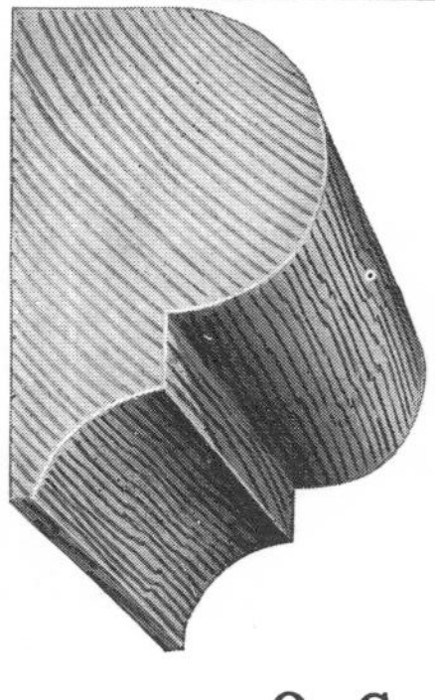

NOSING.

Nosing, made of clear stock. Sold in random lengths only.

No. 63B7769 Clear Soft Wood. Size, 1⅜x2¼ inches.
Price, per 100 feet..... **$1.80**

No. 63B7770 Yellow Pine. Size, 1⅜x2¼ inches.
Price, per 100 feet..... **$1.80**

O. G. BARN BATTENS.

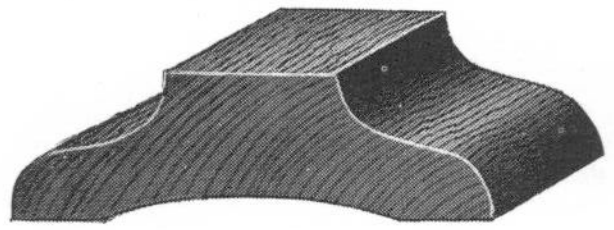

Our Battens are carried in stock in gum (hazel wood) and clear soft wood. Prices are for 100 lineal feet.

Size, inches		$\frac{13}{16}$x2	$\frac{13}{16}$x2½
No. 63B7677	**Gum (Hazel Wood)**	**60c**	**72c**
No. 63B7678	**Clear Soft Wood**	**64c**	**76c**

FLAT BATTENS.

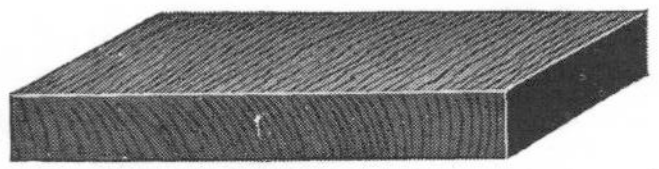

Size, ⅜x3 inches. Prices are for 100 lineal feet.

No. 63B7680 Gum (Hazel Wood) **40c**
No. 63B7679 Clear Soft Wood **44c**

BRICK MOLDING.

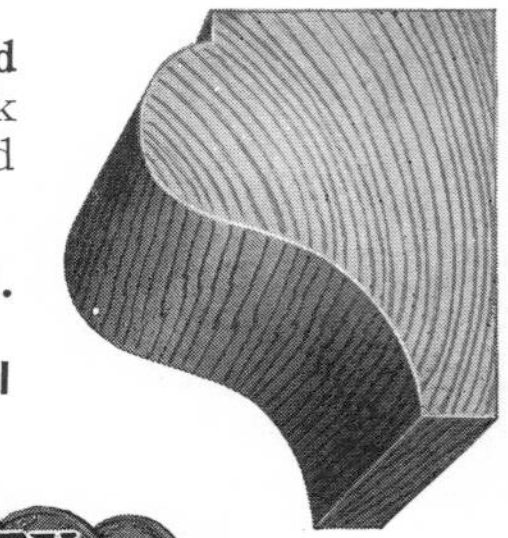

Used as a molding around window and door frames in brick or concrete buildings. Carried in stock in clear soft wood.

No. 63B7771 Clear Soft Wood. Size, 1⅜x1⅝ inches.
Price, per 100 feet..... **$1.31**

QUALITY GUARANTEED

LATTICE.

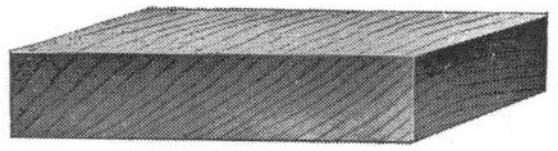

Our Lattice is made of the different soft woods suitable for outside use. We cannot agree to furnish any particular wood at the **very low prices we quote,** but will ship whatever kind we have on hand at the time the order is received.

No. 63B7916 Size, $\frac{5}{16}$x1⅛ inches. Price, per 100 lineal feet. **28c**
No. 63B7917 Size, $\frac{5}{16}$x1⅜ inches. Price, per 100 lineal feet. **33c**
No. 63B7918 Size, $\frac{5}{16}$x1¾ inches. Price, per 100 lineal feet. **44c**

QUARTER ROUND MOLDING.

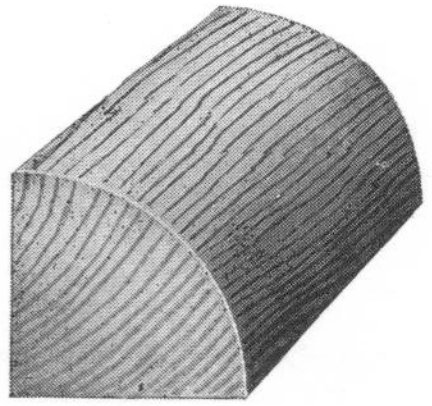

Used for base shoe or to cover joints in corners.

No. 63B7784 Size, ⅝x⅝ in. Price, per 100 lineal feet.... **23c**

SCREEN MOLDING.

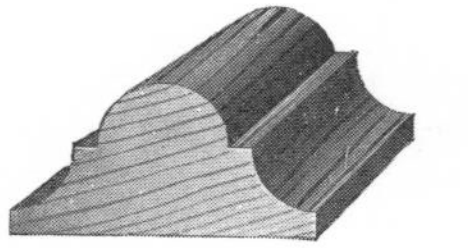

Clear Soft Wood Screen Molding. Size, ⅜x⅝ inch.

No. 63B7935 Price, per 100 lineal feet **32c**

BLIND STOP.

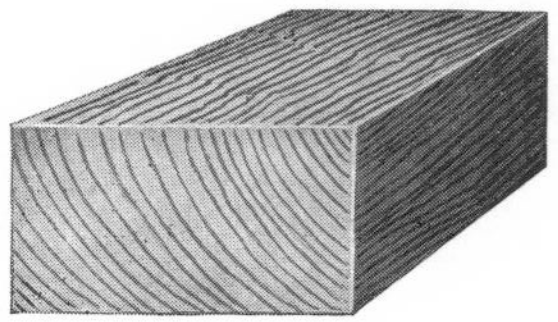

No. 63B7934 Blind Stop is carried in stock in soft wood. Size, $\frac{13}{16}$x1⅜ inches.

Price, per 100 lineal feet in random lengths.... **51c**

PARTING STOP.

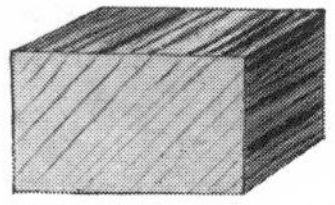

Parting Stop is carried in stock in yellow pine and clear soft wood. Size, ½x$\frac{13}{16}$-inch. Price, per 100 lineal feet in random lengths.

No. 63B7937 Clear Soft Wood, for paint. Price..... **34c**
No. 63B7939 Yellow Pine. Price................. **31c**

GABLE ORNAMENTS

$1 05

75c

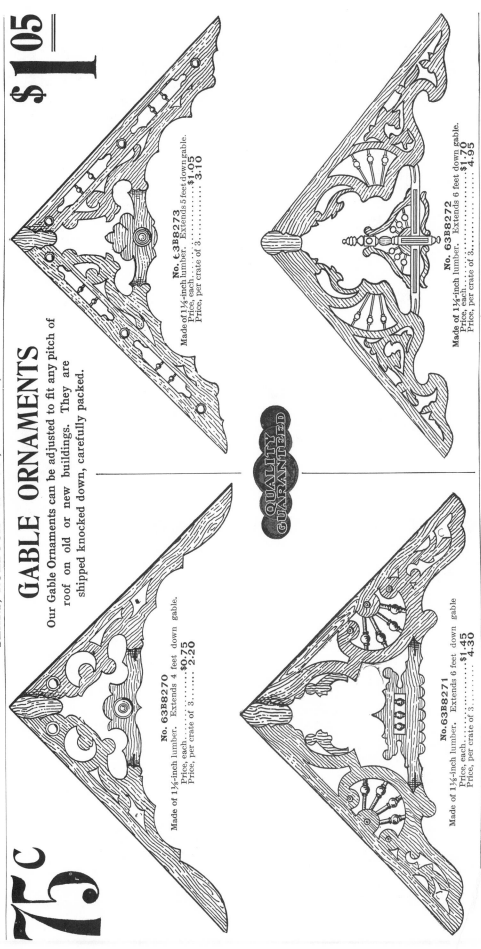

Our Gable Ornaments can be adjusted to fit any pitch of roof on old or new buildings. They are shipped knocked down, carefully packed.

No. 63B8273
Made of 1⅛-inch lumber. Extends 5 feet down gable.
Price, each.................$1.05
Price, per crate of 3........3.10

No. 63B8272
Made of 1⅛-inch lumber. Extends 6 feet down gable.
Price, each.................$1.70
Price, per crate of 3........4.95

No. 63B8270
Made of 1⅛-inch lumber. Extends 4 feet down gable.
Price, each.................$0.75
Price, per crate of 3........2.20

No. 63B8271
Made of 1⅛-inch lumber. Extends 6 feet down gable
Price, each.................$1.45
Price, per crate of 3........4.30

ROOF CRESTING.

Roof Cresting is used as an ornament for the ridge of the roof. The fact that nearly every house now being built uses cresting proves its enormous popularity. We carry it in stock in 6-foot lengths. It may be cut by purchaser to any length required. It is 5¾ inches high and ⅞ inch thick. The post or knob is 1¾x1¾x10 inches. Free from knots and defects.

No. 63B8260 Post or Knob. 1¾x1¾x10 inches.
Price, each................................**$0.05**
No. 63B8261 Roof Cresting. Price, per 6-foot length, without post.....................................**.34**
No. 63B8262 Roof Cresting. Price, per crate of 6 pieces, 6 feet long.............................**1.98**

GABLE DRAPERY.

Gable Drapery is used as an ornament on the gables and eaves of the house. This work looks very nice and is used in enormous quantities throughout the country. We carry it in stock in 6-foot lengths. It may be cut to any required length by the purchaser. It is 5¾ inches deep and ⅞ inch thick. Free from knots and defects.

No. 63B8255 Gable Drapery. Price, per 6-foot piece, **$0.35**
No. 63B8256 Gable Drapery. Price, per crate of 6 pieces, 6 feet long...........................**2.00**

PORCH SPANDRIL.

Porch Spandril is used as an ornament on porches to take the place of spindles and frieze stock. We carry it in stock in 6-foot lengths. It may be cut by purchaser to any length required; it is 9½ inches deep and 1⅛ inches thick, free from knots and defects.

No. 63B8251 Porch Spandril. Price, per 6-foot piece, **$0.85**
No. 63B8252 Porch Spandril. Price, per crate of 6 pieces, 6 feet long.............................**5.00**

HIGHEST GRADE COLONIAL BUILT=UP COLUMNS

No. 63B8070

No. 63B8073

No. 63B8076

No. 63B8079

COLONIAL LOCK JOINT BUILT-UP COLUMNS.

The illustration above shows an end view of our lock joint columns, showing how the staves of these columns interlock, allowing for contraction and expansion.

BUILT-UP COLUMNS—Plain Shaft.

Diameter of Shaft at Base	Height Over All	No. 63B8070 With Plain Cap	No. 63B8073 With Composition Cap	Shipping Weight
6 in.	6 ft.	$1.49	$2.06	27 lbs.
6 in.	8 ft.	1.63	2.23	33 lbs.
6 in.	9 ft.	1.76	2.36	36 lbs.
8 in.	6 ft.	1.65	2.30	40 lbs.
8 in.	8 ft.	2.15	2.80	46 lbs.
8 in.	9 ft.	2.33	2.98	50 lbs.
8 in.	10 ft.	2.55	3.20	53 lbs.
10 in.	6 ft.	2.55	3.50	53 lbs.
10 in.	8 ft.	2.90	3.85	62 lbs.
10 in.	9 ft.	3.05	4.00	66 lbs.
12 in.	10 ft.	5.07	6.25	75 lbs.

Clear in the White.

FOR DIVIDING OR SPLITTING THESE COLUMNS ADD 10c

COLONIAL LOCK JOINT BUILT-UP COLUMNS.

The illustration above shows an end view of our lock joint columns, showing how the staves of these columns interlock, allowing for contraction and expansion.

BUILT-UP COLUMNS—Fluted Shaft.

Diameter of Shaft at Base	Height Over All	No. 63B8076 With Plain Cap	No. 63B8079 With Composition Cap	Shipping Weight
6 in.	6 ft.	$2.49	$3.09	27 lbs.
6 in.	8 ft.	2.63	3.23	33 lbs.
6 in.	9 ft.	2.76	3.36	36 lbs.
8 in.	6 ft.	2.55	3.30	40 lbs.
8 in.	8 ft.	3.15	3.80	46 lbs.
8 in.	9 ft.	3.33	3.98	50 lbs.
8 in.	10 ft.	3.65	4.20	53 lbs.
10 in.	6 ft.	3.90	4.85	53 lbs.
10 in.	8 ft.	4.25	5.20	62 lbs.
10 in.	9 ft.	4.39	5.34	66 lbs.
12 in.	10 ft.	6.41	7.63	75 lbs.

Clear in the White.

FOR DIVIDING OR SPLITTING THESE COLUMNS ADD 10c

We illustrate above four designs of our Colonial Lock Joint Built-Up Columns. These columns are constructed to withstand the worst weather conditions. They are made from selected lumber, practically clear and smooth, thoroughly kiln dried, and if painted immediately upon receiving them they are guaranteed not to check or warp.

A **comparatively small amount of money invested in a porch will add greatly to the selling or rental value of your home,** to say nothing of the added beauty and comfort. You can pick from this catalog the same material that is used on the handsomest porch in your vicinity and you will be surprised at the small cost. The columns with the plain shafts may be cut down to fractional parts of a foot. The columns that we list herewith are strictly the highest grade columns on the market, and when you receive these columns they are in the white or unpainted, so that you will have a chance to see the fine workmanship and lumber used throughout their manufacture.

IMPORTANT: WHETHER YOU BUY THE BUILT-UP COLUMNS OR SOLID COLUMNS, WE WOULD SUGGEST THAT YOU GIVE THEM A GOOD COAT OF PRIMING AS SOON AS RECEIVED TO KEEP OUT MOISTURE.

COLONIAL PORCH COLUMNS AND PORCH NEWELS

$1.29 $1.33   Solid Colonial Porch Columns

The best solid bored column on the market, hand turned from the very best live timber with the heart bored out, with a large hole bored in center which prevents checking. In certain localities solid columns with bored centers are used in preference to built-up columns.

Painted with a good grade of linseed oil paint in a first class manner. These columns are perfect in shape and are architecturally correct. The low prices we ask for these columns include caps and bases, which we pack separately. All columns are protected by strips to prevent damage in shipping.

Diameter at Base of Shaft	Height Over All	No. 63B8100 Price, each	No. 63B8101 Price, each	Approximate Shipping Wt.
6 inches	6 feet	$1.29	$1.33	41 pounds
6 inches	7 feet	1.35	1.43	45 pounds
6 inches	8 feet	1.43	1.48	48 pounds
6 inches	9 feet	1.75	1.83	51 pounds
7 inches	6 feet	1.50	1.58	42 pounds
7 inches	7 feet	1.63	1.71	48 pounds
7 inches	8 feet	1.73	1.78	52 pounds
7 inches	9 feet	2.15	2.23	66 pounds
8 inches	6 feet	1.96	2.01	46 pounds
8 inches	7 feet	2.18	2.23	53 pounds
8 inches	8 feet	2.40	2.45	65 pounds
8 inches	9 feet	2.64	2.69	73 pounds
8 inches	10 feet	2.98	2.98	80 pounds
10 inches	6 feet	2.48	2.53	72 pounds
10 inches	7 feet	2.78	2.83	84 pounds
10 inches	8 feet	3.13	3.18	100 pounds
10 inches	9 feet	3.45	3.50	120 pounds
10 inches	10 feet	3.90	3.95	140 pounds

For dividing or splitting these columns add 10 cents to catalog price.

No. 63B8100   No. 63B8101

$3.75 $6.45   Colonial Built=Up Columns

Our Colonial Lock Joint Built-Up Columns illustrated here will not warp, swell or check, being constructed to withstand the worst weather conditions. They are made from thoroughly kiln dried selected lumber. No.63B8082 column furnished with composition cap like that shown on our No. 63B8092 column, for 70 cents extra. When ordering in this manner mark the word "Special" after the catalog number; or if you would like our No. 63B8092 with a plain cap like that shown on our No. 63B8082, deduct 70 cents from the price of our No. 63B8092 column, being sure to mark the word "Special" after the catalog number.

No. 63B8092   No. 63B8082

Diameter of Shaft at Base	Height Over All	No. 63B8082 Clear, In the White	No. 63B8092 Clear, In the White	Shipping Weight
6 inches	8 feet	$3.75	$6.45	35 lbs.
6 inches	9 feet	4.16	6.75	39 lbs.
8 inches	8 feet	4.68	6.95	50 lbs.
8 inches	9 feet	5.20	7.33	55 lbs.
10 inches	8 feet	5.70	8.45	68 lbs.
10 inches	9 feet	6.26	8.97	72 lbs.

Colonial Built=Up Newel

No. 63B8150

Diameter of Shaft at Base, inches	Length, feet	No. 63B8150 Price, each	Weight, pounds
7	4	$1.50	23

Colonial Balusters.

No. 63B8163

Size, 2⅜x20 in.   Each ..12½c   Per crate of 50 ....$6.15
Size, 2⅜x20 in.
Size, 2¾x24 in.   Each ..$6.13   Per crate of 50...$6.40
Size, 2¾x24 in.

The designs of Colonial Top Porch Rail Nos. 63B8158 and 63B8155 are to be used with our Colonial Baluster No. 63B8163

COLONIAL TOP PORCH RAIL.   COLONIAL TOP PORCH RAIL.

12½c

No. 63B8158   Made up of six members. Size over all, 4x5¾ inches. Knocked down. Price, per lineal foot.......12½c

7¼c

No. 63B8155   Size, 2¾x3½ inches. Price, per lineal foot.......7¼c

Outside Heavy Rail, for 2¾-in. baluster

COLONIAL BOTTOM PORCH RAIL.

No. 63B8159

Size, 1¾x3¾ in. Price, per lineal foot.......4c

We illustrate above a bottom porch rail to be used with our Nos. 63B8158 and 63B8155 Colonial Top Porch Rail.

NEW DESIGNS OF PORCH RAIL AND PORCH SUGGESTIONS

We show below two illustrations of porches, which illustrate the variety of up to date designs which can be built from our line of porch work. Our designs of rail, balusters, columns, etc., are strictly modern and up to date and include designs which are suitable to and used in all parts of the United States. Our prices are about one-half regular prices.

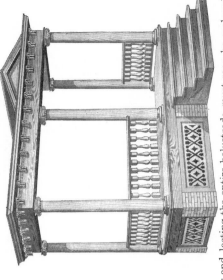

Porch rail is an important item in the construction of a porch. Unless the rail is strong, clear and lasting the entire balustrade must soon be replaced. Our rail is made of good clear quality of fir. Smooth and clean, the best made.

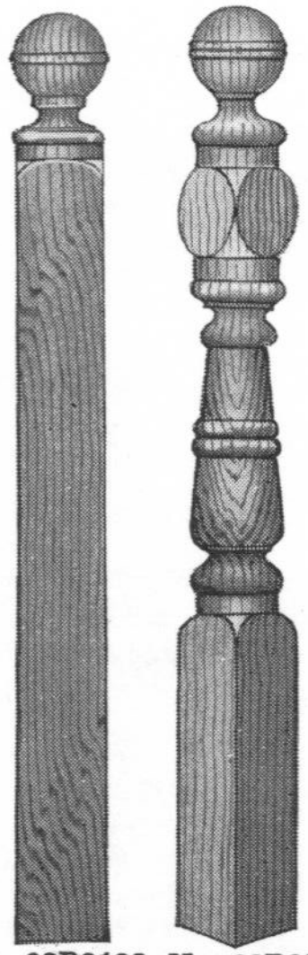

FRIEZE RAIL.

3¼c

No. 63B8196 Size, 1¾x 2⅝ inches. Price, per foot............3c

BALUSTER STOCK OR FRIEZE RAIL.

No. 63 B8206

Porch Baluster or Frieze Stock. Carried in stock in fir, in sizes as listed below. Prices are for 100 lineal feet.

Size, in.	Per 100 ft.
1¾x1⅜	$1.50
1¾x1¾	2.00

TOP PORCH RAIL.

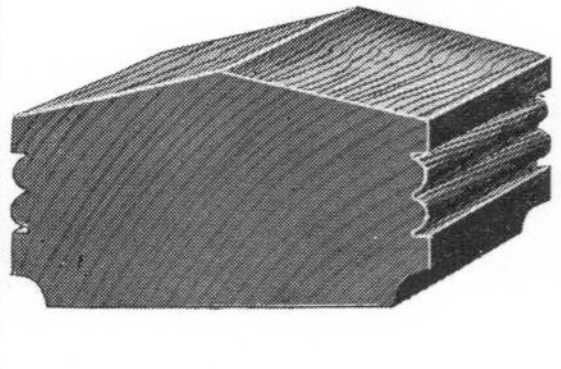

3¼c

No. 63B8191 Size, 1¾x3 inches. Price, per foot............3¼c

BOTTOM PORCH RAIL.

3¼c

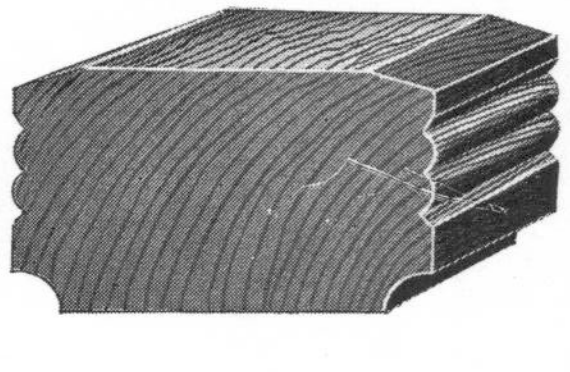

No. 63B8193 Size, 1¾x3 inches. Price, per foot............3¼c

TOP PORCH RAIL.

4c

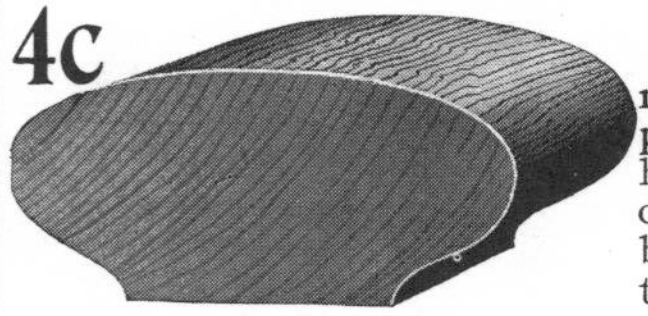

No. 63B8195

This is a new design of porch rail. It has no sharp corners to break, and the curve makes a good water shed. It can be used with No. 63B8193 bottom rail. Size, 1¾x3¾ inches.

Price, per foot............4c

TOP and BOTTOM PORCH RAIL.

No. 63B8187

Top Porch Rail. Size, 1¾x3 inches. Rabbeted for ⅞-inch scroll sawed balusters. Price, per foot....3¼c

No. 63B8189

Bottom Porch Rail. Is carried in stock in the white. Rabbeted for ⅞-inch scroll sawed balusters. Size, 1⅜x3 inches. Price, per foot....1½c

Nos. 63B8187 and 63B8189

SOLID NEWELS.

The turned column and newels illustrated on this page are made from Washington fir, the very best wood known from which to manufacture solid porch columns and newels. It is used throughout the world as masts for ships and in other places where durability and strength are required. Washington fir holds paint well, turns smoothly, will last indefinitely and is not easily affected by climatic changes. By looking at our prices you can see that it costs very little to make improvements on your home that will beautify and increase its rental or selling value.

No. 63B8182 No. 63B8180

Size Shaft	Length, feet	No.63B8180 Price, each	No.63B8182 Price, each	Weight, pounds
4x4	4	37c	33c	11
5x5	4	50c	46c	15
6x6	4	70c	65c	24

SOLID COLUMNS.

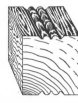

No. 63B8175

Size, inches	Length, feet	Price, each	Weig't, pounds
4x4	8	$0.55	20
4x4	9	.63	21
5x5	8	.86	27
5x5	9	.97	37
5x5	10	1.10	42
6x6	8	1.23	48
6x6	9	1.36	54
6x6	10	1.60	60

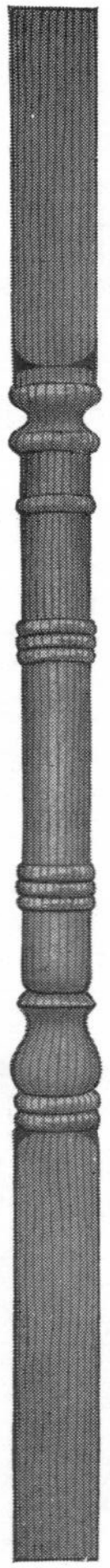

For dividing or splitting this column add 5 cents to catalog price.

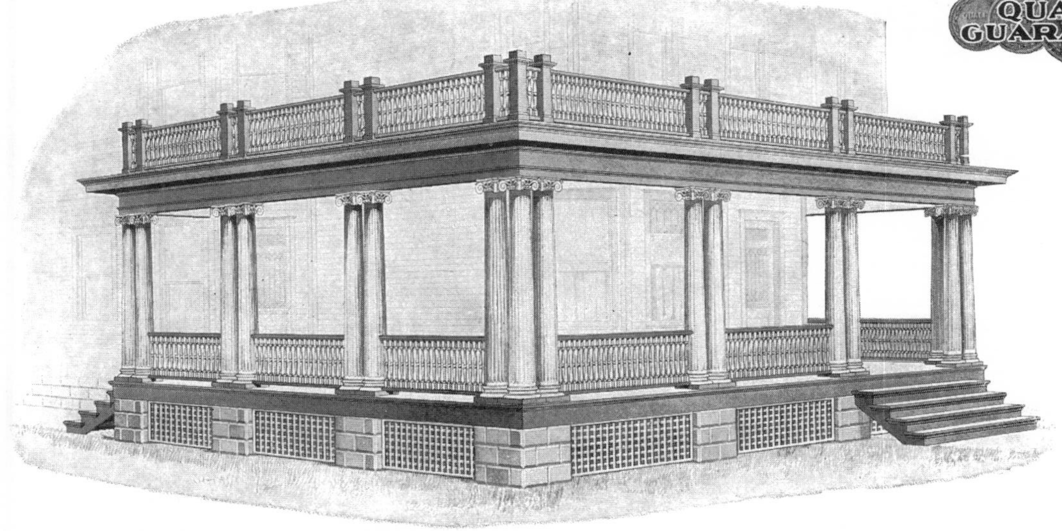

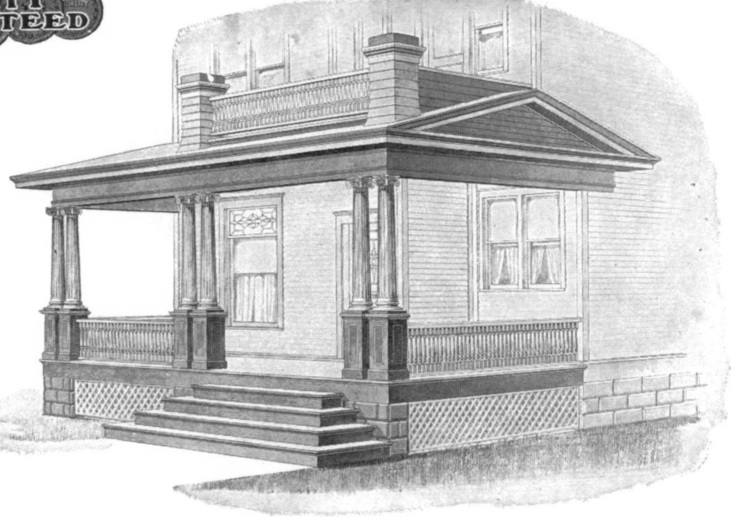

You will find all material used in the building of these porches listed in this catalog, such as columns, balusters, brackets, porch rail, spindles, etc. Remember, QUALITY is GUARANTEED. the prices speak for themselves.

GABLE OR EAVES BRACKETS.

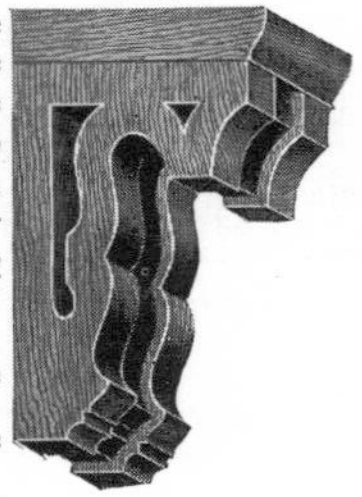

Gable or Eaves Brackets are used under the eaves along the cornice as ornaments. We carry them in stock in two sizes: 14x18 and 16x18 inches, 3½ inches thick and made three-ply for main cornice and in one size, 6x8 inches by 2¼ inches thick, for porch cornice.

No. 63B8200 6x8 in. by 2¼ in. thick. Price............**30c**

No 63B8218 14x18 in. by 3½ in. thick. Price........**50c**

No. 63B8219 16x18 in. by 3½ in. thick. Price........**55c**

TURNED PORCH BALUSTERS.

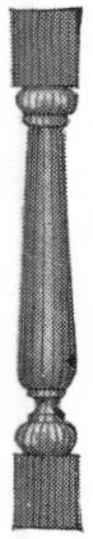

Carried in stock in following sizes:

Catalog Number	Size, inches	Price, each	Price, per Crate of 50
63B8210	1¾x20	4¼c	$1.98
63B8210	1¾x24	4½c	1.99
63B8212	1¾x20	4¼c	1.98
63B8212	1¾x24	4½c	1.99

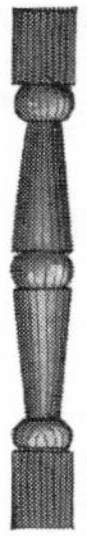

No. 63B8212

No. 63B8210

TURNED PORCH SPINDLES.

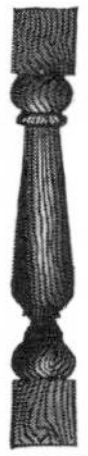

No.63B8220

We carry Turned Porch Spindles in stock in two designs and sizes as listed below. Either design the same price. When ordering specify the catalog number of the design wanted and give size and length. Put up in crates containing 100 spindles. We sell any quantity.

Size, 1⅜x1⅜x 8 inches.
Price, each............**$0.01¼**
Size, 1⅜x1⅜x 8 inches.
Price, per crate of 100.. **1.05**
Size, 1¾x1¾x10 inches.
Price, each............ **.01½**
Size, 1¾x1¾x10 inches.
Price, per crate of 100.. **1.20**

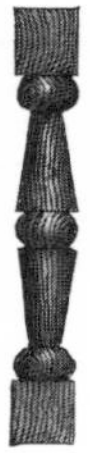

No. 63B8221

SCROLL SAWED BALUSTERS.

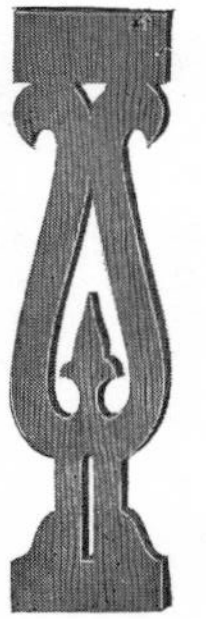

No. 63B8222

We carry Scroll Sawed Balusters (in the white) in stock. Strictly No. 1 quality. Size, ⅞ inch thick, 5¾ inches wide by 20 or 24 inches long.

Catalog No.	Length, inches	Price
63B8222	20	6c
63B8223	24	7c
63B8230	20	6c
63B8231	24	7c

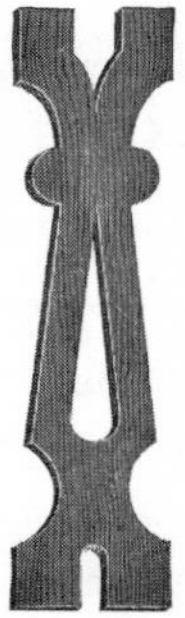

No. 63B8230

PORCH BRACKETS.

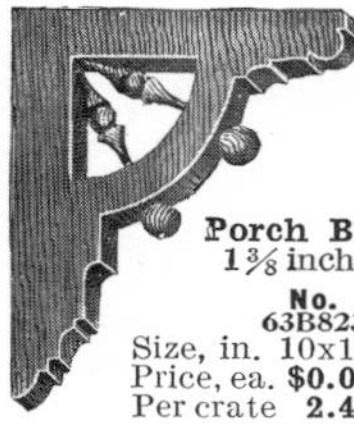

5c

Porch Brackets. 1⅜ inches thick.

	No. 63B8239	No. 63B8240
Size, in.	10x12	12x14
Price, ea.	$0.05	$0.06
Per crate	2.45	2.95

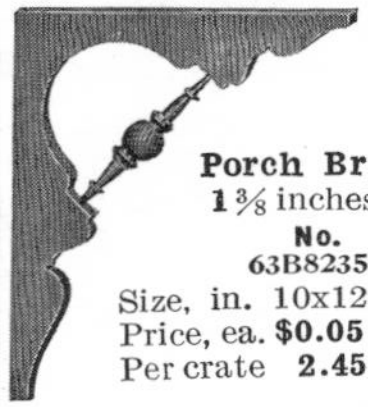

5c

Porch Brackets. 1⅜ inches thick.

	No. 63B8235	No. 63B8236
Size, in.	10x12	12x14
Price, ea.	$0.05	$0.05½
Per crate	2.45	2.65

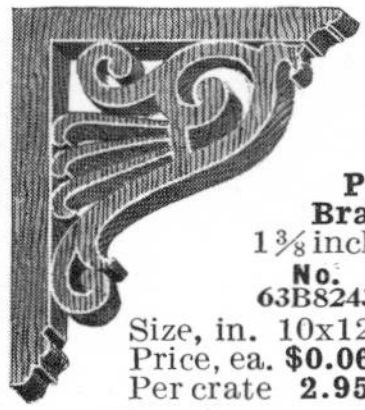

6c

Porch Brackets. 1⅜ inches thick.

	No. 63B8243	No. 63B8244
Size, in.	10x12	12x14
Price, ea.	$0.06	$0.07
Per crate	2.95	3.45

The above brackets are put up in crates containing fifty brackets. We sell any quantity.

FACE BRACKETS.

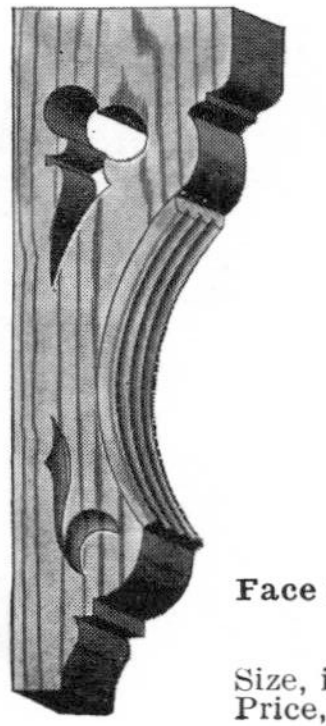

20c

SIZE, 7x22 INCHES.

You have paid double these prices for material which was far below the grade we furnish. We guarantee ours to be the best.

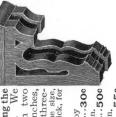

Face Brackets, 1¾ inches thick.

	No. 63B8246	No. 63B8247
Size, in...	7x22	9x28
Price, each	20c	25c

BAY BRACKETS.

Used beneath bay windows and corner bay windows. Made of material suitable for outside use. **Our prices are lowest.**

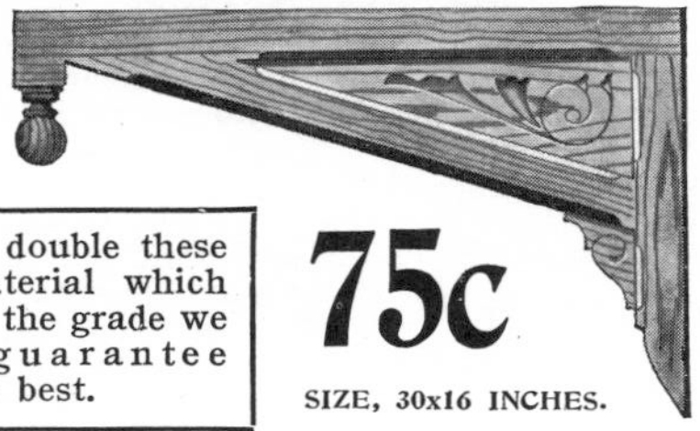

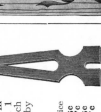

75c

SIZE, 30x16 INCHES.

Bay Brackets, 2¾ inches thick.

	No. 63B8248	No. 63B8249
Size, inches........	30x16	36x13
Price, each.......	75c	$1.00

SAVE FROM $50.00 TO $100.00 ON A FLIGHT OF STAIRS

The Stairwork Business has up to within the last year been in the **hands of a few stair builders throughout the country,** who sell to the sash and door manufacturer or jobber, who in turn sells to the retailer, who in turn sells to the consumer. Everyone has claimed that stairs could not be made correctly by a good carpenter and that it is necessary to buy your stairs knocked down and pay an enormous price for same. Any good carpenter can buy his main starting newels, angle newels, rail, fillet, shoe balusters, stringers, treads and risers (which are the materials required) from us in the form listed and save an enormous amount. By fitting each piece carefully and taking pains with the work, a better flight of stairs may be made, as they are put up by you right on the spot, not some place hundreds of miles away by guesswork. We therefore claim that you not only save money and time by ordering stairwork from us as listed in this catalog, but you will get better satisfaction and more prompt service.

SAVED ONE-QUARTER TO ONE-HALF AND ARE WELL PLEASED WITH THE QUALITY OF OUR MILL WORK.
Box No. 52, Oxford, Mich.
Sears, Roebuck and Co. Chicago, Ill.
Gentlemen:—Would state that we were very much pleased with all our mill work we received from you; we saved 25 cents on the dollar and some things were really half price. We were so well pleased that we recommended your goods to all farmers in this locality.
BURKART & BURKART.

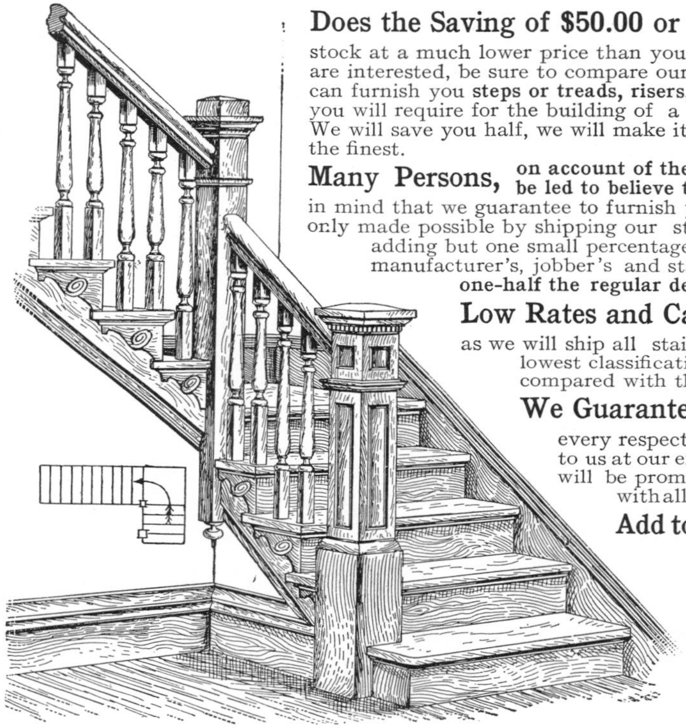

DESIGN No. 15

Does the Saving of $50.00 or More on a flight of stairs interest you? Do you know that you can build a solid oak flight of stairs from our stock at a much lower price than you can buy a cheap grade of pine from your local dealer? If you are interested, be sure to compare our low prices with those you have been paying in the past. We can furnish you **steps or treads, risers, stair balusters, stair rail and stair newels,** in fact, everything you will require for the building of a high grade flight of stairs complete (rough horses excepted). We will save you half, we will make it possible for you to get better stairs, as our workmanship is of the finest.

Many Persons, **on account of the extremely low prices we name for our line of stairwork, may be led to believe that we do not furnish the finest grade of materials.** Please bear in mind that we guarantee to furnish you only the very best grades. Our exceptionally low prices are only made possible by shipping our stairwork and other mill work direct from our factory to you, adding but one small percentage of profit. We save you a chain of profits which includes the manufacturer's, jobber's and stair builder's profits, and as a result are able to sell at about **one-half the regular dealer's price.**

Low Rates and Careful Packing. **Do not let the question of freight charges prevent you from sending us your order** as we will ship all stairwork knocked down, carefully bundled, which takes the very lowest classification, and as a result your freight charges amount to nothing compared with the great amount we are able to save you.

We Guarantee **that you will receive the goods clean and bright,** perfect in every way. If not all we claim, in fact, if not satisfactory in every respect, same can be returned to us at our expense and your money will be promptly returned, together with all transportation charges.

Add to the Beauty of your home **by selecting one of the artistic designs shown on this page.** If you intend to remodel your home, stop and consider how little expense is necessary to install an up to date, high grade flight of stairs at our special low prices.

WE SAVE YOU $50.00 OR MORE ON A FLIGHT OF STAIRS

To demonstrate to you how cheaply we sell high grade stairwork of all kinds we itemize below a flight of stairs of average height which you formerly have paid $75.00 to $100.00 for to your regular dealer. Get an estimate from your local dealer on a complete set of stairs such as we describe below and we know that you will appreciate the wonderful saving we are able to make you. **The table below is only for comparison of prices. Before ordering your stairwork see that quantity of each item is correct.**

DESIGN No. 15 IN YELLOW PINE.

15 Steps or Stair Treads	No. 63B8282 at	$0.40	$6.00
16 Stair Risers	No. 63B8286 at	.20	3.20
1 Starting Newel	No. 63B8309		2.85
2 Angle Newels	No. 63B8321 at	1.62	3.24
26 Balusters (28 and 32-in.)	No. 63B8365		1.99
18 Lineal Ft. Rail	No. 63B8351 at	.09½	1.71
34 Lineal Ft. String Board.	No. 63B8376 at	.06½	2.21
60 Lineal Ft. Cove	No. 63B7817 at	.31	.19
14 Stair Brackets	No. 63B8355 at	.14	1.96
AVERAGE RETAILER'S PRICE			75.00
Our price			23.35
We save you			**$51.65**

QUALITY GUARANTEED

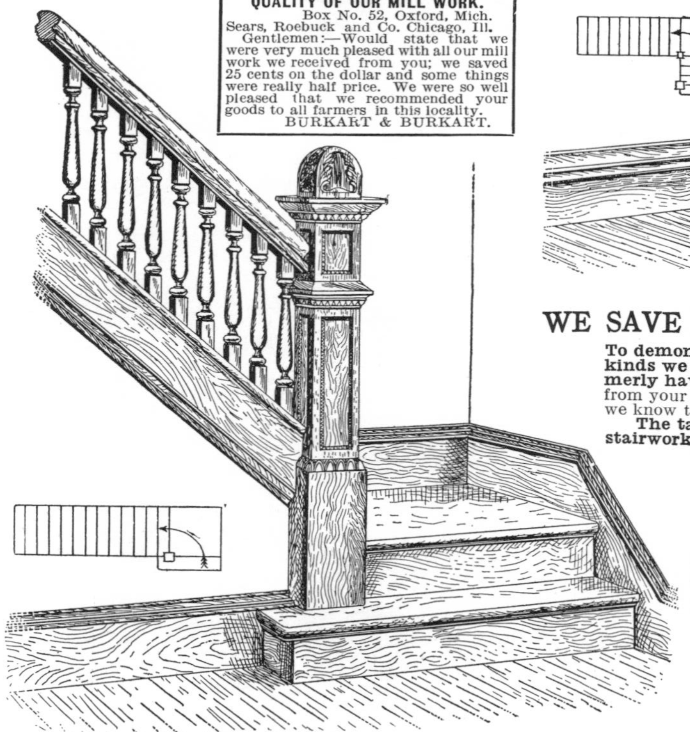

DESIGN No. 10

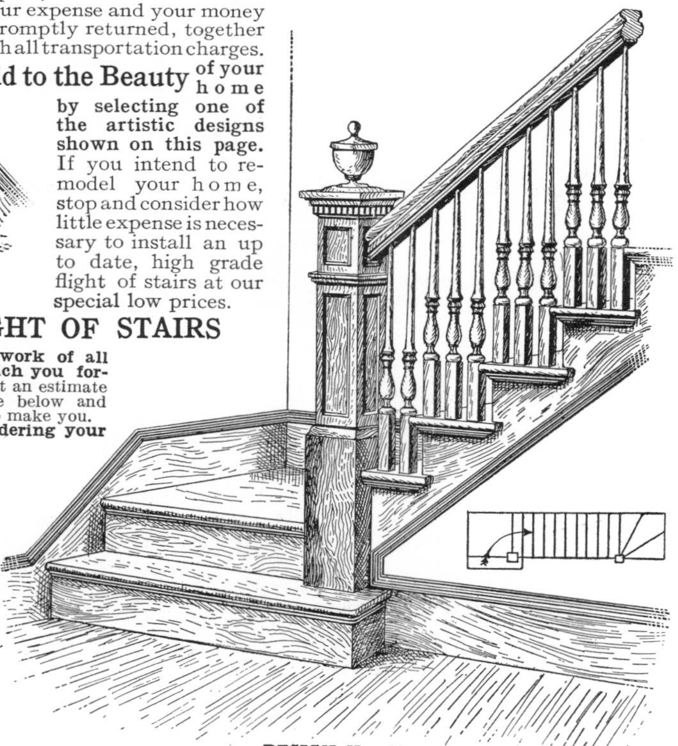

DESIGN No. 20

REMEMBER, we will ship your order for stairwork within five days and will include same with the rest of your mill work order. The average stair builder requires from sixty to ninety days.

SEARS, ROEBUCK AND CO., CHICAGO, ILLINOIS.

HIGHEST GRADE BUILT=UP STAIR NEWELS, LOCK JOINT

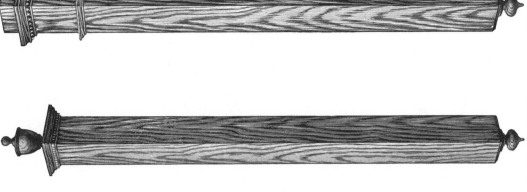

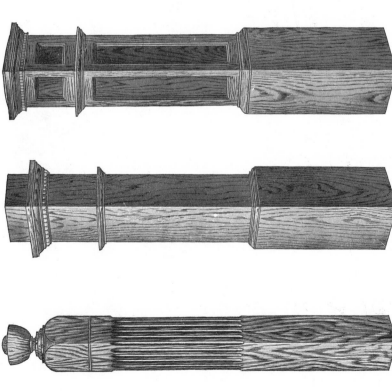

STARTING NEWELS.

No. 63B8300 Plain
Sawed Red Oak...$2.10
No. 63B8301 Yellow
Pine............$1.88

The shaft is 5 inches square; height, 4 feet. The material is first class in every way. Fluted on four sides.

STARTING NEWELS.

No. 63B8304 Plain
Sawed Red Oak...$2.54
No. 63B8305 Yellow
Pine............$2.29

Egg and dart molding is placed under the cap. Size of shaft, 6 inches square. Base, 8 inches square and 18 inches high. Height of post, 4 feet.

STARTING NEWELS.

No. 63B8308 Plain
Sawed Red Oak...$2.96
No. 63B8309 Yellow
Pine............$2.85
No. 63B8306 Birch, 2.95

This paneled newel has shaft 6 inches square. Base, 8 inches square, 18 inches high. Height of post, 4 feet. Paneled on four sides below and on three sides above.

STARTING NEWELS.

No. 63B8312 Plain
Sawed Red Oak...$3.12
No. 63B8313 Yellow
Pine............$2.85

This newel has shaft 6 inches square, paneled on four sides below and on three sides above. The base is 8 inches square, 18 inches high. Trimmed with acorn top. Height of post, including acorn, 4 feet 6 inches.

STARTING NEWELS.

No. 63B8316 Plain
Sawed Red Oak...$5.19
No. 63B8317 Yellow
Pine............$4.84

The shaft is 6 inches square, paneled on four sides below and three sides above. Base is 8 inches square. Base is 8 inches square, 18 inches high. Panels are molded with turned bead moldings. All other moldings are egg and dart design. The cap is hand carved.

ANGLE NEWELS.

No. 63B8324 Plain
Sawed Red Oak...$1.80
No. 63B8325 Yellow
Pine............$1.68

This neat angle newel may be used with any of our starting newels or may be sawed off 4 feet long and used as a cheap starting newel. The shaft is 5 in. square. Length, 5 ft. 6 in. (not measuring the ornaments at top and bottom).

ANGLE NEWELS.

No. 63B8320 Plain
Sawed Red Oak...$1.72
No. 63B8321 Yellow
Pine............$1.62
No. 63B8307 Birch, 1.71

This angle newel is suitable for use with any of our starting newels or may be sawed off 4 feet long and used as a cheap starting newel. The shaft is 5 in. square. Length, 5 ft. 6 in. (not measuring the ornament at bottom). Cap is molded with egg and dart design molding.

WE CAN SAVE YOU
$50.00 TO $100.00 ON
A FLIGHT OF STAIRS
(See page 74).

All of our stair newels are made from thoroughly kiln dried selected stock, 1 inch thick, carefully built, smoothly finished and guaranteed. The 18-inch base on the starting newels may be used for either open or closed string board and will receive either one or two risers. They are carefully wrapped in paper and securely crated for shipment. We carry a large stock on hand at all times and can ship promptly. When others delay your shipments try us.

STAIRWORK  QUALITY GUARANTEED

MADE IN OUR OWN FACTORY BY EXPERT STAIR BUILDERS. READ HOW IT IS POSSIBLE TO SAVE $50.00 ON AN ORDINARY FLIGHT OF STAIRS, WHICH IS EXPLAINED ON PAGE 74.

NOTE—If stairwork is wanted in cypress it will have to be made special to your order and will cost considerably more than the prices we ask for oak or birch; therefore, we recommend your ordering oak, birch or yellow pine in preference to cypress. We will also require about fifteen days in which to ship cypress stairwork.

You can build a flight of stairs with our stair material which will equal, if not surpass, stairwork turned out and put together in the very best stairwork factories. By referring to the illustration you will see how simple and easy it is to build a flight of stairs with our material and at the same time have a strictly first class, high grade job.

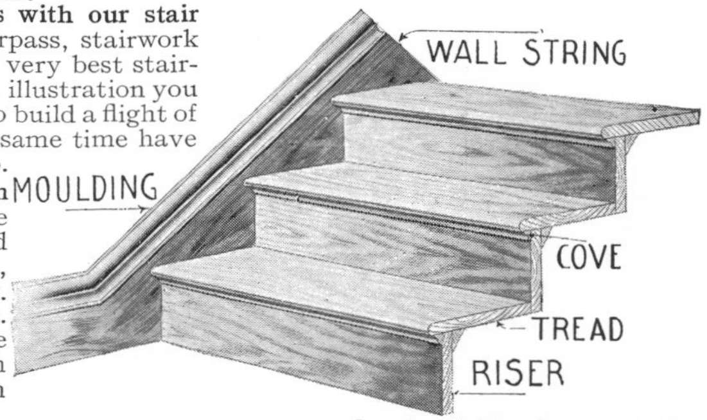

We furnish Treads and Risers in two lengths. This will enable the carpenter to cut to any desired length. Made in yellow pine, birch, or plain red oak. Absolutely clear. Furnished at prices quoted below. The treads and risers may be made narrower to fit any height or length of run. Furnished in 3-foot 5-inch lengths and 4-foot 6-inch lengths.

Labels: WALL STRING — COVE — TREAD — RISER — MOULDING

	Length, 3 ft. 5 in. Price, each	Length, 4 ft. 6 in. Price, each
No. 63B8281 Stair Treads, 1⅛x11 inches, Plain Red Oak	52c	77c
No. 63B8282 Stair Treads, 1⅛x11 inches, Yellow Pine	40c	60c
No. 63B8283 Stair Treads, 1⅛ x 11 inches, Birch	51c	76c
No. 63B8285 Stair Risers, ⅞x7½ inches, Plain Red Oak	25c	37c
No. 63B8286 Stair Risers, ⅞x7½ inches, Yellow Pine	20c	31c
No. 63B8287 Stair Risers, ⅞ x 7½ inches, Birch	24c	36c
No. 63B7819 Stair Cove, ⅝x⅞ inch, Plain Red Oak. Price, per 100 feet		66c
No. 63B7817 Stair Cove, ⅝x⅞ inch, Yellow Pine. Price, per 100 feet		31c
No. 63B7820 Stair Cove, ⅝x⅞ inch, Birch. Price, per 100 feet		48c

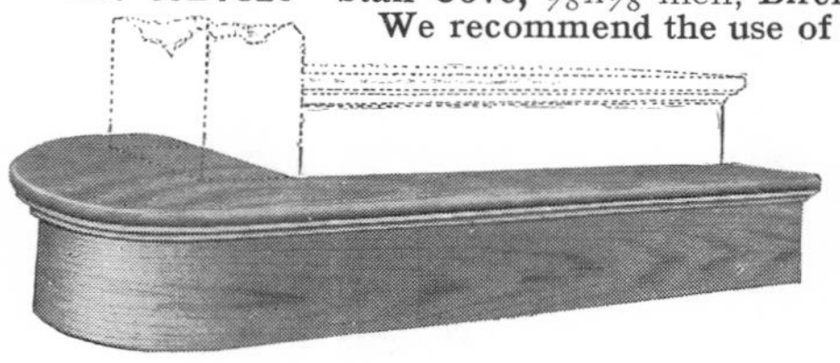

We recommend the use of our Bull Nose or Half Circle End Tread and Riser for the starting of stairs. This half circle work is very carefully manufactured and gives a very attractive finish and appearance to any flight of stairs. We carry these Bull Nose or Half Circle End Treads with both right hand and left hand ends. When ordering be sure to state whether the circle end is at the right hand or left hand side going up the stairs.

	For Stairs 3 feet 5 inches or less	For Stairs 4 feet 6 inches or less
No. 63B7821 Oak. Price, each	$2.95	$3.55
No. 63B7822 Yellow Pine. Price, each	2.90	3.50
No. 63B7823 Birch. Price, each	2.93	3.53

STRING BOARDS.

We carry in stock two styles of String Board in both yellow pine and oak. Style No. 63B8376, No. 63B8377 and No. 63B8378 are of plain design and are intended to be used when the hall is finished with a one-member base. Style No. 63B8379 and No. 63B8380 are two-member string boards and the cap is the same design used with our three-member base which is shown on pages 62 and 64. If the hall is trimmed with our stock three-member base such as shown on pages 62 and 64 this string board and cap will match and will give a very pleasing and harmonious effect.

No. 63B8376 Yellow Pine. Price, per foot 6½c
No. 63B8377 Plain Red Oak. Price, per foot 10c
No. 63B8378 Birch. Price, per foot 10c
No. 63B8379 Yellow Pine. Price, per foot for two-member ... 8c
No. 63B8380 Plain Red Oak. Price, per foot for two-member ...12c

No. 63B8376
No. 63B8377 ONE-MEMBER
No. 63B8378 ⅝x11 inches.
No. 63B8379 TWO-MEMBER
No. 63B8380 ⅝x13 inches over all.

STAIR RAIL.
Size, 2½x3½ inches.

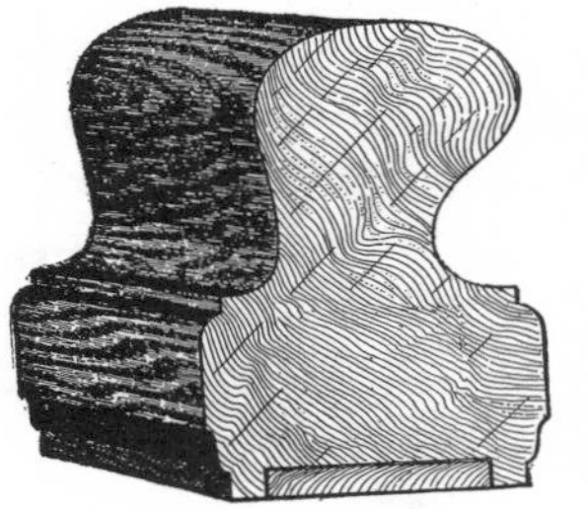

Architects consider this to be the best designed Stair Rail for all purposes that is on the market. The right side of the rail, as you look at it, is especially designed to fit the ends of the fingers when gripped over the rails, as is the custom of most people in going up and down stairs. Made in oak, birch or yellow pine; size, 2½ x 3½ inches. We make this rail plowed for 1¾-inch balusters. Made from selected kiln dried stock, hand smoothed. We do not furnish loose fillet strip to cut between balusters, in order to make a nice finished job, unless ordered separately, in which case we charge 1 cent per lineal foot for fillet.

Stair Rail Without Fillet.

No. 63B8351 Yellow Pine. Price, per foot 9½c
No. 63B8350 Plain Red Oak. Price, per foot 11½c
No. 63B8362 Birch. Price, per foot ..11c
No. 63B8349 Fillet to match. Price, per foot .. 1c

SHOE RAIL.

With Fillet. Size, 1⅜x2¾ Inches. **Rabbeted for 1¾-inch Balusters.**

No. 63B8353 Yellow Pine. Per foot..3c
No. 63B8352 Plain Red Oak. Per foot.4c
No. 63B8363 Birch. Price, per foot..4c

STAIR RAIL. Size, 1¾ x 3⅝ Inches.

This design of Stair Rail is now becoming very popular with housewives, who have found that the fancy rails catch an enormous amount of dust and dirt and that this design need only be wiped off lightly with a cloth and the dust will instantly disappear.

No. 63B8359 Yellow Pine. Per foot. 6½c
No. 63B8358 Plain Red Oak. Per foot, 8½c

STAIR BALUSTERS.

We carry in stock these two designs of Stair Balusters in both oak and yellow pine. These balusters are very carefully turned and sandpapered and are high class in every respect.

No. 63B8364 Plain Red Oak.
1¾x1¾x28 inches. Price, 8½c — Each
1¾x1¾x32 inches. Price, 8¾c

No. 63B8368 Birch.
1¾x1¾x28 inches. Price, 8½c — Each
1¾x1¾x32 inches. Price, 8¾c

No. 63B8365 Yellow Pine.
1¾x1¾x28 inches. Price, 7½c — Each
1¾x1¾x32 inches. Price, 7¾c

No. 63B8366 Plain Red Oak.
1¾x1¾x28 inches. Price, 9c — Each
1¾x1¾x32 inches. Price, 9¼c

No. 63B8367 Yellow Pine.
1¾x1¾x28 inches. Price, 8½c — Each
1¾x1¾x32 inches. Price, 8¾c

No. 63B8364 Oak.
No. 63B8365 Yellow Pine.
No. 63B8368 Birch.
No. 63B8366 Plain Red Oak.
No. 63B8367 Yellow Pine.

SQUARE BALUSTER STOCK.

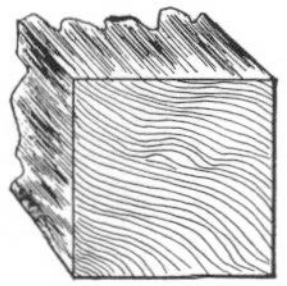

We furnish this square Baluster Stock in plain red oak and yellow pine, clear stock, in random lengths. Size, 1⅛x1⅛ inches.
No. 63B8370 Yellow Pine. Price, per foot 1½c
No. 63B8371 Plain Red Oak. Price, per foot 2c

WALL ROSETTES.

This Rosette or Plate is used at the end of the rail where it leads against a wall and the center portion is large enough to receive our big rail 3½ inches wide.
No. 63B8360 Yellow Pine. Price, each.... 10c
No. 63B8361 Plain Red Oak. Price, each, 14c

STAIR BRACKETS.

Some people like to construct their stairs with a small bracket at the end of each tread. This bracket is placed on the string board below the balusters and adds very much to the appearance of the stairs.
No. 63B8355 Yellow Pine. Price, each.. 14c
No. 63B8356 Plain Red Oak. Price, each. 16c

OUR ROYAL ACME HIGH GRADE HARDWOOD FLOORING

The Best High Grade Flooring Made. There Is None Better No Matter How Much You Pay.

At the reduced prices we name for the finest grades of hardwood flooring anyone can afford to lay a good hardwood floor made of maple, quarter sawed red oak or plain oak instead of using a poor grade of hardwood flooring or common soft wood.

Every modern building today, whether residence, factory, office, warehouse or store, uses maple or oak flooring, as experience has proven that a good hardwood floor made of maple or oak will give much better satisfaction and is cheaper in the long run as it will outwear a dozen soft wood floors. There is nothing which will add more beauty, style and comfort to your home than our Royal Acme Hardwood Flooring.

Our Royal Acme Flooring is made in one of the largest and b st flooring plants in the United States. Every foot of Royal Acme Flooring is treated scientifically, properly cured in kilns and subjected to an average temperature of 212 degrees Fahrenheit.

Every foot of Royal Acme Maple or Oak Flooring is steel polished, which gives it a beautiful satin finish. It is all very carefully end matched and bundled for shipment. The $\frac{13}{16}$-inch is hollow backed and bored for blind nailing.

Freight rates on flooring are very low, whether bought in carloads or less than carload lots. Hardwood flooring in carload lots usually takes 6th class rate, less than carload lots usually takes 4th class rate. We sell a large number of carload orders, which take the lowest freight rate, as it takes only 14,000 feet to make a minimum car.

We sell flooring in any quantity from a hundred feet to carload lots or more and quote you our lowest factory cost prices and ship from the factory in Chicago direct to you, insuring your receiving the lowest possible freight rates, which amount to nothing compared with the wonderful saving we are able to make you on nice, clean, selected high quality flooring.

Oak flooring can also be shipped from Cincinnati, Ohio.

The Above Illustration Shows a Room Floored With Our Royal Acme Hardwood Flooring, the Best Flooring Made.

Maple flooring is invariably used in preference to any other kind of flooring where it is subjected to extremely hard wear. For residences it is used in the kitchen, hallways and quite frequently throughout the entire house. It is an ideal flooring for stores, offices, warehouses, factories and skating rinks, as the longer it is used the better it becomes. As it is practically indestructible, it wears even better than concrete or tile. It is the easiest kind of a floor to keep clean and takes a beautiful oil finish. If you want the best maple flooring made, at factory price, then order our Royal Acme Maple Flooring.

Quarter sawed red oak flooring. We recommend our Royal Acme Quarter Sawed Red Oak Flooring where a floor combining the most beautiful finish and hard wearing qualities is desired. Our Royal Acme Quarter Sawed Red Oak is very carefully selected, bringing out the beautiful flake and grain in such a manner that when varnished it is beautiful to behold. It is extensively used in all high class buildings, residences and offices where the finest kind of a flooring is in demand. We sell quarter sawed red oak flooring to you at factory price, a price but little higher than you have been obliged to pay for common grade plain sawed oak flooring.

Plain sawed oak flooring, which we quote below, is the finest grade plain sawed oak flooring made, being beautiful in grain and color and it will take a beautiful natural or antique finish, in fact, can be finished to harmonize with the interior of the finest building. It is especially adapted for residences, offices and high class stores. Like all of our flooring, it is perfectly made, every foot being steel polished and every piece is end matched, that the joints may be perfect. The $\frac{13}{16}$-inch is hollow backed and bored for blind nailing.

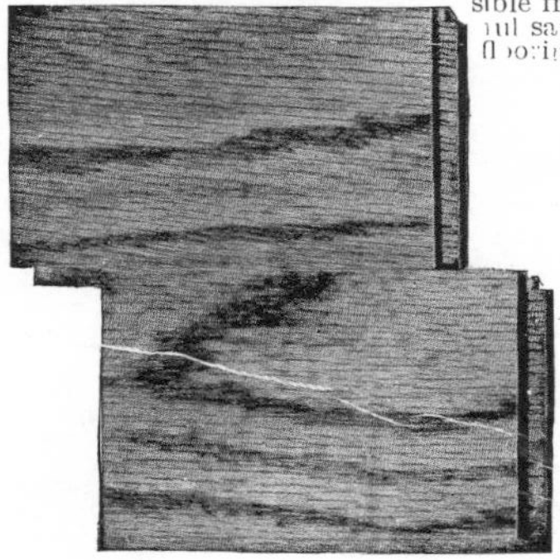

Plain Sawed Oak Flooring.

Rules for Grading Flooring

Our clear grade is absolutely clear, just what the name implies, and is furnished in random lengths from 2 to 16 feet inclusive.

Our select grade is not quite so good as our clear grade but nearly all dealers sell it for clear as it is a very high grade. It will lay with no waste and allows but few defects. Furnished in random lengths from 1 to 16 feet inclusive.

Clear grade allows 8 per cent of lengths 4 feet and under.

Select grade allows a much larger percentage of short lengths.

No. 1 Factory flooring must be of such a character as will lay and make a good serviceable floor, with some cutting. Lengths from 1 to 16 feet inclusive.

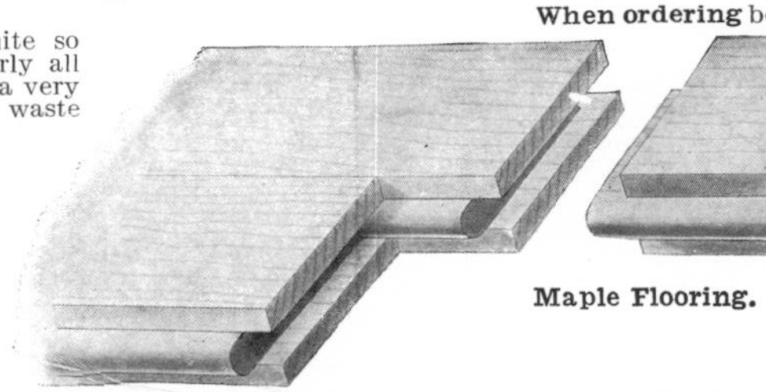

Maple Flooring.

How To Order Flooring

When ordering be sure to bear in mind that flooring with a 2-inch face is figured as 2½ inches wide and flooring with 2¼-inch face is figured as 3 inches wide to allow for tongue and groove. When making up your order it is necessary that you increase the amount you order about 30 per cent more than the actual measurement of the surface to be covered. Also allow a few feet additional for waste as it is always better to have a little too much than too little.

To illustrate, a room 10x12 feet equals 120 square feet. If a flooring with a 2-inch face is ordered, add 30 per cent, which makes about 160 square feet. The same rule applies no matter from whom you buy your flooring.

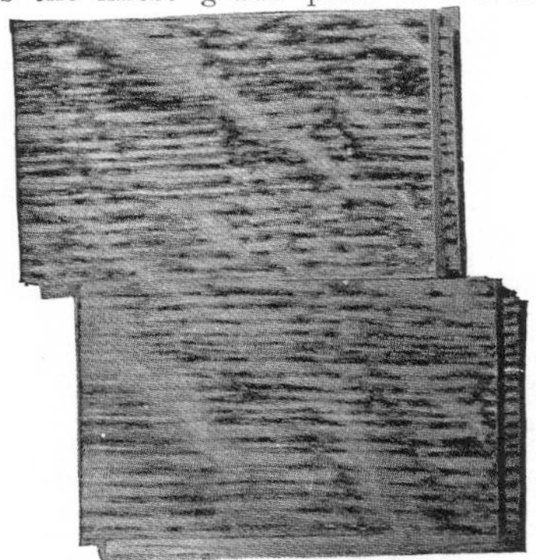

Quarter Sawed Red Oak Flooring.

PLAIN SAWED OAK FLOORING

Catalog No.	Grade	Thickness	Size of Face	Price, per 1,000 Feet
63B7429	Select	⅜ inch	1½ or 2 in.	$30.70
63B7428	Clear	⅜ inch	1½ or 2 in.	43.10
63B7433	Clear	$\frac{13}{16}$ inch	2¼ in.	60.20
63B7434	Select	$\frac{13}{16}$ inch	2¼ in.	44.90

MAPLE FLOORING

Catalog No.	Grade	Thickness	Size of Face	Price, per 1,000 Feet
63B7441	Select	⅜ inch	1½ or 2 in.	$22.80
63B7440	Clear	⅜ inch	1½ or 2 in.	30.80
63B7442	Clear	$\frac{13}{16}$ inch	2¼ in.	44.50
63B7443	Select	$\frac{13}{16}$ inch	2¼ in.	37.60
63B7444	No. 1 Factory	$\frac{13}{16}$ inch	2¼ in.	24.50

QUARTER SAWED RED OAK FLOORING

Catalog No.	Grade	Thickness	Size of Face	Price, per 1,000 Feet
63B7427	Select	⅜ inch	1½ or 2 in.	$40.20
63B7426	Clear	⅜ inch	1½ or 2 in.	60.30
63B7431	Clear	$\frac{13}{16}$ inch	2¼ in.	86.20

IN ORDERING BE SURE TO SPECIFY WIDTH OF FACE WANTED.

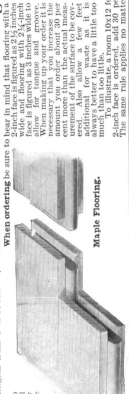

Our "Royal Acme" Gum Flooring, Ceiling, Bevel Siding or Clapboards

SHIPPED FROM LUMBER MILLS IN CHICAGO OR SOUTHERN OHIO OR MILL WORK FACTORY IN EASTERN IOWA.

Ever increasing demand and large sized orders repeated by our customers being received daily is the best proof that the Royal Acme Gum products are giving perfect satisfaction.

Unlike most other gum materials, our Royal Acme Gum products are giving perfect satisfaction simply because we understand the secret of properly treating and curing this kind of wood. It is a standing rule at our factory that all gum lumber which enters into Royal Acme Gum products must be properly air dried for at least twelve months. Most other concerns try to work gum wood regardless of its age and naturally the wood will bend, warp or shrink, making it an unsatisfactory material. **Gum wood is known in some localities as satin walnut, and hazel wood** closely resembles walnut in grain and color, and is being used for pianos, organs and high class furniture as it takes an elegant finish. Gum wood contains no pitch and is an excellent wood for siding, ceiling and flooring, takes a beautiful polish, wears to a smooth even surface and will not splinter or check like many other woods.

WHY NOT MAKE UP A CARLOAD ORDER?

Order your siding, ceiling, flooring and finishing lumber shown on this and on the preceding page with your other mill work. You can in this way make up an order for a carload lot and thereby get the lowest carload freight rate, **reducing your freight charges about one-half.** Everything on this and the preceding page is carried in stock at our mill work factory and can be shipped with our other mill work, such as doors, windows, blinds, frames, moldings, columns, etc. **The freight rate on a carload of mill work is exceedingly low.** Even if you have only a fair sized mill work order, you could have it shipped in a carload by itself, and the freight charges for the car would be practically the same as if you were to have the goods shipped by local freight. In many cases you will find you can get your siding, ceiling, flooring, finishing lumber, etc., without extra freight at all, by having them come with your other goods in a carload lot. There are many advantages in shipping mill work in carloads. We will be glad to give you any additional information upon this subject upon request.

When ordering siding, ceiling or flooring, bear in mind that this material is all figured trade size, that is, 2¼-inch face flooring is quoted 3 inches, 3½-inch siding is quoted 4 inches and 3¼-inch ceiling is quoted 4 inches. All products of this kind are charged on the basis of the width of the rough lumber it will take before it is smoothed or planed, and in ordering the correct amount of siding, ceiling or flooring, it is necessary to add enough extra to allow for the smoothing of edges and also for the tongue and groove on flooring and ceiling and the lap on the siding. In making up your order for this material, figure the number of square feet of surface to be covered and add as follows: 2¼-inch face flooring, add 33 per cent for tongue and groove and smoothing of edges; 3¼-inch face flooring, add 25 per cent for tongue and groove and smoothing of edges; 5¼-inch face flooring, add 15 per cent for tongue and groove and smoothing of edges; 3½-inch finished siding, add 33 per cent to the total area to be covered, not making any deductions for window or door openings; 3¼-inch face ceiling, add 25 per cent for tongue and groove and smoothing of edges. It is always well to have a few feet over to allow for fitting, etc. Our Royal Acme products are carefully graded and bundled, but are not sorted for color. Prices quoted are for random lengths 8 to 16 feet. Specified lengths cannot be furnished in siding, ceiling or flooring.

"ROYAL ACME" GUM FLOORING.

$28.00 and up For 1,000 Feet.

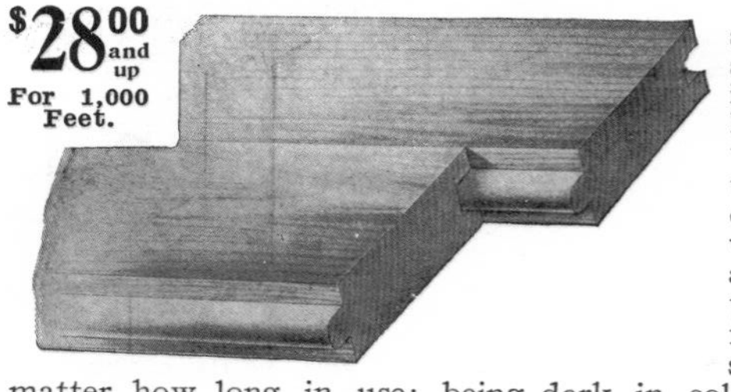

Gum makes an exceptionally fine flooring if properly laid. The wood is of an unusually close grain, very hard and always maintains a perfect, smooth surface, no matter how long in use; being dark in color, somewhat similar to walnut, it takes a beautiful finish. While our "Royal Acme" flooring is guaranteed to be the best air dried gum flooring on the market, we do not guarantee it not to warp. We do guarantee, however, that there is no better gum flooring made. We furnish our "Royal Acme" Gum Flooring in two grades:

Clear grade, exactly what the word implies, allowing no defects of any kind except bright sap.

Select grade may contain defects which can be cut out and not waste more than one-tenth of any one piece and also may have slight imperfections in working.

"ROYAL ACME" GUM FLOORING.

SHIPPED FROM MILLS IN CHICAGO, SOUTHERN OHIO OR EASTERN IOWA.

Catalog No.	Grade	Thickness	Size of Face	Price, per 1,000 feet
63B7395	Clear	13/16 inch	2¼ inches	$33.50
63B7396	Select	13/16 inch	2¼ inches	28.00
63B7397	Clear	13/16 inch	3¼ inches	33.60
63B7398	Select	13/16 inch	3¼ inches	28.10
63B7399	Clear	13/16 inch	5¼ inches	34.80
63B7400	Select	13/16 inch	5¼ inches	29.30

Shipping weight, 2,000 pounds per 1,000 feet.

COMPARE THE LOW PRICES.

$14.40 and up For 1,000 Feet.

we ask for our "Royal Acme" Bevel Siding or Clapboards with the prices you have been paying in the past for pine clapboards. We believe you will find that we can save you from 25 to 33⅓ per cent or more. Gum siding, if properly laid, makes an excellent material for the purpose intended. Due to the high price and scarcity of Northern pine, many architects are now specifying red gum. Our sales on this siding are increasing at an astonishing rate. Many contractors buy it in carload lots. When making up your next order for flooring and other mill work be sure to include at least a trial order of our "Royal Acme" Bevel Siding; we feel sure that you will find it a better value and give you exactly the same good service as the old style pine siding.

"ROYAL ACME" GUM SIDING.

SHIPPED FROM MILLS IN CHICAGO, SOUTHERN OHIO OR EASTERN IOWA.

Catalog No.	Grade	Trade Size	Worked to	Thickness	Price, per 1,000 feet, Surface Measure
63B7385	Clear	4 inches	3½ inches	½ inch	$17.50
63B7386	Select	4 inches	3½ inches	½ inch	14.40
63B7387	Clear	5 inches	4½ inches	½ inch	18.75
63B7388	Select	5 inches	4½ inches	½ inch	15.70
63B7389	Clear	6 inches	5½ inches	½ inch	20.00
63B7390	Select	6 inches	5½ inches	½ inch	16.90

Shipping weight, 900 pounds per 1,000 feet.

"ROYAL ACME" GUM CEILING.

$16.25 and up For 1,000 Feet.

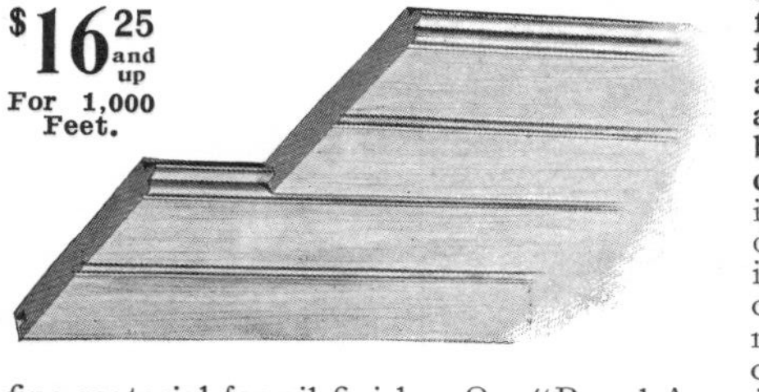

makes a very fine material for ceiling at an exceptionally low price; being dark in color, smooth in finish and due to its having a beautiful close grain, it makes an exceptionally fine material for oil finish. Our "Royal Acme" Gum Ceiling is made from air dried stock and is perfectly machined and well matched. If you have never used this material we recommend that you order one sample order and we feel sure that you will never order anything but our "Royal Acme" ceiling in the future.

Why pay from 25 to 50 per cent more for white pine ceiling when our "Royal Acme" ceiling will answer the purpose just as well in every way? We are selling thousands of feet daily; we sell to the best contractors in the country, many of them ordering it in solid carload lots. We furnish it in one size in two grades, namely: Clear grade, which is perfectly clear allowing sound sap; select grade may have discolored sap, some knots and other defects.

"ROYAL ACME" BEADED CEILING.

SHIPPED FROM MILLS IN CHICAGO, SOUTHERN OHIO OR EASTERN IOWA.

This ceiling double center beaded, as illustrated.

Catalog No.	Grade	Trade Size	Worked to	Thickness	Price, per 1,000 feet, Surface Measure
63B7410	Clear	4 in.	3¼ in.	⅜ in.	$18.75
63B7412	Select	4 in.	3¼ in.	⅜ in.	16.25

Shipping weight, 900 pounds per 1,000 feet, surface measure. Graded exactly the same as flooring listed on this page.

AIR DRIED FINISHING LUMBER, SURFACED OR PLANED ON TWO SIDES.

This finishing lumber is the same grade as the rest of our gum products and is thoroughly suitable for all kinds of outside and inside use. Can be used for porch box frieze work or paneling on the under side of extension roofs; for corner boards, water tables, outside casing; in fact, will take the place of any kind of outside finishing lumber; also can be used on the inside for all kinds of closet trim; also for making china closets, cupboards, etc.

CLEAR GRADE

In ordering be sure to specify widths wanted.

	No. 63B7407 Clear Grade 13/16 inch thick Per 1,000 feet, Board Measure	No. 63B7415 Clear Grade 1⅛ inches thick Per 1,000 feet, Board Measure
Gum, clear grade, 3 or 4 inches wide	$32.40	$34.80
Gum, clear grade, 5, 6, 8 or 10 inches wide	35.40	38.10
Gum, clear grade, 12 inches wide	38.50	41.50
Gum, clear grade, 14, 15 or 16 inches wide	41.50	44.90

All gum products are furnished in random lengths. 15 per cent extra for specified lengths.

SAMPLES FREE

If you doubt the quality of our **Acme Gum products,** write for samples which we will be glad to send you by return mail **free,** postage prepaid.

SELECT GRADE

In ordering be sure to specify widths wanted.

	No. 63B7409 Select Grade 13/16 inch thick Per 1,000 feet, Board Measure	No. 63B7419 Select Grade 1⅛ inches thick Per 1,000 feet, Board Measure
Gum, select grade, 3 or 4 inches wide	$28.10	$30.50
Gum, select grade, 5, 6, 8 or 10 inches wide	31.10	33.90
Gum, select grade, 12 inches wide	34.20	37.20

NOTE:—This lumber will all finish ¼ inch less in width on account of machining.

Cypress Siding, Ceiling, Flooring and Finishing Lumber

For a Great Many Years cypress has been known and recognized as one of the very best woods for outside and inside building purposes. As is generally known, cypress grows in swampy districts and is by nature a natural water resisting wood. There are very few, if any, woods which will last longer and cypress is one of the very last to be affected by rot or decay. For this reason cypress is particularly well adapted for use as siding, ceiling and flooring. Cypress is not susceptible to climatic conditions and is a wood which is used in preference to most other kinds in parts of the country where it is damp, such as along the seashore, the Great Lakes and many parts of the South. Cypress products takes paint perfectly, can also be stained or oiled and we do not hesitate to recommend our cypress products to our customers.

GRADES.

No. 1 Grade. Must be clear with the exception of a small amount of bright sap stain and an occasional very small knot or slight defect.

No. 2 Grade. Will allow any amount of stain, two or three small sound knots and minor defects in machine work.

No. 3 Grade. May contain any amount of stain, several knots and any defects which may be cut out without wasting more than 10 per cent of any one piece.

Note — The above grading rules will apply to finishing lumber up to 5 inches wide. Over this width a greater number of defects will be allowed in proportion to the width. The greater the width, the more difficult it is to get a piece which is free from defects and for this reason finishing lumber in wider widths will allow more defects in proportion.

CYPRESS CEILING. Center Beaded.

Catalog No.	Grade	Trade Size	Finished Size	Thickness	Price, per 1,000 Feet, Surface Measure
63B7220	No. 1	4 inches	3 1/4 inches face	3/8 inch	$29.40
63B7221	No. 2	4 inches	3 1/4 inches face	3/8 inch	28.30
63B7222	No. 3	4 inches	3 1/4 inches face	3/8 inch	22.20

Above prices are for assorted lengths.

CYPRESS SIDING.

Catalog No.	Grade	Trade Size	Finished Size	Thickness	Price, per 1,000 Ft., Surface Square Measure
63B7242	No. 1	4 inches	3 1/4 inches face	1/2 inch	$26.10
63B7243	No. 2	4 inches	3 1/4 inches face	1/2 inch	24.95
63B7246	No. 3	4 inches	3 1/4 inches face	1/2 inch	18.85
63B7252	No. 1	6 inches	5 1/4 inches face	1/2 inch	28.30
63B7253	No. 2	6 inches	5 1/4 inches face	1/2 inch	27.20
63B7254	No. 3	6 inches	5 1/4 inches face	1/2 inch	20.55

Above prices are for assorted lengths.

CYPRESS FLOORING.

Catalog No.	Grade	Trade Size	Finished Size	Thickness	Price, per 1,000 Feet, Board Measure
63B7230	No. 1	3 inches	2 1/4 inches face	13/16 inch	$49.60
63B7231	No. 2	3 inches	2 1/4 inches face	13/16 inch	47.40
63B7233	No. 3	3 inches	2 1/4 inches face	13/16 inch	43.00
63B7236	No. 1	4 inches	3 1/4 inches face	13/16 inch	49.50
63B7237	No. 2	4 inches	3 1/4 inches face	13/16 inch	46.50
63B7238	No. 3	4 inches	3 1/4 inches face	13/16 inch	41.60

Above prices are for assorted lengths.

CYPRESS FINISHING LUMBER. Surfaced and Planed Two Sides.

Thickness	Width	No. 63B7273 No. 1 Grade, Price, per 1,000 Feet, Board Measure	No. 63B7274 No. 3 Grade, Price, per 1,000 Feet, Board Measure
13/16 inch	4 inches	$49.00	$40.80
13/16 inch	5 inches	54.10	48.00
13/16 inch	6 inches	54.00	43.00
13/16 inch	7 inches	54.00	46.90
13/16 inch	8 inches	49.50	46.50
13/16 inch	9 inches	53.55	50.25
13/16 inch	10 inches	50.20	44.15
13/16 inch	12 inches	52.00	48.00

All lumber is cut full even inch width at the mills when it is green, but after being thoroughly air dried and passed through the dry kilns there is more or less shrinkage, and for this reason all thoroughly dry finishing lumber will run a little scant in width.

For 1 1/8-inch finishing lumber add $2.00 per 1,000 feet to the above prices.

Oak Finishing Lumber

We List in the Table Below the principal widths, thickness and kinds of oak used as finishing lumber. We have on hand at all times a very large supply of oak lumber at the factory and ordinarily can furnish any of the stock listed below very promptly and ship with other mill work.

GRADE.

Up to 5 inches in width oak finishing lumber will be practically free from all serious defects. Wider than 5 inches in width will allow a greater number of defects in proportion to the width. This grade will be suitable for finishing purposes and will only contain minor defects such as an occasional small knot, stain and slight imperfection in machine work. Our finishing lumber is better than that furnished by most concerns.

CLEAR GRADE FINISHING OAK LUMBER. Surfaced and Planed Two Sides.

All finishing lumber will finish 1/8 to 1/4 inch scant of the full inch measurement specified below. This is caused by shrinkage of the lumber during the drying process. Hardwood lumber is liable to check and crack and it is better to order a piece a little longer than you want in order that you may trim each end. This material is all surfaced on two face sides, but not on the edges. Sizes not priced cannot be furnished.

Thickness	Width	No. 63B7303 Plain Red Oak or Plain White Oak. Price, per 1,000 Feet, Board Measure	No. 63B7306 Quarter Sawed Red Oak. Price, per 1,000 Feet, Board Measure	No. 63B7308 Quarter Sawed White Oak. Price, per 1,000 Feet, Board Measure
13/16 inch	4 and 6 inches	$64.80	$86.40	$108.00
1 1/16 inch	8 inches	69.60	92.40	114.00
1 5/16 inch	10 inches	92.00	105.60	......
1 9/16 inch	12 inches	74.40	......	......
1 13/16 inch	14 inches	......	......	......

For finishing lumber 1 1/4 inches thick add $5.00 per 1,000 feet to above prices.
For finishing lumber 1 3/8 inches thick add $5.00 per 1,000 feet to above prices.
For finishing lumber 1 3/4 inches thick add $7.50 per 1,000 feet to above prices.

Yellow Pine Ceiling, Flooring and Finishing Lumber

Below We Show a Line of Yellow Pine Ceiling, Flooring and Finishing Lumber for the purpose of serving our customers who wish to order this material with other kinds of mill work. These prices are based on cost, F. O. B. factory in Muscatine, Iowa.

If you have not already placed an order for dimension lumber including timbers, joists, studding, boards, etc., we recommend that you order your yellow pine, ceiling, flooring and finishing material with your lumber, as considerable can be saved in freight charges when shipping in carload lots.

GRADES.

B and Better Grade. The majority of the pieces must show one face practically free of all defects, but slight imperfections are allowable, such as slight torn grain, small pin knots, small pitch pockets and pitch streak and sap stain and small seasoning checks. This is the highest grade usually furnished in ceiling, flooring and finishing lumber.

No. 1 Common Grade. This grade will contain the stock which does not grade B and Better and will contain checks and defects in manufacture in a larger proportion than is allowed to B and Better, shake, torn grain and seasoning sound knots, sap stain, pitch streak, shake, torn grain and seasoning checks. B and Better grade, but on some kinds of work where quality is not an important point, the No. 1 Common grade will probably be satisfactory.

YELLOW PINE CEILING.

Catalog No.	Grade	Trade Size	Finished Size	Thickness	Price, per 1,000 Feet, Surface Square Measure
63B7280	No. 1 Common	4 inches	3 1/4 inches face	3/8 inch	$29.90
63B7283	B & Better	4 inches	3 1/4 inches face	5/8 inch	17.10
		4 inches	3 1/4 inches face	5/8 inch	25.25

YELLOW PINE FLOORING. Flat Grain.

Catalog No.	Grade	Trade Size	Finished Size	Thickness	Price, per 1,000 Feet, Board Measure
63B7285	B & Better	4 inches	3 1/4 inches face	13/16 inch	$33.70
63B7286	No. 1 Com.	4 inches	3 1/4 inches face	13/16 inch	35.00
63B7287	B & Better	4 inches	3 1/4 inches face	13/16 inch	31.00
63B7289	No. 1 Com.	4 inches	3 1/4 inches face	13/16 inch	41.40

YELLOW PINE FINISHING LUMBER. Surfaced Two Sides. Grade B and Better.

All finishing lumber will finish from 1/8 to 1/4 inch less than the full inch width measurements specified below. This is caused by the shrinkage in width when drying. Yellow pine lumber is cut full inch widths at the sawmill, but after it is air dried and passed through the dry kilns it will shrink more or less, which will make all widths measure a little scant of the full inch. In drying there is bound to be more or less checking or cracking and to be on the safe side, it is best in making up your orders to specify a little extra, that you may have enough to allow for trimming, especially at the ends.

Thickness	Width, Inches	Trade Size	Finished Size	No. 63B7288 Price, per 1,000 Feet, Board Measure
13/16 inch	4	4 inches	3 1/4 inches face	$33.70
1 1/16 inch	6 and 8	4 inches	3 1/4 inches face	35.00
1 1/8 inches	5, 10 and 12			39.00
1 1/8 inches	4, 6, 8 and 10			41.40
1 1/4 inches	12			42.55
1 1/4 inches	4 and 6			41.40
1 1/4 inches	8 and 10			42.55
1 1/4 inches	12			43.70

Thickness	Finished Size	Price, per 1,000 Feet, Board Measure
1 1/8 inch	3 1/4 inches face	$23.00
1 1/8 inch	3 1/4 inches face	28.75

Grade B and Better.

The lumber which we use is thoroughly dry and unusual care is taken in machine work. You will find our ceiling, flooring, siding and finishing lumber better manufactured and a nicer class of material than you can get from any other source.

Special lengths will cost 20 per cent extra.

Prices on this page are for assorted lengths.

MISSION SIDEBOARD

This Mission Sideboard is of simple but massive design. When finished with a Mission stain or in golden oak, the effect is rich and imposing.

we are able to quote you these low prices on china closets, sideboards and buffets, by making them up in very large quantities by a well equipped factory.

We employ nothing but the most skilled cabinet makers on this class of work and every piece is perfectly made, well finished and every joint is perfectly fitted.

All our cabinets are perfectly crated to reach destination in good condition.

SPECIFICATIONS.

Width of opening in wall, 6 feet.
Height of opening in wall, 7 feet.
Depth of opening in wall, 5 inches.
Size of bevel plate mirror, 5 feet 3 inches by 1 foot 1 inch.
Doors glazed with leaded crystal sheet glass.
Furnished in oak or yellow pine.
Prices given do not include knobs, hinges and drawer pulls as this hardware should match the rest of the hardware in your house.

No. 63B8635 **Yellow Pine** (not oiled or varnished). Price $39.00
No. 63B8636 **Oak** (not oiled or varnished). Price 40.00
Shipping weight, about 300 pounds.

QUEEN ANNE SIDEBOARD

The Queen Anne Sideboard shown below will impart an air of dignity and distinction to any dining room.

Furnished with leaded crystal sheet glass doors, heavy bevel plate mirrors, and with seven large, roomy drawers, allowing ample room for silver and table linen.

SPECIFICATIONS.

Width of opening in wall, 6 feet.
Height of opening in wall, 7 feet 4 inches.
Depth of opening in wall, 5 inches.
Measurement from front to back, 1 foot 6 inches.
Size of large bevel plate mirror, 2 feet 9 inches by 1 foot 1 inch.
Size of small bevel plate mirrors, 1 foot 3 inches by 1 foot 1 inch.
Size of doors, each, 1 foot 4 inches by 2 feet 4 inches.
Workmanship the best.
Prices do not include knobs, hinges and drawer pulls as these articles should match the rest of the hardware in your house.

No. 63B8645 **Yellow Pine** (not oiled or varnished). Price $38.00
No. 63B8644 **Oak** (not oiled or varnished). Price 39.00
Shipping weight, about 300 pounds.

MEDICINE CASES

No bathroom is really complete without a medicine case built in the wall. Very handy and convenient for shaving and an ideal place for keeping everything of a medicinal nature, where you will always know where they are and where they will be out of the reach of children.

The two designs listed below have proven very popular and they are being installed in most every up to date bathroom. Furnished in oak, birch or yellow pine.

Birch can be stained mahogany or enameled. The yellow pine which we furnish can be enameled or given a beautiful natural finish.

CABINET H.

This Medicine Case is furnished with casing, stool, apron and cap trim, together with the door glazed with mirror. Furnished in oak, yellow pine or birch.

Size of medicine cabinet door, 1 foot 8 inches by 2 feet 1 inch. Sets back in wall, 5 inches.

No. 63B8601 Oak, in the white. Glazed with D.S. glass mirror. Price..**$4.40**

No. 63B8602 Yellow pine, in the white. Glazed with D.S. glass mirror. Price **$4.30**

No. 63B8603 Birch, in the white. Glazed with D. S. glass mirror. Price.......**$4.35**

If beveled plate glass mirror is wanted, add $1.15 extra.

CABINET K.

This Medicine Case is furnished complete with casings, stool, drawer, head casing and door which is glazed with a nice mirror. Underneath the stool there is a fair sized roomy drawer which will be handy for holding razors, brushes, etc. Furnished in oak, yellow pine or birch.

Size of medicine cabinet door, 20x25 inches. Size of drawer in medicine cabinet, 20x5 inches.

No. 63B8608 Oak, in the white. Glazed with D.S. glass mirror. Price..**$4.90**

No. 63B8609 Yellow pine, in the white. Glazed with D. S. glass mirror. Price............**4.80**

No. 63B8610 Birch, in the white. Glazed with D. S. glass mirror. Price....................**4.85**

If beveled plate glass mirror is wanted, add $1.15 extra.

CRAFTSMAN CHINA CLOSET AND BUFFET

A glance at the illustration below of our Craftsman China Closet and Buffet will give you a better idea of its simple elegance and beauty of design than mere words could express, even though we devoted this entire page to that end.

Being installed in high priced flats and the finer class of residences. This combination china closet and buffet is primarily of Craftsman design, but your house does not necessarily have to be finished in the Craftsman style in order to use it, as the design is such as will harmonize perfectly with almost any interior. Another of its advantages is that it can be installed in an old house as readily as in a new one. It is not set back in an offset of the wall as most built in china closets and sideboards are.

SPECIFICATIONS: Width over all, 7 feet 6 inches; height over all, 5 feet 6 inches; measurement from front to back, 1 foot 7 inches; size of doors, 1 foot 5 inches by 4 feet; size of mirror, 3 feet 6 inches by 2 feet. Shipping weight, about 400 pounds.

No. 63B8625 Natural wood (not oiled or varnished), with leaded art glass in doors. Price **$48.50**

No. 63B8626 Natural wood (not oiled or varnished), with clear double strength glass in doors. Price.....**39.75**

CABINET CHINA CLOSET AND SIDEBOARD

CONVENIENT AND ORNAMENTAL

Made in Two Sections, Ready to Set Up

Up to date residences and flats throughout the country are being equipped with combination china closets and sideboards such as we show on these pages. Heretofore it has been necessary to have china closets and sideboards made special according to the architects' plans, and the cost of making them amounted to from $75.00 to $200.00 according to the workmanship and material used in their manufacture. We make up these china closets and sideboards in large quantities, thereby reducing the cost of manufacturing to the point where we can offer this fine up to date sideboard and china closet for the remarkably low price of $17.00, a price that enables you to have a first class sideboard in your house even though you intend building a low priced house.

Consider how much more desirable the flat or house is to the prospective renter or buyer if upon examining it he finds a nice china closet built in the dining room, and nine times out of ten you secure your tenant or buyer on the spot.

Strictly high grade material and workmanship used in the manufacture of this Cabinet China Closet and Sideboard.

SPECIFICATIONS.

Furnished in yellow pine, birch or plain red oak.
Height of opening in wall, 7 feet.
Width of opening in wall, 4 feet 6 inches.
Depth of opening in wall, 1 foot 3 inches.
Height from floor to counter, 2 feet 8 inches.
Size of china closet doors, 1 foot by 2 feet 9½ inches.
Backed with tongued and grooved beaded ceiling.
Shelves are adjustable.
Thickness of counter or shelf, 1⅛ inches.
Shipping weight, about 250 pounds.

We furnish this china closet complete with glass and casing, as shown in illustration, excepting hardware, at the price named.

CABINET CHINA CLOSET AND SIDEBOARD.

No. 63B8615   Yellow Pine.   Price. $17.00
No. 63B8616   Birch.   Price. 18.00
No. 63B8617   Plain Red Oak.   Price. 18.50

We do not furnish drawer pulls or hinges with these sideboards, as the hardware used should match the other hardware in your house.

GRILLES AND COLONNADES AT HALF REGULAR RETAIL PRICES

The grilles and colonnades illustrated on this and other pages of this book are acknowledged by architectural authorities to be correct in style and design. Choose a good grille or colonnade. A few extra dollars spent for a furnishing of this kind adds hundreds of dollars to the value of your building. A good grille or colonnade transforms the interior of an old house into that of a new one. No newly constructed house is complete without a cabinet grand grille. By using the proper kind of grille two rooms can be joined together and the beauty of either room is not lost or screened by doors or curtains. The very best, most modern buildings of today are considered incomplete unless furnished with stylish and up to date colonnades and grilles, such as we illustrate on the pages of this book.

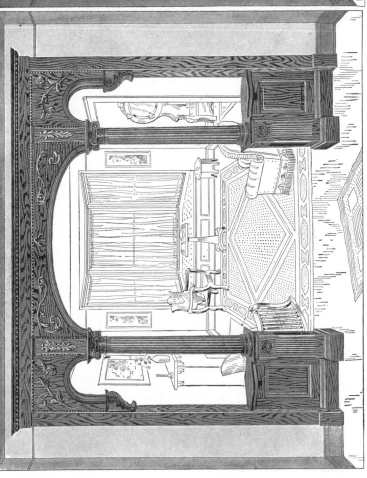

PERFECTION COLONNADE.

The **Perfection Colonnade, which we illustrate above, is considered one of the finest grilles made.** Perfectly proportioned and made by skilled workmen. It will add a tone of refinement and luxury to your home that is afforded by no other piece of furniture. **The illustration in no way does justice to this beautiful colonnade.** To be fully appreciated, it is necessary to see the actual goods. All carvings are in genuine wood, with the exception of the column caps, which, on account of their peculiar artistic shape, are made in composition laid on wood form, and so closely imitate wood that an expert could hardly tell that they were not hand carved wood. **Center segment and two half circles** at the sides are made from bent lumber, which is placed in forms, steamed and held in place until thoroughly dry; it is the only correct way that segments and circles of this kind can be made, and being made in this manner, show the beautiful grain of wood to the best advantage. **Pedestal Base** is 7 inches square, measures 30 inches from the floor to the top of pedestal. **Center Arch**, thickness, 4½ inches; depth in the center, 6 inches; drop at the sides, 34 inches. **Columns**, diameter at base, 6 inches, tapering to 5 inches at the top. **Genuine Wood Hand Carvings.**

No. 63B8160 Perfection Colonnade. Price, 9 feet wide by 9 feet high or less, furnished in plain oak, birch, yellow pine or cypress in the natural wood (not oiled or varnished) **$46.80**

This price does not include jambs, casing, base blocks or cap trim. Shipping weight, 290 pounds.

If filled, shellaced and varnished, $6.00 extra. If made of quarter sawed oak, add $5.00 extra. If ordered finished to match interior woodwork, be sure to say whether light or dark finish is desired. Some of our customers send us a small chip or piece of wood showing grain and color of finish desired, which enables us to send a perfect match.

NOTE—When ordering, be sure to give width and height, the kind of wood wanted and whether the grille is to be finished or in the white.

LORRAINE COLONNADE.

The **Lorraine Colonnade illustrated above is one of the greatest sellers in our line, having found favor everywhere.** Contractors and builders, after sending us a trial order invariably sent us repeated orders, as it is considered one of the best high grade grilles made, and our price is from one-third to one-half less than the same colonnade would cost if bought from regular makers or dealers. Made from the very best selected lumber, very massive and effective, yet arranged in such a way as not to be an obstruction.

Pedestal below column is 7 inches square opposite panel work.

Fluted Column, 6-inch shaft, tapering to 5 inches at top neck. Columns fluted two-thirds length.

Panel Wainscoting measures 30 inches from floor line to top of shelf; distance from jamb to inside of column, 17 inches.

Carvings or Trimmings and Column Capitals are made of the finest kind of composition work, which is a perfect imitation of wood. Side beams extend down 3 feet 8 inches at the bottom of the bracket and are 4 inches thick.

No. 63B8405 Lorraine Colonnade, for 9 feet wide by 9 feet high or less, furnished in oak, birch, yellow pine or cypress in the natural wood (not oiled or varnished) **$36.40**

This price does not include jambs, casing, base blocks or cap trim.

If the beam only is wanted (no columns, pedestals or paneled wainscoting) price will be $14.75.

If filled, shellaced and varnished, add $4.25 extra. If ordered in quarter sawed oak, add $4.00 extra. For grilles larger than the above mentioned size, add for each additional foot or fraction thereof $1.50. Shipping weight, 250 pounds.

Will furnish this carved all wood wood cap in place of the composition cap, if wanted, without extra charge.

Be sure to write the word "Special" after the catalog number if ordering with carved wood cap.

QUALITY GUARANTEED

Arch Grille and Colonnade of the Highest Quality

The Nethersole Grille and Wellington Colonnade are two of our best selling designs. A few dollars spent for an arch grille or colonnade like those illustrated below will increase the value of your building greatly. It transforms the interior of an old house into that of a new house, and no new house is really complete without one of our fine Cabinet Grand Grilles.

NETHERSOLE.

The Nethersole Grille Colonnade illustrated above is an exceptionally fine and massive structure. Columns are extremely massive and are made by the improved lock joint process, insuring durability and strength. The scroll and spindle work is very artistic and tasty and is sure to please the most critical trade. Adapted for any kind of a building. Grilles at $35.00, $40.00 and even $50.00 are not superior in style, workmanship and finish to our Nethersole Grille which we sell for $24.70.

Columns are 6 inches in diameter where fluting starts, tapering to 5 inches at the top.
Pedestal supporting column, 7½ inches in diameter opposite shelf.
Composition capitals of the finest make adorn the columns.
Panel Wainscoting is 15 inches from column to jamb and measures 30 inches from floor line to top of shelf. Panels are raised on both sides.

No. 63B8447 Nethersole Grille Colonnade, for opening 8 feet wide by 8 feet 6 inches high, or less, furnished in oak, birch, yellow pine or cypress (in the natural wood, not oiled or varnished). Price.......................... $24.70

The price quoted above does not include casing, base blocks, cap trim or jambs.
If filled, shellaced and varnished, add $3.00 extra. If ordered in quarter sawed oak, allow $2.50 extra. For grilles larger than the above mentioned size, add for each additional foot or fraction thereof $1.50 extra. Shipping weight, 230 pounds.
If carved wood cap such as we show on the bottom of page 83 is wanted instead of composition cap shown on columns, write the word "Special" after the catalog number.
We will furnish same without any additional charge.

WELLINGTON.

The Wellington Cabinet Grand Colonnade illustrated above is one of the latest and up to date designs on the market. Note the pleasing and artistic appearance of this colonnade; the rich reeded columns which have heretofore only been used on the most expensive of colonnades. These columns are made with lock joint by specially constructed machinery. They will give much better satisfaction, wear longer and there is no possibility of the joints opening. Every inch of this fine cabinet work is made by skilled workmen. Each and every part of the columns and pedestals is smooth and sanded by hand, which assures you receiving as fine a piece of cabinet work as was ever turned out by any manufacturer.
Octagon Base opposite panels, 7¾ inches in diameter. Base at floor, 9¼ inches in diameter.
Cap is 10 inches in diameter.
Column above pedestals is 6 inches at the base, tapering to 5 inches at the top.
Octagon Base on top of shelf on which the reeded column rests is 7¾ inches in diameter. Distance of panel work between column and casing, 16 inches. Top of shelf is 30 inches above the floor line. Finest quality composition capitals adorn the columns.

No. 63B8400 Two columns, pedestals and panel wainscoting, for opening 8 feet 6 inches in height, or less, furnished in oak, birch, yellow pine or cypress (in the natural wood, **$18.00** not oiled or varnished). Price, per pair.
If filled, shellaced and varnished, add $4.00 extra to the above price, which includes two columns, pedestals and wainscoting.
In case only one column and wainscoting is wanted, mark the word "Special" after the catalog number and allow but one-half the price of our regular No. 63B8400, or $9.00.

No. 63B8401 Columns, without wainscoting, for opening 8 feet **$7.50** 6 inches in height or less, furnished in red oak, birch, yellow pine or cypress (in the white). Price, per single column.
Shipping weight, single column, 75 pounds.
The prices quoted above do not include casing, jambs, base blocks or cap trim.
The prices quoted above are to be finished or in the white.

QUALITY GUARANTEED

NOTE—When ordering be sure to specify width and height, the kind of wood wanted and whether it is to be finished or in the white.

CABINET GRAND COLONNADES AND GRILLES

WILL ADD 100 PER CENT TO THE APPEARANCE OF ANY HOUSE.

On this page we illustrate two up to date and attractive designs which will harmonize with the interior of the finest homes. Many people by installing one of our Cabinet Grand Colonnades or Grilles convert the interior of an out of date house into a strictly up to date twentieth century interior. At our extremely low prices anyone can easily afford to install the highest grade and most attractive styles we illustrate on these pages.

Our colonnades and grilles are made of the finest selected material, machined and assembled by expert grille makers, and are the most attractive inside work turned out by any modern factory. All parts, in fact, every inch of surface is carefully sanded by hand and if ordered in the white without varnish can be given a piano finish. Please remember that grilles of equal style and quality in many localities sell at double our prices.

COLONIAL

Our Colonial Cabinet Grand Colonnade illustrated above is a new and attractive design built on Colonial lines and will harmonize with the interior of the finest homes. It can also be used to equally good advantage in any ordinary building as it is in keeping with every kind of architecture. Columns are put together with special lock joint which is guaranteed not to open at the joints or crack.

Pedestal opposite shelf is 7 inches diameter and measures 30 inches from the floor to the top of shelf.

Columns have octagon base at the floor 7½ inches in diameter, 6½ inches at the fluted section of the column tapering to 5½ inches at the top; 6-inch genuine composition capitals at top of columns; wainscoting measures 15 inches from post to the jamb.

No. 63B8452 Colonial Colonnade, for opening 8 feet 6 inches high, or less, furnished in oak, birch, yellow pine or cypress (in the natural wood), not oiled or varnished). Price............. **$17.55**

The price quoted above does not include jambs, casing, base blocks or cap trim.

Shipping weight, 150 pounds.

If filled, shellaced and varnished, add $4.25 extra, and for each additional foot or fraction thereof in height, add 75 cents extra.

If carved wood cap such as we show on the bottom of page 83 is wanted instead of composition cap shown on columns, we will furnish same without any additional charge.

ELITE

The Elite Cabinet Grand Colonnade and Grille illustrated above is one of the best low medium priced colonnades and grilles on the market; in fact, the quality of material and workmanship is executed in the same careful manner as our higher priced grilles, the only difference being that it is not nearly so massive. Identically the same grille is sold in many localities at double our price.

Pedestal opposite shelf is 4½ inches diameter and measures 30 inches from the floor to the top of shelf.

Columns are formed by an octagon base 6 inches in diameter, plain turned part 4½ inches, and the fluted base is 4 inches and is trimmed with genuine wood carved ornament. Wainscoting measures 16 inches from the inside of the post to the jamb.

No. 63B8456 Elite Cabinet Grand Colonnade and Grille, for opening 8 feet wide by 8 feet 6 inches high, or less, furnished in oak, birch, yellow pine or cypress (in the natural wood, not oiled or varnished). Price........... **$15.95**

The price quoted above does not include jambs, casing, base blocks or cap trim.

Shipping weight, 150 pounds.

If filled, shellaced and varnished, add $4.25 extra. For grilles larger than the above mentioned size, add $1.50 extra, for each additional foot or fraction thereof.

GRILLES, COLONNADES AND COLUMNS ARE MADE SPECIAL TO YOUR ORDER.

Items illustrated on this page are shipped direct from the grille factory and cannot be shipped with other mill work and building material. Casings and inside jambs are not a part of the grille, and, therefore, if wanted must be ordered extra. For prices of casing see molding pages in this book.

To insure the best kind of a job, it is necessary to allow from five to ten days to make shipment.

NOTE—When ordering be sure to give width and height, the kind of wood wanted and whether the grille is to be finished or in the white.

ARTISTIC GRILLE COLUMNS AND ARCH GRILLES

Artistic Grill Columns and Arch Grilles designed by grille artists of highest repute. As to workmanship, material and durability, our Cabinet Grand Grilles have no equal. Every part entering into the construction of these beautiful interior ornamentations is finished in a most painstaking manner. We can guarantee any Cabinet Grand Grille to be satisfactory in every way and to be the greatest value that has ever been offered in the grille work line.

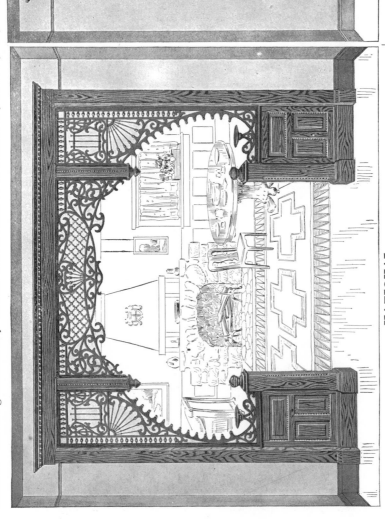

NATIONAL.

Our National Arch Grille illustrated above is acknowledged one of the most pleasing arch patterns ever designed, extremely effective yet very inexpensive. This grille can be used to very good advantage where the opening is low or narrow. Note the fine scroll work, beautiful panels and posts, and you will then appreciate what a wonderful value we offer in our National Arch Grille. All cross grained sections and joints are reinforced by wooden dowels, making it very strong and durable.

Pedestal Column is 5 inches in diameter and measures 34 inches from floor.

Posts, 5 inches square, handsomely ornamented beaded molding on each side and has a hand turned top. Grille work drops from 12 to 15 inches from the head jamb at the center. **Wainscoting** consists of panels which are raised on each side, making a heavy finished appearance.

No. 63B8460 National Colonnade and Grille for opening 9 feet wide by 9 feet high, or less, furnished in oak, birch, yellow pine or cypress (in the natural wood, not oiled or varnished). Price........... **$26.00**

The price quoted above does not include jambs, casing, base blocks or cap trim.

Shipping weight, 180 pounds.

If ordered in quarter sawed oak, allow $3.00. If filled, shellaced and varnished, add $4.25. For grilles larger than the above mentioned size, add for each additional foot or fraction thereof, $1.50 extra.

EXCELSIOR.

Our Excelsior Grille illustrated above is one of the best values in our line. Please note that patterns neatly trimmed with small chamfered base columns, the wainscoting composed of four panels neatly trimmed with small turned beaded molding. Also note the beautiful scroll designs in the grilles, which are handsomely trimmed with hand turned spindles.

Pedestal Column is 5 inches in diameter and measures 32 inches from the floor.

Columns, 5 inches square at the bottom and turned part 4 inches in diameter at the top, tapering to 3 inches, carefully fluted and smoothed.

Carvings and Capitals on the posts made of very best composition work. Side grilles, 32 inches deep. Center grille extends down to post 24 inches.

No. 63B8470 Excelsior Colonnade and Grille for opening 9 feet wide by 9 feet high, or less, furnished in oak, birch, yellow pine or cypress (in the natural wood, not oiled or varnished). Price.......... **$23.50**

Shipping weight, 200 pounds.

The price quoted above does not include jambs, casing, base blocks or cap trim. If filled, shellaced and varnished, add $2.50 extra. For grilles larger than the above mentioned size, allow $2.50 extra. For grilles larger than the above mentioned size, add for each additional foot or fraction thereof, $1.50.

NOTE—When ordering be sure to give width and height, the kind of wood wanted and whether the grille is to be finished or in the white.

SEARS, ROEBUCK AND CO., CHICAGO, ILLINOIS.

Colonnade and Colonial Interior Columns

WILL ADD MATERIALLY TO THE SELLING OR RENTAL VALUE OF ANY HOUSE.

The Roman Colonnade listed below is a neat and massive design suitable for any interior.

Colonial Interior Columns are being specified for fine homes by the leading architects of the country. Never before have they been obtainable at such reasonable prices as we show below.

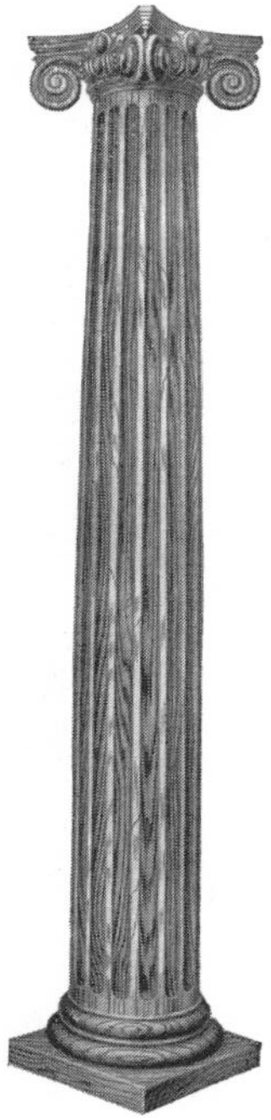

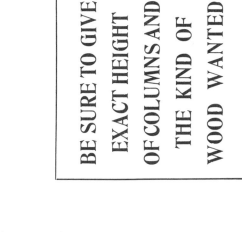

No. 63B8423

No. 63B8422

**BE SURE TO GIVE
EXACT HEIGHT
OF COLUMNS AND
THE KIND OF
WOOD WANTED**

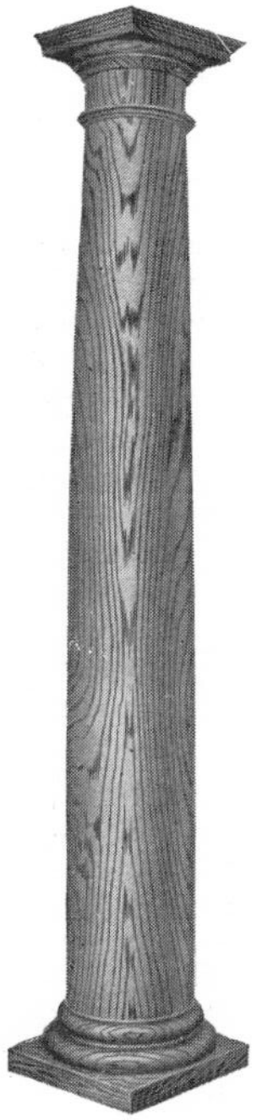

Since the old Colonial architecture has become so popular, interior Colonial columns have become a **very important feature** in all Colonial work, often being used one on each side of a large hall and reaching from floor to an overhead arch, or from the floor to the ceiling. If you are thinking of introducing a touch of the Colonial style in your new home be sure to order a pair of these columns. Furnished with fluted shaft or plain shaft and with composition cap or plain cap. All columns are made 10 inches in diameter and in any height up to 8 feet.

In ordering mention whether wanted with plain or fluted shaft, plain or composition cap, kind of wood, height, and whether it is to be in the white or filled and varnished.

No. 63B8422 Colonial Columns, yellow pine (in the natural wood, not oiled or varnished). Price, each....................................$11.00

No. 63B8423 Colonial Columns, yellow pine (in the natural wood, not oiled or varnished). Price, each............................ 10.00

If wanted filled, shellaced and varnished, add $2.00 extra for each column. If wanted in plain red oak add $1.00 extra for each column. Shipping weight, about 65 pounds, each.

ROMAN COLONNADE.

Made with a solid carved wood cap. (See illustration above.) Height of pedestals and panel work, 20 inches. Top over pedestal and panel work, 10 inches wide and made to fit on each side of jambs 5½ inches wide. The column base resting on the pedestal is 7½ inches in diameter. Size of column at base, 6 inches in diameter. Size of column at top, 5 inches in diameter.

When ordering give exact width of opening from jamb to jamb and exact height from floor to head jamb, being sure to always specify the width first, stating kind of wood wanted and whether it is to be in the white or filled and varnished.

Furnished in plain sawed red oak, birch, cypress or yellow pine at the same price. **State the kind of wood wanted.** Will furnish this colonnade with wood cap as shown on page 83 instead of composition cap at the same price if desired.

No. 63B8455 Roman Colonnade, for opening 8 feet wide by 8 feet 6 inches high, or less (in the natural wood, not oiled or varnished). Price.....................$16.90

If wanted filled, shellaced and varnished, price $4.25 extra. Shipping wt., 200 lbs.

Colonnades and Columns are made special to your order. To insure the best kind of a job, it is necessary to allow from five to ten days to make shipment. Shipped direct from the grille factory and cannot be shipped with other mill work and building material. The casings and inside jambs are not a part of the grille and therefore, if wanted, must be ordered extra. For prices of casing see molding pages in this book.

SEARS, ROEBUCK AND CO., CHICAGO, ILLINOIS.

Artistic Grilles Will Beautify Your Home

THE FINEST LINE MADE. OUR PRICES ARE ABOUT ONE-HALF REGULAR PRICES.

All grilles illustrated and described in the column at the left hand side of this page will be made special to your order at the extremely low prices named directly below illustrations. Extreme care is used in the manufacture of all our grilles; in fact, all special made to order grilles are laid out according to special patterns to fit any special size opening for which you may order. These grilles are carefully sanded by hand and are the most substantially constructed grilles on the market. Our grilles are carefully crated and packed without extra charge. As these grilles are made to order it will take from five to ten days to make shipment. Be very careful to give us the correct measurements, as grilles made special to your order cannot be returned, providing we furnish the size and kind specified.

All grilles illustrated in the column at the right hand side of this page are made with the patented adjustable end shoe (see Fig. I in middle column); simple, easy to fit, a most satisfactory feature. Carpenters, in fact anyone who is handy with a hammer, can fasten this end shoe into place in a few minutes. With the adjustable end shoe it is not necessary to do any sawing or trimming. All that is necessary is to put the grille into place, drive nails in each side of the shoe and the job is complete. The groove in the shoe takes care of all vibration of the frame, prevents cracking or breaking due to expansion or contraction. This excellent feature is only to be found in the grilles illustrated and described in the right hand column of this page, Catalog Nos. 63B8428, 63B8431 and 63B8430.

A STRONG FEATURE

OUR PATENT ADJUSTABLE END SHOE.

SHOE
GRILLE
Fig. I.

So simple a child can fit it into place. The only tool required is a hammer or screwdriver. Makes a perfect job.

Can be taken out and refitted in the same size opening at any time without injury to the grille. Our Patent Adjustable End Shoe is only furnished with

Grille No. 63B8428
Grille No. 63B8431
Grille No. 63B8430

WHEN ORDER-ING GRILLES

please note the prices quoted on this page are for grilles "in the white" just as they come from the woodworker's hands without filler or varnish. If finished grilles are wanted, that is grilles which are filled, shellaced and varnished to harmonize with your interior woodwork, add 15 cents per lineal foot to the price in the white and write the word "finished" after the cat-alog number. In order to insure a perfect match to your wood-work, kindly state whether light or dark finish is wanted, and if possible enclose a sam-ple showing the grain and color.

All grilles shown on this page are shipped direct from the grille factory at Chicago and cannot be shipped with other mill work or build-ing material.

No. 63B8428

EXTENDS DOWN 24 INCHES AT ENDS.

57c

Made in oak, birch, yellow pine or cypress (in the natural wood, not oiled or varnished). Price, per lineal foot.

No. 63B8431

EXTENDS DOWN 24 INCHES AT ENDS.

58c

Made in oak, birch, yellow pine or cypress (in the natural wood, not oiled or varnished) Price, per lineal foot.

No. 63B8430

EXTENDS DOWN 24 INCHES AT ENDS.

59c

Made in oak, birch, yellow pine or cypress (in the natural wood, not oiled or varnished). Price, per lineal foot.

ALL GRILLES ORDERED UNDER 4 FEET WILL BE CHARGED AS IF 4 FEET LONG.

No. 63B8436

EXTENDS DOWN 16 INCHES AT ENDS.

60c

Made in oak, birch, yellow pine or cypress (in the natural wood, not oiled or varnished). Price, per lineal foot.

No. 63B8440

EXTENDS DOWN 16 INCHES AT ENDS.

80c

Made in oak, birch, yellow pine or cypress (in the natural wood, not oiled or varnished). Price, per lineal foot.

No. 63B8443

EXTENDS DOWN 24 INCHES AT ENDS.

$1.10

Made in oak, birch, yellow pine or cypress (in the natural wood, not oiled or varnished). Price, per lineal foot.

No. 63B8444

EXTENDS DOWN 16 INCHES AT ENDS.

89c

Made in oak, birch, yellow pine or cypress (in the nat-ural wood, not oiled or varnished). Price, per lineal foot.

ALL GRILLES ORDERED UNDER 4 FEET WILL BE CHARGED AS IF 4 FEET LONG, except No. 63B8444, which will be charged as 3 feet if shorter than 36 inches.

ATTENTION! CAREFUL HOME BUILDERS!

Wood Mantels and Consoles With Mirrors; Palace Car Finish in Hand Rubbed and Luster Polished Full
Quarter Sawed Oak; Piano Polished Rich Birch, Mahogany Finish; Straight Grain Plain Sawed Solid Oak.

NEW IDEAS IN DESIGN. **ART TILE AND MANTEL GRATES** UNQUESTIONABLE QUALITY.
BEAUTIFUL GRAINED WOODS. EXCEPTIONAL VALUES.

Do not be deceived if told we cannot furnish **full quarter sawed oak mantels with mirrors at from $12.98 to $33.00,** and plain sawed solid oak mantels at from $2.22 to $21.00, but send us your order for one or more and prove it for yourself, remembering that we guarantee them to be all and more than we claim for them, the greatest value you ever saw in like style and finish, or you can hold them subject to our orders for disposal and we will return your money, including any freight charges you may have paid.

Only the clearest, most beautifully grained woods are used, not only in the manufacture of our full quarter sawed, but in our plain straight sawed gloss finish mantels.

These wonderfully low prices are for these mantels safely packed and delivered on board the cars at the factory in Indiana, guaranteed to reach you in perfect condition, free from mar, scratch or injury in transportation, and to be made of the choicest selections of solid oak, free from blemishes of any kind.

Send for our big free Book of Wood Mantels and Consoles. Over half a hundred of artistic halftone photographic illustrations of the most popular styles. We want every contractor, carpenter, home builder and house owner to see this splendidly illustrated Book of Wood Mantels and Consoles. Anyone who contemplates building or remodeling a house should possess this information it contains, know the great values it offers, read the guarantee we give, whether buying from us or elsewhere.

$2.22 When we tell you we can furnish a solid oak base mantel, like No. 61B3413, with shelf and top apron, for $2.22;

$7.49 When we tell you we can furnish you a solid oak elegant mantel with mirror, like No. 61B3406, for $7.49;

$12.98 When we call your attention to that beautiful specimen of velvet rubbed quarter sawed oak, No. 61B3363, and tell you it is solid full quarter sawed golden oak, second to none other at anything like the price of $12.98;

$33.00 When we call your attention to that most magnificent specimen of full quarter sawed, full luster polished mantel, with serpentine pilasters, illustrated on the next page as No. 61B3280, you will know that we make the finest line of full quarter sawed solid oak

mantels, the finest line of medium priced plain sawed solid oak mantels, with or without mirrors and while you are startled with our wonderfully low prices of $2.22 and upward for solid oak mantel bases without mirrors, you will agree with us that you cannot afford to overlook these wonderful values whether you are building a new house, remodeling an old one or dealing in mantels for profit. Our remarkable values in mantel grates are fully described on page 96.

Art tile mantel facings and hearths are fully described on page 97.

Satin or Matte Finish Mantel Tile. This modern, soft satin finish enameling is in the new, novel, attractive solid colors so much favored by architects, decorators and home designers. We furnish it in dark greens, dark olives, browns, chocolates and buffs, a splendid dark red oxblood and a beautiful dull finish ivory white. All are solid colors in matte enameled tile. Satin or matte finish mantel tile will always be furnished 6x1½ inches unless other sizes are ordered. We can furnish them in all the other standard sizes and half sizes when desired. Price in barrel lots, 30 cents per square foot.

Brilliant, Glazed, Iridescent Lustered, Multicolored Tile in beautiful blends and mottles. These are the conventional, brilliant, glazed enamel tiles most popular for mantel facings and hearths. We furnish them in more beautiful shades of mottled tints and solid colors than ever before. We furnish them in the most brilliant enamel glazes, in colors, tints and shades that neither fade nor tarnish. Brilliant, glazed mantel tile will always be furnished 6x1½ inches unless other sizes are ordered. We can always furnish them in the other standard sizes and half sizes when desired. Price in barrel lots, 22½ cents per square foot.

Mission Finish or Dull Brick Unglazed Encaustic Mantel Tile. A wonderfully strong vitreous tile, furnished only in a dull, dark brick red, or a beautiful smooth brick dull buff color. While only two colors can be furnished in this dull Mission finish mantel tile, yet the dark red is in perfect harmony with dark Mission finish woodwork, and the buff brick shade blends beautifully with all natural finish woodwork colors. This vitreous tile is more durable than building brick and far more durable than the more brilliant colored enameled tile. Mission Brick Finish, Unglazed Mantel Tile will be furnished 6x1½ inches and 3x1½ inches only. Price in barrel lots, 18 cents per square foot.

CONSOLES WITH MIRRORS, EXCEPTIONAL VALUES

GRAND DRAWING ROOM CONSOLE.

ROYAL PARLOR CONSOLE.

COTTAGE CONSOLE.

$27.98
Straight Sawed
Solid Oak.

$28.50
Birch, Mahogany
Finish.

Console No. 45, 7 feet 3 inches high by 4 feet 6 inches wide; beveled French plate mirror, 4 feet 2 inches by 2 feet 6 inches; veneered columns, 3½ inches diameter. Shipping weight, 265 pounds. Delivered on cars at the factory in Indiana.

No. 61B3276
Straight sawed solid oak, with mirror. Price reduced to........$27.98
No. 61B3277
Birch, mahogany finish, with mirror. Price reduced to........$28.50
Don't forget that we guarantee to please you or return your money.

CONSOLE No. 45.

$38.95
Full Quarter
Sawed Oak.

$39.45
Piano Polished
Birch, Mahogany
Finish.

Console No. 33, 7 feet 10 inches high by 5 feet wide; beveled French plate mirror, 54 inches high by 34 inches wide; veneered columns, 5 inches diameter. Shipping weight, 315 pounds. Delivered on cars at the factory in Indiana.

No. 61B3272
Quarter sawed oak, with mirror. Price reduced to $38.95
No. 61B3273
Birch, mahogany finish, with mirror. Price reduced to.....$39.45

CONSOLE No. 33.

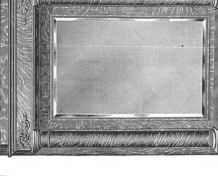

$46.93
Full Quarter
Sawed Oak.

$47.50
Piano Polished
Birch, Mahogany
Finish.

Console No. 34, 8 feet high by 5 feet wide; plain edge French plate mirror, 5 feet high by 3 feet 4 inches wide; pilasters, half round, 9 inches diameter. Shipping weight, 390 pounds. Delivered on cars at the factory in Indiana.

No. 61B3267
Quarter sawed oak, with mirror. Price reduced to $46.93
No. 61B3268
Birch, mahogany finish, with mirror. Price reduced to.....$47.50

CONSOLE No. 34.

Luster Polished Quarter Sawed Oak Mantel, $31.98

The big 5-inch round columns above and beautiful wave line pilasters below are both full quartering veneered. The total height is 7 feet 8 inches by 4 feet 9 inches wide, with wall plates set to full 5 feet. Its plate glass mirror is beveled at the top and ends and measures 42x24 inches. The modern serpentine or wave line pilasters are 5 inches wide, varying from 5 inches deep to 2½ inches deep in the curved line sweeps. Tile opening, 42 inches wide by 39 inches high, requiring a tile hearth 21 inches deep, running the full width of the mantel. Profile, 3 inches. Shipping weight, 315 pounds. Price, delivered on the cars at the factory in Indiana.

No. 61B3283
Full Quarter Sawed Golden Oak Mantel and Mirror Only.
Price reduced to $31.98
Coal and gas grates extra, see page 96.
Tile facings and hearth extra, see page 97.

MANTEL No. 277

Luster Polished Quarter Sawed Oak Mantel, $29.95

Grand value in full quartering sawed and quartering veneered Solid Oak Mantel with mirror, full luster polished. Total height, 7 feet 6 inches; width, 4 feet 11 inches, with wall plates set to full 5 feet. The full length quartering veneered columns are 5 inches in diameter, topped out with beautiful ornamental caps. The o g e e shelf is 7½ inches high, including the molding, and extending the full width of the mantel. The big mirror measures 36x 20 inches, and the lower shelf is 8 inches deep by 4 inches high with rounding quartering veneered face. Tile opening, 42 x 42 inches and requires a tile hearth 24 inches deep, running the full width of the mantel. Profile, 3 inches. Shipping weight, 315 pounds. Price, delivered on the cars at the factory in Indiana.

No. 61B3301
Woodwork and Mirror Only.
Price $29.95
Coal and gas grates extra, see page 96.
Tile facings and hearth extra, see page 97.

MANTEL No. 274

Luster Polished Quarter Sawed Oak Mantel, $31.85

Massive, beautifully grained, full quartering sawed and quartering veneered Solid Oak Mantel with mirror. Total height, 7 feet 8 inches. Furnished 4 feet 9 inches wide, with wall plates set to full 5 feet. 5-inch quartering veneered columns, lower box shelf 6 inches high and 9¾ inches deep; upper box shelf 5½ inches high and 8¾ inches deep. Bevel plate mirror, 42 inches long by 24 inches high. Tile opening, 42 inches high by 39 inches high, requiring a tile hearth 21 inches deep, extending the full width of the mantel. Profile, 3 inches. Shipping weight, 310 pounds. Price, delivered on the cars at the factory in Indiana.

No. 61B3291
Luster Polished Full Quarter Sawed Golden Oak Mantel and Mirror Only
to $31.85

No. 61B3292
Piano Polished Rich Birch, Mahogany Finish Mantel and Mirror Only
to $32.35
Coal and gas grates extra, see page 96.
Tile facings and hearth extra, see page 97.

MANTEL No. 275

$23.50 Luster Polished Piano Birch, Mahogany Finish.
$23.00 Luster Polished Full Quarter Sawed Oak.

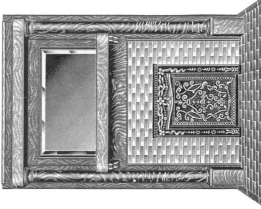

Mantel No. 22, 7 feet 2 inches high and 5 feet wide. Quartering veneered columns 4 inches in diameter. Its beveled plate glass mirror measures 36 by 20 inches. Tile opening 42x39 inches, requiring a tile hearth 21 inches deep, running the full width of the mantel. Profile, 3 inches. Shipping weight, 185 pounds. Prices, delivered on the cars at the factory in Indiana.

No. 61B3306
Full Quarter Sawed and Luster Polished Golden Oak Mantel and Mirror Only.
Price $23.00

No. 61B3307
Piano Polished Rich Birch, Mahogany Finish Mantel and Mirror Only.
Price $23.50
Coal and gas grates extra, see page 96.
Tile facings and hearth extra, see page 97.

MANTEL No. 22

$24.50 Luster Polished Piano Birch, Mahogany Finish.
$24.00 Luster Polished Full Quarter Sawed Oak.

Mantel No. 23, 7 feet 2 inches high and 5 feet wide. Its beveled plate glass mirror measures 36x20 inches. Both upper and lower columns are 4 inches in diameter and are full quartering veneered. Tile opening, 42 inches wide by 39 inches high, requiring a tile hearth 21 inches deep, running the full width of the mantel. Profile, 3 inches. Shipping weight, 200 pounds. Prices, delivered on the cars at the factory in Indiana.

No. 61B3303
Full Quarter Sawed and Luster Polished Golden Oak Mantel and Mirror Only.
Price $24.00

No. 61B3304
Piano Polished Rich Birch, Mahogany Finish Mantel and Mirror Only.
Price $24.50
Coal and gas grates extra, see page 96.
Tile facings and hearth extra, see page 97.

MANTEL No. 23

Luster Polished Quarter Sawed Oak Mantel, $33.00

Mantel No. 276, 7 feet 8 inches high and 4 feet 9 inches wide, with wall plates set to full 5 feet. Profile, 3 inches. Tile opening, 42 inches wide by 39 inches high, requiring a tile hearth 21 inches deep, running the full width of the mantel. Its bevel plate glass mirror is the full width of the mantel. Ser-pentine wave line pilasters 5 inches wide, varying from 5 inches deep to 2½ inches deep in the curve line sweeps, and are full quartering veneered. Its lower box shelf is 6 inches high on the face and 9 inches deep. The upper box shelf is 5½ inches high and 8¾ inches deep. Shipping weight, 310 pounds, delivered on the cars at the factory in Indiana.

No. 61B3280
Woodwork and Mirror Only.
Price $33.00
Coal and gas grates extra, see page 96.
Tile facings and hearth extra, see page 97.

MANTEL No. 276

$27.98 Luster Polished Full Quarter Sawed Oak.

$28.50 Piano Polished Birch, Mahogany Finish.

$27.48 Luster Polished Full Quarter Sawed Oak.

$28.00 Piano Polished Birch, Mahogany Finish.

$26.98 Luster Polished Full Quarter Sawed Oak.

$27.48 Piano Polished Birch, Mahogany Finish.

Mantel No. 15, 7 feet 6 inches high and 5 feet wide. Its plate glass mirror is beveled at the top and ends and measures 36x20 inches. Both upper and lower columns are 5 inches in diameter and are full quartering veneered. Both shelves extend the full width of the mantel. Tile opening from woodwork to woodwork is 42 inches wide by 39 inches high, requiring a tile hearth 21 inches deep, running the full width of the mantel. Profile, 3 inches. Shipping weight, 215 pounds. Prices, delivered on the cars at the factory in Indiana.

MANTEL No. 15.
No. 61B3286 Full Quarter Sawed and Luster Polished Golden Oak Mantel and Mirror Only. Price reduced to..$27.98
No. 61B3287 Piano Polished Rich Birch, Mahogany Finish Mantel and Mirror Only. Price reduced to..........$28.50
Coal and gas grates extra, see page 96.
Tile facing and hearth extra, see page 97.

Mantel No. 14, 7 feet 6 inches high and 5 feet wide. Its full length quartering veneered columns are 5 inches in diameter. Its plate glass mirror is beveled at the top and ends and measures 36x20 inches. Tile opening from woodwork to woodwork is 42x39 inches, requiring a tile hearth 21 inches deep, running the full width of the mantel. Profile, 3 inches. Shipping weight, 200 pounds. Prices, delivered on the cars at the factory in Indiana.

MANTEL No. 14.
No. 61B3293 Full Quarter Sawed and Luster Polished Golden Oak Mantel and Mirror Only. Price reduced to..$27.48
No. 61B3294 Piano Polished Rich Birch, Mahogany Finish Mantel and Mirror Only. Price reduced to..........$28.00
Coal and gas grates extra, see page 96.
Tile facing and hearth extra, see page 97.

Mantel No. 273, 7 feet 3 inches high and 4 feet 9 inches wide, with wall plates set to full 5 feet. The tile opening from woodwork to woodwork is 42 inches wide by 39 inches high, requiring a tile hearth 21 inches deep, running the full width of the mantel. Its plate glass mirror is 36x20 inches. The big quartering veneered columns measure 5 inches in diameter, capped with bric-a-brac shelves 9 inches wide, 8 inches deep and 2½ inches thick. Its full length top shelf is 5 inches high on the face. The lower shelf is 9 inches deep with a face 5½ inches high. Profile, 3 inches. Shipping weight, 300 pounds.

MANTEL No. 273. Prices, delivered on the cars at the factory in Indiana.
No. 61B3311 Full Quarter Sawed and Luster Polished Golden Oak Mantel and Mirror Only. Price reduced to..$26.98
No. 61B3312 Piano Polished Rich Birch, Mahogany Finish Mantel and Mirror Only. Price reduced to..........$27.48
Coal and gas grates extra, see page 96.
Tile facing and hearth extra, see page 97.

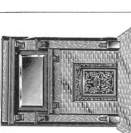

Mantel No. 252, 7 feet 6 inches high and 4½ feet wide, with wall plates set to 5 feet. Tile opening 42x39 inches, requiring a hearth 21 inches deep. Profile, 3 inches. Quartering veneered columns 3 inches in diameter. Beveled mirror, oval or square, 36x18 inches. Shipping weight, 230 pounds. Price, delivered on the cars at the factory in Indiana.

No. 61B3371 Woodwork and Mirror Only. Price..............$17.75
Coal and gas grates extra, see page 96.
Tile facing and hearth extra, see page 97.

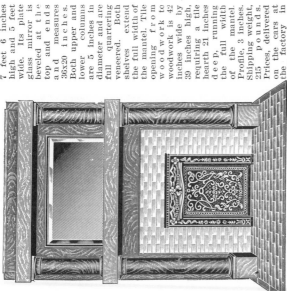

$24.98 Luster Polished Quartered Oak.

$21.90 Luster Polished Quartered Oak.

$21.60 Luster Polished Quartered Oak.

$20.00 Luster Polished Quartered Oak.

$18.98 Luster Polished Quartered Oak.

$17.75 Luster Polished Quartered Oak.

Mantel No. 256, 7 feet 8 inches high and 4 feet to 5 feet 8 inches wide, with wall plates set to 5 feet. Quartering veneered columns 4 inches in diameter, 3 inches in diameter above. Beveled mirror, oval or square, as ordered, 36x18 inches. Tile opening, 42 inches wide by 39 inches high, requiring a tile hearth 21 inches deep. Profile, 2⅝ inches. Shipping weight, 260 pounds. Price, delivered on the cars at the factory in Indiana.

No. 61B3321 Woodwork and Mirror Only. Price.............$24.98
Coal and gas grates extra, see page 96.
Tile facing and hearth extra, see page 97.

Mantel No. 231, 7 feet high and full 5 feet wide. Quartering veneered columns 4 inches in diameter. Arched plate glass beveled mirror 40x18 inches. The opening 36x36 inches, requiring a tile hearth 18 inches deep. Profile, 2⅞ inches. Shipping weight, 250 pounds. Price, delivered on the cars at the factory in Indiana.

No. 61B3331 Woodwork and Mirror Only. Price..............$21.90
Coal and gas grates extra, see page 96.
Tile facing and hearth extra, see page 97.

Mantel No. 263, 7 feet high and 4½ feet wide, with wall plates set to 5 feet. Upper and lower quartering veneered columns 4 inches in diameter. Beveled plate mirror, 36x18 inches. The lower shelf is rounded at the front corners, and is 9 inches deep. Tile opening 36x36 inches, requiring a tile hearth 18 inches deep. Profile, 2⅞ inches. Shipping weight, 260 pounds. Price, delivered on the cars at the factory in Indiana.

No. 61B3351 Woodwork and Mirror Only. Price.............$21.60
Coal and gas grates extra, see page 96.
Tile facing and hearth extra, see page 97.

Mantel No. 255, 7 feet 4 inches high and 4 feet and 10 inches wide, with wall plates set to 5 feet. Quartering veneered columns 4 inches in diameter below the shelf, and 3 inches above. Beveled plate glass mirror is 40x18 inches. Tile opening, 36x36 inches, requiring a tile hearth 18 inches deep. Profile, 3 inches. If desired with tile opening 42x36 inches, it can be furnished, and the profile would be 3¾ inches. Shipping weight, 260 pounds. Price, delivered on the cars at the factory in Indiana.

No. 61B3333 Woodwork and Mirror Only. Price..............$20.00
Coal and gas grates extra, see page 96.
Tile facing and hearth extra, see page 97.

Mantel No. 264, 6 feet 7 inches high and 4½ feet wide, with wall plates set to 5 feet. The square pilasters are capped with handsome bric-a-brac squares. Beveled plate glass mirror 36x18 inches. Tile opening, 42x39 inches, requiring a tile hearth 21 inches deep. Profile, 2¾ inches. Shipping weight, 200 pounds. Price, delivered on the cars at the factory in Indiana.

No. 61B3316 Woodwork and Mirror Only. Price.............$18.98
Coal and gas grates extra, see page 96.
Tile facing and hearth extra, see page 97.

$24.67 Luster Polished Full Quarter Sawed Oak. | $25.25 Piano Polished Rich Birch, Mahogany Finish.

Mantel No. 24, 7 feet 2 inches high and 5 feet wide. Its big pilasters are topped with square bric-a-brac caps. Its plate glass mirror is beveled at the top and ends and measures 36x20 inches. Tile opening from woodwork to woodwork is 42x39 inches, requiring a tile hearth 21 inches deep, running the full width of the mantel. Profile, 3 inches. Shipping weight, 175 pounds, delivered on the cars at the factory in Indiana.

No. 61B3313 Full Quarter Sawed Golden Oak Mantel and Mirror Only. Price reduced to ...$24.67

No. 61B3314 Piano Polished Rich Birch, Mahogany Finish Mantel and Mirror Only. Price ...$25.25

Coal and gas grates extra, see page 96. Tile facing and hearth extra, see page 97.

$23.97 Luster Polished Full Quarter Sawed Oak. | $24.50 Piano Polished Birch, Mahogany Finish.

Mantel No. 18, 7 feet 4 inches high and 5 feet wide. Its plate glass mirror is beveled at the top and ends and measures 36x20 inches. Both upper and lower columns are 4 inches in diameter and are full quartering veneered. Tile opening from woodwork to woodwork is 42x39 inches, requiring a tile hearth 21 inches deep, running the full width of the mantel. Profile, 3 inches. Shipping weight, 210 pounds, delivered at the factory in Indiana.

No. 61B3323 Full Quarter Sawed and Luster Polished Golden Oak Mantel and Mirror Only. Price reduced to ...$23.97

No. 61B3324 Piano Polished Rich Birch Mahogany Finish Mantel and Mirror Only. Price reduced to ...$24.50

Coal and gas grates extra, see page 96. Tile facing and hearth extra, see page 97.

$22.99 Luster Polished Full Quarter Sawed Oak. | $23.50 Piano Polished Birch, Mahogany Finish.

Mantel No. 17, 7 feet 4 inches high and 5 feet wide. Its plate glass mirror is beveled at the top and ends and measures 36x20 inches. Its full length quartering veneered columns are 4 inches in diameter. Tile opening from woodwork to woodwork is 42x39 inches, requiring a tile hearth 21 inches deep extending the full width of the mantel. Profile, 3 inches. Shipping weight, 210 pounds, delivered on the cars at the factory in Indiana.

No. 61B3326 Full Quarter Sawed and Luster Polished Golden Oak Mantel and Mirror Only. to ...$22.99

No. 61B3327 Piano Polished Rich Mahogany Finish Mantel and Mirror Only. ...$23.50

Coal and gas grates extra, see page 96. Tile facing and hearth extra, see page 97.

$20.98 Luster Polished Full Quarter Sawed Oak.

Mantel No. 280, 7 feet high and 5 feet wide. The full length box pilasters measure 4½ inches wide. The mirror is beveled at the top and both ends and measures 40x18 inches. The shelf below the mirror is 10 inches deep. The tile opening from woodwork to woodwork is 42x42 inches, requiring a tile hearth 24 inches deep, extending the full width of the mantel. Profile, 2½ inches. Shipping weight, 240 pounds, delivered on the cars at the factory in Indiana.

No. 61B3341 Full Quarter Sawed and Luster Polished Golden Oak Mantel and Mirror Only. Price reduced to ...$20.98

Coal and gas grates extra, see page 96. Tile facing and hearth extra, see page 97.

$16.98 Luster Polished Full Quarter Sawed Oak.

Mantel No. 282, 6 feet 11 inches high and 4½ feet wide, with wall plates set to 5 feet. Its full length pilasters are 5 inches wide and the lower mantel shelf is 9 inches deep. Its beveled plate glass mirror is 40x18 inches. The tile opening from woodwork to woodwork is 42x42 inches, requiring a tile hearth 24 inches deep, extending the full width of the mantel. Profile, 5 inches. Shipping weight, 220 pounds, delivered on the cars at the factory in Indiana.

No. 61B3343 Full Quarter Sawed and Luster Polished Golden Oak Mantel and Mirror Only. Price reduced to ...$16.98

Coal and gas grates extra, see page 96. Tile facing and hearth extra, see page 97.

$15.00 Luster Polished Full Quarter Sawed Oak.

Mantel No. 279, 6 feet 8 inches high and 4½ feet wide, with wall plates set to 5 feet. Its oval beveled plate mirror is 28x16 inches and the long shelf is 9 inches deep. Its tile opening from woodwork to woodwork is 42x42 inches, requiring a tile hearth 24 inches deep, extending the full width of the mantel. Profile, 4 inches. Shipping weight, 220 pounds. Price, delivered on the cars at the factory in Indiana.

No. 61B3346 Full Quarter Sawed and Luster Polished Golden Oak Mantel and Mirror Only. Price reduced to ...$15.00

Coal and gas grates extra, see page 96. Tile facing and hearth extra, see page 97.

SEARS, ROEBUCK AND CO, CHICAGO, ILLINOIS.

$19.50 FULL QUARTER SAWED GOLDEN OAK.

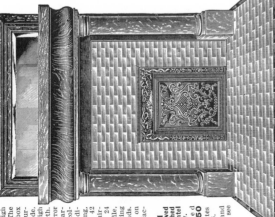

Mantel No. 281M, 6 feet 4 inches high and 5 feet wide. The massive deep ogee box shelf has a top surface 12 inches wide, and is 5 feet high above the hearth. Beveled plate mirror 50x12 inches. Quartering veneered columns 5 inches in diameter. Tile opening, 45 inches high by 42 inches wide, requiring a tile hearth 24 inches deep. Profile, 3 inches. Shipping weight, 200 pounds. Price, delivered on the cars at the factory in Indiana.

No. 61B3361
Full Quarter Sawed and Luster Polished Golden Oak Mantel and Mirror Only.

Price reduced to $19.50

Coal and gas grates extra, see page 96.

Tile facing and hearth extra, see page 97.

$13.67 MODERN LOW TYPE DESIGN IN PLAIN SAWED GOLDEN OAK, WATER RUBBED AND FULL LUSTER POLISHED.

Mantel No. 269, made in the novel new type, and only 5 feet 9 inches high, but measuring full 5 feet wide. Its quartering veneered columns are 4 inches in diameter. The mantel shelf is 9 inches deep and extends the full width of the mantel. Its magnificent beveled mirror is 48 inches long by 12 inches high. The tile opening from woodwork to woodwork is 42x42 inches, requiring a tile hearth 24 inches deep, extending the full width of the mantel. Profile, 2¾ inches. Shipping weight, 175 pounds. Price, delivered on the cars at the factory in Indiana.

No. 61B3366 Water Rubbed and Full Luster Polished Golden Oak Mantel and Mirror Only. Price reduced to....$13.67

Coal and gas grates extra, see page 96.

Tile facing and hearth extra, see page 97.

$12.98 VELVET RUBBED FULL QUARTER SAWED OAK.

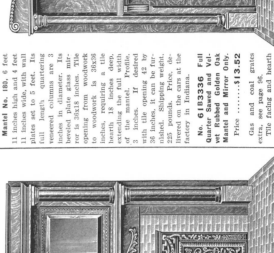

Mantel No. 263 is a choice selection that must be seen to be appreciated. Only the choicest selected quarter sawed oak is used and its design is the most modern. It is made in the modern boudoir height of 6 feet and is 4½ feet wide, with wall plates set to full 5 feet. Its splendid beveled mirror is 42x14 inches. The long mantel shelf is 9 inches deep. The tile opening from woodwork to woodwork is 42x42 inches, requiring a tile hearth 24 inches deep, extending the full width of the mantel. Profile, 1½ inches. Shipping weight, 150 pounds. Price, delivered on the cars at the factory in Indiana.

No. 61B3363 Velvet Rubbed Full Quarter Sawed Boudoir Mantel and Mirror.....$12.98

$13.52 VELVET RUBBED FULL QUARTER SAWED OAK.

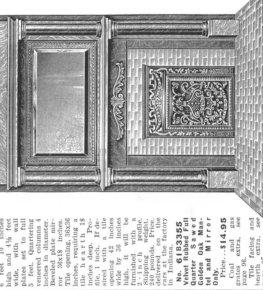

Mantel No. 180, 6 feet 11 inches high and 4 feet 11 inches wide, with wall plates set to 5 feet. Its full length quartering veneered columns are 3 inches in diameter. Its beveled plate glass mirror is 36x18 inches. Tile opening from woodwork to woodwork is 36x36 inches, requiring a tile hearth 18 inches deep, extending the full width of the mantel. Profile, 3 inches. If desired with tile opening 42 by 36 inches, it can be furnished. Shipping weight, 225 pounds. Price, delivered on the cars at the factory in Indiana.

No. 61B3336 Full Quarter Sawed and Velvet Rubbed Golden Oak Mantel and Mirror Only.

Price $13.52

Gas and coal grates extra, see page 96.

Tile facing and hearth extra, see page 97.

$15.99 LUSTER POLISHED FULL QUARTER SAWED OAK.

Mantel No. 244, 6 feet 10 inches high and 4½ feet wide, with wall plates set to full 5 feet. Quartering veneered columns 4 inches in diameter. Oval beveled plate mirror 36x18 inches. Tile opening, 36x36 inches, requiring a tile hearth 18 inches deep. Profile, 1 inch. If desired, this mantel can be furnished with tile opening 42 inches wide by 36 inches high, with a 2-inch profile. Shipping weight, 240 pounds. Price, delivered on the cars at the factory in Indiana.

No. 61B3353 Full Quarter Sawed and Luster Polished Golden Oak Mantel and Mirror Only.

Price....$15.99

Coal and gas grates extra, see page 96.

Tile facing and hearth extra, see page 97.

$14.95 VELVET RUBBED FULL QUARTER SAWED OAK.

Mantel No. 243, 6 feet 10 inches high and 4½ feet wide, with wall plates set to full 5 feet. Quartering veneered columns 4 inches in diameter. Beveled plate mirror 36x18 inches. Tile opening, 36x36 inches, requiring a tile hearth 18 inches deep. Profile, 1 inch. If desired, this mantel can be furnished with tile opening 42 inches wide by 36 inches high, it will be furnished with a 2-inch profile. Shipping weight, 240 pounds. Price, delivered on the cars at the factory in Indiana.

No. 61B3355 Velvet Rubbed Full Quarter Sawed Golden Oak Mantel and Mirror Only.

Price....$14.95

Coal and gas grates extra, see page 96.

Tile facing and hearth extra, see page 97.

$21⁰⁰ Plain Sawed Rubbed and Polished Golden Oak.

Mantel No. 271.

Total height, 6 feet by only 4 feet wide, with wall plates set to full 4½ feet. Full length quartering veneered columns, 3 inches in diameter. Beveled plate mirror, 24x14 inches. Tile opening, 36x36 inches, requiring a tile hearth 18 inches deep, extending the full width of the mantel. Profile, ⅞ inch. Shipping weight, 150 pounds. Price, delivered on the cars at the factory in Indiana.

No. 61B3396 Woodwork and Mirror Only. Price reduced to......$9.50
Coal and gas grates extra, see page 96.
Tile facing and hearth extra, see page 97.

$21⁷⁵ Rubbed and Polished Rich Birch, Mahogany Finish.

Mantel No. 5, 7 feet 3 inches high and 5 feet wide. Its full length quartering veneered columns are 5 inches in diameter. Its plate glass mirror is beveled at the top and ends, and measures 36x18 inches. Tile opening from woodwork to woodwork is 42x39 inches, requiring a tile hearth 21 inches deep, running the full width of the mantel. Profile, 3 inches. Shipping weight, 210 pounds. Prices, delivered on the cars at the factory in Indiana.

No. 61B3296 Plain Sawed, Rubbed and Polished Golden Oak Mantel and Mirror Only.
Price reduced to......$21.00

No. 61B3297 Piano Polished Rich Birch Mahogany Finish Mantel and Mirror Only.
Price reduced to......$21.75

Coal and gas grates extra, see page 96.
Tile facing and hearth extra, see page 97.

Mantel No. 5.

$12²⁹ Plain Sawed Golden Oak.

Mantel No. 241.

Total height, 6 feet 8 inches by 4½ feet wide, with wall plates set to full 5 feet. Its quartering oak veneered columns are 3 inches in diameter. Its beveled plate mirror is 36x18 inches. The tile opening is 36x36 inches, and requires a tile hearth 18 inches deep, extending the full width of the mantel. Profile, 1 inch, or if desired it can be furnished with a tile opening 42x36 inches, with a 2-inch profile. Shipping weight, 210 pounds. Price, delivered on the cars at the factory in Indiana.

No. 61B3383 Woodwork and Mirror Only. Price......$12.29
Coal and gas grates extra, see page 96.
Tile facing and hearth extra, see page 97.

$10²⁵ Plain Sawed Golden Oak.

Mantel No. 248.

Total height, 6 feet 4 inches by 4½ feet wide, with wall plates set to full 5 feet. Its quartering veneered columns are 2½ inches in diameter. Beveled plate mirror, 28x16 inches. Tile opening, 36x36 inches, requiring a tile hearth 18 inches deep, extending the full width of the mantel. Profile, 3 inches. Price, delivered on the cars at the factory in Indiana.

No. 61B3386 Woodwork and Mirror Only. Price......$10.25
Coal and gas grates extra, see page 96.
Tile facing and hearth extra, see page 97.

$9⁹⁹ Plain Sawed Golden Oak.

Mantel No. 284.

Total height, 6 feet 7 inches by 4½ feet wide, with wall plates set to full 5 feet. The shelves and brackets are of semi-Mission construction and the beveled plate mirror, 28x16 inches. Tile opening, 36x36 inches, requiring a tile hearth 18 inches deep, extending the full width of the mantel. Profile, 4 inches. Shipping weight, 200 pounds. Price, delivered on the cars at the factory in Indiana.

No. 61B3401 Woodwork and Mirror Only. Price reduced to......$9.99
Coal and gas grates extra, see page 96.
Tile facing and hearth extra, see page 97.

$9⁷⁵ Plain Sawed Golden Oak.

Mantel No. 270.

Total height, 6 feet 8 inches by 4½ feet wide, with wall plates set to full 5 feet. The columns are set to full 5 feet. The columns are quartering veneered, 3 inches in diameter. Its beveled plate mirror is 28x16 inches. Tile opening, 36x36 inches, requiring a tile hearth 18 inches deep, extending the full width of the mantel. Profile, 2½ inches. Shipping weight, 210 pounds. Price, delivered on the cars at the factory in Indiana.

No. 61B3393 Woodwork and Mirror Only. Price reduced to......$9.75
Coal and gas grates extra, see page 96.
Tile facing and hearth extra, see page 97.

$14⁹⁹ Straight Grain Plain Sawed Solid Oak in Either Mission or Golden Finish, as Ordered.

Mantel No. 278, 7 feet high and 4½ feet wide, with wall plates set to 5 feet. Its columns are 3¾ inches square and 9 inches deep, extending the full width of the mantel. Its bevel plate apex mirror measures 36x18 inches and is beveled at the ends and the edges of the apex top. It extends below the shelf, giving a duplicate reflection of the shelf surface in the glass. The tile opening from woodwork to woodwork is 42 inches wide and 39 inches high, requiring a tile hearth 21 inches deep, extending the full width of the mantel. Profile, 2 inches. Shipping weight, 225 pounds. Price, delivered on the cars at the factory in Indiana.

No. 61B3381 Straight Grain Plain Sawed Gloss Finish Golden Oak Mantel with Mirror Only. Price reduced to......$14.99
Mission finish will be furnished if requested, at the same price.
Coal and gas grates extra, see page 96.
Tile facing and hearth extra, see page 97.

Mantel No. 278.

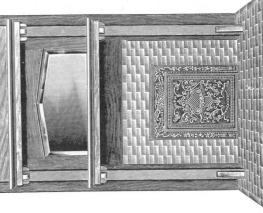

$9⁵⁰ Plain Sawed Golden Oak.

Mantel No. 345.

Total height, 6 feet 5 inches by 4½ feet wide, with wall plates set to 5 feet. Beveled plate mirror, 28x16 inches. Tile opening, 36x36 inches, requiring a tile hearth 18 inches deep, extending full width of mantel. Profile, 3 inches. Shipping weight, 200 pounds. Prices, delivered on the cars at the factory in Indiana.

No. 61B3411 Woodwork and Mirror Only. Price reduced to......$8.99
Coal and gas grates extra, see page 96.
Tile facing and hearth extra, see page 97.

$8⁹⁸ Plain Sawed Golden Oak.

Mantel No. 272.

Total height, 6 feet 2 inches by only 4 feet wide, with wall plates set to full 4½ feet. Beveled plate mirror, 24x14 inches. Tile opening, 36x36 inches, requiring a tile hearth 18 inches deep, extending full width of the mantel. Profile, 2⅝ inches. Shipping weight, 150 pounds. Price, delivered on the cars at the factory in Indiana.

No. 61B3403 Woodwork and Mirror Only. Price reduced to......$8.98
Coal and gas grates extra, see page 96.
Tile facing and hearth extra, see page 97.

$7⁴⁹ Plain Sawed Golden Oak.

Mantel No. 334.

Total height, 6 feet 3 inches by only 4½ feet wide. Long mantel shelf, bric-a-brac shelves and top shelf. Beveled plate mirror, 24x14 inches. Tile opening, 36x36 inches, requiring a tile hearth 18 inches deep, extending full width of mantel. Profile, 3 inches. Shipping weight, 125 pounds. Price, delivered on the cars at the factory in Indiana.

No. 61B3406 Woodwork and Mirror Only. Price......$7.49
Coal and gas grates extra, see page 96.
Tile facing and hearth extra, see page 97.

$16.50 Full Quarter Sawed Solid Oak Mantel Base.

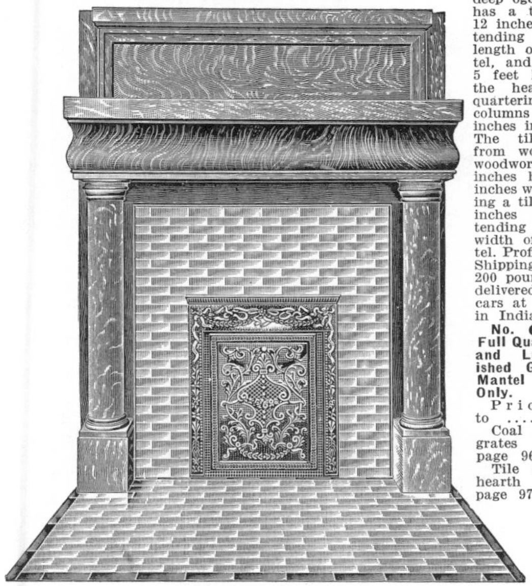

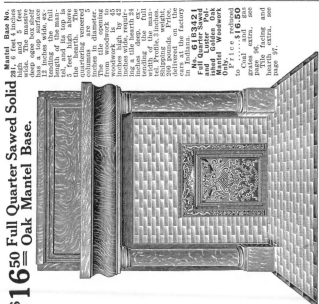

Mantel Base No. 281.

Mantel Base No. 281, 6 feet 4 inches high and 5 feet wide. The massive deep ogee box shelf has a top surface 12 inches wide, extending the full length of the mantel, and its top is 5 feet high above the hearth. The quartering veneered columns are 5 inches in diameter. The tile opening from woodwork to woodwork is 45 inches high by 42 inches wide, requiring a tile hearth 24 inches deep, extending the full width of the mantel. Profile, 3 inches. Shipping weight, 200 pounds. Price, delivered on the cars at the factory in Indiana.

No. 61B3421 Full Quarter Sawed and Luster Polished Golden Oak Mantel Woodwork Only.
Price reduced to **$16.50**

Coal and gas grates extra, see page 96.
Tile facing and hearth extra, see page 97.

$11.50 For This Rich Quartered Beauty Mantel Base, with Back Board.

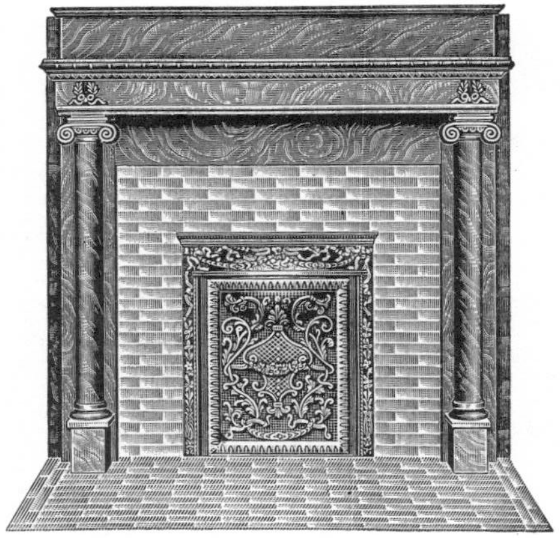

Mantel Base No. 259.

$11.50 for this full quarter sawed and full luster polished Solid Oak Mantel Base, with its 4-inch quartering veneered columns, topped out with beautiful composition caps, surmounted by a deep box shelf and capped with a high back board, all full quarter sawed.

No. 61B3423 Full Quarter Sawed and Full Luster Polished Mantel Base with Back Board. Total height, 4 feet 10 inches. Furnished 4 feet 8 inches wide, with wall plates set to 5 feet. Quartering oak veneered columns, 4 inches in diameter. Tile opening, 39x42 inches, requiring a tile hearth 60x21 inches. Profile, 2⅞ inches. Shipping weight, 150 pounds. Price, delivered on the cars at the factory in Indiana....................................**$11.50**

Coal and gas grates extra, see page 96.
Tile facing and hearth extra, see page 97.

$14.98 Full Mission Straight Grain Plain Sawed Solid Oak.

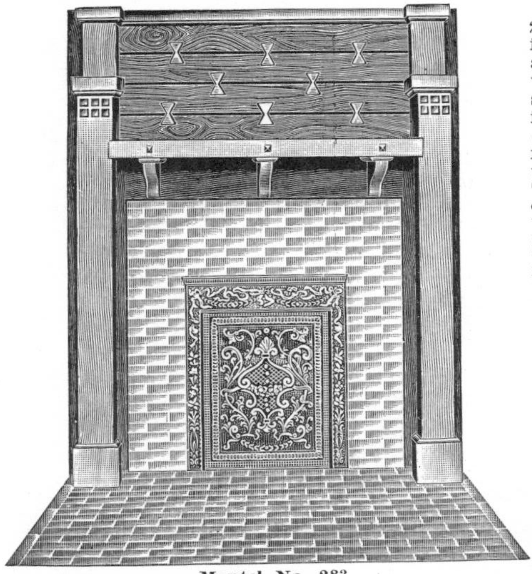

Mantel No. 283.

Mantel No. 283, 6 feet 10 inches high and 5 feet wide. The shelf is 9 inches deep, extending from pilaster to pilaster. The splendid capped pilasters are 5 inches wide. Tile opening from woodwork to woodwork is 42x42 inches, requiring a tile hearth 24 inches deep, extending the full width of the mantel. Profile, 3 inches. Shipping weight, 200 pounds. Price, delivered on the cars at the factory in Indiana.

No. 61B3391 Dark Mission Finish Plain Sawed Solid Oak Mantel Woodwork Only. Price reduced to..............**$14.98**

Gas and coal grates extra, see page 96.
Tile facing and hearth extra, see page 97.

$6.99 Quarter Sawed Mantel Base, with Back Board.

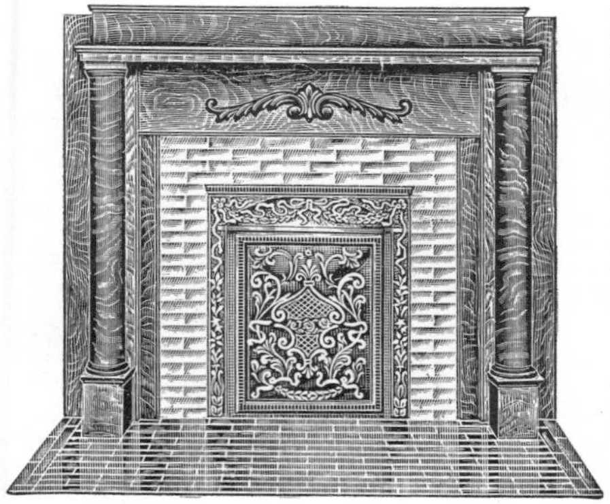

This ever popular style of mantel is furnished in full quarter sawed solid oak, velvet rubbed, the same elegant finish as in our velvet rubbed quarter sawed full mirrored mantels. The workmanship is equal in every particular, the selection of the lumber that goes to make them is the same, the care taken in the cabinet work is fully as great, and in every particular these mantel bases receive the utmost attention from the selection of the lumber to the finishing, packing and shipping.

Quarter Sawed Velvet Rubbed Solid Oak Mantel Base with Back Board. Total height, 4 feet 4 inches. Furnished 4½ feet wide, with wall plates set to 5 feet. Quartering oak veneered columns, 4 inches in diameter. Tile opening, 36x36 inches, requiring a tile hearth 60x18 inches. Profile, ⅞ inch. Shipping weight, 140 pounds. Price, delivered on the cars at the factory in Indiana.

No. 61B3426 Woodwork and Mirror Only.
Price reduced to...**$6.99**

Coal and gas grates extra, see page 96.
Tile facing and hearth extra, see page 97.

$5.49 Solid Oak Mantel Base, with Back Board.

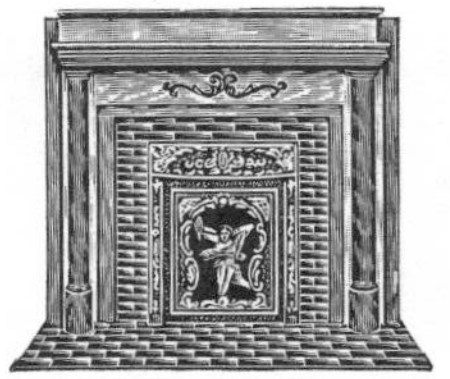

Mantel Base No. 2481.

Choice selected plain sawed golden gloss finish Mantel Base. Total height with back board, 4 feet 6 inches. Furnished 4½ feet wide, with wall plates set to 5 feet. Equipped with 2½-inch quartering veneered columns. Its tile opening from woodwork to woodwork is 36x36 inches, and a tile hearth to match should be 18 inches deep, running the full width of the mantel. Profile, 3 inches. Shipping weight, 130 pounds. Price, delivered on the cars at the factory in Indiana.

No. 61B3417 Woodwork Only. Price...........**$5.49**

Coal and gas grates extra, see page 96.
Tile facing and hearth extra, see page 97.

$4.99 Golden Oak Mantel Base, with Back Board.

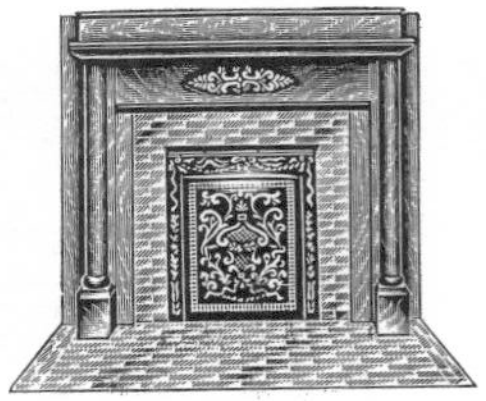

Mantel Base No. 260.

Solid oak plain sawed golden gloss finish Mantel Base. Total height with back board, 4 feet 5 inches. Furnished 4½ feet wide, with wall plates set to 5 feet. Equipped with 3-inch quartering veneered columns. Its tile opening from woodwork to woodwork is 36x36 inches, and a tile hearth to match should be 18 inches deep, running the full width of the mantel. Profile, 2 inches. Shipping weight, 130 pounds. Price, delivered on the cars at the factory in Indiana.

No. 61B3416 Woodwork Only. Price reduced to..**$4.99**

Coal and gas grates extra, see page 96.
Tile facing and hearth extra, see page 97.

$4.30 Golden Oak Mantel Base, with Back Board.

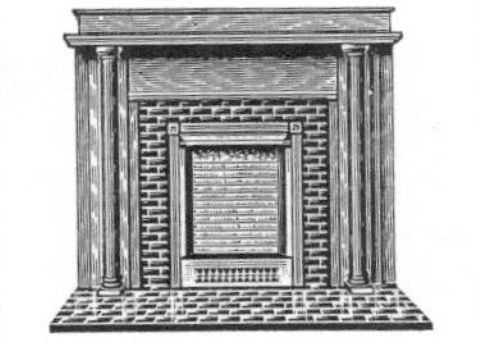

Mantel Base No. 261.

Solid oak plain sawed golden gloss finished Mantel Base, equipped with 3-inch quartering veneered columns. Total height with back board, 4 feet 5 inches. Furnished 4½ feet wide, with wall plates set to 5 feet. Its tile opening from woodwork to woodwork is 36x36 inches, and a tile hearth to match should be 18 inches deep, running the full width of the mantel. Profile, ⅞ inch. Shipping weight, 120 pounds. Price, delivered on the cars at the factory in Indiana.

No. 61B3414 Woodwork Only. Price...........**$4.30**

Coal and gas grates extra, see page 96.
Tile facing and hearth extra, see page 97.

$2.22 Solid Oak Mantel Base, with Back Board.

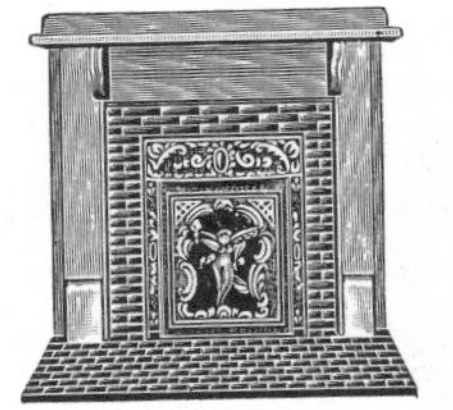

Mantel Base No. 11.

Wonderful value. Golden gloss finish Solid Oak Mantel Base. Total height with top apron, 4 feet 4 inches. Furnished 4 feet or 4½ feet wide, as desired. Its tile opening from woodwork to woodwork is 36x36 inches, and a tile hearth to match should be 18 inches deep, running the full width of the mantel. Profile, ⅞ inch. Shipping weight, 50 pounds. Price, delivered on the cars at the factory in Indiana.

No. 61B3413 Woodwork Only. Price reduced to..**$2.22**

Coal and gas grates extra, see page 96.
Tile facing and hearth extra, see page 97.

$1.68 Acme Beauty Dummy Outfit or Blank Grate Front.

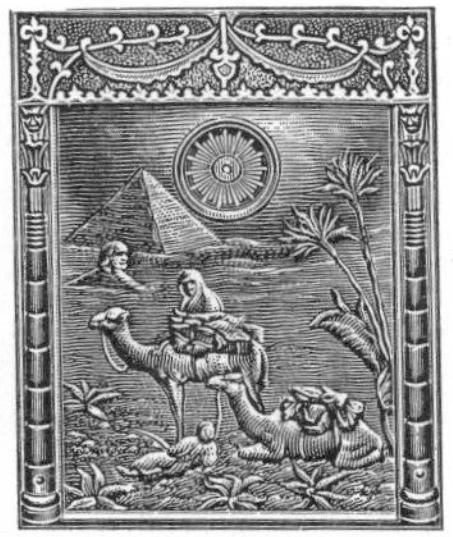

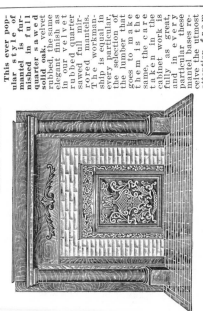

Dummy Grate Front.

This Blank Grate Outfit consists of an artistically designed oxidized copper plated pressed sheet steel, imitation of a grate frame and summer front, 30¼ inches high by 24½ inches wide, all in one piece, as illustrated, to be used for imitating a fireplace against a blank wall. All the decorative advantages of our popular splendid wood mantels are possible where fireplaces are not used by using this outfit against a blank wall. Shipping weight, 15 pounds. Delivered on the cars at the factory in Indiana.

No. 61B3247 Blank Grate Front or Dummy Outfit.
Price **$1.68**

BEST QUALITY MANTEL FIREPLACE GRATES

DURABLE, ATTRACTIVE, REASONABLE. LIVE AND LET LIVE PRICES.

Cast Iron and Pressed Steel Summer Fronts in Oxidized Copper or Brass Finishes, and the Latest Berlin Black Finish. Heavy Cast Iron Frames. Heavy Ribbed Brick Linings Shaking and Dumping Heavy Bottom Grates.

Sunbeam Grand Open Fireplace Mantel Grates

Heavy castings reinforced with extra thick firebrick lining. Elegantly modeled front frame and cast summer piece, either oxidized copper or brass finish. Shaking and dumping bottom grate. Two flue draft regulator dampers, each with separate handle. Prices, complete with summer front, delivered on the cars at the factory in Ohio.

No. 61B3230 Mantel Grate No. 128, 30¾ inches high by 24½ inches wide, with 20-inch fire opening. Shipping weight, 210 pounds. Price.......$10.94
No. 61B3231 Mantel Grate No. 128B, 30¾ inches high by 30½ inches wide, with 24-inch fire opening. Shipping weight, 250 pounds. Price.... 12.97

$12.97 Complete with Cast Summer Front. Fire Opening, 24 inches wide.

No. 128, Open View.

$10.94 Complete with Cast Summer Front. Fire Opening, 20 inches wide.

No. 128, with Summer Front.

Spaulding Royal Open Fireplace Coal Grates.

$8.48 With 20-Inch Opening.

Complete With Cast Summer Front.

Ornamental cast iron frame and cast summer piece in oxidized copper or brass finish. Full deep fireplace with back brick lining. Shaking and dumping grate with shaker handle furnished free. Prices, complete with summer front, delivered on the cars at the factory in Ohio.

No. 61B3234 Mantel Grate No. 78, 30¾ inches high by 24½ inches wide, with 20-inch fire opening. Shipping weight, 185 pounds. Price.........$8.48
No. 61B3235 Mantel Grate No. 78B, 30¾ inches high by 30½ inches wide, with 24-inch fire opening. Shipping weight, 195 pounds.
Price.

No. 78, with Summer Front.

No. 78, Open View.

Acme Beauty Open Fireplace Mantel Grates.

$9.98 With 24-Inch Opening.

Oxidized copper plated cast iron grate frame, 20-inch heavy black grate basket and screen. Pressed steel oxidized copper plated summer front. The basket has V shaped bottom bars and is heavy Fire-brick not included. Prices, with summer front, delivered on the cars at the factory in Ohio.

No. 61B3243 Coal Grate Outfit No. 81, oxidized copper plated, 30¾ inches high by 24½ inches wide, with 20-inch fire opening. Shipping weight, 60 pounds. Price........$9.98

No. 61B3245 Coal Grate Outfit No. 89, oxidized plated, 30¾ inches high by 30½ inches wide, with 24-inch fire opening. Shipping weight, 75 pounds.
Price................. $9.98
No. 61B3246 Cast Frame and Summer Piece Only (grate not included.) Price.........2.11
Without summer front, deduct 50 cents.

Coal Grate No. 81, with Summer Front.

Coal Grate No. 81, Open View.

Coal Grate No. 81, oxidized plated, 30¾ inches. Shipping weight...$2.93
same as above but black, 30¾ inches high by 30½ inches wide. Shipping weight, 75 pounds. Price (grate not included.)....$3.67

Acme Model Open Fireplace Gas Grates.

$7.75 With 25½-Inch Opening.

Complete With Cast Summer Front.

Heavy cast iron open fireplace gas grate with artistic summer piece, as illustrated. Gas back made of heavy pressed steel with asbestos mineral fiber firmly attached. Prices, delivered on the cars at the factory in Ohio.

No. 61B3256 Gas Grate No. 42, 30¾ inches high by 24½ inches wide, with 20-inch fire opening. Shipping weight, 60 pounds, complete with summer front.....$6.47
No. 61B3257 Gas Grate No. 42A, 30¾ inches high by 30½ inches wide, with 25½-inch opening. Shipping Wt., 70 lbs. Price, complete with summer front.$7.75
STATE WHETHER NATURAL GAS OR MANUFACTURED GAS IS USED.

$6.47 With 20-Inch Opening.

Gas Grate No. 42, with Summer Front.

Gas Grate No. 42, Open View.

Acme Beauty Gas Fireplaces.

$4.83

Oxidized copper plated pressed steel openwork fire guard, pressed steel lower guard with air supply openings, artistic summer front and heavy back with asbestos mineral fiber firmly attached. Size, 30¾ inches high by 24½ inches wide, with projecting canopy as illustrated. Shipping weight, 55 pounds. Prices, delivered on the cars at the factory in Ohio.

No. 61B3261 Gas Outfit No. 94, with summer front. Price............$5.33
No. 61B3262 Gas Outfit No. 94, without summer front, as shown. Price.......$4.83

Gas Grate No. 94, without Summer Front.

Berlin Black Beauty Open Fireplace Mantel Grates.

$6.00 With 20-Inch Opening.

Complete With Pressed Steel Summer Front.

Rich design of simple beauty in Berlin black finish. Heavy, durable cast iron structure, complete. Full deep fireplace with convenient dumping bottom grate. Two flue draft regulating dampers. Prices, with summer front, delivered on the cars at the factory in Ohio.

No. 61B3336 Mantel Grate No. 35, 30¾ inches high by 24½ inches wide, with 20-inch fire opening. Shipping weight, 165 pounds. Price.$6.00
No. 61B3337 Mantel Grate No. 35B, 30¾ inches high by 30½ inches wide, with 24-inch fire opening. Price.

Mantel Grate No. 35, with Summer Front. Shipping weight, 195 pounds.

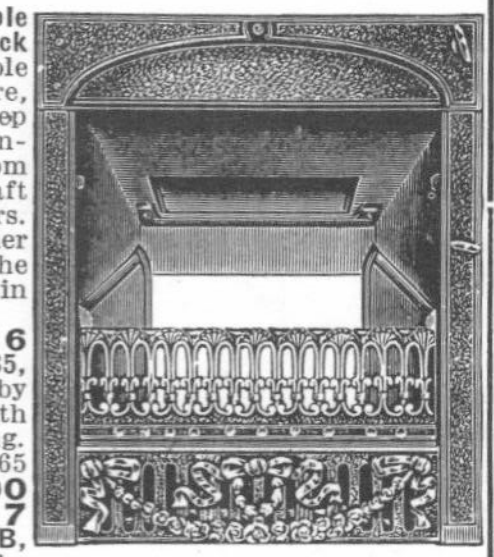

Mantel Grate No. 35, Open View.

Congo Black Open Fireplace Mantel Grates.

$7.50 With 24-Inch Opening.

Complete With Pressed Steel Summer Front.

Coal Grate No. 71, with Summer Front.

Coal Grate No. 71, Open View.

Berlin black finish cast iron grate frame, basket and ash guard, with pressed steel summer piece. Heavy V shaped bottom bars. Firebrick not furnished. Prices, with summer front, delivered on cars at the factory in Ohio.

No. 61B3248 Coal Grate No. 71, black, 30¾ inches high by 24½ inches wide, with 20-inch fire opening. Shipping weight, 60 pounds. Price.......$1.98
No. 61B3249 Coal Grate No. 89, black, 30¾ inches high by 30½ inches wide, with 24-inch fire opening. Shipping weight, 75 pounds. Price.$2.72
Without summer front, deduct 50 cents.

Acme Colonial Open Fireplace Gas Log Grates.

Oxidized copper or brass finish, cast iron grate frame. Adjustable steel lining, asbestos lining. Terra cotta gas logs. Solid brass rod and openwork lower guard. Prices, delivered on the cars at the factory in Ohio.

No. 61B3252 Gas Log Grate No. 26, 30¾ inches high by 24½ inches wide, with 20-inch fire opening. Logs, 16 inches long. Shipping wt., 95 lbs. Price.$9.33
No. 61B3253 Gas Log Grate No. 26B, same as above, 30¾ inches high by 30½ inches wide, with 24-inch opening and 18-inch logs. Shipping weight, 110 pounds. Price.........$10.25

Gas Log Grate No. 26.

ART TILE FOR FIREPLACE FACINGS AND HEARTH

STANDARD SIZES, 6x1, 6x1½, 6x2, 6x3 AND 6x6 INCHES. HALF SIZES, 3x1, 3x1½, 3x2 AND 3x3 INCHES.

Satin or Matte Finish Mantel Tile. This modern soft satin finish enameling is the new, novel, attractive solid color so much favored by architects, decorators and home art designers. We furnish it in dark greens, dark olives, browns, chocolates and buffs, a splendid dark red oxblood and a beautiful dull finish ivory white. All are solid colors in matte enameled tile. Mantel tile will always be furnished 6x1½ inches unless other sizes are ordered. We can furnish them in all other standard sizes and half sizes when desired. Price in barrel lots, 30 cents per square foot.

No. 61B3217 Matte finish, set, complete, to be used in a mantel woodwork opening 36x36 inches, with a hearth 60 inches long by 18 inches deep. Shipping wt., 80 lbs. Price..........**$3.59**

No. 61B3218 Matte finish, set, complete, to be used in a mantel woodwork opening 39x42 inches, with a hearth 60 inches long by 21 inches deep. Shipping wt., 106 lbs. Price..........**$4.50**

No. 61B3219 Matte finish, set, complete, to be used in a mantel woodwork opening 42x42 inches, with a hearth 60 inches long by 24 inches deep. Shipping wt., 116 lbs. Price..........**$5.25**

Brilliant, Glazed, Iridescent Luster, Multicolored Tile in beautiful blends and mottles. These are the conventional, brilliant, glazed enameled tiles most popular for mantel facings and hearth. We furnish them in more beautiful shades of mottled tints than ever before. We furnish them in the most brilliant enamel glazes, in colors, tints and shades that neither fade nor tarnish. Mantel tile will always be furnished 6x1½ inches unless other sizes are ordered. We can always furnish them in the other standard sizes and half sizes when desired. Price in barrel lots, 22½ cents per square foot.

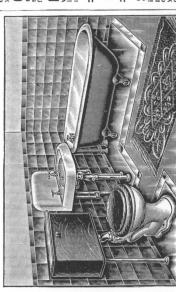

No. 61B3220 Set, complete, to be used in a mantel woodwork opening 36x36 inches long by 18 inches deep. Shipping wt., 80 lbs. Price..........**$2.70**

No. 61B3221 Set, complete, to be used in a mantel woodwork opening 39x42 inches, with a hearth 60 inches long by 21 inches deep. Shipping wt., 106 lbs. Price..........**$3.38**

No. 61B3222 Set, complete, to be used in a mantel woodwork opening 42x42 inches, with a hearth 60 inches long by 24 inches deep. Shipping wt., 116 lbs. Price..........**$3.94**

Mission Finish or Dull Brick Finish Unglazed Encaustic Mantel Tile. A wonderfully strong vitreous tile, furnished only in a dull, dark brick red or a beautiful smooth brick dull buff color. While only two colors can be furnished in this dull Mission finish mantel tile, yet the dark red is in perfect harmony with dark Mission finish woodwork, and the buff brick shade blends beautifully with all natural finish woodwork colors. This vitreous tile is more durable than building brick and far more durable than the more brilliant colored enameled tile. Mission Mantel Tile will be furnished 6x1½ and 3x1½ inches only. Price in barrel lots, 18 cents per square foot.

No. 61B3223 Set, complete, to be used in a mantel woodwork opening 36x36 inches, with a hearth 60 inches long by 18 inches deep. Shipping wt., 106 lbs. Price..........**$2.16**

No. 61B3224 Set, complete, to be used in a mantel woodwork opening 39x42 inches, with a hearth 60 inches long by 21 inches deep. Shipping wt., 106 lbs. Price..........**$2.69**

No. 61B3225 Set, complete, to be used in a mantel woodwork opening 42x42 inches, with a hearth 60 inches long by 24 inches deep. Shipping wt., 116 lbs. Price..........**$3.15**

White Enameled Sanitary Wall Tile, Cove Bases, Door Trims, Stops and Angles

House Owners, Builders, Contractors and Architects: Send us a rough sketch with accurate measurements, or your blue prints, and let us estimate on tiling the bathroom, the kitchen or any room where pure white sanitary wall treatment appeals to you.

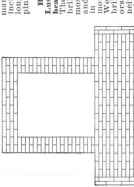

No. 61B3530 White Enameled Wall Tile. Price, per square foot..........**22½c**

While sanitary bases, caps, door trims, stops and angles are all extra, if you will send us a rough sketch with accurate measurements of the room to be tiled, we will send you our estimate free of charge, showing exactly how many square feet of tile and extra trimmings will be required, or if you prefer a plain design of beautiful white tile like we show in the illustration above, in its beautiful, clean, pure simplicity, free from ornamentation, caps or extra trimmings of any kind, you can estimate the number of square feet, sending us your order, and we will be glad to ship it at 22½ cents per square foot after submitting to you our drawings or plan illustrating exactly how we understood you desired it installed. Send for our special Tile Book, giving you thorough, complete instructions in setting wall tile.

While the illustration of the bathroom shown above must be printed in lights and shades, yet this bathroom contemplates a white tile wainscot. We guarantee to please. We guarantee the quality. We save you money.

Send us your sketch with accurate measurements and let us estimate for you.

CERAMIC MOSAIC TILE FLOORS

THE WONDERFUL INCREASE IN OUR SALES of this wonderful material enables us to reduce the price to the heretofore unheard of figure of 14 cents per square foot and upward, according to color design selected from our special Color Plate Book which we furnish on application.

FURNISH YOUR BATHROOM WITH ONE OF THESE BEAUTIFUL CERAMIC MOSAIC TILE FLOORS and your neighbors will never cease to envy you the luxury and beauty of it until they own one like it. It is sweet, clean, washable and can be kept immaculate. Splash as much as you please and the last drop can be wiped away, leaving no trace that the room has ever been used. Its wonderful beauty as the red oxblood and a beautiful dull finish and the whole results in repose but not monotony.

ORDER ONE FOR THE ENTRANCE VESTIBULE, selecting the rich, warm colors we have to offer, and reap the reward of pleasure to yourself in the admiration of your visitors.

ORDER ONE FOR THE KITCHEN, PANTRY OR BUTTERY of simple, cleanly colors and feel the pleasure and comfort of knowing how clean, sweet, pure and sanitary it can be kept with but the use of soap and water without fear of defacing, softening or affecting it in any manner.

DON'T FORGET THAT FLOOR TILES MADE FROM CLAY were in use 2,000 years before the inventors of substitutes were born, and they will be in use 2,000 years after the substitutes have rotted and decayed or have been thrown away as worthless.

14 CENTS AND UPWARD PER SQUARE FOOT

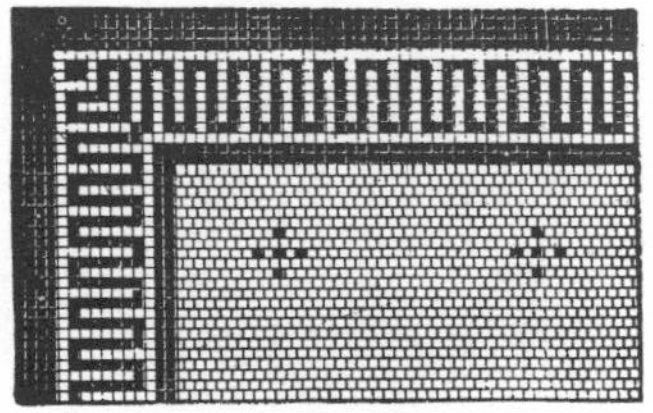

STARTLING AS IT IS, impossible as it may seem, yet we are prepared to tell you all about how you can have a ceramic mosaic tile floor in your vestibule, your bathroom or any other room. We are prepared to furnish this wonderful material in the proper form and design for laying the floor with the help of your local mason or handy workman. We tell you all about how these little ¾-inch adamantine pieces are delivered to you mounted in sheets of 2 square feet ready for placing in position in the design selected without being necessary. They are shipped to you in strips or sheets, say 1 foot wide, and when placed in position the flexible sheet holding them in position is easily removed by moistening. Each and every layer will match complete to fit your vestibule, your bathroom or any other floor whether it is odd shaped or square.

SEND FOR OUR BEAUTIFUL COLOR PLATES showing this wonderful material in beautiful color designs with borders and center pieces, most artistic, in plain white 1-inch hexagons or ¾-inch squares for bathroom floors. We tell you all about how these tiny pieces of ceramic mosaics are of hard, dense, non-porous, unglazed porcelain, burned at a heat of 3,000 degrees; how they are aseptic, sanitary and absolutely fireproof, how they will wear longer than any other flooring you could possibly put in your home vestibule, where passing is the greatest; how they are the cleanest, most wearing wall floors when laid in pure white, and they if what we have said interests you we will tell you all about how this wonderful material has heretofore been controlled by a small organization or association, causing your house contractor to send a long distance for an expert tilewright at great expense to you, whether included in the total amount of your contract or charged for separately. We tell you all about how the simple method of preparing, leveling and laying ceramic mosaic has been kept a mysterious secret by the tilewright only, to the inflated and surrounded price heretofore prevailing, your admiration and obtain from you the excessive contract prices heretofore prevailing.

14 CENTS AND UPWARD PER SQUARE FOOT.

Ask your local contractor what he has had to pay the tile setter who came from a larger city to place this mysteriously secret yet simple material in position.

DRUG STORES, ice cream parlors, banks and saloons, take notice! Why not have the cleanest, most sanitary, the easiest swept floor in the world when it can be had for only 14 cents and upward per square foot, ready for laying? Ceramic mosaic floors are supplanting wooden floors, and even marble mosaic floors, because of their non-absorbing, sweeping and sanitary qualities and the economy with which they can be laid at drug stores, banks, office buildings, schools, churches, hotels, restaurants, saloons, and meat markets, at our heretofore unheard of price of 14 cents per square foot, ready for laying, you cannot afford to use the old wooden floors.

WRITE FOR OUR COLOR BOOKLET showing our beautiful assortment of designs. Make your selection and send us your order with a rough sketch of the floor to be tiled, and we will send you perfect tile, ready to lay. Anyone having a little mason skill can lay it, and we will furnish perfectly plain, printed instructions for leveling the bed and laying the tile so that it can be done as perfectly as if you paid $10.00 per day for the most expert tilewright to come from a distance to do the work for you.

Hot Air Furnaces for Modern Heating and Ventilating—

Hot Air Furnaces Heat your House, Ventilate your House, and Keep the Warm Air Pure and in Constant Circulation.

GREATER VALUES in house heating and ventilating furnaces were never before offered by us or any other furnace manufacturer. We heat your house. We ventilate your house. We keep the warm air pure and in constant circulation. We are manufacturing the best line of hard coal, soft coal and wood furnaces that can be had anywhere, and at prices so low as to attract orders from dealers everywhere on account of the high quality, scientific construction, durability, efficiency in ventilative heating, and the low prices we make. **$25.11 AND UPWARD** according to equipment and fuel used. These money saving and "live and let live" prices are the actual cost of material and labor, with only our one conscientious margin of profit added.

WRITE FOR OUR SPECIAL CATALOG of hot air warming and ventilating furnaces with question blank or information sheet. Or, better still, send us a rough sketch of the floor plan of your house, showing points of the compass or which direction the house fronts, giving careful inside measurements of all rooms in the house, regardless of which are to be heated, showing the location of the doors, stairways, offsets, bay windows, etc. size and sketch of cellar, showing under what rooms it is located, giving location and size of chimney flue and height of cellar, and we will give you an exact estimate of cost, including all wall pipes, basement pipes, registers and everything necessary to heat the house properly to an average of 70 degrees in the coldest weather. If you are building a new house or remodeling an old house you cannot afford to be without our prices. **Get our estimate now** and order early, as it always takes two weeks to get out your order, and in the fall rush it takes from four to six weeks.

ACME TROPIC

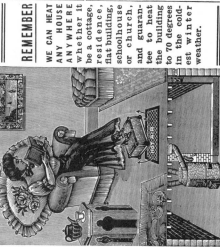

FURNACE FOR HARD (ANTHRACITE) COAL AT

$27.79 to $72.71

without casing; $34.46 to $82.84 with double galvanized casing, tee, check draft and chains; we offer this popular Acme Tropic Hot Air Furnace for hard (anthracite) coal as the most desirable coal burning furnace made. The Acme Tropic is a circular radiator furnace, being equipped with a heavy steel plate dome and radiator, giving the greatest amount of utilized radiating surface above the fire pot and insuring the most economical consumption of fuel.

ACME TROPIC FURNACE FOR HARD (ANTHRACITE) COAL.

Furnace No.	Catalog No.	Diameter Fire Pot, Inches	Diameter Casing, Inches	Heating Capacity, Cubic Feet	Price, Without Casing	Price, with Casing, as Shown
134	61B3209	20	34	6,000 to 9,000	$27.79	$34.46
136	61B3210	22	36	9,000 to 12,500	33.97	41.30
140	61B3211	24	40	12,500 to 16,000	40.13	47.48
144	61B3212	26	44	16,000 to 20,000	48.49	56.40
148	61B3213	28	48	20,000 to 25,000	60.60	69.40
158	61B3214	30	48	25,000 to 30,000	72.71	82.84

$54⁴¹ EQUIPPED THIS HOME WITH A FURNACE

HOT AIR PIPES AND REGISTERS COMPLETE,

AND IS HEATING IT TO AN AVERAGE OF 70 DEGREES IN THE COLDEST ZERO WEATHER.

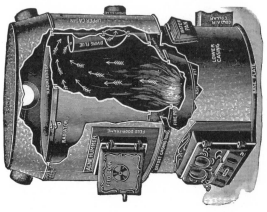

QUALITY GUARANTEED

REMEMBER

WE CAN HEAT ANY HOUSE ANYWHERE whether it be a cottage, residence, flat building, schoolhouse or church, and guarantee to heat the building to 70 degrees in the coldest winter weather.

ACME HUMMER

BITUMINOUS SOFT COAL OR WOOD FURNACE AT

$25.11 to $68.13

without casing; $31.91 to $78.46 with double galvanized iron casing, tee, check draft and chains, cement and bolts; we offer this Acme Hummer Heating and Ventilating Hot Air Furnace with broad top fire pot for soft coal and wood. The fire pot is so broad that long sticks of wood can be put in when you desire to burn this fuel. The Acme Hummer is a dome furnace and has the largest and heaviest wrought steel combustion dome of any furnace on the market, making it a perfect soft coal burning and a thoroughly durable, quick and powerful heater.

ACME HUMMER FURNACE FOR SOFT COAL AND WOOD.

Catalog No.	Furnace No.	Diameter Upper Casing, In.	Diameter Base Plate Inches	Diameter Fire Pot, Inches	Heating Capacity, Cubic Feet	Price, Without Casing	Price, with Casing, as Shown
61B3201	134	34	30	20	6,000 to 9,000	$25.11	$31.91
61B3202	136	36	32	22	9,000 to 12,500	31.40	38.87
61B3203	140	40	40	24	12,500 to 16,000	37.48	44.95
61B3204	144	44	40	26	16,000 to 20,000	45.86	53.86
61B3205	148	48	44	28	20,000 to 25,000	56.00	64.80
61B3206	158	58	48	30	25,000 to 30,000	68.13	78.46

SEARS, ROEBUCK AND CO., CHICAGO, ILLINOIS.

BATH TUBS

We control the making of these goods and guarantee the material and construction throughout. We do not sell B grade or chipped enamel tubs, remember this when comparing prices.

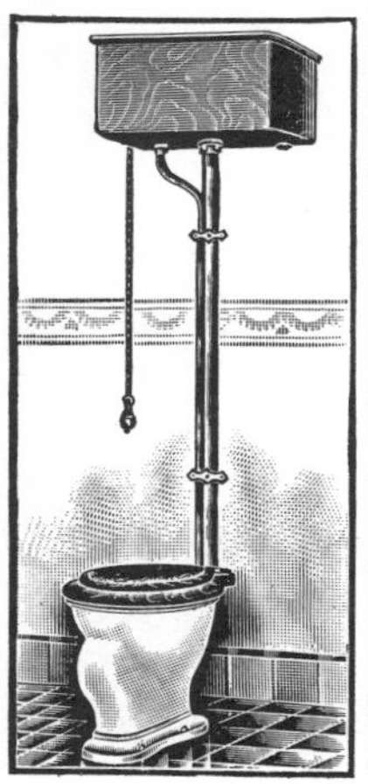

PEERLESS WASH OUT WATER CLOSET, WITH LOOSE BOARD TANK - $11.28

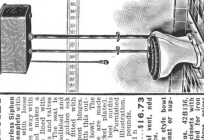

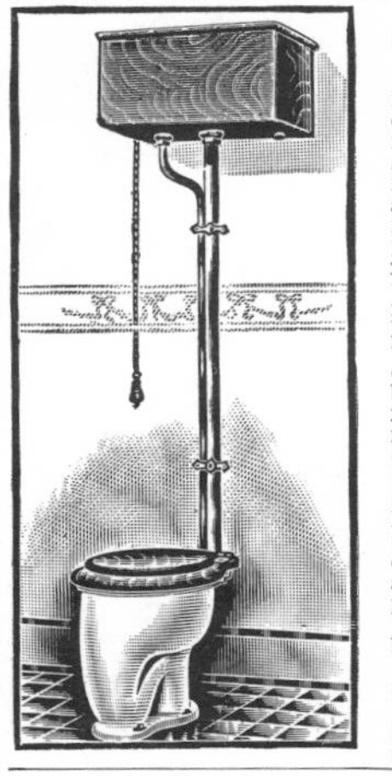

The equal of closets that plumbers sell at $16.00 to $20.00.
No. 42B130 Our Peerless Water Closet is by far the best finished and most up to date closet on the market. It has a round cornered oak 5½-gallon siphon tank. Golden oak finish, with double oak attached seat, 1¼-inch nickel plated supply pipe, with No. 3 front washout; plain earthenware bowl and all fixtures are nickel plated. Tank is copper lined, has patent float cutoff, with chain and pull to flush closet, and with loose board back, brackets and nails as much neater job. It is made of the very best materials throughout and the workmanship and finish are perfect. Furnished complete, ready for use, no fitting or extras required. This closet roughs in at 10 inches from wall. Shipping weight, about 90 pounds.
Price, with plain bowl $11.28
If wanted with vent, add 25 cents to above price.
We can furnish this style bowl only, without tank or seat, for $3.30.

$16.73 PEERLESS SIPHON JET CLOSET

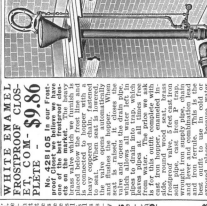

No. 42B141 Peerless Siphon Jet Closet furnished complete with 8-gallon high tank with loose board back which does away with unsightly brackets and makes a very neat job. It is lined with copper, and all fittings and valves are made of brass. The seat is made of oak highly polished and the tank and seat are golden oak finish and is fitted with nickel plated brass post hinges. The bowl furnished with this outfit is a siphon jet bowl. The flush and supply pipe are made of brass heavily nickel plated. This is one of the best outfits that money can buy. Furnished complete as shown in illustration. Shipping weight, 100 pounds.
Price, with plain bowl $16.73
If wanted with local vent, add 25 cents to above price.
We can furnish this style bowl only, without tank, seat or supply pipes, for $7.65.

We can furnish Nos. 42B136, 42B130 and 42B141 closets with all connections threaded for iron pipe at 25 cents extra over prices quoted.

Remember, when comparing prices, that we handle only absolutely new A grade guaranteed plumbing goods. Every article on these pages is guaranteed as such and this is the basis on which you purchase the same.

WHITE ENAMELED IRON HOPPER $4.25 CLOSET

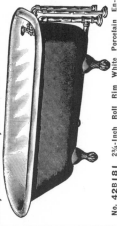

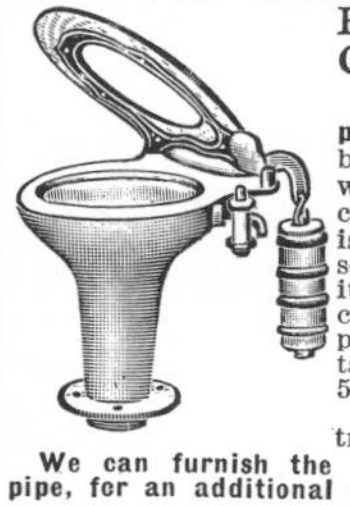

No. 42B100 This is our latest Improved Hopper Closet, complete with brass valve, heavy round seat and iron weight. This closet is intended to be connected to water supply. When seat is lowered, it opens valve and when seat rises, which it does automatically, it shuts off the valve and water. It can be connected with ¾ or 1-inch lead pipe. No waste or supply pipes or tank furnished with this outfit. Weight, 50 pounds.
Price, complete, as shown in illustration $4.25
We can furnish the above closet, tapped for ½-inch pipe, for an additional charge of 50 cents over price quoted.

ENAMELED STEEL BATH TUB - - - $5.48

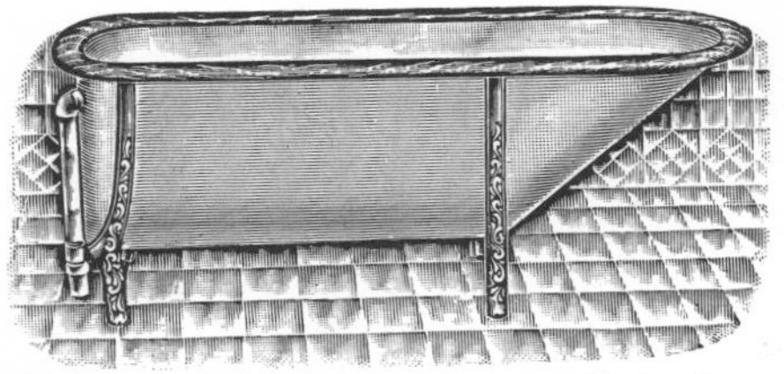

No. 42B114 ROLL RIM WHITE PORCELAIN ENAMELED BATH TUB, COMPLETE, A GRADE $15.81

In our Enameled Steel Bath Tub we are able to offer our customers the best tub of this kind made today, and a tub that is just the thing for those in moderate circumstances who desire the comforts of a bathroom. This tub is made of heavy galvanized sheet steel, is enameled on the inside with white enamel and nicely painted on the outside and tinted in bronze. The top of the tub is capped with a 3-inch wood rim which is nicely finished and varnished, and is furnished with a brass nickel plated waste and overflow. These tubs are fitted for No. 4½ Fuller Bath cocks, but these are not furnished at above prices. Weight direct from factory in Detroit, Michigan, about 90 pounds.

No. 42B160	Size, 4 feet 6 inches. Price........	$5.48
No. 42B161	Size, 5 feet. Price........	5.98
No. 42B163	Size, 5 feet 6 inches. Price........	6.23
No. 42B163	Size, 6 feet. Price........	6.98

The tail pieces on above tubs are threaded for iron pipe connections.
NOTICE—Do not pour boiling water in these tubs. Always run cold water into the tub first, then the hot water.
NOTICE—We can furnish a No. 4½ Fuller Bath Cock to fit above tubs with iron pipe connections for $1.80.

No. 42B181 2¾-Inch Roll Rim White Porcelain Enameled Bath Tub, complete with No. 4½ Fuller Combination Cock. Connected waste and overflow, nickel plated plug and chain; ½-inch nickel plated supply pipes. These are the best tubs on the market. Everything about them is new and up to date. We guarantee the enameling not to crack or peel off, as first class work as is possible to get in any tub, and buy, but Manufactured by our own factory and guaranteed to be perfect in every respect. Enameled inside, painted one coat outside. Price includes everything complete, ready for use. Height on legs, 23 inches; width over all, 30 inches; depth inside, 17 inches. Shipped from our factory in Southeastern Wisconsin. Roughs in: Supplies, center to center, 7 inches; center of supplies to center of waste, 3½ inches.

Size of tub..	4 feet	4½ feet	5 feet	5½ feet	6 feet
Wt. about..	.225 lbs	250	300 lbs.	330	400 lbs.
Price	$15.81	$16.40	$17.58	$19.34	$22.87

Can furnish above tub with compression bath cocks if desired at the same price, or can furnish the above tub with all connections threaded for iron pipe at an additional cost of 50 cents to above prices.

ROLL RIM PORCELAIN ENAMELED IRON BATH TUB, A GRADE - $11.76

No. 42B177 Best Grade Porcelain Enameled Bath Tub, extra heavy weight enameling, put on by a patent process, which we guarantee not to flake or peel off. We furnish the tub with 2¾-inch wide enameled roll rim. There is no article on the market where more real good values are disposed of than in these tubs. We guarantee all these tubs to be strictly A grade goods; remember this when comparing prices. Enameled inside, painted one coat outside. Height on legs, 23 inches; width over all, 30 inches; depth inside, 17 inches. Shipped from our factory in Southeastern Wisconsin. Prices quoted are for tubs only, without any fittings.

Size of tub..	4 feet	4½ feet	5 feet	5½ feet	6 feet
Wt. about..	.225 lbs	255	300 lbs.	335	400 lbs.
Price	$11.76	$12.34	$13.52	$15.29	$18.82

Our special Plumbing Goods Catalog shows a complete line of Nickeloid and Copper Lined Bath Tubs.

We can furnish a common overflow and waste plug for above bath tub for 80 cents.

WHITE ENAMEL FROSTPROOF CLOSET, COMPLETE - $9.86

No. 42B105 In our Frostproof Closet we believe we have one of the best frostproof closets on the market. The heavy brass valve which we furnish is placed below the frost line and is connected to hopper with a heavy coppered chain, fastened to seat. When seat is lowered, the valve opens automatically and flushes the hopper. When seat is raised, it closes the valve and opens the drain pipe, which allows all water left in the pipes to drain into trap, which leaves pipes at all times free from water. The price we ask for this outfit completed with cast iron hopper, enameled inside, round wood seat, brass frostproof valve, 5 feet cast iron wrought iron supply pipe, chain and lever and combination lead and iron ferrule. This is the best outfit to use in cold or frosty places, because no water is always below frost line. No closet tank is furnished or needed with this outfit. Weight, 110 lbs. Price, complete $9.86

Peerless Combination Hopper and Trap Closet, with Loose Board Tank $11.98

No. 42B136 Combination Hopper and Trap or Wash Down Closet. This makes one of the best, low priced outfits we carry. The tank is a 4½-gallon tank, made of oak, golden oak finish. The pipe and fittings are the same as described in our No. 42B130 closet. Everything is first class. Could not work better nor last longer at any price. A great many prefer this combination hopper to the regular No. 3 front washout, as shown. The hopper is fitted with a much neater and better job than tanks furnished with brackets. This closet roughs in 9 inches from wall. Shipping weight 95 pounds.
Price, complete ready ..$11.98
If wanted with local vent, add 25 cents to above price.
We can furnish this style bowl only, without tank, seat or supply pipes, for $4.07.

LOW DOWN OUTFIT $15.40 WITH CHINA TANK

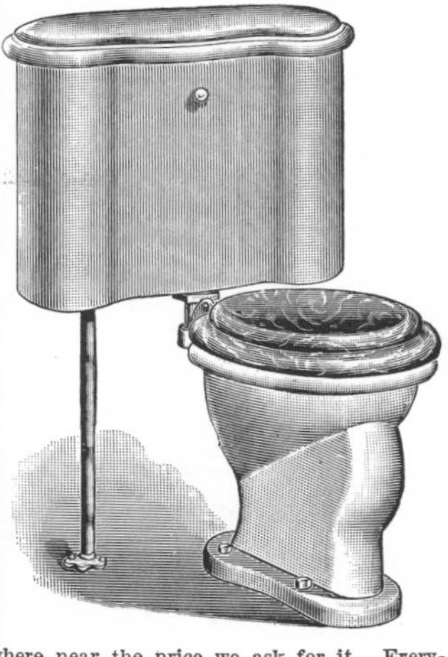

No. 42B112
One of the most up to date closets both in appearance and efficiency. The tank is made of heavy earthenware, highly polished and glazed. It is fitted with the latest improved Douglas Ball Valve. All fittings are made of heavy brass and copper. The tank is furnished with china push button in front of tank, a slight push on which releases the valve and causes a positive flush of the bowl. The seat is golden oak with heavy brass nickel plated post hinges, complete with cover. The bowl is a siphon action wash down closet bowl, made of the highest grade vitreous earthenware. This closet cannot be duplicated at anywhere near the price we ask for it. Everything first class in every respect. This closet roughs in at 12 inches. Shipping wt., about 120 lbs. Price........$15.40
No. 42B114 Same as above, except furnished with Siphon Jet Bowl. Price........$17.75

LOW TANK COMBINATION CLOSET, WITH SIPHON JET BOWL $15.25

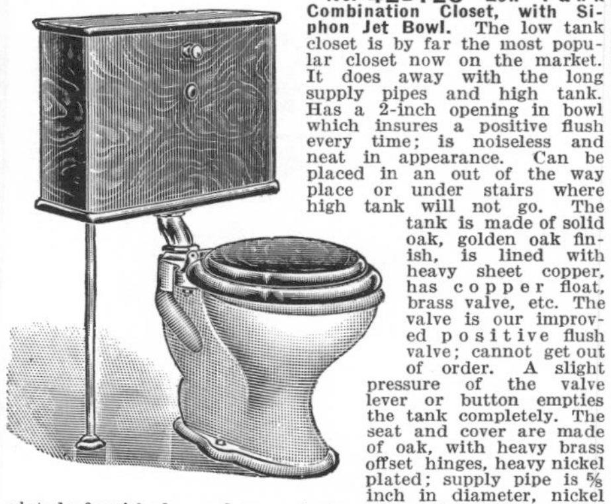

No. 42B120 Low Tank Combination Closet, with Siphon Jet Bowl. The low tank closet is by far the most popular closet now on the market. It does away with the long supply pipes and high tank. Has a 2-inch opening in bowl which insures a positive flush every time; is noiseless and neat in appearance. Can be placed in an out of the way place or under stairs where high tank is made of solid oak, golden oak finish, is lined with heavy sheet copper, has copper float, brass valve, etc. The valve is a full improved, positive flush valve; cannot get out of order. A slight pressure of the valve lever or button empties the tank completely. The seat and cover are made of oak, with heavy nickel plated supply pipe is % inch in diameter, and is connected to heavy brass frostproof valve, cast iron % trap.
Price, complete, with plain earthenware bowl........$15.25
No. 42B125 Quarter Sawed Oak Outfit, same as above, except the tank and seat are made of quarter sawed oak with plano polish. Price........$16.10

CONNECTED BATH WASTE $1.35 AND OVERFLOW

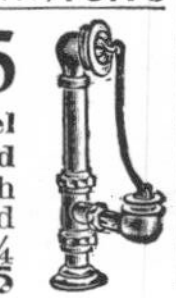

No. 42B1002 Extra Heavy Nickel Plated Brass Connected Bath Waste and Overflow, with elbow top, complete, with fittings. Size, 1% inches. To be used with bath tubs shown above. Weight, 3¼ pounds. Price........$1.35

PORCELAIN WHITE ENAMEL IRONWARE

In buying Enameled Sinks, Lavatories, Tubs, Etc., from us remember that you get first quality goods, no seconds, and any piece found imperfect in any way can be returned to us at our expense. Our low prices may lead you to believe there is something wrong in the quality. All we ask is a trial order. There is no better ware made—quality, style and finish considered—than the following line of enameled ware. It is made in one of the most modern and complete foundry and enameling plants. Only skilled workmen employed who have had years of experience in enameling. Our prices are low because they are based on actual factory cost, with just our one small profit added.

All the following Enameled Cast Lavatories, unless otherwise ordered. This bracket always insures a rigid, firm lavatory, as this board can be nailed on to studding when less otherwise ordered. This bracket can be screwed on to the board. It is not always possible to strike a studding when bracket is screwed to the wall.

WHITE PORCELAIN ONE-PIECE LAVATORY, A GRADE — $4.32

No. 42B286 Porcelain One-Piece Half Circle Lavatory, with patent brackets, sanitary soap dish, brass soap dish, sanitary soap dish, waste plug and coupling, nickel plated chain stay, nickel plated rubber stopper, patent overflow, 10x13 inches; height of back, 8 inches; size of slab, 20 inches; patent brackets. Shipped from our factory in Southeastern Wisconsin.
Enameled inside, bronzed outside. Price............$4.32
NOTICE—The above prices do not include faucets, traps or supply pipes, etc.
No. 42B281 Same as above, except furnished complete as shown in illustration, with two nickel plated compression basin cocks with cross handles and 1¼-inch nickel plated S trap with waste to floor and vent to wall, two nickel plated supply pipes with flanges. Everything complete, as shown in illustration. Price.....$7.98
Enameled inside, bronzed outside. Price...........$8.40
Shipping weight, about 69 pounds. Shipped from our factory in Southeastern Wisconsin.
Enameled inside, bronzed outside. Price........$9.60
We can furnish the above with connections threaded for iron pipe at an extra cost of 75 cents from prices quoted.

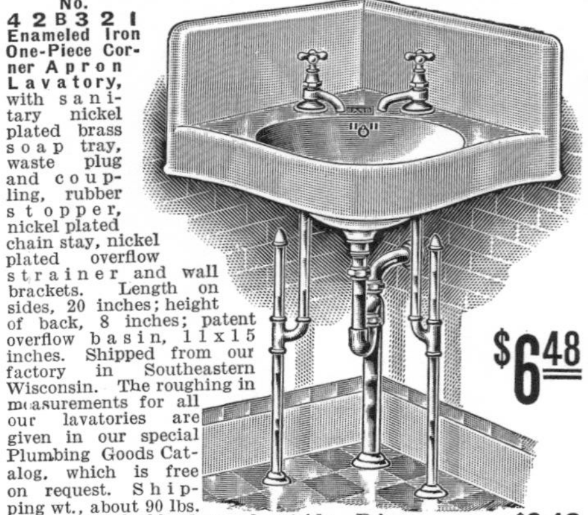

WHITE ENAMELED ONE-PIECE CORNER APRON — $6.48

No. 42B326 Same as above, except furnished complete with two low down compression basin cocks, one 1¼-inch nickel plated S trap with waste to floor and vent to wall, two nickel plated brass straight supply pipes to floor, everything complete as shown in illustration. Price....................$12.22
Enameled inside, bronzed outside. Price..........$12.42
We can furnish these lavatories with all connections threaded for iron pipe at an extra cost of 75 cents over prices quoted. If above lavatory is wanted without revent on trap, deduct 15 cents from prices quoted.

ENAMELED IRON ONE-PIECE CORNER LAVATORY, A GRADE — $4.14

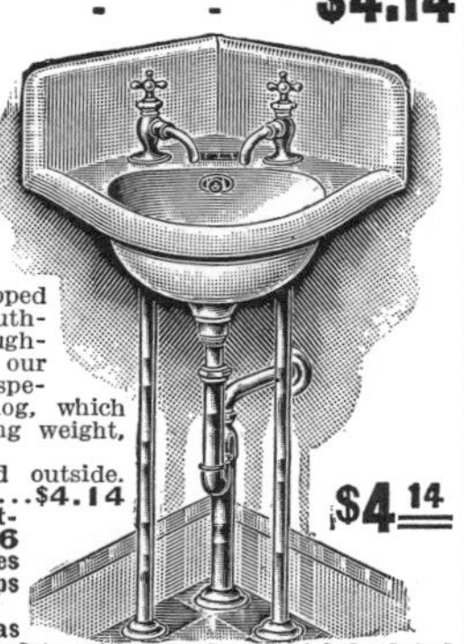

No. 42B311 Enameled Iron One-Piece Corner Lavatory, with sanitary nickel plated brass soap dish, waste plug and coupling, rubber stopper, chain stay, nickel plated chain stay and strainer and wall brackets. Length, 11x15 inches; back 6 inches high. Size of patent overflow bowl, 10x13 inches. Shipped from our factory in Southeastern Wisconsin. The roughing in measurements for all our lavatories are given in our special Plumbing Goods Catalog, which is free on request. Shipping weight, about 60 pounds.
Enameled inside, bronzed outside. Price.............$4.14
NOTICE—The above prices do not include faucets, traps or supply pipes.
No. 42B316 Same as above, furnished complete with two brass nickel plated compression basin cocks, 1¼-inch nickel plated trap with waste to floor and vent to wall, two brass nickel plated supply pipes to floor with flanges. Everything complete, as shown in illustration. Price............$9.90
Enameled inside, bronzed outside. Price............$10.30
We can furnish the above with connections threaded for iron pipe at an extra cost of 75 cents above prices quoted.

ENAMELED ONE-PIECE APRON LAVATORY, WITH MODEL WASTE, A GRADE — $9.96

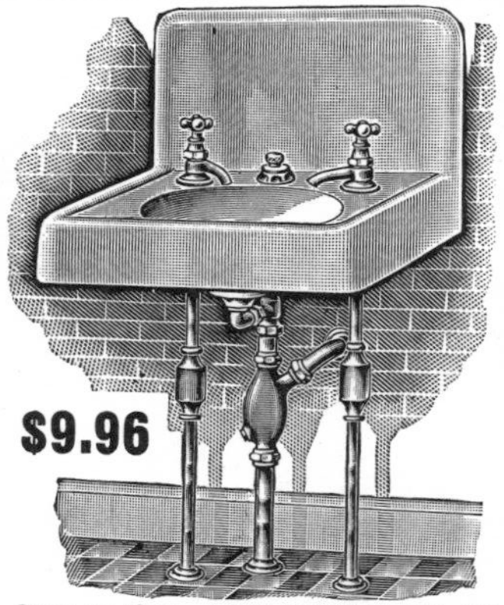

No. 42B375 Enameled One-Piece Apron Lavatory, with nickel plated model waste and wall brackets. Size of slab, 18x24 inches; height of back, 12 inches; size of bowl, 11x15 inches. Shipped from our factory in Southeastern Wisconsin. Shipping weight, about 140 lbs.
Enameled inside, bronzed outside. Price $9.96
Enameled outside, inside and outside. Price......$10.46
NOTICE—The above prices do not include faucets or supply pipes.

ENAMELED ONE-PIECE APRON LAVATORY, A GRADE — $7.38

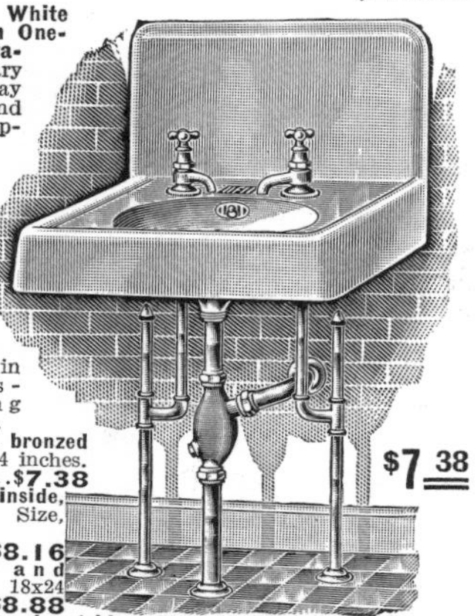

No. 42B370 White Enameled Iron One-Piece Apron Lavatory, with sanitary nickel plated soap tray with waste plug and coupling, rubber stopper, nickel plated overflow strainer and wall brackets. Made in two sizes. 18x24 inches, and 20x24 inches, with 12-inch back; size of patent overflow bowl 11x15 inches and 12x16 inches. Shipped from our factory in Southeastern Wisconsin. Shipping wt., about 140 lbs.
Enameled inside, bronzed outside. Size, 18x24 inches. 20x24 inches.
Enameled inside, bronzed outside. Size.
Price.............................$8.16
Price...........................$8.88
Enameled inside and outside. Size, 18x24 inches.............$8.88
Enameled inside and outside. Size, 20x24 inches...........$9.38

No. 42B380 Same as above, except furnished with two low down compression basin cocks with cross handles and china tops, one nickel plated bottle trap, with waste to floor and vent to wall, two straight air chamber supply pipes to floor. Everything complete as shown in illustration. The roughing in measurements for all our lavatories are given in our special Plumbing Goods Catalog, which is free on request.
Enameled inside, bronzed outside, 18x24 in. Price....$16.32
Enameled inside, bronzed outside, 20x24 in. Price....$16.32
Enameled inside and outside, 18x24 inches. Price....$17.34
Enameled inside and outside, 20x24 inches. Price....$17.84
We can furnish the above with connections threaded for iron pipe at an extra cost of 75 cents above prices quoted.

ONE-PIECE SQUARE WHITE PORCELAIN LAVATORY, A GRADE — $5.64

No. 42B291 Enameled One-Piece Square Lavatory, with sanitary nickel plated brass patent overflow and waste plug and coupling, rubber stopper, chain stay, nickel plated brass patent overflow bowl 11x15 and 12x16 inches. Shipped from our factory in Southeastern Wisconsin. The roughing in measurements for all our lavatories are given in our special Plumbing Goods Catalog, which is free on request. Shipping weight, about 110 pounds.
Enameled inside, bronzed outside. Price...$5.64
Enameled inside, bronzed outside. Price...$6.74
Enameled inside and outside. Price...$6.74
No. 42B296 Same as above, except furnished complete with two low down compression cocks with china tops, one 1¼-inch nickel plated S trap with waste to floor and two straight supply pipes to floor with flanges. Everything complete, as shown in illustration.
Enameled inside, bronzed outside, 18x24 in. Price.$9.72
Enameled inside and outside, 20x24 in. Price.$10.52
Enameled inside and outside, 18x24 inches. Price.$5.74
Enameled inside and outside, 20x24 inches. Price.$6.00
NOTICE—The above prices do not include faucets, traps or supply pipes, etc.

HALF-CIRCLE WHITE ENAMELED IRON APRON LAVATORY, A GRADE — $5.46

No. 42B345 Enameled Iron Lavatory, with sanitary soap tray, waste plug and coupling, rubber stopper, chain stay and nickel plated brass overflow and brackets. Size, 18x21 inches with 8-inch lavatory is 18x21 inches with 8-inch back, is furnished with patent overflow basin 10x14 inches, and is made with china stay and one basin which it is thoroughly sanitary. It is made of the highest grade of gray cast iron, and is enameled by a process which we will guarantee not to shake or peel off. The roughing in measurements in illustration, as shown in illustration.
Enameled inside, bronzed outside. Price..........$5.46
Enameled inside and outside. Price...........$6.66
NOTICE—The above prices do not include faucets, traps or supply pipes.
No. 42B350 Same as above, except furnished complete with two low down compression cocks with china tops, one 1¼-inch nickel plated S trap with waste to floor and vent to wall, two nickel plated brass straight supply pipes to floor, everything complete as shown in illustration.
Enameled inside, bronzed outside. Price........$9.59
Enameled inside and outside. Price.............$10.94
We can furnish the above with connections threaded for iron pipe at an extra cost of 75 cents over prices quoted.

WHITE ENAMELED ONE-PIECE CORNER LAVATORY, A GRADE — $4.50

No. 42B317 Enameled One-Piece Corner Lavatory, with sanitary soap tray, nickel plated waste plug and coupling, china stay, nickel plated overflow strainer and wall brackets. Length of sides is 19½ inches; height of back, 10x14 inches. Shipped from our factory in Southeastern Wisconsin. Shipping weight, about 90 pounds.
Enameled inside, bronzed outside. Price..........$4.50
Enameled inside, bronzed outside, 8-inch back. Price..........$4.80
Enameled inside and outside, 6-inch back. Price..........$5.74
Enameled inside and outside, 8-inch back. Price..........$6.00
NOTICE—The above prices do not include faucets, traps or supply pipes.
No. 42B318 Same as above, except furnished complete with nickel plated S trap with waste to floor and vent to wall. Nickel plated nickel plated supply pipes with floor and two low down compression nickel plated cocks, one 1¼-inch nickel plated S trap with waste to floor, which is free on request. The roughing in measurements for all our lavatories are given in our special Plumbing Goods Catalog, which is free on request.
Enameled inside, bronzed outside, 6-in. back. Price.$8.58
Enameled inside, bronzed outside, 8-in. back. Price.$8.94
Enameled inside and outside, 6-inch back. Price.$9.78
Enameled inside and outside, 8-inch back. Price.$10.14
We can furnish the above with connections threaded for iron pipe at an extra cost of 75 cents above prices quoted.

PORCELAIN ENAMELED IRON ROLL RIM KITCHEN SINKS, A GRADE.

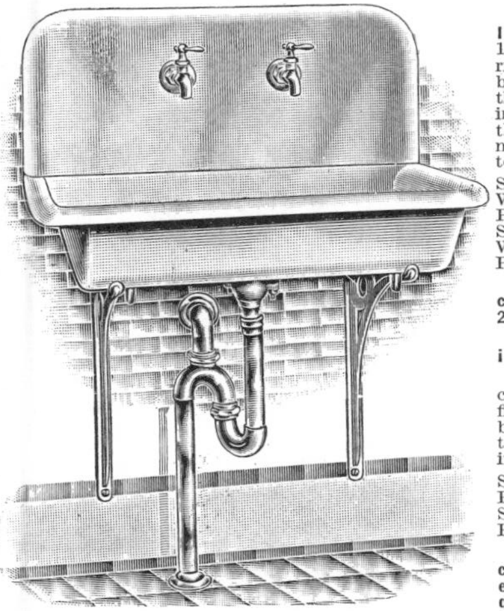

No. 42B495 Porcelain Enameled Iron Roll Rim Kitchen Sinks, with 12-inch high back, and 2¼-inch roll rim, nickel plated brass strainer and bronzed brackets. We can furnish these sinks in five sizes, but the 20x30-inch is the one most generally used and the size which we recommend for ordinary purposes. Shipped from our factory in Southeastern Wisconsin.

Size, inches	18x24	18x30	20x30
Weight, lbs.	110	140	150
Price	$5.16	$6.08	$6.36

Size, inches	20x36	20x40
Weight, lbs.	170	200
Price	$7.56	$8.16

We can furnish the above with all connections threaded for iron pipe at 25 cents above prices quoted.

NOTICE—The above prices do not include faucets or trap.

No. 42B505 Same as above, except furnished with two nickel plated flanged faucets, nickel plated 1½-inch brass trap with vent to wall and waste to floor, everything complete, as shown in illustration.

Size, inches	18x24	18x30	20x30
Price	$8.70	$9.60	$9.90

Size, inches	20x36	20x40
Price	$11.10	$11.70

We can furnish these sinks with all connections threaded for iron pipe at an extra cost of 75 cents over prices quoted.

PORCELAIN ENAMELED IRON ROLL RIM CORNER KITCHEN SINKS, A GRADE.

$7.20

No. 42B516 Porcelain Enameled Roll Rim Corner Kitchen Sinks, with 12-inch high back with 2¼-inch deep roll rim. Bronzed bracket. Furnished with either right or left hand end piece. Illustration shows left hand. We can furnish these sinks in five sizes, but the 20x30-inch is the one most generally used and the size which we recommend for ordinary purposes. Shipped from our factory in Southeastern Wisconsin. **Be sure to state whether right or left hand end piece is wanted.**

Size	Weight	Price
18x30 inches	150 pounds	$7.20
18x36 inches	170 pounds	8.34
20x30 inches	180 pounds	7.80
20x36 inches	180 pounds	8.64
20x40 inches	190 pounds	9.42

We can furnish the above with connections threaded for iron pipe at 25 cents above prices quoted.

NOTICE—The above prices do not include faucets or trap.

No. 42B526 Same as above, except it is furnished complete with two nickel plated Fuller flanged bibbs and one 1½-inch nickel plated trap with waste to floor and vent to wall. Everything complete, as shown in illustration.

Size	Price
18x30 inches	$10.74
18x36 inches	11.88
20x40 inches	11.34
20x36 inches	12.18
20x40 inches	12.96

If above sink is wanted without revent on trap, deduct 15 cents from prices quoted. We can furnish these sinks with all connections threaded for iron pipe at an extra cost of 75 cents over prices quoted.

EXTRA HEAVY CAST IRON SINKS.

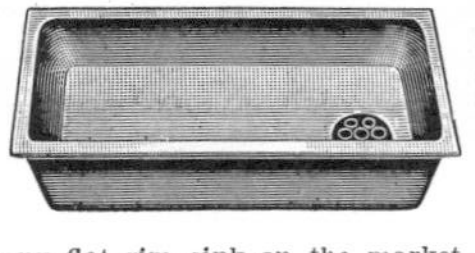

No. 42B385 Extra Heavy Cast Iron Sinks. Made of high grade gray iron, painted or white enameled inside. Do not compare these sinks with some of the light enameled sinks now on the market. These are made in our own factory, and we guarantee them the equal of any flat rim sink on the market. We can furnish these sinks in six sizes, but the 18x30-inch is the one most generally used and the size which we recommend for ordinary purposes. Fitted for 1¼-inch lead pipe.

Size, inches	Weight, pounds	Painted	White Enameled Inside, Painted Outside
16x24x6	35	$0.87	$2.04
18x30x6	40	1.20	2.16
18x36x6	50	1.44	2.94
20x30x6	50	1.45	2.52
20x36x6	60	1.79	3.30
20x40x6	70	1.92	3.90

We can furnish these sinks with all connections threaded for iron pipe at an extra cost of 25 cents over prices quoted.

SEAMLESS WROUGHT STEEL SINK WITH FLAT RIMS.

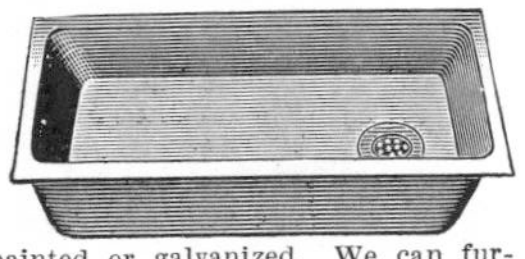

Wrought Steel Kitchen Sinks. These sinks are made from one plate of steel and are superior to cast iron sinks in every particular, being lighter, stronger and more durable; are fitted for 1¼-inch lead or 1½-inch iron pipe. Please state which is wanted. Come painted or galvanized. We can furnish these sinks in six sizes, but the 18x30 is the one most generally used and the size which we recommend for ordinary purposes.

No. 42B390 Painted inside and outside.

Size, in.	Wt., lbs.	Price	Size, in.	Wt., lbs.	Price
16x24x6	7	$1.32	20x30x6	13	$1.85
18x30x6	12½	1.62	20x36x6	15½	2.22
18x36x6	13½	1.98	20x40x6	19	2.55

No. 42B391 Galvanized inside and outside.

Size, in.	Wt., lbs.	Price	Size, in.	Wt., lbs.	Price
16x24x6	9	$1.62	20x30x6	15	$2.20
18x30x6	14½	1.97	20x36x6	18	2.58
18x36x6	15½	2.32	20x40x6	20	2.90

ROLL RIM ONE-PIECE ENAMELED SINKS, A GRADE.

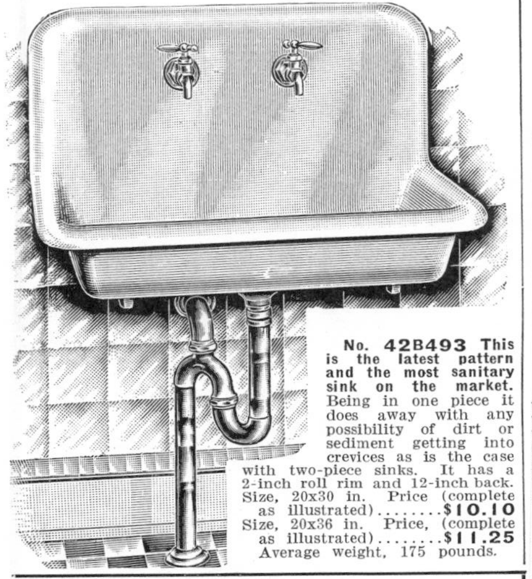

No. 42B493 This is the latest pattern and the most sanitary sink on the market. Being in one piece it does away with any possibility of dirt or sediment getting into crevices as is the case with two-piece sinks. It has a 2-inch roll rim and 12-inch back.

Size, 20x30 in. Price (complete as illustrated)........$10.10

Size, 20x36 in. Price, (complete as illustrated)........$11.25

Average weight, 175 pounds.

PORCELAIN ENAMELED IRON ROLL RIM KITCHEN SINK, A GRADE.

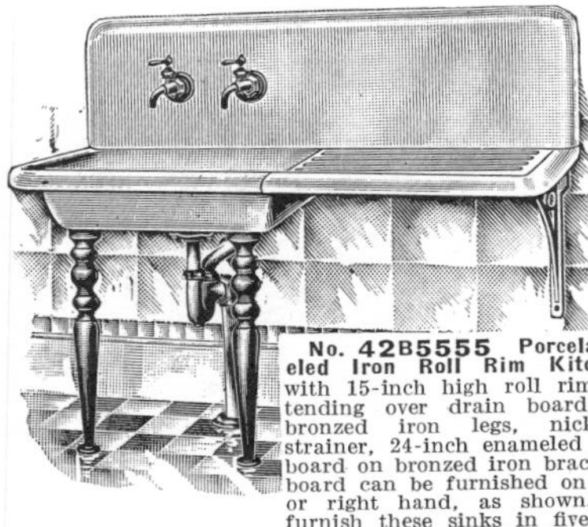

No. 42B5555 Porcelain Enameled Iron Roll Rim Kitchen Sink, with 15-inch high roll rim back extending over drain board, has two bronzed iron legs, nickel plated strainer, 24-inch enameled iron drain board on bronzed iron bracket. Drain board can be furnished on either left or right hand, as shown. We can furnish these sinks in five sizes, but the 20x30-inch is the one most generally used and the size which we recommend for ordinary purposes. Shipped from our factory in Southeastern Wisconsin. **Be sure to state whether right or left hand drain board is wanted.**

Size, inches	18x30	18x36	20x30	20x36	20x40
Price	$12.60	$14.40	$13.86	$15.06	$15.96

We can furnish the above with all connections threaded for iron pipe at 25 cents above prices quoted.

NOTICE—The above prices do not include faucets or trap.

No. 42B5655 Same as above, except furnished with two nickel plated Fuller flanged faucets and one 1½-inch nickel plated trap with waste to floor and vent to wall. Everything complete as shown in illustration. **Be sure to state whether right or left hand drain board is wanted.**

Size, inches	18x30	18x36	20x30	20x36	20x40
Weight, lbs.	200	230	220	250	300
Price	$16.14	$17.94	$17.40	$18.60	$19.50

We can furnish these sinks with all connections threaded for iron pipe at an extra cost of 75 cents over prices quoted.

If above sink is wanted without revent on trap, deduct 15 cents from price quoted.

If wanted with ash drain board in place of enameled iron deduct $1.00 from above prices.

KITCHEN SINK OUTFITS SHOULD BE IN EVERY HOME.

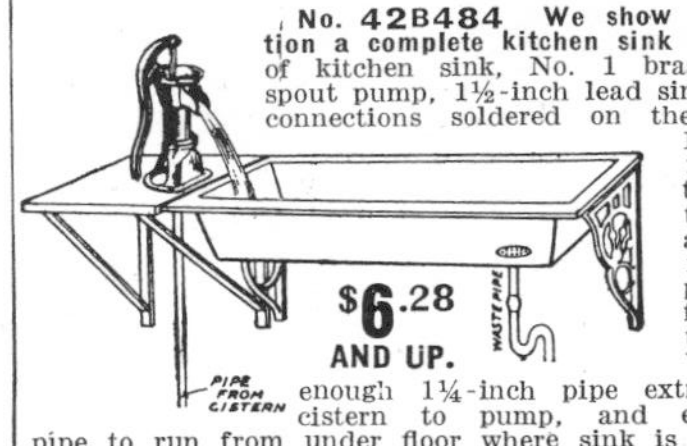

$6.28 AND UP.

No. 42B484 We show in this illustration a complete kitchen sink outfit, consisting of kitchen sink, No. 1 brass lined pitcher spout pump, 1½-inch lead sink trap with iron connections soldered on the same; enough 1½-inch galvanized iron pipe to run from sink through floor, and enough 1¼-inch galvanized pipe to reach from pump through floor. You must order enough 1¼-inch pipe extra to run from cistern to pump, and enough 1½-inch pipe to run from under floor where sink is placed to where you want the waste water to run. All connections are for iron pipe and anybody can set it up. For prices on iron pipe see page 1114.

Size, 18x30 in. Weight, 68 lbs. **Enameled Sink, complete,** with brass lined pump, trap and pipe to floor. Price..**$6.28**

Size, 18x36 in. Weight, 81 lbs. **Enameled Sink, complete,** with brass lined pump, trap and pipe to floor. Price..**$7.12**

Size, 20x30 in. Weight, 75 lbs. **Enameled Sink, complete,** with brass lined pump, trap and pipe to floor. Price..**$6.81**

Size, 20x36 in. Weight, 90 lbs. **Enameled Sink, complete,** with brass lined pump, trap and pipe to floor. Price..**$7.59**

Size, 20x40 in. Weight, 98 lbs. **Enameled Sink, complete,** with brass lined pump, trap and pipe to floor. Price..**$8.19**

SEAMLESS WROUGHT STEEL SINK WITH ROLL RIM.

Seamless Wrought Steel Sinks with turned edges. This sink is adapted for exposed or open plumbing and has improved brass strainer couplings. They are made of one piece of steel, and are finely finished and one of the strongest sinks made. Cannot crack or rust out. We can furnish these sinks in six sizes, but the 20x30 is the one most generally used and the size which we recommend for ordinary purposes. Fitted for 1¼-inch lead pipe or 1½-inch iron pipe. Furnished in two finishes and sizes as follows:

No. 42B392 Painted inside and outside.

Size, in.	Wt., lbs.	Price	Size, in.	Wt., lbs.	Price
16x24x6	8	$1.38	20x30x6	13	$1.89
18x30x6	13	1.61	20x36x6	15½	2.16
18x36x6	15	1.98	20x40x6	19	2.58

No. 42B393 Galvanized inside and outside.

Size, in.	Wt., lbs.	Price	Size, in.	Wt., lbs.	Price
16x24x6	9	$1.60	20x30x6	15	$2.22
18x30x6	14	1.98	20x36x6	17½	2.59
18x36x6	16	2.35	20x40x6	19	2.95

No. 42B394 White enameled inside, blue enameled outside. One of the prettiest and most serviceable sinks on the market.

Size, in.	Wt., lbs.	Price	Size, in.	Wt., lbs.	Price
16x24x6	9	$3.22	20x30x6	16	$4.30
18x30x6	14	3.87	20x36x6	17½	4.75
18x36x6	16	4.35	20x40x6	20	5.30

WHITE ENAMELED IRON SINK BACKS.

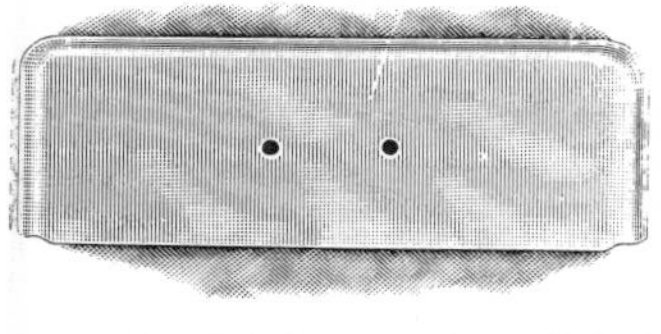

No. 42B465 White Porcelain Enameled Iron Sink Backs, for flat rim sinks, 12 inches high and 1¾ inches deep.

Length	Weight	Price
24 inches	18 lbs.	$1.44
30 inches	26 lbs.	1.68
36 inches	32 lbs.	2.10
40 inches	34 lbs.	2.40
42 inches	36 lbs.	2.58
48 inches	42 lbs.	3.00

No. 42B470 Same as above, 12 inches high and 2¼ inches deep.

Length	24 in.	30 in.	36 in.	40 in.	42 in.	48 in.
Weight	26 lbs.	30 lbs.	35 lbs.	33 lbs.	39 lbs.	55 lbs.
Price	$1.62	$1.92	$2.28	$2.70	$2.76	$3.48

No. 42B480 Same as above, 15 inches high and 2½ inches deep.

Length	24 in.	30 in.	36 in.	40 in.
Weight	29 lbs.	35 lbs.	46 lbs.	50 lbs.
Price	$2.10	$2.64	$3.00	$3.42

CAST IRON FLAT RIM SINK WITH ROLL BACK.

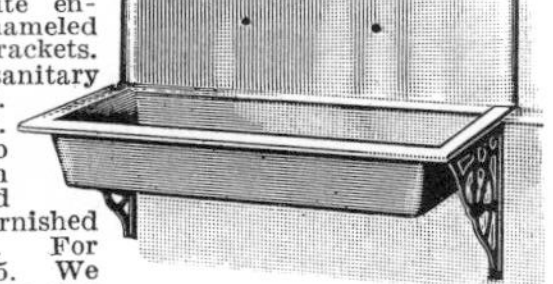

No. 42B485 Porcelain Enameled Cast Iron Flat Rim Roll Back Sinks. White enameled inside with enameled back; and painted brackets. This makes a very neat sanitary sink at a small cost. Backs are 12 inches high. Made with holes for two faucets. Complete with all connections and strainer. Faucets not furnished at prices given below. For faucets, see No. 42B1345. We can furnish these sinks in five sizes, but the 18x30-inch is the one most generally used and the size which we recommend for ordinary purposes.

Size, inches	18x30	18x36	20x30	20x36	20x40
Weight, lbs.	79	86	82	94	100
Price	$4.32	$5.90	$5.20	$6.50	$7.50

We can furnish these sinks with connections threaded for iron pipe at an extra cost of 25 cents over prices quoted.

SINK COUPLINGS.

No. 42B440 Cast Sink Couplings to connect sink to lead pipe. Weight, 4 oz. Price....**10c**

No. 42B445 Same as above, to connect sink to iron pipe, 1¼ or 1½ inches. Weight, 8 oz. Price **25c**

SEAMLESS WROUGHT ROLL RIM STEEL SINK BACKS.

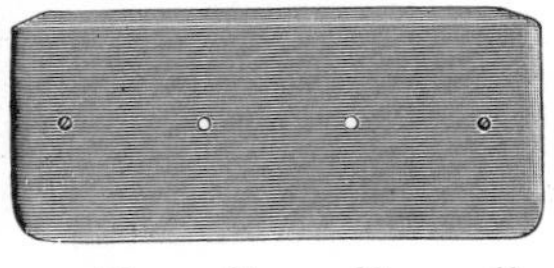

No. 42B395 Our Seamless Wrought Steel Sink Backs to be used in connection with our steel sinks. These backs have a 2½-inch roll rim and can be used only on Nos. 42B392, 42B393 and 42B394, or, in other words, on a turned edge sink.

Width, inches	24	30	36	40
Weight	6 lbs.	8 lbs.	10 lbs.	12 lbs.
Painted. Price	$0.69	$0.86	$1.08	$1.40
Galvanized. Price	.92	1.05	1.32	1.60
White enameled. Price	1.55	1.82	2.16	2.60

PIPE HOOKS.

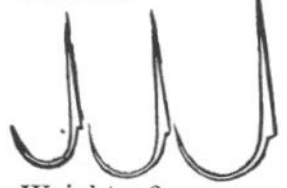

Pipe Hooks for Soil Pipe.
No. 42B1620 Weight, 6 oz. Price........ 4c
No. 42B1621 Size, 4 inches. Weight, 6 ounces. Price........ 5½c

SERVICE OR STOP COCK BOXES.

Made of cast iron, japanned.
No. 42B1650 Size, 2½ inches to run from waste pipe.
42B1650 Size, 2½ inches in diameter; extends from 36 to 54 inches. Weight, 22 pounds. Price........ 83c
No. 42B1707 Size, 2½ inches in diameter; extends from 51 to 66 inches. Price........ $1.10

CAST CESSPOOLS.

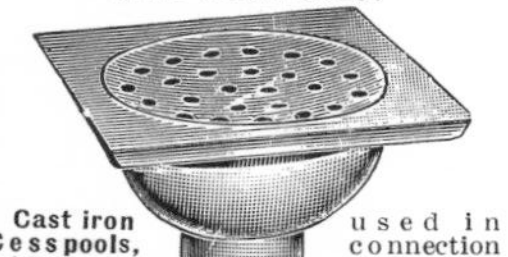

No. 42B1706 Size, 2½ inches in diameter; extends from 36 to 54 inches. Weight, 22 pounds.
used in connection with soil pipe.
No. 42B1685 Size, 6x6 inches. Price........ 41c
Size, 9x9 inches. Price........ 52c
No. 19 lbs. Size, 13x13 inches. Price........ 78c

Cast iron Cesspools with bell trap head.

PIPE HYDRANTS.

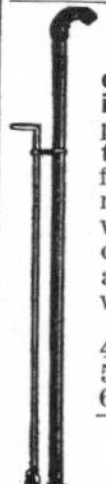

No. 42B1720 When a cheap but serviceable hydrant is desired, we recommend our underground pipe hydrant. It attaches to the underground pipe below freezing point and is furnished with a brass shut off valve, the drip from which drains the hydrant as soon as it is turned off and prevents injury from frost.

No. 42B1710 Size, ¾ in. 1 in. 1¼ in.
4 ft. long $1.37 $1.44 $1.48
5 ft. long 1.74 2.78 2.48
6 ft. long 2.68

HYDRANTS.

No. 42B1725 All parts of this hydrant with which water comes in contact are at bottom out of the way. The waste operates perfectly, emptying the valve from rising pipe when the valve is closed and closing the waste when valve is open. Valve may be pulled out at top when in repairs, thus avoiding the necessity of digging up. Weight, about 55 lbs.

4 ft. long 3 ft. 4 ft.
To set in ground 3 ft. 4 ft.
$2.98 $3.27 $6.65 $7.18

HANDY FORCE PUMP, WITH VALVE, 29 CENTS.

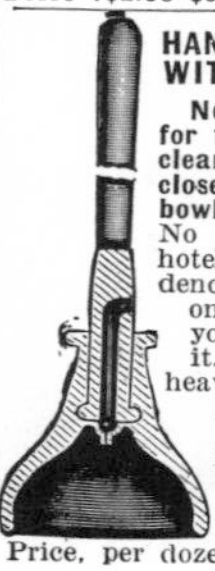

No. 42B1880 Used for forcing stoppages out of cleaning waste pipes, closets, sinks, wash bowls, bath tubs, etc. No plumber, janitor, hotel, restaurant or residence should be without one. One stoppage of your pipes will pay for it. It is made with a heavy rubber cup on the 3-foot wooden handle, furnished with valve. Price, each........ $0.29
valve. Price, per dozen........ 3.25

RUNNING TRAPS.

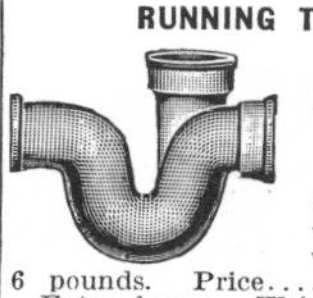

Cast iron Running Trap for soil pipe.
42B1700 Standard. Size, 2 inches with vent. Weight, 9 pounds.
6 pounds. Price........ 38c
Size, 4 inches. Weight, 28 pounds.
No. 42B1701 Standard. Size, 2 inches with 4-inch vent. Weight, 4 inches. Weight, 28 pounds.
Price........ 47c
Extra heavy. Price........ 70c
Price........ 90c

THREE-QUARTER S TRAP WITH VENT.

No. 42B1641 Three-Quarter S Trap with vent. Made of cast iron. Size, 4 inches.
Standard. Price........ 60c
Extra heavy. Weight, 29 pounds.
Price........ 80c

HALF S TRAP WITH HAND HOLE AND COVER.

No. 42B1686 Standard. Size, 4 inch hand hole and cover.
20 pounds. Price........ 60c
Extra heavy. Weight, 29 pounds. Price........ 80c

LONG INCREASERS.

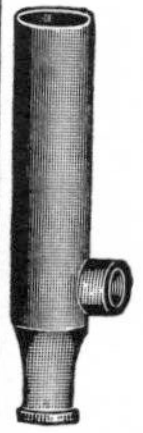

Cast iron Long increasers for soil pipe, for calking; tapped on side. Our increasers are used at the top of soil pipe going through the roof, in order to let the air get a better chance to destroy all foul gas or other foul odors.
No. 42B1605 Standard. Size, 2 to 4x24 inches. Weight, 23 pounds. Price........ 77c
No. 42B1606 Standard. Size, 4 to 4x24 inches. Weight, 40 pounds. Price........ 90c
No. 42B1607 Standard. Size, 5x30 inches. Weight, 33 pounds. Price........ 93c
No. 42B1608 Extra heavy. Size, 4 to 5x30 inches. Weight, 40 pounds. Price........ $1.10

CLEAN OUT Y WITH BRASS SCREW COVER.

For Standard and Extra Heavy Pipe, to be placed in waste pipe, so that soil pipe may be cleaned out at any time without destroying soil pipe. Be sure to give catalog number and size wanted.
No. 42B1703 Standard. Size, 2 inches. Weight, 10 pounds. Price........ 55c
No. 42B1703 Extra heavy. Weight, 13 pounds. Price........ 88c
No. 42B1704 Standard. Size, 4 inches. Weight, 23 pounds. Price........ 58c
No. 42B1704 Extra heavy. Weight, 25 pounds. Price........ 92c

RUNNING TRAP WITH HAND HOLE AND COVER.

No. 42B1702 Standard. Running trap with hand hole and cover. Size, 4 inches. Weight, 15 pounds.
Standard. Price........ 60c
Extra heavy. Price........ 80c
Weight, 30 pounds.

PIPE RESTS.

No. 42B1625 Pipe Rests for Soil Pipe. Standard grade. Weight.
Size, 2 inches. Standard. Weight........ 8c
Size, 2 inches. Extra heavy. Weight........ 15c
Size, 4 inches. Standard. Weight........ 15c
Size, 4 inches. Extra heavy. Weight........ 17c

CAST S TRAPS.

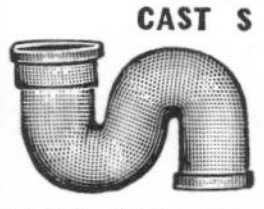

Our traps are used in the ground and on top for closets, such as No. 42B924 and 42B100 closets, which have no local sewer gas and stench coming through the closet bowl. Cast S Traps for Soil Pipe.
Cast S Traps for Soil Pipe. Plain.
Size, 4 inches.
No. 42B1630 Standard. Weight, 19 pounds. Price........ 40c
No. 42B1631 Extra heavy. Weight, 28 pounds. Price........ 60c

CAST THREE-QUARTER S TRAPS.

No. 42B1632 Three-Quarter S Trap. Plain. Size, 4 inches.
Standard. Weight, 18 pounds. Price........ 40c
No. 42B1633 Extra heavy. Size, 4 inches. Weight, 27 pounds. Price........ 60c

CAST HALF S TRAPS.

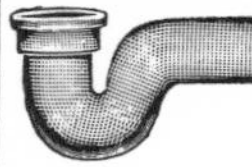

Cast Half S Traps for Soil Pipe. Size, 4 inches.
No. 42B1635 Standard. Weight, 18 pounds. Price........ 40c
No. 42B1636 Extra heavy. Weight, 27 pounds. Price........ 60c

CAST S TRAP WITH VENT.

Cast S Trap with Vent. Size, 4 inches with 2-inch vent.
No. 42B1645 Standard. Wt. Weight, 21 pounds. Price........ 55c
Extra heavy. Weight, 30 pounds. Price........ 75c

THREE-QUARTER S TRAP WITH HAND HOLE AND COVER.

No. 42B1687 Three-Quarter S Trap with hand hole and cover. Size, 4 inches.
Standard. Wt. 21 pounds. Price........ 60c
Extra heavy. Weight, 30 pounds. Price........ 80c

HALF S TRAP WITH VENT.

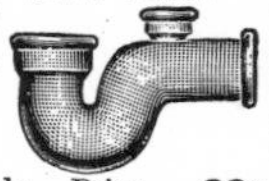

No. 42B1640 Half S or P Trap with vent. Made of cast iron. Size, 4 inches, with 2-inch vent.
Standard. Weight, 20 pounds. Price........ 60c
Extra heavy. Weight, 29 pounds. Price........ 80c

FULL S TRAP WITH HAND HOLE AND COVER.

No. 42B1688 Full S Trap with hand hole and cover. Size, 4 inches.
Standard. Weight, 21 pounds. Price........ 60c
Extra heavy. Weight, 30 pounds. Price........ 80c

Y BRANCHES.

CAST SANITARY T BRANCHES, TAPPED FOR IRON PIPE.

Cast Sanitary T Branches, tapped for iron pipe.
Size. Weight.
4x1½ inches. Weight, 7 pounds. Price........ 44c
No. 42B1550 Size, 4x2 inches. Weight, 8 pounds. Price........ 45c

No. 42B1680 Cast Y Branches for soil pipe, are used for connecting the waste of lavatories, tubs, sinks and closets to soil pipe.

Size	Wt. lbs.	Price
Standard 2x2 in.	8	14c
Standard 4x2 in.	13	36c
Standard 4x4 in.	13	21c
Extra heavy 2x2 in.	10	21c
Extra heavy 4x2 in.	23	48c
Extra heavy 4x4 in.	25	49c

OFFSETS.

No. 42B1690 Cast Offsets for soil pipe, and are used to run the soil pipe over any distance to avoid any obstructing article.

Size inches	Standard	Extra Heavy
2x2	17c	30c
2x6	30c	38c
4x4	31c	48c
4x12	49c	68c

T BRANCHES.

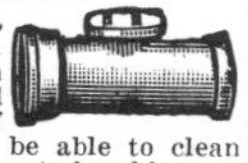

Cast T Branches with cleanout cap. These T branches with cleanouts are on any length of soil pipe, so as to be able to clean out the pipe without breaking or destroying any pipe.
No. 42B1594 Size, 2 inches, with 2-inch screw. Standard. Weight, 3½ pounds. Price........ 31c
No. 42B1595 Extra heavy. Weight, 6½ pounds. Price........ 44c
No. 42B1596 Size, 4 inches, with 2-inch screw. Standard. Weight, 12 pounds. Price........ 54c
No. 42B1601 Size, 4 inches, with 4-inch screw, extra heavy. Price........ 60c

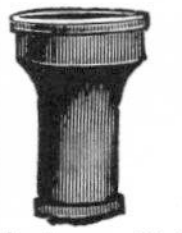

TAPPED INCREASERS.

No. 42B1690 Tapped for soil pipe over iron. Small opening, threaded for iron.
Standard. Size, 4x4 inches. Price........ 28c
No. 42B1601 Size, 4x2 inches. Standard. Size, 4x2 inches. Price........ 30c
Extra heavy. Weight, 7 pounds. Price........ 35c
Extra heavy. Size, 4x2 inches. Price........ 37c

TAPPED CROSSES.

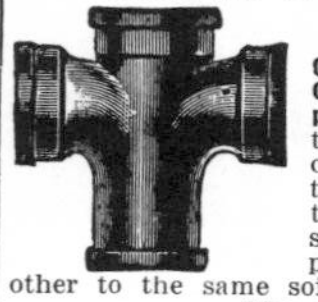

No. 42B1685 Cast Sanitary Crosses for soil pipe are used to connect two closets, lavatories, sinks or same floor on each side of opposite each other to the same soil pipe.

	Size	Wt. lbs.	Price
Standard	2x2 in.	10	28c
Standard	4x2 in.	10	40c
Standard	4x4 in.	12	52c
Extra heavy		21	53c
Extra heavy		24	73c

SANITARY CROSSES.

CAST DOUBLE HUBS.

No. 42B1612 Cast Double Hubs for Soil Pipe.
Size, 2 inches. Weight, 3 pounds. Price........ 7c
Extra heavy. Size, 2 inches. Weight, 7 pounds. Price........ 10c
Standard. Size, 4 inches. Weight, 9 pounds. Price........ 14c
Extra heavy. Size, 4 inches. Weight, 8 pounds. Price........ 19c

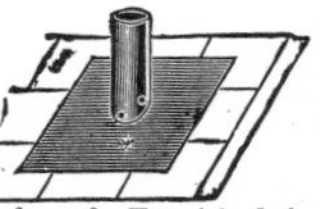

VENTILATING CAPS.

No. 42B1660 Cast Iron Ventilating Caps. Our ventilating caps are used in connection with our No. 42B1701 Ventil trap, which is run outside the house in the ground and up to the top of the vent cap.
Standard. Size, 4x6 inches long. Weight, 7 pounds. Price........ 25c
Extra heavy. Size, 4x6 inches long. Weight, 15 pounds. Price........ 35c

TAPPED CROSSES.

No. 42B1572 Cast Iron Cross for soil pipe. Side Opening, tapped for iron pipe. Our tapped crosses are used to connect sinks or lavatories to one on each side of partition.
Standard. Weight, 9 pounds.
Size, 4x1½-inch opening. Price........ 68c
Standard. Size, 4x2-inch opening. Price........ 69c
Extra heavy. Size, 4x1¼-inch opening. Weight, 12 pounds. Price........ 88c
Extra heavy. Size, 4x2-inch opening. Weight, 12 pounds. Price........ 89c

CAST SANITARY CROSSES.

No. 42B1573 Cast Sanitary Cross for soil pipe, side opening, tapped for 1½ and 2-inch iron pipe.
Standard. Size, 4x1½ inches. Price........ 68c
Standard. Size, 4x2-inch. Price........ 88c
Extra heavy. Size, 4x1½ inches. Price........ 69c
Extra heavy. Size, 4x2 inches. Price........ 89c

ROOF FLASHING.

Galvanized Flashing. be connected to soil pipe.
No. 42B1665 Cast Roof Plate, for soil pipe. Size, 4 inches. Standard. Weight, 10 pounds. Price........ 16c

ROOF PLATES.

No. 42B1665 Cast Roof Plate, for soil pipe. Size, 4 inches. Standard. Weight, 8 pounds. Price........ 16c
Extra heavy. Weight, 8 pounds. Price........ 16c
No. 42B1666 Size, 4 inches. Price........ 16c
No. 42B1667 Size, 5 inches.

CAST IRON SOIL PIPE.

Single Hub Cast Iron Soil Pipe. best grade; comes in 5-foot pieces.
42B1552 2-inch soil pipe is used for the roof of house. Our No. 42B1550 and No. 42B1551 4-inch soil pipe is used to run from closet to sewer, or from sewer to roof.
No. 42B1550 Standard, 2-inch size. Price, per foot........ 9c
No. 42B1551 Standard, 4-inch size. Price, per foot........ 15c
No. 42B1552 Extra heavy, 2-inch. Price, per foot........ 12c
No. 42B1553 Extra heavy, 4-inch. Price, per foot........ 25c
2-inch standard pipe weighs 17½ pounds per 5-foot length.
4-inch standard pipe weighs 32½ pounds per 5-foot length.
2-inch extra heavy pipe weighs 27½ pounds per 5-foot length.
4-inch extra heavy pipe weighs 65 pounds per 5-foot length.

DOUBLE HUB SOIL PIPE.

No. 42B1558 Double Hub Soil Pipe. Best grade. Sold in 5-foot pieces.
Our No. 42B1558 2-inch and 4-inch soil pipe has a hub on both ends, and is used because it can be used on any length you desire to run or waste any pipe.
Standard. 2-inch. Price, per foot........ 11c
Standard, 4-inch. Price, per foot........ 17c
Extra heavy, 2-inch. Price, per foot........ 17c
Extra heavy, 4-inch. Price, per foot........ 25c
2-inch standard pipe weighs 17½ pounds per 5-foot length.
4-inch standard pipe weighs 32½ pounds per 5-foot length.
2-inch extra heavy, 27½ pounds per 5-foot length.
4-inch extra heavy, 65 pounds per 5-foot length.

SOIL PIPE FITTINGS. CAST EIGHTH BENDS.

No. 42B1562 Eighth Bends are used to avoid a right angle to a brick wall or joist.
Standard, 2-inch. Weight, 3 pounds. Price........ 9c
Standard, 4-inch. Weight, 6 pounds. Price........ 14c
Extra heavy, 2-inch. Weight, 2¾ pounds. Price........ 14c
Extra heavy, 4-inch. Weight, 6½ pounds. Price........ 28c

CAST QUARTER BENDS.

No. 42B1565 Cast Quarter Bends for Soil Pipe are used at the bottom of soil pipe running to the roof, to connect to the sewer on the outside.
Standard, 2-inch. Weight, 4 pounds. Price........ 9c
Standard, 4-inch. Weight, 8 pounds. Price........ 14c
Extra heavy, 2-inch. Weight, 4 pounds. Price........ 14c
Extra heavy, 4-inch. Weight, 12 pounds. Price........ 28c

CAST QUARTER BENDS.

No. 42B1567 Extra heavy. Weight, 4 pounds. Price........ 21c
No. 42B1568 Extra heavy. Weight, 12 pounds. Price........ ...

QUARTER BENDS WITH HEEL OUTLET.

No. 42B1576 Cast Quarter Bends, with side outlet, with right or left hand. Be sure to state kind wanted. Size, 4 inches with 2-inch side outlet.
Standard. Weight, 12 pounds. Price........ 58c
Extra heavy. Weight, 12 pounds. Price........ 70c

CAST T BRANCHES, TAPPED FOR IRON PIPE.

No. 42B1670 Cast T Branches, Tapped for iron pipe. Standard.
Weight, 7 pounds. Price........ 25c
Extra heavy. Weight, 12 pounds. Price........ 60c

SANITARY T BRANCHES.

No. 42B1580 Sanitary T Branches for soil pipe are used in connection with soil pipe to connect the waste of lavatories, sinks and closets.
Standard. Size, 2x2 inches. Price. Standard, 4x4. Price........ 25c
No. 42B1581 Standard. Price, each........ 20c
No. 42B1582 Extra heavy. Size, 2x2. Weight, 7 pounds. Price, each........ 35c
No. 42B1583 Extra heavy. Size, 4x4. Weight, 14 pounds. Price, each........ 43c
No. 42B1584 Standard. Size, 4x2. Weight, 8 pounds. Price, each........ 35c
No. 42B1585 Extra heavy. Size, 4x2. Weight, 20 pounds. Price, each........ 48c

SANITARY T BRANCHES.

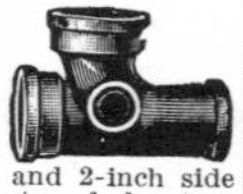

No. 42B1590 Sanitary T Branches, with 2-inch side outlet, either right or left hand. Made of cast iron, to be used with soil pipe. Size, 4 inches with 2-inch side opening is for waste of closet, and 2-inch side opening is for waste of lavatory or bath tub. Size, 4 inches, either right or left side outlet. Be sure to state kind wanted.
Standard. Weight, 12 pounds. Price........ 58c
Extra heavy. Weight, 12 pounds. Price........ 70c

VENTILATING BRANCHES.

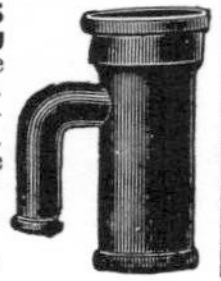

No. 42B1655 Cast Iron Ventilating Branches, with side outlets for soil pipe.
Size, 2x1½ in. Price........ 45c
Size, 4x1½ in. Price........ 45c
Size, 4x2 in. Price........ 60c

CAST REDUCERS.

No. 42B1616 Cast Reducers for Soil Pipe.
Standard. Size, 4x2 inches. Weight, 6 pounds. Price........ 18c
Extra heavy. Size, 4x2 inches. Weight, 6 pounds. Price........ 25c

LEAD PIPE.

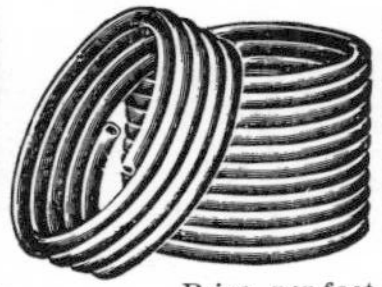

No. 42B1870 Lead Pipe. Prices subject to change without notice.

Lead Pipe.		Price, per foot
½ in. diam., 10 oz.	to ft..	4¼c
¾ in. diam., 1 lb.	to ft..	6¾c
1 in. diam., 1½ lbs.	to ft..	10¼c
1¼ in. diam., 2 lbs.	to ft..	13½c
1½ in. diam., 3 lbs.	to ft..	20½c
2 in. diam., 3 lbs.	to ft..	21c

STRONG LEAD PIPE.

No. 42B1875

Lead Pipe.		Price, per foot
½ in. diam., 1¼ lbs.	to ft..	8½c
⅝ in. diam., 2 lbs.	to ft..	13½c
¾ in. diam., 2¼ lbs.	to ft..	15¼c
1 in. diam., 3¼ lbs.	to ft..	20c

SHEET LEAD AND ZINC.

No. 42B1885 Sheet Lead furnished in two sizes. Thicknesses, 1-32 and 1-16 inch; 1-32-inch weighs 2 pounds to the square foot; 1-16-inch weighs 4 pounds to the square foot. Always state thickness wanted.

Price, 1-32-inch, per pound, 8½c
Price, 1-16-inch, per pound, 8c

No. 42B1890 Best Grade Sheet Zinc. Cannot sell less than half sheet, 26-gauge, No. 9, 36 inches wide by 84 inches long. Weight, about 14 pounds.

Price, per sheet........$1.50
Price, per half sheet..... .80

PLUMBERS' SOLDER.

No. 42B1900 High Grade Plumbers' Refined Metal Solder. Comes in bars of about 1½ pounds each. We do not sell less than a bar. Our solder is so rich in tin that 1 pound of our composition will do the same work as 2 pounds of most of the refined and wiping solder on the market, consequently it is the cheapest solder you can buy.

Price, per pound........19½c
Price for 50 pounds, per pound 19c

PIG LEAD.

No. 42B1905 Genuine Pig Lead. Comes in pigs of about 80 pounds each and ingots 7 pounds each.

Price, per pound, in 80-pound pigs 6¼c
Price, per pound, in 7-pound ingots 6½c

ACME BLOW TORCH.

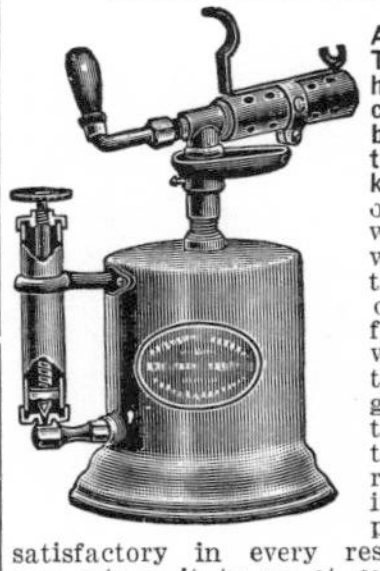

In our Acme Blow Torch we have secured the best on the market and one which we know will give the best of satisfaction. All we ask is that you give the torch a test at our risk, and if it is not perfectly satisfactory in every respect, you can return it to us at our expense and we will willingly return your money, together with any transportation charges. Do not let our low price lead you to believe this torch is not strictly up to date. We know it is the best torch on the market. It is made of heavy brass, and every torch is equipped with soldering copper attachment.

No. 42B1770 Capacity, 1 pint. Price $2.62
No. 42B1771 Capacity, 1 quart. Price $2.85

LEAD S TRAPS WITH IRON PIPE CONNECTIONS.

No. 42B1493 Size, 1¼ inches. Weight, 3 pounds. Price ...$1.25
No. 42B1494 Size, 1½ inches. Weight, 4 pounds. Price.....$1.40

DRAWN LEAD TRAPS.

Full S Standard Heavy Drawn Lead Traps for Sinks, Basins, Etc.

No. 42B1490 Size, 1¼ inches. Weight, 2⅝ pounds. Price 27c
No. 42B1491 Size, 1½ inches. Weight, 4 pounds. Price 42c
No. 42B1492 Size, 4 inches. Weight, 16½ lbs. Price $1.53

EXTRA LONG S LEAD TRAPS.

Extra Long Standard S Lead Traps for Sinks, Basins, Etc.

No. 42B1497 Size, 1¼ inches. Weight, 4 pounds. Price 43c
No. 42B1498 Size, 1½ inches. Weight, 6 pounds. Price 62c

LONG S LEAD TRAPS, VENTED.

Long S Lead Traps, Vented, as per illustration.

No. 42B1502 Size, 1¼ inches. Weight, 4½ pounds. Price 80c
No. 42B1503 Size, 1½ inches. Weight, 7 pounds. Price $1.05

HALF S LEAD TRAPS.

Standard Heavy Half S Lead Traps, to be used in connection with sinks, basins, etc.

No. 42B1504 Size, 1¼ inches. Weight, 4½ lbs. Price 24c
No. 42B1505 Size, 1½ inches. Weight, 7 lbs. Price 35c
No. 42B1506 Size, 4 inches. Weight, 12 pounds. Price..$1.17

THREE-QUARTER S LEAD TRAPS.

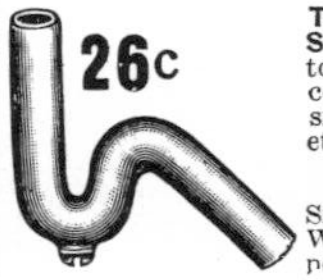

Standard Three-Quarter S Lead Traps, to be used in connection with sinks, basins, etc.

No. 42B1508 Size, 1¼ inches. Weight, 1¾ pounds. Price 26c

No. 42B1509 Size, 1½ inches. Weight, 3⅛ pounds. Price..38c

PIPE BENDER.

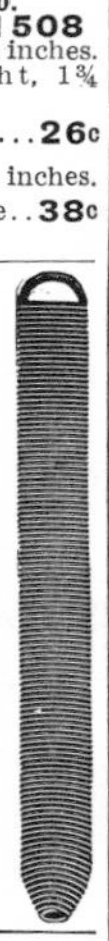

Pipe Bender, to be placed inside lead pipe when bending to avoid kinks in pipe. Made of a high grade spring steel.

No. 42B1795 Size, 1¼ inches. Weight, 2¾ pounds. Price 25c

No. 42B1796 Size, 1½ inches. Weight, 3¼ pounds. Price 35c

COMBINATION LEAD BENDS AND FERRULES.

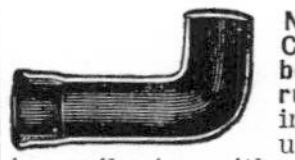

No. 42B1514 Combination lead bends and ferrules. With 5½-inch inlet to be used in connecting soil pipe with closet bowl.

Size, inches.	4x12	4x14	4x18
Weight	9½ lbs.	10¼ lbs.	12 lbs.
Price	$1.03	$1.13	$1.31

IMPROVED GASOLINE BULB BLAST FURNACE, $3.32.

No. 42B1768 Improved Bulb Furnace with improved coils, which will produce a blue and hot flame and which is equal to any furnace on the market for melting metals. Furnished with shield to hold melting pot, but no pot furnished at this price. Weight, 17 pounds.

Price ...$3.32

MELTING POT.

No. 42B1769 To fit above furnace. Weight, 3 pounds. Price 18c

SHORT BENDS.

Lead Short Bends, standard grade and sizes.

Cat. No.	Size	Weight	Price
42B1522	2 in.	2⅞ lbs.	27c
42B1524	4 in.	7½ lbs.	70c

LONG BENDS.

Standard Grade and Sizes Long Bends.

No. 42B1542 Size, 2 inches. Weight, 4¼ pounds. Price.37c
No. 42B1544 Size, 4 inches. Weight, 9 pounds. Price....90c

LEAD DRUM TRAPS.

No. 42B1530 Lead Drum Traps. Diameter, 4 inches; length, 9 inches, with brass top and screw. Weight, 4¼ pounds. Price....95c

No. 42B1536 Same as above, except with nickel plated top and screw. Weight, 4¼ pounds. Price..............$1.08

No. 42B1535 Lead Drum Traps, with connection and brass screws. Weight, 4¼ pounds. Price $1.64

IRON DRUM TRAP.

No. 42B1532 With deep seal. All connections threaded so that 1¼ or 1½-inch iron pipe can be used. State which size is wanted. Weight, 6½ pounds. Price $1.28

TAP BORER.

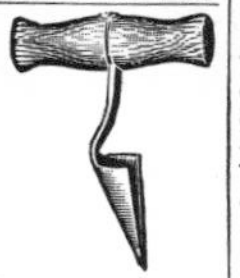

No. 42B1835 Plumbers' Tap Borer. Made of high grade English steel. Weight, 5 ounces. Price 18c

WIPING CLOTH.

No. 42B1845 Plumbers' Wiping Cloth. Neat and compact, made of the very best ticking. Weight, 1 ounce. Price 6c

ALCOHOL LAMP.

No. 42B1855 Gas Fitters' Alcohol Lamp. Made of tin, finely finished. Weight, about 10 ounces. Price 39c

SPUN OAKUM.

No. 42B1866 Oakum, for calking iron pipe, soil pipe and fittings.

Price, per pound......$0.05½
Price, per bale, about 50 pounds 1.75

ACME BRAZING TORCH.

No. 42B1772 The best Brazing Torch on the market. No pump to get out of order. Gives 2,500 degrees of heat, suitable for all purposes for which an intense amount of heat is required. Can be held in any position. Turned cast metal container adapted for rough wear. No loose parts. Capacity, ¾ pint. Price....$3.10

TURNING PINS.

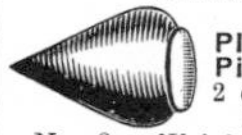

No. 42B1810 Plumbers' Turning Pins. No. 1. Weight, 2 ounces. Price 18c
No. 2. Weight, 3 ounces. Price 19c
No. 3. Weight, 4 ounces. Price 20c

DRIFT PLUGS.

No. 42B1811 Boxwood Drift Plugs. Weight, about 1 ounce.

Sizes, inches.......	1	1¼	1½
Price..............	9c	11c	13c

ASBESTOS LEAD JOINT RUNNERS.

No. 42B1815 Asbestos, being unaffected by heat, is admirably adapted for making joint runners for running lead or molten metal in soil, water or gas pipe. The accompanying illustration shows the runners as applied to pipe. Weight, 1½ pounds.

No. 2, ¾-inch. Round, for 4, 5 and 6-inch pipe. Price, each..............$1.22

BENDING PIN.

No. 42B1820 Plumbers' Bending Pin. Weight, 1 pound. Price 9c

YARNING IRON.

No. 42B1825 Plumbers' Yarning Iron. Weight, 10 ounces. Price 20c

CALKING CHISEL.

No. 42B1831 Plumbers' Calking Chisel. Made of high grade steel. Can furnish straight, right or left hand offset. Weight, 1¼ pounds. Price..............13c

GEM BIBB SEAT DRESSER, $1.10

No. 42B1790 The Gem Bibb Seat Dresser is the most practical tool of its kind on the market. Cutters are rose pattern and the inside of bell is threaded for the purpose of screwing in top of bibb. Cannot grind crooked. Weight, 9 ounces. Price $1.10

HERCULES GAS MACHINE

LIGHT YOUR HOME LIKE A CITY RESIDENCE WITHOUT THE USE OF LAMPS—SIMPLE, SAFE AND SAVING.

Of course you are tired of lamps; everybody is, and also of the dingy, dirty smoky light that emanates from them. Previous to this time you were, of course, compelled to use them, as nothing better was at hand, but with our **Hercules Gas Machine** we are glad to offer our customers relief from this nuisance. Think of what it means to own your own gas plant. Think of what it means to be able to strike a match at any hour of the night or day and illuminate your home, not with the kind of light you have been using, but with a clear 100-candle power light that will illuminate every nook and corner in the various rooms of your home.

IT IS A GEM FOR COOKING. It produces a hotter flame than city gas and at less expense. Think of the convenience when arising in the morning, instead of waiting for a fire to burn up, to say nothing of the hauling of wood and coal and the emptying of ashes, to merely strike a match, touch it to the gas stove and the morning meal is being prepared.

The gas is made or generated by this machine by allowing the gasoline to pass from the storage tank through the small pipe on the side of the tank into the carburetor, the carburetor being equipped with a float valve which allows the gasoline to flow only as it is generated. The carburetor has also a perforated section between the air section and gasoline, causing the air from the blower to pass through the gasoline and up to the pipes throughout the house. The float valve in the carburetor can be regulated to take care of a certain quantity of gasoline, and as the gas is used from the fixtures more gasoline flows into the carburetor to take the place of that used. Thus, it is readily seen, the flow of gasoline into the carburetor is regulated by the amount used at the different fixtures. The air pipe from blower is connected to the regulator to regulate the pressure of air entering into the carburetor, the air being forced up through the gasoline through the perforated partitions, causing the gasoline to generate, and forces it into gas chambers. It is then forced through the pipes to the fixtures.

This machine requires about 4 gallons of gasoline to manufacture 1,000 cubic feet of gas, making the cost about 90 cents a thousand. But, for cooking purposes it will go much farther than city gas, inasmuch as gasoline gas is about 20 per cent hotter than manufactured coal or water gas. We quote prices below for this machine, as shown in illustration, but if you contemplate placing this outfit in your home, kindly draw a rough sketch of your building, giving us the number and size of the various rooms you desire to light. Whether you desire to light with this outfit only or cook with it as well, we will be glad to furnish you a complete estimate as to what it will cost you for this machine complete, together with necessary piping to install it in your home. These estimates are free for the asking and place you under absolutely no obligation to us to purchase an outfit.

No. 42B6999 **Outfit complete,** as shown in illustration, for 15-light plant, with 70-gallon tank. Price..........$54.00
No. 42B7000 **Outfit complete,** as shown in illustration, for 20-light plant, with 70-gallon tank. Price.......... 57.50
No. 42B7001 **Outfit complete,** as shown in illustration, for 30-light plant, with 70-gallon tank. Price.......... 60.00
No. 42B7002 **Outfit complete,** as shown in illustration, for 40-light plant, with 134-gallon tank. Price.......... 68.75

Notice—The regulating tank is not needed or furnished with 15, 20 or 30-light plant.

PLUMBERS' OR MELTING LADLES.

No. 42B1780 Steel bowl with wrought iron handle.

Size across bowl, inches.	3	4	5
Weight....	12 oz.	1 lb.	1¼ lbs.
Price......	11c	13c	17c

BOXWOOD DRESSER.

No. 42B1800 Plumbers' Boxwood Dresser. Weight, 1 pound. Price 45c

OVAL SHAVE HOOK.

No. 42B1805 Plumbers' Oval Shave Hook. Steel blade. Weight, 4 ounces. Price....18c

SPRING GAUGE PROVING OUTFIT.

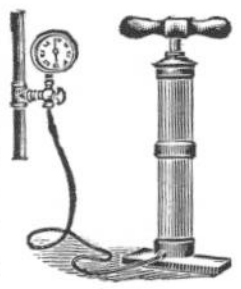

No. 42B1750 Spring Gauge Proving Outfit, for testing gas pipes. Complete as shown in illustration. Weight, 6 pounds. Price, per set $6.75

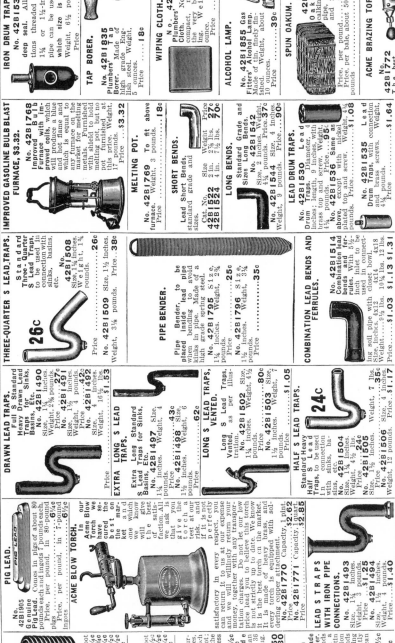

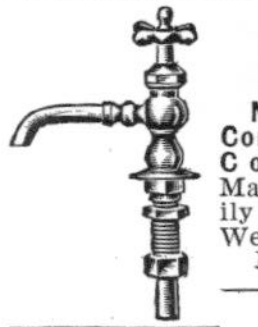

COMPRESSION BASIN COCKS.

No. 42B1267 Compression Basin Cocks, T handle. Made of brass. Heavily nickel plated. Weight, 1 pound. Price.........**51c**

NICKEL PLATED BASIN COCKS.

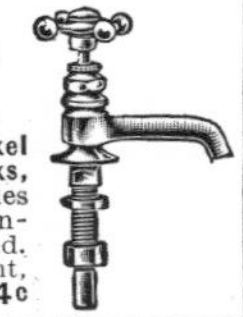

No. 42B1272 Low Down Nickel Plated Basin Cocks, with cross handles and china tops, indexed hot and cold. Quality, A1. Weight, 1 pound. Price..**74c**

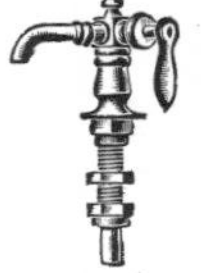

FULLER BASIN COCKS.

No. 42B1277 High Grade Fuller Basin Cocks, furnished complete, nickel plated. In ordering single faucets be sure to state whether left or right hand is wanted. Weight, 1¼ lbs. Price **70c**

COMBINATION BATH COCKS.

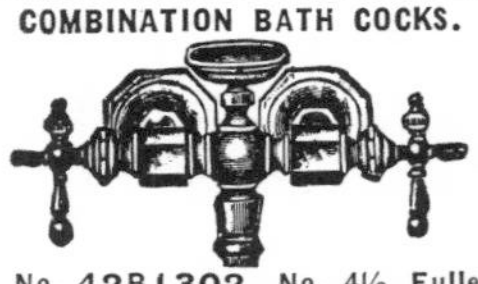

No. 42B1302 No. 4½ Fuller Cast Brass Combination Hot and Cold Bath Cocks. Nickel plated, complete, ready for use. One of the heaviest and best finished cocks on the market; nothing cheap about it but the price. Weight, 4 pounds. Price **$1.80**

COMPRESSION BATH COCKS.

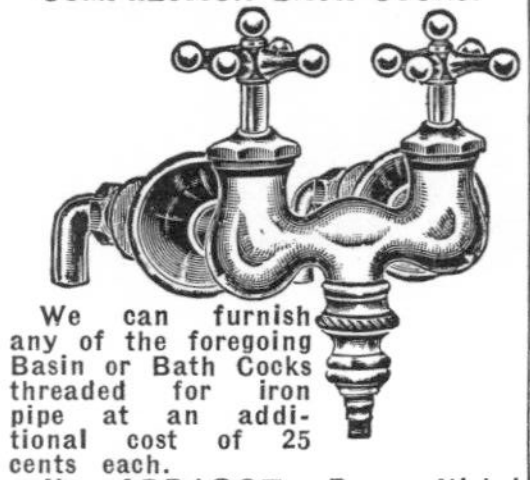

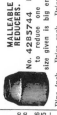

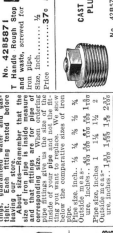

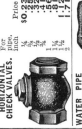

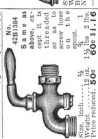

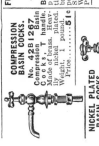

We can furnish any of the foregoing Basin or Bath Cocks threaded for iron pipe at an additional cost of 25 cents each.

No. 42B1307 Brass Nickel Plated Compression Bath Cocks. Combination hot and cold. A heavy well made cock. Complete as shown in illustration. Weight, 2¾ pounds. Price.........**$1.80**

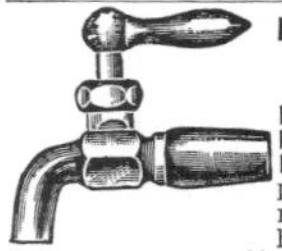

FULLER BIBBS, PLAIN.

No. 42B1365 Plain Fuller Bibbs, for lead pipe connection, made of brass, highly polished.

Size, inch....	½	¾	1
Weight	12 oz.	1¼ lbs.	2 lbs.
Price	**40c**	**48c**	**95c**

RUBBER BALLS FOR FULLER BIBBS.

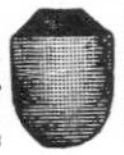

Average weight, ½ ounce. **No. 42B1380** Size for bibbs, ½ inch, **5c**; ¾ inch, **5c**; 1 inch.......**6c**

FULLER HOSE BIBBS.

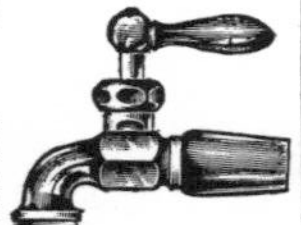

No. 42B1370 Fuller Hose Bibbs, for lead pipe connections. Made of brass, highly polished.

Size, in.....	½	¾	1
Weight	12 oz.	1¼ lbs.	2 lbs.
Price	**44c**	**52c**	**$1.03**

BIBBS.

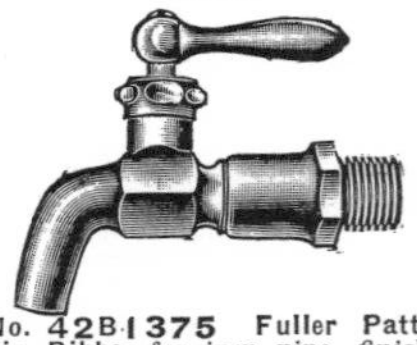

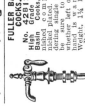

No. 42B1375 Fuller Pattern Plain Bibbs, for iron pipe, finished brass.

Size, inch...........	½	¾
Weight	11 oz.	1 lb.
Price	**44c**	**52c**

FULLER PATTERN HOSE BIBBS.

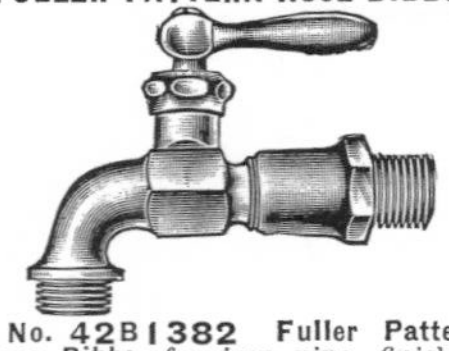

No. 42B1382 Fuller Pattern Hose Bibbs, for iron pipe, finished brass.

Size, inch...........	½	¾
Weight	13 oz.	1 lb.
Price	**48c**	**54c**

GROUND KEY BIBBS FOR IRON PIPE.

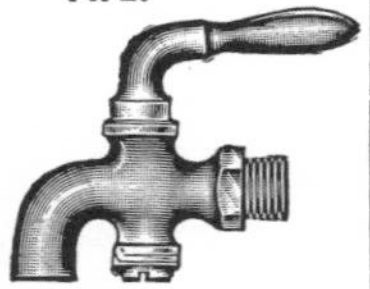

No. 42B1385 Plain Ground Key Bibbs, made entirely of brass. No rubber washers to wear out. Highly polished.

Size, inch....	½	¾	1
Weight	12 oz.	1½ lbs.	2 lbs.
Price reduced.	**45c**	**54c**	**$1.05**

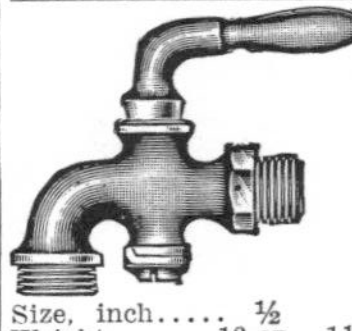

No. 42B1384 Same as above, except it is threaded so as to screw hose on the spout.

Size, inch.....	½	¾	1
Weight	12 oz.	1½ lbs	2 lbs.
Price reduced.	**50c**	**60c**	**$1.16**

COMPRESSION HOSE BIBBS.

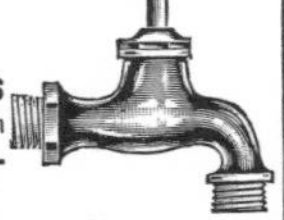

No. 42B1386 Screwed for iron pipe with shoulder; finished.

Size, inch....	½	¾	1
Weight	12 oz.	1¼ lbs.	2½ lbs.
Price reduced.	**40c**	**48c**	**$1.12**

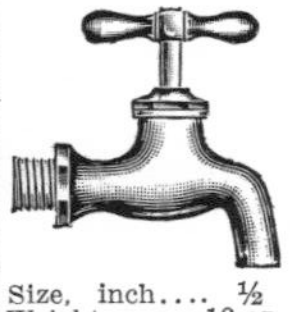

COMPRESSION PLAIN BIBBS.

No. 42B1390 Compression Plain Bibbs, screwed for iron pipe, with shoulder; finished.

Size, inch....	½	¾	1
Weight	12 oz.	1¼ lbs.	2½ lbs.
Price reduced.	**35c**	**44c**	**$1.10**

COMPRESSION PLAIN BIBBS WITH FLANGE.

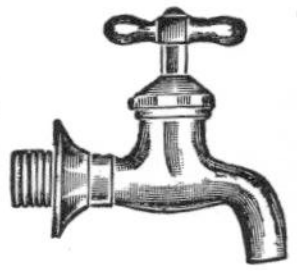

No. 42B1325 Plain Compression Bibbs with flange, screwed for iron pipe. Made of brass, finely finished.

Size, inch..	½	¾	1
Weight	1 lb.	1¼ lbs.	2¼ lbs.
Price reduced	**48c**	**60c**	**$1.30**

COMPRESSION HOSE BIBBS WITH FLANGE.

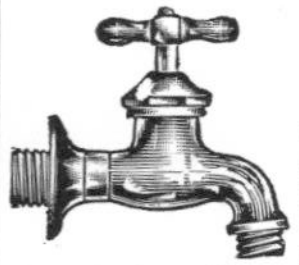

No. 42B1330 Compression Hose Bibbs with flange, screwed for iron pipe. Made of brass, finely finished.

Size, inch..	½	¾	1
Weight	1¼ lbs.	1¾ lbs.	2¾ lbs.
Price reduced	**53c**	**67c**	**$1.50**

FULLER BIBBS, PLAIN, WITH FLANGE.

At Reduced Prices.

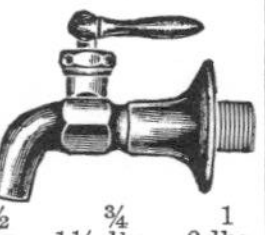

No. 42B1345 Fuller Bibbs, plain, with flange, screwed for iron pipe. Made of brass, highly finished.

Size, inch....	½	¾	1
Weight	14 oz.	1½ lbs.	2 lbs.
Brass finished	**52c**	**60c**	**$1.40**
Nickel plated.	**62c**	**72c**	**1.65**

FULLER HOSE BIBBS WITH FLANGE.

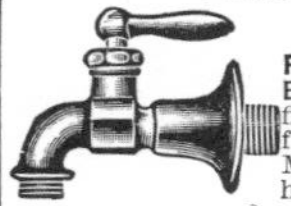

No. 42B1350 Fuller Hose Bibbs, with flange, screwed for iron pipe. Made of brass, highly finished.

Size, inch....	½	¾	1
Weight	15 oz.	1 lb.	2 lbs.
Brass finished	**59c**	**61c**	**$1.40**
Nickel plated.	**69c**	**80c**	**1.60**

STANDARD WEIGHT BRASS GLOBE VALVES.

No. 42B5826

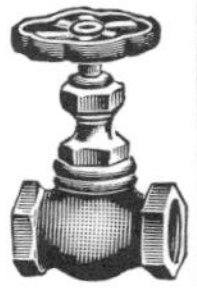

For pipe, in.	¼	⅜
Price	..$0.26	$0.27
For pipe, in.	½	¾
Price	.. .35	.45
For pipe, in.	1	1¼
Price	.. .63	.90
For pipe, in.	1½	2
Price	.. 1.22	1.90

STANDARD WEIGHT BRASS ANGLE VALVES.

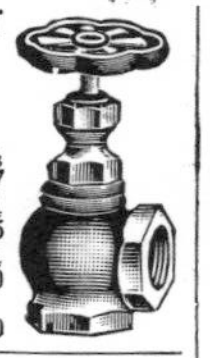

No. 42B5828

For pipe, in.	¼	⅜
Price	....$0.26	$0.27
For pipe, in.	½	¾
Price	.... .35	.45
For pipe, in.	1	1¼
Price	.... .63	.90
For pipe, in.	1½	2
Price	.... 1.22	1.90

STANDARD WEIGHT HORIZONTAL CHECK VALVES. No. 42B5832

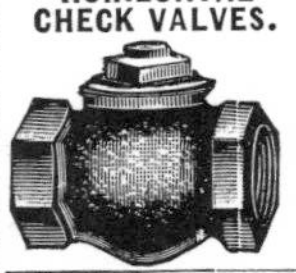

For pipe, inch	Price
¼	**$0.23**
⅜	**.25**
½	**.32**
¾	**.41**
1	**.56**
1¼	**.81**
1½	**1.12**
2	**1.71**

WATER PIPE STOPS.

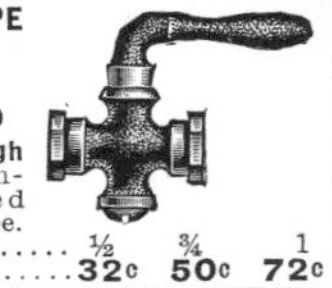

No. 42B5870 Brass Rough Stop, lever handle, screwed for iron pipe.

Size, inches......	½	¾	1
Price, plain......	**32c**	**50c**	**72c**

CHECK AND WASTE.

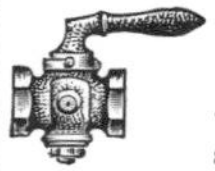

No. 42B5872 All Brass Check and Waste, lever handle, screwed for iron pipe.

Size, in.	½	¾	1	1¼	1½
Price...	36c	53c	78c	$1.23	$1.83

ROUGH BRASS STOP, T HANDLE.

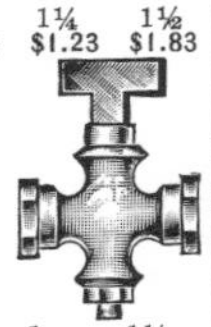

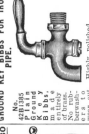

No. 42B5874 Rough Brass Stop, T Handle, screwed for iron pipe.

Size, in..	½	¾	1	1¼
Price ...	**33c**	**49c**	**72c**	**$1.17**

MALLEABLE IRON PIPE FITTINGS.

We handle only the best pipe fittings, guaranteed water and gas-tight. Each fitting tested before leaving our store.

About sizes—Remember that the size of iron pipe is inside measure and that fittings are for pipe of corresponding size. When ordering pipe fittings give us the size of the inside of your pipe and not the fitting you want to replace. We show below the comparative sizes of iron pipe.

Pipe size, inch..	⅛	¼	⅜	½	¾
Outside measure, inches..	$\frac{40}{100}$	$\frac{54}{100}$	$\frac{67}{100}$	$\frac{84}{100}$	$1\frac{5}{100}$
Pipe size, inches	1	1¼	1½	2	
Outside measure, inches..	$1\frac{31}{100}$	$1\frac{66}{100}$	$1\frac{9}{10}$	$2\frac{37}{100}$	

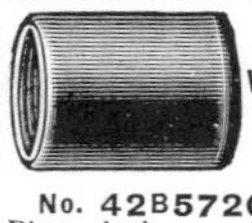

WROUGHT IRON COUPLINGS.

No. 42B5720 Black.

Pipe, inch......	¼	⅜	½	¾
Black, each.....	4c	4c	4c	4c
Black, per doz..	44c	44c	45c	45c
Pipe, inches.....	1	1¼	1½	2
Black, each.....	5c	6c	7c	8c
Black, per doz..	54c	65c	76c	85c

No. 42B5721 Galvanized.

Pipe, inch......	¼	⅜	½	¾
Galv., each......	4c	5c	5c	5c
Galv., per doz..	44c	54c	54c	54c
Pipe, inch......	1	1¼	1½	2
Galv., each......	6c	7c	9c	10c
Galv., per doz..	65c	76c	98c	$1.08

MALLEABLE TEES.

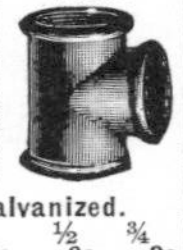

No. 42B5732 Black.

Pipe, inch	Price, each	Price, dozen
¼	**4c**	**$0.44**
⅜	**4c**	**.44**
½	**4c**	**.44**
¾	**6c**	**.65**
1	**9c**	**.98**
1¼	**11c**	**1.18**
1½	**17c**	**1.80**
2	**22c**	**2.36**

No. 42B5733 Galvanized.

Pipe, inches.	¼	⅜	½	¾
Price, each..	5c	5c	6c	8c
Price, per doz.	53c	54c	65c	87c
Pipe, inches.	1	1¼	1½	2
Price, each..	$0.14	$0.18	$0.26	$0.36
Price, per doz.	1.52	1.95	2.80	3.95

STANDARD WROUGHT STEAM, GAS AND WATER PIPE.

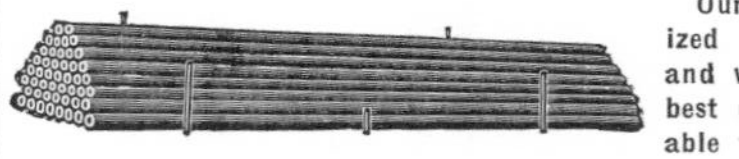

Our black and galvanized wrought steam, gas and water pipe is the very best grade of pipe we are able to secure. For carrying steam, gas or water it will give perfect satisfaction, as it is made in the best pipe mills in the country. It is free from imperfections of any nature and is guaranteed by us to be the very highest grade. Remember, we sell only new first class pipe. Do not compare our pipe with the second hand pipe sold by some concerns. **Prices given below are for pipe in random or regular stock lengths as they come from the mill.** This does not mean exact 16 or 20-foot lengths, but in lengths as they come from the mill. When pipe is ordered in this way one coupling is furnished free with each piece. Where you specify exact lengths we charge for the threads on both ends as per price list below, and we do not furnish couplings with the pipe cut into exact lengths.

No. 42B5710 Black Pipe.
No. 42B5711 Galvanized Pipe.

Inside Diam.	Lbs., per ft.	Blk., per ft.	Galv., per ft.	Extra thr'ds, per cut
⅛-inch	¼	2c	.....	2½c
¼-inch	⅜	2c	3¼c	2½c
⅜-inch	½	2c	3¼c	2½c
½-inch	4-5	2¾c	4c	2½c
¾-inch	1 1-10	3⅛c	4¾c	2½c
1 -inch	1⅜	4½c	6¾c	3c
1¼-inch	2¼	6¼c	9¼c	3½c
1½-inch	2¾	7½c	10¾c	5c
2 -inch	3⅜	10c	14½c	5c
2½-inch	5¾	15¾c	23c	5c
3 -inch	7½	20¾c	30c	7c
3½-inch	9	26¼c	38¼c	10c
4 -inch	10 2-3	30c	43½c	12c
4½-inch	12½	36c	52½c	18c
5 -inch	14½	40c	58½c	27c
6 -inch	18¾	52c	75½c	35c

Be sure to allow for cost of cutting threads when pipe is ordered cut to exact lengths. PRICES ON PIPE ARE SUBJECT TO FLUCTUATIONS OF THE MARKET.

T HANDLE ROUGH STOP AND WASTE.

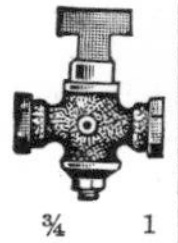

No. 42B5871 T Handle Rough Stop and waste, screwed for iron pipe.

Size, inch........	½	¾	1
Price	**37c**	**53c**	**80c**

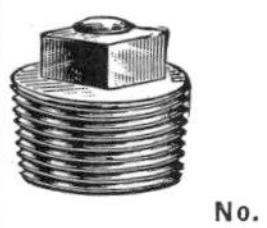

CAST IRON PLUGS.

No. 42B5748 Black.

Pipe, inch........	¼	⅜	½	¾
Price	**2c**	**2c**	**2c**	**2c**
Pipe, inches......	1	1¼	1½	2
Price	**3c**	**4c**	**4c**	**5c**

No. 42B5749 Galvanized.

Pipe, in.	¼	⅜	½	¾	1	1¼	1½	2
Price...	3c	3c	3c	3c	4c	5c	6c	7c

MALLEABLE UNIONS.

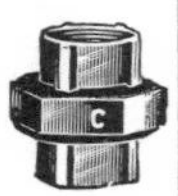

No. 42B5740 Black.

Pipe, inch	Price, each	Price, dozen
¼	**7c**	**$0.76**
⅜	**8c**	**.85**
½	**8c**	**.87**
¾	**9c**	**.98**
1	**11c**	**1.09**
1¼	**16c**	**1.73**
1½	**20c**	**2.16**
2	**25c**	**2.70**

No. 42B5741 Galvanized.

Pipe, inch...	¼	⅜	½	¾
Price, each..	$0.10	$0.11	$0.12	$0.15
Price, per doz.	1.08	1.10	1.30	1.62
Pipe inches..	1	1¼	1½	2
Price, each..	0.17	0.25	0.31	0.39
Price, per doz.	1.80	2.70	3.35	4.22

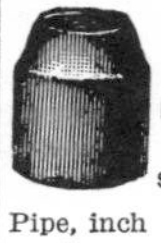

MALLEABLE REDUCERS.

No. 42B5744 Black. to reduce one size—size given is big end.

Pipe, inch	Price, each	Price, doz.
¼	**3c**	**$0.32**
⅜	**3c**	**.33**
½	**3c**	**.33**
¾	**5c**	**.54**
1	**6c**	**.65**
1¼	**7c**	**.75**
1½	**11c**	**1.09**
2	**17c**	**1.84**

No. 42B5745 Galvanized.

Pipe, inch......	½	¾	1
Price, each......	$0.05	$0.07	$0.09
Price, per doz...	.54	.76	.98
Pipe, inches.....	1¼	1½	2
Price, each......	0.13	0.17	0.27
Price, per doz...	1.40	1.84	2.92

MALLEABLE ELBOWS.

No. 42B5724 **Black.**

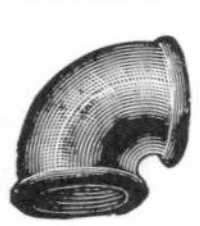

Pipe, inch.	Black, each.	Black, dozen
¼	**3c**	**$0.33**
⅜	**4c**	**.44**
½	**4c**	**.44**
¾	**6c**	**.65**
1	**8c**	**.85**
1¼	**9c**	**.90**
1½	**13c**	**1.45**
2	**18c**	**1.95**

No. 42B5725 Galvanized.

Pipe, inch.	¼	⅜	½	¾	1	1¼
Galv., each	4c	5c	6c	8c	12c	15c
Galv., doz.	44c	54c	65c	90c	$1.35	$1.72

Pipe, inches.......	1½	2
Galv., each........	**22c**	**31c**
Galv., per dozen...	**$2.38**	**$3.36**

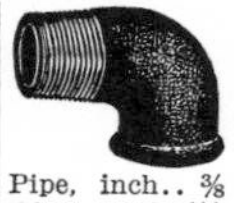

STREET ELBOWS.

No. 42B5726 Malleable Iron Street Elbows.

Pipe, inch..	⅜	½	¾	1	1¼
Black, each.	4½c	5¼c	8c	10c	16c
Black, doz..	49c	57c	85c	$1.08	$1.73

No. 42B5727 Galvanized.

Pipe, inch.....	⅜	½	¾
Galv., each....	**5c**	**7½c**	**11c**
Galv., per doz.	**54c**	**68c**	**$1.19**
Pipe, inches........		1	1¼
Galv., each........		**13¼c**	**22c**
Galv., per dozen...		**$1.44**	**$2.42**

Be sure to state size wanted.

45-DEGREE MALLEABLE ELBOWS.

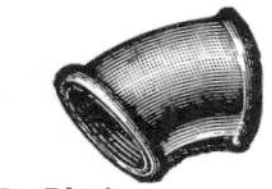

No. 42B5728 Black.

Pipe, inch...	¼	⅜	½	¾
Black, each..	5c	5c	6c	7c
Black, doz...	54c	54c	65c	76c
Pipe, inches..	1	1¼	1½	2
Black, each..	10c	13c	20c	30c
Black, doz...	$1.08	$1.41	$2.16	$3.24

No. 42B5729 Galvanized.

Pipe, inch...	¼	⅜	½	¾
Galv., each..	6c	6c	8c	9c
Galv., doz...	65c	65c	85c	98c
Pipe, inches..	1	1¼	1½	2
Galv., each..	15c	18c	30c	52c
Galv., doz...	$1.62	$1.95	$3.24	$5.60

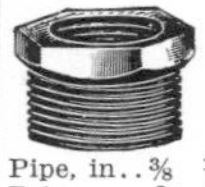

BUSHINGS.

Reducing one size, largest size is given.

No. 42B5725 Black.

Pipe, in..	⅜	½	¾	1	1¼	1½	2
Price.....	3c	3c	3c	4c	4c	4c	6c

No. 42B5753 Galvanized.

Pipe, in..	⅜	½	¾	1	1¼	1½	2
Price.....	4c	4c	5c	6c	6c	8c	11c

LOCK NUTS.

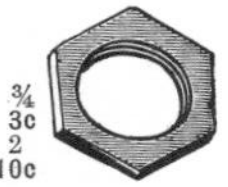

No. 42B5755

Pipe, in.	¼	⅜	½	¾
Price....	2c	3c	3c	3c
Pipe, in.	1	1¼	1½	2
Price....	3c	4c	6c	10c

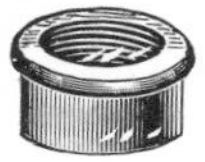

PIPE CAPS.

No. 42B5758 Black.

Pipe, in.	¼	⅜	½	¾
Price....	3c	4c	4c	4c
Pipe, in.	1	1¼	1½	2
Price....	5c	6c	10c	12c

No. 42B5759 Galvanized.

Pipe, in..	¼	⅜	½	¾	1	1¼	1½	2
Price.....	4c	4c	4c	5c	7c	9c	15c	20c

NIPPLES.

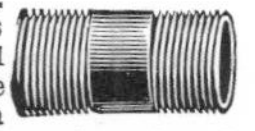

State length wanted. All nipples 6 inches long or over will be charged at price per foot of iron pipe with cost of cutting threads added. Short nipples are 2½ inches or under. Long nipples are over 2½ inches long.

Size, in.	No. 42B5763 Black short, price	No. 42B5764 Galv'd short, price	No. 42B5765 Black long, price	No. 42B5766 Galv'd long, price
¼	**3c**	**4c**	**4c**	**5c**
⅜	**3c**	**4c**	**4c**	**5c**
½	**3c**	**4c**	**4c**	**5c**
¾	**3c**	**4c**	**4c**	**5c**
1	**3c**	**4c**	**4c**	**5c**
1¼	**4c**	**5c**	**5c**	**8c**
1½	**5c**	**6c**	**6c**	**10c**
2	**6c**	**7c**	**8c**	**12c**

MALLEABLE IRON PIPE VISE WITH TOOL STEEL JAWS, 94 CENTS.

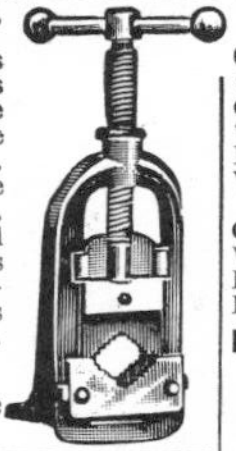

Steamfitters, plumbers and gasfitters will find this the handiest vise on the market. The jaws are made of the best tool steel, accurately machined. Frame is made of malleable iron, is strong, well proportioned and nicely finished. Weighs only 7 pounds. Can be carried in tool chest. Takes pipe from ⅛ to 2 inches.

No. 42B5968

Price 94c

OPEN HINGE, MALLEABLE IRON PIPE VISE, SIZE NO. 1, $1.15.

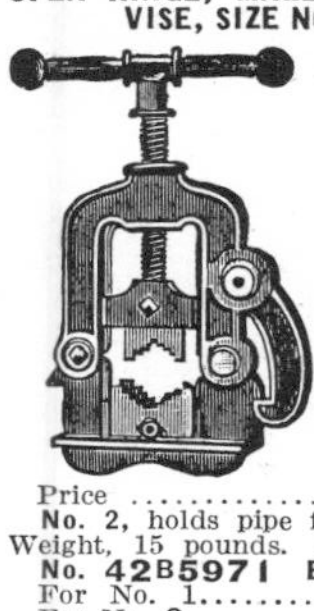

Has interchangeable cut steel jaws and self locking latch, and is constructed to do the heaviest work. Great care has been taken in manufacturing the various parts, putting the strength where most needed. Jaws are warranted.

No. 42B5970

No. 1, holds pipe from ¼ to 2½ inches. Weight, 11½ pounds.

Price $1.15

No. 2, holds pipe from ¼ to 3 inches. Weight, 15 pounds. Price........$1.60

No. 42B5971 Extra Jaws.

For No. 1.......................... .65

For No. 2.......................... .90

GENUINE SMITH COMBINATION PIPE VISE, SIZE NO. 1, $4.56.

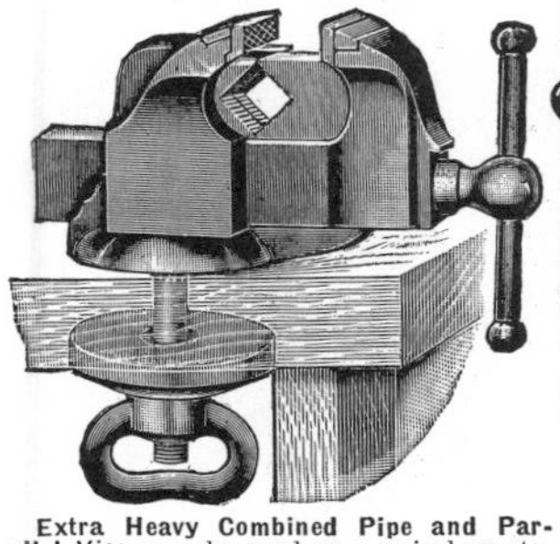

Extra Heavy Combined Pipe and Parallel Vise, can be used as a swivel or stationary bottom. Has heavy steel slide bar and steel removable jaws. Material and workmanship A1. Best vise for the money sold by anyone.

No. 42B5976 Size 1, weight, 45 pounds; takes pipe ⅛ to 2 inches.

Price $4.56

Size 2, weight, 72 pounds; takes pipe ¼ to 3 inches. Price...............$5.71

THREE-WHEEL PIPE CUTTER, SIZE NO. 1, 81 CENTS.

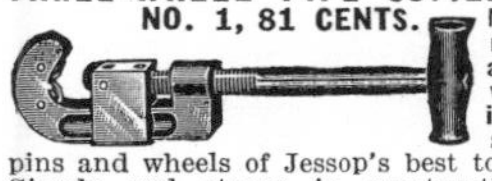

Made of malleable and wrought iron with steel pins and wheels of Jessop's best tool steel. Simple and strong in construction and cuts rapidly and easily.

No. 42B5987	No. 1	No. 2	No. 3
Cuts pipe.	⅛ to 1 in.	½ to 2 in.	1½ to 3 in.
Wt., lbs...	2¾	5½	9
Price	81c	$1.09	$1.83
Ex. wheels.	4½c	.05½	.07½

OUR HEATING ESTIMATES ARE FREE FOR THE ASKING. SEND FOR OUR HEATING CATALOG.

SAUNDERS' PATTERN IMPROVED PIPE CUTTER, SIZE NO. 1, 62 CENTS.

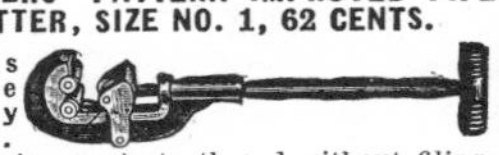

Cuts square every time.

Leaves pipe ready to thread without filing. Weight, 3¾ to 6¾ pounds.

No. 42B5996	No. 1	No. 2	No. 3
Cuts pipe...	⅛ to 1 in.	½ to 2 in.	2 to 3 in.
Weight, lbs.	3½	7	13
Price	62c	92c	$2.24
Ex. wheels..	5c	6½c	.12

BROWN'S ADJUSTABLE PIPE TONGS, SIZE NO. 1, 58 CENTS.

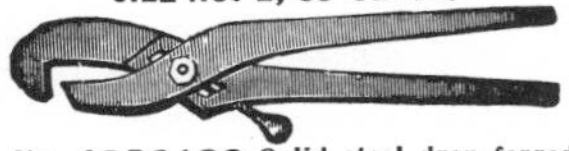

No. 42B6122 Solid steel drop forged.

Number...	1	1½	2	3	4
Takes pipe from, in..	⅛to¾	⅜to1	½to1¼	1to2	1¼to3
Wt., lbs.	2¼	3¾	6	11	21
Price ...	58c	69c	82c	$1.14	$2.55

TWIST DRILLS FOR RATCHET DRILL STOCK.

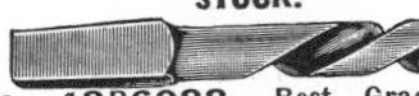

No. 42B6088 Best Grade Twist Drills for our No. 42B6075 Ratchet Drill Stocks shown on this page. Made extra heavy.

Diam.	Length	Price
¼ inch	5 inches	60c
5-16 inch	5 inches	62c
⅜ inch	6 inches	72c
7-16 inch	6¼ inches	75c
½ inch	6½ inches	78c
9-16 inch	6½ inches	81c
⅝ inch	6½ inches	84c
¾ inch	6½ inches	93c

ECONOMY PIPE STOCK AND DIES WITH STEEL CUTTERS.

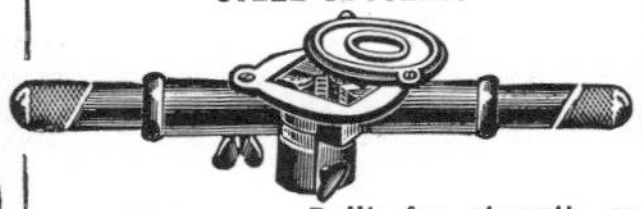

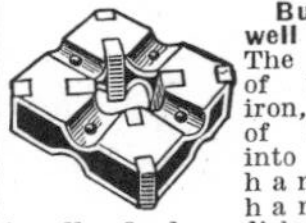

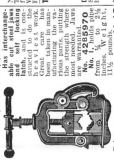

Built for strength as well as economy in price. The center part is made of the best malleable iron, handles are made of steel pipe screwed into stock. The knurled handles prevent the hands from slipping; handle finely polished, center part dark finish. They are true to size, light and fully guaranteed. Average weight, 20 lbs.

The dies are made of four cutters of the best steel. Interlocked with two homogeneous steel plates. Stock, dies and bushings in sets.

Catalog No.	No.	Cuts Pipe, inches	Dimension of Dies	Price
42B6006	0	⅛, ¼, ⅜, ½	2x2x½	$1.97
42B6007	1	¼, ⅜, ½, ¾, 1	2½x2½x¾	3.10
42B6008	1½	¾, 1, 1¼	3x3x¾	2.75
42B6009	2	1¼, 1½, 2	4x4x⅞	4.00
42B6011	1A	½, ¾, 1	2½x2½x¾	2.25
42B6012	1½ B.	¼, ⅜, ½, ¾, 1, 1¼	3x3x¾	4.48
42B6013	1¾ B.	½, ¾, 1, 1¼, 1½	3x3x¾	4.05

No. 42B6010 Extra Dies.

Cut Pipe, inches	Dimension of Dies	Fit Stock No.	Price
⅛, ¼, ⅜, ½	2x2x½	0	31c
⅛, ¼, ⅜, ½, ¾, 1	2½x2½x¾	1	41
¾, 1, 1¼	3x3x¾	1½ & 1¾	52c
1¼, 1½, 2	4x4x⅞	2	70c

LIGHTNING PUMP REPAIRERS' DIES AND STOCK.

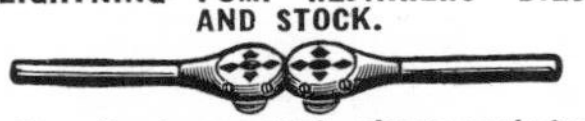

Two dies in one stock, always ready for use without changing dies. Made of the very best materials and fully warranted. Will cut a full thread. Size dies, ⅜ and 7-16 inch. Weight, 2 pounds.

No. 42B6095 Price.........$1.92

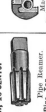

$3.18 ARMSTRONG PATTERN No. 2 ADJUSTABLE STOCK AND DIES FOR THREADING PIPE.

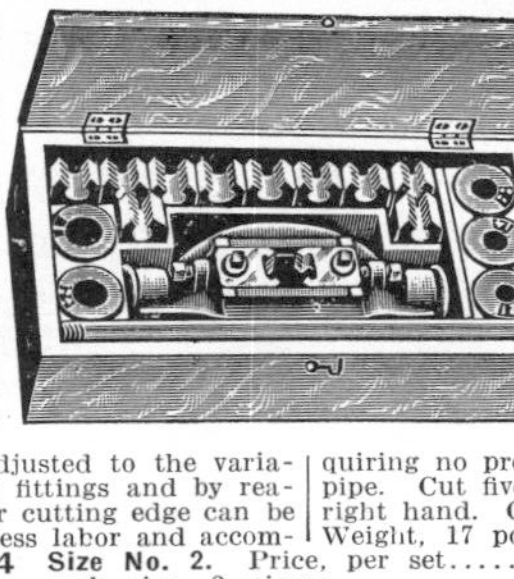

The best known pipe cutting tool on the market. They are made of highest grade material throughout, have tool steel cutters, are easily adjusted and are the most satisfactory pipe stock and dies ever constructed. More of them have been sold in the past fifteen years than any other make. The dies can be adjusted to the variations in the size of fittings and by reason of their peculiar cutting edge can be worked with much less labor and accomplish the desired results in less time than with other dies. The dies have a double taper; that is, the taper at the entrance for the first few threads is greater in degree than the standard taper which forms a lead to the dies, causing them to start on the pipe without filing, even when there is a swell or burr, and requiring no pressure to start dies on the pipe. Cut five sizes, ¼ inch to 1 inch, right hand. Complete in hardwood box. Weight, 17 pounds.

No. 42B6014 Size No. 2. Price, per set.........................$3.18

Extra pipe dies, each size, 2 pieces............................... .50

$3.25 ARMSTRONG PATTERN No. 2½ ADJUSTABLE STOCK AND DIES FOR THREADING PIPE.

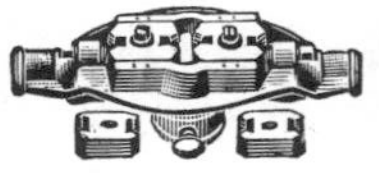

Made of the same high grade material and in the same careful manner as our No. 42B6014, described above. No. 2¾ Pipe Stock, complete with four dies cutting ½, ¾, 1 and 1¼ inches, right hand. Illustration shows head only. Furnished with handles, dies and guides, complete in hardwood case. Weight, 17½ pounds.

No. 42B6015 Size No. 2½. Price, per set.$3.25

Extra pipe dies, each size, 2 pieces............ 1.08

$5.35 ARMSTRONG PATTERN No. 3 ADJUSTABLE STOCK AND DIES FOR THREADING PIPE.

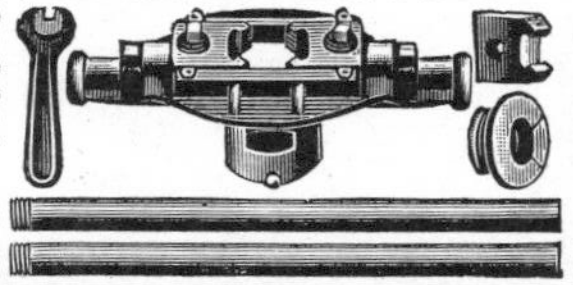

Made of the same material and in the same manner as the other Armstrong pattern pipe sets shown above. No. 3 Pipe Stock, complete with three sizes of dies cutting 1¼ to 2 inches. Right hand; furnished with handle, dies and guides, complete. Weight, 29 pounds.

No. 42B6016 Size, No. 3.

Price, per set...................$5.35

Extra pipe dies, each size, 2 pieces 1.35

MALLEABLE IRON PIPE STOCK WITH SOLID STEEL DIES.

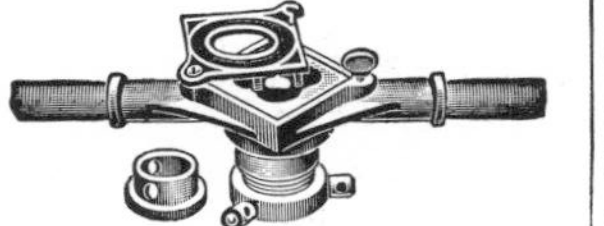

The most satisfactory stock and dies on the market at anything like our price. They are light, strong, convenient and fully guaranteed to do the work we claim for them. Nos. 2 and 3 furnished with leader screw as shown in illustration. We do not furnish leader screws with other sizes. We do not furnish taps with these sets. See No. 42B6060 for taps. Average weight, about 20 pounds.

No.	42B6000	42B6001	42B6002
Pipe size	No. 0	No. 1	No. 1½
of dies.	⅛, ¼, ⅜, ½	¼, ⅜, ½, ¾, 1	¾, 1, 1¼
Dimension of dies.	2x½	2½x¾	3x¾
Complete with dies......	$2.38	$2.83	$2.58
Extra dies, each.	.33	.42	.65
Ex. guides, each.	.07	.08	.10

No.	42B6003	42B6004	42B6005
Pipe size	No. 1¾	No. 2	No. 3
of dies......	1, 1¼, 1½	1¼, 1½, 2	2½, 3
Dimension of dies......	3x¾	4x⅞	5x1¼
Complete with dies.....	$2.60	$2.80	$11.50
Extra dies, each	.65	.83	2.50
Ex. guides, each	.08	.09	.28

These are the finest tools of their kind manufactured or sold by anyone regardless of price.

COMBINATION DROP FORGED EXTRA TOOL STEEL GAS PLIERS.

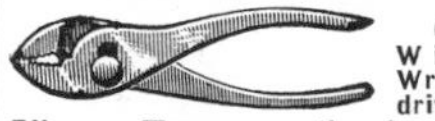

Combination Wire Cutter, Wrench, Screwdriver and Gas Pliers. These are the handiest pliers made, very strong and durable, nicely finished.

6-inch pliers take up to ¾-inch pipe; 8-inch and 10-inch take up to 1-inch pipe.

No. 42B6136 Black Finish.

Size, inches.....	6	8	10
Price, each.....	$0.32	$0.37	$0.41
Weight, oz......	½	10	16
Per dozen......	3.40	4.30	4.65

No. 42B6137 Nickel Plated.

Size, inches......	6	8	10
Price, each.....	$0.36	$0.50	$0.54
Per dozen......	3.65	4.65	5.25

ACME LIGHTNING COMBINATION WRENCH AND PLIERS.

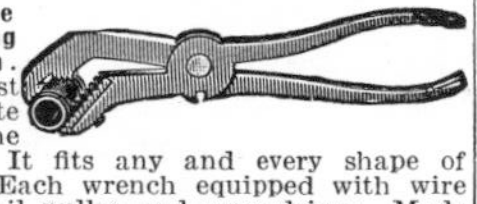

Acme Lightning Wrench. The most up to date tool on the market. It fits any and every shape of article. Each wrench equipped with wire cutter, nail puller and screwdriver. Made of the finest grade of drop forged steel, oil tempered. 6-inch are nickel plated; 8-inch and 12-inch polished. Cheap in price only.

No. 42B6139

Size	Weight	Price
Size, 6 inch.	6 oz.	Price.....46c
Size, 8 inch.	1 lb.	Price.....59c
Size, 12 inch.	2¼ lbs.	Price.....68c

HIGH GRADE PIPE TAPS AND REAMERS, SIZE ⅛ INCH, 16 CENTS.

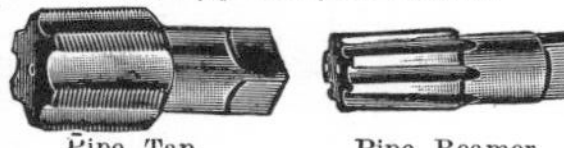

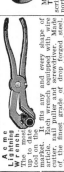

Pipe Tap. Pipe Reamer.

No. 42B6060 Pipe Tap.

No. 42B6062 Pipe Reamer.

Taps or reamers are the same price.

Size, inch......	⅛	¼	⅜	½	¾
Weight, oz......	⅓	2	4	5	10
Price	16c	19c	22c	27c	36c

Size, inches...	1	1¼	1½	2
Weight, lbs...	1	1½	2¼	3½
Price	45c	54c	65c	89c

HIGH GRADE TOOL STEEL LIGHTNING BURRING REAMER.

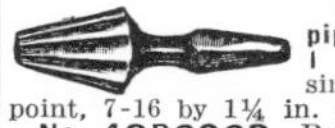

Used for reaming pipe from ½ inch to 1 inch, also countersinking. Size at point, 7-16 by 1¼ in. at base. Wt., 4 oz.

No. 42B6063 Price 69c

No. 42B6064 Same as above, except it can be used on pipe ⅛ to 1¼ inches. Weight, 8 ounces.

Price 98c

SOLID DROP FORGED STEEL GAS PLIERS.

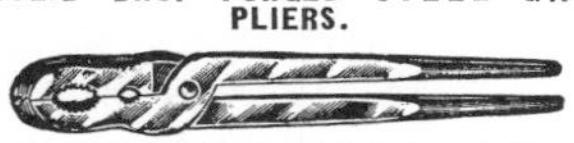

No. 42B6130 Polished and blued.

Length, inches...............	8	10
Weight, ozs.................	12	16
Price	24c	34c

YANKEE ADJUSTABLE PIPE WRENCH JAWS, SIZE NO. 1, PER PAIR, 19 CENTS.

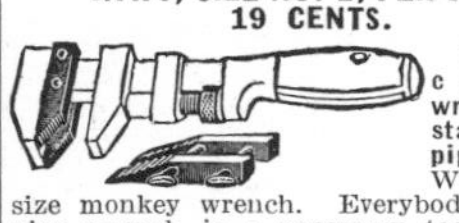

Change a common wrench instantly into a pipe wrench. Will fit any size monkey wrench. Everybody knows a pipe wrench is a necessary tool to have, but is expensive; now everybody can have one. It can be adjusted to fit pipe or bolts from ⅛ to 3 inches. Made of high grade steel. Will last a lifetime. Prices are for jaws only. Weight, about 7 oz.

No. 42B6140 No. 1, fits wrench 6 inches to 10 inches in size. Price.... 19c

No. 2, fits wrench 10 inches to 24 inches in size. Price................23c

DROP FORGED ALLIGATOR PIPE WRENCH, 5¾ INCHES LONG, 9 CENTS.

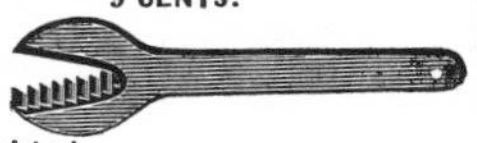

Made of a high grade tool steel, nicely finished.

No. 42B6145

Length, in.	5¾	9	16	22	27
Takes pipe	⅛to⅜	⅜to¾	½to1¼	1¼to2	2to3
Weight ...	3 oz.	12 oz.	3½ lbs.	7 lbs.	9 lbs.
Price ...	9c	21c	43c	65c	$1.10

GENUINE STILLSON PIPE WRENCH, 10-INCH, 64 CENTS.

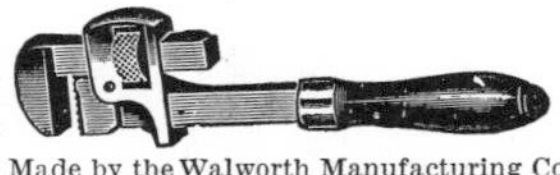

Made by the Walworth Manufacturing Co. **Too well known** to require a lengthy description. They are made of the best imported steel, finely finished and will give satisfaction.

No. 42B6149

Length, open, inches.	6	8	10
Takes pipe from..	⅛ to ½	⅛ to ¾	⅛ to 1
Price	53c	55c	64c
Length, open, inches.	14	18	24
Takes pipe from.....	¼to1½	¼to2	¼to2½
Price	89c	$1.18	$1.78

GENUINE TRIMO PIPE WRENCH, 10-INCH, FOR 68 CENTS.

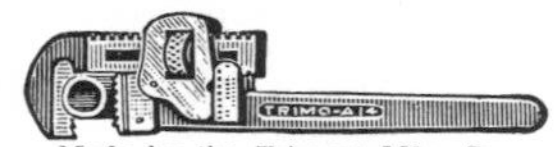

Made by the Trimont Mfg. Co.

This wrench is drop forged from bar steel, is interchangeable in all its parts, does not lock upon the pipe, but releases its hold readily; grips the pipe firmly without lost motion; does not crush the pipe or slip. The movable jaw and the nut are made with a round top and bottom thread, guaranteed not to strip or burr. An inserted jaw is placed in the handle, which can be renewed at little expense when dull or worn.

No. 42B6147

Length, open, inches....	6	8
Takes pipe..............	⅛ to ½	⅛ to ¾
Weight	6 oz.	10 oz.
Price	58c	60c

Length, open, in..	10	14	18	24
Takes pipe..	⅛to1	¼to1½	¼to2	¼to2½
Weight, lbs.	1½	2½	4¼	8
Price	68c	89c	$1.19	$1.79

BEMIS & CALL'S COMBINATION NUT AND PIPE WRENCH, 10-INCH, $1.18.

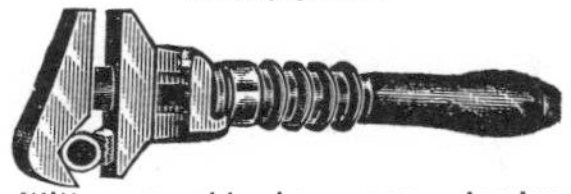

With wrought bar, case hardened throughout, parts interchangeable; furnished with **long nut,** every wrench guaranteed.

No. 42B6164 10-inch, takes pipe ½ to 1 inch in diameter. Weight, 2 lbs.

Price $1.18

12-inch, takes pipe ½ to 1¾ inches in diameter. Wt., 3½ lbs. Price......$1.34

15-inch, takes pipe ½ to 2¼ inches in diameter. Weight, 4½ lbs. Price...$1.89

BROCK'S STANDARD PIPE WRENCH.

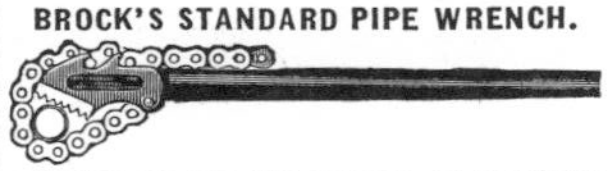

Gotten up for the purpose of supplying a first class wrench at a reasonable price. It is forged out of bar steel in one piece. The teeth are milled and tempered. The chain is made of special steel. The handle is made oblong shape and has greater resisting power against a bending strain than wrenches with handles made of round or hexagon steel. By swinging the chain from one side to the other this wrench will take more intermediate sizes of pipe than any other wrench made. We guarantee every wrench against defects and to be as good a wrench as you have ever used, or money returned.

No. 42B6167 Size No. 1, capacity, ¼ to 2 inches; length, 20 inches. Weight, 19 lbs. Price...................$1.58

Size No. 2, capacity, ¼ to 3 inches; length, 27 in. Wt., 5 lbs. Price....$2.34

Size No. 3, capacity, ¾ to 6 inches; length, 37 in. Wt., 9½ lbs. Price..$3.23

THE KEYSTONE DOUBLE ACTING RATCHETS.

For Square Shank Drills only.

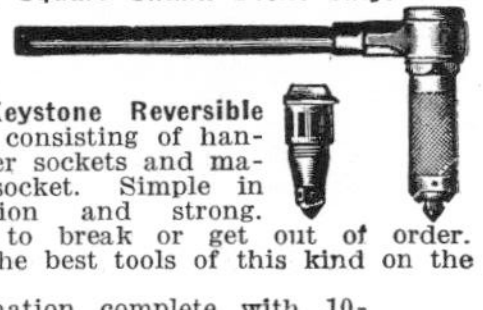

No. 42B6075

The Keystone Reversible Ratchet, consisting of handle, boiler sockets and machinist socket. Simple in construction and strong. Nothing to break or get out of order. One of the best tools of this kind on the market.

Combination complete with 10-inch handle. Wt., 4 lbs. Price.....$5.20

Combination complete with 14-inch handle. Wt., 8½ lbs. Price... 6.00

Combination complete with 16-inch handle. Wt., 13½ lbs. Price.. 6.80

GAS AND ELECTRIC FIXTURES IN THE NEWEST STYLES

The selection of Gas and Electric Fixtures for the modern home is exceedingly important as fixtures have so much to do with the appearance and proper lighting of the rooms. Careful home builders are becoming more particular in this matter; their demands are more exacting each year. In selecting your fixtures we ask you to consider the fact that they will be a part of your home as long as it lasts. One should not be too considerate of the money if it is at a sacrifice of quality and appearance. We have a large variety to select from, including inexpensive and showy fixtures, as well as those that display richness and simple elegance. We can save you so much on these goods, owing to the fact that they are sold on larger profits elsewhere, that you can readily afford to buy our very best grades.

We show you a number of our popular styles in their actual colors on page 50, but all these fixtures are described and illustrated in the following pages as well.

While we have a large variety of designs and styles and a considerable range of prices, the quality of our fixtures is uniformly good throughout; only the finest quality of solid brass of extra heavy gauge (weight) is used in their construction. The finish of fixtures Nos. 3B2200 to 3B2314 is polished brass relieved by brass gilt ornaments. The finish of fixtures Nos. 3B2400 to everything 3B2586 is rich satin brass (brush brass) buffed and polished by hand. No pains or expense have

been spared to make the details of construction perfect. The connecting joints, sockets, etc., are thoroughly cemented; each part fits perfectly and the embossing and workmanship are faultless. We guarantee our electric fixtures to be properly wired and insulated, and all gas fixtures to hold gas without leakage. They all conform in every way with the requirements of the Board of Insurance Underwriters. No better fixtures are made at any price.

Our prices are for the fixtures absolutely complete, ready to hang, which includes complete electric wiring, Edison key socket, brass shade rings, glass shades, gas pillars, lava tips and insulating joints where necessary according to the descriptions and illustrations. These parts add one-fourth to the value of the chandelier.

We invite comparison of our values with those offered by other dealers. It is a matter of common knowledge that these goods are sold on large profits elsewhere. It is in the case of such merchandise as this that our economical methods of business show our customers the largest savings. We price these goods on exactly the same basis as we price the most common, everyday household article. Our well known guarantee of quality applies to these goods as to everything else we sell.

No. 3B2200

No. 3B2202

No. 3B2200 Stiff Gilt Gas Bracket, 6-inch. Price....13c
No. 3B2202 Swing Gilt Gas Bracket, 11-inch. Price.......28c

No. 3B2236

No. 3B2235 1-Light Polished Brass 30-Inch Gas Pendant, no glassware. Price....36c
No. 3B2236 Same as No. 3B2235, 36 inches long. Price 49c

No. 3B2210

No. 3B2212

No. 3B2210 Double Swing Gilt Brass Bracket. Price..........45c
No. 3B2212 Single Swing Gilt Polished Brass Bracket. Extends 11½ inches. Star pattern glass shade. 75c

No. 3B2225 2-Light Polished Brass 36-Inch Gas Pendant, no glassware. Price 95c

No. 3B2214

No. 3B2218

No. 3B2214 Double Swing Square Polished Brass Bracket. Extends 21 inches. Star pattern glass shade. Price 95c
No. 3B2218 Polished Gilt Electric Bracket. Extends 6 inches. Fancy star pattern glass shade. Price.........69c

No. 3B2220

No. 3B2220 2-Light Combination Bracket. One gas and one electric. Extends 8 inches. Fancy star pattern glass shades. Price..........$1.18

No. 3B2232 1-Light Polished Brass 36-Inch Gas Pendant. Fancy brass ornament. Star pattern glass shade. Price 97c

No. 3B2238 1-Light 36-Inch Fancy Gas Pendant, fluted cup and leaf ornament. Star pattern glass shade. Price $1.18

No. 3B2240 1-Light Polished Brass Electric Pendant, 42 inches to end of lamp. Star pattern glass shade. Price...$1.65

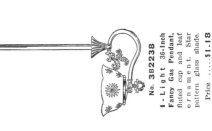

No. 3B2242 2-Light Combination 36-Inch Polished Brass Fixture. One gas and one electric light. Star glass shades. Price $1.98

SPECIAL VALUES IN SHOWY GAS AND ELECTRIC FIXTURES

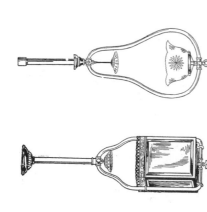

No. 3B2252
Square Polished Brass Hall Fixture. Beveled plate glass sides, Fancy brass crown smoke bell
Price $3.35

No. 3B2250
Polished Brass 30-Inch Gas Hall Fixture. Smoke bell and star pattern glass shade.
Price $1.25

No. 3B2248
Polished Brass Combination Hall Pendant, electric opal glass ball shade and gas candle.
Price..$3.25

No. 3B2266   **No. 3B2269**
FANCY POLISHED BRASS CHANDELIERS. Fluted ball center with cup. Loop arms, half fluted tubing, ceiling canopy and fancy star pattern shades.
No. 3B2265 2-Light Gas Chandelier. Price...................$1.67
No. 3B2266 3-Light Gas Chandelier. Price................... 2.25
No. 3B2268 2-Light Electric Chandelier. Price............. 2.48
No. 3B2269 3-Light Electric Chandelier. Price............. 3.45
No. 3B2270 4-Light Combination Chandelier. Price....... 3.98

No. 3B2274   **No. 3B2279**
FANCY RICH GILT CHANDELIERS. Ornamented with embossed center ball body and cup, fluted tubing and fancy canopy. The arms are fitted with gilt cast brass ornaments. Fancy star pattern shades.
No. 3B2273 2-Light Gas Chandelier. Price...................$2.18
No. 3B2274 3-Light Gas Chandelier. Price................... 2.95
No. 3B2278 2-Light Electric Chandelier. Price............. 2.91
No. 3B2279 3-Light Electric Chandelier. Price............. 4.38

No. 3B2297   **No. 3B2302**
RICH MAT GILT BRASS CHANDELIERS. Partly fluted tubing, with ceiling plate. Large pineapple center with mat. gilt band surmounted by a small ball and fluted cup. Fancy cast mat gilt brass ornaments on the arms and on bottom of body. Star pattern glass shades.
No. 3B2295 2-Light Gas Chandelier. Price...................$3.25
No. 3B2301 3-Light Gas Chandelier. Price................... 4.27
No. 3B2302 2-Light Electric Chandelier. Price............. 4.25
No. 3B2304 3-Light Electric Chandelier. Price............. 5.45
No. 3B2304 4-Light Combination Chandelier. Price....... 5.75
No. 3B2305 6-Light Combination Chandelier. Price....... 7.48

No. 3B2309   **No. 3B2312**
RICH MAT GILT AND POLISHED BRASS CHANDELIERS. Half reed tubing. Large center body with cast mat gilt ornaments and a beaded cup. Heavy mat gilt castings on each arm. Embossed silver frosted shades in Cupid design. The best of the low priced fixtures.
No. 3B2308 2-Light Gas Chandelier. Price...................$3.45
No. 3B2309 3-Light Gas Chandelier. Price................... 4.68
No. 3B2311 2-Light Electric Chandelier. Price............. 4.50
No. 3B2312 3-Light Electric Chandelier. Price............. 5.75
No. 3B2314 4-Light Combination Chandelier. Price....... 6.25

OUR FINEST FIXTURES BEGIN HERE

We can furnish brackets Nos. 3B2403, 3B2404, 3B2405 and 3B2406 fitted with shades to match the glassware on any of our fixtures without extra charge.

No. 3B2400
1-Light Satin Brass Gas Bracket. Extends 8 inches. Wreath pattern shade. Price...**78c**

No. 3B2401
1-Light Satin Brass Electric Bracket. Extends 10¾ inches. Wreath pattern shade. Price...**95c**

No. 3B2403
1-Light Satin Brass Gas Bracket. Extends 10 inches. Large wall canopy. Silver frosted blown shade, chrysanthemum pattern. Price...**$1.15**

No. 3B2404
1-Light Satin Brass Electric Bracket. Extends 12 inches. Large wall canopy. Silver frosted blown shade, chrysanthemum pattern. Price...**$1.28**

No. 3B2405
1-Light Upright Satin Brass Electric Bracket. Extends 10¾ inches. Large wall canopy. Silver frosted blown shade, chrysanthemum pattern. Price...**$1.18**

No. 3B2406
2-Light Combination Satin Brass Bracket. Extends 8 inches. Large wall canopy. Silver frosted blown shades, chrysanthemum pattern. Price...**$1.95**

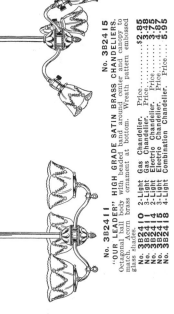

No. 3B2415

No. 3B2411

"OUR LEADER" HIGH GRADE SATIN BRASS CHANDELIERS. Octagonal ball body with beaded band around center and canopy to match. Acorn brass ornament at bottom. Wreath pattern embossed glass shades.

No.			Price
No. 3B2410	2-Light	Gas Chandelier.	$2.85
No. 3B2411	3-Light	Gas Chandelier.	3.48
No. 3B2414	2-Light	Electric Chandelier.	3.77
No. 3B2415	3-Light	Electric Chandelier.	4.85
No. 3B2418	4-Light	Combination Chandelier.	5.95

No. 3B2446

Because of damage to the page, the caption and one of the drawings of the "Radiant Diana" Rich Fluted Satin Brass Chandeliers have been deleted.

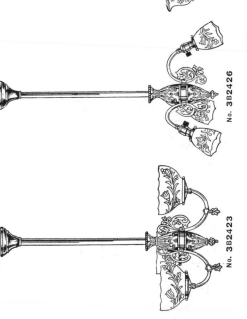

No. 3B2434

No. 3B2431

"CHRYSANTHEMUM" SATIN BRASS CHANDELIERS. Large center body of spun brass with ornamental casting at bottom. Spun floral canopy. The gracefully curved arms are fitted with handsome floral ornaments in chrysanthemum designs at the top. Fancy gas brass keys. Silver frosted blown shades with etched chrysanthemum pattern.

No.			Price
No. 3B2430	2-Light	Gas Chandelier.	$4.45
No. 3B2431	3-Light	Gas Chandelier.	5.48
No. 3B2433	2-Light	Electric Chandelier.	5.25
No. 3B2434	3-Light	Electric Chandelier.	6.49
No. 3B2436	4-Light	Combination Chandelier.	7.88
No. 3B2437	6-Light	Combination Chandelier.	9.98

No. 3B2426

No. 3B2423

"QUEEN LOUISE" RICHLY EMBOSSED SATIN BRASS CHANDELIERS. Center body beautifully embossed in raised flower design with cast ornament at the bottom and embossed cup at the top. Large ceiling canopy. Arms fitted with rich patina finish cast brass ornaments. Fancy gas keys and embossed flower pattern shades.

No.			Price
No. 3B2422	2-Light	Gas Chandelier.	$4.75
No. 3B2423	3-Light	Gas Chandelier.	5.95
No. 3B2425	2-Light	Electric Chandelier.	5.48
No. 3B2426	3-Light	Electric Chandelier.	6.75
No. 3B2428	4-Light	Combination Chandelier.	7.98

RICH AND BEAUTIFUL HIGH GRADE CHANDELIERS

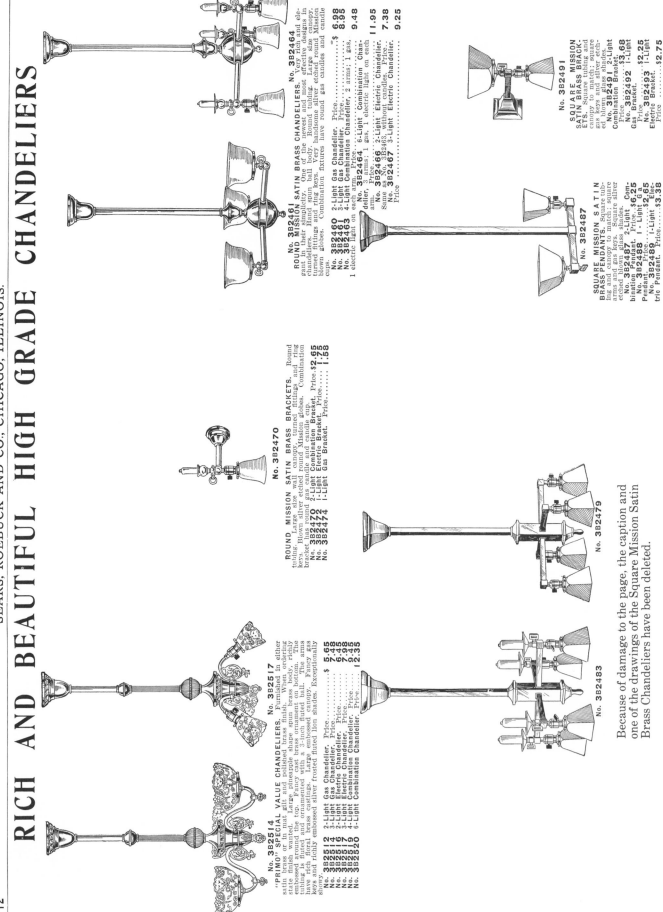

No. 3B2514

No. 3B2517

"PRIMO" SPECIAL VALUE CHANDELIERS. Furnished in either satin brass or in mat gilt and polished brass finish. When ordering state finish wanted. Large pineapple shape spun brass body, richly embossed around the top. Fancy cast brass ornament on bottom. The tubing is fluted and ornamented with a 3-inch fluted ball. The arms have rich floral brass castings. Large embossed canopy. Fancy gas keys and richly embossed silver frosted fluted lion shades. Exceptionally showy.

No. 3B2512	2-Light Gas Chandelier. Price............	$ 5.65
No. 3B2514	2-Light Gas Chandelier. Price............	7.48
No. 3B2517	3-Light Electric Chandelier. Price.......	6.98
No. 3B2519	3-Light Electric Chandelier. Price.......	9.45
No. 3B2520	4-Light Combination Chandelier. Price....	9.45
	6-Light Combination Chandelier. Price....	12.35

No. 3B2470

ROUND MISSION SATIN BRASS BRACKETS. Round tubing. Large size wall canopy, turned fittings and ring keys. Blown silver etched round Mission globes. Combination bracket has round gas candle and candle cup.

No. 3B2470	2-Light Combination Bracket. Price.$2.65
No. 3B2472	1-Light Electric Bracket. Price......	1.75
No. 3B2474	1-Light Gas Bracket. Price........	1.58

No. 3B2464

No. 3B2461

ROUND MISSION SATIN BRASS CHANDELIERS. No. 3B2464. Very rich and elegant in their simplicity. One of the newest and most effective designs in chandeliers. Hand spun, ball body. Round tubing. Large size canopy, turned fittings and ring keys. Very handsome silver etched round Mission blown globes. Combination fixtures have round gas candles and candle cups.

No. 3B2460	2-Light Gas Chandelier. Price............$	6.98
No. 3B2461	3-Light Gas Chandelier. Price............	8.95
No. 3B2463	4-Light Combination Chandelier, 2 arms; 1 gas. Price............	9.48
No. 3B2464	6-Light Combination Chandelier. 7 arms, 1 gas, 1 electric light on each arm. Price............	11.95
No. 3B2466	2-Light Electric Chandelier. Same as No. 3B2463, without candles. Price............	7.38
No. 3B2467	3-Light Electric Chandelier. 1 electric light on each arm. Price............	9.25

No. 3B2491

SQUARE MISSION SATIN BRASS BRACKETS. Square tubing and canopy to match; square keys and silver etched blown glass shades.

No. 3B2491	2-Light Combination Bracket. Price............$3.68
No. 3B2492	1-Light Gas Bracket. Price............	$2.25
No. 3B2493	1-Light Electric Bracket. Price............	$2.75

No. 3B2487

SQUARE MISSION SATIN BRASS PENDANTS. Square tubing and canopy to match; square arms and gas keys. Square silver etched blown glass shades.

No. 3B2487	2-Light Combination Pendant. Price............$6.25
No. 3B2488	1-Light Gas Pendant. Price............	$2.65
No. 3B2489	1-Light Electric Pendant. Price............	$3.38

No. 3B2479

No. 3B2483

Because of damage to the page, the caption and one of the drawings of the Square Mission Satin Brass Chandeliers have been deleted.

THE NEWEST IDEAS IN CHANDELIERS

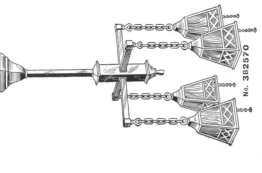

No. 3B2501

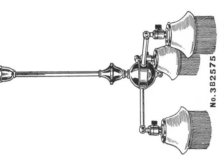

No. 3B2505

"VENUS" FANCY SATIN BRASS CHANDELIERS. Exceptionally rich and elegant. Extra large hand spun body of Grecian design, ornamented at top and bottom with carved brass. Tubing is reeded half way up the stem. Large spun ceiling canopy. The gracefully curved arms project out of carved ornaments fastened to the center body. Fancy gas keys. Silver frosted blown shades etched with tulip design.

No. 3B2501	3-Light Gas Chandelier. Price......	$ 9.85
No. 3B2502	4-Light Gas Chandelier. Price......	11.58
No. 3B2505	3-Light Electric Chandelier. Price....	9.48
No. 3B2506	4-Light Electric Chandelier. Price....	11.65
No. 3B2507	4-Light Combination Chandelier. Price....	11.98
No. 3B2508	6-Light Combination Chandelier. Price....	15.50

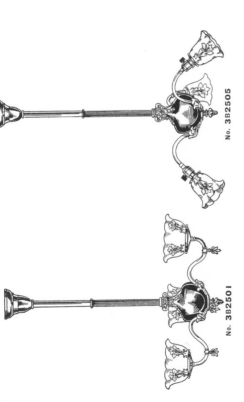

No. 3B2530 ORNA- MENTAL HALL LIGHT. Length, 36 inches. ⅞- inch satin brass tubing. Chain pull socket, opal glass ball shade. Fancy ceiling canopy.

Price $2.43

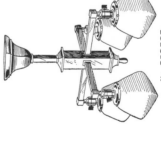

No. 3B2585

No. 3B2585 SQUARE FOUR-LIGHT MISSION ELEC- TRIC CEILING FIXTURE. Satin brass. Large square Mis- sion body 7 inches long, and four 8-inch arms. On each arm is a large octagon shape silver frosted closed bottom mission glass globe. Keyless sockets. Exceptionally attractive parlor or hall chan- delier. Extends 20 inches. Price. Extends 20 inches..$13.50
No. 3B2586....Exactly the same as No. 3B2585, but fitted with two lights only.
Price $9.75

No. 3B2575 THREE-LIGHT ROUND MISSION COLONIAL PARLOR CHANDELIER. Satin brass. Large spun ball center, surmounted by an oblong ball ornament. Three 8-inch round Mission arms, with silver frosted Colonial 6-inch shades, with 4- inch transparent silver crystal fringe. Length to bottom of fringe, 46 inches.
Price $10.75
No. 3B2576 Exactly the same as No. 3B2575, but with two lights only. Price..$8.85

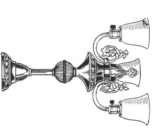

No.3B2575

No. 3B2580 THREE-LIGHT ELECTRIC CEILING FIXTURE. Very newest method of lighting. The chandelier is out of the way and the light is diffused over the entire room. Satin brass. Has spun pineapple shape body, richly embossed with fancy orna- ment at bottom. Three stalactitic arms, ornamented with floral brass castings. Extends 18 inches from the ceiling. Has four round silver frosted glass shades. Keyless sockets. Price..$6.95

No.3B2580

No. 3B2570

No. 3B2570 FANCY FOUR-LIGHT ART SQUARE MISSION PARLOR OR DINING ROOM CHANDELIER. Exceptionally rich and ornamental chandelier. Embodies the very newest ideas in art shade lighting. Satin brass with square body 7 inches long. Four 8-inch square arms. At end of arm hangs an 18-inch brass chain and 8-inch amber colored cathedral glass shade mounted on cut out Mission brass frame. Chain pull sockets. Length to bottom of shade, 48 inches. Retail price, $50.00. Our price..........$29.75
No. 3B2571 Exactly the same as No. 3B2570, but fitted with two lights only. Price..........$18.98

No. 3B2555 SIX-LIGHT COMBINATION ART DOME SHADE. Made of satin brass, fitted with 16-inch amber colored cathedral art glass with 5-inch transparent beaded fringe to match. Has four outside lights; two fancy gas arms, fitted with fancy embossed shades, and two electric arms with fancy embossed shades. There are also two electric lights inside of dome. The stem is richly orna- mented. Length to bottom of fringe, 48 inches. Price.....$18.75

WE OFFER YOU HIGH GRADE DOMES AT UNUSUALLY LOW PRICES

Art glass domes, like everything else, are manufactured in several grades and thus vary in quality and appearance. There are on the market many cheap and poorly constructed domes which will look shabby and fall to pieces after being used for a short time. Such domes are cheap in price in the beginning, but very expensive in the long run. We do not handle such goods at all. Our purpose is to give the best possible value your money can buy. We are quoting you the lowest possible prices for reliable quality and construction.

We have succeeded in assembling a line of art glass domes which positively represents the greatest values on the market, considering the material, construction, symmetry and artistic effects. Our domes are patterned after the exceedingly expensive art glass domes in luxurious residences of the country. When the wealthy build expensive homes or a municipality builds a

costly public building, well known artists are usually employed on the art glass features of the buildings. Our domes reflect the same points of excellence as are to be found in many of the most expensive homes in the country.

Our large sales enable us to buy these goods in big quantities at rock bottom prices. There is no necessity for your accepting the common, cheaply made varieties offered on the market elsewhere when you can get these beautiful art glass domes, as described and illustrated in this catalog, at such very low prices. We guarantee these goods. If you receive any dome from us that does not please you or does not come up to our description and guarantee in every particular, we will be glad to have you return it to us at our expense and we will refund to you both the price and any transportation charges you paid.

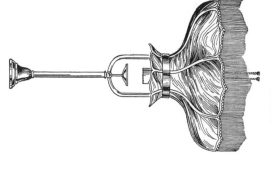

No. 3B2535 **Hall or Porch Ceiling Light.** Mission style, c o p p e r ceiling canopy and large frosted octagonal electric ball lined with black to represent leaded glass.

Price. **$2.95**

No. 3B2542 **Gas Art Dome Light.** Exactly the same as No. 3B2540, except fitted for gas instead of electricity. Complete with 100-candle power incandescent gas burner, mantle, chimney and patent by-pass, which lowers the gas without turning off. State whether you want green or amber glass. Price. **$15.75**

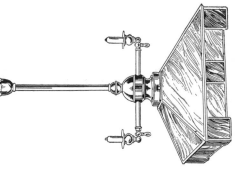

No. 3B2560 **Four-Light Combination Square Art Dome Light.** Fitted with 20-inch square amber colored cathedral art glass shade, which has a 3-inch amber glass curtain around edge, instead of fringe. Curtain has green art glass corners and center squares. Satin brass frame and stem. The two electric lights are inside of glass dome. The gas lights are on outside round Mission arms, with round white candles and candle cups. Length to bottom of curtain, 48 inches. Retail price, $30.00.

Our price. **$17.98**

Art Glass Library Dome Shades

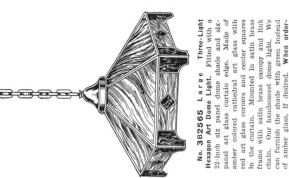

No. 3B2543 **Five-Light Combination Art Dome Shade.** Exactly the same as No. 3B2540, but fitted with two round Mission gas arms, projecting out of the crown of the shade, these arms fitted with round white gas candles and candle cups; three electric lights under dome shade. State whether you want green or amber glass. Price. **$18.95**

BEAUTIFUL ART GLASS DOME SHADES

No. 3B2537 **Mission Art Glass Hall Light.** Satin brass. Length, 36 inches; ¾-inch square tubing with square canopy to match, with 8-inch square amber colored cathedral glass shade mounted in cut out brass frame. Chain pull socket.

Price **$5.78**

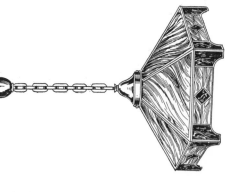

No. 3B2565 **Large Three-Light Hexagon Art Dome Light.** Fitted with a 22-inch six panel dome shade and six-panel art glass curtain edge. Made of amber colored cathedral art glass with red art glass corners and center squares in the curtain. Mounted in satin brass frame with satin brass canopy and link chain. Our handsomest dome light. We can furnish the shade with green instead of amber glass, if desired. When ordering state color wanted. Length to bottom of curtain, 48 inches. Retail price, $35.00.

Our price. **$21.50**

Art Glass Dining Room Dome Shades

No. 3B2540 **Three-Light Electric Art Dome Light.** Length, 48 inches. The shade is 22 inches in width with eight panels of bent cathedral art glass, either green or amber colored, transparent beaded fringe to match. It is ornamented with fancy bent art glass crown in satin brass frame, surrounded by satin brass band. Has ⅝-inch satin brass tubing and large spun canopy. A truly big value. State whether you want green or amber glass. Retail price, $25.00.

Our price. **$16.50**

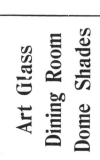

DOMES, INCANDESCENT GAS BURNERS, MANTLES AND GLASSWARE

No. 3B2545

No. 3B2545 TWO-LIGHT ELECTRIC SQUARE DOME LIGHT. Length, 48 inches. 14-inch dome shade of green cathedral art glass with 6-inch transparent green beaded fringe to match. Mounted in satin brass frame with ceiling canopy and square link chain made of satin brass. Retail price, $20.00. Price $14.98

No. 3B2549

No. 3B2549 ROUND GAS DOME LIGHT with 14-inch dome shade of cathedral art glass mounted in embossed satin brass frame and ⅞-inch tubing. 6-inch transparent green beaded fringe. This dome is surmounted with an ornamental cut out embossed brass crown. Fitted complete with 80-candle power incandescent burner, mantle, chimney and patent by-pass. Price....$11.75

No. 3B2547

No. 3B2547 TWO-LIGHT ROUND ELECTRIC DOME LIGHT with 14-inch dome shade of amber colored cathedral art glass and 6-inch transparent amber beaded fringe to match. Mounted in satin brass frame with round link chain and ceiling canopy made of satin finished brass. Price $14.45

CRYSTAL GAS AND ELECTRIC SHADES.

No. 3B2316 Crystal Pebbled Glass Gas Shade. In star pattern. Fancy edge. Fits 4-inch holder. Price.............12c

No. 3B2317 Star Pattern Electric Gas Shade. Fits 3-inch holder. Price.....9c

No. 3B2104 Strictly high grade Pebbled Crystal Gas Shade. Beautiful wreath pattern. Fits 4-inch holder. Price.....8c

No. 3B2102 Wreath Pattern Electric Shade. Fits 3-inch shade ring. Price.......13c

No. 3B2106 Silver Frosted Blown Gas Shade. Etched in beautiful carnation pattern, fitted edge. Fits 4-inch holder. Price...29c

No. 3B2107 Electric Carnation Blown Shade. Fits 3-inch holder. Price..........25c

INCANDESCENT GAS MANTLES.

We handle only the best grade of mantles, guaranteed to give a bright, standard light.

No. 3B2380 No. 1. Standard Grade Mantle, 60-candle power. Price........8c

No. 3B2384 No. 5. Extra Grade Post Mantle, 100-candle power. Price........13c

No. 3B2386 No. 6. Heavy Weave, especially for high pressure gasoline lamps; 5 inches long; nothing better made. Price.........18c

No. 3B2390 Our Triple Weave Double Post Cap Mantle, 100-candle power. Price....17c

No. 3B2392 Genuine Sears Special Double Post Cap Mantle, extra double strength, 100-candle power. Nothing better made at any price. Price 21c

No. 3B2385 Our Special Cross Weave Inverted Gas Mantle. Made extra heavy to stand high pressure. Price..........11c

No. 3B2387 Best Quality Triple Weave Inverted Mantle. Extra light producing surface of exceptional durability. Price.........13c

No. 3B2391 Highest Grade Soft Inverted Mantle. Extra strong. For artificial gas and high pressure gasoline systems. Price.........8c

No. 3B2399 Genuine Rico Mantle. Made of double woven imported Ramie fiber, strong, durable and exceptionally high candle power. Price.........21c

INCANDESCENT GAS BURNERS.

FOR NATURAL OR ARTIFICIAL GAS.

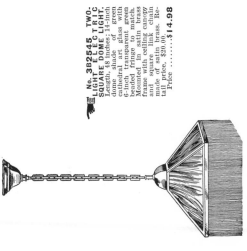

No. 3B2367 "SUNBEAM" UPRIGHT ADJUSTABLE GAS BURNER. Made of polished brass, complete with mica airhole chimney, star pattern glass shade, 3¼-inch brass shade ring and mantle. Burns 1 foot of gas per hour. Price.........35c

No. 3B2368 "Sunbeam" Burner, with chimney and mantle but without glass shade. Price..........25c

No. 3B2370 "BANNER" ADJUSTABLE GAS BURNER. Polished brass. Best quality mantle and opal airhole globe. Price.........45c

No. 3B2372 "SOLAR" ADJUSTABLE GAS BURNER. Polished brass. Gas regulated by patent air shutter. Best quality mantle and opal airhole globe. Fancy Perforated body. Price...........65c

No. 3B2374 "MAGIC" INVERTED BURNER. Polished brass air regulator, mantle and half frosted glass globe. Price..........48c

No. 3B2376 "EUREKA" INVERTED GAS BURNER. Highly polished with patent side screw regulator and air adjustment. Inverted gas mantle and half frosted globe. Price..........78c

No. 3B2378 "RADIANT" INVERTED GAS BURNER, satin brass. Ornamental crown detachable goose neck. Patent gas adjustment. Best quality mantle, frosted globe. Price..........$1.17

No. 3B2381 PATENT BY-PASS, permitting gas to be lowered to a speck without turning off. In ordering state catalog number of burner on which it is to be used. Price..........35c

RAMSDELL INVERTED GAS LAMPS.

Graceful appearance, efficient in operation, simple in construction, economical and durable, lever air shutter, no flash back.

No. 3B2398 RAMSDELL MARVEL 50-CANDLE POWER INCANDESCENT GAS LAMP. So constructed that there is nothing to get out of order. Complete with airhole globe and imported Rico mantle. Satin brass finish. A high grade lamp at the price of an ordinary one. Price.........68c

No. 3B2394 RAMSDELL NO. 7 65-CANDLE POWER INCANDESCENT GAS LAMP. Complete with full silver frosted globe, imported Rico mantle, adapter, and porcelain heat protector. Satin brass finish. This is the very best inverted gas lamp that is made. Price.........$1.35

No. 3B2396 RAMSDELL No. 8 BIJOU INCANDESCENT GAS LAMP. Giving 35-candle power on 1 foot of gas per hour. Complete with silver frosted shade, imported mantle and adapter, porcelain cone and bracket protector. Satin brass finish. Ideal lamp for bedroom, den, etc. Price.........$1.08

No. 3B2860 Adjustable Desk Light. Length, 40 inches. Made of polished brass with heavy weighted base and spiral flexible stem which enables the light to be placed in any position desired. Fitted with 6 feet of silk cord, detachable plug, Edison key socket and green reflecting aluminum lined shade. Shipping weight, 10 pounds. Price.........$3.45

GAS AND ELECTRIC PORTABLES FROM $1.48 UP

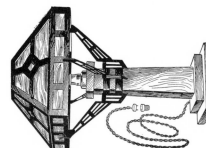

No. 3B2835 "TULIP" Electric Portable. Height, 22 inches. Heavy solid satin brass cast column in rich rococo design. The shade is made of pink and green art glass mounted in an embossed brass frame in the shape of a tulip. Has Edison chain pull socket, 6 feet of silk electric cord and detachable plug. Shipping weight, 23 pounds. Price.....$9.95

No. 3B2820 "MISSION" Electric Portable. Height, 26 inches. Made of solid dark weathered oak with four metal arms, 12-inch green art glass shade, metal edges and grille work. 6 feet electric cord, plug and Edison key socket. Weight, 25 pounds. Price.....$3.98

No. 3B2822 Exactly the same as No. 3B2820, but fitted for gas with 80-candle power incandescent burner, mantle and chimney. 6 feet of gas tubing and brass goose neck.

No. 3B2890 Table Candlestick with Shade. Height, 15 inches. Polished brass Colonial design. Fitted complete with candle, shade holder and hand painted rose design shade. The edges of the shade are of strong green fiber. Weight, 3 pounds. Price, complete......98c

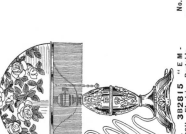
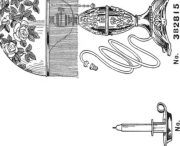
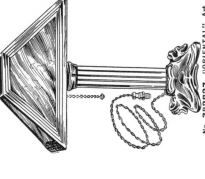
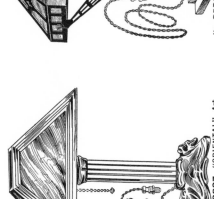

No. 3B2815 "EMPRESS" Electric Portable. Height, 18 inches. Made of satin brass, richly embossed in flower design. Full patina finish. Has 6 feet of silk cord, plug, chain pull Edison socket, 12-inch full tinted shade, decorated with pink rose and bud with their green foliage, with 4-inch green beaded fringe. Weight, 20 pounds. Price...$7.48

No. 3B2827 "ORIENTAL" Art Electric Portable oxidized bronze finish. Heavy ribbed metal stem, mounted on richly embossed base, fitted with 14-inch metal bound green cathedral art glass shade. Height, 21 inches. Has 6 feet of electric cord, plug and Edison key socket. Weight, 30 pounds. Price.....$3.98

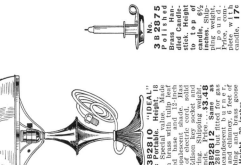
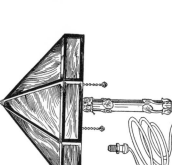

No. 3B2875 Polished Brass Handled Candlestick. Height to top of candle, 6½ inches. Shipping weight, 1 pound. Price, complete with candle, 17c

No. 3B2810 "IDEAL" Electric Portable. Height, 18 inches. Special value. Made of satin brass with tulip leaf embossed base and 12-inch straw opalescent shade. Has 6 feet of electric cord, solid plug, Edison key socket and shade ring. Shipping weight, 18 pounds. Price.....$3.48

No. 3B2812 Same as No. 3B2810 but fitted for gas with incandescent burner, mantle and chimney, 6 feet of gas tubing and brass goose neck. Price.....$3.45

No. 3B2880 Polished Brass Colonial Candlestick. Height to top of candle, 10 inches. Shipping weight, 1½ pounds. Price, complete with candle, 21c

No. 3B2855 "OUR FINEST" Electric Portable. Height, 32 inches. Made of satin brass. The beautiful 14-inch leaded shade has ten panels of cathedral glass in the softest green and amber tints. The concave base is extra large and richly carved, while the stem is ornamented with applied cast brass leaves and stems. All the metal part is full patina finish. Has 6 feet of silk cord, detachable plug and two Edison chain pull sockets. Shipping weight, 30 pounds. Retail price, $25.00. Our price.....$14.98

No. 3B2805 "PEERLESS" Gas Portable. Height, 21 inches. Made of embossed metal with fancy base, finished in a rich black, with polished brass band and burner. Complete with 80 candle power incandescent gas burner, chimney, mantle, 10-inch porcelain lined green shade, shade ring, 4-inch beaded fringe, 6 feet green mohair tubing and goose neck. Weight, 19 pounds. Price.....$2.98

No. 3B2840 "REGENT" Electric Portable. Height, 25 inches. Made of extra heavy richly embossed and elaborately carved polished brass column mounted on very heavy ornamental footed base. The shade is made of six panels of bent amber colored art glass with ornamental crown surrounded by cast brass band. Complete with 5-inch transparent amber beaded fringe, 6 feet of silk electric cord and detachable plug and Edison chain pull socket. Shipping weight, 26 pounds. Price.....$11.75

No. 3B2842 Exactly the same as No. 3B2840, but fitted for gas with 80 candle power incandescent burner, mantle and chimney, 6 feet of silk gas tubing and goose neck. Price.....$11.75

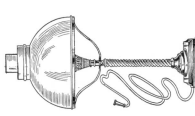

No. 3B2800 "OUR LEADER" Gas Portable. Height, 20 inches. Made of rope brass tubing with square iron base enameled black. Fitted complete with 80-candle power incandescent gas burner, tripod, shade ring, mantle, chimney and 10-inch opal dome shade, 6 feet of green mohair tubing and brass goose neck. Weight, 16 pounds. Price.....$1.48

No. 3B2830 "CUPID" Gas Portable. Height, 30 inches. An elegant, massive portable. Cupid figure on an ornamental footed base. Rich copper bronze finish. 80-candle power incandescent gas burner, mantle and chimney, and richly tinted 12-inch shade, decorated with pink roses, 4-inch ruby beaded fringe, 6 feet of silk gas tubing, and brass goose neck. Weight, 25 pounds. Price.....$7.98

RIM DOOR LOCKS—JAPANNED IRON CASES

THESE LOCKS ARE ALL REVERSIBLE for right or left hand doors, and are furnished complete with screws and japanned keyhole escutcheons.

Japanned Iron Upright Rim Locks.

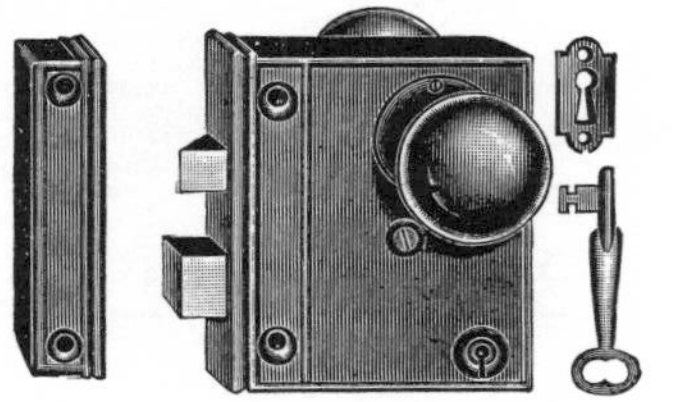

With stop, iron bolts and tinned iron key. Size, 3¾x3⅛ inches.
No. 9B45980 Complete as illustrated, with brown mineral knobs.
Price, per dozen sets, **$1.66**; per set..**14c**
No. 9B45982 Complete as illustrated, with jet black knobs.
Price, per dozen sets, **$1.88**; per set..**17c**
No. 9B46001 Locks only, as illustrated, but without knobs or spindle.
Price, per dozen, **95c**; each............**8c**

Japanned Iron Upright Rim Locks.

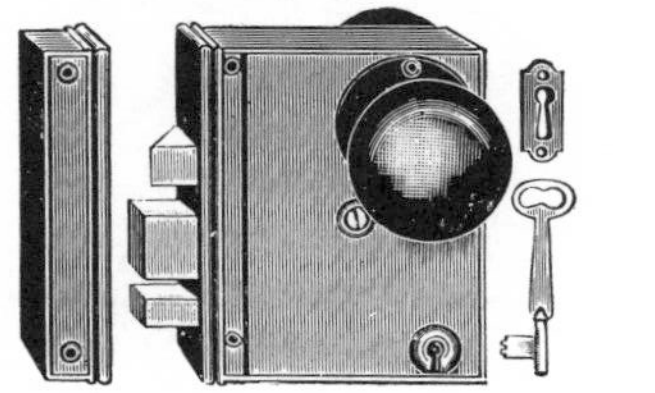

With three brass bolts and nickel plated steel key. Size, 4x3⅛ inches.
No. 9B45988 Complete as illustrated, with brown mineral knobs.
Price, per dozen sets, **$3.19**; per set..**27c**
No. 9B45990 Complete as illustrated, with jet black knobs.
Price, per dozen sets, **$3.41**; per set..**30c**
No. 9B46005 Locks only, as illustrated, but without knobs or spindle.
Price, per dozen, **$2.48**; each.........**21c**

Japanned Iron Horizontal Rim Locks.

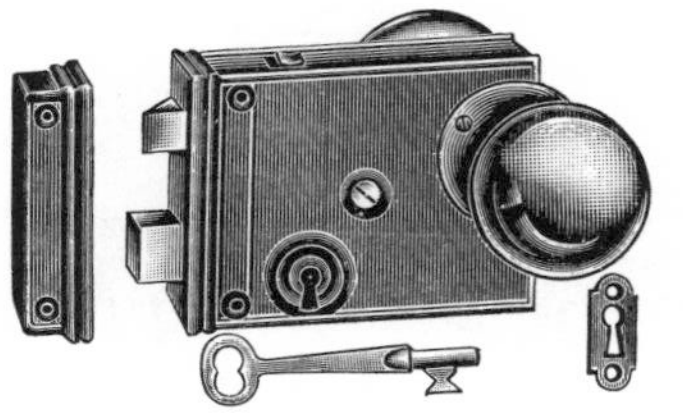

With stop, iron bolts and tinned iron key. Size, 3¼x4¼ inches.
No. 9B45981 Complete as illustrated, with brown mineral knobs.
Price, per dozen sets, **$1.77**; per set..**15c**
No. 9B45986 Complete as illustrated, with jet black knobs.
Price, per dozen sets, **$1.99**; per set..**18c**
No. 9B46003 Locks only, as illustrated, but without knobs or spindle.
Price, per dozen, **$1.06**; each..........**9c**

Japanned Iron Horizontal Rim Locks.

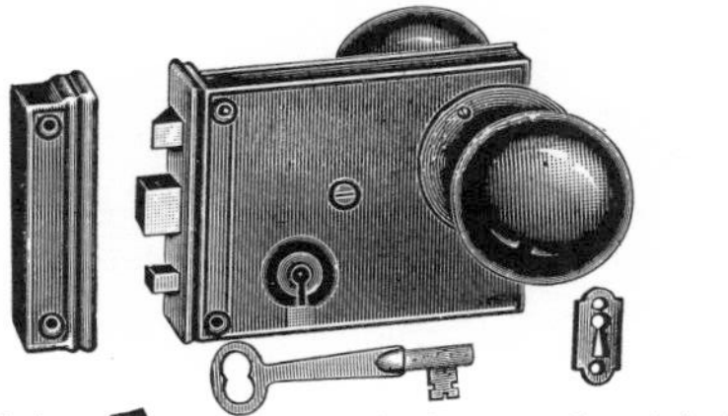

With three brass bolts and nickel plated steel key. Size, 4⅛x3¼ inches.
No. 9B45992 Complete as illustrated, with brown mineral knobs.
Price, per dozen sets, **$3.31**; per set..**28c**
No. 9B45994 Complete as illustrated, with jet black knobs.
Price, per dozen sets, **$3.53**; per set..**31c**
No. 9B46009 Locks only, as illustrated, but without knobs or spindle.
Price, per dozen, **$2.60**; each **22c**

RIM DOOR LOCKS—IVORY BLACK STEEL CASES

THESE LOCKS EASILY REVERSIBLE for right or left hand doors, and are packed complete with screws and keyhole escutcheons to match. Strong and substantial. Not easily broken. Black finish, will not peel or wear off, and effectually prevents lock from rusting.

Ivory Black Steel Upright Rim Locks.

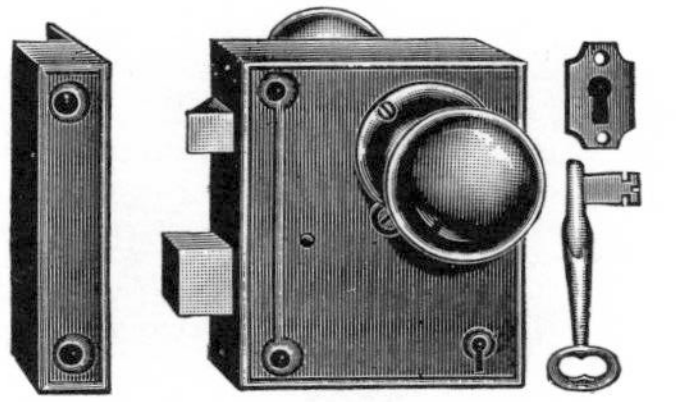

With stop, iron bolts and tinned iron key. Size, 4x3⅛ inches.
No. 9B46010 Complete as illustrated, with brown mineral knobs.
Price, per dozen sets, **$2.49**; per set..**21c**
No. 9B46012 Complete as illustrated, with jet black knobs.
Price, per dozen sets, **$2.71**; per set..**24c**
No. 9B46013 Locks only, as illustrated, but without knobs or spindle.
Price, per dozen, **$1.78**; each.........**15c**

Ivory Black Steel Upright Rim Locks.

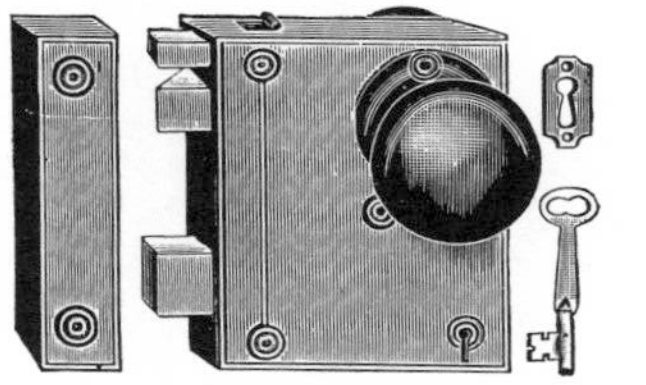

With three iron bolts and nickel plated steel key. Size, 4x3⅛ inches.
No. 9B46014 Complete as illustrated, with brown mineral knobs.
Price, per dozen sets, **$4.29**; per set **36c**
No. 9B46016 Complete as illustrated, with jet black knobs.
Price, per dozen sets, **$4.51**; per set..**39c**
No. 9B46015 Locks only, as illustrated, but without knobs or spindle.
Price, per dozen, **$3.58**; each.........**30c**

Ivory Black Steel Horizontal Rim Locks.

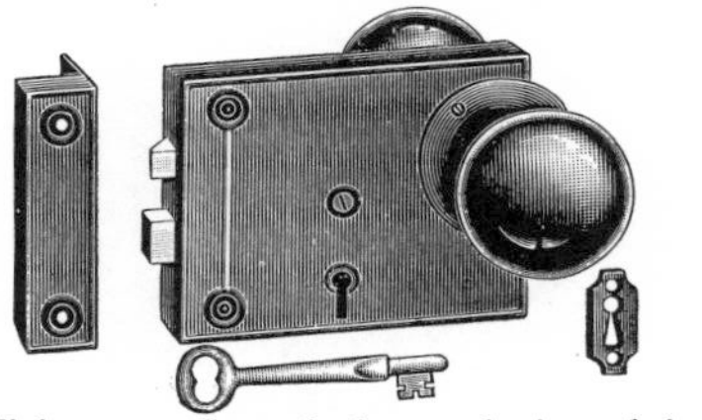

With stop, iron bolts and tinned iron key. Size, 4¼x3¼ inches.
No. 9B46018 Complete as illustrated, with brown mineral knobs.
Price, per dozen sets, **$2.95**; per set..**25c**
No. 9B46020 Complete as illustrated, with jet black knobs.
Price, per dozen sets, **$3.17**; per set..**28c**
No. 9B46019 Locks only, as illustrated, but without knobs or spindle.
Price, per dozen, **$2.24**; each.........**19c**

Ivory Black Steel Horizontal Rim Locks.

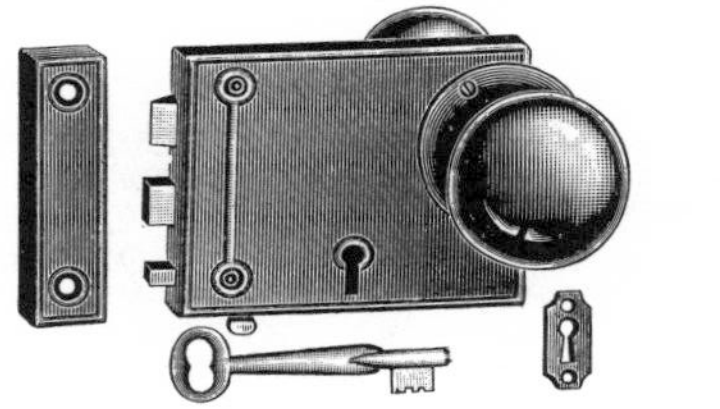

With three brass bolts and nickel plated steel key. Size, 4¼x3¼ inches.
No. 9B46022 Complete as illustrated, with brown mineral knobs.
Price, per dozen sets, **$5.69**; per set..**48c**
No. 9B46024 Complete as illustrated, with jet black knobs.
Price, per dozen sets, **$5.91**; per set..**51c**
No. 9B46021 Locks only, as illustrated, but without knobs or spindle.
Price, per dozen, **$4.98**; each.........**42c**

Door Knobs for Rim and Mortise Locks.

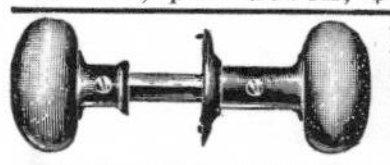

Pair of Rim Knobs and Spindle.

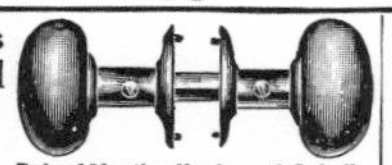

Pair of Mortise Knobs and Spindle.

Fit any of our knob locks and latches. Knobs are 2¼ inches in diameter, with 5-16-inch spindle. Price quoted is for one pair of knobs with connecting spindle. Mineral knobs are mottled brown; porcelain knobs are white, and jet knobs are black. All have japanned shanks and roses.
No. 9B46301 Mineral Knobs. For rim locks.
Price, per dozen, **71c**; per pair...............**6c**
No. 9B46303 Porcelain Knobs. For rim locks.
Price, per dozen, **93c**; per pair...................**8c**
No. 9B46305 Jet Knobs. For rim locks.
Price, per dozen, **93c**; per pair...................**9c**
No. 9B46307 Mineral Knobs. For mortise locks.
Price, per dozen, **71c**; per pair...................**6c**
No. 9B46309 Porcelain Knobs. For mortise locks.
Price, per dozen, **93c**; per pair...................**8c**
No. 9B46311 Jet Knobs. For mortise locks.
Price, per dozen, **93c**; per pair...................**9c**

Store Door Rim Dead Lock.

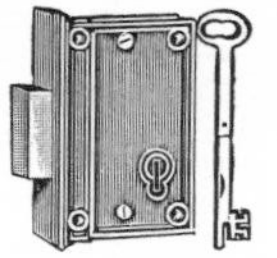

No. 9B46069 Strong, heavy, very durable. For stores, barns or other buildings where great security is desired; japanned iron case, 5x3½ inches; two nickel plated folding steel keys, heavy iron bolt. Price.....**54c**

Rim Door Latch.

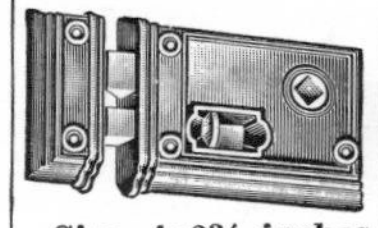

Size, 4x2¾ inches. Iron bolts, japanned; with screws.
No. 9B46025 With brown mineral knobs. Per set..**16c**
Dozen sets.**$1.89**
No. 9B46026 With jet black knobs. Per set..**19c**
Dozen sets.**$2.11**
No. 9B46023 Latch only, without knobs. Each....**10c**
Per dozen..**$1.18**

Cylinder Rim Night Latch.

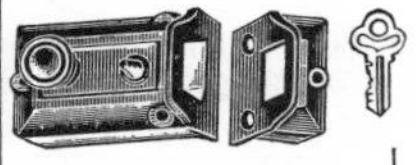

No. 9B46049 Strongest and best latch made. Japanned iron case, 2½x3¾ inches. Has genuine bronze bolt, escutcheon and cylinder, three Yale pattern German silver keys. For either right or left hand doors ⅞ to 3 inches thick; with screws.
Price **99c**

Tubular Rim Night Latch.

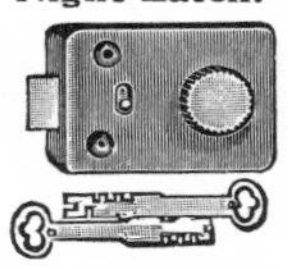

No. 9B46059 A good night latch for very little money. Has japanned iron case, size 3 x 2 inches. For doors up to 1¾ inches thick. Bronze escutcheon, plated bolt, knob and two flat steel keys.
Price **21c**

Mortise Knob Locks and Latches.

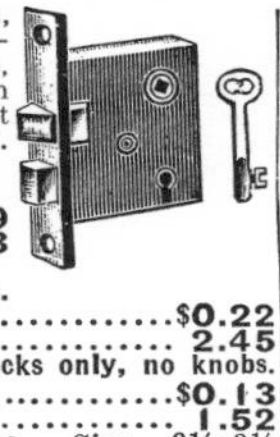

Mortise Door Locks, japanned case and keyhole escutcheons. Size, 3⅝x3¼ inches. Iron bolts, lacquered front and strike, tinned key.
No. 9B46108 With mineral knobs.
Per set.......**$0.19**
Dozen sets... **2.23**
No. 9B46110 With jet or black knobs.
Per set.........................**$0.22**
Dozen sets.......................**2.45**
No. 9B46111 Locks only, no knobs.
Each **$0.13**
Per dozen.........................**1.52**
Mortise Door Locks. Size, 3½x3¼ inches. Brass front and bolts, nickel plated steel key.
No. 9B46112 With mineral knobs. Dozen sets, **$3.56**; per set.......**31c**
No. 9B46114 With black knobs. Dozen sets, **$3.78**; per set.......**34c**
No. 9B46113 Locks only, no knobs. Per dozen, **$2.85**; each.........**25c**

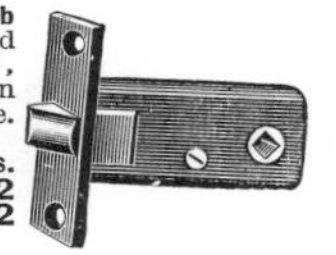

Mortise Knob Latches, japanned iron case. Size, 1¼x3⅛ inches, iron bolt, front and strike.
No. 9B46098 With mineral knobs.
Per set.....**$0.12**
Dozen sets. **1.42**
No. 9B46100 With black knobs.
Per set.........................**$0.15**
Dozen sets.......................**1.64**
No. 9B46101 Latches only, no knobs.
Each **6c**
Per dozen........................**71c**
Mortise Knob Latches, japanned iron case. Size, 1¼x3⅛ inches. Brass front, bolt and strike.
No. 9B46102 With mineral knobs. Dozen sets, **$2.36**; per set.......**20c**
No. 9B46104 With black knobs. Dozen sets, **$2.58**; per set.......**23c**
No. 9B46103 Latch only, no knobs. Per dozen, **$1.65**; each.........**14c**

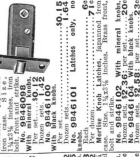

STRATFORD DESIGN BUILDERS' HARDWARE

STRATFORD DESIGN CYLINDER FRONT DOOR LOCK SETS

ONE SET IN A BOX, WITH SCREWS TO MATCH.

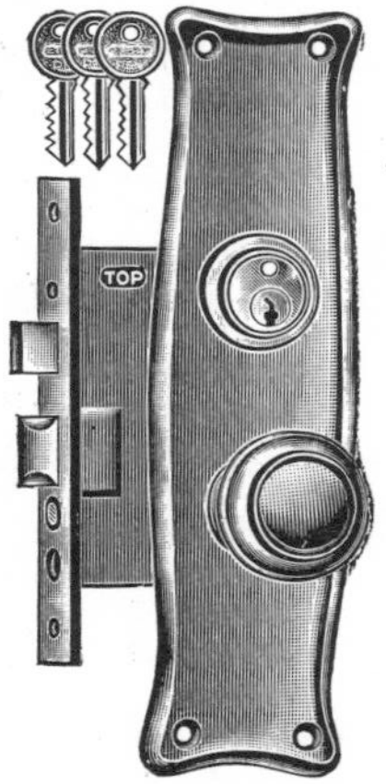

LOCK. For doors 1⅜ to 2¼ inches thick. Reversible. Size, lock, 5½x4 inches; face, 7¾x1¼ inches.

ESCUTCHEONS. Bronze metal, size 3x12 inches outside, 7¾x2½ inches inside.

KNOBS. Bronze metal, size 2¼ inches, on ⅜-inch swivel spindle.

BRONZE METAL bolts, face and cylinder.

KEYS. Three German silver.

Cat. No.	Finish	Price, per Set
9B44802	Antique Copper Polished	$5.47
9B44809	Old or Lemon Brass	5.49

STRATFORD DESIGN DOOR BELLS

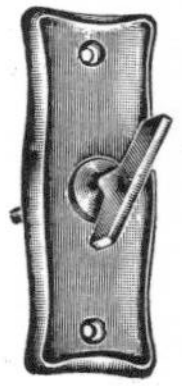

ONE IN BOX, WITH SCREWS AND FIXTURES.

GONG. Nickel plated bell metal, size 3½ inches.

ESCUTCHEON. Bronze metal, size 3¾x1½ inches.

Cat. No.	Finish	Price
9B44862	Antique Copper Polished	73c
9B44869	Old or Lemon Brass	73c

A HANDSOME EXTRA SIZE COLONIAL DESIGN

in two of the most popular finishes made. Our Stratford design is strong and simple in outline and very pleasing in appearance. Escutcheons are extra large size, with ribbed and beveled edges. Made in antique copper polished finish and old or lemon brass finish. Antique copper is a standard polished mottled finish that is very durable and very popular. It is particularly suitable for light and dark oak, chestnut, maple, etc. Old or lemon brass is a highly polished lemon brass color finish that wears well and is particularly suitable for dark wood trim, as Flemish, Spanish and Mission oak, mahogany, rosewood and cherry; also on white enamel.

All hardware on this page packed complete with screws to match.

STRATFORD DESIGN FRONT DOOR LOCK SETS

ONE SET IN A BOX, WITH SCREWS TO MATCH.

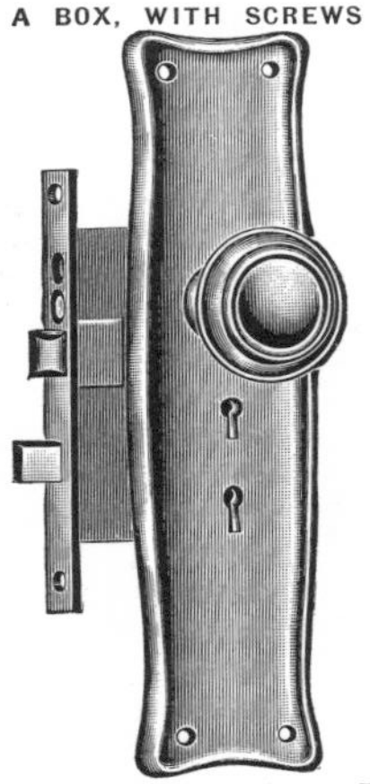

LOCK. Easy spring action. Reversible. Size, 5x3½ in. Face, 7x1 in. Japanned.

ESCUTCHEONS. Bronze metal, size 3x12 inches outside, 7¾x2½ inches inside.

KNOBS. Bronze metal, size 2¼ inches; on 5-16-inch swivel spindle.

BRONZE METAL face, bolts and strike.

KEYS. Nickel plated steel, two for latch bolt and one for lock bolt.

Cat. No.	Finish	Price, per Set
9B44812	Antique Copper Polished	$1.97
9B44819	Old or Lemon Brass	1.99

STRATFORD DESIGN INSIDE DOOR LOCK SETS

ONE SET IN A BOX, WITH SCREWS TO MATCH.

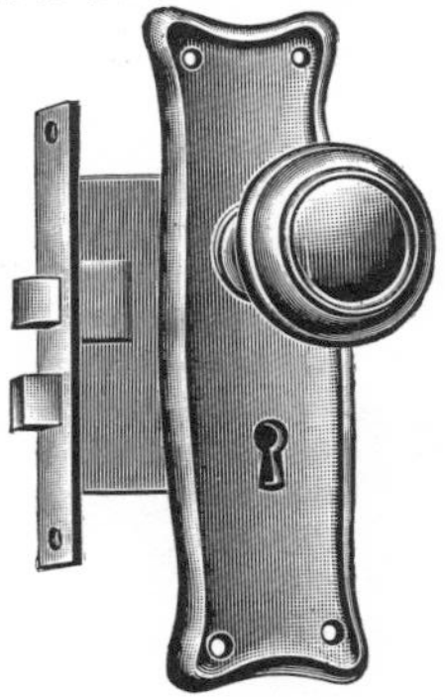

LOCK. Easy spring action. Reversible. Size, lock, 3¾x3¼ inches; face, 5⅜x⅞ inch.

ESCUTCHEONS. Bronze metal, size 7¾x2½ inches.

KNOBS. Bronze metal, 2¼ inches.

BRONZE METAL front and bolts.

KEY. Nickel plated steel.

Cat. No.	Finish	Price, per Set
9B44822	Antique Copper Polished	97c
9B44829	Old or Lemon Brass	99c

Same as above, except with electro bronze plated steel face, knobs, escutcheons and bolts.

Cat. No.	Finish	Price, per Set
9B44832	Antique Copper Polished	52c
9B44839	Old or Lemon Brass	53c

STRATFORD DESIGN SLIDING DOOR LOCK SETS

ONE SET IN A BOX, WITH SCREWS TO MATCH.

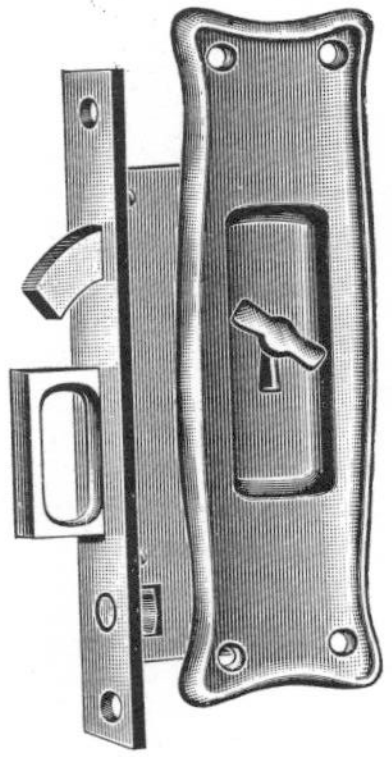

LOCK. Flat face only. With extension pull operated by stop on face. Size, lock, 5½x3¼ inches; face, 1x7⅜ inches.

ESCUTCHEONS. Bronze metal, flush pattern. Single lock sets have two escutcheons, double lock sets have four.

BRONZE METAL front, bolts and strike.

KEY. Bronze metal, extension pattern.

No. 9B44842 Antique Copper Polished Finish.
For single doors. Price, per set........$1.37
For double doors. Price, per set........ 1.97

No. 9B44849 Old or Lemon Brass Finish.
For single doors. Price, per set........$1.39
For double doors. Price, per set........ 1.98

STRATFORD DESIGN PUSH PLATES

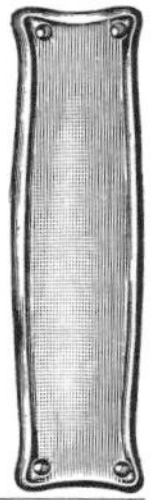

BRONZE METAL. Size, 3x12 inches.

PACKED with screws to match.

Cat. No.	Finish	Price, each
9B44852	Antique Copper Polished Finish	62c
9B44859	Old or Lemon Brass Finish	63c

Window, Door and Cupboard Trimmings to Match our Stratford Design

Finished Polished Antique Copper or Old Brass, to match our Stratford Design. These goods, together with butts and other trimmings to match this design, are fully described and quoted on pages 124 to 126.

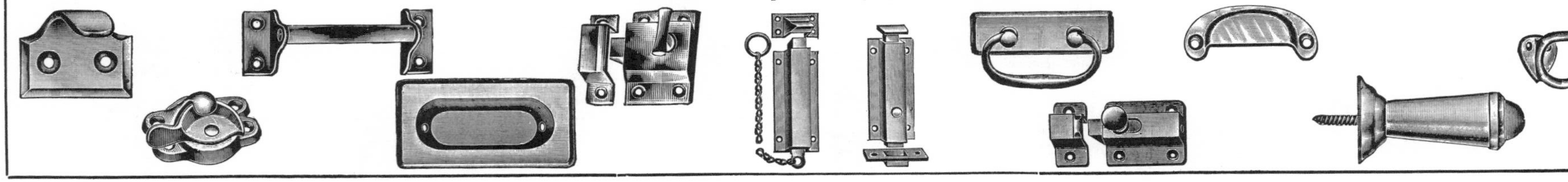

ASTORIA DESIGN HARDWARE TRIM

A PLEASING GREEK PATTERN, VERY POPULAR WITH HOME BUILDERS ON ACCOUNT OF ITS BEAUTY, STRENGTH AND DURABILITY.

One of the prettiest and most popular patterns you could put on your house. Simple in outline, but not too severe, elegant but not too prominent; our Astoria is the kind of trim that appeals to people of refinement everywhere.

Astoria Design Hardware is made in two finishes, polished antique copper and old or lemon brass. Polished antique or mottled copper is a standard, widely used, durable finish. It particularly suits light or dark polished oak, chestnut, maple, etc. Old or lemon brass has a highly polished lemon brass colored smooth surface with a dark antique brass colored border or background. Oldbrass finish hardware is especially suitable for dark or dull wood trim, as weathered oak, mahogany, rosewood or cherry.

ASTORIA DESIGN CYLINDER FRONT DOOR LOCK SETS

ONE SET IN BOX, COMPLETE WITH SCREWS TO MATCH.

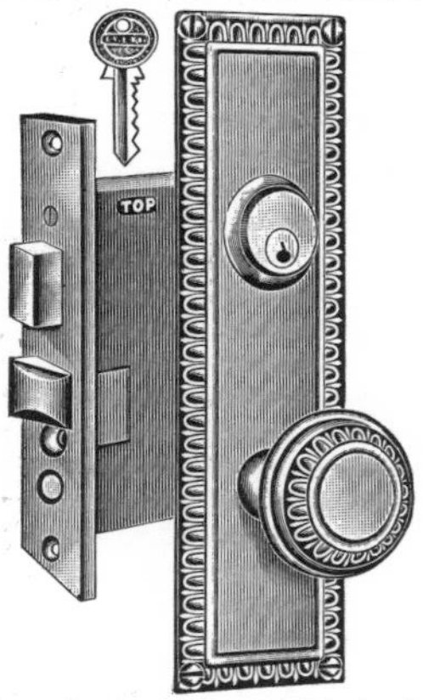

LOCK. For doors 1⅜ to 2¼ inches thick. Reversible. Size, lock, 5½x4 inches; face, 7¾x1¼ inches.
ESCUTCHEONS. Bronze metal. Size, 3x10 inches outside, 2½x7 inches inside.
KNOBS. Bronze metal. Size, 2⅝ inches outside, 2¼ inches inside, on ⅜-inch swivel spindle.
BRONZE METAL bolts, face, strike and cylinder.
KEYS. Three German silver.

No. 9B44902 Antique copper polished finish. Price, per set........$5.20
No. 9B44909 Old or lemon brass finish. Price, per set........5.22

ASTORIA DESIGN DOOR BELLS

ONE IN BOX, WITH SCREWS AND FIXTURES.

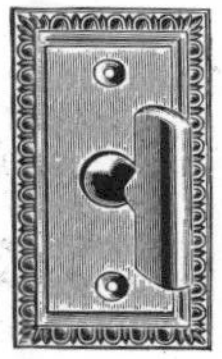

GONG. Nickel plated bell metal. Size, 3½ inches.
ESCUTCHEON. Bronze metal. Size, 3¾x1½ inches.

No. 9B44962 Antique copper polished finish. Price, each...78c
No. 9B44969 Old or lemon brass finish. Price, each........79c

ASTORIA DESIGN FRONT DOOR LOCK SETS

ONE SET IN BOX, WITH SCREWS TO MATCH.

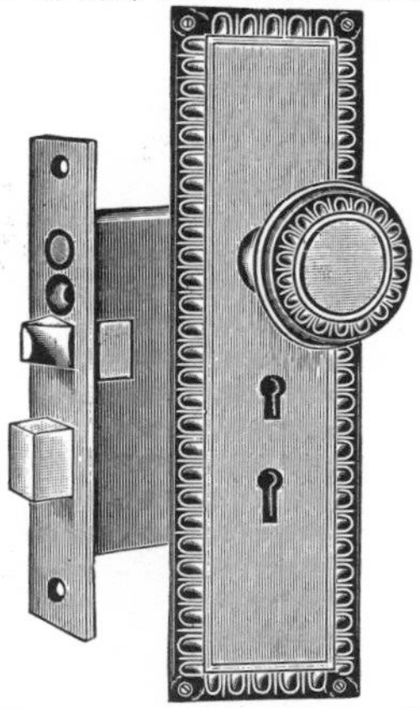

LOCK. Easy spring action. Japanned. Reversible for right or left hand doors. Size, lock, 5x3½ inches; face, 7x1 inch.
ESCUTCHEONS. Bronze metal. Size, 3x10 inches outside; small inside escutcheon.
KNOBS. Bronze metal. Size, 2¼ inches, on 5-16-inch swivel spindle.
BRONZE METAL face, bolts and strike.
KEYS. Nickel plated steel, two for latch bolt and one for lock bolt.

Cat. No.	Finish	Price, per set
9B44912	Antique copper polished	$1.77
9B44919	Old or lemon brass	1.79

ASTORIA DESIGN INSIDE DOOR LOCK SETS

ONE SET IN BOX, WITH SCREWS TO MATCH.

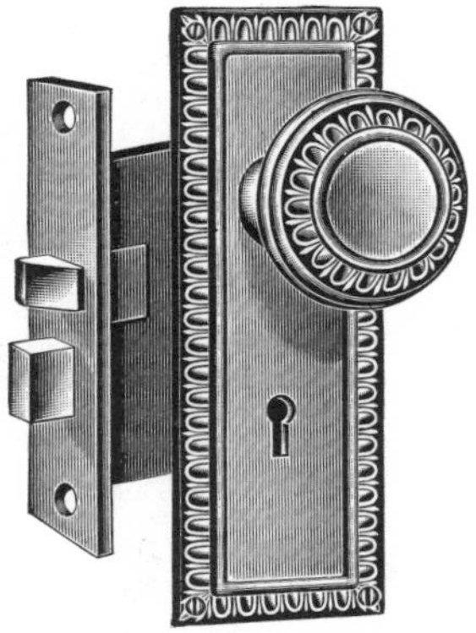

LOCK. Easy spring action. Reversible. Size, lock, 3¾x3¼ inches; face, 5¼x⅞ inch.
ESCUTCHEONS. Bronze metal. Size, 7x2½ inches.
KNOBS. Bronze metal. Size, 2¼ inches.
BRONZE METAL front and bolts.
KEY. Nickel plated steel.

No. 9B44922 Antique copper polished finish. Price, per set........86c
No. 9B44929 Old or lemon brass finish. Price, per set........87c
Same as above, except with electro bronze plated steel face, knobs, escutcheons and bolts.
No. 9B44932 Antique copper polished finish. Price, per set........42c
No. 9B44939 Old or lemon brass finish. Price, per set........43c

ASTORIA DESIGN SLIDING DOOR LOCK SETS

ONE SET IN BOX, WITH SCREWS TO MATCH.

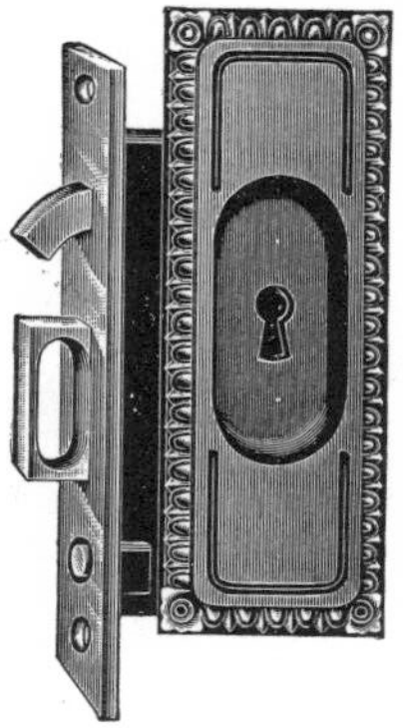

LOCK. Flat face only with extension pulls, operated by stop on face. Size, lock, 5½x3¼ inches; face, 1x7⅜ inches.
ESCUTCHEONS. Bronze metal, flush pattern. Single lock sets have two escutcheons, double lock sets have four. Size of escutcheons, 2½x7 inches.
BRONZE METAL front, bolts and strikes.
KEY. Bronze metal, extension pattern.

No. 9B44942 Antique copper polished finish.
For single doors. Price, per set........$1.23
For double doors. Price, per set........1.78
No. 9B44949 Old or lemon brass finish.
For single doors. Price, per set........$1.24
For double doors. Price, per set........1.79

ASTORIA DESIGN PUSH PLATES.

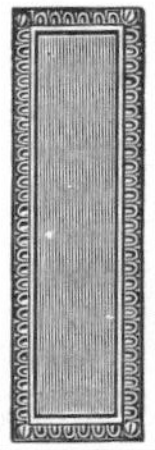

PACKED WITH SCREWS TO MATCH.

BRONZE METAL. Size, 3x10 inches.

No. 9B44952 Antique copper polished finish. Price, each........55c
No. 9B44959 Old or lemon brass finish. Price, each........56c

Trimmings for Windows, Doors and Cupboards, Finished to Match Our Astoria Design

Finished Polished Antique Copper or Old Brass, to match our Astoria Design. These goods, together with butts and other trimmings to match our Astoria Design, are fully described and quoted on pages 124 to 126.

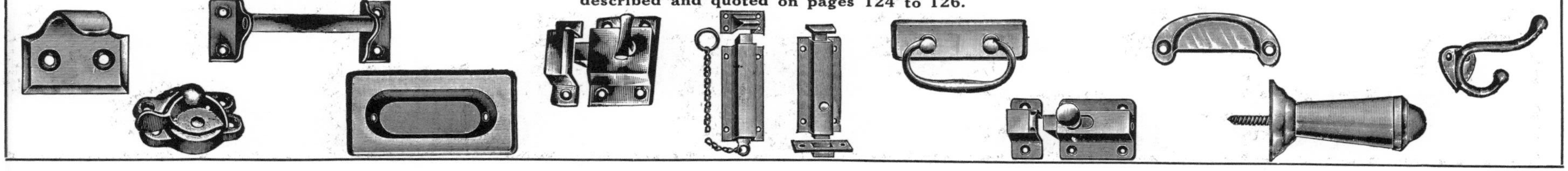

EMERALD DESIGN LOCKS AND HARDWARE

EMERALD DESIGN CYLINDER FRONT DOOR LOCK SETS

ONE SET IN BOX, WITH SCREWS TO MATCH.

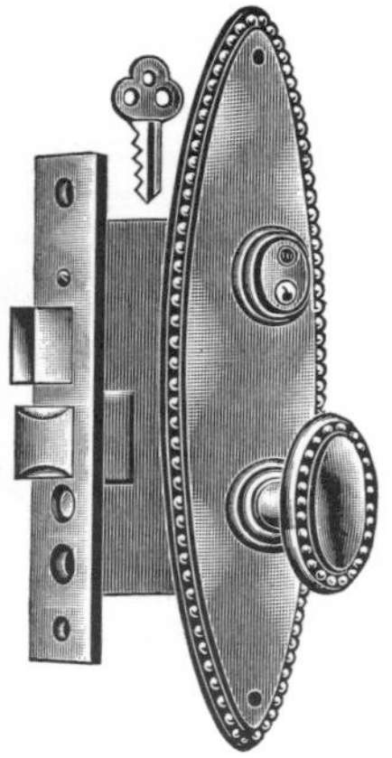

LOCK. For doors $1\frac{3}{8}$ to $2\frac{1}{4}$ inches thick. Reversible. Size, lock, $5\frac{1}{2}$x4 inches; face, $7\frac{3}{4}$x$1\frac{1}{4}$ inches.

ESCUTCHEONS. Bronze metal. Size, 10x$2\frac{3}{4}$ inches outside, $6\frac{3}{4}$x$2\frac{1}{4}$ inches inside.

KNOBS. Bronze metal. Size, 3 inches outside, $2\frac{5}{8}$ inches inside, on $\frac{3}{8}$-inch swivel spindle.

BRONZE METAL face, bolts, strike and cylinder.

KEYS. Three German silver.

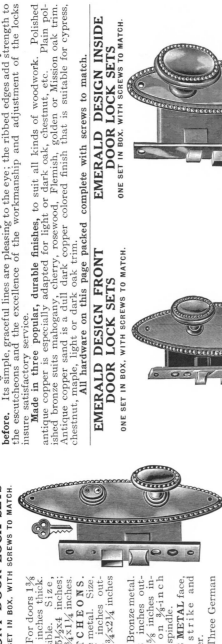

Cat. No.	Finish	Price, per set
9B45002	Antique copper polished	$5.30
9B45004	Plain polished bronze	5.25
9B45006	Antique copper sand	5.35

EMERALD DESIGN DOOR BELLS

ONE IN BOX, WITH SCREWS AND FIXTURES.

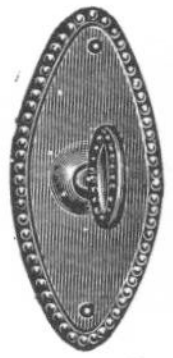

ESCUTCHEON. Bronze metal. Size, $4\frac{5}{8}$x$2\frac{1}{8}$ inches.

GONG. Electro copper plated, cast gong. Size, 3 inches.

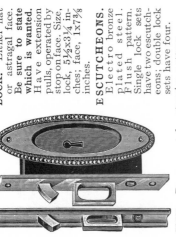

Cat. No.	Finish	Price, each
9B46662	Polished antique copper	52c
9B46664	Plain polished bronze	52c
9B46666	Antique copper sand	52c

Same as above, except with $3\frac{1}{2}$-inch nickel plated bell metal gongs.

Cat. No.	Finish	Price, each
9B46672	Antique copper polished	73c
9B46674	Plain polished bronze	73c
9B46676	Antique copper sand	73c

A NEAT COLONIAL PATTERN THAT IS VERY POPULAR.

This design has been on the market for years and is in more demand today than ever before. Its simple, graceful lines are pleasing to the eye; the ribbed edges add strength to the escutcheons and the excellence of the workmanship and adjustment of the locks insure satisfactory service.

Made in three popular, durable finishes, to suit all kinds of woodwork. Polished antique copper is especially adapted for light or dark oak, chestnut, etc. Plain polished bronze suits mahogany, cherry, rosewood, Flemish, golden or Mission oak trim. Antique copper sand is a dull dark copper colored finish that is suitable for cypress, chestnut, maple, light or dark oak trim.

All hardware on this page packed complete with screws to match.

EMERALD DESIGN FRONT DOOR LOCK SETS

ONE SET IN BOX, WITH SCREWS TO MATCH.

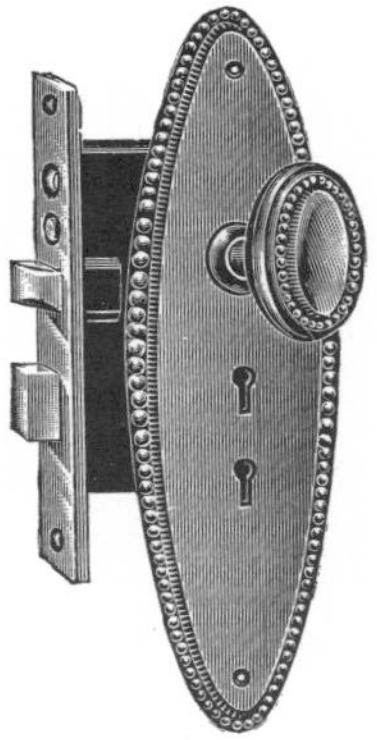

LOCK. Easy spring action. Reversible for right or left hand doors. Japanned. Size, lock, $4\frac{3}{4}$x$3\frac{5}{8}$ inches; face, 7x1 inch.

ESCUTCHEONS. Bronze metal. Size, $2\frac{7}{8}$x10 inches outside, small inside escutcheon.

KNOBS. Bronze metal. Size, $2\frac{3}{8}$ inches, on 5-16-inch swivel spindle.

BRONZE METAL face, bolts and strike.

KEYS. Nickel plated steel; two for latch bolt and one for lock bolt.

Cat. No.	Finish	Price, per set
9B45092	Antique copper polished	$1.64
9B45094	Plain polished bronze	1.63
9B45096	Antique copper sand	1.65

EMERALD DESIGN INSIDE DOOR LOCK SETS

ONE SET IN BOX, WITH SCREWS TO MATCH.

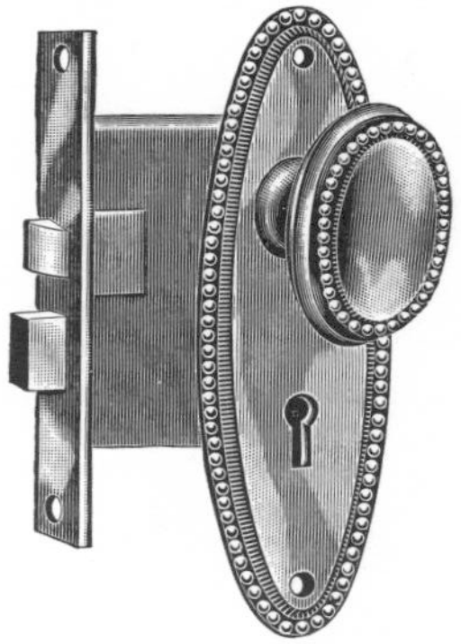

LOCK. Easy spring action. Reversible. Size, lock, $3\frac{1}{2}$x$3\frac{1}{4}$ inches; face, $5\frac{1}{4}$x$\frac{7}{8}$ inch.

ESCUTCHEONS. Bronze metal. Size, $2\frac{1}{8}$x7 inches.

KNOBS. Bronze metal. Size, $2\frac{3}{8}$ inches.

BRONZE METAL front and bolts.

KEY. Nickel plated steel.

Catalog No.	Finish	Price, per set	Doz. sets
9B45202	Antique copper polished	89c	$ 9.95
9B45204	Plain polished bronze	88c	9.86
9B45206	Antique copper sand	92c	10.05

Same as above, except with electro bronze plated steel face, knobs, escutcheons and bolts.

Catalog No.	Finish	Price, per set	Dozen sets
9B45212	Antique copper polished	48c	$5.60
9B45214	Plain polished bronze	47c	5.50
9B45216	Antique copper sand	49c	5.70

EMERALD DESIGN SLIDING DOOR LOCK SETS

ONE SET IN BOX, WITH SCREWS TO MATCH.

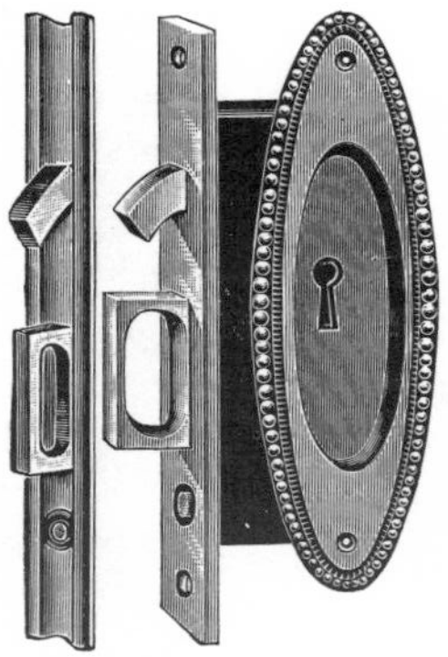

LOCK. Either flat or astragal face. **Be sure to state which is wanted.** Have extension pulls, operated by stop on face. Size, lock, $5\frac{1}{2}$x$3\frac{1}{4}$ inches; face, 1x$7\frac{3}{8}$ inches.

ESCUTCHEONS. Electro bronze plated steel. Flush pattern. Single lock sets have two escutcheons; double lock sets have four.

KEY. Bronze metal, extension pattern.

No. 9B45402 Antique copper polished finish.
For single doors, flat front. Price, per set $1.08
For double doors, flat front. Price, per set 1.62
For double doors, astragal front. Price, per set 1.76

No. 9B45404 Plain polished bronze finish.
For single doors, flat front. Price, per set $1.07
For double doors, flat front. Price, per set 1.61
For double doors, astragal front. Price, per set 1.75

No. 9B45406 Antique copper sand finish.
For single doors, flat front. Price, per set $1.09
For double doors, flat front. Price, per set 1.72
For double doors, astragal front. Price, per set 1.89

EMERALD DESIGN PUSH PLATES

PACKED, WITH SCREWS TO MATCH.

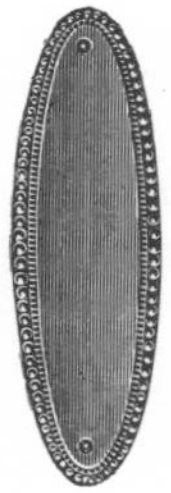

BRONZE METAL. Size, $2\frac{3}{4}$x$9\frac{1}{2}$ inches.

Cat. No.	Finish	Price, each
9B46602	Antique copper polished	56c
9B46604	Plain polished bronze	55c
9B46606	Antique copper sand,	57c

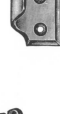

Miscellaneous Hardware Trimmings Finished to Match Our Emerald Design

Antique Copper Polished, Antique Copper Sand or Plain Polished Bronze Finish, to match our Emerald Design. These items, together with butts and other trimmings to match our Emerald Design, are fully described and quoted on pages 124 to 126.

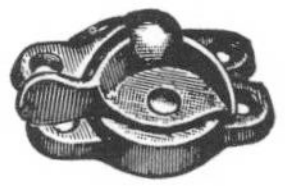
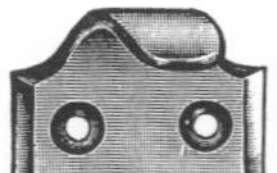
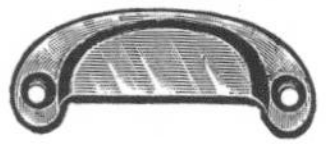
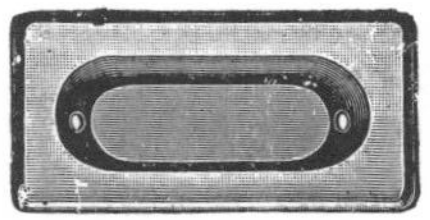
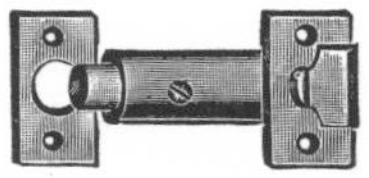
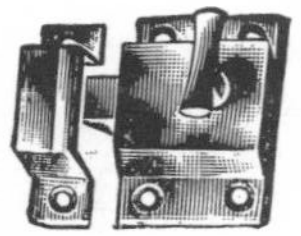
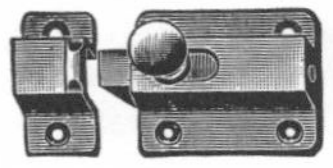

OUR CHICAGO OR PLAIN DESIGN HARDWARE

A STANDARD PATTERN, PLAIN, SERVICEABLE AND SUBSTANTIAL

This well known design is handled by many hardware dealers, but few of them carry a class of goods that will compare with ours. Our Chicago design hardware is made of sheet bronze or steel of a thicker gauge than is ordinarily used. It measures full size, is handsomely finished and the bevel edge makes it extra strong. Finished in polished antique copper and plain polished bronze. Antique copper is adapted for light or dark oak, chestnut, etc. Plain polished bronze suits mahogany, cherry and golden or Mission oak.

CHICAGO DESIGN CYLINDER FRONT DOOR LOCK SETS

ONE SET IN BOX, WITH SCREWS TO MATCH.

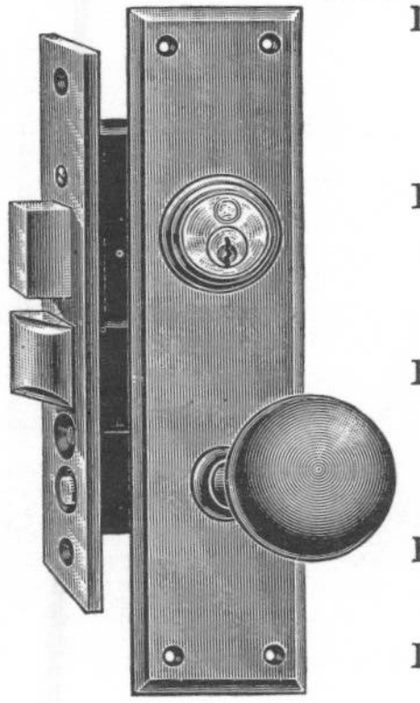

LOCK. For doors $1\frac{3}{8}$ to $2\frac{1}{4}$ inches thick. Reversible. Size, lock, $5\frac{1}{2}$x4 inches; face, $7\frac{3}{4}$x$1\frac{1}{4}$ inches.
ESCUTCHEONS. Bronze metal. Size, $9\frac{1}{2}$x$2\frac{1}{2}$ inches outside, $5\frac{1}{2}$x$1\frac{3}{4}$ inches inside.
KNOBS. Bronze metal. Size, $2\frac{1}{2}$ inches outside, $2\frac{1}{4}$ inches inside. On $\frac{3}{8}$-inch swivel spindle.
BRONZE METAL face, bolts, cylinder and strike.
KEYS. Three German silver.

Cat. No.	Finish	Price, per set
9B45022	Antique copper polished	$4.82
9B45024	Plain polished bronze	4.79

CHICAGO DESIGN DOOR BELLS

ONE IN BOX, WITH SCREWS AND FIXTURES.

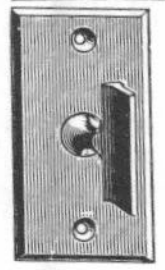

ESCUTCHEONS. Bronze metal. Size, $3\frac{1}{2}$x$1\frac{7}{8}$ inches.
GONG. Electro copper plated cast gong. Size, 3 inches.

Cat. No.	Finish	Price, each
9B46682	Antique copper polished	52c
9B46684	Plain polished bronze	52c

Same as above, except with $3\frac{1}{2}$-inch nickel plated bell metal gongs.

Cat. No.	Finish	Price, each
9B46692	Antique copper polished	73c
9B46694	Plain polished bronze	73c

Your door is no better than the lock that fastens it. On the strength and security of the hardware depends the safety of the whole house. Order your locks from us and get the secure, dependable kind.

CHICAGO DESIGN FRONT DOOR LOCK SETS

ONE SET IN BOX, WITH SCREWS TO MATCH.

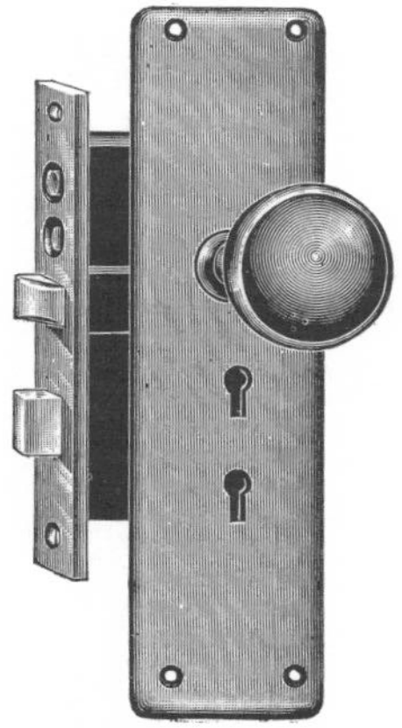

LOCK. Easy spring action, reversible for right or left hand doors, japanned. Size, lock, 5x$3\frac{1}{2}$ inches; face, 7x1 inches.
ESCUTCHEONS. Bronze metal. Size, $2\frac{3}{4}$x10 inches outside, small inside escutcheon.
KNOBS. Bronze metal. Size, $2\frac{1}{4}$ inches, on 5-16-inch swivel spindle.
BRONZE METAL face bolts and strike.
KEYS. Three nickel plated steel.

Cat. No.	Finish	Price, per set
9B45102	Antique copper polished	$1.67
9B45104	Plain polished bronze	1.66

Same as above, except with electro bronze plated steel face, knobs, escutcheons and bolts.

Cat. No.	Finish	Price, per set
9B45112	Antique copper polished	$1.26
9B45114	Plain polished bronze	1.25

CHICAGO DESIGN INSIDE DOOR LOCK SETS

ONE SET IN BOX, WITH SCREWS TO MATCH.

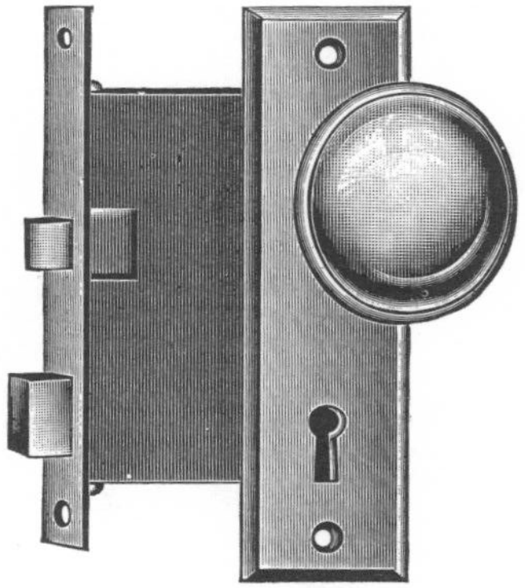

LOCK. Easy spring action. Reversible. Size, lock, $3\frac{1}{2}$x$3\frac{1}{4}$ in.; face, $5\frac{1}{4}$x$\frac{7}{8}$ in.
ESCUTCHEONS. Bronze metal. Size, $1\frac{5}{8}$x$5\frac{1}{2}$ inches.
KNOBS. Bronze metal. Size, $2\frac{1}{4}$ inches.
BRONZE METAL front and bolts.
KEY. Nickel plated steel.

Cat. No.	Finish	Per Set	Doz. Sets
9B45222	Antique copper polished	84c	$9.90
9B45224	Plain polished bronze	83c	9.60

Same as above, except with electro bronze plated steel face, knobs and escutcheons.

Cat. No.	Finish	Per Set	Doz. Sets
9B45232	Antique copper polished	42c	$4.90
9B45234	Plain polished bronze	41c	4.80

Same as above, except with electro plated steel face and escutcheons, and jet or black knobs.

Cat. No.	Finish	Per Set	Doz. Sets
9B45252	Antique copper polished	32c	$3.65
9B45254	Plain polished bronze	31c	3.55

CHICAGO DESIGN SLIDING DOOR LOCK SETS

ONE SET IN BOX, WITH SCREWS TO MATCH.

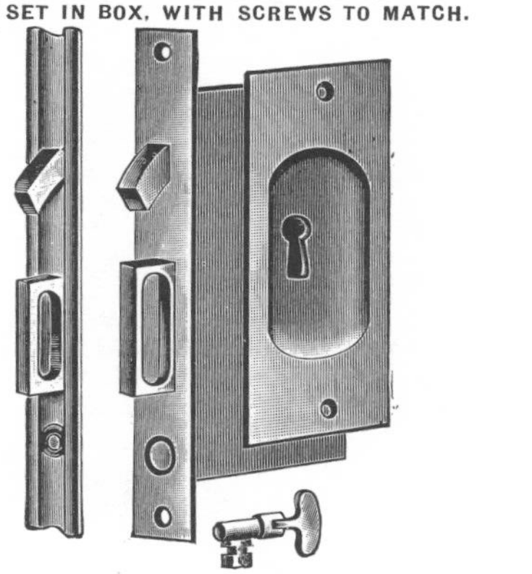

LOCK. Either flat or astragal face. **Be sure to state which is wanted.** Have extension pulls; operated by stop on face. Size, lock, $5\frac{1}{2}$x$3\frac{1}{4}$ inches; face, 1x$7\frac{3}{8}$ inches.
ESCUTCHEONS. Electro bronze plated steel, flush pattern. Single lock sets have two escutcheons, double lock sets have four. Size of escutcheons, $2\frac{1}{8}$x4 inches.
KEY. Bronze metal, extension pattern.

No. 9B45462 Antique copper polished finish.
For single doors, flat front. Price, per set..$1.01
For double doors, flat front. Price, per set.. 1.46
For double doors, astragal front. Price, per set......1.62

No. 9B45464 Plain polished bronze finish.
For single doors, flat front. Price, per set..$1.00
For double doors, flat front. Price, per set.. 1.45
For double doors, astragal front. Price, per set......$1.61

CHICAGO DESIGN PUSH PLATES

PACKED WITH SCREWS TO MATCH.

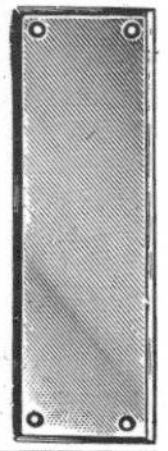

BRONZE METAL. Size, $2\frac{3}{4}$ x $9\frac{1}{2}$ inches.

Cat. No.	Finish	Price, each
9B46612	Antique copper polished	54c
9B45514	Plain polished bronze	52c

Window, Door and Cupboard Trimmings to Match Our Chicago Design

Finished Polished Antique Copper or Plain Polished Bronze to Match Our Chicago Design. These Goods, Together With Butts and Other Trimmings to Match This Handsome Design, Are Fully Described and Quoted on Pages 124 to 126.

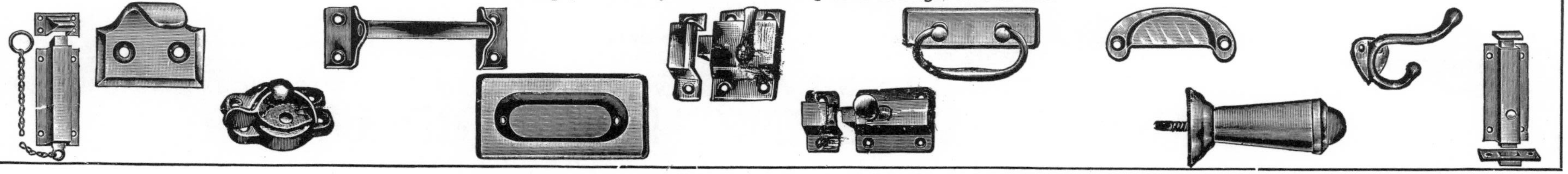

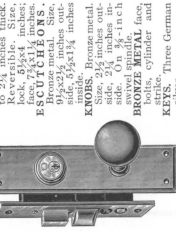

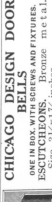

MAYFAIR DESIGN BUILDERS' HARDWARE
A POPULAR, MEDIUM PRICED PATTERN

A GREAT FAVORITE WITH CONTRACTORS AND BUILDERS

Our Mayfair design hardware is attractive in appearance, rather ornamental and at the prices we quote, cannot be equaled.

The raised surfaces as shown by white lines in illustrations, are polished bronze finish; background is dull black. This polished bronze makes a handsome contrast with the dull black background, producing a pleasing effect.

All hardware quoted on this page is packed complete with screws to match.

MAYFAIR DESIGN STORE DOOR LOCK AND HANDLE

ONE SET IN BOX, WITH SCREWS AND FIXTURES.

For front doors of stores, hotels, apartment houses, public halls, etc. A secure and satisfactory fastening for large doors.

FINISH. Electro plated; raised surfaces polished bronze finish; background, dull black.

LOCK. Easy acting spring, brass bolts. Reversible for right or left hand doors. Japanned. Size, 3x4¼ inches.

FACE. Polished bronze finish. Size, 1⅛x6⅜ inches.

ESCUTCHEONS. Extra large size. Electro plated cast escutcheons. Complete with handle and thumb latch. Size of escutcheons, 13¼x2½ inches.

KEYS. Two flat steel, nickel plated.

No. 9B45748 Price, per set.............$1.68

MAYFAIR DESIGN DOOR BELLS

ONE IN BOX, WITH SCREWS AND FIXTURES.

FINISH. Electro plated; raised surfaces polished bronze finish; background, dull black.

ESCUTCHEONS. Bronze metal. Size, 1¾x3⅝ inches.

No. 9B46708 With 3-inch electro copper plated cast gong. Price......52c

No. 9B46718 With 3½-inch nickel plated bell metal gong. Price......73c

MAYFAIR DESIGN SLIDING DOOR LOCK SETS

ONE SET IN BOX, WITH SCREWS TO MATCH.

FINISH. Electro plated; raised surfaces polished bronze finish; background, dull black.

LOCK. Either flat or astragal face. Be sure to state which is wanted. Have extension pulls operated by stop on face. Size, lock, 5½x3¾ inches; face, 1x7⅜ inches.

ESCUTCHEONS. Electro bronze plated steel, flush pattern. Size, 2⅛x4 inches. Single lock sets have two escutcheons. Double lock sets have four.

KEY. Bronze metal, extension pattern.

No. 9B45568 Mayfair Design Sliding Door Lock Sets.   Per set
For single doors, flat front $1.00
For double doors, flat front..........1.47
For double doors, astragal front........1.58

MAYFAIR DESIGN INSIDE DOOR LOCK SETS

ONE SET IN BOX, WITH SCREWS TO MATCH.

FINISH. Electro plated; raised surfaces polished bronze finish; background, dull black.

LOCK. Easy spring action. Reversible. Size, lock, 3½x3¾ inches; face, 5¼x⅞ inch.

ESCUTCHEONS. Bronze metal. Size, 1¾x5½ inches.

KNOBS. Bronze metal. Size, 2¼ inches.

BRONZE METAL front and bolts.

KEY. Nickel plated steel.

No. 9B45268 Price, per set.......$0.74
Per dozen sets.............8.80
Same as above, except with electro bronze plated steel front, bolts, knobs and escutcheons.
No. 9B45278 Price, per set.......$0.39
Per dozen sets.............4.50
Same as above, except with electro bronze plated front, bolts and escutcheons and with jet or black knobs.
No. 9B45298 Price, per set.......$0.29
Per dozen sets.............3.46

MAYFAIR DESIGN FRONT DOOR LOCK SETS

ONE SET IN BOX, WITH SCREWS TO MATCH.

FINISH. Electro plated, raised surfaces polished bronze finish; background, dull black.

LOCK. Easy spring action. Reversible for right or left head doors. Japanned. Size, 5x3½ inches.

FACE. Cast bronze metal, with stop work to set latch bolt. Size, 7x1 inch.

ESCUTCHEONS. Bronze metal. Size, 2x7 inches outside; small inside escutcheon.

KNOBS. Bronze metal. Size, 2¼ inches, on 5-16-inch swivel spindle.

BRONZE METAL bolts and strike.

KEYS. Nickel plated steel; two for latch bolt and one for lock bolt.

No. 9B45138 Price, per set.........$1.20
No. 9B45148 Same as above, except with electro bronze plated front, bolts, knobs and escutcheons. Price, per set.........$1.05

MAYFAIR DESIGN CAST BUTTS

No. 9B47758 Electro plated iron. raised surfaces polished bronze finish; background, dull black, with screws to match.

Size, inches	Price, per pair
3x3	23c
3½x3½	26c
4x4	31c
4½x4½	35c

Mayfair Design Window, Door and Cupboard Trimmings

Match our other Mayfair hardware in design. These trimmings are fully described and quoted on pages 124 to 126.

OUR REGAL DESIGN

A graceful ornamental design, first quality in every respect, a design that pleases the most exacting. Made with genuine bronze metal trimmings throughout and finished in antique copper sand blast finish, a finish that is handsome in appearance and very durable. If you want a strictly first class line of hardware at a reasonable price, you will make no mistake in ordering this Regal design. Contractors and builders whose specifications call for genuine bronze trimmings on their hardware will find our prices on this Regal design hardware very attractive. **All the goods on this page are packed complete with screws to match.**

REGAL DESIGN FRONT DOOR LOCK SET

ONE SET IN A BOX, WITH SCREWS TO MATCH.

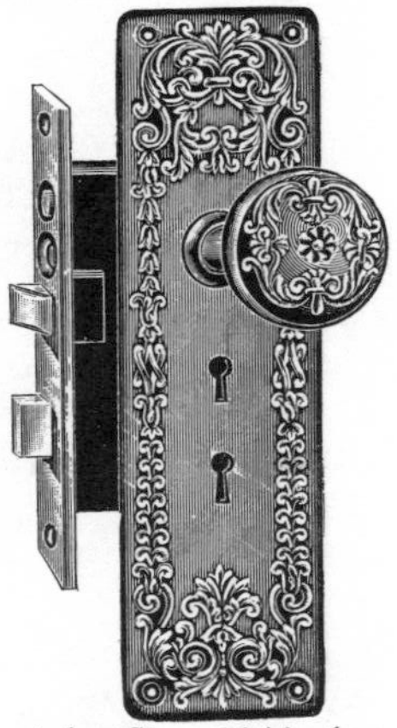

FINISH. Antique copper sand finish only.
LOCK. Easy spring action. Reversible for right or left hand doors. Size, 5x3½ inches. Japanned.
FACE. Bronze metal, with stop work to set latch bolt. Size, 7x1 inch.
ESCUTCHEONS. Bronze metal. Size, 2¾x10 inches outside, small inside escutcheon.
KNOBS. Bronze metal. Size, 2¼ inches, on 5-16-inch swivel spindle.
BRONZE METAL bolts and strike.
KEYS. Nickel plated steel, two for latch bolt and one for lock bolt.
No. 9B45116 Price, per set..........$1.59

REGAL DESIGN INSIDE DOOR LOCK SETS

ONE SET IN A BOX, WITH SCREWS TO MATCH.

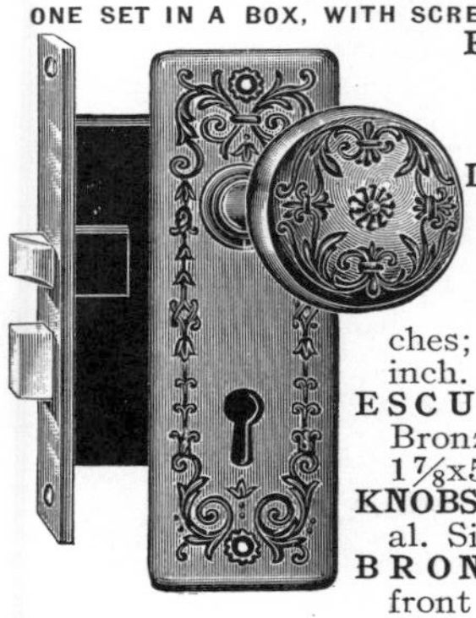

FINISH. Antique copper sand finish only.
LOCK. Easy spring action, reversible. Size lock, 3½x3¼ inches; face, 5¼x⅞ inch.
ESCUTCHEONS. Bronze metal. Size, 1⅞x5¾ inches.
KNOBS. Bronze metal. Size, 2¼ inches, **BRONZE METAL** front and bolts.
KEYS. Nickel plated steel.
No. 9B45256 Price, per set..........$0.83
Per dozen sets.......................... 9.65

REGAL DESIGN SLIDING DOOR LOCK SETS

ONE SET IN A BOX, WITH SCREWS TO MATCH.

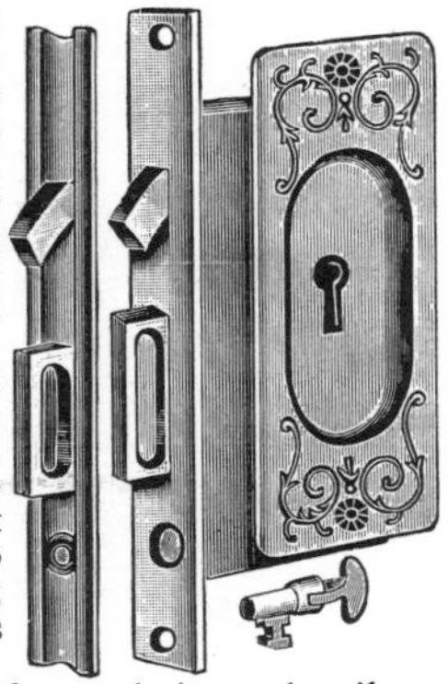

LOCK. Either flat or astragal face. **State which is wanted.** Has extension pulls, operated by stop on face. Size lock, 5½ x 3¼ inches; face, 1x7⅜ inches.
ESCUTCHEONS. Bronze metal, flush pattern. Size, 2⅜x5½ inches. Single lock sets have two escutcheons; double lock sets have four.
BRONZE METAL fronts, bolts and strikes.
KEY. Bronze metal, extension pattern.
No. 9B45486 Antique copper sand finish.
For single doors, flat front. Price, per set...$1.06
For double doors, flat front. Price, per set... 1.66
For double doors, astragal front. Price, per set.................................. 1.82

REGAL DESIGN DOOR BELLS

ONE IN A BOX, WITH SCREWS AND FIXTURES.

ESCUTCHEON. Genuine bronze metal. Size, 1⅞x3¾ inches.
FINISH. Antique copper sand finish only.
No. 9B46686 With 3-inch electro copper plated cast gong. Price..52c
No. 9B46706 With 3½-inch nickel plated bell metal gong. Price..........................73c

Sand Finished Antique Copper Plated Trimmings and Butts to Match Our Regal and Fulton Hardware are described and quoted on pages 124 to 126.

OUR FULTON DESIGN

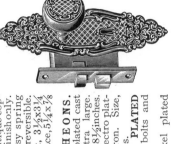

A rather unusual pattern with extra large escutcheons. Strong and massive in appearance. Our Fulton is a very substantial line of hardware in a finish that wears well. It is a low priced high grade line that makes a good showing for a little money. Contractors and builders who put up houses to sell can add more real value to their houses by using our Fulton design in preference to most of the patterns usually offered in regular stores. Made in antique copper sand finish only, a finish that looks well on any woodwork and that for durability and wearing qualities is unexcelled. **All the hardware on this page is packed complete with screws to match.**

FULTON DESIGN FRONT DOOR LOCK SET

ONE SET IN A BOX, WITH SCREWS TO MATCH.

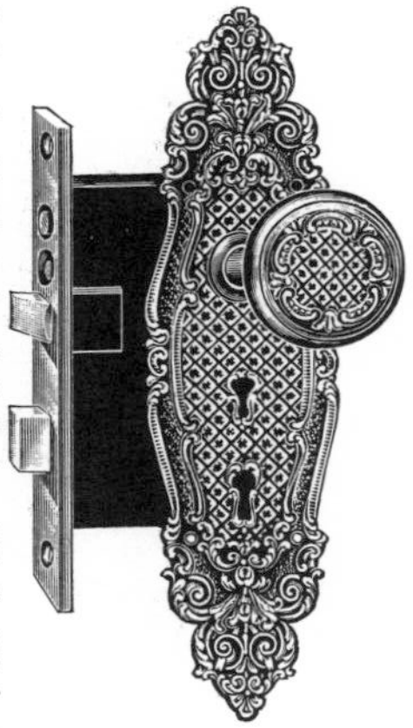

FINISH. Antique copper sand finish only.
LOCK. Easy spring action, reversible for right or left hand doors. Size, 5x3½ inches. Japanned.
FACE. Electro plated with stop work to set latch bolt. Size, 7x1 inch.
ESCUTCHEONS. Electro plated iron. Extra large; size, 2¾x11 inches outside; small inside escutcheon.
KNOBS. Electro plated cast iron. Size, 2¼ inches, on 5-16 inch swivel spindle.
ELECTRO PLATED bolts, strike and trimmings.
KEYS. Nickel plated steel, two for latch bolt and one for lock bolt.
No. 9B45156 Price, per set..........$1.27

FULTON DESIGN DOOR BELLS

ONE IN A BOX, WITH SCREWS AND FIXTURES.

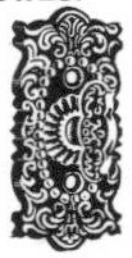

FINISH. Antique copper sand finish only.
ESCUTCHEON. Bronze metal. Size, 3⅜x1½ inch.
No. 9B46696 With 3-inch electro copper plated cast gong. Price..........................52c
No. 9B46716 With 3½-inch nickel plated bell metal gong. Price....................73c

FULTON DESIGN FLUSH SASH LIFTS

FINISH. Antique copper sand finish only.
ELECTRO PLATED cast iron. Size, 3x1¼ inches.
PACKED with screws to match.
No. 9B46546 Price, each..................6c
Per dozen....................................68c

FULTON DESIGN INSIDE DOOR LOCK SETS

ONE SET IN A BOX, WITH SCREWS TO MATCH.

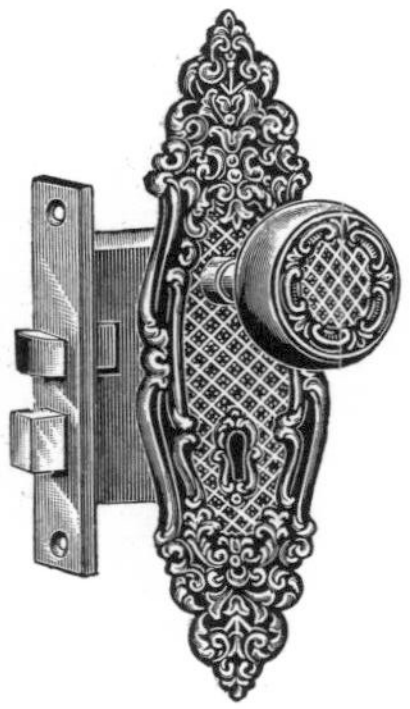

FINISH. Antique copper sand finish only.
LOCK. Easy spring action, reversible. Size lock, 3½x3¼ inches; face, 5¼x⅞ inch.
ESCUTCHEONS. Electro plated cast iron, extra large. Size, 2⅜x8½ inches.
KNOBS. Electro plated cast iron. Size, 2¼ inches.
ELECTRO PLATED front, bolts and strike.
KEY. Nickel plated steel.
No. 9B45306 Price, per set..........$0.52
Per dozen sets.............................. 6.10

FULTON DESIGN SLIDING DOOR LOCK SETS

ONE SET IN A BOX, WITH SCREWS TO MATCH.

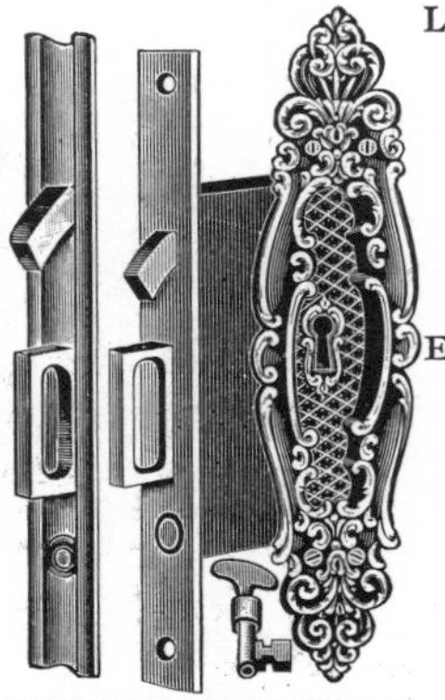

LOCK. Either flat or astragal face. **State which is wanted.** Has extension pulls, operated by stop on face. Size lock, 5½x3¼ inches; face, 1x7⅜ inches.
ESCUTCHEONS. Electro plated cast iron, flush pattern. Size, 2⅜ x 8¾ inches. Single sliding door locks have two escutcheons; double sliding door locks have four.
ELECTRO PLATED front, bolts and strike.
KEY. Bronze metal, extension pattern.
No. 9B45596 Antique copper sand finish only.
For single doors, flat front. Per set....$1.05
For double doors, flat front. Per set.... 1.71
For double doors, astragal front. Per set 1.89

WINDOW, TRANSOM AND BLIND HARDWARE

Small But Important Items Finished to Match Our Various Designs and Quoted at Prices That Mean a Saving to You on Every Article.

Hook Sash Lifts.

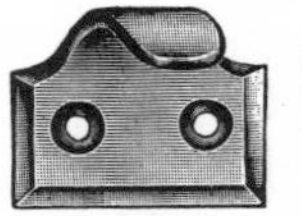

Have bevel edges and are nicely finished. No better goods made. Size, 1½ inches. Complete with screws to match.

Genuine Wrought Bronze Metal.

No. 9B46432 Antique Copper Polished Finish. Per doz., **44c**; each **5c**
No. 9B46434 Plain Polished Bronze Finish. Per doz., **43c**; each **5c**
No. 9B46436 Antique Copper Sand Finish. Per doz., **45c**; each.. **5c**

Bronze Plated Wrought Steel.

No. 9B46442 Antique Copper Polished Finish. Per doz., **18c**; each.. **2c**
No. 9B46444 Plain Polished Bronze Finish. Per doz., **17c**; each **2c**
No. 9B46446 Antique Copper Sand Finish. Per doz., **19c**; each.. **2c**
No. 9B46449 Old or Lemon Brass Finish. Per doz., **18c**; each **2c**

Bar Sash Lifts.

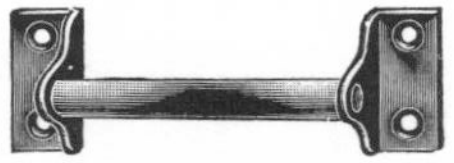

Most convenient sash lifts made. Electro plated wrought steel, with screws. Length handle, 3 inches, long enough to get all four fingers under. Length over all, 4¼ inches.

No. 9B46392 Polished Antique Copper Finish.
Price, per dozen, **68c**; each.... **6c**
No. 9B46394 Plain Polished Bronze Finish.
Price, per dozen, **68c**; each.... **6c**
No. 9B46399 Old or Lemon Brass Finish.
Price, per dozen, **68c**; each.... **6c**

Flush Sash Lifts.

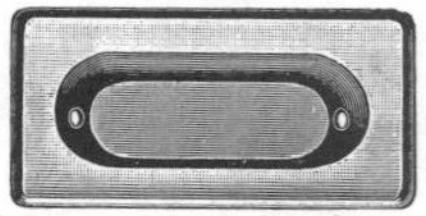

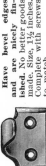

Very neat and strong. Electro plated wrought steel, with screws. Size, 3x1½ inches.

No. 9B46502 Polished Antique Copper Finish.
Price, per dozen, **46c**; each.... **4c**
No. 9B46504 Plain Polished Bronze Finish.
Price, per dozen, **46c**; each.... **4c**
No. 9B46509 Old or Lemon Brass Finish.
Price, per dozen, **46c**; each.... **4c**

Fulton Design Flush Sash Lifts.

No. 9B46546 Electro plated antique copper sand finish. A strong, neat looking sash lift in a very durable finish. Size, 3x1¼ inches. With screws to match.
Price, per dozen, **68c**; each.... **6c**

Crescent Pattern Sash Fasteners.

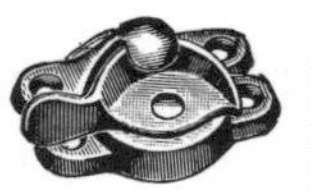

Strong and secure, hold fast and prevent rattling. Most popular pattern sash fasteners made. Electro plated, wrought steel, with screws.

No. 9B46882 Antique Copper Polished Finish.
Price, per dozen, **49c**; each.... **5c**
No. 9B46884 Plain Polished Bronze Finish.
Price, per dozen, **48c**; each.... **5c**
No. 9B46886 Antique Copper Sand Finish.
Price, per dozen, **54c**; each.... **5c**
No. 9B46889 Old or Lemon Brass Finish.
Price, per dozen, **53c**; each.... **5c**

Standard Pattern Sash Fasteners.

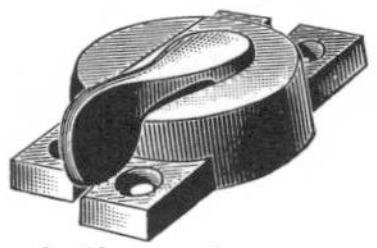

Hold sash securely, prevent rattling. Malleable iron, electro plated, with screws.

No. 9B46872 Antique Copper Polished Finish.
Price, per dozen, **58c**; each.... **6c**
No. 9B46874 Plain Polished Bronze Finish.
Price, per dozen, **57c**; each.... **6c**
No. 9B46876 Antique Copper Sand Finish.
Price, per dozen, **68c**; each.... **6c**

Ornamental Design Sash Fastener.

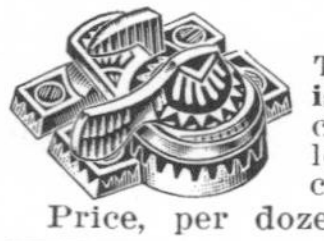

No. 9B46918
Tuscan bronze finished iron. A first class fastener at a low price. Full size, complete with screws.
Price, per dozen, **43c**; each.... **4c**

Side Sash Fasteners.

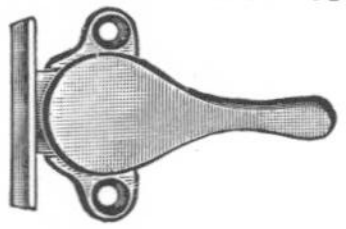

No. 9B46842 Prevent rattling and hold sash at any height. Excellent for ventilation, can be used on windows not equipped with weights. Electro plated antique copped polished finish, with screws to match.
Price, per dozen, **56c**; each.... **6c**

Stop Bead Screws and Washers.

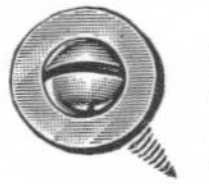

Round head screws, bevel edge washers, electro plated steel.

No. 9B47022 Antique Copper Polished Finish.
Price, per gross, **68c**; per dozen. **6c**
No. 9B47024 Plain Polished Bronze Finish.
Price, per gross, **64c**; per dozen. **6c**

Ventilating Sash Fasteners.

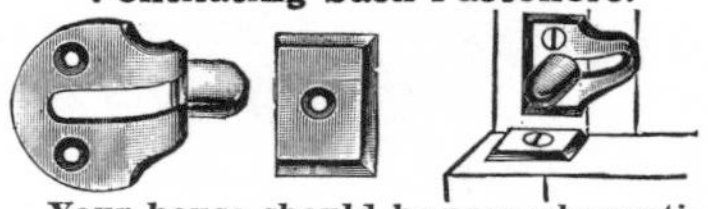

Your house should be properly ventilated. Physicians and health officers recommend it, but you don't like to leave your windows open and allow a burglar to come in. These ventilating fasteners allow windows to be left open at top, bottom or both top and bottom, wide enough for thorough ventilation, but not wide enough to permit a person to come in. Simple, strong and safe. Easily operated; quickly applied. Electro bronze plated, with screws to match.

No. 9B47012 Antique Copper Polished Finish.
Price, per dozen, **$1.41**; each.. **12c**
No. 9B47014 Plain Polished Bronze Finish.
Price, per dozen, **$1.40**; each.. **12c**
No. 9B47019 Old or Lemon Brass Finish.
Price, per dozen, **$1.42**; each.. **12c**

Porcelain Shutter Knobs.

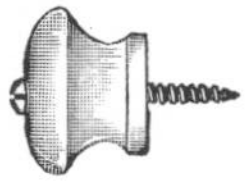

No. 9B47817 White porcelain knobs, with round head tinned screws. Used on shutters, door and window screens, as drawer pulls, cupboard pulls, etc.

Size, inch.	¾	1	1¼	1½
Per dozen.	7c	$0.09	$0.11	$0.13
Per gross.	82c	1.05	1.29	1.53

Window Spring Bolts.

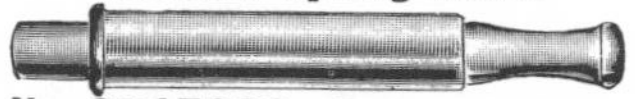

No. 9B47003 Japanned bolt, tin case. Put in by simply boring hole in sash. Made especially for windows without weights, but can be used on any window. A very secure fastening.
Price, per gross, **92c**; per dozen.. **8c**

Self Locking Outside Blind Hinges.

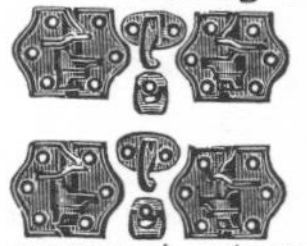

No. 9B47865 For frame houses; made of best gray iron; throws blind 1¼ inches from casing. Set includes four hinges and two fasteners, but does not include screws. A set requires thirty No. 8 flat head screws. For screws see page 128.
Price, per set.................. **5c**
Per dozen sets.................. **59c**

Adjustable Outside Blind Fasteners.

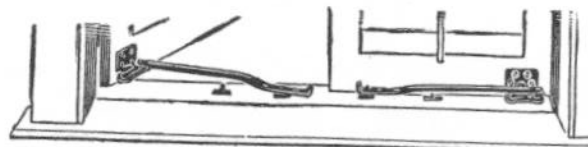

No. 9B47867 For storm sash or outside blinds. Securely fastens and locks blinds at any angle. Made of cold rolled steel. Finish, electro galvanized plated. Unbreakable and rustproof, with screws to match. Length, 13 inches. Price, per pair........ **18c**

Spring Sash Balances.

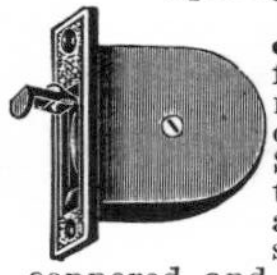

Take the place of sash cords and weights. The first cost is the only cost, no cords to renew, no carpenters' bills to pay. Springs made of finest tempered steel, guaranteed to retain their strength. Springs are coppered and will not rust. Full directions with each set. Price is per set of four balances, enough for upper and lower sash. **Be sure to order the size to suit your sash.**

No. 9B47551 Spring Sash Balances. State size wanted.

Size No.	Weight of window (2 Sash)	Height, each Sash	Weight, per Set of 4 Balances	Price, per Set of 4
6	8 to 12 lbs.	34 in.	6 lbs.	$0.94
8	12 to 16 lbs.	34 in.	6 lbs.	1.04
10	16 to 20 lbs.	34 in.	7 lbs.	1.14
12	20 to 24 lbs.	44 in.	7 lbs.	1.24
14	24 to 28 lbs.	44 in.	7½ lbs.	1.34
16	28 to 32 lbs.	44 in.	7½ lbs.	1.48
18	32 to 36 lbs.	48 in.	9½ lbs.	1.63
20	36 to 40 lbs.	48 in.	10 lbs.	1.78
22	40 to 44 lbs.	48 in.	11 lbs.	1.98
24	44 to 48 lbs.	48 in.	13 lbs.	2.17
26	48 to 52 lbs.	50 in.	13 lbs.	2.27
28	52 to 56 lbs.	50 in.	13½ lbs.	2.37
30	56 to 60 lbs.	50 in.	14 lbs.	2.47
32	60 to 64 lbs.	50 in.	14 lbs.	2.57
34	64 to 68 lbs.	50 in.	14 lbs.	2.72
36	68 to 72 lbs.	50 in.	14 lbs.	2.92

Automatic Sash Holder.

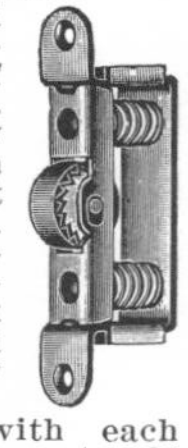

No. 9B47575 Hold windows up at any point desired. Take place of weights, cords or springs. Adaptable for old or new windows. Do away with pockets, grooves and a lot of time, labor and material. Just the thing for old windows with no weight pockets. Easy to place, work automatically, save time and labor putting in. Strongly made. Size, 3¼x⅞x1⁵⁄₁₆ inches. Full directions with each set. For sash weighing up to 30 pounds each. Per set of 4..... **$0.76**
Per dozen sets............... **8.70**

Common Sense Cast Iron Sash Pulleys.

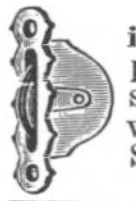

No. 9B47563 Mortised in with a 1⅛-inch bit. Rapidly put in place, firmly held by screws and easily removed when necessary. 2-inch wheel. Screws not included.
Price, per dozen......... **18c**

Steel Sash Pulleys.

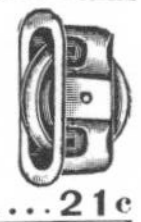

No. 9B47561 The unbreakable steel kind. Require no screws, save time and labor; just bore three holes and drive the pulley in; 2-inch wheel. Price, per dozen........... **21c**

Noiseless Sash Pulleys.

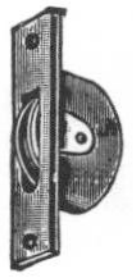

No. 9B47572 Heavy, first quality, finely finished goods. Have steel axles and 2¼-inch turned wheels, for ⅜-inch rope or smaller. Wheels are properly adjusted, run easily and without noise. **Polished antique copper finished face.** Size face, 5⅝x1⅛ inches.
Price, per dozen..... **$1.08**

Transom Catches.

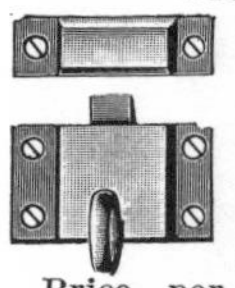

Self fastening, with ring for cord or hook. Electro plated steel, bronze metal ring, with screws. Size, 2⅛x1¼ inches.

No. 9B47462 Antique Copper Polished Finish.
Price, per dozen, **98c**; each.... **9c**
No. 9B47464 Plain Polished Bronze Finish. Per doz., **98c**; each. **9c**
No. 9B47469 Old or Lemon Brass Finish. Per doz., **98c**; each. **9c**

Electro Plated Transom Butts.

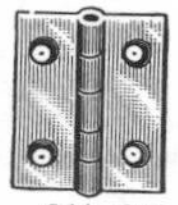

Electro plated wrought steel, heavy pattern, fast joints with screws to match.

No. 9B47742 Antique Copper Polished Finish.

Size, inches....	2½x2½	3x3	3½x3½
Per pair.......	18c	22c	27c

No. 9B47744 Polished Bronze Finish.

Size, inches....	2½x2½	3x3	3½x3½
Per pair.......	17c	20c	27c

Transom Pivots or Sash Centers.

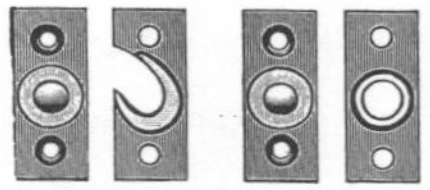

No. 9B47445 For pivoting transoms or sash. Very desirable in barns, warehouses, and other buildings where thorough ventilation is desired. Made of iron, japanned. Size, ⅞x2¼ inches. Prices are without screws. Price, per set of four pieces, as illustrated, **3c**; per dozen sets......... **31c**

Transom Lifters.

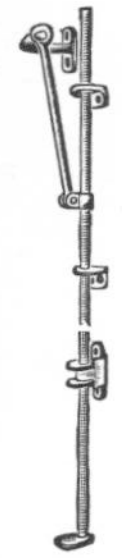

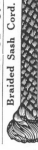

For use on transoms hinged at top, bottom, or pivoted in the middle. Transom may be easily lowered, raised or locked in any position with these lifters. Makes it possible to properly ventilate any room. The 3 and 4-foot lengths are made of ¼-inch round rod; 5 and 6-foot lengths are made of 5-16-inch round rod. **Our coppered finish** is ordinarily sold by others as bronze plated or electro copper plated finish. Prices below include screws to match.

No. 9B47441 Coppered Finish.

Length, feet.	3	4	5	6
Price........	9c	11c	21c	26c

No. 9B47442 Electro Bronze Plated Antique Copper Finish.

Length, ft.	3	4	5	6
Price......	18c	21c	32c	37c

Braided Sash Cord.

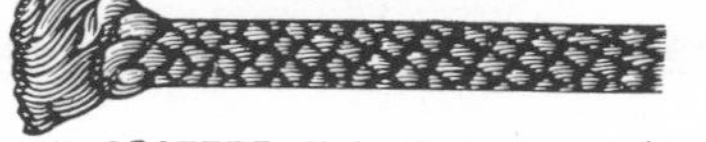

No. 9B47555 Made of extra quality long fiber cotton, smoothly braided. Not made with a jute center and cotton braided on the outside, but made of best white cotton throughout. There is no better cord made than this and our price saves you money. Size, No. 8, 8-32-inch diameter. Put up in bundles of 100 feet.
Price, per bundle...................... **67c**

TRIMMINGS FOR DOORS, CUPBOARDS AND CLOSETS

First quality goods, finished to match our design hardware and unexcelled for wearing quality or appearance by any similar line on the market.

Improved Safety Door Guard.

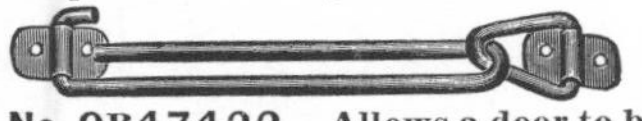

No. 9B47422 Allows a door to be partly opened but holds it so that a person cannot force his way in. For outside doors, apartment houses, etc. Keeps out burglars, tramps, agents and solicitors. Stronger, better and more convenient than chain door guards. Instantly unhooked when door is closed. A great protection for women who stay at home alone. Neat in appearance, nicely finished, quickly and easily put on. Made of steel, electro plated, antique copper finish. With screws to match and directions for putting on. Price..........15c

Plain Pattern Chain Bolts.

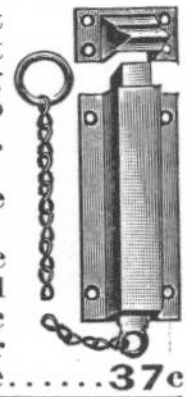

This chain bolt in connection with the foot bolt shown below makes a neat and very secure fastening for double doors. Electro bronze plated, 6-inch bolt, 2-foot chain, with screws.
No. 9B47392 Antique Copper Polished Finish. Price..........36c
No. 9B47394 Polished Bronze Finish. Price..35c
No. 9B47399 Old or Lemon Brass Finish. Price......37c

Plain Pattern Foot Bolts.

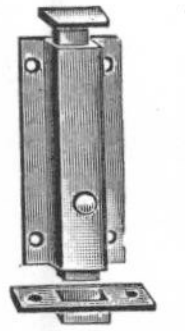

To be used in connection with chain bolt shown above. Electro bronze plated, spring release, 6 inches long, with screws to match.
No. 9B47382 Antique Copper Polished Finish. Price..........33c
No. 9B47384 Polished Bronze Finish. Price..32c
No. 9B47389 Old or Lemon Brass Finish. Price......34c

Mayfair Design Chain Bolt.

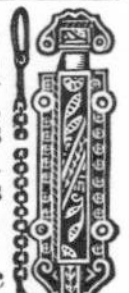

Electro bronze plated. Raised surfaces polished bronze finish, background dull black. Has coppered chain 2 feet long. Length, 6 inches, with screws to match.
No. 9B47408
Price, complete..........24c

Mayfair Design Foot Bolt.

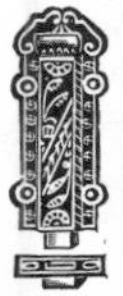

Electro bronze plated. Raised surfaces polished bronze finish, background dull black. Length, 6 inches. Furnished complete with socket and screws to match.
No. 9B47418 Price...23c

Enameled Thumb Latches and Handles. 6c

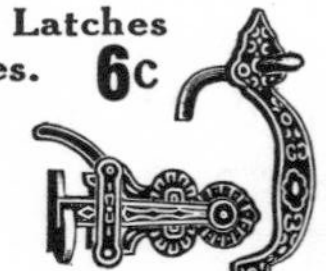

Packed complete with screws. Suitable for doors ⅞ to 1½ inches thick.
No. 9B48501
Price, each..... 6c
Per dozen......68c

Electric Ring Door Bell.

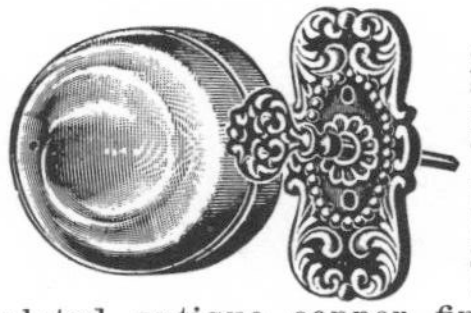

Best bell on the market for the price. Has 3½-inch nickel plated steel gong and 3½x1½-inch electro plated antique copper finished turnplate. Easy to turn and makes a clear loud ring. The usual 50 to 65-cent kind elsewhere.
No. 9B46642 Price, complete..........28c

Rubber Tipped Door Holders.

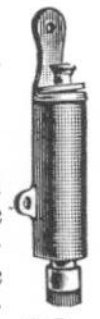

Operated with foot. Quickly set or released. Holds door in any position. Cannot injure floor or carpet. Simple and durable. Strongly made, good quality rubber tip.
No. 9B47811 Japanned Finish. Price..........42c
No. 9B47812 Antique Copper Polished Finish. Price..47c
No. 9B47814 Plain Polished Bronze Finish. Price.........48c

Rubber Tipped Metal Base Knobs.

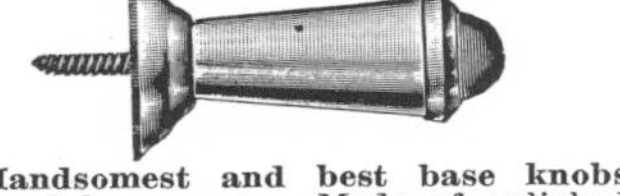

Handsomest and best base knobs offered by anyone. Made of polished wrought steel, electro bronze plated. First quality rubber tips, extra strong screws. Length, 2¾ inches.
No. 9B46362 Antique Copper Polished Finish.
Price, per dozen, 76c; each.....7c
No. 9B46364 Polished Bronze Finish. Price, per dozen, 75c; each,7c
No. 9B46369 Old or Lemon Brass Finish.
Price, per dozen, 77c; each.....7c

Rubber Tipped Birch Base Knobs.

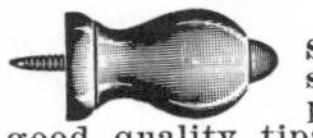

No. 9B46353 Smoothly turned from selected stock. Have perfect screws and good quality tips. Usual 25-cent per dozen value.
Price, per dozen, 13c; each.....2c

Mortise Door Bolts.

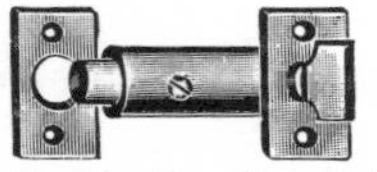

With T handle thumbpiece and plate. Electro plated plates and face, complete with screws to match.
No. 9B47332 Antique Copper Polished Finish. Price..........13c
No. 9B47334 Polished Bronze Finish. Price..........12c
No. 9B47336 Antique Copper Sand Finish. Price..........14c

Drop Handles With Plates.

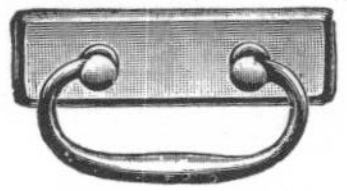

A neat handsome pattern in solid bronze; a first quality handle at a medium price. These handles finished to match practically every kind of woodwork. Plate is made of wrought bronze, size, 1¼x3¾ inches, handles made of cast bronze, width, 3⅛ inches. With screws to match.
No. 9B47202 Antique Copper Polished Finish.
Price, per dozen, $2.98; each..27c
No. 9B47204 Plain Polished Bronze Finish.
Price, per dozen, $2.86; each..26c
No. 9B47209 Old or Lemon Brass Finish.
Price, per dozen, $3.10; each..28c

Plain Pattern Drawer Pulls.

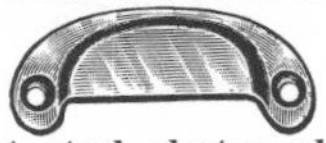

Wrought steel electro plated, with screws to match. Length, 3⅝ inches.
No. 9B47212 Antique Copper Polished Finish.
Price, per dozen, 29c; each......3c
No. 9B47214 Polished Bronze Finish. Price, per dozen, 28c; each, 3c
No. 9B47216 Antique Copper Sand Finish.
Price, per dozen, 30c; each....3c
No. 9B47219 Old or Lemon Brass Finish.
Price, per dozen, 28c; each....3c

Mayfair Design Drawer Pull.

No. 9B47238 Electro plated iron; raised surfaces polished bronze finish, background dull black. With screws to match. Length, 3½ inches.
Price, per dozen, 36c; each....4c

Wrought Barrel Bolts.

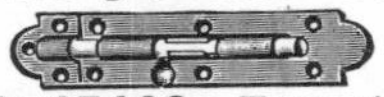

No. 9B47423 Very strong and secure. Polished steel bolt with brass knob.

Length of bolt, in..	3	4	5	6
Price, each........	3c	4c	5c	6c
Per dozen........	35c	45c	55c	65c

Plated Barrel Bolts.

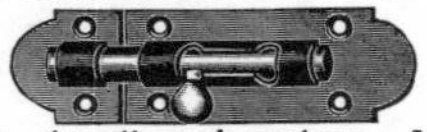

Combines strength and neatness. Made of electro plated wrought steel. Furnished complete with screws to match. All three finishes the same price.
No. 9B47402 Antique Copper Finish.
No. 9B47404 Polished Bronze Finish.
No. 9B47409 Old or Lemon Brass Finish.

Length of bolt, inches........	3	4
Price, each....................	7c	8c
Per dozen....................	79c	86c

Plain Pattern Cupboard Turns.

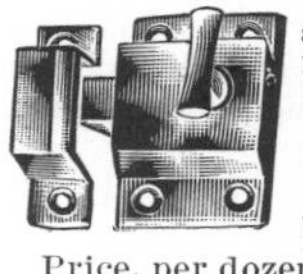

Self fastening, neat and substantial. Finished to match all kinds of wood trim. Wrought steel, electro plated, with screws.
No. 9B47082 Antique Copper Polished Finish.
Price, per dozen, $1.14; each..11c
No. 9B47084 Polished Bronze Finish.
Price, per dozen, $1.12; each..11c
No. 9B47086 Antique Copper Sand Finish.
Price, per dozen, $1.18; each..11c
No. 9B47089 Old or Lemon Brass Finish.
Price, per dozen, $1.04; each..9c

Mayfair Design Cupboard Turns.

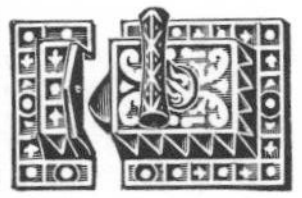

No. 9B47078
Electro plated; raised surfaces polished bronze finish, background dull black. Size, 1¾x2⅛ inches. Complete with screws to match.
Price, per dozen, $1.28; each..11c

Plain Pattern Cupboard Catches.

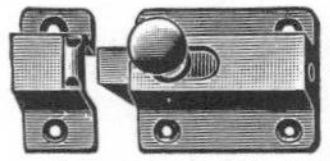

Self fastening, easy acting, nicely finished. Wrought steel, electro plated with screws to match.
No. 9B47042 Antique Copper Polished Finish.
Price, per dozen, 65c; each....6c
No. 9B47044 Polished Bronze Finish. Price, per dozen, 64c; each, 6c
No. 9B47046 Antique Copper Sand Finish.
Price, per dozen, 68c; each....6c
No. 9B47049 Old or Lemon Brass Finish.
Price, per dozen, 65c; each....6c

Mayfair Design Cupboard Catches.

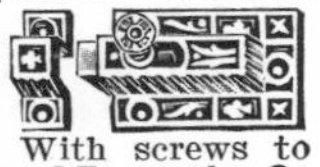

No. 9B47048
Electro plated; raised surfaces polished bronze finish, background dull black. With screws to match. Price, per doz., 65c; each..6c

Japanned Cupboard Catches.

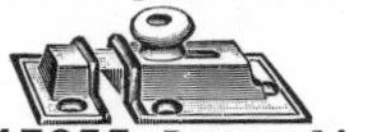

No. 9B47055 Japanned iron, with white porcelain knobs. Screws not included.
Price, per dozen, 34c; each....3c

Japanned Elbow Catches.

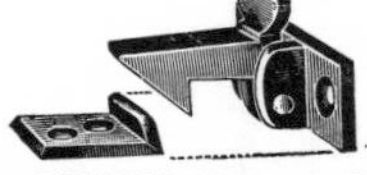

No. 9B47057 Japanned iron. For use on double cupboard doors.
Price, per dozen, 22c; each....3c

Coat and Hat Hooks.

A number of patterns for you to choose from, ranging in price from the cheapest to the best.

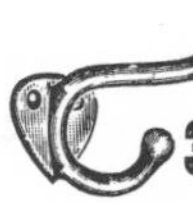

3c

Electro plated iron. Complete with screws to match. Length, 3½ inches.
No. 9B47482 Antique Copper Polished Finish. Per doz., 34c; each...3c
No. 9B47484 Plain Polished Bronze Finish. Per doz., 33c; each.3c
No. 9B47489 Old or Lemon Brass Finish. Per doz., 34c; each.......3c

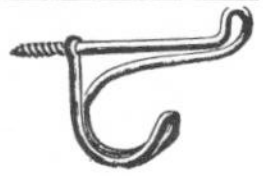

No. 9B47501 Made of spring steel wire, nicely coppered. No tools required to put them up. Lighter than iron hooks and not easily broken. Length, 3 inches.
Price, per gross, 58c; per doz..6c

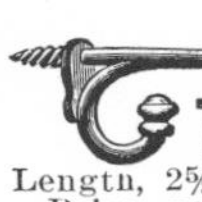

7c

No. 9B47505 Extra strong, japanned iron. A good substantial hook at a reasonable price. No screws required to put up. Length, 2⅝ inches.
Price, per gross, 81c; per doz..7c

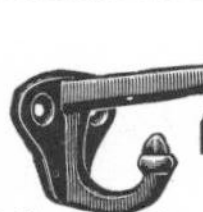

18c

No. 9B47515 Japanned Iron Schoolhouse or Heavy Coat and Hat Hook. Extra strong. Length, 3 inches.
Price, per gross,$1.98; per doz.18c

Coppered Wire Wardrobe Hooks.

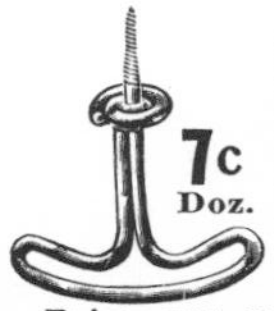

7c Doz.

No. 9B47521 Light, strong, convenient; require no screws, never rust and will not break. The most convenient hook made to screw into tops or underneath shelves in wardrobes, closets, lockers, etc. Length, 2 inches.
Price, per gross, 78c; per doz...7c

Cloak, Coat, Hat and Umbrella Hooks.

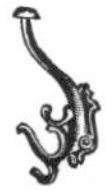

No. 9B47522 Single pattern. Neat, strong and durable. One of the handiest barber shop hooks on the market. Electro plated iron, polished antique copper finish, with screws. Height, 7 inches; projects from wall, 4 inches.
Price, each..........11c
Price, per dozen..........$1.25

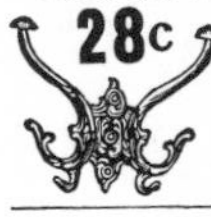

28c

No. 9B47532 Double pattern. These hooks largely used on hall trees and hall racks. Height, 9 inches; projects from wall, 4½ inches; spread, 10 inches.
Price, each..........$0.28
Price, per dozen.......3.30

Japanned Door Buttons.

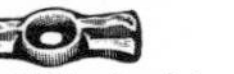

No. 9B48505 Without plates or screws. State size.

Length		Per gross	Per dozen
1½ inches.	Price..........	24c	3c
2 inches.	Price..........	36c	4c

HOUSE DOOR BUTTS AND HINGES

A COMPLETE LINE OF THE DIFFERENT STYLES AND FINISHES. ALL OUR BUTTS AND HINGES ARE FULL SIZE, FULL STRENGTH AND QUOTED AT MONEY SAVING PRICES

Wrought Steel Loose Pin Butts.

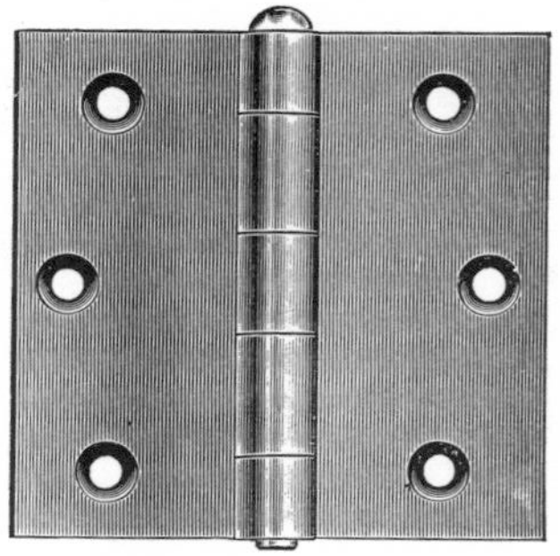

No. 9B47773 Heavy pattern, plain finish. Full size, full weight goods; we do not handle the skimped light weight butts sometimes offered. These high grade goods usually sell at one-third to one-half more than we ask. Prices below are for butts without screws. For screws see page 128.

Size, inches	Takes Screws	Per pair	Doz. pairs
2½x2½	No. 8	5c	$0.53
3 x3	No. 9	6c	.62
3½x3½	No. 10	8c	.90
4 x4	No. 10	10c	1.10
4½x4½	No. 11	12c	1.36

Japanned Loose Pin Steel Butts.

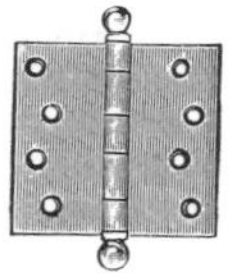

No. 9B47775 Same high class butts as quoted above except with ball tips and japanned. Prices are without screws. For screws see page 128.

Size, inches	Takes Screws	Per pair	Doz. pairs
2½x2½	No. 8	6c	$0.71
3 x3	No. 9	7c	.83
3½x3½	No. 10	9c	.99
4 x4	No. 10	11c	1.20
4½x4½	No. 11	14c	1.49
5 x5	No. 12	16c	1.85

Fast Joint Narrow Steel Butts.

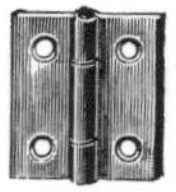

No. 9B47777 Wrought steel, plain finish, tight pins. For boxes, cupboards, transoms, etc. Prices quoted are without screws. For screws see page 128.

Length, inches	Takes Screws	Doz. pairs
1	No. 3	11c
1¼	No. 3	14c
1½	No. 5	17c
2	No. 6	22c
2½	No. 6	29c
3	No. 7	37c

Electro Plated Transom Butts.

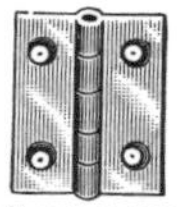

Electro plated wrought steel, heavy pattern, fast joints, with screws to match.

No. 9B47742 Antique Copper Polished Finish.

Size, inches	2½x2½	3x3	3½x3½
Per pair	18c	22c	27c

No. 9B47744 Polished Bronze Finish.

Size, inches	2½x2½	3x3	3½x3½
Per pair	17c	20c	27c

Mayfair Design Cast Butts.

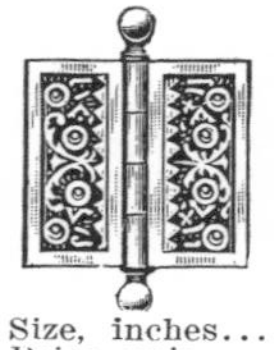

No. 9B47758 Electro bronze plated iron; raised surfaces polished bronze finish, background dull black. Matches our other Mayfair design hardware. With screws to match.

Size, inches	3x3	3½x3½
Price, pair	23c	26c
Size, inches	4x4	4½x4½
Price, pair	31c	35c

Fulton Design Cast Butts.

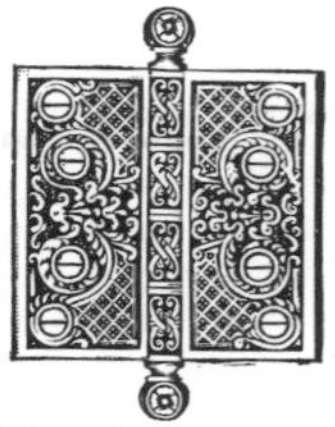

No. 9B47766 Electro bronze plated iron; antique copper sand finish. With screws to match.

Size, inches	Price, per pair
3x3	26c
3½x3½	29c
4x4	35c
4½x4½	40c

Steeple Tipped Cast Butts.

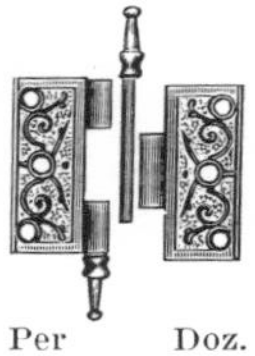

No. 9B47771 Loose pin, plain finish. Prices do not include screws. See page 128 for screws.

Size, inches	Takes Screws	Per pair	Doz. pairs
2 x2	No. 8	3c	29c
2½x2½	No. 9	4c	39c
3 x3	No. 10	5c	51c
3½x3½	No. 10	6c	66c
4 x4	No. 11	7c	79c

Electro Plated Polished Wrought Steel Butts.

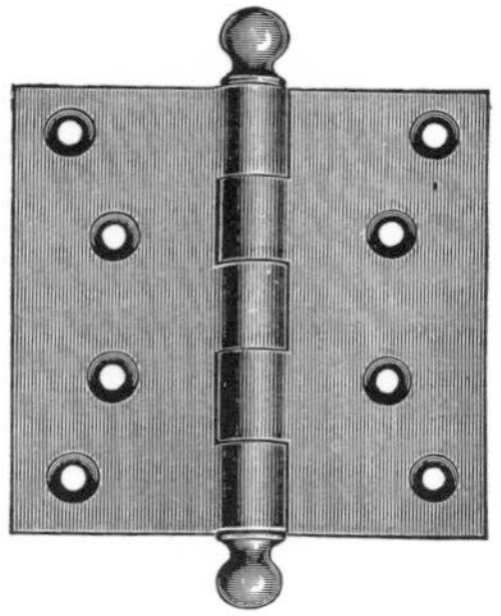

Heavy high grade loose pin butts. Finest finished butts made. Our prices save you money on these extra polished butts. Furnished with screws to match.

No. 9B47722 Antique Copper Polished Finish.

Size, in.	3x3	3½x3½	4x4	4½x4½	5x5
Per pair	26c	30c	34c	38c	42c

No. 9B47724 Polished Bronze Finish.

Size, in.	3x3	3½x3½	4x4	4½x4½	5x5
Per pair	25c	29c	33c	37c	41c

Electro Plated Planished Wrought Steel Butts.

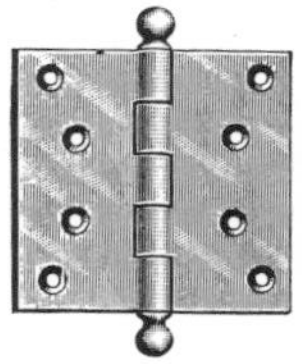

Full size and strength. Pins are ball tipped and removable. These butts are electro plated and planished and commonly sold by dealers as the polished butt. The same grade of steel as the polished, but not as finely finished. Furnished with screws to match.

No. 9B47732 Antique Copper Finish.

Size, inches	2½x2½	3x3	3½x3½	4x4
Per pair	13c	15c	17c	19c

No. 9B47734 Plain Bronze Finish.

Size, inches	2½x2½	3x3	3½x3½	4x4
Per pair	12c	14c	16c	18c

No. 9B47736 Antique Copper Sand Finish.

Size, inches	2½x2½	3x3	3½x3½
Per pair	14c	16c	18c
Size, inches	4x4	4½x4½	5x5
Per pair	20c	28c	35c

No. 9B47739 Old or Lemon Brass Finish.

Size, inches	3x3	3½x3½	4x4
Per pair	15c	17c	19c

Ornamental Half Mortise Butts.

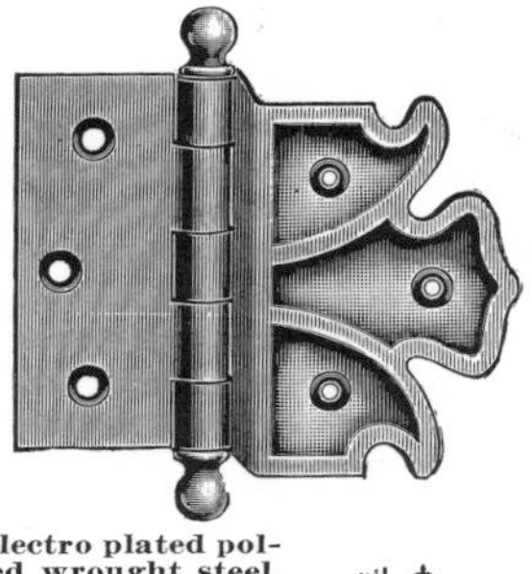

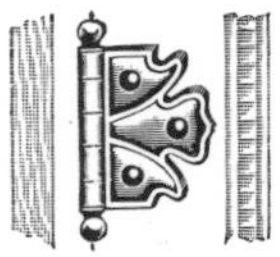

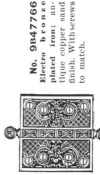

Electro plated polished wrought steel. Very handsome, strong and durable. These butts are becoming very popular and are fast taking the place of old style butts. We quote them in three of the most popular finishes and a full range of sizes. They are very easy to put on, many carpenters declaring they save at least half the time and labor in hanging doors. Reversible for right or left hand doors. Sizes, 1½, 2 and 2½-inch intended for boxes, cabinets, cupboards, etc. Larger sizes for house doors. 3-inch size for 1⅛-inch doors or thinner, 3½-inch size for 1⅜-inch doors and 4-inch size for 1¾-inch doors. Size 1½-inch fast pin, not ball tipped; other sizes loose pin, ball tipped. Size given is length of joint. Furnished with screws to match. All three finishes same price.

No. 9B47762 Antique Copper Finish.
No. 9B47764 Polished Bronze Finish.
No. 9B47769 Old or Lemon Brass Finish.

Size, in.	1½	2	2½	3	3½	4
Per pair	9c	13c	17c	20c	23c	28c

Fast Joint Wrought Brass Butts.

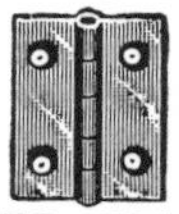

No. 9B47779 Light Pattern, smoothly finished. Intended for boxes, cupboards, cabinets, etc. Our prices are without screws. Brass screws to fit quoted on page 128.

Length, inches	Takes Screws	Doz. pairs
1	No. 2	$0.19
1¼	No. 3	.23
1½	No. 4	.29
2	No. 5	.45
2½	No. 6	.73
3	No. 8	1.32

Ball Bearing Double Acting Floor Spring Hinges.

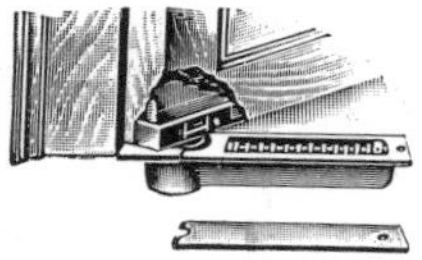

Hinge sets in floor and is almost invisible. It is easy to put in, readily adjusted, works noiselessly and is dust and rust proof. Door can be quickly removed without disturbing the hinge or its spring tension. Doors cannot sag. Provided with best steel ball bearings. Price includes pivot for top of door and all necessary screws. The best floor hinges made. Directions with each set.

No. 9B47790 Japanned Finish.
For ordinary doors..........$1.28
For heavy doors..........1.62

No. 9B47793 Old Copper Finish.
For ordinary doors..........$1.67
For heavy doors..........2.36

Niles Double Acting Spring Hinges.

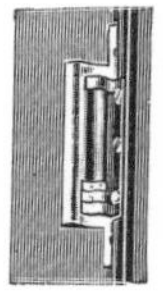

Swing both ways; require no jamb strip. They are easily put on, have adjustable tension, and doors cannot sag. For a set we furnish one spring hinge and pivot for top of door. Be sure to order right size hinges to suit your doors.

Thickness, Doors	No. 9B47801 Iron, Japanned	No. 9B47802 Antique Copper Finish
⅞ in. to 1$\frac{1}{16}$ in.	$0.67	$1.20
1⅛ in. to 1¼ in.	.91	1.44
1⅜ in. to 1½ in.	1.17	1.68
1¾ in. to 1⅞ in.	1.48	1.94

Adjustable Tension Double Acting Spring Butts.

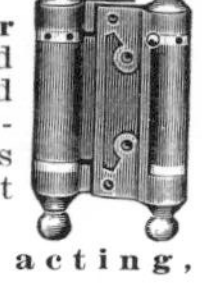

Reversible for right or left hand doors. Japanned iron. Tension quickly and easily adjusted. The largest hinge that the thickness of the door will permit works best.

No. 9B47781 Double acting, swing both ways.

Size	For doors	Per pair
3 in.	¾ to 1 inch thick	$0.80
4 in.	⅞ to 1¼ inches thick	1.03
5 in.	1 to 1½ inches thick	1.26
6 in.	1⅛ to 1¾ inches thick	1.73

Self Locking Outside Blind Hinges.

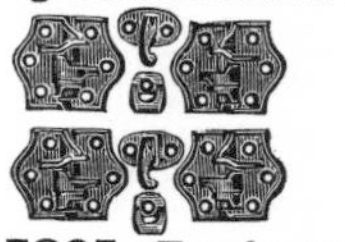

No. 9B47865 For frame houses; made of best gray iron; throw blind 1¼ inches from casing. Set includes four hinges and two fasteners but does not include screws. A set requires thirty No. 8 flat head screws. Price, per doz. sets, **59c**; per set, **5c**

HEAVY DOOR AND GATE HINGES AND HANGERS

Regular Standard Goods, Full Size and Full Weight, Quoted at Money Saving Prices, Which No Careful Buyer Can Afford to Overlook.

Light Wrought Steel T Hinges.

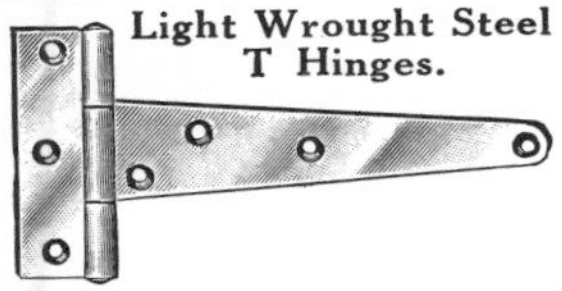

No. 9B47851 Made of standard gauge wrought steel, full size and weight. At these low prices you save on every size. Size given is measurement from joint to end of hinge. Price quoted is without screws. For screws see page 128.

Size, inches	3	4	6	8
Takes Screws No.	6	7	8	9
Price, per pair	3c	3c	4c	5c
Per dozen pairs	27c	34c	45c	56c

Extra Heavy Wrought Steel T Hinges.

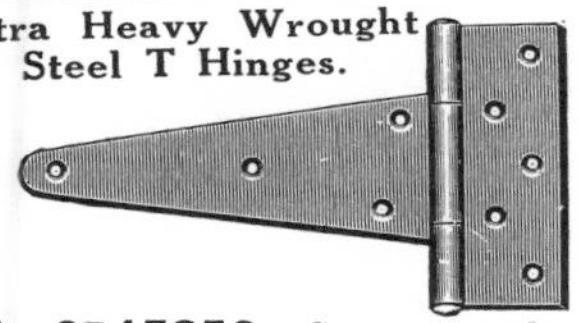

No. 9B47853 Compare these prices with the prices of other dealers and remember that these are not the skimped, under sized kind sometimes offered. Size given is measurement from joint to end of hinge. Our prices do not include screws. For screws see page 128.

Size, inches	6	8	10	12	14
Takes Screws No.	9	10	10	12	12
Price, per pair	8c	$0.13	$0.18	$0.27	$0.30
Per dozen pairs	87c	1.46	2.18	3.16	3.48

Light Wrought Steel Strap Hinges.

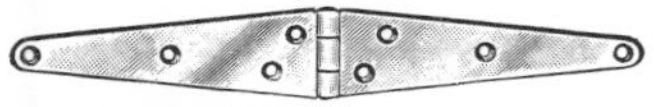

No. 9B47855 Full standard size and weight, the same high grade hinges sold by others at one-third more than we ask. Size given is measurement from joint to end of hinge. Without screws. For screws see page 128.

Size, in.	3	4	5	6
Takes Screws No.	6	7	8	9
Price, per pair	3c	3c	4c	5c
Per dozen pairs	26c	32c	40c	48c

Heavy Wrought Steel Strap Hinges.

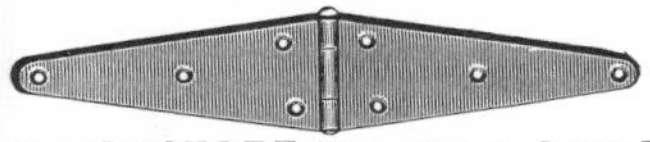

No. 9B47857 The strong dependable kind, hinges that you can hang a door on and know it will stay hung. Note our low prices on these goods. Size given is length from joint to end of hinge. Our prices do not include screws. For screws see page 128.

Size, in.	6	8	10	12	14
Takes Screws No.	10	12	12	14	16
Price, per pair	6c	9c	$0.14	$0.20	$0.22
Per dozen pairs	68c	98c	1.58	2.28	2.58

Wrought Steel Screw Strap Hinges.

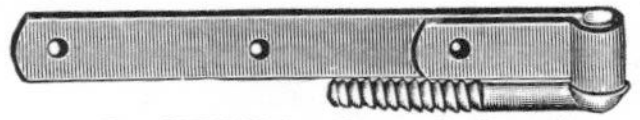

No. 9B47861 One of the strongest pattern hinges made for heavy doors and gates. A set requires two ⅜-inch and four 5-16-inch bolts to put them on. Bolts not included. See bottom of this page or our big General Catalog for bolts.

Size, in.	10	12	14
Price, per pair	$0.17	$0.22	$0.27
Per doz. pairs	1.98	2.48	2.97

Self Closing Gate Hinges.

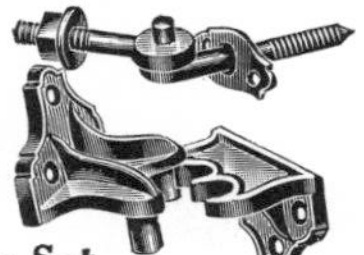

24c Per Set.

No. 9B48953 Swing both ways, need no spring or weight to keep gate closed. Nicely japanned. Wrought upper hinge, cast lower hinge.

Price, per set....................24c

Gate Latch.

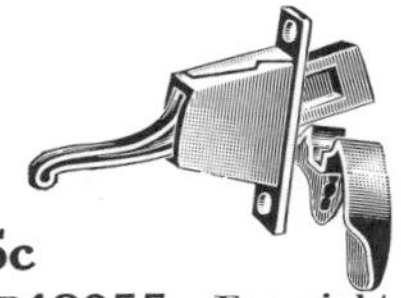

5c

No. 9B48955 For right or left hand gates or gates that swing both ways. Especially recommended for use with above hinges though it can be used on any gate.

Price 5c

"Sure Catch" Gate Latch and Hinges.

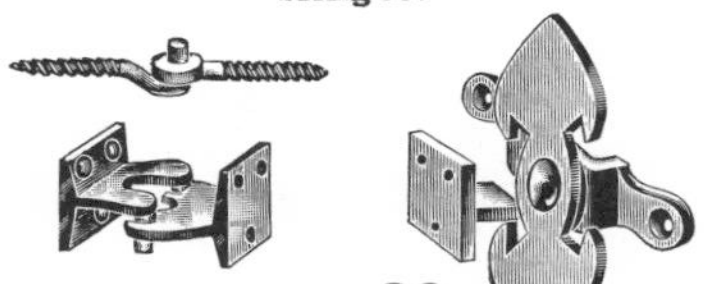

26c

No. 9B48947 Simple, strong and substantial. Swing both ways. Gate cannot be lifted from hinges when closed. Made entirely of steel and malleable iron, outlast half dozen sets of the ordinary gray iron kind. Nicely japanned. Require no cutting or mortising. A regular 50-cent value in any hardware store.

Price, per set, complete with screws 37c

No. 9B48949 Gate Latch only, without hinges. With screws.

Price 26c

Trolley Roller Bearing Steel Barn Door Hangers.

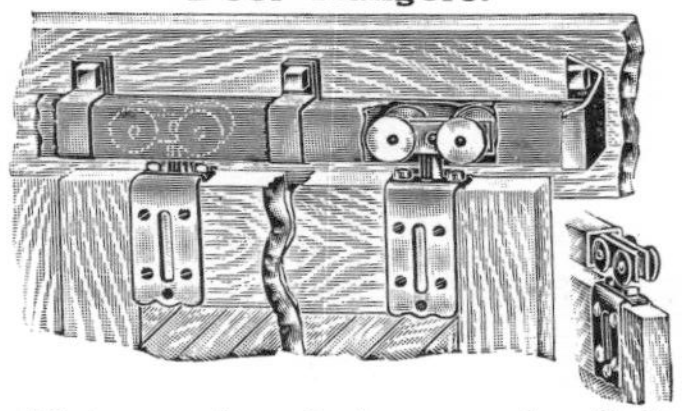

Waterproof and jumpproof. Suitable for doors weighing up to 400 pounds and from 1½ to 2¼ inches thick. This is one of the strongest and most durable outfits of barn door hangers and track possible to construct. Largely used on store and warehouse doors, or wherever great strength and security are required. Set consists of two hangers, two end brackets, one center bracket and the necessary bolts and screws.

No. 9B48829 Price, per set, complete, without track.......$1.26

No. 9B48831 Trolley Track for hangers above. Price does not include brackets.

Length, feet	4	5	6	8	10
Price, per length	40c	50c	60c	80c	$1.00

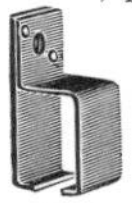

No. 9B48833 Center Track Brackets for Trolley Track. Wrought steel, japanned. Center brackets should not be more than 3 feet apart. Price includes lag screw for attaching.

Price, each.......................10c

Double Pivoted Gate Hanger.

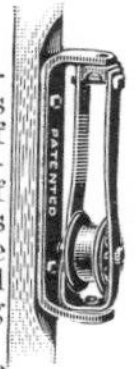

No. 9B48959 Strong, convenient and durable. Works easily and cannot get out of order. Only one hanger required for a gate. Weight of gate hangs on center and at its strongest point. Hanger made of steel, nicely japanned, and fastened to post with two lag bolts. Lag bolts included.

Price 38c

49c FOR 100 FIRST QUALITY ASSORTED CARRIAGE BOLTS.

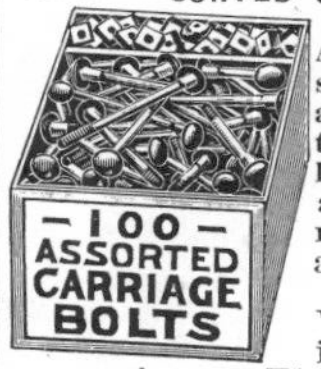

—100— ASSORTED CARRIAGE BOLTS

No. 9B31174 Assortment consists of 17 lengths and sizes from 1½ to 5 inches in length by ¼, 5-16 and ⅜-inch diameter. Needed about every shop, barn and home. Worth three times its cost for its convenience. Elsewhere you would pay at least 85 cents for this assortment. Don't fail to include this lot of bolts in your next order.

Our price..................49c

Full line of all kinds bolts, nuts and washers shown in our big General Catalog.

Roller Bearing Barn Door Hangers.

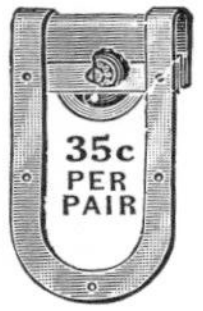

35c PER PAIR

Cold rolled steel axle and anti-friction bearings, fully covered to protect them from the weather. With the exception of the wheel, this hanger is made entirely of wrought steel. A first class hanger at a very low price. Bolts not furnished at prices quoted. For bolts see bottom of this page or our big General Catalog.

No. 9B48837 For ordinary doors. Pair requires six 5-16-inch bolts. Frame, 4¾x11½ inches.

Price, per pair..................35c

No. 9B48839 For heavy doors. Frame, 6¼x12¼ inches. Pair requires eight 5-16-inch bolts.

Price, per pair..................43c

No. 9B48841 For extra heavy doors. Frame, 7x14 inches. Pair requires eight 5-16-inch bolts.

Price, per pair..................52c

Anti-Friction Barn Door Hangers.

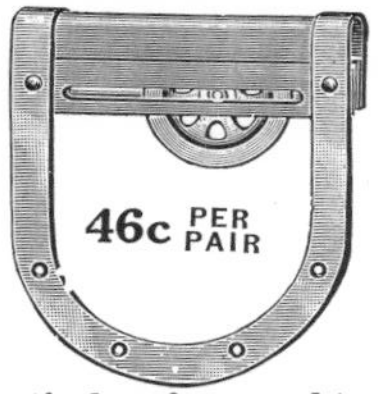

46c PER PAIR

Made entirely of wrought steel, except the wheel, fully covered to protect from snow and ice. Run smoothly and are built to stand hard service. Wheel has a deep groove to prevent jumping the track. Our prices on these high grade hangers save you at least one-third. Bolts not furnished at prices quoted. For bolts see bottom of this page or our big General Catalog.

No. 9B48851 For ordinary doors. Frame, 9x10¼ inches. 3-inch wheel, 6-foot run. Pair requires eight 5-16-inch bolts.

Price, per pair..................46c

No. 9B48853 For wide doors. Frame, 11x11¾ inches. 4-inch wheel for 8-foot run. Pair requires eight ⅜-inch bolts.

Price, per pair..................58c

No. 9B48855 For wide and heavy doors. Frame, 12x12¼ inches, 5-inch wheel for 10-foot run. Pair requires eight ⅜-inch bolts.

Price, per pair..................79c

Standard Barn Door Track.

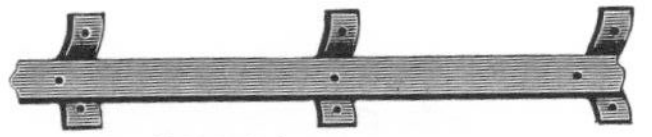

No. 9B48861 Solid and strong; will carry any ordinary door. Size, 3-16x1 inch. To attach requires two ¼-inch bolts or No. 12 screws to each foot. Screws and bolts not included.

Length, feet	4	6	8	10
Price, per length	13c	19c	25c	32c

"Perfect" Barn Door Hanger.

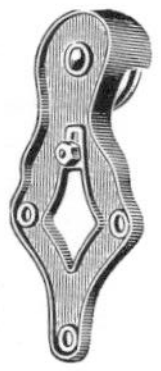

No. 9B48835 Made of tough malleable iron, which is practically unbreakable, with ½-inch steel axle and case hardened roller bearings. Wheel, 2¾ inches diameter, turned perfectly true and has deep groove. Equipped with adjustable "stay-on" attachment, making it positively jumpproof. Runs on any size standard track from 1 to 1½ inches wide. For prices of track see our No. 9B48861 or 9B48873 track quoted on this page. "Perfect" hangers are nicely finished and heavily japanned to prevent rust. Price includes bolts for attaching.

Price, per pair, without track..59c

Rockwell Hinge Joint Barn Door Hanger.

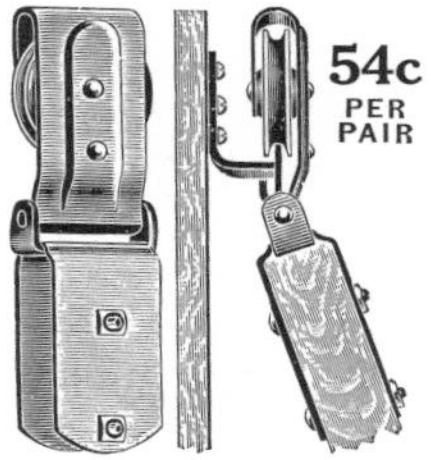

54c PER PAIR

No. 9B48871 Has hinge joint, which prevents binding when door is swung in or out, and guard that runs under and inside track makes it impossible for hanger to jump off. Made entirely of steel, except the wheel; has steel roller bearings and hood to protect wheel from storms. Made extra strong at hinged joint, the point where most hangers of this pattern are weak. Complete with bolts. Made in one size only, for doors 1¾ inches thick, and strong enough for any door. Will not run on common track; for track, see next number.

Price, per pair..................54c

Heavy Standard Barn Door Track.

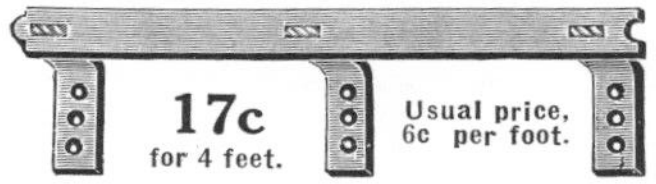

17c for 4 feet.
Usual price, 6c per foot.

No. 9B48873 For the Rockwell or any other barn door hanger. Made of round edge steel, 1¼x3-16 inches. Strong enough to carry the heaviest door. To put track up requires three ¼-inch bolts or No. 12 screws to each foot. Screws and bolts not included.

Length, feet	4	6	8	10
Price, per length	17c	26c	34c	42c

IRON AND BRASS SCREWS FOR WOOD

A COMPLETE ASSORTMENT OF DIFFERENT SIZES, PATTERNS AND FINISHES TO SUIT PRACTICALLY EVERY KIND OF WORK. NOTE OUR LOW PRICES AND REMEMBER WE GUARANTEE THE QUALITY OF THESE SCREWS TO BE EQUAL TO ANY MADE.

OUR SCREWS ARE MADE OF BEST TOUGH STOCK

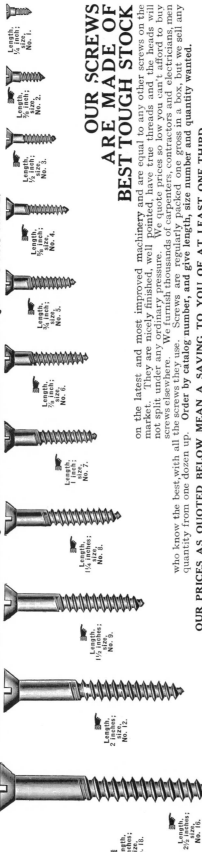

Length, 1/4 inch; size, No. 1.
Length, 3/8 inch; size, No. 2.
Length, 1/2 inch; size, No. 3.
Length, 5/8 inch; size, No. 4.
Length, 3/4 inch; size, No. 5.
Length, 7/8 inch; size, No. 6.
Length, 1 inch; size, No. 7.
Length, 1 1/4 inches; size, No. 8.
Length, 1 1/2 inches; size, No. 9.
Length, 2 inches; size, No. 12.
Length, 2 1/2 inches; size, No. 16.
Length, 3 inches; size, No. 18.

on the latest and most improved machinery and are equal to any other screws on the market. They are nicely finished, well pointed, have true threads and the heads will not split under any ordinary pressure. We quote prices so low you can't afford to buy screws elsewhere. We furnish thousands of carpenters, contractors and electricians, men who know the best, with all the screws they use. Screws are regularly packed one gross in a box, but we sell any quantity from one dozen up. Order by catalog number, and give length, size number and quantity wanted.

OUR PRICES AS QUOTED BELOW MEAN A SAVING TO YOU OF AT LEAST ONE-THIRD.

17C PER GROSS WELL ASSORTED FLAT HEAD BRIGHT IRON WOOD SCREWS, 1/2, 5/8, 3/4, 7/8, 1, 1 1/4 AND 1 1/2 INCHES LONG. ALL BRIGHT NEW GOODS, SELECTED FROM OUR REGULAR STOCK. NO CULLS OR SECONDS. Needed in every home, on every farm, in every shop. Include a package in your order. **17c**

1 GROSS ASSORTED SCREWS 1/2 TO 1 1/2 IN. LONG **17c**

No. 9B48550   Price, per gross (144 screws)   **17c**

No. 9B48551 FLAT HEAD BRIGHT IRON SCREWS.

Length	Per doz.	Size, No. 1	2	3	4	5	6	7	8
1/4 inch	1c	6c	7c	8c	9c	10c	11c		
3/8 inch	1c		7c	8c	9c	10c	11c		
1/2 inch	1c		7c	8c	9c	10c	11c		

Length	Per doz.	Size, No. 5	6	7	8	9	10	12
5/8 inch	2c	9c	11c	12c	13c	14c		
3/4 inch	2c	10c	11c	12c	13c	14c		
7/8 inch	2c	10c	11c	12c	13c	14c		
1 inch	2c	11c	12c	13c	14c	15c	16c	16c
1 1/4 inch	3c	14c	15c	17c	19c	21c		
1 1/2 inch	3c	17c	19c	21c	23c	26c		
2 inch	4c	22c	26c	31c	36c			
2 1/2 inch	5c	37c	45c	52c	62c	74c		
3 inch	10c	43c	52c	74c	87c	96c		

No. 9B48555 FLAT HEAD JAPANNED SCREWS.

Length	Per doz.	Size, No. 8	9	10	12
7/8 inch	3c	19c	20c	21c	24c
1 inch	3c	20c	21c	24c	27c
1 1/4 inch	3c	21c	22c	24c	29c
1 1/2 inch	3c	24c	26c	29c	

No. 9B48553 ROUND HEAD BLUED SCREWS.

Length	Per doz.	Size, No. 4	5	6	7
1/2 inch	2c	10c	11c	12c	
3/4 inch	2c	12c	13c	14c	
7/8 inch	2c	13c	14c	15c	

Length	Per doz.	Size, No. 8	9	10	12
1 inch	3c	14c	16c	17c	19c	21c
1 1/4 inch	3c	16c	18c	19c	21c	23c
1 1/2 inch	3c	22c	24c	26c	28c
2 inch		26c	28c	30c	32c

No. 9B48557 ROUND HEAD IRON SCREWS, NICKEL PLATED.

Length	Per doz.	Size, No. 3	4	5	6	7	9
7/8 inch	2c	17c	18c	20c	21c	23c	
1 inch	2c	18c	19c	20c	21c	23c	
1 1/4 inch	3c	21c	23c	24c	25c	26c	
1 1/2 inch	4c	24c	25c	27c	28c	34c	38c
2 inch	5c	29c	37c	39c	41c	46c	

No. 9B48559 ROUND HEAD BRASS SCREWS.

Length	Per doz.	Size, No. 2	3	4	5	7	9
3/8 inch	3c	Price, per gro.... 19c	22c	24c	26c		
1/2 inch	3c	19c	23c	24c	28c	31c	
5/8 inch	3c			26c	30c	36c	
3/4 inch	4c					36c	43c

Length	Per doz.	Size, No. 6	7	9	10	12
7/8 inch	5c	36c	40c	47c	54c	
1 inch	6c	39c	45c	53c	60c	67c
1 1/4 inch	6c		52c	61c	67c	74c	96c
1 1/2 inch	10c			71c	78c	90c	99c

No. 9B48561 FLAT HEAD BRASS SCREWS.

Length	Per doz.	Size, No. 2	3	4	5	7
3/8 inch	3c	18c	20c	22c	24c	
1/2 inch	3c	19c	22c	24c	27c	31c
5/8 inch	3c		24c	25c	28c	33c
3/4 inch	3c				28c	33c	40c

Length	Per doz.	Size, No. 6	7	8	9	10	12
7/8 inch	4c	32c	39c	41c	47c	51c	
1 inch	6c	34c	46c	45c	51c	59c	
1 1/4 inch	8c			52c	59c	67c	86c
1 1/2 inch	3c			62c	69c	81c	98c

Bright Wire Screw Eyes.

No. 9B48601 Standard goods, none better. Size wire is in proportion to length, the larger screw eyes being made of heavier wire. Be sure to state size wanted.

Size No.	Length inches	Price per doz.	Per gross
105	2	4c	34c
108	1 5/8	2c	20c
110	1 1/4	2c	16c
112	1 1/8	2c	12c
114	1	2c	11c
214	7/8	2c	10c

Bright Wire Screw Hooks.

Straight Pattern. Bent Pattern. Full size, first quality standard goods. State catalog number and length wanted.

No. 9B48609 Straight.   No. 9B48605 Bent.

Length, inches	Straight Per doz.	Per gross	Bent Per doz.	Per gross
1 1/4	2c	18c	2c	21c
1 1/2	2c	21c	2c	24c
1 3/4	2c	30c	3c	30c
2 3/8	3c	44c	4c	44c
3	6c	65c	6c	65c
3 1/2			12c	
4 3/4	10c			

Per doz.	Per gross
2c	$0.16
2c	.18
2c	.21
3c	.29
4c	.42
6c	.56
12c	1.39

Screw and Cup Hooks.

Solid brass, polished. Best quality, full size, standard goods. Both styles, same price. State size.

No. 9B48615 Screw Hooks.   No. 9B48619 Cup Hooks.

Size, inches	Price, per dozen	Price, per gross
1/2	6c	63c
5/8	6c	66c
3/4	7c	69c
7/8	7c	76c
1	8c	87c

Brass Picture Chains With Hooks.

Safer and neater than cord. Length, 36 inches. Can be taken apart at any link and shortened if desired.

No. 9B49458 For heavy frames. Per pair......$0.12. Per dozen pairs......$1.35
No. 9B49460 For light frames. Price, per pair......9c. Per dozen pairs......99c

Picture Wire.

No. 9B48617 Braided wire, silvered finish. Full strength, No. 2 size, in coils of full 75 feet. With most dealers 75 feet really means about 60 or 65 feet.
Price, per coil (75 feet)......4c
Price for 6 coils (75 feet each)......23c

Picture Nails and Hooks.

White porcelain heads, gilt rims. Heads come off for nail to be driven.
No. 9B48611 Price, per dozen......8c

No. 9B48613 Solid brass. Put up with an ordinary wire nail. Round plate comes off for nail to be driven. Price does not include nails.
Price, per dozen......16c

Picture Knobs.

No. 9B48621 White porcelain, complete with round head screws. Full regular size. Price, per dozen......13c. Dozen......16c

NAILS, BRADS, TACKS AND SMALL CHAINS

STAPLE STANDARD ARTICLES, HANDLED BY ALL HARDWARE DEALERS ON A VERY CLOSE MARGIN. EVEN ON THESE SMALL PROFIT ITEMS OUR SAVING TO YOU IS CONSIDERABLE.

FIRST QUALITY WIRE NAILS

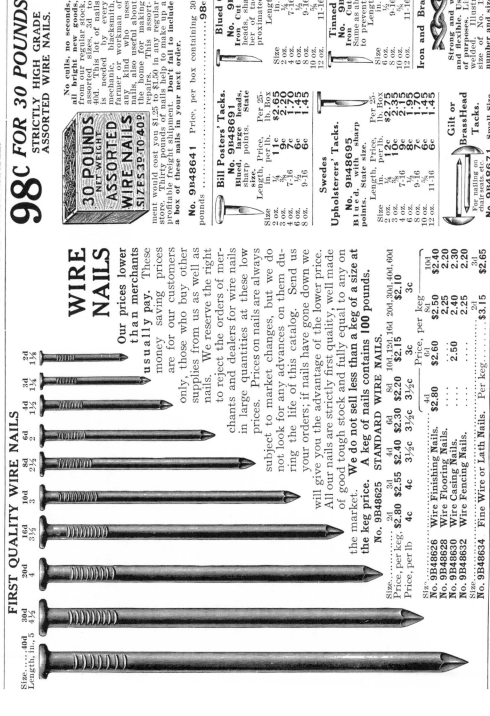

Size	40d	30d	20d	16d	10d	8d	6d	4d	3d	2d
Length, in.	5	4½	4	3½	3	2½	2	1½	1¼	1⅛

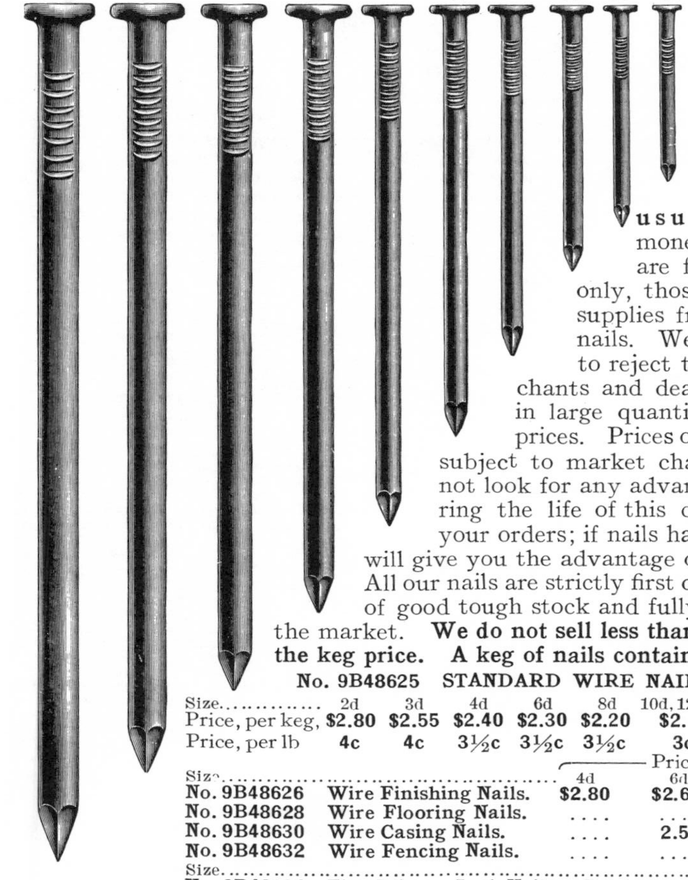

WIRE NAILS

Our prices lower than merchants usually pay. These money saving prices are for our customers only, those who buy other supplies from us as well as nails. We reserve the right to reject the orders of merchants and dealers for wire nails in large quantities at these low prices. Prices on nails are always subject to market changes, but we do not look for any advances on them during the life of this catalog. Send us your orders; if nails have gone down we will give you the advantage of the lower price. All our nails are strictly first quality, well made of good tough stock and fully equal to any on the market. **We do not sell less than a keg of a size at the keg price. A keg of nails contains 100 pounds.**

No. 9B48625 STANDARD WIRE NAILS.

Size	2d	3d	4d	6d	8d	10d, 12d, 16d	20d, 30d, 40d, 60d
Price, per keg	$2.80	$2.55	$2.40	$2.30	$2.20	$2.15	$2.10
Price, per lb	4c	4c	3½c	3½c	3½c	3c	3c

Size		Price, per keg 4d	6d	8d	10d
No. 9B48626	Wire Finishing Nails.	$2.80	$2.60	$2.50	$2.40
No. 9B48628	Wire Flooring Nails.	....	....	2.25	2.20
No. 9B48630	Wire Casing Nails.	....	2.50	2.40	2.30
No. 9B48632	Wire Fencing Nails.	....	....	2.25	2.20

Size		2d	3d
No. 9B48634	Fine Wire or Lath Nails. Per keg	$3.15	$2.65

Slim Wire Nails.

No. 9B48661 In 1-pound packages.

Length, inches	¾	⅞	1	1¼	1½
Gauge wire	18	17	16	15	15
Per pound	7c	6c	6c	5c	5c

Wire Brads.

No. 9B48653 In 1-pound packages.

Length, inches	½	⅝	¾	⅞	1	1¼	1½
Gauge wire	19	18	18	17	16	15	15
Per pound	11c	9c	7c	6c	6c	5c	5c

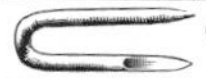

Galvanized Fencing Staples.

No. 9B45355

Size, inches	1	1¼	1½
No. in pound, about	120	100	80
Price, per pound	$0.03½	$0.03½	$0.03½
Price, per keg	2.88	2.87	2.86

Galvanized Netting Staples.

No. 9B45350 First quality. Well Finished.

Size, inches	¾	1
Number in pound, about	550	230
Price, per pound	$0.04½	$0.04½
Price, per 100 pounds	3.96	3.95

98c FOR 30 POUNDS

STRICTLY HIGH GRADE ASSORTED WIRE NAILS.

No culls, no seconds, all bright new goods, from our regular stock, assorted sizes, 3d to 40d. This lot of nails is needed by every mechanic, blacksmith, farmer or workman of any kind who uses nails, also useful about the home for making repairs. This assortment would cost you $1.25 to $1.50 in any regular store. Thirty pounds of nails help to make up a profitable freight shipment. **Don't fail to include a box of these nails in your next order.**

No. 9B48641 Price, per box containing 30 pounds **98c**

83c FOR THIS COMPLETE OUTFIT OF NAILS, SCREWS, TACKS, RIVETS, ETC.

No. 9B415 Sixteen packages of strictly first quality household supplies in quantities and sizes as shown in illustration. You need them in your home. Sell for $1.50 to $1.75 in any regular store. Shipping wt., about 15 lbs. Price **83c**

Bill Posters' Tacks.

No. 9B48691 Blued, large heads, sharp points. State size.

Size	Length, in.	Price, per lb.	Per 25-lb. Box
2 oz.	¼	11c	$2.65
3 oz.	⅜	9c	2.20
4 oz.	7-16	7c	1.70
6 oz.	½	6c	1.45
8 oz.	9-16	6c	1.45

Swedes Upholsterers' Tacks.

No. 9B48695 Blued, with sharp points. State size.

Size	Length, in.	Price, per lb.	Per 25-lb. Box
2 oz.	¼	12c	$2.75
3 oz.	⅜	10c	2.35
4 oz.	7-16	9c	2.15
6 oz.	½	8c	1.95
8 oz.	9-16	7c	1.70
10 oz.	⅝	6c	1.45
12 oz.	11-16	6c	1.45

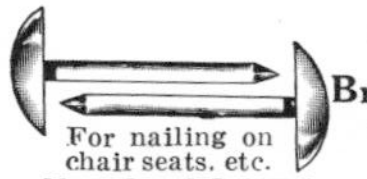

For nailing on chair seats, etc.

Gilt or BrassHead Tacks.

No. 9B48671 Small Size.
100 nails. Price 6c
1,000 nails. Price 52c

No. 9B48673 Large Size.
100 nails. Price 9c
1,000 nails. Price 80c

Double Pointed Tacks or Matting Staples.

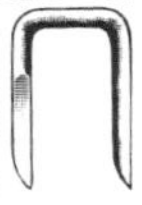

No. 9B48685 Blued. For matting, oilcloth, etc. Size, as illustrated. In papers of 100 tacks.
Price, per dozen papers. **8c**

Blued Carpet Tacks.

No. 9B48681 Blued Iron Cut Tacks. Medium heads, sharp points. Number of tacks to paper approximated. State size.

Size	Length, in.	No. in Paper	Per doz. Papers
2 oz.	¼	370	11c
4 oz.	7-16	350	14c
6 oz.	½	375	17c
8 oz.	9-16	410	20c
10 oz.	⅝	410	26c
12 oz.	11-16	400	31c

Tinned Carpet Tacks.

No. 9B48683 Tinned Iron Cut Carpet Tacks. Same as above, except tinned to prevent rust. State size.

Size	Length, in.	No. in Paper	Per doz. Papers
6 oz.	½	375	20c
8 oz.	9-16	410	26c
10 oz.	⅝	410	30c
12 oz.	11-16	400	35c

Iron and Brass Jack Chains.

Strong and well made, smooth and flexible. Useful for a variety of purposes. Links closed but not welded. Illustration shows half size of No. 12. **State catalog number and size.**

No. 9B49451 Iron.

Size No.	Length Link	Price, per yd.	Per doz. yds.
8	1⅛ in.	4c	44c
12	⅞ in.	3c	22c
16	⅝ in.	2c	17c
20	⅜ in.	2c	14c

No. 9B49453 Brass.

Size No.	Length Link	Price, per yd.	Per doz. yds.
8	1⅛ in.	20c	$2.26
12	⅞ in.	8c	.90
16	⅝ in.	4c	.39
20	⅜ in.	3c	.23

Brass Ladder or Safety Chain.

No. 9B49457 Well made, nicely finished and the best pattern safety chain made. Illustration shows half size of No. 18, the size we furnish.

Price, per yard 5c
Per dozen yards 53c

Bright Wire Coil Chain.

No. 9B49461 One of the strongest patterns on the market; links made without welds. Wire will break before links will pull apart. Illustration shows half size No. 2.

Size No.	Length, Link	Price, per foot	Per 100 feet
000	2½ in.	3c	$2.79
0	2 in.	2½c	2.08
2	1¾ in.	2c	1.66
6	1⅜ in.	2c	1.34

Flat Steel Coil Chain.

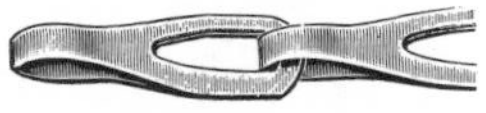

No. 9B49465 Each link is cut from steel, making a strong, smooth, flexible chain. Illustration shows half size No. 0. **State size.**

Size No.	Length, Link	Price, per foot	Per 100 feet
000	1⅞ in.	4c	$3.56
0	1¾ in.	3c	2.60
2	1½ in.	2½c	1.94
6	1 in.	2c	1.64

ROPE, TACKLE BLOCKS AND HOISTS

CONTRACTORS, BUILDERS AND OTHERS WHO USE THESE GOODS: NOTE OUR LOW PRICES; NOTE ALSO THAT WE GUARANTEE THE QUALITY OF EVERY ARTICLE QUOTED ON THIS PAGE.

Steel Strapped Metal Tackle Blocks.

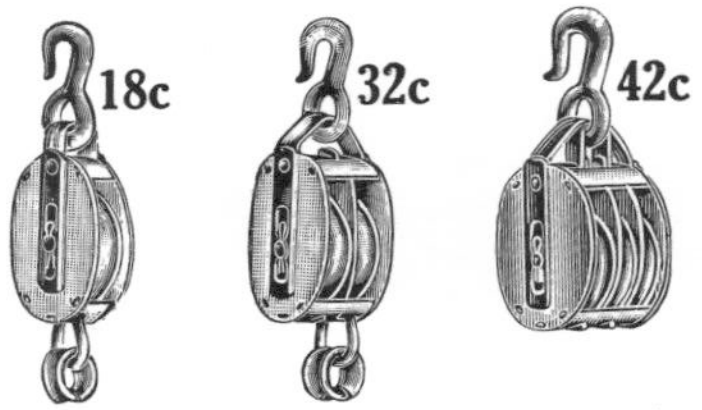

Regular standard quality, full size and full strength. No better blocks sold by anyone. Have steel shells, straps and pins, wrought iron hooks and gray iron sheaves. Edges are rounded to prevent wearing of rope; straps extend below the pins, making them extra strong. Heavily japanned to prevent rust. These tackle blocks are intended to be used with rope only and cannot be used with chain. Same price with or without beckets. **When two blocks are ordered for a set, one should be with becket and the other without.**

No. 9B49631 Without becket.
No. 9B49633 With becket.

Size of Shell, inches	For Rope, inches	Single Pulley, Price	Double Pulley, Price	Triple Pulley, Price
3	⅜	18c	$0.32	$0.42
4	½	20c	.39	.51
5	⅝	22c	.43	.55
6	¾	27c	.48	.71
7	⅞	32c	.57	.83
8	1	40c	.68	1.00
10	1⅛	66c	1.08	1.48

Metal Snatch Blocks.

Recommend themselves for their strength, durability and convenience. They are almost as light as wood blocks, and yet 30 per cent stronger and stiffer.

No. 9B49641

Length of Shell, inches	For Diameter Rope, inches	Size of Sheave, inches	Price
7	¾ to ⅞	3½x1¼	$1.86
8	1 to 1⅛	4 x1½	2.18
10	1¼ to 1⅜	5½x1⅞	3.12
12	1½ to 1⅝	7 x2	3.89

FULTON GOOD SERVICE TOOLS

Fulton Tools are like old friends, they wear well. Full line Fulton mechanics' tools in our Free Special Hardware and Tool Catalog.

PURE MANILA ROPE

Made of long manila fiber, unmixed with sisal, jute or inferior material of any kind. It is full weight, full size, fresh, new stock and will stand 25 to 50 per cent more strain than the ordinary rope sold by most dealers. We guarantee every foot of rope we send out to be the finest grade, made of pure manila fiber and to be satisfactory in every way.

Contractors and builders require the very best rope made, for on the strength and wearing qualities of their hoisting ropes often depend the lives and limbs of their employes. It is therefore very essential that the rope they buy should be of the very best quality made. Our manila rope is especially recommended for contractors and builders, as it is made of the very best material, runs absolutely uniform and is guaranteed full strength.

Manila rope is never measured exact diameter, one-third of the circumference being considered the diameter. Can furnish in one piece any length up to 1,200 feet. **State size wanted.**

No. 9B71298 Pure Manila Rope. State size wanted.

Size, inches	3-16	¼	5-16	⅜	½	⅝	¾	⅞	1	1⅛	1¼	1½
Price, per foot	¼c	⅜c	½c	¾c	1c	1¾c	2½c	3c	4c	5c	6c	7c

Regular Iron Strapped Wood Tackle Blocks.

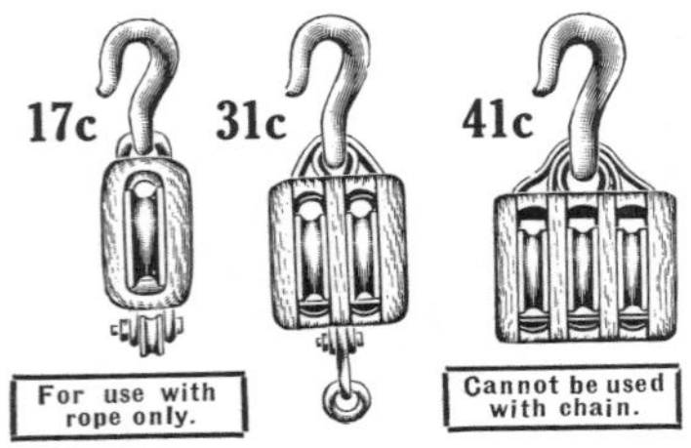

Standard goods, full size and full strength, no better blocks sold by anyone. Iron strap with iron sheaves and steel pins. Strap extends below the pins, making them extra strong. Edges are rounded, preventing wear on the rope. Wood is best tough seasoned stock, filled with varnish to prevent being affected by the weather. Quality considered, you save at least one-third when you buy your tackle blocks from us. Blocks with or without beckets are the same price.

When two blocks are ordered for a set, one should be with becket and the other without.

No. 9B49601 With becket.
No. 9B49603 Without becket.

Size of Shell, inches	For Rope, inches	Single Pulley, Price	Double Pulley, Price	Triple Pulley Price
3	⅜	$0.17	$0.31	$0.41
4	½	.19	.38	.50
5	⅝	.21	.42	.54
6	¾	.26	.47	.70
7	⅞	.31	.56	.82
8	1	.39	.67	.99
10	1⅛	.65	1.07	1.47
12	1¼	1.05	1.74	2.49
15	1½	1.90	3.10	4.20

Security Automatic Hoist.

Convenient, powerful and safe; hoists, lowers, locks and unlocks without the bother of a trip rope. The heavier the load the tighter it locks. Can be used in any position, horizontal or perpendicular. With this hoist one man can easily lift 600 pounds. Just the thing for erecting windmills, pumps, bridges, etc. Made of best malleable iron and fully warranted. All sizes have double lower block. The best hoist ever offered at prices so low. **Prices quoted do not include rope.**

No. 9B49691 Takes ⅜-inch rope. Capacity, 1,000 pounds. Price, without rope........74c

No. 9B49693 Takes ½-inch rope. Capacity, 1,500 pounds. Price, without rope........$1.49

No. 9B49695 Takes ¾-inch rope. Capacity, 2,500 pounds. Price, without rope........$2.37

Differential Chain Hoist.

Weston Pattern, the most powerful hoist ever constructed to sell at anything like our price. Handles heavy loads quickly and safely. Automatically holds load in any position. No brake or locks required. Made throughout of the very best material. Each pulley and chain is carefully tested to its full capacity before being shipped. Our prices on these high class hoists at least one-third less than regular supply dealers ask.

No. 9B49699

Capacity in Tons	Lift in Feet	Net Weight Complete, Pounds	Price Complete with Chain as Illustrated	Extra Chain, Price per Foot
½	7	29	$ 7.35	26c
1	8	50	9.45	28c
1½	8½	87	12.75	30c
1	9	123	16.25	32c

Four feet extra chain required for every foot of extra lift.

Burr Steel Safety Lift.

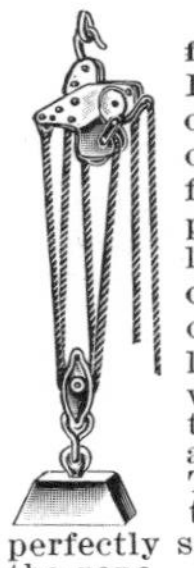

Made of the best material for standing hard service. Recommended for contractors, bridge builders and others who require a powerful hoist that can be depended on. No part of the lift can be worn out by ordinary use, and it is far cheaper than the common lock blocks, as it has no wedge, eccentric, springs or teeth to get out of order and need constant repairs. The brake against which the rope is locked being perfectly smooth, can in no way injure the rope. Prices quoted include upper and lower blocks **but do not include rope.** We recommend our pure manila rope quoted above for use with this lift.

No. 9B49651 Size 3. For ⅜-inch rope; one man can hoist 300 pounds. Double lower block. Weight, 4⅛ pounds; capacity, 800 pounds.
Price, without rope............93c

No. 9B49655 Size 4. For ½-inch rope; one man can hoist 350 pounds. Double lower block. Weight, 6½ pounds; capacity, 1,500 pounds.
Price, without rope..........$1.74

No. 9B49659 Size 5. For ⅝-inch rope; one man can hoist 400 pounds. Double lower block. Weight, 11 pounds; capacity, 2,000 pounds.
Price, without rope..........$2.20

No. 9B49663 Size 6. For ¾-inch rope; one man can hoist 450 pounds. Double lower block. Weight, 17 pounds; capacity, 2,500 pounds.
Price, without rope..........$2.68

No. 9B49667 Size 4½. For ½-inch rope; one man can hoist 600 pounds. Triple lower block. Weight, 10 pounds; capacity, 3,000 pounds.
Price, without rope..........$3.15

No. 9B49671 Size 5½. For ⅝-inch rope. one man can hoist 700 pounds. Triple lower block. Weight, 20 pounds; capacity, 3,500 pounds.
Price, without rope..........$3.75

No. 9B49675 Size 6½. For ¾-inch rope; one man can hoist 850 pounds. Triple lower block. Weight, 28 pounds; capacity, 5,000 pounds.
Price, without rope..........$4.37

"Boston" Self Locking Roller Bearing Safety Hoist.

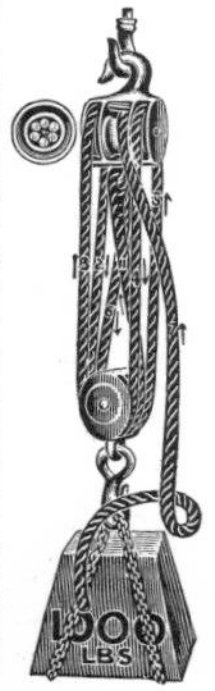

The latest improved and most practical hoist made. Enables one man to raise one-third to one-half more weight than any other rope hoist on the market. With a "Boston" hoist there is no lost energy, every inch of pull counts. If rope should slip, load would not drop as the block would lock automatically. Loosening the rope or leading it slightly to the right locks the block and holds the strain or load at any point. When block is locked, load cannot possibly slip, as the heavier the load the tighter it is locked. To lower, raise load an inch or two and hold rope slightly to left of block. Invaluable for painters, wire fence builders, machinery and piano movers, factory and dock use. "Boston" hoists can be used horizontally as well as vertically, a feature that will be readily appreciated by linemen, safe movers and others. Shells are made of one piece of galvanized malleable iron. Sheave castings are solid and have patent steel roller bushings, which greatly reduce the friction and stand twice the strain of ordinary sheaves. "Boston" hoists are reeved straight, without twists as in old style hoists, which saves wear on the rope and causes it to last much longer. Prices below for upper and lower blocks, **but do not include rope.** We recommend our pure manila rope quoted above for use with this hoist.

No. 9B49643 For ⅜-inch rope, 3-inch blocks, double upper and single lower. Capacity, 600 pounds.
Price, without rope..........$2.15

No. 9B49645 For ½-inch rope, 4-inch double upper and lower blocks. Capacity, 1,200 pounds.
Price, without rope..........$2.85

No. 9B49647 For ¾-inch rope, 6-inch blocks, triple upper and double lower. Capacity, 2,500 pounds.
Price, without rope..........$4.60

No. 9B49649 For 1-inch rope, 8-inch triple upper and lower. Capacity, 5,000 pounds.
Price, without rope..........$7.80

FULTON GOOD SERVICE TOOLS

The word Fulton on a mechanic's tool is a positive guarantee of good service. Full line of Fulton mechanics' tools in our Free Special Hardware and Tool Catalog.

HANGERS AND TRACK

First quality easy running hangers and strong substantial track. Full size, full weight standard goods, the kind handled by the best dealers and usually sold at prices at least one-

BALL BEARING TROLLEY PARLOR DOOR HANGERS AND TRACK.

Ball Bearing Vulcanized Fiber Wheels. Best steel trolley track. Track is rigid and firm. Hangers made of steel and are adjustable. This is the best parlor door equipment made and you make no mistake in sending us your orders for these hangers and track. Complete directions packed with each set. Prices include track.

No. 9B47655 For Double Doors.

Size opening, ft.	5	6	7
Per set....$3.14	$3.22	$3.34	$3.47

No. 9B47657 For Single Doors.

Size opening, ft.	3	5	6
Per set....$1.63	$1.84	$2.13	$2.53

FIBER TREAD NOISELESS BALL BEARING PARLOR DOOR HANGERS AND TRACK.

$2.99 SET

Our prices save you money on these high quality goods. Made of steel with fiber tread rollers. Price includes hangers, guides, stop screws and track. Cheap imitations of this hanger are sold as low as $2.50. Our hangers are heavier, stronger and worth far more than the difference we ask in price. Takes less than half the time usually required to put up other styles.

No. 9B47661 For Double Doors, complete with 14 feet of steel track. Per set....**$2.99**

No. 9B47663 For Single Doors, complete with 8 feet of steel track. Per set....**$1.54**

WEATHER STRIPS

Soon save you more in fuel bills than the original cost of the strip, to say nothing of making your home more comfortable. Not necessary to have a carpenter to put it on; a woman with a box of tacks and a hammer can strip a door or window in a short while.

Rubber Weather Strip.

Keeps out the cold, keeps in the heat. Made of best quality rubber, tough and durable. Narrow width for windows, medium width for tops and sides of doors. Quickly and easily applied; only tool necessary is a hammer. Put up 50 feet in package.

	Width	Per ft.	Per pkg.
No. 9B48735	½ inch	2c	$0.72
No. 9B48737	¾ inch	2½c	.96
No. 9B48739	1 inch	3c	1.22

All Felt Weather Strip.

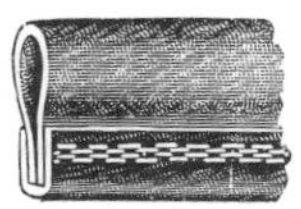

Made of black wool felt, closely woven and very durable. Narrow width for windows. Medium width for sides and tops of doors, widest for bottoms of doors. Put up 50 feet in package.

	Width	Per ft.	Per pkg.
No. 9B48745	½ inch	1¼c	$0.52
No. 9B48747	¾ inch	2c	.89
No. 9B48749	⅞ inch	2½c	1.04

Cast Aluminum Letters and Figures.

CAB 642

Highly polished. Will not rust or tarnish. With prongs for fastening to wood. Prongs easily cut or filed off and letters or figures glued to glass. Used extensively for signs, house numbers, room numbers, automobile numbers, etc. Be sure to state which letters and figures you want—write plainly.

No. 9B47600	Size, 2 inches, any letter. Price, each................5c
No. 9B47602	Size, 3 inches, any letter. Price, each................7c
No. 9B47609	Commas. Price, each....2c
No. 9B47611	Periods. Price, each....2c
No. 9B47604	Size, 2 inches, any figure. Price, each................5c
No. 9B47606	Size, 3 inches, any figure. Price, each................6c
No. 9B47608	Size, 4 inches, any figure. Price, each................8c

FULTON GOOD SERVICE TOOLS Full line Fulton (Good Service) Mechanics' Tools quoted at Money Saving Prices in our Free Special Hardware Catalog. Write for it.

Wrought Steel Shelf Brackets.

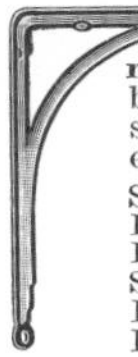

Much better than the old time common cast iron shelf brackets, which are brittle and unreliable. Corrugated and stiffened. Finished in rustproof baked enamel. Without screws.

	4x5	6x8	7x9
Size, inches........	4c	6c	8c
Price, per pair.......	39c	72c	87c
Per dozen pairs....			
	8x10	10x12	12x14
Size, inches........	$0.09	$0.13	$0.18
Price, per pair.	1.02	1.44	2.12
Per doz. pairs.			

Ash Pit or Fuel Doors.

No. 9B48771

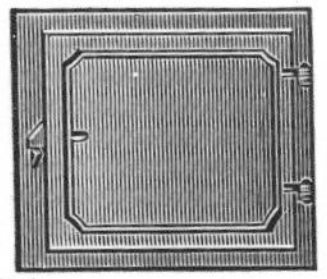

Heavy cast iron, well made, nicely finished, fit tight. Intended to be set in walls, etc. These fuel doors ordinarily sell at from 75 cents to $1.25 each. Our price includes door and frame complete, as shown.

Size of opening	Weight, about	
8x 8 inches	10 pounds	38c
8x10 inches	12 pounds	43c
10x12 inches	15 pounds	49c
10x14 inches	20 pounds	57c

PADLOCKS

A complete line, from the cheapest padlocks on the market that are really worth using, to the best cylinder padlocks, the highest grade made.

$1.06

Best padlock you can buy. Rustproof and burglar proof. Strong and secure. Heavy cast bronze metal case, bronze solid bronze metal shackle, pin tumbler cylinder and two gold plated keys, different for each lock. Size 2x3 lock, 1¾x2¾ inches.

No. 9B49002 Price, as shown.................**$1.06**
No. 9B49003 With bronze metal chain. Price..**$1.17**

33c

No. 9B49037 **A very popular pattern** and one of the strongest, most secure locks ever offered. Genuine gun bronze metal case, phosphor bronze springs, solid brass inside works. Guaranteed full 6-lever and absolutely rustproof. Width, 2¼ inches; height, including shackle, 2½ inches. Price.............**33c**

43c

No. 9B49039 **Same as above,** except has extra long shackle and 3-inch nickel plated chain. No danger of losing nor being stolen. Width, 2¼ inches; height, including shackle, 3 inches. Price.................**43c**

87c

A handsome, secure, self locking cylinder padlock. Rustless black iron case, solid bronze metal shackle, rivets, cylinder and inside works. Price includes two gold plated cylinder keys, different for each lock. Size, 2x2⅜ inches. Weight, 10 ounces.
No. 9B49006 Price, as shown.................**87c**
No. 9B49007 With bronze metal chain. Price...**98c**

36c

No. 9B49057 **Cast bronze metal case and shackle.** One of Corbin's very best padlocks. Has two keys, self locking and can never rust. Size, 2x3 inches. A regular 75-cent value. Price.................**36c**

MACHINERY

We issue a free special Catalog of Wood and Metal Working Machinery for foot, hand and belt power. If interested in machinery, write for this catalog.

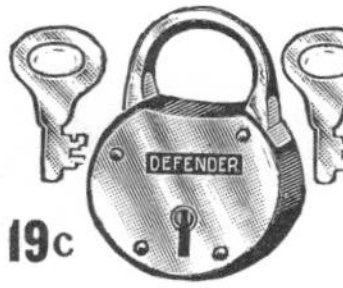

19c

No. 9B49004 **Made of solid brass, is self locking,** has three secure levers, heavy spring shackle and two flat steel keys. Will outlast half a dozen ordinary iron locks and will never rust. Especially recommend for outdoor use. Width, 2 inches; height, including shackle, 2⅞ inches. Price.................**19c**

17c

No. 9B49043 **Handsome, strong and secure.** A good lock for indoor use and an excellent value at our low price. Case and shackle made of malleable iron; brass plated inside and out. Has six secure brass levers, is self locking and has two flat steel keys. Width, 2¼ inches; height, including shackle, 2½ inches. Price.................**17c**

26c

No. 9B49005 **Extra strong and heavy,** not easily picked or smashed. A lock you can depend on to stop almost any thief. Made of heavy wrought steel, brass plated inside and out. Is self locking, has extra heavy brass plated spring shackle and two double bitted keys. Width, 2½ inches; height, including shackle, 3½ inches. A regular 50-cent value. Price **26c**

15c

No. 9B49025 **This lock is considered a bargain generally at 25 cents.** It is strong and secure, made of wrought steel, heavily brass plated, is self locking and has a spring shackle. Has six secure levers and two double bitted keys. Width, 2 inches; length, 3½ inches. Excellent value at our price. Price.................**15c**

32c

No. 9B49053 **High grade, large sized, low priced.** Rustproof black iron case, bronze metal shackle, two flat steel keys. Extra strong, easy working, self locking. Size, 2x3 inches. Usually sells for 50 cents. Our price.................**32c**

FLY SCREEN WIRE CLOTH, SCREEN DOOR AND WINDOW HARDWARE

SCREEN WIRE CLOTH

We Quote Wire Cloth, Hinges, Springs, Catches, Brackets, Etc., everything you need for making, repairing and putting up screen windows and doors, except the wood frames, which you can easily procure at any planing mill. Our prices save you money, and better goods than we offer cannot be had anywhere.

DOUBLE SELVAGE FLY SCREEN CLOTH

For window and door frames. Doctors and health officers everywhere declare that screens are necessary, as they keep out flies, mosquitoes and other insects which are not only annoying but positively dangerous, as they spread disease germs and filth. All our screen wire cloth is highest grade, with true square mesh and double selvage. Our painted and galvanized wire cloth runs 12 wires to the inch each way, which is the ordinary size mesh and same as illustrated. Our bronze wire cloth is made with a finer mesh, running 14 wires to the inch each way. There is no better wire cloth made than this we quote; a lower price elsewhere means lower quality. All our screen wire cloth is put up in rolls of 50 and 100 running or lineal feet. We cannot cut rolls. Below we give approximate weights of painted and galvanized wire cloth in full rolls of 100 feet in length. Bronze wire cloth weighs slightly heavier than below.

Width, inches	24	26	28	30	32	36	42	48
Weight, per 100 feet, pounds	19	21	23	24	26	29	35	40

Painted Black Fly Screen Cloth. 12 Wires to Inch Each Way. Thoroughly coated with best black paint. Will not crack nor peel off. Our prices on this high grade wire cloth save you money.

Width	No. 9B4200 50-foot roll	No. 9B4205 100-foot roll
24 inches. Price	$1.48	$2.76
26 inches. Price	1.59	2.99
28 inches. Price	1.70	3.22
30 inches. Price	1.84	3.45
32 inches. Price	1.95	3.68
36 inches. Price	2.18	4.14
42 inches. Price	2.53	4.83
48 inches. Price	2.88	5.52

Galvanized Fly Screen Cloth. 12 Wires to Inch Each Way. Electro-galvanized, not painted with aluminum paint. Does not keep out light like painted screen wire and dust and dirt do not readily stick to it.

Width	No. 9B4210 50-foot roll	No. 9B4215 100-foot roll
24 inches. Price	$2.02	$3.84
26 inches. Price	2.18	4.16
28 inches. Price	2.34	4.48
30 inches. Price	2.50	4.80
32 inches. Price	2.66	5.12
36 inches. Price	2.98	5.76
42 inches. Price	3.46	6.72
48 inches. Price	3.94	7.68

Genuine Bronze Fly Screen Cloth. 14 Wires to Inch Each Way. Made of genuine bronze wire, will not rust like steel, corrode nor discolor as badly as brass or copper. Best screen wire cloth you can buy.

Width	No. 9B4230 50-foot roll	No. 9B4235 100-foot roll
24 inches. Price	$4.95	$9.60
26 inches. Price	5.35	10.40
28 inches. Price	5.75	11.20
30 inches. Price	6.15	12.00
32 inches. Price	6.55	12.80
36 inches. Price	7.35	14.40
42 inches. Price	8.55	16.80
48 inches. Price	9.75	19.20

Adjustable Screen Door Braces.

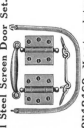

No. 9B48475 Can be used on any screen door, and will cure and prevent sagging, so that the door will swing freely and close tightly. If your door sags, raise it to the position in which it should hang, screw on the brace and it is held securely. Doubles the life of an ordinary screen door. Price, per dozen, 62c; each....6c

Japanned Iron Window Screen Corner Brackets.

No. 9B48471 For window screen frames, packed with screws. Do away with mortises, save time, labor and trouble. Make old frames strong as new, prevent new screens from sagging. With these brackets anyone can make a strong, neat window frame. Four brackets to a set. Complete with screws. Price, per doz. sets, 47c; per set..4c

Japanned Screen Door Brackets.

No. 9B48473 Improve the appearance of any door. Save time cutting mortises. With these brackets any person who is handy with tools can make a door frame, and with but little labor. Make a strong job. Complete with screws. Four large corner pieces and two center pieces to a set. Per dozen sets, $1.78; per set. 15c

Hold Back Screen Door Set.

No. 9B48465 Consists of 1 pair japanned hold back spring hinges, 1 steel door pull and 1 hook and eye, all complete with screws. Price, per set.............7c

Our Leader Screen Door Set.

No. 9B48467 Consists of 1 pair of japanned spring hinges, 1 steel door pull and 1 hook and eye, all complete with screws. Price, per set............10c

All Steel Screen Door Set.

No. 9B48469 Most substantial screen door set made. Also an excellent outfit of 1 pair wrought steel, loose pin japanned butts 2¼x2½ inches, 1 wrought null, 1 hook and eye and 1 heavy spiral door spring with hooks and screws. Price, per set.............12c

Bronze Plated Door Pulls or Window Lifts.

No. 9B48392 Wrought steel, antique copper finish. Much neater and a more durable finish than the ordinary coppered door pulls usually offered. Size, 4⅞ inches. Price, per dozen, 23c; each....2c

Screen Door Catches.

No. 9B48401 For use on inside of doors opening out. Tuscan bronze finish. With stop, knobs and screws.
Each ..$0.11
Dozen 1.30

No. 9B48408 Electro Bronze Plated Ornamental Iron. Raised surfaces polished bronze finish, background dull black, with screws to match. Price, per dozen, $2.70 each.23c

Screen Wire Cloth Staples.

No. 9B4250 Handier and better than ordinary tacks. Two points enter the wood and they lap over three wires, hence hold the wire better, and not so many tacks required. Blued steel, sharp points. Illustration shows actual size. About 2,000 staples to the pound. Price, per pound.......15c

Japanned Iron Screen Door Spring Hinges.

No. 9B48461 Extra heavy and will not get out of order. Not the frail, easily broken kind usually offered. Neatly finished in baked japan. May be used on either right or left hand doors. Price does not include screws. See page 128 for screws. Usual 10-cent value. Per dozen pairs, 58c; per pair..5c

Warner Screen Door Springs.

No.9B48451 An effectual easily applied door spring. Extra strong, made of rust-proof coppered wire. Complete as illustrated, but without screws. Price, per dozen, 58c; each....5c

Spiral Door Springs.

Made of oil tempered crucible steel, nicely japanned. Has loop at each end and screw hooks to fasten to door and casing. Properly adjusted, the most effective door springs made. Length, 16 inches.
No. 9B48441 Size, ¼-inch. For light and medium screen doors. Price, per dozen, 20c; 4 for....7c
No. 9B48443 Size, 9-32 inch. For heavy screen or inside doors. Price, per dozen, 26c; 4 for....9c
No. 9B48445 Size, 11-32inch. For outside doors. Price, per dozen, 32c; 4 for..11c
No. 9B48447 Size, ⅜ inch. For heavy outside doors. Price, per dozen, 36c; 4 for..13c
No. 9B48449 Size, 17-32 inch. For extra heavy doors and gates. Price, per dozen, 45c; 4 for..17c

Screen or Numeral Nails.

No. 9B48480 For marking screen doors, storm sash, outside blinds, etc., in order to match them, which should always be done. Also useful for a great many other purposes. Illustrations are actual sizes. Heads made of copper. Points about ⅜ inch long. Sold only in packages of 25 nails as below, or packages of 100 numbered consecutively.
Pkgs ....1 to 25 26 to 50 51 to 75 76 to 100
Price, pkg., 18c 18c 18c 18c
Packages of 100, any consecutive series from 1 to 999.
Price, per 100 tacks............68c

MISCELLANEOUS HARDWARE AND CONTRACTORS' SUPPLIES

WE WANT ALL YOUR HARDWARE BUSINESS. We can save you money on small items as well as large, and it will pay you to get into the habit of sending to us for everything you need in this line. The prices we quote on this page are but a fair sample of the low prices all through our hardware line.

BELL BOTTOM JACK SCREWS

Wrought iron screws, lathe turned threads, cast iron stands. High class, well made, nicely finished, powerful and durable. We do not furnish levers with these screws. **Capacity.—1¼-inch screws, 10 tons; 1½-inch screws, 12 tons; 1¾-inch screws, 16 tons; 2-inch screws, 20 tons; 2½-inch screws, 28 tons.**

No. 9B31355 Bell Bottom Jack Screws.

Diam. of Screw, inches	Height of Stand, inches	Length of Screw, inches	Height, over all, inches	Weight, about, pounds	Price, each
1¼	8	7½	11¼	11	$0.89
1¼	8	7½	11½	15	1.15
1½	10	9¼	13½	12	1.29
1½	12	11½	15	20	1.41
1½	12	9½	13¾	21	1.57
1¾	12	9½	15½	26	1.68
2	8	7½	11¼	23	1.59
2	10	9½	14¼	27	1.82
2	12	11½	16¾	30	1.98
2	14	13½	18	35	2.19
2½	14	13½	18	39	2.48
2½	16	15½	19¾	51	3.21
2½	18	17½	22½	56	3.86

CAST IRON JACK SCREWS.

Strong and powerful, will last indefinitely and give satisfaction. Made of best cast iron with seamless threads, which make them very smooth and uniform. Recommended for house movers, contractors, builders and all others who require a strong, dependable screw. Used extensively for raising roofs, porches, etc. Price includes cap as shown.

No. 9B31365

Diam. of Screw	Height Over All	Price
3 inches	20 inches	$1.69
3 inches	24 inches	1.93
3 inches	30 inches	2.29
3 inches	36 inches	2.68

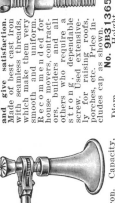

$1.69

ACME RATCHET JACK SCREW.

Handiest, quickest and best ratchet jack screw made. Lifts a load in half the time required with an old style screw and without pulling out lever. Can be used in places where an ordinary jack will not work. Screw is made of tough wrought iron, threads are lathe turned. Stand is cast iron. Capacity, 25 tons. Diameter of base, 9 inches; diameter of screw, 2 inches; height over all, closed, 15¾ inches; open, 23 inches. **No. 9B31375** Price, each, without lever.................$2.79

CONTRACTORS AND BUILDERS

Write for our free special Machinery Catalog which illustrates, describes and quotes low prices on Foot, Hand and Belt Power Wood Working Machinery

BLACKSMITHS

We issue a catalog especially for you, quoting money saving prices on goods you use. WRITE FOR THIS BLACKSMITHS' TOOL AND SUPPLY CATALOG. IT'S FREE

SECURITY COMBINED HOOK AND HASP.

No. 9B48975 The most popular hasp on the market. Length, 8 inches. Price, 2 for..................7c Per dozen..................39c

POLISHED WROUGHT STAPLES.

No. 9B48991 Assorted lengths, 1½ to 3 in. Nicely finished, well pointed. Six dozen in a box. Price, per box...15c

BRIGHT WIRE HOOKS AND EYES.

No. 9B48967
Length, inches....... 2
Price, 3 for..............2c
Per dozen................6c

| | 4 | 6 | 8 |
| 3c | 5c | 6c | 10c |

WROUGHT STEEL HINGE HASPS.

No. 9B48979 Complete as shown. Without screws. For screws see page 128.
Length, inches... 3 6 8
Price, each...... 3c 5c 6c
Per dozen......34c 54c 70c

3c

HASPS AND STAPLES.

No. 9B48973 Wrought steel.
Length, inches. 6 8 10
Price, 3 for.... 5c 6c 9c
Per dozen.....15c 19c 27c

5c

WROUGHT HOOKS AND STAPLES.

No. 9B48965 Standard goods, none better.
Length, inches....... 4 6
Price, 3 for......... 4c 6c
Per package, 3 doz..38c 47c

FENCE OR ROOF ORNAMENTS.

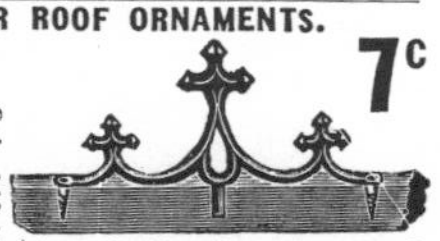

No. 9B48935 Malleable iron, japanned. Length, 12 inches; height, 5 inches. Used extensively for tops of fences and partitions, on cornices, veranda roofs, etc. Often used inverted for ornaments under veranda roofs. Without screws. Weight, about 1 pound. Price, per 100, $6.50; each...7c

7c

TINNED MALLEABLE GATE HOOKS AND STAPLES.

No. 9B48969
Length, inches..... 4 6
Price, each........ 4c 6c
Per dozen.........47c 64c

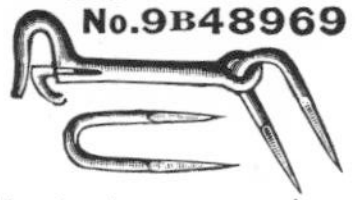

BARN DOOR STAY ROLLER.

No. 9B48926 Adjustable to any thickness door. Stays in line. Price..............7c

7c

STEEL JOIST HANGERS OR STIRRUPS.

14c

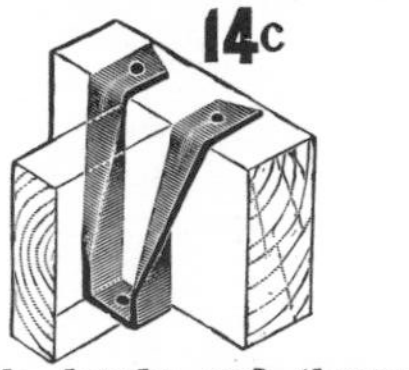

A quick, handy and thoroughly practical device for connecting timbers to walls, to each other or to steel I beams. Require no boring, cutting, mortising or tenoning. Make a job stronger than any other known construction. Save their cost in labor alone, as compared with other methods of hanging joists and sleepers. Invaluable for use around stairways, elevator shafts and fireplaces. Made of very best tough wrought steel, painted with first quality rustproof paint. These steel joist hangers are absolutely safe, as they will stand more strain than any size joist that can be used with them. **No. 9B48772 Steel Joist Hangers.** State size joists hangers are to be used with.

		Price, Per
Takes Size	Safe strain	each dozen
joists, steel, each hang-	Wt.,	
in. in.	doz., lbs.	
2x10 2 x3-16	7,500 32 lbs.	14c $1.64
2x12 2 x3-16	7,500 38 lbs.	18c 2.11
4x10 2½x3-16	9,380 46 lbs.	24c 2.83
4x12 2½x3-16	9,380 64 lbs.	29c 3.42

REGISTERS, BORDERS AND FACES

For Use in Floors or Walls on Hot Air Pipes, Furnaces, Ventilators, Etc.

Unbreakable Wrought Steel
Black Japanned Registers.
6x8-inch size for
42c 6-inch pipe.

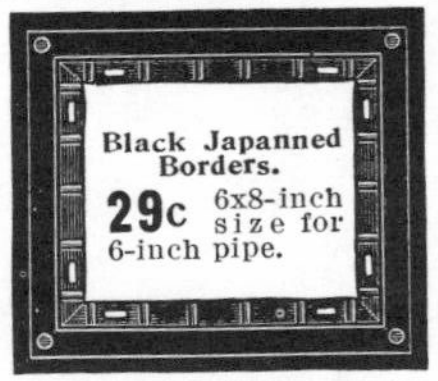

Black Japanned Borders.
6x8-inch size for
29c 6-inch pipe.

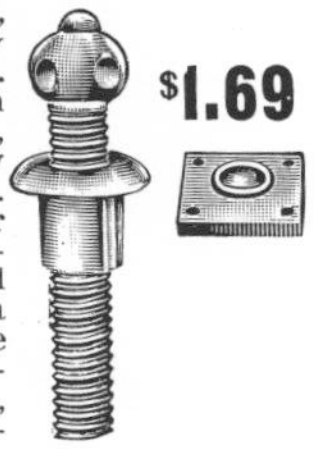

White Japanned Faces.
6x8-inch size for
34c 6-inch pipe.

Our Prices Save You Money.

Why Pay More Elsewhere?

Our Wrought Cold Rolled Steel Unbreakable Registers, Borders and Faces are in every way superior to the brittle cast iron goods usually offered. They will stand as much weight and strain as cast iron registers without twisting or bending and they cannot break. Made of two-ply cold rolled wrought steel, very strong and rigid. Size register required is governed by the size hot air pipe leading to it. Fit either in floor or side wall. Registers, black japanned. Can be used in floor or side wall. Borders of the same dimensions. Match registers described above. Measurements are inside.

Borders, black japanned. Fit in price of registers.

Register Faces, white japanned. Used in ceilings and side walls as ventilators.

Size, inches.......	6x8	8x10	9x12	10x12	12x15
To fit pipe size, inches...	6	8	9	10	12
No. 9B23310 Registers. Price.....	42c	48c	64c	74c	$1.36
No. 9B23312 Borders. Price.....	29c	34c	43c	49c	.76
No. 9B23314 Register Faces. Price..34c	34c	39c	51c	58c	.94

SAVES HEAT COMBINATION FLOOR AND CEILING REGISTER AND VENTILATOR.

$1.28

No. 9B23316. Makes one stove do the work of two. Keeps that cold room upstairs warm and comfortable with the heat that is ordinarily wasted near the ceiling of the room below. Quickly pays for itself in the saving of fuel. Consists of a black floor register with valves, a white ceiling plate and an adjustable sheet metal box connecting the two. Easily and quickly put into position; just cut the holes in floor and ceiling, place the register and ceiling plate in position and hook the two coil springs that hold them together. **Adjustable to fit any floor or ceiling from 7 to 12 inches apart.**

Size opening......	8x10	10x12	12x15
Price, each........	$1.28	$1.64	$2.86

WROUGHT JAPANNED BARN DOOR BOLT.

14c

No. 9B48891 Extra heavy bolt. 8 inches. Price......14c

BARN DOOR PULL.

No. 9B48899
Heavy cast iron, japanned. Price...................2c

FULTON TOOLS

FULTON GOOD SERVICE TOOLS are like old friends. They wear well.

Fulton Mechanics' Tools are quoted at money saving prices in our free special Hardware and Tool Catalog

YANKEE DOOR CATCH.

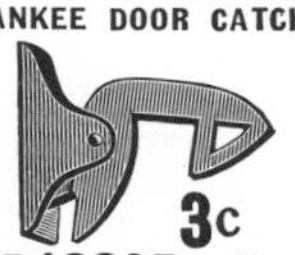

3c

No. 9B48895 To hold swing doors open. Made of cast iron, japanned. Price.......3c

BARN DOOR LATCH.

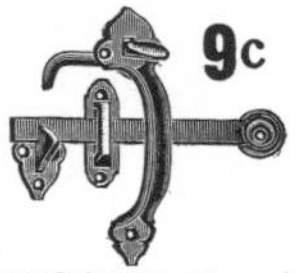

9c

No. 9B48885 Japanned iron, heavy, strong and durable wrought latch. Price.......9c

CABINET AND MISCELLANEOUS HARDWARE

EVEN IN THE "LITTLE THINGS" OUR HARDWARE BUSINESS EXCELS. HOW MANY STORES DO YOU KNOW OF WHERE YOU HAVE SUCH AN ASSORTMENT OF CABINET HARDWARE TO SELECT FROM, AND HOW MANY THAT SELL EVEN WHAT THEY HAVE AT SUCH LOW PRICES AS WE DO?

No. 9B47873 Brass Box Hinges. Size open, 3x1 inch.
Per pair............ 7c
Dozen pairs.........73c

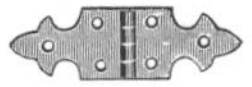

No. 9B47875 Brass Box Hinges. Size open, 1⅝x½ inch.
Per pair............ 3c
Dozen pairs.........27c

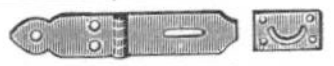

No. 9B47879 Brass Hinge Hasps. Size open, 3x9-16 inch.
4 for...............18c
Per dozen..........48c

No. 9B47881 Brass Hinge Hasps. Size, open, 1¾x⅝ inch.
4 for...............15c
Per dozen..........36c

No. 9B47909 Brass Box Corners. Size, 1⅞x 1⅝ inches.
4 for...............19c
Per dozen..........56c

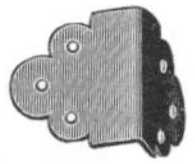

No. 9B47917 Brass Box Corners. Size, 2½x 2½ inches.
4 for...............34c
Per dozen.........98c

No. 9B47927 Cast Brass Lifting Handles. Size, 2½ inches.
Each $0.10
Per dozen.. ..... 1.17

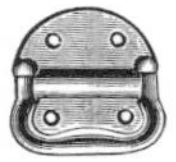

No. 9B47943 Japanned Iron Chest Handles. Size, 4 inches.
Per pair........... 8c
Per dozen pairs....94c

No. 9B47951 Japanned Steel Chest Handles. Size, 4 inches.
Per pair.........$0.11
Per dozen pairs.. 1.28

No. 9B47952 Antique Copper Finished Steel Chest Handles. Size, 4 inches.
Per pair.........$0.17
Per dozen pairs.. 1.98

No. 9B47981 Brass Drawer Handles. Bolts, 3 inches center to center.
4 for............... 8c
Per dozen..........20c

No. 9B47985 Brass Drawer Handles. Bolts, 3 inches center to center.
4 for...............12c
Per dozen..........33c

No. 9B47987 Brass Drawer Handles. Bolts, 3 inches center to center.
4 for...............21c
Per dozen..........59c

No. 9B47990 Cast Brass Drawer Handles. Bolts, 3 inches center to center.
4 for...............24c
Per dozen..........69c

No. 9B47995 Cast Brass Drawer Handles. Bolts, 3 inches center to center. 4 for.........31c
Per dozen..........86c

No. 9B48011 Drawer Handles, brass plate, 1½-inch brass plated ring.
4 for............... 9c
Per dozen..........25c

No. 9B48021 Drawer Handles, brass plate, **ebonized wood handle.** ....
4 for...............14c
Per dozen..........39c

No. 9B48033 Cast Brass Knob, ¾-inch.
4 for............... 9c
Per dozen..........23c

No. 9B48035 Cast Brass Knob, 1 inch.
4 for...............16c
Per dozen..........44c

No. 9B48039 Cast Brass Knobs, 1¼ inches.
4 for...............11c
Per dozen..........30c

No. 9B48043 Cast Brass Knobs, 1¼ inches.
4 for...............14c
Per dozen..........33c

No. 9B48047 Cast Brass Knobs, 1½ inches.
4 for...............19c
Per dozen..........55c

No. 9B48067 Brass Keyhole Escutcheons, with pins for attaching.
Per dozen........... 6c

No. 9B48070 Cast Brass Keyhole Escutcheons, with pins for attaching. 4 for............8c
Per dozen..........21c

No. 9B48101 Chest Lock. Brass case, single link, size 1¼x⅞ inches. Keys all alike. Each.. 6c
Per dozen..........69c

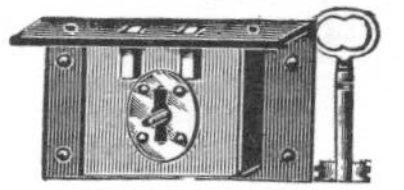

Self Locking Iron Chest Locks with brass keyhole escutcheon. Double bitted keys.
No. 9B48107 Width, 2⅜ inches. Each...$0.32
Price, per dozen.. 3.82
No. 9B48109 Width, 4 inches. Each.....$0.39
Price, per dozen.. 4.65

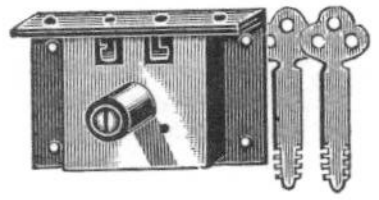

No. 9B48123 Self Locking Solid Brass Chest Lock. Two nickel plated flat steel keys. For wood 1 inch thick. Width, 3½ inches. Best chest lock made. Usual $1.00 value.
Our price..........64c

No. 9B48147 Steel Drawer Locks with brass cylinder. For wood ⅞ inch thick. Two nickel plated steel keys. 1¾ inch wide.
Price, each......$0.16
Per dozen........ 1.90

No. 9B48151 Solid Brass Cylinder Drawer Locks. Put on without cutting wood. Size, 1⅝ inches wide. Two nickel plated steel keys. For wood ⅞ inch thick.
Price, each......$0.22
Per dozen........ 2.60

No. 9B48173 Wardrobe or Cupboard Locks. Width, 1¼ inches; length, 2⅝ inches. One iron tumbler, 1 key.
Price, each.......... 3c
Per dozen..........35c

No. 9B48177 Width, 1⅜ inches; length, 2⅞ inches. Heavy iron bolt, 2 levers. Price, each $0.22
Per dozen........ 2.60

ASSORTED KEYS.

We quote below three assortments of keys in various shapes and kinds. These assortments are made up of the keys and blanks most commonly used and we cannot change the assortments or sell less than a full box. Locksmiths, property owners, janitors, hotel men, housekeepers or anyone who uses keys, our prices below save you half.

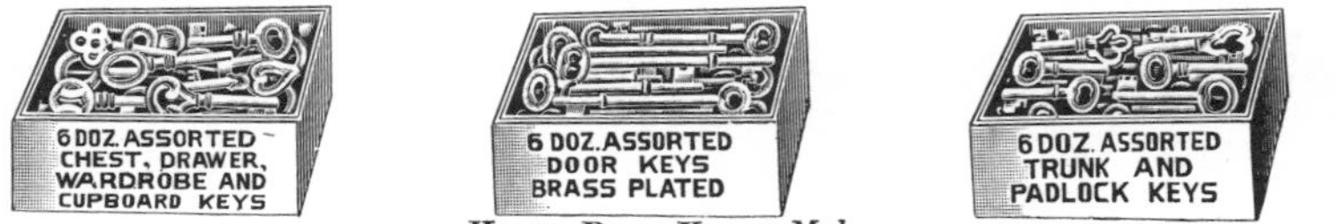

Cabinet Lock Keys. Barrel, solid bit and flat; blank and fitted; well assorted. Full boxes only.
No. 9B48225 Per box of 6 dozen keys.......76c

House Door Keys. Malleable Iron, brass plated; fitted, skeleton and blank. A good assortment. Full boxes only.
No. 9B48228 Per box of 6 dozen keys......68c

Trunk and Padlock Keys. Flat, barrel, single and double bit; blank and fitted. Full boxes only.
No. 9B48231 Per box of 6 dozen keys.......72c

No. 9B48191 Nickel Plated Brass Suit Case or Box Locks. Size, 1⅝ inches.
Each $0.12
Per dozen........ 1.42

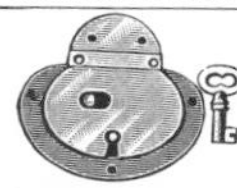

No. 9B48193 Nickel Plated Brass Suit Case or Box Locks. Size, 2¼x2 inches. Each $0.15
Per dozen........ 1.70

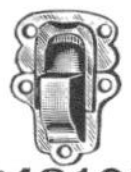

No. 9B48197 Nickel Plated Brass Suit Case or Box Catches. Length, 2½ inches.
2 for...............11c
Per dozen..........64c

No. 9B48201 Japanned Wrought Steel Trunk Catches, tinned loop, 4½ inches long.
2 for............... 8c
Per dozen..........46c

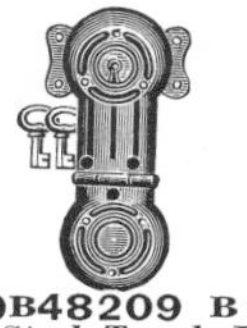

No. 9B48209 Brass Plated Steel Trunk Locks. Extra strong. Size, 6½x 1⅜ inches.
Each $0.19
Per dozen........ 2.26

No. 9B48211 Solid Brass Trunk Lock. Size, 5½x5 inches. Has two secure levers and two steel keys. Extra quality, $1.25 value.
Price 73c

STORMPROOF RUBBER THRESHOLD.

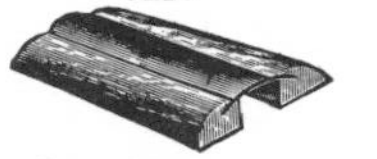

No. 9B48755 Prevents the cold and snow from coming in. Made of hardwood strips with rubber center. Length, 3 feet, but can be cut to make shorter if desired.
Price 59c

IRON STORM THRESHOLDS.

No. 9B48761 Snow and rain cannot beat under your door in the most severe weather if you use one of these thresholds. Size given is length between jambs.

Size, in.	28	30	32	34	36
Price	43c	46c	50c	54c	57c

JAPANNED FOOT SCRAPER.

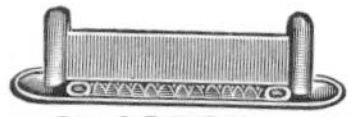

No. 9B48795 Best cast iron.
Price, each............3c

JAPANNED STEEL FOOT SCRAPER.

No. 9B48791 Tough steel, very rigid, not easily broken, 6 inches wide.
Price 6c

IRON LADDER SOCKETS.

No. 9B48801 By use of these sockets ladders can be made much lighter and stronger. Hole in socket 1 inch in diameter.
Price, 24 for........29c
Price, 100 for.......89c

WROUGHT STEEL CORNER IRONS.

No. 9B48995 For strengthening and repairing boxes, chests, etc. Very strong and rigid. Size given is length of each side, and width. Price does not include screws.

Size, inches..	1x½	2x⅝	3x¾	4x⅞
Price for 4...	4c	7c	9c	12c
Per dozen....	10c	18c	25c	32c

Did You Ever Stop to Figure the Difference in Cost Between Our Prepared Felt Roof and a Shingle Roof?

A Comparison of the Cost of a Roof With Felt or Shingles. Good wood shingles are scarce on account of the exorbitant price of lumber. The better grades of lumber that some years ago were sawed into shingles are now put into interior finish or used up for manufacturing purposes and the shingles are sawed from stuff that can't be cut up into anything else.

Prepared Felt Roofing Has Attained a Point of Perfection where it can be depended upon, in any climate, on any kind of a building, and its life on the roof is practically

dependent on the construction of the building itself. Provided it is taken care of properly, the life of any roofing is prolonged by a good coat of paint or coating at intervals of from three to five years.

Below We Submit a Statement showing the comparative cost and life of prepared felt and shingle roofs, also the approximate cost of laying same. Note the saving in price where our Best-ov-al Rubber Asphalt Felt Ready Roofing is used.

OUR FREE SAMPLES Of Roofing and Building Paper

This Illustration shows the big line of samples of which we will be glad to send to you free. Felt Roofing and Building Paper Contractors and builders who are well acquainted with the technical terms, weights, etc., used in roofing felts, building papers, etc., will readily understand from the printed description just what the article is they are going to get. If you are not familiar with the different kinds and styles of roofing felts and building papers or if you are in doubt which brand will best serve your purpose, you should write us for our free samples of felt and building papers and we will be very glad to send them to you by mail, postpaid. These samples are from our regular goods taken from our stock, showing exactly what the goods are and each sample has a catalog number, price, description, etc. We will be very glad to send these samples to you so that their quality may be compared with samples offered by other firms or your home dealer, because such comparison plainly shows the wonderful value and high standard of quality of every article of this character sold by us.

Be sure to state whether roofing or building paper samples are wanted.

We Here Illustrate a House which is being covered with Best-ov-al Prepared Felt Roofing, which is described on page 137. Size of the main building is 22x26 feet, "L" or wing addition is 12x16 feet and a porch 6x22 feet. To cover this roof we will figure out the area as noted below. By following the same rule it is an easy matter to ascertain the exact amount required for covering any roof.

Right hand side of the roof, 17x28 feet (17-foot rafters)	476 square feet
Left hand side, 17x28, less the amount of surface covered by gable (102 feet)	.374 square feet
Two sides of the roof on the "L" or wing addition, 12x16 feet, plus the pitch or gable extending on the main roof (12-foot rafters)	.390 square feet
Size of roof on porch, 9x24 feet	.216 square feet
Allowing one roll for covering the bay window, making valley, chimney flashings, etc.	.100 square feet
Total number of square feet	1,556, or 16 squares or rolls

We Have Taken This Average Size House as a basis for giving you a comparative cost for roofing a building with shingles and prepared felt roofing of various grades and costs.

To Ascertain the Area of a Plain Gable Roof, first multiply the entire length of the rafters by the length of the building, including the projection of eaves or cornices. This gives one side of the roof. Doubling this amount will give the total number of square feet on both sides of the roof. To ascertain the area or covering space of a gable roof, take the extreme length of the outside or longest rafter and multiply this by the width of the roof at a point half way between the gable and eaves. This will give you the total amount of square feet on one side of the gable, and taking double this amount will give you the number of square feet on both sides of the gable roof.

Below We Furnish a Table Showing the Difference in Cost to You between shingles and our Best-ov-al Prepared and Asphalt Felt and Marble Coat Rubber Roofing. Felt Roofing, THE BEST ROOFING MADE, in which case the average covering space of a shingle is 16 square inches. Shingles are usually laid 4½ inches to the weather, in square feet or a space 10x10 feet square. We have used two grades of shingles to cover a square of roofing containing 108 today. We believe the cost for labor as given is a good fair average wage. and the price is the retail price in Chicago

NOTE—WE CAN SAVE YOU $60.00 on an average roof of 16 squares and furnish you with a roof which is more satisfactory in every way.

Kind of Roofing	Quantity Required for One Square	Price, per Square	Cost of Laying, per Square	No. of Square Feet in Roof of House and Porches	Cost of Labor and Material	Total Cost	Estimated Life of Roof
Star Shingles...	900 Shingles or 3½ Bundles	$4.00	$1.40	1,556 or 16 squares	Shingles, $64.00 Nails, 2.25 Labor, 20.40	$86.65	From 10 to 15 Years
"AA" Shingles...	900 Shingles or 3½ Bundles	$3.50	$1.40	1,556 or 16 squares	Shingles, $56.00 Nails, 2.25 Labor, 20.40	$78.65	From 8 to 10 Years
Marble Coat Rubber Roofing	One Roll	$2.25	30c	1,556 or 16 squares	Roofing, $36.00 Labor, 4.80	$40.80	From 10 to 15 Years
Best-ov-al Three-Ply Rubber	One Roll	$1.80	30c	1,556 or 16 squares	Roofing, $28.80 Labor, 4.80	$33.60	From 10 to 15 Years
Flint Surfaced Asphalt, Three-Ply..	One Roll	$1.79	30c	1,556 or 16 squares	Roofing, $28.64 Labor, 4.80	$33.44	From 8 to 12 Years

Compare Our Goods With Those of Your Local Dealer. Compare the thickness and weight of our felt roofing and building papers with that of other concerns, and at the same time compare the prices they ask you for their goods of similar weight and grade, and you will be astonished at the saving you can make by buying from us. We have studied the roofing and building paper situation carefully for years and have paid particular attention to the materials used in their manufacture, to the machinery and method of making, and we know that it would be impossible for any other concern to make or sell as good a grade of roofing and building paper as we do for the same amount of money.

QUALITY GUARANTEED

Valleys and Flashings for Prepared Felt Roofings are or should be made of the same material as used for roofing. A roll of roofing is 32 inches wide and splitting a part of a roll making two strips, each 16 inches wide, makes a most satisfactory width for valleys on gable roofs. Valleys for shingle roofs are sometimes made of tin or galvanized iron. However, both of these materials are being rapidly replaced by rubber asphalt felt roofing. The standard two-ply or extra heavy Best-ov-al Felt Roofing makes a most desirable valley, even though shingles or slate are used for the roof. Three-ply Best-ov-al Prepared Felt Valleys will outlast the best grade of tin or galvanized iron possible for you to obtain.

$25 MARBLE COAT ROOFING

HIGHEST GRADE ROOFING MADE OF ONE SOLID PIECE OF PURE ALL WOOL FELT

ONE WEIGHT, ONE GRADE, ONE QUALITY—ALWAYS THE BEST

PER ROLL

We Especially Recommend Our Marble Coat Prepared Felt Roofing **for high class residences or for other buildings where highest quality and best appearance are desired.** The demand for roofing similar to our Marble Coat Roofing is becoming greater every day. People have learned by experience that a high grade prepared felt roofing gives much better satisfaction and costs less to lay than shingles, but have a slight objection to using the regular prepared felt roofing on account of its color or the appearance it presents. Our Marble Coat will beautify the appearance of your home, it will add richness and style to the building as no other roofing will do, as it is finished in a beautiful silver gray color, being coated with marble spar, which not only adds to its appearance but to its fireproof qualities as well.

Best-ov-al Rubber and Asphalt Felt Roofings Have Been Used for Years and are given most excellent satisfaction, but the contractor and the home builder want something for a new residence that looks better; the owner of a house that needs a new roof wants something dependable and lasting, but doesn't want the same kind of a roof on a $5,000.00 or $10,000.00 residence as now used on lower priced residences or barns and other outbuildings. It is only fitting and proper that there should be a demand for a better looking roofing, a roof with all the good qualities of our high grade Best-ov-al Rubber Felt Roofing, and with a coating or finish in keeping with the building; something that will not only look nice and always appear pleasing to the eye, but something that has quality and is in every way dependable. **Marble Coat Roofing is made especially for this purpose and to meet this demand.**

Marble Coat Roofing is of the Highest Quality. fiber pure wool felt that is used in making our Best-ov-al Rubber Felt Roofing, only that the felt is all of one weight and thickness and first of all is treated with a pure mineral rubber or wax compound which is absolutely without any animal oil and it is rolled or compressed a little more at the time the saturation is put in. We use the same compound or saturation as is used in our Best-ov-al Roofing, which is waterproof and fireproof, after which it is coated with a strictly pure mineral asphalt and is then surfaced or covered with a fine marble spar which makes it the most attractive roofing made, and at the same time this additional coating of fine white marble adds to its fireproof qualities.

There is No Roofing More Beautiful Than Marble Coat Roofing. The color of the roofing is of light silver gray or clean marble color, making it especially desirable for the finest residence. This beautiful silver gray color effect is lasting, it will not fade away nor lose its rich color, rains serving to keep it washed clean. On a country residence or any building situated away from the dirt and smoke of cities and factories this roofing will hold its color for a long time.

We Furnish Free with every roll plenty of large headed galvanized nails (which does away with the use of the tin cap), plenty of waterproof cement for lapping the edges and seams, also a can of marble coating for sprinkling along the edges after the cement has been used and the roof nailed down. Your roof will then appear as one solid mass of silvery white color, no seams nor tin caps showing. The nails being galvanized will never rust.

MARBLE COAT RUBBER ROOFING

WILL WEAR TWELVE YEARS. Each roll contains 108 square feet, enough to cover a space 10 feet by 10 feet, or a square, and have 8 square feet to allow for a 2-inch overlap at all the seams; complete with large headed galvanized nails, cement, etc.

Catalog No.	Grade	Width	Covering Space	Weight	Price, per Roll
63B3030	Extra Heavy	32 inches	1 square, 100 square feet	58 pounds	$2.25

TO REDUCE YOUR FREIGHT CHARGES AND TO AVOID DELAYS IN TRANSIT, we will ship your order from our factory or one of our warehouses nearest you. Warehouses in Cincinnati, Ohio, Pittsburg, Penn., Kansas City, Mo., and factory at Chicago, Ill. The price is the same no matter from which point your roofing is shipped. **NOTE**—See page 141 for price on our pure imported especially prepared Asphalt Coating and Roof Preservative. Marble Coat Roofing does not require a heavy coat put on but should be recoated every three or four years with our Asphalt Roof Preservative.

FULL ILLUSTRATED DIRECTIONS FOR LAYING PACKED INSIDE OF ROLLS. NO EXPERIENCE NECESSARY.

WHAT OTHER PEOPLE SAY ABOUT OUR PREPARED FELT ROOFING

OUR ROOFING AT $1.17 A ROLL, BETTER THAN OTHER ROOFING AT $2.00 A ROLL.

Sears, Roebuck and Co., Chicago, Ill.   R. F. D. No. 1, Louisburg, Wis.
Gentlemen—The roofing I bought from you six years ago is very satisfactory. It is as good now as it was the day I bought it. About two years ago I ordered from another dealer and paid $2.00 a roll and it is nowhere near the quality of the roofing I purchased from you for $1.17 a roll; I saved nearly $1.00 a roll.
Yours truly,   ANTON BUSH.

HAS ROOFED SIX BUILDINGS WITH OUR BEST-OV-AL AND SAYS IT IS THE BEST.

Sears, Roebuck and Co., Chicago, Ill.   874 Manning Avenue, Collinwood, Ohio.
Gentlemen—I put on your three-ply Best-ov-al Roofing on an apartment house flat roof and I figure it will last much longer than metal roofing of any kind. I think it is better than the roofing sold by local dealers at $2.50 per square, it is one-ply thicker. I saved about 35 per cent after paying freight charges and consider I have a much better and heavier roofing. I have used your roofing on six buildings and like it very much.
Yours very truly,   J. M. HART.

HE TELLS A STORY OF SATISFACTION FROM BEGINNING TO END.

Sears, Roebuck and Co., Chicago, Ill.   Evansville, Wis.
Gentlemen—Concerning the question of roofing, will say that yours is the best. After looking at samples of several different kinds of widely advertised roofing, yours stood the tests best of all. As to price, it is a great deal cheaper than any I saw of the same grade. Our local dealer handles Reberold Roofing, and yours is far better and very much cheaper. I employed a carpenter to put it on and he said it was the best he ever saw, and he has laid prepared roofing for many years as smooth as glass on the roof, is wind and water proof and was easily laid. I am well pleased with it and calculate I saved about $8.00 on my job of eighteen rolls, as compared with prices of other brands. Wishing you all success, I am, respectfully yours,
CLINTON W. MOORE.

HE SAVED 33 PER CENT BY GETTING HIS ROOFING FROM US.

Sears, Roebuck and Co., Chicago, Ill.   R. F. D. No. 1, Box 66, Appleton, Wis.
Gentlemen—I am well pleased with your roofing. Having seen several kinds and grades sold here and elsewhere, yours is much better both as to quality and durability. I saved at least 33 per cent by buying direct of your house, and in the future shall remember you with my roofing orders.
Yours truly,   NIELS C. TOLVERSON.

BEST-OV-AL IS ABSOLUTELY SATISFACTORY.

Sears, Roebuck and Co., Chicago, Ill.   620 S. Lincoln Avenue, Hastings, Neb.
Gentlemen—This is to certify that I, B. F. Iveson of this city, purchased of Sears Roebuck and Co. of Chicago, five rolls of Extra Heavy Best-ov-al Felt Roofing at $2.38 per roll (our reduced price now is $1.80 per roll), and can say it has given splendid satisfaction, not a particle of trouble in any way, shape or form. I recently gave it one coat of paint and found it was not suffering for that, and will gladly recommend it to anyone against any other make of felt roofing that I have ever seen or had to do with, for twice the price.
Yours truly,   B. F. IVESON.

SAVED ONE-THIRD BY BUYING FROM US.

Sears, Roebuck and Co., Chicago, Ill.
Gentlemen—Some time ago I received from you an order of Prepared Felt Roofing and it is with pleasure that I testify of its good quality. It has given good results, it is easy to put on and does not require a mechanic to put it on. Anyone with hammer and nails can put the Prepared Felt Roofing on and I would recommend it to any one as a good cheap roof, and I saved about one-third of the price in buying from you, in comparison with others.
Yours respectfully,   CRAWFORD S. COCHRAN.

$1 25 Per Roll of 108 Square Feet

BETTER THAN THE KIND $2 50 USUALLY SOLD FOR . .

For the BEST ROOFING ON EARTH
BEST-OV-AL RUBBER FELT ROOFING

IT IS FIREPROOF AND WATERPROOF. IT IS BETTER AND CHEAPER AND WILL OUTWEAR TIN, TAR AND GRAVEL OR ANY OTHER KIND OF ROOFING.

Why Our Best-ov-al Rubber Felt Roofing Is the Best.

Looks like rubber, feels like rubber, but wears better and longer than rubber. If you want the best roofing made, insist on getting the celebrated Best-ov-al Rubber Felt Roofing. It is made of heavy and strong wool felt which is thoroughly saturated with a composition which not only gives it a heavy body, but makes it entirely waterproof. The roofing is elastic, pliable, strong and tough. It is not affected by changes in climate, vapors, steam or gas, and will not rust. It is also free from odor which is so commonly found with other roofings which are made with petroleum or coal tar products. It can be used on either steep or flat roofs. It will not shrink or crack if properly nailed down. Best-ov-al Rubber Felt Roofing will not impart any taste and will not discolor water. Best-ov-al Rubber Felt Roofing requires no coating when first put on a roof.

Best-ov-al Rubber Felt Roofing Is Better Than Shingles, because if properly cared for it will wear longer, is warmer in winter and cooler in summer. Best-ov-al Rubber Felt Roofing makes an airtight roof—it holds the heat in the building—makes the building easier to heat.

Best-ov-al Rubber Felt Roofing Is the Easiest to Apply. The standard and heavy grades are put up in rolls containing one square (108 square feet), allowing ample material for lapping joints, etc., and are also put up in double rolls containing two squares (216 square feet) to the roll. Many of our customers prefer the larger size rolls, which are easy to handle on the roof and usually show a saving of time and labor. The only tool required to lay this roofing is a hammer. Best-ov-al Rubber Felt Roofing can be put on any old roof over shingles.

Best-ov-al Rubber Felt Roofing Will Outwear Any Other Prepared Felt Roofing, because it is made of the very best felt and composition, insuring the greatest possible strength, and is better prepared to withstand heat and cold, rain or snow than any other prepared roofing on the market. It is provided with a heavy coating of waterproofing material on both sides and the same material is also mixed with the compound with which the felt is saturated and rolled. This composition is forced into and through the felt under great pressure and at an enormous heat as it passes through heavy rollers, thus producing a wonderful strength and flexibility.

We Furnish Free With Every Roll of our Best-ov-al Rubber Roofing large headed galvanized roofing nails and plenty of cement for lapping the seams or joints. Note that we furnish a galvanized nail with large head which costs 100 per cent more than the old style wire roofing or shingle nail and tin cap used by many concerns. We know that a good roof depends on its being firmly secured to the roof boards. Galvanized nails will last for many years. No matter what kind of roofing you buy, insist on using galvanized roofing nails with large heads.

Our Prices for Best-ov-al Rubber Felt Roofing Are Very Low. Many dealers will ask $2.50 to $3.00 (per roll of one square) for roofing which is not equal in quality to our Standard Grade Best-ov-al Rubber Roofing which we sell at only $1.25. Our low prices on this, the finest grade of felt roofing are only made possible by our controlling the output of the largest and most modernly equipped roofing plant in the United States. We sell direct from factory to customer. This enables us to save for our customers the manufacturer's profit, the jobber's profit and the small dealer's profit. All we ask is one small profit over the manufacturer's net cost, hence we sell you our roofing at less than wholesale price. **NO TOOLS NECESSARY. ANYONE CAN LAY IT. WRITE FOR FREE SAMPLES OF ALL KINDS OF READY ROOFINGS.**

Best-ov-al Rubber Felt Roofing Is Practically Fireproof; in fact, in certain localities insurance companies consider Best-ov-al Rubber Roofing a better risk than shingles. The composition used in the manufacture of Best-ov-al Rubber Felt Roofing does not easily burn, cannot be set on fire by flying coals or embers. There is absolutely no tar or pitch used in the preparation of this roofing, as is commonly found in many other kinds of roofing. **WE GUARANTEE EVERY ROLL OF BEST-OV-AL ROOFING TO OUTWEAR ANY OTHER PREPARED FELT ROOFING MADE.**

SOLD IN THREE DIFFERENT WEIGHTS, VIZ.:

One-Ply or Standard Grade is a most excellent covering for barns, sheds and all buildings where a moderate priced roofing is wanted. There is no better one-ply roofing made than our Best-ov-al. One-ply is very largely sold throughout the country and with proper care it will last years.

Two-Ply or Heavy Grade is made of a very much heavier felt the better class buildings and on any job where a good, durable roof is wanted. Our Two-Ply Heavy Grade Best-ov-al Rubber Roofing when properly taken care of will outwear shingles. You will find our Two-Ply Best-ov-al Rubber Roofing to be a splendid grade, and with coating applied every three or four years it will last many years.

Three-Ply or Extra Heavy Best-ov-al Rubber Roofing is positively the best grade of roofing made. This roofing when properly cared for will last almost as long as the building. This grade of roofing is used on the finest and largest buildings in the country and where quality is desired you will find that money invested in our Three-Ply Extra Heavy Grade Best-ov-al Rubber Roofing will be a splendid investment. We especially recommend it for roofing houses. Felt roofing takes a low freight rate.

There Are Many Kinds and Brands of so called Rubber Roofing on the market, some of them are no better than ordinary pasteboard or heavy paper with a coating of some kind applied to make it look like roofing. **Remember.** Do not let anybody talk you into buying an inferior grade because they offer it to you a few cents cheaper than Best-ov-al Rubber Roofing.

To Reduce Your Freight Charges and to Avoid Delays in transit, we will ship your order from our factory or one of our warehouses nearest you. Warehouses in Cincinnati, Ohio, Pittsburg, Kansas City and factory at Chicago, Illinois. The price is the same no matter from which point your roofing is shipped. We carry a large stock of all kinds of roofing, hence can ship roofing with other goods in one lot.

BEST-OV-AL RUBBER FELT ROOFING.					
Complete with Large Headed Galvanized Nails, Roofing Cement, etc. Width, 32 Inches.					
Catalog No.	Weight and Grade	Thickness	Covering Space in Square Feet	Square Feet in Roll	Price, per Roll
63B3031	36 Pounds, Standard Grade	One-Ply	100	108	$1.25
63B3032	46 Pounds, Heavy Grade	Two-Ply	100	108	1.25
63B3033	56 Pounds, Extra Heavy Grade	Three-Ply	100	108	1.50
DOUBLE ROLLS OF BEST-OV-AL RUBBER FELT ROOFING FOR EXTRA LONG ROOFS.					
Complete with Large Headed Galvanized Nails, Roofing Cement, Etc. Width, 32 Inches.					
Catalog No.	Weight and Grade	Thickness	Covering Space in Square Feet	Square Feet in Roll	Price, per Roll
63B3034	72 Pounds, Standard	One-Ply	200	216	$2.45
63B3036	92 Pounds, Heavy	Two-Ply	200	216	2.95

This is positively the highest grade of prepared rubber felt roofing made. Refer to the weights and you will note Best-ov-al is heavier and thicker than other kinds of rubber roofing. Full illustrated directions for laying, packed inside of rolls. No experience necessary.

1-Ply STANDARD. Will wear 7 years. Sectional View showing Cement and Nails packed inside. **REMEMBER, WE USE GALVANIZED ROOFING NAILS.**

2-Ply HEAVY. Will wear 10 years.

3-Ply EXTRA HEAVY. Will wear 12 years.

$1.15 PER ROLL FLINT SURFACED ASPHALT ROOFING
(108 SQUARE FEET)
THE BEST FLINT COATED ASPHALT ROOFING ON THE MARKET, REGARDLESS OF PRICE.

With Large Headed GALVANIZED ROOFING NAILS

OUR FLINT SURFACED ASPHALT READY ROOFING is heavily coated with flint sand on both sides, adding much to its fireproof qualities. The strong feature of any gravel coated roof is its protection against fire. This roofing being flint sanded on the top side makes it especially desirable from that standpoint because flying embers or coals are not liable to set it on fire from the top of the roof, while the same coating of flint sand on the under side of the roof makes a splendid resistance against fire from the inside of the building. There is absolutely no tar or pitch used in the preparation of our Asphalt Roofing. Our Flint Surfaced Roofing is 32 inches wide.

OUR FLINT SURFACED ASPHALT READY ROOFING is guaranteed to be made from a long fiber pure wool felt and saturated with an asphalt composition which is treated with a pure mineral rubber. It is positively without any animal oil and is absolutely weatherproof, guaranteed not to melt or run during the summer time, nor crack or break in the winter time, and the fact that it is surfaced on both sides with a good clear sharp sand embedded in the coating under heavy pressure makes it practically fireproof, at least the best fire resisting roofing ever made or sold. We guarantee this roofing to wear better than any other flint or sand coated roofing on the market. It positively requires no coating when first put on the roof. Our three-ply should be coated with our asphalt roof preservative within from three to five years and again at intervals of three years (depending upon the pitch of the roof). Three-ply Asphalt Felt Roofing, if treated in this manner, will outwear all others and will last about twelve years. Two-ply should be coated at about the same intervals, in which case it will wear from eight to nine years. One-ply should be coated within two years from the time first laid and at intervals of two years thereafter, in which case with good care it ought to last from five to six years, at which time when coating the roofing you should apply a good sharp fine sand, sprinkling as much over the roofing as will adhere to the coating. Half-ply (sometimes sold for one-ply) is recommended only for use on temporary buildings, sheds, etc.; it is not intended for long life and durability.

THERE IS POSITIVELY NO COAL TAR IN THIS ROOFING. This fact alone helps to make it fireproof and the waterproofing qualities of our coating give it a good heavy body, make it very strong and flexible and it positively will not crack or break in either heat or cold and neither will it run nor drip when exposed to the rays of the sun.

Flint Surfaced Asphalt Ready Roofing

requires no coating when first put on the building. We absolutely guarantee our Flint Surfaced Asphalt Sanded Roofing to be the strongest and best roofing ever made. The sand is evenly applied on both sides of the roofing and is thoroughly embedded in the coating under heavy pressure, thus insuring against being washed or blown away by rain or wind. The surface of the roofing is so evenly covered and protected with this coating that it will outwear any sand and gravel roof, besides the weight is but little more than that of the rubber or smooth roofing, hence the freight charges on our Flint Surfaced Asphalt Roofing will be very much less than on the heavy gravel and tar roofings sold by other concerns.

WE FURNISH FREE WITH EVERY ROLL of our Flint Surfaced Asphalt Felt Ready Roofing galvanized barbed roofing nails with large head, and plenty of cement, together with all necessary directions for laying the roofing. We use the large headed galvanized nail in the place of a galvanized cap, because it will more firmly secure the roofing. Note that we furnish a galvanized nail with large head which costs 100 per cent more than the old style wire roofing or shingle nail and tin cap used by many concerns. We know that a good roof depends on its being firmly secured to the roof boards. Galvanized nails will never rust, hence it will last for many years. No matter what kind of roofing you buy, insist on using galvanized roofing nails with large heads.

Write for Free Samples of All Kinds of Ready Roofings.

TO REDUCE YOUR FREIGHT CHARGES AND TO AVOID DELAYS

IN TRANSIT, WE WILL SHIP YOUR ORDER FROM OUR FACTORY OR ONE OF OUR WAREHOUSES NEAREST YOU. WAREHOUSES IN CINCINNATI (OHIO), PITTSBURG, KANSAS CITY, AND FACTORY AT CHICAGO, ILLINOIS. THE PRICE IS THE SAME NO MATTER FROM WHICH POINT YOUR ROOFING IS SHIPPED. **IMPORTANT.** Our one, two and three-ply roofing is thicker and heavier than the one, two and three-ply usually furnished. We give you more pounds of HIGH GRADE ROOFING for the price than any other concern.

REDUCED PRICES OF FLINT SURFACED ASPHALT FELT READY ROOFING.
COMPLETE WITH LARGE HEADED GALVANIZED BARBED ROOFING NAILS AND CEMENT.

Catalog No.	Weight and Grade		Thickness	Covering Space in Sq. Ft.	Square Ft. in Roll	Price, per Roll
63B3018	50 Pounds,	Standard Grade	Half-Ply	100	108	$1.15
63B3016	60 Pounds,	Medium Grade	One-Ply	100	108	1.24
63B3015	70 Pounds,	Heavy Grade	Two-Ply	100	108	1.49
63B3011	80 Pounds,	Extra Heavy Grade	Three-Ply	100	108	1.79

Freight Charges on Flint Surfaced Asphalt Felt Ready Roofing are nothing compared with the wonderful saving we make you. Felt roofing takes fourth class rate (less than 25 cents per 100 pounds) going to most points within a radius of 500 miles. To nearer points, from 10 to 15 cents per square or roll. **NO EXPERIENCE NECESSARY. FULL ILLUSTRATED DIRECTIONS FOR LAYING PACKED INSIDE OF ROLLS.**

READ WHAT OTHER PEOPLE SAY
About Our Asphalt Roofing.
It Is the Strongest Proof We Can Offer.

SAVED $6.00 ON SIX ROLLS OF ASPHALT ROOFING.
R. F. D. No. 4, Brodhead, Wis.
Sears, Roebuck and Co., Chicago, Ill.
Gentlemen:—I got a lot of roofing of you from you a year ago and I like it very much; it was just like the samples you sent me and I saved about $6.00 on the order of six rolls.
Yours truly, HELLICK OLSON.

PAYS SAME FOR OUR HEAVIEST GRADE (THREE-PLY) ROOFING THAT HIS DEALER ASKED FOR HIS LIGHTEST GRADE OF ONE-PLY PREPARED ROOFING.
R. F. D. No. 1, Marathon, Wis.
Sears, Roebuck and Co., Chicago, Ill.
Dear Sirs:—Your roofing is all right, just as good as elsewhere. I found out I pay for three-ply here at home what other dealers for the lightest grades.
Yours truly, MAX KOLBE.

HE SAVES ONE-THIRD (33½ PER CENT) AND WILL RECOMMEND OUR ASPHALT ROOFING TO HIS FRIENDS.
R. F. D. No. 2, Potosi, Wis.
Sears, Roebuck and Co., Chicago, Ill.
Dear Sirs:—I am very much pleased with the roofing received from you and will kindly recommend it to my friends. Besides we saved one-third of the cost by sending to your firm. We will likely send for another order soon.
GEO. STOLL.

HE TELLS US OUR ROOFING AT $1.75 A ROLL IS BETTER THAN ROOFING SOLD FOR $2.75 AND $3.00 A ROLL.
Chicopee, Kan.
Sears, Roebuck and Co., Chicago, Ill.
Dear Sirs:—I will say that the Felt Roofing that I received from you some time ago has given every satisfaction. I have compared it with roofing bought here for $2.75 and $3.00 a roll, but I would not exchange with them, as I think that what I got from you was so much better in quality, and if I have any more buildings to put up I will use your felt roofing, as I prefer it to shingles and it is more easily put on.
Yours respectfully, J. B. BRAITHWAITE.

THE FINEST ROOFING HE EVER SAW AND RECOMMENDS IT TO HIS FRIENDS.
Oshkosh, Wis.
Sears, Roebuck and Co., Chicago, Ill.
Dear Sirs:—Your roofing is the finest I have ever seen. My carpenters said that your roofing was the best they have ever handled for the price and they wanted to know where I bought the roofing, and I told them where to get it.
Yours truly, JOHN MACHO.

SAVED 25 PER CENT AND GOT ENTIRE SATISFACTION.
R. F. D. No. 3, Cuyahoga Falls, Ohio.
Sears, Roebuck and Co., Chicago, Ill.
Gentlemen:—The roofing I received from you has given entire satisfaction and I find that the saving to me over the price asked by local dealers is about 25 per cent. Whenever I am in the market again I shall be pleased to give you my order.
Very respectfully, V. E. FERRICT.

SEE PAGE 136 FOR MORE LETTERS FROM OUR CUSTOMERS.

WE HAVE THOUSANDS OF LETTERS from some of the best people in the United States; they all tell us that our Best-of-all and Flint Surfaced Asphalt Roofing is the best they have ever seen and that our prices are about one-third less than prices quoted by the regular dealer.

GRAVEL BURLAP ROOFING

$2.69 PER ROLL OF 108 SQUARE FEET.

A Roofing of the First Quality. Needs No Coating. Waterproof, Hailproof and Fireproof

BEST ROOFING MADE FOR USE OVER OLD SHINGLES.

Gravel Burlap Roofing Is Just What the Name Implies, roofing made of base, burlap center, asphalt and gravel surface. The wool felt and burlap center are thoroughly saturated with asphalt at a temperature of 325 degrees Fahrenheit and formed into one solid piece, then heavily coated with a thick layer of asphalt compound and gravel coated with washed lake pebbles.

An Ideal Roofing for Laying Over Shingles, because it is heavier and has makes of roofing. The burlap gives added strength and equalizes contraction and expansion caused by sudden and extreme changes in temperature. It is the heaviest prepared roofing made and is sold in one weight (one thickness) only. Weight, 85 pounds, hence is warmer in winter and cooler in summer than shingles, slate, steel or other prepared roofings.

Gravel Burlap Roofing Is Hailproof because it is made with a strong burlap cloth center, making it sufficiently strong to withstand sleet, hail, snow and the heaviest downpour of rain. It never needs coating or painting, as the exposed surface is heavily covered with a thick layer of asphalt compound and further protected with gravel. As a result it will wear ten years without coating or repairing. While a trifle more expensive to commence with, it is cheapest in the end, and when once laid your roofing troubles cease.

Suitable for Any Pitch of Roof. It can be used on any kind or style of roof, "from a mansion to a henhouse." It is being extensively laid on buildings used for stores, offices, factories and warehouses which are located in districts where flying embers are a menace to the average roofs, or in localities where steel roofs have been considered the only fire protection. Can be laid on roofs with the slightest pitch (nearly flat) because it is made with a **2-inch border** free from gravel, permitting a tightly cemented and waterproof seam.

We Furnish Free with every roll sufficient large headed galvanized nails and cement, and full and complete directions for laying. Anyone can lay it. No experience required. The only tools required are a common jack knife and a hammer.

Can Be Laid in One-Fourth the Time it takes to lay shingles and at at a total cost of less than one-half the cost of the commonest grades of wood shingles.

When Used Over Shingles, be sure that there are no projecting nails or loose shingles. If laid on a new building, the building should be sheathed with dry, well seasoned lumber and laid closely together.

If You Are Having Trouble with your old shingle roof do not attempt to patch it up so that it will last possibly another six months, but send in your order for a sufficient amount of gravel burlap roofing to cover your roof right over the old shingles. If you do this it means that your roofing troubles are over. No painting or coating is necessary, either at the time you lay the roofing or after it is laid.

SEND FOR SAMPLES. THEY ARE FREE AND WILL BE MAILED ON REQUEST. POSTAGE PREPAID.

Furnished in Rolls Containing 108 Square Feet, covering surface 100 feet. Price includes all necessary large headed galvanized nails and waterproof seam cement, and full directions for laying.

Catalog No.	Ply or Thickness	Rolls Contain	Covering Space	Weight	Price, per Roll or Square
63B3026	Extra Heavy	108 Sq. ft.	100 Sq. ft.	85 Pounds	$2.69

Shipped from Chicago factory or Waukegan, Ill., warehouse, from which points customer pays the freight. Cannot be shipped from Kansas City, Mo., or Pittsburg, Penn., warehouses.

Washed Lake Gravel
Asphalt Compound
Burlap Center
Asphalt Compound
Heavy Wool Felt

OUR "CENTURY" BRAND PREPARED TARRED FELT ROOFING

CENTURY BRAND PREPARED TARRED ROOFING 3 PLY

77c A ROLL
— OF —
108 SQUARE FEET

A Good Roofing for 3/4 CENT a Square Foot.

CENTURY BRAND PREPARED TARRED ROOFING 2 PLY

49c A ROLL
— OF —
108 SQUARE FEET

A Good Roofing for 1/2 CENT a Square Foot.

THE OLD RELIABLE BRAND THAT HAS BEEN TESTED FOR YEARS AND FOUND SATISFACTORY. SO SIMPLE TO APPLY, A BOY CAN LAY THIS ROOFING. A HAMMER, BRUSH AND KNIFE ARE THE ONLY TOOLS NECESSARY.

A Satisfactory Prepared Ready Roofing at an Unusually Low Price.

"Century" Brand Prepared Tarred Felt Ready Roofing is the best two and three-ply prepared tarred felt roofing made, regardless of price. **Every ounce of material used in** this roofing **has waterproof qualities** and does not contain clay or other cheap mineral substances which are so often used by many manufacturers who **aim to get weight** (heavier rolls), but who care little or nothing about the wearing quality. While our "Century" Brand Prepared Tarred Felt Roofing is the best prepared tarred felt roofing made, we only recommend it to customers who are looking for a low cost roofing to last but a few years. If you want tarred felt roofing, such as has been used during the past twenty-five years, you make no mistake in ordering our famous "Century" Brand Prepared Tarred Felt Roofing, as it is equal to other tarred roofing selling at 33⅓ to 50 per cent more in price.

Why Our Prices for Prepared Tarred Felt Roofing are so Much Below Regular Prices.

Selling as we do, over 400,000 squares of roofing per year, we are one of the largest buyers of felt roofing in the country and are in a position to make very favorable contracts with dry felt mills for a better grade of saturating felt than is usually put in tarred felt roofings. The tar compound used in saturating our roofing is bought in million gallon lots at a price

THREE-PLY "CENTURY" BRAND PREPARED TARRED FELT ROOFING is made of three sheets or layers of wool felt which are thoroughly saturated at a very high temperature with a distilled tar waterproof compound, rendering the felt absolutely water proof.

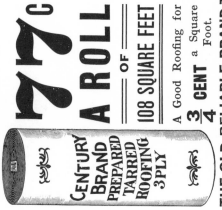

This illustration shows a section of our Three-Ply "Century" Brand Prepared Tarred Felt Roofing.

and weather proof. Between these three layers are two layers of high grade waterproof binding cement and when applied the roofing is run through heated rollers under hydraulic pressure, which makes three layers of felt and two layers of cement in one solid waterproof flexible sheet. There being three layers of felt and two layers of cement, the thickness and the quality of the roofing is thereby increased 50 per cent over the two-ply. The three-ply, therefore, will wear the longer.

far below regular market prices. It is shipped in latest improved steel tank cars which reduces the freight charges on the raw materials and eliminates all waste, and also the cost and losses usually incurred by other concerns who are obliged to buy in less quantities. Besides naming you a much lower price than any other concern offers the inferior grade at, **we guarantee this roofing to outwear and give better satisfaction in every way than any similar brands of tarred felt roofing now on the market at much higher prices.** Don't forget that every ounce of material used in the making of this roofing has a wearing quality and is not loaded with clay or other mineral substances to make it weigh 5 or 6 pounds more per roll. This would simply mean additional freight charges to our customers on pounds of material which in no way would add to the life of the roof.

To Properly Lay Two or Three - Ply "Century" Brand Roofing

you will require 1 pound of tin caps, 1 pound of common barbed roofing nails and 1¼ to 2 gallons of roof coating to each roll or square. Each roll contains 108 square feet, which, after allowing for a 2-inch lap, will cover 100 square feet. When laid this roofing should have a good coat of Duck Brand Roof Coating and then be heavily surfaced with coarse sand or fine gravel immediately after the coating is applied, which will make you a good gravel or sand roof. Some of our customers use hot pitch for coating this kind of roofing. If you are prepared to heat the pitch it will answer the purpose of coating or recoating very well. "Century" Brand Prepared Tarred Felt Roofing, like other tarred felt roofing, should be coated as soon as laid, and every two or three years thereafter, and recoated with sand or gravel as explained above. Our Duck Brand Roof Coating, catalog No. 63B3035, shown on the following page, is specially made to be used on "Century" Brand Prepared Tarred Felt Roofing.

Shipped from our Chicago factory or from our Chicago store if ordered with other merchandise.

TWO-PLY "CENTURY" BRAND PREPARED TARRED FELT ROOFING is made of two sheets or layers of wool felt which are thoroughly saturated at a very high temperature with a distilled tar waterproof compound which renders the felt absolutely water and weather proof. Between these two layers of saturated felt is a layer of high grade waterproof binding cement, and when applied the roofing is run through heated rollers under hydraulic pressure, which makes both layers of felt and the layer of cement into one solid waterproof and flexible sheet. (See illustration showing plies.)

Compare These Prices,

then compare the quality of our roofing and remember if we have not saved you money and given you roofing which is equal to or better than you could buy elsewhere, return it at our expense and we will immediately return your money, together with any transportation charges you have paid. **Each roll is 32 inches wide.**

Catalog Number	Grade	Thickness	Square Ft.	Weight	Price, per roll
No. 63B3102	Medium	Two-Ply	108	40 Pounds	49c
No. 63B3103	Heavy	Three-Ply	108	60 Pounds	77c

Each roll of 108 square feet will cover 100 square feet of roof surface.

The above prices on "Century" Brand Prepared Tarred Felt Roofing do not include caps, nails or coating. For each roll of 108 square feet you should order extra, 1 pound tin caps, 1 pound roofing nails and 1¼ to 2 gallons of roof coating.

No. 63B3028 ⅞-Inch Common Barbed Nails. Price, per pound $0.04
Price, per keg of 100 pounds 3.75
No. 63B3029 Tin Roofing Caps. Price, per pound 05
No. 63B3035 Duck Brand Roof Coating. (See following page.)

WE SPECIALLY RECOMMEND OUR BEST-OV-AL MARBLE COAT OR FLINT SURFACED ASPHALT FELT ROOFING TO THOSE WHO DESIRE A ROOFING WHICH WILL LAST AS LONG AS SHINGLES. THESE ROOFINGS ARE FULLY DESCRIBED ON THE OTHER PAGES of this book.

QUALITY GUARANTEED   NO EXPERIENCE NECESSARY.

FULL ILLUSTRATED DIRECTIONS FOR LAYING PACKED INSIDE OF ROLLS.

ROOFING PITCH

65c PER 100 LBS.

A genuine straight run American coal tar roofing pitch. We use the best grade of roofing pitch that we can obtain. We have a large sale among roofers and contractors on this material. It is put up in barrels weighing from 300 to 400 pounds each. It is in a solid state, and requires melting and is the proper consistency for gravel roofers' use. Architects are now specifying the use of a sheet of roofing fabric as a damp course in walls and foundations. It prevents the wall from absorbing moisture from the ground by capillary attraction. It should be put on the outside walls of the foundation while hot and with a mop, generally about two or three coatings, and then a good layer of heavy felt roofing and another coating of hot pitch. Foundations of structures below the ground will be practically waterproof after having been heavily coated with this roofing pitch. We do not sell less than full barrels which weigh 300, 350 and 400 pounds.

No. 63B3056   Roofing Pitch.   Price, per 100 pounds....65c

Length	Price, per lb.	Price, per Keg
⅞ in.	4c	$3.75
1¾ in.	4c	3.60
1 in.	6c	5.60

BARBED ROOFING NAILS AND TIN CAPS.

The tin cap should be used with tarred roofing felt. Practically makes a large head for the nail and prevents it being pulled through the felt. The barbed nail holds better than a smooth nail, and if kept well protected with coating never rusts. Use plenty of tin caps and barbed roofing nails with Tarred Felt and Duck Brand Prepared Tarred Felt Roofing. They are necessary to do a lasting job. For Best-ov-al and Asphalt Felt Roofing we recommend the use of a large headed galvanized barbed roofing nail and not the use of a tin cap. We recommend the galvanized barbed roofing nail.

Catalog No.	Kind of Nail	Price, per lb.
63B3028	Common Barbed	4c
63B3088	Common Barbed	4c
63B3041	Large Headed Galvanized Barbed	6c

No. 63B3029   Tin Roofing Caps. (1 lb. required for each roll or square of felt roofing or siding). Price, per pound....5c
No. 63B3087   Dry Red Mineral Paint for Steel Roofing.
Requires 1 pound for each square of steel roofing. Price, per pound...2c

ROOFING BRUSHES.

Our brushes are made of good stock, are bound with wire and carefully cemented into a head of hard maple, thoroughly seasoned and will not check or crack. A good brush and well made. Quality fully guaranteed.

No. 63B3038   Roof Paint Brushes.
Price, two knots, each................33c
Price, three knots, each................50c
Price, four knots, each................68c

MY-TE-GOOD LEAK MENDER.

BIG STICK
A SURE CURE FOR LEAKS IN ANY OLD THING

My-Te-Good Leak Mender is a sure cure for leaks in any old thing. It mends leaks in any kind of roofing material, wood or felt. Mends gutters, valleys, chimney flashings, sky-lights, flashings, iron, wood or metal roofing, brushes, wood boats, either wood, steel or canvas, etc. There are so many uses to which this mender can be applied that space will not permit us to mention them all. Our customers daily write us of many uses they have discovered for our leak mender. It can be used in hot or cold weather, on wet or dry surfaces. An old knife is the only tool required. It is put up in a round package 10 inches long, about 1½ inches in diameter. Full directions are on each package.

No. 63B3037   My-Te-Good Leak Mender.   Price, per package....15c

BEST-OV-AL ROOFING STANDS THE TEST OF FIRE.
Sauk City, Wis.

Sears, Roebuck and Co., Chicago, Ill.
Gentlemen:—I cannot say how thankful and well satisfied I am with your Best-ov-al Roofing. It certainly fireproof. Lightning struck one of my buildings, a log house, and set the log house on fire, but where the Best-ov-al Roofing we could check the fire, when otherwise it would have taken the rest of the buildings on the farm. I built a new hog house this fall and covered it with your Best-ov-al Roofing and certainly don't care for anything better. During the fire there was no signs of the Best-ov-al Roofing catching fire, everything that was there would have been shingles on that building I would have lost several hundred dollars at least. I intend to put it on a square after deducting the freight charges and the roofing is better than I could get of our dealer here.

Yours truly,
CHAS. C. BECKER.

SAVE YOUR ROOF BY USING OUR Celebrated Prepared Roof Preservative

PREPARED ROOF PRESERVATIVE.

Any roof, whether made of tin or other metals, wood shingles or any kind of prepared asphalt felt, will not give the best satisfaction, in fact will not give you one-half its real wear unless properly coated with our Prepared Roof Preservative at intervals ranging from two to five years. This roof coating is made from the same high grade waterproof and asphalt coating as is contained in our Best-ov-al and Asphalt Felt Roofings. It forms a heavy yet flexible and pliable coating and is especially adapted for any kind of roof. For steel structures such as bridges, iron fences, steel siding or metal structures of any kind which are exposed to the weather, it is by far the best preservative on the market. It is frequently used on old wood shingle roofs where the coating is found not only a most excellent preservative of the wood but it closes up any cracks or leaks in an old shingle roof. It drys with a fine black, glossy luster and will not crack or blister. It is not affected by either heat or cold. A good preservative to use for painting any kind of fence posts before putting into the ground. **It is guaranteed to be free from coal tar or any by-product of coal tar.** We furnish it in the following packages. Packed in barrels and half barrels, jacket tin cans, also shipped in barrels and half barrels.

PRICES OF PREPARED ASPHALT PRESERVATIVE.
Shipped from Cincinnati, Ohio, Kansas City, Mo., or Chicago, Ill.

Catalog No.	Size	Weight	Price, per Package
63B3017	1 gallon	8 pounds	$ 0.54
63B3017	2 gallons	16 pounds	.90
63B3017	3 gallons	25 pounds	1.20
63B3017	5 gallons	41 pounds	1.93
63B3017	10 gallons	80 pounds	3.60
63B3017	25 gallons, ½ barrel	250 pounds	6.67
63B3017	50 gallons, full barrel	475 pounds	12.50

(Packed in flat top wood jacket tin cans)

We especially recommend our pure imported especially Prepared Asphalt Preservative for recoating our Celebrated Best-ov-al and Asphalt Felt Roofing after it has been laid for about two years and recommend its use every two or three years thereafter.

DUCK BRAND ROOF COATING.

Duck Brand Ready Roof Coating is especially prepared for coating felt roofs. It is distilled from low heat, straight run American coal tar, and is more durable and far superior in every way to coatings made from the common kind of tar. Naturally our price for Duck Brand Ready Roof Coating is higher than inferior grades are sold for, but, durability considered, Duck Brand Roof Coating is cheapest to use.
The coating is the life of the roof, keeping it soft and pliable, avoiding cracking in extremely cold weather and protecting the felt from the heat of the sun and the wear of storms and rain. Do not try to economize by not putting on two coats of Duck Brand Roof Coating as directed. Should be coated when laid, and plenty of clean sand used. Do not wait until your roof leaks or is in bad shape before renewing the coating. The roof should be inspected about one year after it is first laid, and any defects or bad joints should be made good. Afterward apply a coat of Duck Brand Roof Coating every two or three years.

PRICES OF DUCK BRAND ROOF COATING.
Shipped from Cincinnati, Ohio, or Chicago.

Catalog No.	Size	Weight	Price, per Package
63B3035	2-gallon can	22 pounds	$0.49
63B3035	5-gallon can	50 pounds	.95
63B3035	10-gallon can	100 pounds	1.69
63B3035	25-gallon barrel	290 pounds	2.60
63B3035	35-gallon barrel	400 pounds	3.60
63B3035	40-gallon barrel	495 pounds	3.90
63B3035	50-gallon barrel	575 pounds	4.80

COMPOSITION ROOFING

89c A ROLL

A PRICE FAR BELOW WHAT OTHERS WILL CHARGE FOR THE VERY SAME ROOFING WHICH MAY BE SOLD UNDER SOME SPECIAL LABEL.

Composition Roofing is sold by us for the purpose of meeting the demands of those who want an Asphalt Ready Roofing because it is low in price, and who are not so particular about its wearing qualities. This roofing is not manufactured for us in any of our regular roofing factories, but we buy it of a concern which claims it to be good roofing.

We Sell This Cheap Roofing for just what the manufacturers claim it to be and, while we do not warrant it, yet we do believe that it is as good a grade of roofing as is sold by any concern in the country at prices ranging from 75 cents to $1.50 a roll higher than our prices. It is made of standard felt, saturated with an asphaltic composition and is finished on one side with a smooth asbestos rubber coating and the other side is coated with fine sand. Some roofers prefer to use the rubber surface while others prefer the sanded surface up to the weather. This roofing can be used with either side up according to the wishes of the purchaser.

89c
FOR A ROLL OF 108 SQUARE FEET.
RUBBER FINISH ON ONE SIDE, SAND FINISH ON THE OTHER SIDE.

THIS ROOFING IS 36 INCHES WIDE, FURNISHED COMPLETE WITH NAILS, CAPS AND CEMENT

Why Not Buy the Best Roofing, such as Best-ov-al Asphalt Felt Roofing? It will wear many years longer than any other make, and the price for these high grades, fully guaranteed roofings is only a little higher than the cheaper grades.

We By All Means Recommend that you buy our guaranteed Best-ov-al or Asphalt Felt Roofings, even in preference to our Composition Roofing, because you get better value for your money; but if you want a cheap roof for a short time, then buy our Composition Roofing.

Composition Roofing is shipped direct from factory in Chicago, therefore cannot be shipped with other goods.

PRICES ON COMPOSITION ROOFINGS.

Catalog Number	Kind	Weight	Price, per Roll of 108 square feet
63B3111	One-Ply	34 pounds	$0.89
63B3112	Two-Ply	44 pounds	1.19
63B3113	Three-Ply	54 pounds	1.39

Be sure to read what our customers have to say about Best-ov-al and Asphalt Felt Roofing on pages 136, 138 and 139.

TARRED FELT AND BUILDING PAPER

When You Build Use Plenty of Good Sheathing

Paper or Tarred Felt. The cost is very little and you will save this cost every season in your fuel bills; the added comfort you have will be clear profit. Every year people are using better and better sheathing paper. We especially recommend tarred felt for sheathing purposes. We can safely say that you will make no mistake in buying a strong, heavy sheathing paper or tarred felt. Free samples will be sent on application.

OUR ROLLS OF BUILDING PAPER RUN FULL WEIGHT. For many years it has been the custom of manufacturers, jobbers and retail dealers to sell "trade weights." For instance, rolls labeled 50-pound sheathing paper, according to "trade weight," would weigh from 44 to 46 pounds for 500 square feet; also 40, 30 and 20-pound rolls with a corresponding shortage of weight. Paper sold according to the "trade weight" methods, as above described, **would mean a loss to you of from 10 to 15 per cent in weight alone. To insure your getting full weights we have instructed the manufacturer in all cases to make a 50-pound roll weigh 50 pounds, and make a 40-pound roll weigh 40 pounds,** and so on in the various weights, in order to give you exactly what you pay for. In some instances our rolls run 2 per cent over specified weights, whereas, in other cases not more than 2 per cent below, but we guarantee to a customer buying ten rolls of 50-pound building paper that he will receive a total of 500 pounds full weight. Whether you buy your paper from us or from any other source of supply, protect your own interests by insisting upon getting full weight. If we were to sell our building paper at "trade weights," we could sell it to you at 15 per cent less than we do.

COMPARE THESE PRICES WITH THE PRICE YOUR DEALER ASKS. WE SAVE YOU AT LEAST ONE-THIRD

We Do Not Cut Rolls of Tarred Felt or Building Paper, as we quote the lowest factory price.

Half rolls ordinarily would cost more than the price we ask for full rolls. The prices quoted on this page are the same for single rolls or carload lots.

Freight Charges on Tarred Felt and Building Paper amount to almost nothing, as they take fourth and fifth class freight rates when going to points in most parts of the United States. In many instances freight charges amount to less than 5 cents a roll for rolls weighing from 50 to 60 pounds.

TARRED FELT

USED FOR ROOFING, SHEATHING OR GENERAL BUILDING PURPOSES.

Tarred Felt is the Best Kind of Building Paper. All up to date architects and contractors specify and recommend the use of tarred felt in the construction of a first class building. While its first cost is a trifle higher than cheaper grades of building papers, it is much cheaper in the long run as it adds warmth and comfort to the building, more than saving its cost the first year's fuel bills will, more than saving its cost in the difference between the Tarred Felt and the lower priced building papers such as Red Rosin Sheathing or any other kind of building papers.

About the Quality of Tarred Felt. Tarred felt is made of carefully selected wool felt and is thoroughly saturated with a by-product of coal tar, heated to 220 degrees Fahrenheit, thus forcing the necessary amount of saturation into the felt to make it soft and pliable, but not overloaded with saturation.

This Felt is Used Extensively for roofing sheds and temporary buildings; there is also much of it used on inner lining in lumber camps and any outdoor building that might need protection of this kind; it is still used in roofing of large buildings where the specifications require about three to five layers of tarred felt, each layer of which is thoroughly coated with Pitch, or our Elastic Roof Coating. After the several layers of tarred felt have been placed on these large buildings they are then covered to the depth of an inch or more with sand and gravel.

We Recommend No. 1 Tarred Felt for all first class jobs. It is a good grade of felt for sheathing purposes, also for putting between floors where a good job is wanted. As a Sheathing paper for putting under weatherboard it is equal to any.

No. 2 Tarred Felt. This grade of tarred felt is also used for gravel roofing where four or more layers are specified. It can be used in any place where the No. 1 grade is used, but it is lighter weight (not so thick), and where a medium grade of work is required a No. 2 Tarred Felt will be found very satisfactory.

No. 3 Tarred Felt. This is the heavier grade made with much thinner. This grade of felt is used for gravel roofing where a cheap light roof is required. Many contractors and builders especially recommend it as a sheathing paper and it is always a good investment when put under slate, shingles or metal roofing and, in fact, for general sheathing purposes.

PRICES ON TARRED FELT.

Catalog No.	Grade	No. of Square Feet per Roll	Width, inches	Approximate Weight	Price, per Roll
63B3050	No. 1	250	32	60 lbs.	90c
63B3054	No. 2	400	32	60 lbs.	90c
63B3055	No. 3	500	32	60 lbs.	90c

TARRED STRAWBOARD SHEATHING PAPER.
Tarred Strawboard is used for sheathing purposes and for lining the interior of barns, poultry houses, sheds and other outbuildings. Comes in rolls weighing from 60 to 75 pounds, and 32 inches wide. Weighs about 16 pounds to the square (100 square feet). Our price is very low and the quality of this paper first class. **No. 63B3009** Tarred Strawboard, 32 inches wide, in rolls weighing from 60 to 75 pounds each. Price, per pound..............1½c

Red Rosin Sized Building Paper for Sheathing Purposes

We Carry a Complete Line of Red Rosin Sized Building Paper in only the very best grades. Due to our controlling the entire output of one of the largest and best mills in this country, we are able to guarantee the maximum quality of Red Rosin Sized Building Paper.

Our Prices are so Extremely Low for this high grade building paper that many of the largest contractors throughout this broad country are continually sending us orders for large quantities of this paper. In many instances we receive orders for two and three hundred rolls for a single shipment.

If You are a Builder or Contractor or if you are building your own home do not overlook the economy of properly lining your building with plenty of this high grade paper. It will save its reduction in your fuel bills, saying nothing of the added comfort to your home.

About Quality. Red Rosin Sized Building Paper, which we quote below, is made with a well calendered body and is faced on both sides with a well calendered stock that is thoroughly rosin sized, rendering it dampproof and vermin proof. We sell four different weights of this paper. We recommend for ordinary building purposes our Leader Brand, as it is of sufficient thickness to give entire satisfaction.

Our Fulton Brand is made with exactly the same stock, but is considerably heavier than our Leader Brand and for the difference in price we would by all means recommend that you buy our Fulton Brand.

Our Acme Brand is a fair grade, similar to the kind sold by any other concern. It is light in weight, as it runs only 4 pounds to the square, and will be satisfactory in the construction of a low priced building.

Our Competition Brand is a lighter weight paper, no better or heavier Red Rosin Sized Paper made by any other concern. It is of the same quality as our Leader, except that it is much thinner.

PRICES ON RED ROSIN SIZED SHEATHING PAPER.

Catalog No.	Brand	No. of Sq. Feet per Roll	Weight, pounds	Width, inches	Price, per Roll
63B3001	Fulton	500	50	36	75c
63B3000	Leader	500	40	36	60c
63B3002	Acme	500	30	36	45c
63B3007	Competition	500	20	36	30c

FULTON BRAND BLUE PLASTER BOARD.

Our Fulton Brand Blue Plaster Board is a strong, tough paper, used for sheathing under clapboards and on walls and ceiling in the place of plaster. It makes a very durable substitute for plaster. It can be nailed direct to the studding. It is put on with an ordinary bill poster's tack, or any heavy tack will do, and then cover with wall paper. The color is a nice shade of blue and produces a very pleasant effect. Our Fulton Brand Blue Plaster Board has a good, hard, well finished surface and can be painted any color with good results. (Use any of our Seroco Brand of house paints.) Fulton Brand Blue Plaster Board is made only in "AA" grade. Blue Plaster Board is made from carefully selected all rag stock and makes a sheet exceedingly heavy, very strong and durable. We know that our Fulton Brand Blue Plaster Board will please you.

Catalog No.	Number of Square Feet per Roll	Width, inches	Weight, pounds	Price, per Roll
63B3012	250	36	30	$0.62
63B3013	500	36	60	1.20

COMPETITION BRAND BLUE PLASTER BOARD.

We have an occasional call for a cheaper grade of Blue Plaster Board and while we do not recommend the use of "B" grade material, we can furnish it. This "B" grade Blue Plaster Board is not finished as well, is not as tough and strong as our "AA" grade Fulton Brand Blue Plaster Board, and for the difference in price we would by all means recommend that you buy our Fulton Brand "AA" grade Blue Plaster Board.

Catalog No.	No. of Square Feet per Roll	Width, inches	Weight, about, lbs.	Price, per Roll
63B3020	250	36	30	$0.56
63B3021	500	36	60	1.10

SEROCO BRAND WOOL DEADENING FELT.

Deadening Felt is used in modern buildings to deaden the sound between the floors and in walls throughout the building. This deadening felt is run through the machines without being calendered and is thus soft and pliable and will add very much to the warmth of your building. Seroco Brand Deadening Felt should be under every floor. The price of this material is so low that you cannot afford to put up a building without placing a layer of our Leader Brand, as our Wool Deadening Felt is made in two weights; About 1 pound to the square yard and put up in rolls weighing about 25 to 50 pounds to each; the heavier stock weighs 1½ pounds to the square yard, and is put up in rolls weighing about 37 to 75 pounds each. Rolls 36 inches wide.

Catalog Number	Brand	Width	Weight per Square Yard	Approximate Weight	Price, per Roll
63B3004	Seroco	36 inches	1 pound	50 pounds	$1.05
63B3005	Seroco	36 inches	1 pound	25 pounds	1.55
63B3006	Seroco	36 inches	1½ pounds	75 pounds	1.58
63B3008	Seroco	36 inches	1½ pounds	37 pounds	1.80

We Have Endeavored to give such an accurate description of our tarred felt, building and sheathing papers, blue plaster board, etc., that even though you are not entirely familiar with the various weights and grades of these materials, it will not be necessary that you delay your order to write for samples. Every item or article on this page is the best of its kind or grade. However, if you are not able to judge from the description the weight or the thickness that your work will require, then write for our free samples of building paper and they will be sent to you by return mail, free of charge.

ROLL AND CAP ROOFING

Our Roll and Cap Roofing is used on all kinds of buildings, and with entire satisfaction. It is easy to put on, the only tools necessary being a pair of edging tongs, a pair of squeezing tongs, a wooden mallet or hammer and a pair of tinners' snips. It can be laid safely on rafters and on very flat roofs; in fact, can be used on a roof with only 2 inches fall to the foot. It is therefore especially adapted for either flat or steep roofs and is extensively used on old roofs where it may be placed over the shingles or on uneven surfaces. The most distinctive feature of this roofing is the locking of the cleat into the caps, which holds it firmly to the standing seam. The construction is simple and it is easily and rapidly laid. A roll is 26¼ inches wide and contains 50 lineal feet, which covers one square or 100 square feet. With each order we furnish 50 side cleats which should be placed every 12 or 14 inches apart, and we also furnish 51 lineal feet of caps.

Our Roll and Cap Roofing is easiest to apply. To lay this roofing, first turn up the edge by the use of your edging tongs which will form a standing seam 1 inch high on each side of the roll shown by figure A. Commence at the left hand bottom side of the roof, lay the first sheet on the left hand edge of the roof, running from top to bottom. After you have turned up the standing seam on each side, proceed to nail on the cleats, which are used on the same as shown in the illustration on this page of our Pressed Standing Seam Roofing; then lay up the next sheet with the standing seams formed and flatten the cleat over two by two, two sheets together; now place the cap over the seam and use the squeezing tongs or hammer and mallet for locking the standing seam.

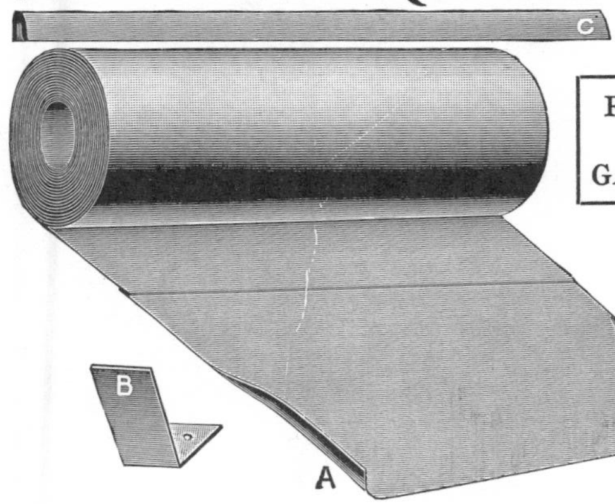

You will get fine results with Plain Roll and Cap Roofing for any kind of work where steel roofing can be applied. To properly apply this roofing you will need the tools mentioned above, which we are prepared to furnish at practically actual cost (see prices at bottom of this page). Plain Roll and Cap Roofing is sold only in full rolls containing one square or 100 square feet, which covers a space 10 feet by 10 feet square. This allows for forming the standing seam and for locking the end joints. Made of 28-gauge steel, either painted or galvanized on both sides. We cannot cut or sell a part of a roll.

Our reduced prices are much lower than steel roofing has been for the last two years. You can safely send us your order at these prices, and if there should be a further decline, we will reduce our prices and return the difference in money to you. Roll and Cap Roofing is shipped direct from the steel mills in Central Ohio.

No. 63B3070 Roll and Cap Roofing, painted, 28-gauge. Weight, 72 lbs. Price........$2.40
No. 63B3071 Roll and Cap Roofing, galvanized, 28-gauge. Weight, 89 lbs. Price, 4.48

$2.40 PER SQUARE

FULL 28 GAUGE

EDGING TONGS.

Edging Tongs are used for turning 1-inch edger or standing seam on roll cap roofing. This tool has two parallel round jaws which will permit the edge of the sheet of steel to enter the right depth, producing a 1-inch standing seam. This tool has a wooden handle and will do the work for which it is intended, and our price barely represents the manufacturing cost. Can be shipped either from our Chicago store or from the steel mills with steel roofing. 
No. 63B3090 Edging Tongs. Weight, 3¼ pounds. Price............40c

SQUEEZING TONGS.

Squeezing Tongs are used for pressing or squeezing the standing seam on either roll cap or pressed standing seam or double cap roofing. The heavy cast iron jaws of this tool are about 14 inches long, and it is sufficiently strong to press the cap seam, and it will do the work of a $3.00 tool and we charge you only actual cost. Can be shipped either from our Chicago store or steel mills with steel roofing.
No. 63B3093 Squeezing Tongs. Weight, 7½ pounds. Price............45c

PRESSED STANDING SEAM ROOFING

Pressed Standing Seam or Double Cap Roofing is made from the same high grade steel as our other roofing and is very simple in its application and effective in its construction. It is a universal roofing used on all kinds of buildings. Its distinctive feature is the outside cleat, which has many points to recommend it, chiefly among which is the rapidity with which it can be laid on the roof and its adaptability to any kind or shape of roof, it being easy to lay on porches, etc. It is easily cut and fitted with a pair of snips.

The sheets are formed with a cap on each side, which makes a stronger and better roof than when separate caps are used, such as are sold by quite a number of other steel mills and dealers. Our Pressed Standing Seam Roofing can be applied by any ordinary laborer, and the only tools required are a pair of squeezing tongs, a jointer, pair of snips and a mallet. It is stronger, neater, more durable and less liable to need repairs than a tin roof.

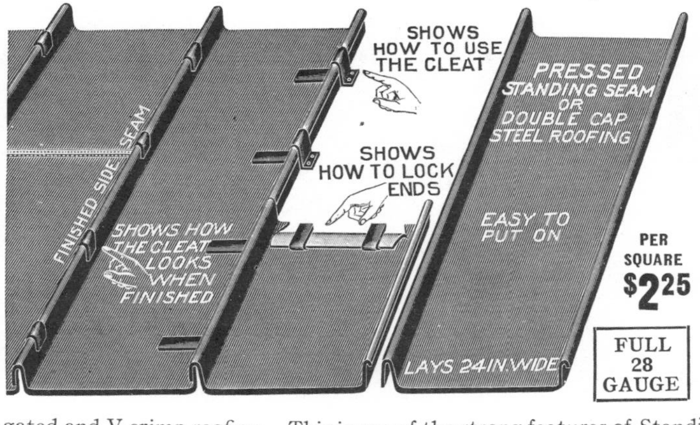

Our Pressed Standing Seam Roofing is firmly held to the sheathing by the use of outside cleats which are nailed at intervals of 12 or 14 inches. This style of fastening is considered the best for metal roofing. The cleats are nailed on the sheathing, making it very strong, and the wind cannot easily blow off your roof. Remember, in using this style of roofing with these cleats that we make no hole in the sheets, as is necessary when laying corrugated and V crimp roofing. This is one of the strong features of Standing Seam Roofing.

Cover your buildings with sheets of such lengths as will cut to the best advantage without loss to you. This roofing comes in six different lengths of sheets, ranging from 5 to 10 feet, inclusive, and lays 24 inches from center to center. We furnish the necessary cleats to lay the roofing.

This roofing can be used over shingles or nailed directly to the rafters. By covering an old shingle roof with steel it will make the building cooler in summer and warmer in winter. Shipped direct from the steel mills in Central Ohio.

No. 63B3075 Pressed Standing Seam Roofing, made of 28-gauge sheet steel, painted both sides. Width of sheets, 24 inches. Weight, per square, about 71 pounds. Price, per square..........$2.25

| Length of sheet, feet.......... | 5 | 7 | 9 | 10 |
| Price, per sheet.......... | 24c | 34c | 43c | 48c |

No. 63B3076 Pressed Standing Seam Roofing, made of 28-gauge steel, thoroughly galvanized. Width of sheets, 24 inches. Weight, per square, 89 pounds. Price, per square..........$3.80

| Length of sheet, feet.......... | 5 | 7 | 9 | 10 |
| Price, per sheet.......... | 29c | 38c | 57c | 81c |

| Length of sheet, feet.......... | 6 | 8 | | |
| Price, per sheet.......... | 41c | 49c | 65c | 73c |

You will require ½ pound ⅞-inch Barbed Roofing Nails and 1 pound Dry Mineral Paint for each square of this roofing.

JOINTERS.

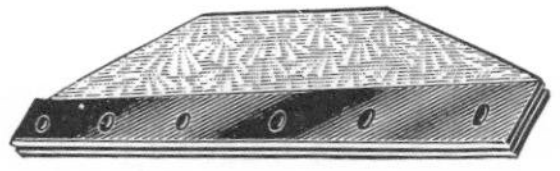

Jointers are used for making the end laps or lapping seams on V Crimp and Pressed Standing Seam as well as other kinds of roofing. This tool is about 20 inches long. A splendid tool that will enable you to fold and make end laps on most any kind of roofing excepting corrugated sheets. Can be shipped either from our Chicago store or from the steel mills with steel roofing.
No. 63B3095 Jointer and End Locker. Weight, 3¼ pounds. Price..........35c

A Complete Set of Roofing Tools, same as described above, consisting of 1 pair edging tongs, 1 pair squeezing tongs and 1 pair steel laid tinners' snips, length 10 inches. These three tools are all that are required for putting on either Roll or Cap or Standing Seam Roofing. Others ask more than double for same tools.

TINNERS' SNIPS.

The Fulton Tool Co.'s guaranteed brand Tinners' Snips are forged from a solid piece of steel and laid full length with finest cutlery steel, fully tempered and every pair fully warranted. A pair of tinners' snips will pay for themselves in the first hour's work. We can ship tinners' snips either from the Chicago store or from the steel mills with steel roofing.

No. 63B3091 Tinners' Snips, 10 inches long; length of cut, 2½ inches. Weight, about 1¼ pounds. Price, complete..........80c

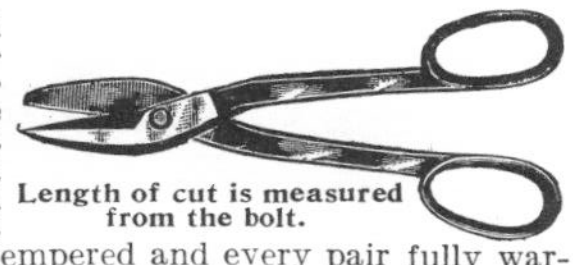

Length of cut is measured from the bolt.
No. 63B3096 Tinners' Snips, 12 inches long; length of cut, 3¼ inches. Weight, about 1½ pounds. Price, complete..........$1.64

The Old Reliable Two and Three=V Crimp Steel Roofing at Reduced Prices

Two and Three-V Crimp Steel Roofing has been performed more extensively used than any other kind of steel roofing. In fact, the sales of V Crimp Roofing are greater than all of the other styles combined. This is accounted for by the fact that it is the oldest steel roofing and for many years was confined to one or two large steel mills and manufacturers.

V Crimp Roofing is in Many Respects the Best of all the various styles of metal roofing. It may be laid over sheathing, shingles, or can be nailed direct to the rafters, which should be placed 24 inches from center to center, and can be used on either a pitch roof or flat roof; in fact, can be used on any roof having more than 2 inches fall to the foot. The ends of the sheets can either be lapped 3 inches or more or can be put together with lock joint as desired. We recommend that you use the lap joint at the end of the sheets instead of lock joint, as it will positively prevent the rain, snow or wind from blowing in under the sheet.

FULL 28-GAUGE.

It is So Easily Laid and has so many advantages over other kinds of steel roofing that it is especially adapted for factories, barns, sheds or temporary buildings and, as it requires no soldering and folding or hammering of seams or joints, anyone who has ordinary mechanical ability can put it on. It has a neat appearance and is the most economical and the cheapest style or kind of steel roofing made.

Save Money on Your Building by laying the roofing direct to the rafters without sheathing. Set the rafters 24 inches from center to center and nail the V wood strips on the top surface of the rafters. Place cross pieces between the rafters to support and nail the end of the top sheet; begin at the lower left hand corner of the roof and lay the sheets from eaves to the ridge, allowing at least 3 inches for the end laps and one crimp for the side laps. Use 1¼-inch barbed roofing nails, which should be driven into the top of the crimp and through the V strip about every 8 or 10 inches. At the end laps use nails every 4 or 5 inches.

Above illustration shows the manner or method of nailing either Two or Three-V Crimp Roofing along the eaves of the roof. With a pair of snips and a hammer a good tight joint can be made that will look well and prevent rain or snow from getting under the roof. The ridge of the roof can be finished very easily by lapping the end of one sheet over the ridge, hammering it down and nailing it, or you can allow the roofing to come up to the ridge on each side, then hammer down the V crimps on the V crimps for the top of use either our angle ridge cap or roll ridge cap, as shown on page 102.

V Crimp Roofing requires a triangular wood strip, size ⅞ inch on each side, to be used under the crimps. These wood V strips are shipped from the steel mills with the steel roofing and sold in any quantity. The Two-V Crimp Roofing requires 50 lineal feet for each square (100 square feet, or a space 10 feet square) while Three-V Crimp Roofing requires 100 lineal feet for each square. These wooden V strips should be nailed on the rafters or sheathing for each crimp. Shipped with roofing direct from the mills in Central Ohio.

No. 63B3081   **Wood V Strips for V Crimp Roofing.** Price, per 100 lineal feet..............19c

We Illustrate to the Left a sheet of Two-V Crimp Steel Roofing which has a covering width of 24 inches after lapping one crimp over the other. This roofing comes in different lengths ranging from 5 to 10 feet inclusive. In laying V Crimp Roofing, the ends of the sheets should be lapped not less than 3 inches and used on roofs having a fall of not less than 2 inches to the foot. The two-V crimp sheet appears to be the more popular because it is less work to lay it on the roof, as it can be put directly on the rafters, which should be spaced 24 inches from center to center. The V wood strips should be nailed on the top surface of the rafter; you should put a cross piece between the rafters wherever there is a joint or lap; they should be well coated with paint under the lap and nailed down to the cross head between the rafters. We illustrate above the manner in which V Crimp Roofing should be folded and nailed to the eaves of the roof; also note an easy method of securely fastening the sheets at the comb or ridge of the building. These are the two places most necessary for a good, neat and lasting job of work.

TWO-V CRIMP ROOFING IS SHIPPED DIRECT FROM THE STEEL MILLS IN CENTRAL OHIO.

PRICES ON TWO-V CRIMP STEEL ROOFING.

Two-V Crimp Roofing weighs, painted, 70 lbs.; galvanized, 85 lbs. per square.

No. 63B3077	Two-V Crimp			PRICE, PER 100 SQUARE FEET		$2.05	
Roofing, 28-gauge, painted both sides.							

Length of sheet, feet.......	5	6	7	8	9	10
Price, per sheet............	22c	26c	31c	35c	40c	44c
Roofing, 28-gauge, galvanized. Price, per 100 sq. ft. $3.65						
Length of sheet, feet.......	5	6	7	8	9	10
Price, per sheet............	39c	46c	54c	60c	69c	77c

The above prices are for roofing only and do not include strips, nails or paint. See page 141 for prices on nails and paint.

It requires 50 feet of wood V strips for a square of the above roofing and 1 pound of dry paint and 1 pound barbed roofing nails for each square of roofing.

We Illustrate to the Right a sheet of Three-V Crimp Steel Roofing which has a covering width of 24 inches from center to center of two outside crimps. The center crimp adds much to the strength of the sheet, as it stiffens the iron, prevents the sheets from rattling and furthermore adds to the appearance of the roofing, closely imitating batten boards. Three-V Crimp Roofing can be laid directly on the rafters by placing them 24 inches from center to center, but, in order to obtain the full value and strength of these sheets, they would perhaps better serve you to lay them on sheathing or over old shingles or on a smooth surface where you can place a wood V strip to support the center crimp. In putting Three-V Crimp Roofing on a new roof it is only necessary to place sheathing boards at intervals of, say, every 2 feet, this being close enough to allow the V strips to properly support and strengthen the center of the sheets.

V Crimp Roofing is Much Used for Siding on barns, sheds and outbuildings. The three-V can be more securely fastened to the walls of the building than the two-V can be painted, any color and with ordinary care will last for many years. Note the illustration above showing the method of fastening Three-V Crimp Roofing along the eaves of the roof. This can be accomplished with a hammer and a pair of tinners' snips and makes a very neat appearance and positively prevents the rain or wind from blowing in under the sheets. We also explain an easy way of finishing the comb or ridge of a roof covered with V crimp sheet steel.

THREE-V CRIMP ROOFING IS SHIPPED DIRECT FROM THE STEEL MILLS IN CENTRAL OHIO.

PRICES ON THREE-V CRIMP STEEL ROOFING

Three-V Crimp Roofing weighs, painted, 72 lbs.; galvanized, 88 lbs. per square.

No. 63B3085	Three-V Crimp Roofing, 28-gauge, painted both			PRICE, PER 100 SQUARE FEET		$2.20	
sides.							

Length of sheet, feet.......	5	6	7	8	9	10
Price, per sheet............	24c	28c	33c	38c	42c	47c
No. 63B3086 Three-V Crimp Roofing, 28-gauge, galvanized. Price, per 100 sq. ft. $3.80						
Length of sheet, feet.......	5	6	7	8	9	10
Price, per sheet............	40c	48c	56c	64c	72c	80c

The above prices are for roofing only and do not include strips, nails and paint. See page 141 for prices on nails and paint.

It requires 100 lineal feet of wood V strips, 1 pound dry mineral paint and 2 pounds of barbed roofing nails for each square of the above roofing.

PRICES ON STEEL ARE RAPIDLY ADVANCING. ORDER NOW. PRICES ON THIS PAGE NOT GUARANTEED BEYOND JULY 1, 1910.

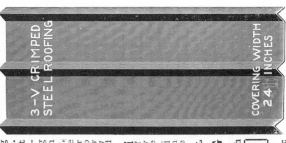

2-V CRIMPED STEEL ROOFING

LAYS 24 IN. CENTER TO CENTER

3-V CRIMPED STEEL ROOFING

COVERING WIDTH 24 INCHES

FULL 28-GAUGE.

QUALITY GUARANTEED

PRESSED CORRUGATED STEEL ROOFING AND SIDING AT REDUCED PRICES

Pressed Corrugated Steel Roofing is the strongest known of sheet metal and is adapted for roofing, siding, ceiling, fire doors and fire shutters, awnings, etc. It is used extensively for siding and is especially well and favorably known for roofing purposes.

Corrugated Roofing is Cheapest and Easiest to Lay. It requires only a hammer and a pair of tinners' snips to lay this kind of roofing either on a roof or side of a building. When you take into consideration the expense of labor, etc., you will find that this roofing is especially desirable where a large quantity is used. In putting on corrugated sheet steel the nails should always be driven through the crown or the highest point of the corrugation. Do not hammer the nail down hard enough to batter or flatten the sheet.

We Can Ship Your Order Promptly and guarantee standard goods of standard weight and gauge, and in making up your order for this roofing ascertain first the different lengths of sheets that you can use with the least cut or waste.

Our 2½-Inch Corrugated Steel Roofing comes in sheets 26 inches wide and the 1¼-inch corrugated in sheets 25 inches wide, but after being lapped on to the adjoining sheet has a covering space of only 24 inches. In figuring the number of square feet in each sheet it is necessary to figure them full width, that is, 26 inches for the 2½-inch corrugated and 25 inches for the 1¼-inch corrugated; but they cover only 24 inches in width.

We Recommend Corrugated Sheets especially for roofing, siding, ceiling and particularly for fireproof buildings, and it is only necessary to suggest the advantage of using sheet metal for such protection. **Corrugated siding is especially desirable** for grain elevators, mills, barns and high buildings where insurance amounts to a considerable figure. Not only do they use corrugated sheets for siding on these large buildings, but also for the roofs.

Corrugated Steel Roofing is Shipped to You Direct from the steel mills in Central Ohio.

Full 28-Gauge

Full 28-Gauge

Above Illustration shows our corrugated sheet steel with corrugations 2½ inches from center to center and ⅝ inch deep and made of No. 28-gauge steel. We can furnish these sheets either painted or galvanized at prices quoted below. Our painted sheets receive a good heavy coat of the best dry mineral paint mixed with linseed oil, while the galvanized sheets are thoroughly well galvanized. We recommend the use of the galvanized sheets where a permanent roof or building is wanted. Sheets when corrugated measure 26½ inches wide and cover 24 inches from center to center of the outside corrugation. 2½-inch corrugated sheets are the standard for a covering purpose, whether for roof or for siding. The ceiling width of all of our corrugated sheets is the covering width with allowance for laps, etc. Corrugated sheets are shipped direct from the steel mills in Central Ohio.

Above illustration shows a large factory building to be covered entirely with corrugated sheet steel. You will note that the roof and all of the sides are covered with this material by nailing it direct on to the studding and rafters. There is no sheathing used on either the roof or sides of the building. We recommend the use of tarred roofing felt on all roofs covered with sheet steel. This tarred felt should be immediately under the steel roofing. It adds to the life of the steel.

The Above Illustration shows our corrugated sheet steel with corrugations 1¼ inches from center to center and ⅜ inch deep, made of No. 28-gauge steel. The painted sheets have one coat of paint made from dry mineral paint mixed with linseed oil and should have another coat after being put on the building. Our 1¼-inch corrugated sheets are used for all covering purposes, whether on a roof or for siding. We carry in stock at the steel mill a large quantity of different lengths of sheets. These sheets have a covering width of 24 inches. We will ship No. 28-gauge steel in 8-foot lengths when not otherwise specified. We advise that you first measure the roof and ascertain the length of sheets that will best cover the building with the least cutting. Corrugated sheet steel is shipped direct from the steel mills in Central Ohio.

> PRICES ON STEEL ARE RAPIDLY ADVANCING. ORDER NOW. PRICES ON THIS PAGE NOT GUARANTEED BEYOND JULY 1, 1910.

PRICES OF 2½-INCH CORRUGATED STEEL ROOFING.

No. 63B3105 Corrugated Sheets, 28-gauge, with 2½-inch corrugations, painted both sides. Weighs, painted, 68 pounds per square. Price, per square.......................$2.05

Length of sheet, feet	5	6	7	8	9	10
Price, per sheet	24c	29c	33c	38c	43c	48c

No. 63B3106 Corrugated Sheets, 28-gauge, with 2½-inch corrugations, galvanized. Weighs, galvanized, 85 pounds per square. Price, per square.......................$3.65

Length of sheet, feet	5	6	7	8	9	10
Price, per sheet	42c	50c	58c	67c	75c	83c

Above prices do not include paint or nails. See page 141 for prices.

PRICES OF 1¼-INCH CORRUGATED STEEL ROOFING.

No. 63B3107 Corrugated Sheets, 28-gauge, with 1¼-inch corrugations, painted both sides. Weighs, painted 72 pounds per square. Price, per square.......................$2.15

Length of sheet, feet	5	6	7	8	9	10
Price, per sheet	25c	30c	35c	40c	45c	50c

No. 63B3108 Corrugated Sheets, 28-gauge, with 1¼-inch corrugations, galvanized. Weighs, galvanized, 87 pounds per square. Price, per square.......................$3.70

Length of sheet, feet	5	6	7	8	9	10
Price, per sheet	43c	51c	60c	69c	77c	85c

Above prices do not include paint or nails. See page 141 for prices.

NUMBER OF SQUARE FEET OF CORRUGATED SHEETS REQUIRED TO COVER ONE SQUARE.

As no allowance is made for laps, the following table gives the number of square feet of corrugated sheet steel necessary to cover one square. This table is based on using sheets 26 inches wide (covering width 24 inches) and 96 inches (8 feet) long.

End Laps.........................3 inches		
Side Lap, 1 Corrugation.........112 feet		
Side Lap, 2 Corrugations........125 feet		

The following table shows the exact number of sheets shipped for each square of either galvanized or painted corrugated roofing, 2½-inch or 1¼-inch corrugation.

2½-INCH CORRUGATED SHEETS.

Length of sheet	5 ft.	6 ft.	7 ft.	8 ft.	9 ft.	10 ft.
No. sheets per square	9¼	7¾	6⅝	5¾	5⅛	4⅝

1¼-INCH CORRUGATED SHEETS.

Length of sheets	5 ft.	6 ft.	7 ft.	8 ft.	9 ft.	10 ft.
No. sheets per square	9⅝	8	6⅞	6	5⅓	4⅞

Sears, Roebuck and Co., Chicago, Ill.   R. F. D. No. 2, Plattsmouth, Neb.

Gentlemen:—We have received the steel roofing from the freight house. There were 15 bundles or 145 sheets in all of 28-gauge 2½-inch corrugation, painted, and all in 8-foot lengths, which makes 2,515 square feet. At the time I ordered the roofing from you we did not ask our local dealer about his roofing or prices, but we did so a few days ago and learn that the prices from our local dealer on 28-gauge 2½-inch corrugated roofing, painted on both sides, will cost us at home 3 cents a square foot. You will therefore see that 2,500 square feet at home would cost me $75.00. I paid Sears, Roebuck and Co. $35.00 for this order, including 25 pounds of nails, and the freight charges on the whole thing were $8.50, making a total cost of $63.50; therefore, you will see that our saving was $11.50 on this order by buying it from you. We always paint steel roofing before it is put on and think it never should be laid on a roof without being painted again.

Yours truly,   C. F. NORD.

NOTE—WHEN ORDERING BE SURE TO ORDER ENOUGH EXTRA FOR LAPS.

PRESSED STEEL BRICK, STONE AND WEATHERBOARD SIDING AT REDUCED PRICES

Cover Your Outbuildings with a Fireproof Material, and at the same time have them appear modern and up to date, with some of our steel pressed brick or stone siding, which is made from the very best soft or mild steel that enables the sheet to be stamped so as to form a perfect imitation of the finest Philadelphia or Milwaukee pressed brick or rock face brick; also a splendid imitation of rock face stone which has been dressed into the proper size to show up best.

Sheet Steel Siding Costs Very Little to Put Up, because **it can be applied** nailed either on to the sheathing, weatherboarding or directly on to the studding, which should be placed 16 inches from center to center.

Brick or Stone Steel Siding Will Outwear Any Wood Siding. At the present time the **better grades of lumber are worked up into interior trimmings** and only the cheaper grades of stuff are used for sawing into weatherboarding, drop siding, etc. **if given a coat of paint every two or three Sheet Steel Siding Will Last For Years** years. We furnish this brick siding and weather-

boarding in both painted and galvanized sheets and recommend the use of galvanized sheets on permanent buildings. Our galvanized sheets are well coated in a thoroughly up to date galvanizing plant and are given a heavy coat of spelter which preserves the sheets from rusting so that they will last for years.

Our Painted Sheet Steel Siding Is Well Painted with an oil paint made from pure linseed oil, and the sheets are well coated on both sides.

The Best Nails to Use with sheet steel siding are a ⅞-inch barbed roofing nail or a four- penny common wire nail, either of which may be readily driven through the grooves in the sheet without the use of a punch. Always use a nail set to drive nails home. It requires about ¾ pound of these nails to a square of siding. See page 141 for barbed roofing nails.

Architects, Builders and Contractors will readily see the advantage of using rock face brick and stone siding for siding purposes on dwellings, schoolhouses, business blocks, factories, etc., in preference to the old style corrugated, beaded and other metal sidings.

PRESSED BRICK STEEL SIDING.

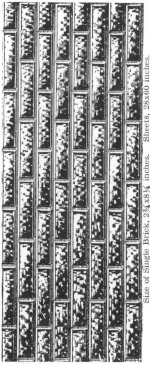

26c PER SHEET PAINTED

OR

45c PER SHEET GALVANIZED

WARRANTED FULL 28-GAUGE.

Size of Single Brick, 2¾x8½ inches. Sheets, 28x60 inches.

Pressed Brick Steel Siding can be put on the building by any workman so that it will lay perfectly smooth: after painting it cannot be distinguished from the finest pressed brick. The sheets should be painted a red brick color and striped for the mortar lines, which you will do after it is put on the building, and this paint covers up the nail holes and a short distance away cannot be told from a brick building. This material costs no more than the best wood siding and less than one-fourth the price of brick. Sold only in full sheets painted a maroon red or galvanized as quoted below. Pressed Brick Steel Siding is shipped direct from the steel mills in Eastern Ohio. A square consists of 8½ sheets.

No. 63B3116 Pressed Brick Steel Siding, painted red. Price, per sheet........26c
No. 63B3117 Pressed Brick Steel Siding, galvanized. Price, per sheet........45c

PRICE, PER SQUARE
Painted........$2.15
Galvanized.....$3.75

ROCK FACE STONE STEEL SIDING.

27c PER SHEET PAINTED

OR

46c PER SHEET GALVANIZED

WARRANTED FULL 28-GAUGE.

This is something comparatively new in sheet metal siding. It imitates rock face stone to perfection. On a building the counterpart of a finely finished rock face stone, it makes the most attractive and handsomest sheet metal covering so far produced or offered the building trade.

It is unquestionably, an elegant facing for store fronts and cannot help but take with the trade and is more easily applied, because it is cheaper, makes a handsomer front and is more durable. Rock Face Stone Steel Siding is shipped direct from the steel mills in Eastern Ohio. A square consists of 8½ sheets.

Size of Single Stone, 7x12 inches. Sheets, 28x60 inches.

No. 63B3142 Rock Face Stone Steel Siding, painted a drab color. Price, per sheet..27c
No. 63B3143 Rock Face Stone Steel Siding, galvanized. Price, per sheet.....46c

PRICE, PER SQUARE
Painted......$2.25
Galvanized...$3.85

ROCK FACE BRICK STEEL SIDING.

28c PER SHEET PAINTED

OR

47c PER SHEET GALVANIZED

WARRANTED FULL 28-GAUGE.

Size of Single Brick, 2¾x8¾ inches. Sheets, 28x60 inches.

Rock Face Brick Steel Siding in beauty of appearance has no equal. This material should be painted again after it is put on the building, the color desired, and then striped between the brick to represent the mortar line, which makes an especially fine looking building. The bricks are of the standard size and we furnish these sheets either painted red, sandstone color or galvanized as specified below. We do not cut sheets. Rock Face Brick Steel Siding is shipped direct from the steel mills in Eastern Ohio. A square consists of 8½ sheets.

No. 63B3139 Rock Face Brick Steel Siding, painted red. Price, per sheet......28c
No. 63B3140 Rock Face Brick Steel Siding, painted sandstone color. Price, per sheet.....28c
No. 63B3141 Rock Face Brick Steel Siding, galvanized. Price, per sheet.....47c

PRICE, PER SQUARE
Painted......$2.30
Galvanized...$3.90

WEATHERBOARD STEEL SIDING.

40c PER SHEET PAINTED

OR

67c PER SHEET GALVANIZED

WARRANTED FULL 28-GAUGE.

Each sheet shows six boards 4 inches wide. Sheets, 96 inches long.

Used extensively as siding on frame buildings. Cheap, durable and fireproof, and a desirable substitute for wood weatherboarding. Six and one-quarter sheets 24x96 inches to the square, which will lay 100 square feet on building, less the laps at the ends of the sheets. Each sheet shows six boards 4 inches wide. Can be applied directly to studding either 16 inches from centers or on rough sheathing. In order to provide for 1-inch end laps, place every sixth stud 15 inches from centers. When applying to sheathing, place nails 4 to 6 inches apart along the horizontal laps and immediately under the projecting crimp. When applying to studding, nail each stud. Nail end laps at the upper edge of each face or board. Sheets may be cut to fit as desired with ordinary tinners' snips. Steel Weatherboard Siding is shipped direct from the steel mills in Eastern Ohio.

No. 63B3131 Weatherboard Steel Siding. Price, per sheet, painted......40c
No. 63B3132 Weatherboard Steel Siding. Price, per sheet, galvanized....67c

PRICE, PER SQUARE
Painted......$2.40
Galvanized...$4.10

QUALITY GUARANTEED

PRICES ON STEEL ARE RAPIDLY ADVANCING. ORDER NOW. PRICES ON THIS PAGE NOT GUARANTEED BEYOND JULY 1, 1910.

PLAIN ROOF GUTTER.

Made of No. 28-Gauge Galvanized Iron.

The accompanying illustrations show our style "B" Roof Gutter. The hangers are applied in such a manner as to leave no exposed nail or screw heads (as pictures readily show); therefore, there can be no leaks from splitting or nail holes, as in the old style way with wood fronts and wood brackets.

This gutter is by far the best produced, and is sold at prices that make it much cheaper than those made of wood lined with tin.

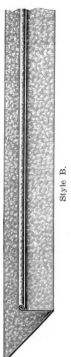

Style B.

Style B.

No. 63B3822 Plain Galvanized Roof Gutter, in lengths of 10 feet. End pieces and drops must be made by workman who puts up the gutter and all joints must be soldered. Shipped from Chicago.
Price of 15-inch sheet, ⅝-inch bead, galvanized. Per length of 10 feet...**64c**

No. 63B3821 Hangers for above trough. Each, 3c; per dozen.......**29c**

TINNERS' PEINING HAMMERS.

No. 63B3245 Tinners' All Steel Peining Hammer. Made of high grade tool steel. Well finished. Weight does not include handle.

No.	1	2	3	4
Size of steel, inches	¾	⅞	1	1⅛
Weight, ounces	8	12	16	20
Price	25c	25c	30c	30c

THE HANDY PIPE CRIMPER.

No. 63B3268 This is a convenient and very practical crimper and fills a long felt want for a low priced hand crimper to be sent out on jobs and for shop use. Weight, 13 ounces. Price.........**25c**

BLACK SHEET STEEL.

No. 63B3222 Black. Size of sheet, 28x96 inches. State gauge wanted.

Gauge	Average Weight per Bundle, pounds	Number of Sheets in a Bundle	Price, per Sheet	Price, per Bundle
16	140	3	$1.20	$3.45
18	149	4	.98	3.76
20	140	5	.74	3.53
22	117	5	.67	3.03
24	131	7	.50	3.39
26	112	8	.39	2.95
27	116	9	.36	3.13
28	117	10	.35	3.30

Prices on black sheets are subject to changes in the market. Shipped direct from the Sheet Steel Mills in Eastern Ohio.

GALVANIZED SHEETS.

Absolutely Flat and Free from Buckles. Every Sheet Warranted of Finest Working Quality.

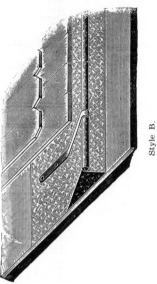

No. 63B3225 Galvanized Sheets. Size of sheet, 28x96 inches.

Gauge	Average Weight per Bundle, pounds	Number of Sheets in a Bundle	Price, per Sheet	Price, per Bundle
16	149	3	$1.53	$4.38
18	161	4	1.31	5.03
20	155	5	1.01	4.84
22	132	5	.87	4.36
24	151	7	.74	4.98
26	135	8	.63	4.78
27	142	9	.63	5.37
28	146	10	.61	5.87

Prices on galvanized sheets are subject to the changes of the market. Shipped direct from the Sheet Steel Mills in Eastern Ohio.

WHY OUR PRICES ARE SO LOW. Don't think that because our prices are so very low finish or make of our roofing is in any way lacking. Please understand that we are quoting you prices that just include the actual cost of manufacturing with our one small margin of profit added, so you can plainly see that these goods are all worth a much higher price, judging by the standard of prices ruling on the market.

PRICES ON STEEL ARE RAPIDLY ADVANCING. ORDER NOW. PRICES ON THIS PAGE NOT GUARANTEED BEYOND JULY 1, 1910.

EAVES TROUGHS AND CONDUCTOR PIPE AT LESS THAN MANUFACTURERS' PRICES

Our Eaves Troughs and Conductor Pipe are First Class in Every Respect.
They are made for us by one of the largest manufacturers in this country, on the latest and most improved machinery, thereby reducing the cost of labor; and being made at the steel mills from sheets rolled from raw iron, all under the same roof, means a saving in the cost of manufacture that is worthy of your consideration.

You Do Not Have To Be a Tinner to get the benefit of these low prices. Anyone can put up our Slip Joint Eaves Troughs. Our low prices are made possible by large and favorable contracts, saving in the cost of shipping and handling and insuring you at all times new, bright, clean goods that are perfectly made from well galvanized standard gauge steel used for that purpose.

SLIP JOINT EAVES TROUGHS. No soldering required.

We recommend the use of Slip Joint Eaves Troughs for general purposes. One end is fitted with a folded seam into which the plain end of the other length can easily be slipped and it locks itself securely so as to make it absolutely watertight. This does away with the expense and inconvenience of soldering and is especially adapted for country use or on buildings where you do not require the services of a tinner. Slip Joint Eaves Troughs are made in 10-foot lengths without a seam and with a single bead and either right hand or left hand. Right hand means that the water is to be discharged at the right hand end of the trough; left hand that the water is to discharge at the left hand end. The illustration shown is that of a right hand length of eaves trough. The size is the width taken inside of the bead. Sold only in 10-foot lengths. (See following page for extras and attachments used in putting it up.) Shipped from Chicago or from factory in Eastern Ohio.

When ordering Slip Joint Eaves Troughs state whether right or left is wanted.
No. 63B3148 Slip Joint Eaves Trough. Right hand.
No. 63B3149 Slip Joint Eaves Trough. Left hand.

Size, inches	3½	4	4½	5	6
Price, per 10-foot length	$0.25	$0.28	$0.32	$0.33	$0.40
Price, per crate containing 25 lengths (250 feet)	6.00	6.75	7.75	8.00	9.75

LAP JOINT EAVES TROUGHS.

Lap Joint Eaves Troughs are generally used by contractors, builders, roofers and tinsmiths. Lap joint eaves trough are made of standard gauge material well galvanized and come in 10-foot lengths in single bead and without a cross seam. Shipped from Chicago or from factory in Eastern Ohio.

No. 63B3150 Galvanized Lap Joint Eaves Troughs.

Size, inches	3½	4	4½	5	6
Weight, per length, pounds					8
Price, per 10-foot length	$0.23	$0.27	$0.30	$0.32	$0.38
Price, per crate containing 25 lengths (250 feet)	5.50	6.50	7.25	7.75	9.25

CORRUGATED ROUND EXPANDING ELBOWS AND SHOES.

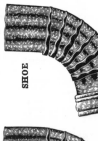

ANGLE No. 1   ANGLE No. 2   ANGLE No. 3   SHOE

Our Galvanized Corrugated One-Piece Elbows are well made from standard gauge sheet steel and well galvanized after being made. These elbows when sold by jobbers and wholesale dealers under the manufacturer's name bring a higher price than we ask for them. Corrugated elbows are made in three different angles, as shown above. Be sure to specify angle wanted and catalog number of same. **Round Corrugated Conductor Shoe** made same as elbows with exception of having a heavy metal band around one end which adds strength and prevents it from being battered up.

No. 63B3181 Corrugated Elbow, Angle No. 1.   No. 63B3183 Corrugated Elbow, Angle No. 3.
No. 63B3182 Corrugated Elbow, Angle No. 2.   No. 63B3184 Corrugated Conductor Shoe.

Size, inches	3	4	5	6
Conductor Elbows. Price, each	6c	7c	$0.09	$0.18	$0.22
Conductor Elbows. Price, per dozen	60c	70c	1.00	1.90	2.40
Conductor Shoes. Price, each	7c	8c	.13	.25	.31

Our Prices on This Line of Goods Are Much Lower than most dealers pay for their eaves troughs and conductor pipe which we guarantee to be exactly the same gauge, namely, standard or 11½-ounce sheets.

If You Are a Carpenter, Contractor or Builder or if you have new eaves troughs or conductor pipe, you can save money by buying this material from us. Our prices are absolutely the lowest and the quality the best.

These Goods are Shipped From Chicago or from factory in Eastern Ohio and in any quantity. Full crates of eaves troughs consist of 25 pieces. We will ship either a full crate of right hand or left or will pack the crates half right hand and half left when so ordered.

GALVANIZED CORRUGATED ROUND EXPANDING CONDUCTOR.

Galvanized Corrugated Conductor is the best made because it is made without cross seam and being corrugated is stiffer than the plain round pipe, easily put together and is most commonly used.

Galvanized Corrugated Round Conductor will not burst when full of ice, the corrugation allowing the metal to expand making it absolutely safe from frost and ice. Each length is a perfect straight piece made from standard gauge steel that is well galvanized and made with a folded lock seam that will not open up. Made and sold only in 10-foot lengths. We cannot cut or furnish a part of a length.

You should order conductor pipes of a suitable size for your eaves trough. They are made to fit the following combinations. Shipped from Chicago or from factory in Eastern Ohio.

Size of eaves troughs, inches	3½	4	4½	5	6
Size of conductor, inches	2	3	3	4	5

No. 63B3180 Round Corrugated Galvanized Conductor.

Size, inches	2	3	4	5	6
Price, per length	$0.27	$0.33	$0.43	$0.54	$0.65
Price, per crate containing 25 lengths (250 feet)	6.50	7.75	10.50	13.25	16.00

GALVANIZED PLAIN ROUND CONDUCTOR PIPE.

We offer this plain round conductor pipe at prices that are much below the regular wholesale price as quoted by hardware jobbers and dealers. Plain round conductor pipe is especially adapted for ventilating purposes, hot and cold pipes, etc. Each piece of pipe made from one sheet and with a good lock seam. Made in 10-foot lengths. We do not cut lengths. Shipped from Chicago or from factory in Eastern Ohio.

No. 63B3826 Galvanized Plain Round Lock Seam Conductor.

Size, inches	2	3	4	5	6
Price, per length of 10 feet	27c	30c	41c	51c	61c

CORNERS OR MITERS—SINGLE BEAD—GALVANIZED.

Inside Corner Miter.   Outside Corner Miter.

These Miters are made complete, ready for use, for both inside and outside bead, either slip or lap joint. If slip joints are ordered be sure to state if wanted right or left.

Inside Corner Miter.
No. 63B3158 Inside Corner, slip joint. Right hand.
No. 63B3159 Inside Corner, slip joint. Left hand.
No. 63B3154 Inside Corner, lap joint.

Size of eaves troughs, inches	3½	4	4½	5	6
Price, each, slip joint	15c	16c	17c	18c	20c
Price, each, lap joint	14c	15c	16c	17c	18c

Outside Corner Miter.
No. 63B3162 Outside Corner, slip joint.
No. 63B3163 Outside Corner, slip joint.
No. 63B3156 Outside Corner, lap joint.

ROUND RIDGE ROLL CAP.

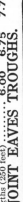

No. 63B3151 Round Ridge Roll Cap. Diameter of roll, 2 inches; width of apron, 2½ inches; girt, 10 inches, in lengths of 10 feet.
Price, per length, painted **32c**
Price, per length, galvanized 39c

No. 63B3152 Round Ridge Roll Cap, same as described under preceding number.
Price, per length, 10 feet, galvanized.

V ANGLE RIDGE CAP.

It is used on steel roofs as well as slate and shingle roofs. Comes in 10-foot lengths.

No. 63B3166 V Angle Ridge Cap, 4-inch apron. Price, per length, 10 feet, painted **28c**
No. 63B3167 V Angle Ridge Cap, 4-inch apron. Price, per length, 10 feet, galvanized 33c

Notice—The word "girt" signifies the width of the flat sheet from which the shape is formed.

PRICES ON STEEL ARE RAPIDLY ADVANCING. ORDER NOW.   PRICES ON THIS PAGE NOT GUARANTEED BEYOND JULY 1, 1910.

ADJUSTABLE OUTLETS FOR EAVES TROUGHS.

This illustration represents outlet in position. End of trough closes with slip joint end cap. Anyone can put this on. No soldering needed. For prices of end caps see No. 63B3161.

No. 63B3160 Adjustable Outlet.

To fit eaves troughs, size, in. 3½ 4 4½ 5 6
Fitted for conductor, size... 2 in. 2 in. 3 in. 3 in. 4 in.

	3½	4	4½	5	6
Price, each	$0.10	$0.11	$0.12	$0.13	$0.15
Price, per dozen	1.20	1.30	1.40	1.50	1.75

END CAP FOR EAVES TROUGHS.

No. 63B3161 End Cap, Slip Joint, for either eaves troughs or our adjustable outlet.

To fit eaves troughs,

Size, inches	3½	4	4½	5	6
Price, each	6c	7c	8c	8c	9c
Price, per dozen	60c	72c	80c	85c	95c

RAIN WATER CUT-OFF.

GALVANIZED, DURABLE, SIMPLE AND CHEAP.

No. 63B3193 For Corrugated Conductor. The strongest and best rain water cut-off ever placed on the market. Thoroughly galvanized.

Size, in.	2	3	4	5	6
Each	$0.18	$0.20	$0.28	$0.52	$0.65
Per doz.	2.00	2.30	3.20	6.00	7.20

CONDUCTOR FUNNEL.

No. 63B3187 Conductor Funnel, for running two conductors into one. Size indicates size of lower spout. Made of galvanized steel.

Size, inches	2	3	4	5	6
Price, each	16c	20c	25c	30c	40c

GALVANIZED WIRE CONDUCTOR OR STRAINERS.

No. 63B3194 Galvanized Wire Conductor Strainers, placed in the outlet of eaves trough, prevent leaves, etc., from entering or stopping up the conductor. The size given designates the size outlet strainer will fit.

Size, inches	2	3	4	5	6
Price, each	4c	5c	6c	9c	$0.11
Per dozen	35c	46c	65c	90c	1.20

WIRE EAVES TROUGH HANGERS.

SIMPLE, SUBSTANTIAL, DURABLE, CHEAP.

It is made of best galvanized steel wire, can be quickly and easily adjusted to trough and is the only wire hanger forming a complete brace as well as hanger, thus holding the trough in shape as well as place.

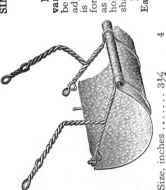

No. 63B3170 Wire Eaves Trough Hanger.

Size, inches	3½	4	4½	5	6
Price, per dozen	$0.14	$0.14	$0.16	$0.17	$0.18
Per gross	1.60	1.65	1.80	1.85	2.10

ADJUSTABLE STEEL EAVES TROUGH HANGERS.

The Greatest Labor Saving Hanger. Made with Galvanized Cross Bar.

No soldering required. Four pounds of solder and one-half day's labor saved on every gross of our hangers. Ice cannot affect them. They serve both as a brace and a hanger. Unequaled in their strength. The cross bar is galvanized. Will not rust.

No. 63B3172 Adjustable Eaves Trough Hangers, complete with rods and nuts.

Size, inches	3½	4	4½	5	6
Price, per dozen	$0.27	$0.30	$0.32	$0.35	$0.37
Per gross	2.88	3.06	3.14	3.24	3.60

No. 63B3173 Hanger Tongs and Wrench combined. Price, each.................25c

CORRUGATED HINGED HOOKS.

Galvanized Conductor Hooks, for round corrugated conductor.

Size, inches...... 2 3 4 5 6

No. 63B3185
For wood, per doz..40c 52c 65c 95c $1.10
No. 63B3186
For brick, per doz..42c 54c 66c 95c $1.15

TIN SHINGLES OR FLASHINGS.

No. 63B3199 Made of a good grade of roofing tin and cut to exact sizes. Useful for repairing old roofs and making a tight joint around chimney, etc. Painted on one side.

Size, 5x7 inches. Price, each $0.01
Per 100............ .65
Size, 7x10 inches. Price, each............ .02
Per 100............ 1.35

RIDGE ROLL FINEAL.

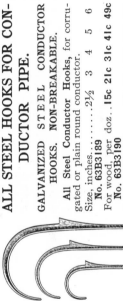

To the right we illustrate a Galvanized Iron Fineal to be used with our Ridge Roll, Catalog No. 63B3151 and No. 63B3152. This fineal is to be used at the ends of the ridge. As you will see from the illustration, this is just the article needed to put a finish on your roof. At this extremely low price every one using ridge roll should have at least two of these fineals.

No. 63B3153 Standard Gauge Galvanized Fineal.
Price, each.................25c

ALL STEEL HOOKS FOR CONDUCTOR PIPE.

GALVANIZED STEEL CONDUCTOR HOOKS. NON-BREAKABLE.

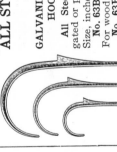

All Steel Conductor Hooks, for corrugated or plain round conductor.

Size, inches.....2½ 3 4 5 6

No. 63B3189
For wood, per doz...15c 21c 31c 41c 49c
No. 63B3190
For brick, per doz...17c 24c 36c 47c 57c

LOWEST PRICES ON BEADED CEILING

$2.25 PER SQUARE FOR BEADED CEILING OR SIDING

Covering Width, 2 feet.

Sheets when beaded cover 24 inches from center to center of outside beads. The beads are small corrugations 3/8 inch wide and 1/8 inch deep and 3 inches from center to center. This style of ceiling is very desirable in stores, churches, warehouses, factories, engine rooms, boiler rooms, public halls, paper mills, glass factories, etc. It is fireproof, and can be easily cleaned with plain soap and water when necessary. Made from the best quality steel, painted on both sides. The sheets should be lapped 1 or 2 inches at ends and over one crimp at side. They can be applied perpendicularly or horizontally (as desired) to boards, studding or joists placed the proper distance apart, or can be put on over old plaster. Shipped from steel mill in Central Ohio.

	4	5	6	7	8	9	10
Length, feet	19c	24c	29c	34c	38c	43c	48c

No. 63B3115   Beaded Siding or Ceiling.   Length, feet........   19c   24c   29c   34c   38c   43c   48c
Painted. Price, per square, $2.25; per sheet.........

TIN ROOFING AND VALLEY TIN

CONTINUOUS TIN ROOFING

No. 63B3200   Made in IC tin plate, locked and soldered together by hand. Put up in rolls containing 120 lineal feet, 20 inches wide, containing 200 square feet. The strips are perfectly straight and ready to lay on the roof. Is especially adapted for use in covering roofs of porches, bay windows, etc. Is also used for long runs of valley where a good wide valley tin is wanted. This is a good grade of tin for laying tin roofs, etc. We would not recommend covering a large roof with tin; we would rather refer you to our 28-gauge steel roofing or our felt roofing. We believe our Marble Coat, Best-ov-al or Flint Surfaced Asphalt Felt Roofing is superior to this for covering buildings. The fact that our Continuous Tin Roofing is put up in long rolls makes it especially desirable and easy to handle. Considered the best and most convenient form of roofing tin ever placed on the market. Painted on under side. Weight, per roll, 105 pounds. We cannot sell less than a full roll.

Price, per roll of two squares.................$6.00

VALLEYS—IN ROLLS

No. 63B3198   Made of a good grade of tin plate in a continuous strip, locked and soldered. Put up in rolls. Full lengths are 50 feet, but we can furnish any quantity. Painted on one side. Shipped from Chicago store.

Width, inches	Price, per Lineal Foot	Price, per 50-Foot Length	Weight, per 50-Foot Length
14	4c	$1.75	29 lbs.
20	6c	2.50	41 lbs.
28	8c	3.50	58 lbs.

No. 63B3197   Galvanized Steel Valley.   Put up in rolls. Made of 28-Gauge Steel, 14 inches wide. Lock seam and soldered. For valleys and flashings.

	25-Foot Roll		50-Foot Roll	
	Price	Weight	Price	Weight
	$1.25	20 lbs.	$2.45	40 lbs.

HIP SHINGLES

Hip Shingles are designed for the covering of hips of roofs, either straight or curved. These shingles are intended to take the place of plain tin strips, wood or metal rolls, etc. They can be adjusted to the different widths shown to the weather and make a very ornamental hip finish.

The drifting of snow and the curling of shingles are overcome by the use of these hip shingles.

There is no need to make close joints in the shingles at the hips, as the offset or shoulder at the sides (which fits snug against the butt of the shingle) forms a gauge and guide by which to keep them straight.

They may be used with shingles, slate, felt or any of the flat styles of metal roofings.   Size, 4 x 9 inches.   Sold only in full crates of 250 shingles.

Our Hip Shingles are shipped direct from the steel mills in Central Ohio with steel roofing or from our Chicago store with other goods.

No. 63B3133   Steel Hip Shingles, painted on both sides. Crate containing 250 shingles.   Weight, 75 pounds.
Price, per crate.................$2.00

No. 63B3135   Tin Hip Shingles, painted on both sides. Crate containing 250 shingles.   Weight, 60 pounds.
Price, per crate.................$2.85

No. 63B3137   Steel Hip Shingles, galvanized.   Crate containing 250 shingles.   Weight, 75 pounds.
Price, per crate.................$3.28

Hip Shingle.

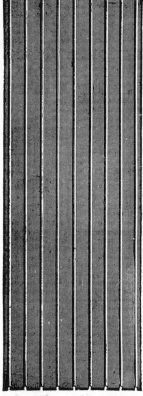

CLUSTER SHINGLES

Cluster Shingles are made of No. 28-gauge steel, painted or galvanized. Made in sheets 60 inches long; covering width, 24 inches, and are used for roofing, siding and finishing gable ends on all styles of buildings.

The sheets for roofing are furnished with pressed standing seam sides and applied with cleats in the same manner as pressed standing seam roofing.

The sheets for siding and finishing gable ends are made to lap one-half shingle at sides.

Cluster Shingles are shipped from steel mill in Central Ohio, from which point the customer pays the freight. Cannot ship from Chicago. Size of sheet, 24x60 inches.

CLUSTER SHINGLES FOR ROOFING.

No. 63B3127   Painted.   Price, per sheet.................**24c**

PAINTED CLUSTER SHINGLES, PER SQUARE,	**$2.30**

No. 63B3128   Galvanized.   Price, per sheet.................41c

GALVANIZED CLUSTER SHINGLES, PER SQUARE,	**$3.90**

CLUSTER SHINGLES FOR SIDING.

No. 63B3129   Painted.   Price, per sheet.................24c

No. 63B3130   Galvanized.   Price, per sheet.................41c

Cluster Shingles for Roofing.

STEEL CEILING

POSITIVELY THE HIGHEST GRADE OF STEEL CEILING EVER FURNISHED AT THIS EXTREMELY LOW PRICE, $2.60 A SQUARE.

This neat and tasty design of steel ceiling is used very extensively for stores, storage rooms, basements, lofts, etc. The advantages of metal decorations as are just as suitable for old buildings as for new. They applied to interior of buildings are numerous. They used in new buildings no plaster need be applied to the walls or ceiling, thus effecting a saving in material and labor. The weight of metal ceiling is trifling; consequently the strain on the joists is much reduced. In case of fire much protection is afforded by metal coverings through their resistance to the spread of flames. From a sanitary point of view metal ceilings have the advantage of being free from infectious germs. It is very easy to keep ceilings and walls clean when metal is used as a covering and they are in no way liable to damage through leaks in the roof. A leak will fill plaster with water and weaken it, to say nothing of the large unsightly blotch on the ceiling. Metal ceilings are nailed on and they are not affected by shrinking of timbers or settling of the building. Their durability makes them the most economical ceiling in existence. This design is made from sheet steel with a pattern clearly and sharply stamped so that every line of the design is displayed to advantage.

The ceiling illustrated is of a neat small pattern which will be appropriate for any room, whether it be large or small.

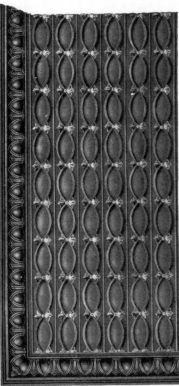

No. 63B3114   Steel Siding or Ceiling Covering. Size of sheets, 24 inches by 96 inches, which includes allowance made for side and end laps as beaded on the sheets. Weight, per square, 74 pounds. Painted a light drab color on both sides. Shipped only from Central Ohio.
Price, per sheet, **42c;** per square **$2.60**
No. 63B3118   Egg and Dart Design Border. Width, 3 inches.
Price, per lineal foot 2¼c

THINK OF THE REDUCTION IN YOUR INSURANCE RATES BY USING STEEL CEILING OR SIDING.

This popular pattern may be used to beautify store buildings, billiard halls or any other building of this kind. Another great advantage in the use of steel ceiling is the simple manner in which it can be applied, either over the old plaster or, in a new building, directly upon the joists. You should also take into consideration the saving made by using steel ceiling instead of plaster. Think of the difference between covering 100 square feet of ceiling at $2.60 and the cost of the same number of square feet covered with plaster! And there is no danger of the steel ceiling ever falling, while a poor job of plastering sometimes will last but six months. The Egg and Dart Border, illustrated to the left, is all that is needed to give this ceiling the appearance of being an elegant high priced ceiling.

Most manufacturers make a design similar to this, using a light gauge sheet steel which lessens the durability of the ceiling and for which they charge from $3.00 to $4.00 per square. Our steel ceiling is made only of standard gauge steel and our design is such that each plate or sheet can be cut to fit any space, and you will have a ceiling that will always be respected for its high standard of workmanship, quality and imposing. elegance, at a price far below that charged by other dealers.

SEND FOR OUR FREE METAL CEILING CATALOG

If you intend building a store building, hall or any other building of this kind, let us send you our **Metal Ceiling Catalog,** beautifully illustrated with full page halftone reproductions of our steel ceilings. We handle a complete line of ceilings in Renaissance, Louis XIV, Empire, Colonial and other designs. In the right hand corner of this page we have a small illustration of one of our French Renaissance Ceiling Designs. While it will give you some idea of our ceilings, it does not begin to do justice to their beauty and workmanship. Steel ceilings such as we handle are now being used extensively for the finest residences as well as public buildings. Before you do any building be sure to send for our free Metal Ceiling Catalog.

Concrete Building Block Machinery

We bind ourselves to protect every customer in every way as to any claimed infringement of patents, trade marks or copyrights on any goods bought from us in the past, or that may be bought from us in the future.

However, it is your own pocket you want to look out for, and if you buy from us you will save about one-half the price of your machine. Our machines are all made of the best materials, and while we have but little call for repair parts, owing to the excellent quality, the same can be had in almost every neighborhood at practically factory cost and to ship promptly. Any time in the future that you want a repair part or extra for a machine bought from us, we will be able to furnish it at practically factory cost, and we accept your order with that understanding.

As a Side Line concrete products are very profitable to carry. Lumber dealers can profitably handle concrete blocks, porch materials and tile. We have sold a great many machines to people who work during the day and make up blocks during the evening and are selling them on the side, realizing an extra income.

Our Prices Are Much Lower than others ask, but this is merely because we are selling machinery to you direct, from the factory at a small margin of profit. When you buy elsewhere there are three or four profits added to the original cost of the machinery, so that the extra price you pay when you buy direct represents extra profits and not extra quality.

Quality is our standby and every machine that does not come up to our standard of quality is rejected by the factory inspector.

Concrete Products Are Being Used Everywhere for building homes, churches and other buildings.

This is no longer an experiment, concrete having been proven to be one of the most desirable and durable materials for building purposes. Concrete blocks are much cheaper than stone or brick, and as they can be made up in various designs of faces, buildings more attractive in appearance can be built from concrete blocks than from any other material. It produces better fire protection, requires no repair expense or painting, thus making it very economical. It gets stronger with age, as has been proven by the many buildings, monuments, walls, etc., which were constructed in ancient times and which, after thousands of years, are in an almost perfect state of preservation.

But Little Capital Needed to start in this business in which there are big profits.

For $63.75 you can purchase a complete outfit of machinery, molds and accessories for making three sizes of blocks, and a complete line of porch materials, as shown on pages 154 and 155. This outfit is sufficient to make up all products for which there is an ordinary demand. If you don't care to start in with a line as complete as what we offer in this outfit, you can buy only one machine as a starter and build up from this. Our Wizard Cement Block Machine at $42.50 makes a fine beginner and it compares with other machines sold at $100.00, or one of our Triumph Machines at $16.95 will enable you to make an excellent start. Although our prices are about one-half what others ask, remember that we guarantee the quality and the workmanship to be of the very best.

No Experience Necessary to start in this most profitable business.

We furnish a complete direction book for operating the machine and for selecting and handling the materials, so that even though you have never done any concrete work you can, by following our simple instructions, make the very best of blocks and other products that command a good profit. We have sold hundreds of outfits to people who have never handled concrete materials and they report that after following our instructions they have been very successful and have made more money at the business than ever before.

Our Unparalleled Offer. We sell our machinery subject to trial and if you are not perfectly satisfied after trying it out carefully you may return the machinery or mold to us and we will pay the return freight and will return the price you paid for the machinery, together with any freight charges you paid. You are therefore perfectly safe in buying from us, as we guarantee to please you or money back. No other concern will do this and if we were not sure that we had the very best machinery we could not afford to make an offer like this.

Low Cost of Materials. The raw materials for making concrete blocks and brick are now very low in cost.

You can buy good Portland cement at prices ranging from $1.25 to $2.50 a barrel, depending upon local conditions. The big cement companies have distributing points all over the country, shipping it to these points by the carload, so that they can sell at a very close figure. Sand or gravel can be had in almost every neighborhood at prices ranging from 50 to 75 cents a cubic yard, and in a great many instances can be had for the cost of the hauling. To make a good concrete block, use a mixture of one part cement, two parts sand and four parts clean gravel or crushed stone. One barrel of cement mixed with two barrels of sand and four barrels of gravel will make forty-eight 8x8x16-inch blocks, figuring cement at $2.00 a barrel and sand and gravel at 75 cents a cubic yard and labor at $2.00 a day, each block would then cost you, for labor and material, from 15 to 20 cents each, giving you a handsome margin of profit. Porch columns, porch balusters, etc., you can make a better a good price at a handsome profit. On porch materials such as columns, caps, balusters, etc., you can make a better profit, as they sell at higher prices.

Don't Worry About Repairs or Extras. A great many agents in the cement machinery business knowing we have beaten them in prices and quality will tell you that you cannot get repairs if you buy from us. Their statements are false and are made to get your order. The agent doesn't want you to buy from anyone else but him, because every machine he sells means that much in his pocket.

OUR UNIQUE PORCH OUTFITS

All these molds are made from the best gray iron castings properly fitted together and we guarantee them to be made of the very best materials and to be put together in a workmanlike manner.

Shipped From Factory in Central Ohio.

The Size of each mold is made to match the other molds in the outfit, so the completed porch will be symmetrical. Each outfit contains the following molds:

1 Combination Plain and Fluted Column Mold. | 1 Pier Body Mold. (State design wanted.)
1 Baluster Mold. | 1 Pier Cap Mold. (State design wanted.)
1 Baluster Pallet. | 1 Pier Base Mold.
1 Ornamental Capital Mold. (State design wanted.) | 1 Top Rail Mold. (State design wanted.)
1 Column Base Mold. | 1 Bottom Rail Mold.

See below for complete description of each mold.

NOTICE—When ordering BE SURE to give designs wanted.

No. 11B5830 Unique Porch Outfit complete for 10-inch column. Shipping weight, 632 pounds. Price..$54.95
No. 11B5831 Unique Porch Outfit complete for 12-inch column. Shipping weight, 760 pounds. Price..$63.25

Description and Price List of Separate Unique Porch Molds

Combination Plain and Fluted Column Molds

can be used for making plain or fluted columns, the flutes being obtained by means of separate strips, pallet and guide ring, as shown in illustration to the left. A stop off ring is also furnished for forming stop off of flutes in column base and cap. Be sure to order the size you want.

No. 11B5835 Combination Plain and Fluted Column Mold for 10-inch column. Height, 24 inches. Shipping weight, 150 pounds. Price..........$11.25
No. 11B5845 Combination Plain and Fluted Column Mold for 12-inch column. Height, 24 inches. Shipping weight, 155 pounds. Price.......... 13.40

Baluster Mold.

A very artistic bell shape design, exactly as shown in illustration above. Makes a baluster 3½ inches in diameter at bell and 17 inches high.
No. 11B5855 Baluster Mold. Shipping weight, 26 pounds. Price.......... $2.08

Baluster Pallet.

One pallet is needed for every baluster you make. A day's run is necessary to leave the baluster in the pallet, to preserve its shape until set.
No. 11B5857 Baluster Pallet. Shipping weight, 13 pounds. Price.......... $1.04

Ornamental Capital Molds.

We can furnish these in either the Gothic or Ionic design as shown in the illustrations. These designs are very artistic and make a beautiful cap. When used in connection with our column mold and by following the directions we furnish, you can make a handsome porch column with cap, so near like cut stone in appearance that it will take an expert to detect that it is of concrete. The design is deep and well formed, but is so shaped that the mold releases easily. The mold is in four parts, which are held together by a simple yet effective latch that is quickly released. Others ask from $25.00 to $35.00 for these molds. Be sure to tell us what design you want and order the right size.

No. 11B5836 Ornamental Capital Mold for 10-inch column. Shipping weight, 80 pounds. Price..........$ 8.62
No. 11B5846 Ornamental Capital Mold for 12-inch column. Shipping weight, 100 pounds. Price.......... 10.35

Pier Cap Molds,

for forming stone that is to top off or plain molding design or egg and dart design, as desired. Be sure to tell us which you want. The mold is 4¾ inches high and is made in four sections which lock together to make blocks that are perfectly true. The egg and dart ornamentations are well defined and this design makes a very handsome pier cap.

No. 11B5839 Pier Cap Mold for 10-inch column. Measures 4¾ inches high, 14 inches square at bottom and 17 inches square at top. Shipping weight, 60 pounds. Price..........$8.25
No. 11B5849 Pier Cap Mold for 12-inch column. Measures 4¾ inches high, 16 inches square at bottom and 19 inches square at top. Shipping weight, 75 pounds. Price.......... 9.45

O. G. Pier Base Molds.

Well fitted and used for making square base stones for porch and gate piers.
No. 11B5837 O. G. Pier Base Mold to match 10-inch column. Measures 5% inches high, 14 inches square at top and 17 inches square at bottom. Shipping weight, 70 pounds. Price..........$6.92
No. 11B5847 O. G. Pier Base Mold to match 12-inch column. Measures 5% inches high, 16 inches square at top and 19 inches square at bottom. Shipping weight, 95 pounds. Price.......... 8.30

Pier Body Molds,

made of all perfect castings in four parts which latch together solidly and squarely and make a perfectly shaped block. The mold opens up entirely so that it is easily released from the block. Can be furnished in any of the following designs: Rock, plain, panel, tooled, tooled edge rock, tooled edge bushhammer and cobblestone. Furnished complete with core. Be sure to order proper size and design wanted.

No. 11B5838 Pier Body Mold to match 10-inch column. Measures 7% inches high, 14 inches square. Be sure to state design wanted. Shipping weight, 65 pounds. Price..........$5.54
No. 11B5848 Pier Body Mold to match 12-inch column. Measures 7% inches high, 16 inches square. Be sure to state design wanted. Shipping weight, 85 pounds. Price.......... 6.22

O. G. Column Base Molds

form a round base stone in the popular O. G. pattern. Made so that the mold releases easily and without destroying the finish of the stone. Can also be used for making a cap stone on cheap work.

No. 11B5834 O. G. Column Base Mold for 10-inch column. Measures 5% inches high, 14 inches in diameter. Shipping weight, 40 pounds. Price..........$3.90
No. 11B5844 O. G. Column Base Mold for 12-inch column. Measures 5% inches high, 16 inches in diameter. Shipping weight, 60 pounds. Price.......... 5.18

Top Rail Mold.

This makes a perfect porch rail that can be used with either size column. Mold is fitted together accurately and released easily and leaves a perfect stone. Can be furnished in either egg and dart or plain design. Be sure to tell us which you want.

No. 11B5856 Top Rail Mold. Makes stone 4% inches high, 24 inches long, 5 inches high. Shipping weight, 70 pounds. Price..........$6.05

Bottom Rail Mold.

This mold forms a perfect bottom rail, one size being used for either 10 or 12-inch columns. With each mold is furnished a small square block for forming square blocks to raise the bottom rail from the floor of the porch to permit shedding of water. We also furnish the small square blocks or stop offs to make recesses in which to place the end of the baluster stones. Furnished in plain design only.

No. 11B5854 Bottom Rail Mold. Makes stone 5% inches high, 24 inches long, 5 inches wide. Shipping weight, 65 pounds. Price..........$5.22

NOTICE—When ordering any of the above please be sure to give us design and size wherever necessary. We cannot fill your order promptly if you don't do this. Please help us to be prompt by giving all of the necessary information.

No. 11B5839 Pier Cap—Egg and Dart.

No. 11B5839 Pier Cap—Plain.

No. 11B5838 Pier Body.

No. 11B5837 O. G. Pier Base.

No. 11B5856 Top Rail—Egg and Dart.

No. 11B5856 Top Rail—Plain.

No. 11B5854 Bottom Rail.

No. 11B5857 Baluster Pallet.

No. 11B5855 Baluster Mold.

No. 11B5836 Gothic.

No. 11B5836 Ionic.

Fluted Attachments.

No. 11B5835 Column.

No. 11B5834 O. G. Column Base.

$63.75 STARTS YOU IN

ASSURING YOU LARGER PROFITS THAN ON OUTFITS COSTING $200.00

Manufacturing Concrete Building Materials complete for general building purposes is now an established and profitable business in almost every section of the country. The outfits we show on these pages are complete in every detail. We furnish everything so that you can start right in this profitable business with but small outlay for equipment. Each outfit includes the necessary machinery and accessories for making concrete building blocks, window and door sills, window and door caps, steps, porch piers, porch columns, chimneys, etc. There is a good market for these lines and you can furnish all of the materials necessary for building an ordinary dwelling, barn or handsome residence. Our porch outfit, included in either equipment, enables you to make up a handsome line of porch materials, which can be used for remodeling old buildings, work of this kind commanding a good price and a bigger profit than ordinary building materials. The tools we furnish for laying the blocks enable an unskilled workman to do an expert job in less time and at less expense than an expert can do it.

Compare Our Outfits With Others and consider their value for the money we ask. Certainly you have never before been offered an outfit so complete for anything near our price. No dealer offers anything like it under twice our price. It includes everything you require to go into this profitable business—tools and all—so all you need to provide is sand, gravel and cement.

Get Into This Business and you are sure to make big money. When working for others have you ever stopped to consider your net earnings in wages at the end of a year? Let us do a little figuring. The average laborer who works ten hours a day and gets $1.50 earns $450.00 in 300 working days. The average mechanic earns $2.50 a day or $750.00 a year.

THE FOLLOWING TABLE SHOWS YOU THE DAILY EARNINGS in making each of the various kinds of concrete products with our $63.75 outfit. Each line of the table shows the output of one man per day in that particular product, but as you can work four or five men with our outfit, you can readily see that a day's profit is big. In the first item alone your profits are $8.00 a day, and this is making allowance for your labor at $2.00 per day, for that is figured in the cost. Your profits in that item alone for 300 working days would be $2,400.00; but making it $3,000.00 you will allow for cost of the various items—for example as follows: Take the first item in the table, 100 8x8x16-inch concrete blocks, made in the proportion of one part cement to five of sand and gravel, requires two barrels of cement at $2.00 a barrel, $4.00; 1½ yards of sand and gravel at 75 cents a cubic yard, $1.00; and allowing yourself $2.00 a day for labor, $2.00; total, $7.00. Divide this by 100 blocks and your cost is 7 cents per block. The cost of the other items in the table are figured on the same basis.

PRODUCT	Cost, each	Selling Price, each	Price, each	One Man's Daily Output	Total Daily Output
Block, 8x 8x16 inches.....	$0.07	$0.15	$0.08	100	$ 8.00
Block, 8x10x16 inches.....	.09	.20	.13	90	9.90
Block, 8x12x16 inches.....	.11	.24	.13	80	10.40
Porch Columns complete.....	2.40	7.00	4.30		23.00
Sill, 5x8 inches wide, 8 inches high, 5 feet long.....	.45	1.00	.55	20	11.00
Cap, 10 inches wide, 8 inches high, 5 feet long.....	.45	1.00	.55	20	11.00
Steps, 10 inches wide, 8 inches high, 5 feet long.....	.45	1.00	.55	20	11.00
Lintel, 10 inches wide, 8 inches high, 5 feet long.....	.45	1.00	.55	20	11.00
Water Table, 10 inches wide, 8 inches high, 5 feet long.....	.45	1.00	.55	20	11.00
Chimney Block.....	.13	.30	.17	30	5.10
Pier Block.....	.13	.30	.17	30	5.10

$63.75 Starts You in This Profitable Business with positive assurance of success. No matter what your present occupation is, whether mechanic, laborer, farmer, merchant or professional man, you can make good profits right from the start. It is not even necessary to take an active part in the business yourself. You can hire reliable and competent men, or if you have a son or dependable relative, you can give him the management of the business and you can attend to your regular work, merely overseeing the affairs of the concrete business.

We Guarantee Our Machines to be standard, durable and equal to every test to which a concrete machine should be subjected. You take no risk whatever, for if any of these machines fail to do the work thoroughly and perfectly, if you are not satisfied, you are at liberty to return it to us at our expense, and we will return both the price and the freight charges. We take all the risk. You cannot lose a penny.

The Illustrations at the right of the opposite page show the various products you can make with this outfit. Beginning at the top we note the various styles and sizes of blocks made on the Triumph Machine. Next, a column complete with its cap, fluted column and ring, column base and pier; also chimney blocks, water table and sill. These are examples of what you can make with our outfits.

We Furnish Free with each outfit or machine a book of instructions, describing the operation of our various machines, so that you will have no trouble in securing the best results from each. It is a book of general information, describing the various processes of mixing, proportioning, waterproofing, coloring and making of the various concrete building materials. It is valuable information to anyone in the concrete construction business.

Read What a Few of the Many Customers Say Who Used the Triumph Machine Furnished With This Outfit.

J. C. TWEEDLE, Delhi, N. Y. "The Triumph Block Machine I purchased from you is O. K. I have operated machines that cost $200.00 and they made no better blocks than this one. Am very much pleased with the Triumph."

CHAS. W. LASHER, Montague, Mich. "The Triumph is the best machine on the market regardless of price. I am perfectly satisfied with it and I know you will get more orders from this neighborhood."

FRANK BLEYTING, Downing, Mo. "The Triumph Block Machine I purchased from you is strong, durable and easy to operate and very rapid. I can turn out 200 blocks in ten hours. I have run thirty-one in a single hour. Saved about $30.00 in my purchase. I stand ready to recommend every time."

ABOUT FACE PLATES FURNISHED WITH MACHINES IN OUTFIT OR WITH MACHINES WHEN ORDERED SEPARATELY.

Unless otherwise specified we furnish the rock face design plate on the Triumph Machine and the plain face plate on the Badger Adjustable Sill and Cap Machine. If you want a different face plate with any of these machines when ordered in the complete outfit we will send any of the following in place of the one regularly furnished, as above stated; and if you want additional face plates we furnish them as extras at prices quoted on opposite page. The following designs of face plates and return doors to match can be furnished for the Triumph Concrete Block Machine: Panel face, plain face, broken ashlar, rock face of two designs, tooled face, cobblestone face, scroll face designs. See page for illustrations of designs. We can furnish the following rock face design plates for the Badger Adjustable Sill and Cap Machine: Rock face, tooled face, tooled margin bushhammer face and panel face. Price, each....$5.18

No. 11B5810
Badger Adjustable Sill and Cap Machine.

No. 11B5759
Flask Attachment for 8x12x16-Inch Blocks, Double Core.

No. 11B5758
Flask Attachment for 8x10x16-Inch Blocks, Double Core.

No. 11B5759
Flask Attachment for 8x12x16-Inch Blocks, Single Core.

No. 11B5758
Flask Attachment for 8x10x16-Inch Blocks, Single Core.

No. 11B5720
Triumph Block Machine, Double Core.

No. 11B5720
Triumph Block Machine, Single Core.

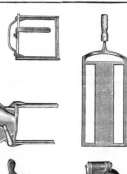

No. 11B5750
Pier and Chimney Mold.

No. 11B5770
Fluted Column Mold.

No. 11B5773
Column Ring Mold.

No. 11B5834
Column Cap and Base Mold.

No. 11B5775
Concrete Block Laying Tools.

No. 11B5811 Extra Face Plates for Sill and Cap Machine. Price, each....$5.18

YOU RUN NO RISK

We Guarantee Perfect Satisfaction or your money returned. We guarantee the material and workmanship of our machinery and we agree to protect you against any claims of infringement of patents. Our concrete machinery is as good or better than you can buy from any concern, although our prices are only about one-half what others are asking. Send us your order for any machinery you want, and if after receiving it you do not feel that you are perfectly satisfied and have saved a great deal by placing your order with us, simply write us where to ship the machinery and will return your money, including the freight charges you paid.

BUSINESS MAKING CONCRETE BUILDING MATERIALS

PRICE FOR COMPLETE OUTFIT $63.75

SEARS, ROEBUCK AND CO, CHICAGO, ILLINOIS.

TO $300.00 ELSEWHERE. WE GUARANTEE EVERY OUTFIT.

No. 11B5790 Complete Outfit as described below, shipped from factory in Central Ohio. Shipping weight, about 800 pounds.
Price............

State whether single or double core is wanted; if not otherwise specified with your order we ship single core block machines and flask attachments.

THIS OUTFIT INCLUDES THE DIFFERENT MACHINES AND ATTACHMENTS LISTED BELOW. WE WILL SELL SEPARATE ITEMS AT PRICES SHOWN

PRODUCTS OF OUR $63.75 OUTFIT.

8x10x16-Inch Block. — 8x8x16-Inch Block. — 8x12x16-Inch Block. — Half and Quarter Blocks. — Joist and Gable Blocks can be made in three sizes. — A Pretty Column. — Porch Pier or Chimney. — Cap, Sill and Water Table Stones.

The attachments and accessories we furnish with this outfit.

No. 11B5720 The Improved Triumph Block Machine, either single or double core, as you choose, furnished with a flask to make 8x8x16-inch blocks. This is the same machine we have sold for several years, but it has been strengthened and improved, making it better than ever before. Makes blocks face down. The equal of block machines sold by others at from $75.00 to $100.00. We have hundreds of letters from customers reporting that they have made from 100 to 150 perfect blocks a day on this machine. Please understand we do not give you both the single and double core machines. We give you but one of these machines with the outfit and you must tell us whether you want the single or double core style; fitted with standard rock face plate for whole blocks. Shipping weight, 170 pounds.
Price, when ordered separate from outfit............$16.95

No. 11B5758 Triumph Flask Attachment for making blocks 8x8x16 inches. Consists of necessary parts to attach to an improved Triumph Block Machine of any size to make blocks 8x10x16-inch blocks. You can have this flask attachment either in the single core or double core style. We don't give you both with the outfit. In ordering the outfit be sure to state whether you want this flask attachment in the single core or double core style. Shipping weight, 60 pounds.
Price, when ordered separate from outfit............$4.00

No. 11B5759 Triumph Flask Attachment to make 8x12x16-inch concrete blocks. Consists of necessary parts to attach to change an Improved Triumph Block Machine of any size to make blocks 8x12x16 inches. In ordering the outfit be sure to state whether you want this flask attachment in the single core or double core style. Shipping weight, 70 pounds.
Price, when ordered separate from outfit............$4.90

No. 11B5810 The Badger Adjustable Sill and Cap Machine, known the country over as the simplest and most efficient ever produced. We have sold hundreds and every one has proved satisfactory. Made entirely of iron and steel. Makes a sill or cap 2 feet to 5 feet in length, 10 inches to 14 inches in width and 3¾ inches high. Is adjusted with ease and does not require any pallets. No sills made on the floor, machine being easily taken from the block. Shipping weight, 180 pounds.
Price, when ordered separate from outfit............$12.95

No. 11B5770 Triumph Column Mold, 10-inch. Made with a plain and defined impression. Makes column sections 10 inches in diameter and 12 inches high. Is released from block in four sections, each part giving a true and perfect impression. Equal to column molds others sell at from $10.00 to $15.00. We furnish fluted design in the outfit but can furnish plain if desired. State which you want. Shipping weight, 45 pounds.
Price, when ordered separate from outfit............$4.10

No. 11B5769 Triumph Pier and Chimney Molds. 16 inches square, 7¾ inches high with 8x8-inch core. A popular size and one that should sell for $10.00. Rock design furnished with the outfit. Can furnish plain or brick design. State which you want. Shipping weight, 90 pounds.
Price, when ordered separate from outfit............$6.20

No. 11B5834 Unique O. G. Column Cap and Base Mold for 10-inch column, similar to the one in our famous Unique Column Pier and Base Mold Outfit on page 153. Makes a beautiful cap and base; a fitting ornament for most any style of column. Shipping weight, 40 pounds.
Price, when ordered separate from outfit............$3.90

No. 11B5773 Triumph Column Ring Mold for 10-inch column. Made entirely of iron. Makes a perfect concrete ring, used for intersecting the fluted columns. (See illustration showing complete column on this page.) Shipping weight, 20 pounds.
Price, when ordered separate from outfit............$2.40

No. 11B5680 Our Wizard Concrete Block Laying Tools. The latest invention and best tools for laying concrete building blocks perfectly. Any inexperienced person who has never laid a block can make just as true and perfect a wall with these tools as the most skilled mason. You will find these of great value. Constructed entirely of metal, and machined to size, so there is no chance to lay blocks wrong. Such tools could not be purchased elsewhere under $15.00 a set. We furnish set for 8x8x16-inch blocks. Shipping weight, 25 pounds.
Price, when ordered separate from outfit............$8.95

ATTACHMENTS AND ACCESSORIES. These are furnished with the various machines and molds and consist of face plates for making half and quarter blocks for the Triumph Block Machine, rock face return end corners, gable plates, gable block plates and wall plugs for 8x8x16, 8x10x16 and 8x12x16-inch blocks. We also furnish joist block attachments and double end tamper.

EXTRAS.

No. 11B5730 Triumph Concrete Block Machine with outfit, to make block 8x10x16 inches. Shipping weight, 200 pounds. Price............$20.85
No. 11B5740 Triumph Concrete Block Machine with outfit, to make block 8x12x16 inches. Shipping weight, 225 pounds. Price............$24.75
Extra Face Plates for whole block, will fit any size. Weight, 12 pounds. Price............$1.37
No. 11B5721 Face Plate for whole block. State design wanted. Weight, 12 pounds. Price............$1.45
No. 11B5722 Face Plate for half and two quarter blocks. State design wanted. Weight, 12 pounds. Price............
No. 11B5728 Circle Face Plate for 4-Inch Course Block.

	For 8x8x16-Inch Machine			For 8x10x16-Inch Machine			For 8x12x16-Inch Machine		
SPECIAL ATTACHMENTS	Catalog No.	Weight, pounds	Price, each	Catalog No.	Weight, pounds	Price, each	Catalog No.	Weight, pounds	Price, each
Return End Door, right or left	11B5733	6	$0.75	11B5733	8	$0.95	11B5743	8	$1.20
Bay Window Attachment	11B5734	30	2.90	11B5736	35	3.95	11B5744	40	3.95
Four-Inch Course Block Attachment	11B5726	40	4.23	11B5737	45	6.27	11B5747	50	7.55
Dividing Pallets for 4-Inch Course Block	11B5727	6							

NOTICE: When ordering face plates, bay window and 4-inch course block attachments, state what design is wanted; radius and what design is wanted; and when ordering return end doors, state whether plain or rock design is wanted. All Triumph face plates are interchangeable with the different sizes of Triumph machines.

All these goods are shipped from factory in Central Ohio.

OUR WIZARD OUTFIT OF CONCRETE MACHINERY $79.95
No. 11B5795 Wizard Outfit of Machinery. Complete as described below. Shipping weight, 1010 pounds.
Price............

We furnish you with the outfit described above, but with our 8x8x16-inch Wizard Block Machine and twenty-five pallets, Catalog No. 11B5601 place of the Triumph Block Machine for $79.95. This gives you an outfit which will enable you to increase your output about 50 per cent over what you can do on the Triumph Machine. The Wizard Block Machine is fully described on page 156 and is a much faster machine than the Triumph in every way. We strongly advise you to buy this outfit, as the majority of our customers buy the Wizard Machine and you can do much faster work on it. This of course means more money for you as you can turn out the same number of blocks in less time. The porch outfit and block laying tools furnished with the Wizard outfit are exactly the same as furnished with the Triumph outfit. The Wizard outfit should have at least 100 pallets to start with, which will give you a capacity of 100 blocks per day. We can furnish extra pallets, Catalog No. 11B5537, at 24 cents each or $24.00 per 100. If you want to make differ-

ent sizes of blocks we can furnish you with additional flask attachments. Write for special catalog of Concrete Block Machinery.

EXTRAS. We can furnish a full line of extras, such as face plates, bay window attachments, corner posts, block attachments, etc., as shown on page 157. Should you want any of these with the outfit, be sure to give us catalog number, design, size and price.

CHANGES. Should you desire an outfit for making sizes other than 8x8x16-inch, simply add the difference in cost between the two machines, as shown on page 156, to the cost of the change desired. Remember that this outfit with the Wizard Machine includes two designs of face plates, rock and plain, together with the complete equipment, just as described on page 157.

$42.50 WIZARD FACE DOWN CONCRETE BLOCK MACHINE

THE ONLY AUTOMATIC ELLIPTICAL CORE BLOCK MACHINE MADE.
— WILL DOUBLE YOUR OUTPUT AND PROFITS. —

FULLY GUARANTEED AND SHIPPED ON 30 DAYS' TRIAL. Send us your order, enclose our price, and we will ship the machine with the understanding that you can try it thirty days and if not satisfactory return it to us and we will return your money and freight charges.

No. 11B5501
8X8X16 INCHES COMPLETE WITH BIG OUTFIT.

125 BLOCKS A DAY FOR ONE MAN.
250 BLOCKS A DAY FOR TWO MEN.
$10.00 A DAY PROFIT FOR ONE MAN.
$20.00 A DAY PROFIT FOR TWO MEN.

QUALITY GUARANTEED

THE LARGE ILLUSTRATION on this page shows our Wizard Face Down Concrete Block Machine with the cores withdrawn from the mold box ready to receive the face mixture, which should be placed in the flask box by stepping on the floor lever and then the flask is filled with the coarser mixture.

THE PROCESS OF MAKING CONCRETE BLOCKS on this machine is shown by the five small illustrations below and you will note by observing the same that the operator is tamping the material in the first illustration, this tamping being all done without refilling the flask. In the following illustrations you will note that the complete process of releasing the block, and you will note here that the complete process is done with the action of the levers and requires only three separate and distinct acts. First.—In turning the flask over, thereby placing the block on its pallet. Second.—By releasing the end doors, the end doors swing away from the machine. Third—By grasping the handles in the pallet, this feature being known to our machine only, as other machines require a carrying device when lifting the block away from the machine.

THE CONSTRUCTION of the Wizard is mechanically perfect. The best quality of iron and fitted together in such a form that all work smoothly and accurately, giving the operator perfect dimensions, corners and impressions for every block that he makes.

THE STAND is heavy, well supported with ribs and braces, making it rigid, so that it does not twist, shift or sag when making a block.

THE FLASK is made on the face down principle and all parts of the flask swing from perfect centers, so that the mold will open with ease. Not only that, the perfect shape when closed and open will interfere with the block when releasing and cause any damage.

THE CORES are two in number on the 16-inch length; three on the 24-inch length. They are elliptical in shape and are proportioned so as to give a ratio of 33⅓ per cent air space to 66⅔ per cent. bearing area, thus being the standard requirements of the core.

THE LEVERS are attached to the flask in such a way that they work all parts that require shifting.

THE AUTOMATIC CORE EXTRACTOR is attached to the cores and frame, so that when tilting the machine to relieve the block the cores are withdrawn automatically and do not require separate handling.

THE SHELF can be placed on either side of the machine, making it convenient to place the tools not in use when operating the machine.

THE PALLET is constructed of iron, very light and well made, with holes for the cores to pass through, and handles so that the block can be lifted away from the machine without a carrying device. We furnish twenty-five of these pallets with each machine, but it is necessary for the operator to have as many pallets as he will make blocks per day.

THE WIZARD IS A BIG PROFIT MAKER.

It is a machine that is setting a pace for all others in that it makes more blocks per day for each man, and better blocks.

FEW OPERATIONS AND EVERY OPERATION AUTOMATIC, ALL DONE SIMPLY BY THE DIFFERENT MOVEMENTS OF THE LEVER.

FIRST OPERATION. Tamping the Material, Face Down.

SECOND OPERATION. Turning Flask.

THIRD OPERATION. Spreading End Doors.

FOURTH OPERATION. Releasing Block.

FIFTH OPERATION. Lifting Out Block.

Building ordinances generally approve the 8x9x16-inch blocks made on our No. 11B5502, listed below.
We recommend No. 11B5502, listed below, as the most popular size. It makes a block 8x9x16 inches.

PRICES OF WIZARD MACHINES

No. 11B5501 Wizard Machine complete, with outfit to make 8x8x16-inch blocks. Shipping weight, 610 pounds. Price......**$42.50**

No. 11B5502 Wizard Machine complete, with outfit to make 8x9x16-inch blocks. Shipping weight, 635 pounds. Price......**$47.50**

No. 11B5503 Wizard Machine complete, with outfit to make 8x10x16-inch blocks. Shipping weight, 700 pounds. Price......**$52.50**

No. 11B5504 Wizard Machine complete, with outfit to make 8x12x16-inch blocks. Shipping weight, 875 pounds. Price......**$57.50**

THE ILLUSTRATION TO THE RIGHT

shows the complete outfit furnished with each Wizard Machine, which consists of face plates and attachments for making the five styles of blocks shown to the left of this page.

THE OUTFIT CONSISTS OF THE FOLLOWING:

1 Set of Face Plates and End Doors for making whole, half and quarter standard plain face blocks.
1 Set of Face Plates and End Doors for making whole, half and quarter standard rock face blocks.
1 Pair of Dividing Plates for making plain ends on half and quarter blocks.
1 Pair of Dividing Plates for making gable blocks.
1 Pair of Core End Doors.

1 Face Plate for making inside corners.
25 Cast Iron Pallets.
1 Set of Joist Block Attachments.
1 Dividing Plate for making a block.
1 Steel Striker.
1 Double End Tamper.
2 Wall Plugs.
1 Iron Hopper.
2 Pallet Plugs.

THIS OUTFIT CONTAINS only such parts as are absolutely necessary for making five standard styles of concrete blocks in plain and rock face designs. Should you desire any of the special styles of blocks, we illustrate such special designs the various designs and special attachments below on this page. The reason we do not include the various designs and special attachments with this outfit is because a person in buying a block machine does not always require a variety of designs of plates and special attachments for making bay windows, 4-inch course blocks and circle blocks. In order not to burden the average purchaser with a big lot of unnecessary parts we furnish only such parts as are absolutely necessary for the making of a standard block, and should you require a special design or style of block, such as illustrated below, you can order the same together with your machine and outfit or at any other time. Be sure to state the design of face plate when ordering face plates, 4-inch course blocks, bay window attachments, and the design of face plate and radius when ordering a circle block plate, and be sure to allow our catalog price for each design or attachment when ordering.

THE ILLUSTRATIONS BELOW show the various special designs of face plates and end doors that we can furnish with either the Wizard or Triumph Block Machine.

IF DESIRED we can also furnish the plain face, rock face, panel face, tool face, machine tool face for bay window attachment, and we can furnish plain face and rock face designs for the circle block plate.

THE ILLUSTRATIONS ABOVE

show the face plates and extra attachments that we furnish with each size of Wizard Concrete Block Machine.

For price list of face plates and extras for Triumph Machine, see page 155.

Four-Inch Course Block.

Tool Marginal Bushhammer Face.

Whirlwind Scroll Face.

WHEN ORDERING END DOORS it is advisable to order both right hand and left hand end doors. Should you not desire both end doors, be sure to state what design is wanted, and whether left or right hand end door is wanted.

ALL OUR FACE PLATES are of the latest design and pattern. We are continually changing these designs so as to keep abreast with the times. Our rock face designs are taken by impressions from the natural stone, and other ornamental designs as illustrated above are made by expert stone cutters, and the impression is taken from their design. We aim to keep a full line of face plate designs on hand at all times, and it may possess, you can readily fit any style of designs to either the Wizard or the Triumph Block Machine. Prices on the above designs of face plates and end doors are given in the list to the left. Be sure, when ordering in addition to those regularly furnished with the outfit, that you allow our full catalog price for each.

Rock Face Whole Block.

Rock Face Fractional Block.

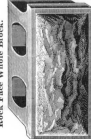

Rock Face Joist Block.

Rock Face Inside Corner Block.

THESE FIVE ILLUSTRATIONS

show the five different styles of blocks that can be made with the regular Wizard Machine and Outfit. The Wizard outfit contains face plates to make these five different style blocks in the rock face design as illustrated, also in the plain face design.

Rock Face Gable Block.

Medium Rock Face.

Broken Ashlar. Style A.

Broken Ashlar. Style B.

Tool Marginal Rock Face.

Plain Face.

Panel Face.

Machine Tool Face.

Cobblestone Face.

Rope Face.

ADDITIONAL DESIGNS FOR THE WIZARD OR TRIUMPH

WHICH YOU MAY ORDER AS EXTRAS.

EXTRAS FOR THE DIFFERENT SIZES OF THE WIZARD MACHINE AS QUOTED ON PRECEDING PAGE

No. 11B5521 16-Inch Face Plate of any design shown above. State design wanted. Weight, 17 lbs. Price......$1.72
No. 11B5522 16-Inch Face Plate of any design shown above. State design wanted. Weight, 17 lbs. Price......1.74
No. 11B5523 Circle Block. Face plate for circle blocks rock or plain design. Weight, 17 lbs. Price......1.75

SPECIAL ATTACHMENTS	For 8x8x16-Inch Machine			For 8x9x16-Inch Machine			For 8x10x16-Inch Machine			For 8x11x16-Inch Machine			For 8x12x16-Inch Machine		
	Catalog No.	Weight	Price	Catalog No.	Weight	Price	Catalog No.	Weight	Price	Catalog No.	Weight	Price	Catalog No.	Weight	Price
Right Hand End Door	11B5531	7 lbs.	$1.24	11B5541	9 lbs.	$1.32	11B5551	11 lbs.	$1.40				11B5561	16 lbs.	$1.48
Left Hand End Door	11B5532	7 lbs.	1.25	11B5542	9 lbs.	1.34	11B5552	11 lbs.	1.34				11B5562	16 lbs.	1.50
Bay Window Attachment	11B5533	26 lbs.	4.25	11B5543	30 lbs.	4.40	11B5553	30 lbs.	4.55				11B5563	32 lbs.	4.50
Four-Inch Course Block Attachment	11B5535	62 lbs.	6.65	11B5545	62 lbs.	6.80	11B5555	62 lbs.	6.95				11B5565	62 lbs.	7.10
Dividing Pallet for 4-Inch Course Block	11B5536	7 lbs.	.36	11B5546	8 lbs.	.29	11B5556	8 lbs.	.34				11B5566	11 lbs.	.40
Extra Cast Iron Pallets	11B5537	7 lbs.	.24	11B5547	9 lbs.	.27	11B5557	10 lbs.	.32				11B5567	11 lbs.	.38

NOTICE. WHEN ORDERING FACE PLATES, BAY WINDOW AND 4-INCH COURSE BLOCK ATTACHMENTS BE SURE TO STATE DESIGN WANTED, AND WHEN ORDERING CIRCLE BLOCK PLATE STATE RADIUS AND DESIGN WANTED. FACE PLATES ARE INTERCHANGEABLE; THAT IS, ANY 16-IN. WIZARD FACE PLATE CAN BE USED WITH ANY 16-IN. WIZARD MACHINE.

ONE=MINUTE CONCRETE BATCH MIXER

$24⁹⁵

Has Proven Under the Severest Tests

to be the most thorough and most rapid hand power mixer ever made. Batches of concrete have been mixed with the One-Minute Mixer in less than one minute's time, and the result has been perfect. We will send you one of our One-Minute Mixers on your order and permit you to test and compare it with other mixers for a period of thirty days. Should you find that it does not prove satisfactory and that it does not comply with our representation, we will ask you to return it to our factory at our expense and we will cheerfully return your money, together with transportation charges you paid on it.

The Construction of our One-Minute Hand Power Mixer is **the best that labor and material can produce. The receptacle** is made entirely of iron, built to form a triangle shape drum with rounded corners. **The drum heads** are of cast iron; the left hand drum head has a cold rolled steel journal, chilled to the center, which runs in a solid box on the stand; the gear is also fastened to this journal. The right hand drum head has a perforated cast journal to permit a water pipe to pass through. The pipe runs directly across the center of the drum and enters a bearing on the opposite head. The water pipe is perforated at the bottom for the purpose of permitting the flow of water to distribute evenly throughout the batch when the drum is in action. **The shelf** is made of 14-gauge cold rolled iron and is riveted to the flanges on the base of each angle. Inside the drum, running across the center of the base of each angle, is a 1-inch angle iron that carries the mixture to an elevated position. **The cover** is hinged directly to the drum and is locked with three separate latches. **The water tank** is connected with a ½-inch pipe and stands on a bracket connected to the frame. A ½-inch globe valve regulates the flow of water. **The power** is produced by two small gears and four to one dimension. **The crank** is attached to the small gear and has a sweep of 30 inches. The gears permit easy power and fifteen revolutions of the drum per minute. **The frame** is made of 3x3-inch wood timbers, well fitted and bolted with long rods. Under the drum is a hopper sufficiently large to hold two batches of 3 cubic feet each. The mixer is painted two coats, the iron is black, the wood is red.

The Mixing is made complete in one minute or fifteen revolutions of the drum. The perfect mixing of the materials is secured by elevating them to a position where they will fall and strike the angle irons on the side of the drum. The mixer can be reversed or run in either direction at the will of the operator. In discharging the batch the door is opened and the drum revolves slowly. The drum can be loaded from either side. One man can easily operate this mixer and supply two or three block machines. Slush concrete can be mixed as well as dry concrete, and this mixer has been proven indispensable among gutter and sidewalk builders. If you consider the construction and efficiency of this mixer and compare it in price with others, you will find that we are saving you over one-half and at the same time giving you a mixer second to none.

SPECIFICATIONS—Length of drum, 30 inches; circumference, 72 inches; diameter, 23 inches; height over all, 4 feet 4 inches; length over all, 4 feet 2 inches; capacity, 3 to 4 cubic feet. Shipped from Central Wisconsin.

No. 11B5760. One-Minute Hand Power Concrete Batch Mixer. Shipping weight, 275 pounds. Price..$24.95

WIZARD CEMENT TILE MACHINE

After Many Months of Careful Experimenting and Testing

our concrete machinery factory has perfected a hand tile machine that will make perfect concrete tile faster than any other hand tile machine now on the market. This new machine is so fast that two of them, representing an investment of $83.00, with a crew of five men, will turn out as many tile as some power outfits costing from $1,200.00 to $1,500.00 operated by a crew of seven men.

The Biggest Money Maker of All. **Concrete tile is superseding clay tile all over the country.** It has been proved beyond all doubt that concrete tile is far superior to clay tile in every respect. Concrete tile can be made and sold at a much lower price than clay tile, but at the same time the profits in its sale are much larger. Better order one of these machines at once and be the first in the field.

A Simple Quick Acting Machine. The illustration shows the position of the machine when ready to make a tile. The machine is exceedingly simple and is entirely free from all complicated parts, so there is absolutely nothing about it to get out of order. The stand is made up of heavy castings securely fastened together. The best grade gray iron castings and cold rolled steel are used in the construction of the machine, giving it great strength. All parts are made interchangeable and can be replaced very easily if broken through accident. Any defective part will be replaced free of charge.

Capacity. **The daily capacity of our Wizard Tile Machine is much greater than any other hand tile machine on the market.** Two men and a boy can turn out from 900 to 1,100 perfect tile per day. Where a concrete mixer is used and racks for convenient handling of tile are built, this capacity can be increased. There is no need for you to invest $1,500.00 to $2,000.00 in a power machine and engine to turn out a large quantity of tile. Buy two of our Wizards and a concrete mixer and with four or five men and two boys you will have a plant capable of turning out on an average of 1,800 to 2,000 tile per day. You can make 4-inch concrete tile for less than 2 cents each and can easily sell them at from 6 to 8 cents each. Think of the big profit you make. You are losing money every day you are without this machine.

COST OF TILE ON THE WIZARD TILE MACHINE.

Two barrels of cement and 2 cubic yards of sand will make about 650 perfect 4-inch tile. This is a good strong tile made up of a mixture, one part cement to three and one-half parts sand. Figure cement at $2.00 a barrel, sand at 75 cents a cubic yard and labor $2.00 a 10-hour day.

Cement (2 barrels at $2.00)................................	$4.00
Sand (2 cubic yards at 75 cents)........................	1.50
One man (8 hours each at 20 cents an hour)......	3.20
One boy (8 hours at 10 cents an hour)...............	.80
Total	$9.50

Your 650 Tile Will Cost You $9.50

Farmers Make Your Own Tile On One Of Our Wizard Tile Machines and supply your neighbors. You can make tile in your spare time, and as they are made very rapidly you will be able to make more than enough for your own needs and can supply your neighbors, furnishing them with a first class tile at less than they would have to pay for inferior clay tiles. In a short time you will be able to make the machine pay for itself. After that all the tile you sell will be profit over and above what the material costs you and this does no amount to very much.

Concrete Tile Are By Far Better Than Clay Tile. **Don't let anyone tell you that concrete tile are not superior to clay tile.** It has been brought to our attention that a number of dealers in clay tile have been making statements that concrete tile were not lasting and would have to be replaced much sooner than clay tile. This is not so and the fact that all cities and towns are commencing to use concrete pipe in preference to clay or iron pipe for sewerage purposes is sufficient evidence that there is nothing better than concrete tile. When you put a clay drain tile in the ground you have no assurance that it is going to last. It may last a season or two or it may last a little longer, but there is no telling when it will give out and then you have the expense of retiling the ground all over again. When you put a concrete tile in the ground it gets stronger with age and at the end of three years it is much stronger than it was when first put in. Concrete tile is everlasting and there is no better or cheaper material for making drain tile. Concrete tile are not injured by freezing, where clay tile when subjected to frost will either crack or break and be worthless. We might go on and tire you out by telling you all the advantages concrete tile have over clay tile, but it has been proven so many times by various authorities that we feel it is unnecessary. You can take our word for it, "there are no better tile than concrete tile."

Construction. **Our Wizard Tile Machine is made throughout of the best quality gray iron castings and steel shafting.** When closed the cast iron jacket is securely held in position with core perfectly centered and no amount of tamping or jarring will displace it. A movement of the lever on the retaining hopper shears off the top of the tile ready for releasing. The side lever is then brought forward, which strips the tile from the core and the tile is carried away in the jacket. The other jacket is immediately placed in the machine ready for making another tile. Two jackets are furnished with each machine, so that one man can be kept busy at the machine while another carries away the finished tile in the jackets. The tile are released from the jacket immediately after making. Four measures are furnished with each machine. The measures are just the right size to contain enough material for one tile. This is without a doubt the best tile machine that has ever been placed on the market and you are bound to meet with success with it. No repair expense and no engine is required, but still you have almost the capacity of a power plant. If you are not perfectly satisfied we will take the machine back and return your money, together with freight charges, so that you run absolutely no risk in placing your order. Shipping weight, 275 pounds. Price....................$41.50

No. 11B5870 Four-Inch Tile Machine. Shipped from factory in Central Ohio.

OUR GUARANTEE OF QUALITY

READ IT. IT PROTECTS YOU AGAINST INFERIOR QUALITY AND GUARANTEES YOU A BIG SAVING. YOU TAKE NO RISK.

If our mill work and building material, including sash, doors, blinds, moldings, stairwork, etc., are not found better in quality and lower in price than the same standard grades can be bought for in your city, even after paying freight charges, send them back at our expense and we will return your money and pay freight charges both ways.

——We Cordially Invite You to Inspect Our Sample Room at Our Chicago Store——

JUST ONE LOOK WILL TELL YOU THAT OUR STANDARD OF QUALITY IS FAR ABOVE THE GRADES SUPPLIED BY THE RETAIL DEALER

The Illustration Below is Reproduced From an Actual Photograph of One of the Sample Showrooms in Our Chicago Store.

ON ACCOUNT OF OUR PRICES BEING SO VERY LOW, in many instances lower than the average dealer is obliged to pay at wholesale, the retail dealers or lumber yards men offer as an argument in their own defense that Sears, Roebuck and Co. furnish goods in lower quality than they (the retail dealers) furnish. Such a statement, no matter by whom it is made, is absolutely false, and as a protection to anyone who buys from us **we make the above broad and liberal guarantee, backed by our entire institution.**

IF IN DOUBT ABOUT THE QUALITY OF OUR GOODS, or if you would become better satisfied by seeing our line of **Doors, Windows, Stairwork, Moldings, Mantels, Furnaces, Hardware, Plumbing Goods, Heating Plants, Paints and other Building Material** before giving us your order, we cordially invite you to inspect our complete line of Building Material which is displayed in our Chicago showrooms. You will save your railroad fare and a great many dollars besides. We will be glad to give you any expert advice which would enable you to construct a better building and at the same time lower its cost. In our showrooms we carry our entire line, which is composed of goods taken from our regular stock. Every item we sell you we guarantee to be equal to or better than the goods shown in our showrooms. If you intend to build, or if you are a carpenter or contractor and have not seen or used any of our goods within the past six months, you have no idea of the great improvement we have made in our line and how much we have bettered its quality.

YOU CAN FIGURE YOUR RAILROAD FARE TO CHICAGO WILL COST YOU NOTHING when buying from us. We save you on an average bill of mill work not only $5.00 to $16.00 (the amount some concerns may allow you for railroad fare), but we make you a big saving besides, perhaps $50.00 or more on a **$100.00 bill of materials.** Some concerns, in order to get business, may offer to pay your railroad fare from points within 50 to 150 miles from Chicago, on condition that you give them a carload order. Railroad fare costs money and, you may be sure, must be added to the cost of your material. Since we name you the lowest factory cost for the finest grade of mill work, you get the lowest prices and the cost of railroad fare goes into your pocket, not the railroads. Hundreds of persons who have come to Chicago at "some dealer's expense" incidentally called on us and to their surprise found that by buying their supplies from us they not only saved their railroad fare many times over, but were convinced beyond a doubt that the quality of goods we furnished was so far superior to the goods shown by dealers who pay prospective customers' railroad fare, that we got their entire order, saved them from 25 to 50 per cent, saved them their railroad fare by quoting the lowest factory prices and gave them materials—doors, windows, moldings, etc., in a fine quality which could not be duplicated elsewhere.

PLEASE UNDERSTAND IT IS NOT NECESSARY TO COME TO CHICAGO TO SELECT YOUR MATERIAL. Nine hundred and ninety-nine customers out of every thousand make up their orders from the illustrations and descriptions shown in this special catalog and always find that the goods come up to their expectations in every way. We guarantee that every item illustrated and described in our Special Home Builders' Catalog will be exactly as represented and that the prices printed in this extra Builders' Catalog are from 10 to 50 per cent lower than any other catalog house in America, and that the prices named are the same low prices printed in our regular Home Builders' Catalog on orders amounting to $5,000.00 or more. In order to make it possible for us to furnish the goods of such quality, however, if you are going to place a large order of mill work and other building material and do not feel perfectly at ease in sending us your order without first inspecting our goods, we by all means recommend that, rather than place your order elsewhere at exorbitant prices, you come to Chicago and see our line, as we guarantee that the saving we will make you will repay you many times the amount you will pay out for railroad fare.

COMPLETE ORDERS SHIPPED THE SAME DAY AS RECEIVED

IN NEARLY EVERY INSTANCE

THE PROMPTNESS WITH WHICH WE COMPLETELY FILL AND SHIP OUR ORDERS amazes the average contractor and builder. (Read but one of the thousands of letters testifying to our prompt and satisfactory service printed below.) We fill the average house bill of mill work, including windows, doors, moldings, etc., within ten working hours after it has been entered at the factory. Such service is really phenomenal, especially when you consider that it has been the practice of the average mill to demand from thirty to sixty days.

IN ORDER TO SHIP SO PROMPTLY we have been obliged to manufacture and place in our five enormous warehouses over $500,000.00 worth of manufactured stock. We have at our command the best shipping organization of its kind in the United States for prompt handling of mill work orders, making a combination that cannot be beat.

JUST THINK OF IT: $500,000.00 worth of stock in readiness to ship on a minute's notice. We give you better service than anyone else.

ALL OUR MILL WORK IS VERY CAREFULLY PACKED. To the left we illustrate a bundle of glazed sash and a crate of balusters simply to show how carefully we pack and crate our material. All exposed parts are carefully protected and the glass is also carefully protected by sound ½-inch lumber. We do not use No. 4 or No. 5 boards that are full of worm holes and dry rot, such as the average manufacturer and wholesale dealer uses, but we buy a special grade of white pine and gumwood lumber that is sound and strong and which will stand the roughest handling while in transit.

A TOUGH GRADE OF PAPER IS USED to cover our doors, balusters, newels, etc., to protect them from dust and dirt. The material you will receive from us will be spotless and much easier to work than other sources. The amount you will save on labor by using our goods will more than repay you your freight charges.

Shipping Department No. 3.   Especially equipped for handling less than carload orders.   Capacity, ten carloads per day.

The above illustrations show the careful manner and the excellent material that is used for packing all our mill work.

Shipping Department No. 1.   Especially equipped for handling carload orders.   Capacity, twenty carloads per day.

THERE IS NO ORDER TOO LARGE, there is no order too small for us to handle. We are equipped for handling orders amounting to from $500.00 to $10,000.00 just as promptly as orders amounting to from $5.00 to $10.00. In order to maintain the excellent service in the way of prompt shipment we are now giving our customers we have been obliged to divide our shipping department into two separate departments: No. 1, known as the carload shipping department, is especially equipped for handling big orders which amount to from $500.00 to $10,000.00, or more. No. 2, our less than carload lot department, is especially equipped for prompt handling of orders amounting to from $500.00 down to the smallest kind of an order.

WE USE A PLAIN SHIPPING TAG on all our crates and bundles, which makes it impossible for anyone to tell by whom the goods were shipped. Contractors or carpenters who buy our goods to sell at a profit to themselves need have no fear that their customers will know where the goods come from; but we guarantee that they will be more than surprised at the excellent quality of the material, which we guarantee to far excel that of the average retail dealer.

SIMPLEX PORTABLE OR "READY MADE" HOUSES AND GARAGES

SPECIALLY ADAPTED FOR SUMMER RESORTS, CAMPING, WESTERN FARMS, MINING DISTRICTS, SUBURBAN TOWNS, AND FOR AUTOMOBILE GARAGES.

WE MAKE YOU A BIG SAVING.

Simplex Portable or Ready Made Houses and Garages are exactly what the name implies, as simple in construction they can be put together by anyone. Ready made, because we ship Simplex houses in sections which are so constructed that they can be put together or erected within a few hours, the only tools required being a wrench, hammer and screwdriver. Where sections or parts are joined together, holes are bored of the proper size to fit bolts and screws, thus doing away with the nuisance of fitting together, sawing, boring or nailing; simply place the sections together, insert the bolts or screws and screw on the nuts with your wrench and the joint is made absolutely tight and secure, and in a more workmanlike manner than the average carpenter could do it by building a house to order.

The portable house is no longer in the experimental stage. The Simplex Portable House is a perfected house, the best portable or ready made house on the market. It is not a light, poorly fitted together, flimsy structure, as a good many persons would believe, but a house that is strong and durable, waterproof, windproof and built in such a manner and of such material that it will last for twenty-five years or more. We furnish both ornamental and plain portable houses, and believe that we give you practically the same satisfaction and wear as a permanent house, built by a first class carpenter.

Our Simplex Portable Houses make ideal houses for the lakeside or summer resort; they are also in great demand in every locality where carpenter aid lumber are scarce or high in price. Within the last few years thousands of portable houses have been used in the mining districts or on the Western farms and even in the suburbs of the large cities and have been found suitable in every climate. If you want a house made of the very best materials by the highest class workmen at the lowest possible cost and a house which can be erected the same day that it is received, you will make no mistake in ordering one of the Simplex Portable Houses illustrated and described on these two pages.

Simplex houses are portable. They can be taken apart as readily as they can be put together. Anyone owning a portable house or garage can move it, with little or no expense, from one place to another, or it can be taken down and stored away for future use. To take apart, all that is necessary is to simply unbolt the various sections, which are interchangeable, making it possible to lengthen the house at any time by adding other sections. Most other manufacturers of portable houses use No. 2 or No. 3 quality. The mill work, including the sash, doors, etc., is strictly high grade. Hardware and other materials are of the best grade. We employ only thoroughly skilled workmen who have profited by the mistakes of others and have made a specialty of portable house building for the past ten years. (See complete specifications and description of each house on these two pages.)

Why our prices are from 20 to 40 per cent lower than those of other manufacturers or dealers. Our prices are 20 to 40 per cent lower than those of portable houses, largely on account of the cost of lumber, as three-quarters of the entire cost or expense is this ore item alone. We own our lumber at a much lower price than the average manufacturer, as we control the timber supply ourselves and are independent of the lumber trust. By controlling the cost of lumber from the time the tree is felled until it is manufactured into Simplex houses, we are able to save you the big chain of profits which ordinarily go to the timber man, the saw mill, the wholesale lumber dealer and the retail lumber man. Our method of "from stump to consumer" saves you all these profits, which amount to from 20 to 40 percent. Which we make you a saving. No. 63 Simplex Portable House and modern methods of manufacturing Simplex houses, as we make our control of the output of the best managed and modernly equipped factory, and by making our houses in big quantities we are able to reduce the manufacturing cost to the very lowest. All this saving goes to the customer who buys the Simplex Portable House, either in the way of lowering the price or by bettering the quality

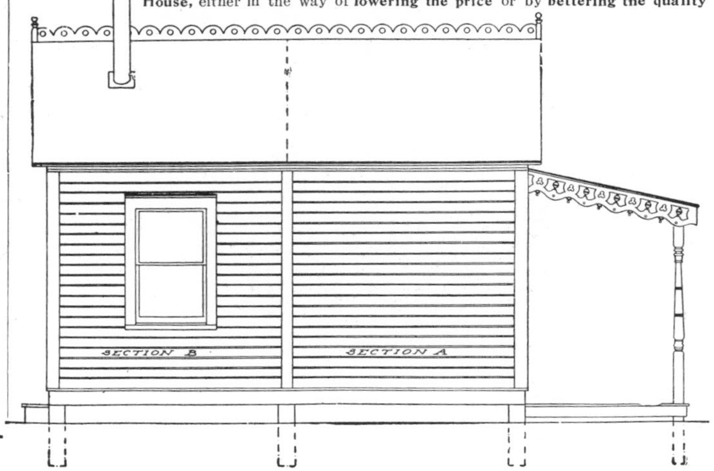

$95.00 BUYS THIS $125.00 Ready Made Portable House With a 4x12-Foot Porch.

SPECIFICATIONS FOR HOUSE No. 5.

ONE ROOM—12 x 10 ft. PORCH—4 x 12 ft. Three 12x20-in. 4-light windows, opng. 4 ft. 4 in., by 3 ft. 10 in. One 5-panel painted door, 2 ft. 6 in. by 6 ft. 6 in., 1¾ in. thick. FOUNDATION—House rests on eight 6-in. by 2-ft. posts (furnished with house). SILLS—2x6 in., yellow pine. WALL SECTIONS—2x2 in., dressed yellow pine, with No. 1 yellow pine drop siding. ROOFING BOARDS—2x3 in., yellow pine, dressed two sides, and beaded on the under side. Window and door frames, doors and windows are already hung. ROOFING—Two-Ply Best-ov-al Rubber Felt Roofing, fully guaranteed. FLOORING—⅞ in. thick by 4-in. face, No. 2 dressed and matched yellow pine. Nails furnished, also paint to give your portable house the first class outside coat of paint. CHIMNEY—28-gauge galvanized sheet steel to fit 6-in. pipe. Pipe extends 24 in. above roof. **$95.00**

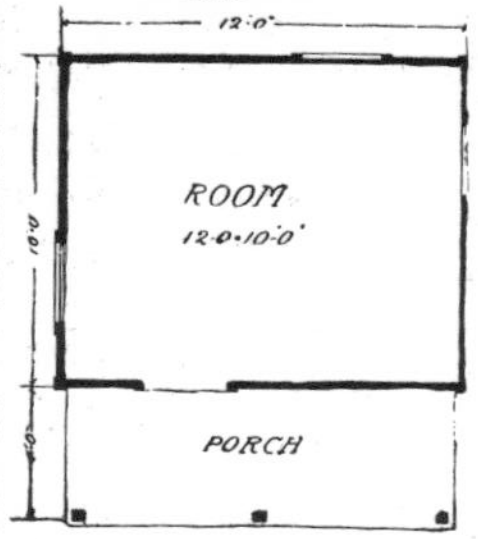

No. 63B5 Simplex Portable House. Price. Shipping weight of complete house, packed and bundled in sections, 3,100 pounds. Shipped from factory in Southern Michigan, from which point the customer pays the freight.

$258.00 BUYS THIS Large Three-Room Portable Ready Made Cottage, Fully Worth from $325.00 to $350.00.

SPECIFICATIONS FOR HOUSE No. 3.

THREE ROOMS: Living Room—9x16 ft. Kitchen—9x11 ft. Bedroom—7x11 ft. PORCH—36 ft. long by 5 ft. wide. Six 12x20-in. 4-light windows, opng. 3 ft. 4½ in. by 3 ft. 10 in. Two 5-panel painted doors, 2 ft. 6 in. by 6 ft. 6 in., 1¾ in. thick. Two inside 4-pane painted doors. FOUNDATION—House rests on eighteen 6-in. by 2-ft. posts (furnished with the house). SILLS—2x6 in., yellow pine. WALL SECTIONS—2x2 in., dressed yellow pine, with No. 1 yellow pine drop siding. PARTITION WALLS—⅞ in. select ceiling, beaded. Made of ⅞-in. select ceiling one side, dressed four sides. ROOF RAFTERS—2x3 ft. wide, pine, dressed two sides, and beaded on sides. ROOFING BOARDS—No. 1 yellow pine, dressed two sides, and beaded on the under side. ROOFING—Two-Ply Best-ov-al Rubber Felt Roofing. CHIMNEY—28-gauge galvanized sheet steel to **$258.00**

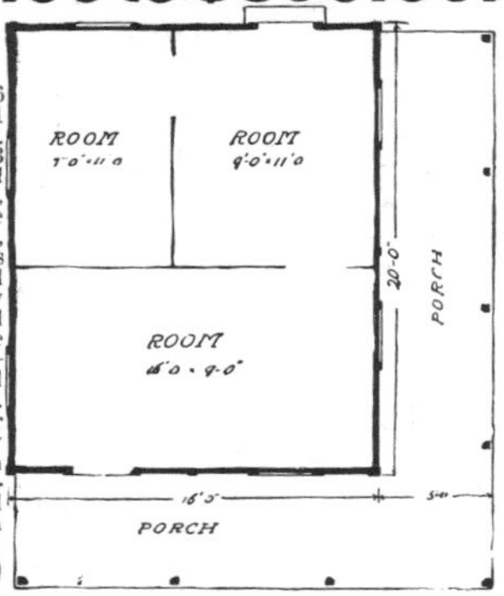

No. 63B3 Simplex Portable House. Price. Shipping weight of complete house, packed and bundled in sections, 7,000 pounds. Shipped from factory in Southern Michigan, from which point the customer pays the freight.

$146.25 Buys this Two-Room Simplex Ready Made Cottage. $220.00 is the Price Regularly Charged for a House of this Size, Made of Same Quality of Material.

SPECIFICATIONS FOR HOUSE No. 4.

TWO ROOMS: Living Room—12 ft. 4 in. by 7 ft. 4 in. Bedroom—12 ft. 4 in. by 7 ft. 4 in. PORCH—5 ft. by 12 ft. 6 in. Four 12x20-in. 4-light windows, opng. 3 ft. 4½ in. by 3 ft. 10 in. Two 5-panel painted doors, 2 ft. 6 in. by 6 ft. 6 in., 1¾ in. thick. FOUNDATION—House rests on thirteen 6-in. by 2-ft. posts (furnished with the house). SILLS—2x6 in., yellow pine, with No. 1 yellow pine dropsiding. PARTITION WALLS—⅞ in. select ceiling, beaded one side, dressed the other side. ROOF RAFTERS—2x3 in., dressed four sides. ROOFING BOARDS—No. 1 yellow pine, dressed two sides, and beaded on the under side. Window and door frames, doors and windows are already hung. ROOFING—Two-Ply Best-ov-al Rubber Felt Roofing, fully guaranteed. FLOORING—⅞ in. thick by 4 in. face, No. 2 dressed and matched yellow pine. FLOOR JOISTS—2x4 in., hung in patent steel stirrups. PAINTING—Entire house primed on outside with one coat of paint. CHIMNEY—28-gauge galvanized sheet steel to fit 6-in. pipe. Pipe extends 24 in. above roof. **$146.25**

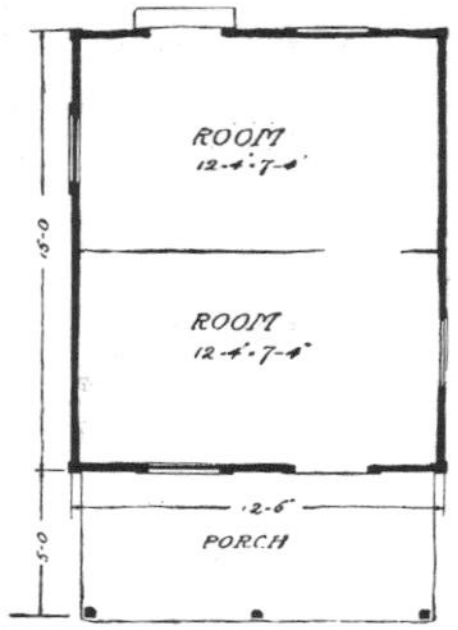

No. 63B4 Simplex Portable House. Price. Shipping weight of complete house, packed and bundled in sections, 4,100 pounds. Shipped from the factory in Southern Michigan, from which point the customer pays the freight.

COMPLETE SET OF INSTRUCTIONS FURNISHED FREE, SHOWING HOW THE SECTIONS (SIDES, ROOF AND PORCH) ARE PUT TOGETHER.

QUALITY GUARANTEED

GUARANTEED TWO-GRADE MATERIAL

SECTION A

SECTION B

SIMPLEX HOUSE

ON ITS WAY FROM THE RAILROAD STATION

Our terms are net cash. The prices printed here are net cash, from which there is no discount, no matter how large the order may be. These prices are based on a cost based on one house making one hundred houses at a time; therefore, the prices are exactly the same for one house as they would be in carload lots.

We guarantee safe delivery and will replace broken glass or make good any damage providing the freight agent, stating the condition for damage bill with a notation signed by the freight agent, stating the condition for damages.

Simplex Portable or Ready Made Houses, such as are illustrated on these pages, are made from the best quality of materials and are guaranteed to be the greatest bargains ever offered in portable houses. Carefully read our specifications printed opposite the illustration of each of the Simplex houses and you will at once appreciate the fact that our houses include much better material than is used by the average portable house manufacturer.

Carefully note detail sketches. Note how simple in construction yet how substantial and perfect all joints are made, simply bolted together (bolt nut on the inside). Anyone can put them up in a few hours' time.

DETAIL SKETCHES OF A SIMPLEX PORTABLE HOUSE.

The outline sketches shown on these two pages show Simplex Portable House No. 4. One of the sketches shows the side elevation in such a way that you can get a good idea of how the side wall sections A and B are formed, also shows how the Simplex houses are set on a solid foundation.

We also show a floor plan and a corner detail and the joining of sections A and B. All our Simplex houses are constructed in the same manner; there are no complicated parts; every part of this house is built along the simplest lines, yet good and substantial, no experience being required to put the house together.

Sections are interchangeable. This enables anyone who buys a Simplex house to keep adding a section or two when they need additional room, or the building can be shortened by taking out a section providing you want to make the building smaller.

Campers desiring a change of location can move these houses from one place to another by wagon or by boat without injury to the house.

All sections are made in a practical size, none being too large to be shipped inside an ordinary box car, and as a result command the lowest possible freight rate.

Please send your order direct with instructions to ship at a later date. This will enable us to deliver it without a day's delay.

The extremely low prices that we name for our Simplex houses are sure to sell more than our big factory can make, and we therefore recommend that you place your order for the portable house at an early date.

Section Sketch. Manner of Wall Construction. Foundation.

SECTION A 15'0"
SECTION B
CORNER DETAIL SCALE 3':1'0
ROOM 12'-4" x 7'-4"
JOINING OF SECTIONS A B SCALE 3':1'0
SECTION A
SECTION C
SECTION B
ROOM 12'-4" x 7'-4"
PORCH
STEP

Floor Plan, showing the manner in which sections are joined together. Note corner detail. It shows how sections are interchangeable. Also shows how bolts securely bind corners, making a tight joint.

FREIGHT RATES ON MILL WORK

FREIGHT CHARGES AMOUNT TO VERY LITTLE, ESPECIALLY AS COMPARED WITH THE GREAT SAVING WE MAKE YOU AS EXPLAINED ON OPPOSITE PAGE. DON'T FAIL TO OBSERVE THE EXTRA SAVING YOU CAN MAKE BY HAVING YOUR GOODS SHIPPED IN CARLOAD LOTS.

The tables on opposite page tell you what the freight rates are to towns in different sections in every state, figured from our mill work factory in Muscatine, Iowa. These tables make it plain and simple. The rate for 100 pounds to your station is almost, if not exactly, the same as it is to the town nearest you, found in the list on the opposite page. Freight charges must always be paid at the station when you get the goods.

As an Example of How to Figure Freight Charges

we submit an order received from one of our customers living in Springfield, Missouri, a distance of about 500 miles from our factory. We plainly show the items ordered and the weight of each item, which can be easily ascertained by referring to the approximate shipping weights shown opposite our prices on all doors, windows, etc. For weights of molding and items not shown opposite prices we submit a table of weights on miscellaneous mill work. After ascertaining the total weight, refer to the freight classification on this page and it is an easy matter to find the proper classification which determines the rate per hundred pounds; when added up it gives you the total freight charge on the entire shipment.

The freight on this good sized shipment actually figures less than ONE-THIRD OF ONE CENT A MILE.

Catalog Number	Quantity	ARTICLE	Size	Weight, each	Total Weight	Takes Class	Rate per 100 pounds	Total Freight Charges
	3	Nona Soft Pine Doors	2-8x6-8x1⅜	35 pounds	105 pounds	4th	32c	$0.34
	6	Windows, 2 light, Check Rail, Gla. S. S.	24x28	22 pounds	132 pounds	3rd	40c	.53
	1000 feet	Molding	1⅛ inches	6 lbs. per 100 feet	60 pounds	3rd	40c	.24
	1	Glazed Front Doors	2-6x6-6x1⅜	58 pounds	58 pounds	4th	32c	.19
	110	Spindles	1⅛ inches		24 pounds	3rd	40c	.10
	12	Brackets	10x12		12 pounds	3rd	40c	.05
								$1.45

Panel Doors.	1⅜ inches thick: Nona Pine	1⅜ inches thick: Yellow Pine	1¾ inches thick: Nona Pine	1¾ inches thick: Yellow Pine
2 ft. by 6 ft.	27 pounds	33 pounds	32 pounds	39 pounds
2 ft. 8 in. by 6 ft. 8 in.	38 pounds	48 pounds	46 pounds	58 pounds
3 ft. by 7 ft.	43 pounds	53 pounds	52 pounds	64 pounds

The above are approximate weights.

Table of Approximate Molding Weights.

	⅞x1-inch, weight per 100 feet lineal	⅞x3-inch, weight per 100 feet lineal	⅞x5-inch, weight per 100 feet lineal	⅞x8-inch, weight per 100 feet lineal
Nona Pine	12 pounds	36 pounds	60 pounds	96 pounds
Yellow Pine	15 pounds	45 pounds	75 pounds	120pounds
Oak	18 pounds	54 pounds	90 pounds	144pounds

FREIGHT CLASSIFICATION

1 stands for First Class.
2 stands for Second Class.
3 stands for Third Class.
4 stands for Fourth Class.
1½ stands for 1½ times First Class.
D 1 stands for 2 times First Class.

The Railroads Charge for Freight according to its classification. For example: Lumber takes fourth class rate. By referring to opposite page you will find the fourth class rate to the nearest town in your state. Multiply the weight of the article (which you can get from our catalog, or estimate pretty closely) by the rate, and you will be able to figure the freight charges almost to a cent. If the following table does not contain the article you want, you can, as a rule, use the rate given on some article of a similar nature.

Merchandise Classification is Governed by Locality. It varies according to the section of the country. For example: Doors, paneled, etc., take fourth class freight rates to sections of the country designated "A," but take the third class freight rate to sections of the country designated "B." Blinds take third class freight rate to sections designated "A," first class to sections designated "B," and fourth class freight rate to sections with the "C," "D" or "E" classifications.

We Pack and Ship our goods in a manner that secures for you the lowest freight charges.

Why Not Have Your Mill Work Shipped in Carload Lots. The carload rates we show on the opposite page are the very lowest rates of freight at which this material can be shipped. A good sized house bill will fill a carload and by ordering all of your material from us you can take advantage of this exceptionally low freight rate and have your material all shipped in one car, which will avoid handling as a local shipment and will insure the goods reaching you more promptly and in better shape. We are shipping carloads of mill work every day to our customers who are taking advantage of these exceptionally low carload freight rates. If your order is not sufficiently large to ship in a car by itself and take the carload rate, we suggest you order additional material or get some friend or neighbor to order material with you and in this way have your material shipped as a carload.

Minimum Carload Weights and Rules Governing. Opposite the carload rates shown to the different sections of the country we have shown the minimum carload weight. The minimum carload weight means the lowest weight that a railroad company will haul a car for. In some parts of the country the minimum carload weights are according to the size of the car used. To points where this minimum weight governs, or to points where any other minimum weight applies, except as shown opposite the rates under the heading of **"minimum weights,"** will be shown a rule number which governs that part of the country to which the shipment is going. By reading these rules carefully you will be able to figure almost to a cent just what it will cost you to get a carload of mill work from our factory in Iowa to your shipping point. Remember that we always ship our goods so that our customers will secure the lowest freight charges. Where the minimum weights are governed by the size of the car used **in every case** we load our cars in such a manner as to secure for our customer the very lowest freight charges.

Rule 1—Minimum weight 30,000 pounds except when car is loaded to full visible space capacity, when actual weight will govern with a minimum weight of 24,000 pounds.

Rule 2—Minimum weight for 30-foot car and under, 20,000 pounds; over 30-foot and under 34-foot inside measurement, 24,000 pounds; in cars 34-foot and over in length, 30 000 pounds.

HOW TO USE CLASSIFICATION TABLE BELOW.

In the Table Below you will find five columns marked "A" (West), "B" (East), "C" (South), "D" (Iowa), "E" (Illinois) respectively, and in each column is shown what classification or rate of freight the merchandise takes in that section. For example, stair rail you will note in the table below goes as third class freight to the section marked "A;" takes second class freight rate to the section marked "B" and fourth class freight rate for the section marked "C," "D" and "E."

On the Opposite Page we show opposite each town just what section it belongs to, that is, whether it is "A," "B," "C," "D" or "E." When you look up your nearest town in the list on the opposite page and find the letter that designates the territory, then refer to the table below and you will find what class freight the articles take; then refer again to the table on opposite page and find what the rate is for that class to your town and then figure at that rate per hundred pounds, according to the weight given in the description of the goods. For example, suppose you are figuring the freight on stair rail and you live in Mason City, Iowa, or Mason City is the nearest town to you. If you will refer to Mason City, Iowa, on the opposite page, you will find that this is designated as "D." Referring to table below you will find that the stair rail takes the fourth class rate in "D" territory. Referring back to the opposite page you find that the fourth class freight rate to Mason City is 22 cents per hundred pounds, therefore the freight on stair rail to Mason City will be 22 cents per hundred pounds.

ARTICLES	Classification of Merchandise: A (West)	B (East)	C (South)	D (Iowa)	E (Illinois)
Balusters	3	2	4	4	4
Blinds	3	1	4	4	4
Blocks	3	3	4	4	4
Brackets	3	3	4	4	3
Columns, built up or solid, ornamental parts crated	4	3	4	4	4
Door and Window Frames, knocked down	3	3	4	4	4
Doors, glazed, crated, glass covered by boards ½ inch thick	4	1	3	4	4
Doors, glazed, leaded or stained glass, glass covered by boards ½ inch thick	D1	1	2	2	2
Doors, glazed, plain or figured glass (not plate)	4	1	3	3	4
Doors, glazed, plate glass	1	1	1	2	2
Doors, paneled, also Sash Doors without glass	4	3	4	4	4
Gable Ornaments	3	1	4	4	4
Glass, boxed, common window, colored, enameled or ground, leaded	1½	1	1	1	1
Glass, boxed, common window, colored, enameled or ground, not leaded	4	3	3	4	4
Glass, boxed, exceeding 68 inches and under 86 inches	2	3	3	2	3
Glass, boxed, under 68 inches	4	3	3	4	4
Glass, boxed, common window in package exceeding 86 inches united measurement	1	3	3	1	3
Grilles, finished	D1	1	1	D1	1
Grilles, in white	1½	1	1	1½	1
Lumber (Studding, Sheathing, etc.), write for special carload rates	......	......	......	......	......
Lumber, finishing, listed in this catalog	4	4	4	4	4
Moldings (unfinished)	3	3	4	4	4
Newels, built up or solid	3	3	4	4	4
Painted Panel Doors and Painted Sash Doors without glass	4	3	4	4	4
Sash, glazed with common or plain glass	3	1	3	4	4
Sash, not glazed	2	1	4	4	4
Sash Weights in bundles	4	4	6	4	4
Spindles	3	3	4	4	4
Stair Newels	3	2	4	4	4
Stair Rail and Porch Rail	3	2	4	4	4
Sash, glazed with leaded glass not exceeding 20 united feet (length and width added)	1½	1	2	1	2

WRITE FOR FREIGHT RATES ON LUMBER. WE WILL NAME YOU A DELIVERY PRICE TO YOUR CITY.

FREIGHT RATES ON MILL WORK TO TOWNS IN THE DIFFERENT SECTIONS OF EVERY STATE.

Have no fear of the freight charges as they amount to very little, especially as compared with the wonderful saving we make for you on all mill work by quoting you prices that just include the actual manufacturing cost with but one small margin of profit added and shipping direct to you from our factory, thus cutting out all but one handling expense and all the profits to wholesale and retail dealers.

Refer to Preceding Page for Freight Classification **to which the articles you are ordering belong, find the approximate weight as quoted on the page where the articles are quoted,** and then refer to this page and find under your state the name of the town nearest you, and the freight rate to that town will be found to be almost if not exactly the same as the freight rate to your own station.

Our Mill Work Factory is Centrally Located **for timber supply, and by so locating it and controlling the supply of timber from the time it is felled in the forest to the time it is finished in our factory,** and by shipping direct to you from our factory, there being only one handling on the finished product, and by quoting you a price which just includes the actual manufacturing cost with only our one small margin of profit added, we make you a most wonderful saving over and above any freight charges. The freight charges amount to very little as compared with the big saving we make for you on mill work by handling it on the direct from the factory to you basis.

We Guarantee to Make You a Big Saving on Mill Work **over and above any freight charges, and upon receiving your goods,** if you don't consider you have made a wonderful saving over and above any freight charges paid, you are perfectly at liberty to return them to us at our expense and we will return both the price and any transportation charges you paid. You will not be out one cent.

To Our Customers Living East of Chicago **we have this to say, that the extra freight for the distance that our factory is west of Chicago does not add a single cent to the cost of your mill work** more than it would be if we shipped it from our Chicago store, because you must remember that if we shipped from Chicago we would first be obliged to have our mill work come from our factory to Chicago on which we would have to pay the freight, charges for cartage and extra handling, which we would, of course, be obliged to add to the price. We are actually making you a saving on freight alone (to say nothing of the saving in the cost of your mill work) by shipping from our factory though it is west of Chicago.

Always Remember This Point About Freight Charges **that no matter from whom you buy** you must pay the freight, because if you do not pay it to the freight agent, you pay it to the dealer, as he always adds to the cost in figuring his selling price.

Steel Roofing, Prepared Felt Roofing, Pipe, Gutter and Building Papers will be shipped from Chicago, Illinois, or from some one of our factories or warehouses in your vicinity which will enable us to give you much quicker delivery and the benefit of the LOWEST FREIGHT CHARGES.

	Classification	1st class freight per 100 lbs	2nd class freight per 100 lbs	3rd class freight per 100 lbs	4th class freight per 100 lbs	Carload freight per 100 lbs	Minimum carload wt., lbs.
ALABAMA—							
Birmingham	C	$1.20	$1.04	$0.84	$0.65	$0.36	30,000
Decatur	C	1.20	1.04	.84	65	.39	24,000
Livingston	C	1.48	1.28	1.03	.85	.59½	24,000
Mobile	C	1.10	.90	.75	.58	.31	24,000
Montgomery	C	1.39	1.22	1.04	.80	.36	30,000
ARIZONA—							
Holbrook	A	3.54	3.19	2.60	2.05	.91	Rule 2
Kingman	A	3.70	3.20	2.60	2.05	1.01	Rule 2
Phoenix	A	3.56	3.10	2.84	2.28	.86	30,000
Tucson	A	3.17	2.74	2.50	2.12	.71½	30,000
Yuma	A	3.54	3.09	2.69	2.12	.76	30,000
ARKANSAS—							
Arkansas City	C	1.10	.90	.75	.58	.31	24,000
Jonesboro	A	.96	.80	.63	.50	.24	24,000
Little Rock	A	1.15	.97	.74	.56	.27	24,000
Marshall	A	1.48	1.26	1.07	.90	.29	30,000
Texarkana	A	1.42	1.27	1.13	.93	.38	26,000
CALIFORNIA—							
Alturas	A	5.20	4.80	4.40	4.10	1.26	30,000
Hanford	A	3.58	3.15	2.72	2.39	1.08	30,000
Los Angeles	A	3.00	2.60	2.20	1.90	.85	30,000
Redding	A	3.61	3.16	2.70	2.32	1.12	30,000
San Francisco	A	3.00	2.60	2.20	1.90	.85	30,000
COLORADO—							
Creede	A	3.20	2.70	2.20	1.67	.68	30,000
Denver	A	1.85	1.45	1.15	.92	.37	30,000
Glenwood Sp'gs	A	3.22	2.67	2.12	1.64	.68	30,000
Julesburg	A	1.55	1.35	1.15	.92	.35	30,000
La Junta	A	1.85	1.45	1.15	.92	.37	30,000
CONNECTICUT—							
Hartford	B	1.04	.91	.71	.51	.41	24,000
New Haven	B	1.04	.91	.71	.51	.41	24,000
DELAWARE—							
Dover	B	.97	.85	.66	.47	.38	24,000
FLORIDA—							
Dade City	C	2.10	1.82	1.61	1.38	.77	30,000
De Funiak Sp'gs	C	1.66	1.37	1.05	.92	.56	24,000
Jacksonville	C	1.36	1.15	1.01	.88	.40	30,000
Miami	C	2.47	2.12	1.81	1.61	1.01	30,000
Tallahassee	C	1.88	1.61	1.36	1.11	.58	30,000
GEORGIA—							
Atlanta	C	1.39	1.22	1.04	.81	.40	30,000
Augusta	C	1.44	1.25	1.07	.83	.40	30,000
Cuthbert	C	1.69	1.47	1.26	1.00	.38	30,000
Nashville	C	2.12	1.83	1.60	1.39	.73	30,000
Savannah	C	1.36	1.15	1.01	.88	.40	30,000
IDAHO—							
Lewiston	A	3.00	2.59	2.16	1.79	.86	24,000
Mountain Home	A	3.00	2.59	2.16	1.79	.76	Rule 1
Pocatello	A	2.75	2.28	1.91	1.59	.66	Rule 1
Saint Anthony	A	3.09	2.57	2.15	1.79	.76	Rule 1
ILLINOIS—							
Cairo	E	.49	.41	.32	.25	.15	24,000
Carthage	E	.37	.29	.22	.18	.07	24,000
Danville	E	.41	.33	.26	.21	.10	24,000
Effingham	E	.43	.35	.28	.22	.11	24,000
Peoria	E	.34	.26	.21	.16	.07	24,000
INDIANA—							
Crown Point	B	.52	.47	.37	.26	.15	24,000
Fort Wayne	B	.53	.47	.37	.26	.17	24,000
Indianapolis	B	.53	.47	.37	.26	.15	24,000
Logansport	B	.52	.47	.37	.26	.15	24,000
Vincennes	B	.59	.50	.40	.29	.16	24,000
IOWA—							
Clinton	D	.23	.19	.15	.11	.06	24,000
Des Moines	D	.33	.26	.20	.16	.08	24,000
IOWA—Continued							
Mason City	D	$0.48	$0.35	$0.27	$0.22	$0.10	24,000
Spencer	D	.59	.43	.33	.28	.12	24,000
KANSAS—							
Abilene	A	1.11	.91	.73	.57	.25	Rule 2
Independence	A	1.01	.83	.70	.52	.22	Rule 2
Oberlin	A	1.44	1.20	1.03	.85	.32	Rule 2
Pratt	A	1.34	1.12	.92	.75	.33	Rule 2
Scott	A	1.46	1.22	1.05	.91	.33	Rule 2
KENTUCKY—							
Catlettsburg	B	.69	.61	.48	.34	.29	24,000
Hopkinsville	C	.97	.82	.70	.57	.33	30,000
Louisville	B	.61	.52	.42	.31	.18	24,000
Morganfield	C	.87	.74	.60	.47	.28	24,000
Richmond	C	.97	.83	.68	.52	.36	24,000
LOUISIANA—							
Alexandria	A	1.40	1.20	1.04	.85	.38	26,000
Lake Charles	A	1.55	1.30	1.07	.90	.38	26,000
Monroe	A	1.40	1.20	1.04	.85	.38	26,000
New Orleans	C	1.10	.90	.75	.58	.31	24,000
Shreveport	A	1.40	1.20	1.04	.85	.38	26,000
MAINE—							
Bangor	B	1.04	.91	.71	.51	.41	24,000
Bath	B	1.04	.91	.71	.51	.41	24,000
Farmington	B	1.04	.91	.71	.51	.41	24,000
Houlton	B	1.42	1.18	.92	.71	.56	24,000
Machias	B	1.22	1.06	.83	.61	.50	24,000
MARYLAND—							
Baltimore	B	.94	.82	.63	.44	.35	24,000
La Plata	B	.97	.85	.65	.46	.37	24,000
Salisbury	B	.97	.85	.66	.47	.38	24,000
MASSACHUSETTS							
Barnstable	B	1.04	.91	.71	.51	.41	24,000
Boston	B	1.04	.91	.71	.51	.41	24,000
Northampton	B	1.04	.91	.71	.51	.41	24,000
MICHIGAN—							
Detroit	B	.55	.50	.40	.29	.18	24,000
Escanaba	B	.65	.55	.44	.28	.18	30,000
Kalamazoo	B	.55	.50	.40	.29	.24	24,000
Petoskey	B	.75	.65	.50	.41	.33	24,000
Sault St. Marie	A	.75	.65	.48	.38	.25	30,000
MINNESOTA—							
Crookston	A	1.19	.99	.79	.55	.31	Rule 2
Duluth	A	.65	.55	.44	.28	.17	Rule 2
Marshall	A	.73	.63	.52	.36	.20	Rule 2
Minneapolis	A	.60	.50	.40	.25	.14	Rule 2
Wadena	A	1.00	.84	.67	.45	.27	Rule 2
MISSISSIPPI—							
Columbus	C	1.30	1.07	.85	.72	.40	30,000
Corinth	C	1.12	.96	.79	.65	.39	30,000
Hattiesburg	C	1.38	1.16	.95	.79	.57	30,000
Jackson	C	1.18	.99	.80	.67	.32	30,000
Liberty	C	1.92	1.56	1.26	1.06	.75	24,000
MISSOURI—							
Chicopee	A	1.08	.90	.72	.61	.16	30,000
Jefferson City	A	.71	.58	.42	.29	.17	30,000
Kirksville	E	.60	.45	.35	.24	.13	24,000
Saint Louis	E	.40	.33	.26	.21	.10	24,000
Springfield	A	.62	.52	.40	.32	.15	30,000
MONTANA—							
Dillon	A	2.85	2.35	1.95	1.60	.66	24,000
Helena	A	2.85	2.40	1.98	1.60	.65	30,000
Kalispell	A	2.99	2.53	2.07	1.68	.86	30,000
Miles City	A	2.29	1.88	1.52	1.30	.65	30,000
Missoula	A	2.96	2.51	2.05	1.67	.70	30,000
NEBRASKA							
Alliance	A	$1.61	$1.38	$1.15	$0.92	$0.37	Rule 2
Broken Bow	A	1.31	1.09	.92	.74	.32	Rule 2
Fairbury	A	.96	.76	.62	.49	.22	Rule 2
Omaha	A	.60	.45	.35	.27	.14	Rule 2
Valentine	A	1.44	1.21	1.01	.82	.33	Rule 2
NEVADA—							
Austin	A	5.02	4.34	3.79	3.13	1.45	30,000
Carson City	A	4.54	3.98	3.47	3.02	1.33	30,000
Elko	A	4.07	3.41	2.87	2.40	.91	30,000
Pioche	A	4.28	3.63	3.02	2.53	1.20	30,000
Tonopah	A	5.35	4.75	4.05	3.33	1.20	30,000
N. HAMPSHIRE—							
Keene	B	1.04	.91	.71	.51	.41	24,000
Lancaster	B	1.04	.91	.71	.51	.41	24,000
Ossipee	B	1.04	.91	.71	.51	.41	24,000
NEW JERSEY—							
Cape May Ct. H.	B	1.02	.90	.71	.52	.43	24,000
Flemington	B	.97	.85	.66	.47	.38	24,000
Toms River	B	1.02	.90	.71	.52	.43	24,000
NEW MEXICO—							
Clayton	A	1.85	1.45	1.15	.92	.37	Rule 2
Roswell	A	1.82	1.60	1.37	1.24	.72	Rule 2
Santa Fe	A	2.12	1.90	1.70	1.47	.68	Rule 2
Silver City	A	2.29	2.08	1.90	1.73	.80	Rule 2
Socorro	A	2.12	1.90	1.70	1.47	.72	Rule 2
NEW YORK—							
Albany	B	.93	.82	.64	.45	.37	24,000
Buffalo	B	.69	.61	.48	.34	.26	24,000
New York	B	.97	.85	.66	.47	.38	24,000
Plattsburg	B	1.04	.91	.71	.51	.41	24,000
Utica	B	.89	.78	.61	.43	.35	24,000
N. CAROLINA—							
Ashboro	C	1.41	1.21	.96	.71	.37	30,000
Halifax	C	1.33	1.13	.90	.65	.36	30,000
Marion	C	1.57	1.37	1.12	.85	.52	30,000
Newbern	C	1.19	.99	.78	.59	.41½	30,000
Wilmington	C	1.23	1.03	.79	.59	.37	24,000
N. DAKOTA—							
Bismarck	A	1.58	1.32	1.05	.74	.43	Rule 2
Medora	A	1.94	1.64	1.34	.99	.57	Rule 2
Pembina	A	1.27	1.06	.85	.59	.36	Rule 2
Valley City	A	1.30	1.08	.87	.60	.37	Rule 2
Williston	A	1.99	1.66	1.36	1.01	.60	Rule 2
OHIO—							
Cincinnati	B	.59	.50	.40	.29	.18	24,000
Cleveland	B	.66	.57	.44	.31	.20	24,000
Columbus	B	.62	.51	.40	.29	.19	24,000
Marietta	B	.69	.61	.48	.34	.26	24,000
Tiffin	B	.62	.51	.40	.29	.19	24,000
OKLAHOMA—							
Guthrie	A	1.30	1.09	.97	.82	.35	Rule 2
Lawton	A	1.40	1.17	1.05	.96	.42	Rule 2
McAlester	A	1.20	1.00	.85	.69	.31	Rule 2
Tahlequah	A	1.12	.97	.78	.62	.23	Rule 2
Woodward	A	1.30	1.09	.97	.90	.37	Rule 2
OREGON—							
Eugene	A	3.46	3.02	2.59	2.23	.96	30,000
Grants Pass	A	4.07	3.53	3.06	2.70	1.05	30,000
Pendleton	A	3.00	2.59	2.16	1.79	.86	24,000
Portland	A	3.00	2.60	2.20	1.90	.85	30,000
Vale	A	3.15	2.72	2.27	1.90	.84	30,000
PENNSYLVANIA—							
Erie	B	.69	.61	.48	.34	.26	24,000
Lock Haven	B	.94	.82	.63	.44	.35	24,000
Philadelphia	B	.95	.83	.64	.45	.36	24,000
Pittsburg	B	.69	.61	.48	.34	.26	24,000
Scranton	B	.95	.83	.64	.45	.36	24,000
RHODE ISLAND—							
Providence	B	$1.04	$0.91	$0.71	$0.51	$0.41	24,000
SO. CAROLINA—							
Charleston	C	1.36	1.15	1.01	.88	.37	30,000
Greenville	C	1.57	1.42	1.12	.85	.42	30,000
Lancaster	C	1.53	1.33	1.08	.83	.40	30,000
Marion	C	1.53	1.33	1.08	.83	.40	30,000
Sumter	C	1.55	1.35	1.10	.83	.41	30,000
SO. DAKOTA—							
Aberdeen	A	1.04	.90	.64	.48	.33	Rule 2
Bellefourche	A	1.89	1.57	1.32	1.08	.56	Rule 2
Hot Springs	A	1.80	1.52	1.27	1.04	.48	Rule 2
Mitchell	A	.90	.78	.57	.45	.31	Rule 2
Pierre	A	1.22	1.04	.80	.60	.31	Rule 2
TENNESSEE—							
Chattanooga	C	1.17	1.00	.83	.65	.33	30,000
Helenwood	C	1.04	.90	.78	.57	.41	24,000
Memphis	C	.85	.65	.55	.43	.27	24,000
Nashville	C	.81	.70	.56	.43	.27	24,000
Paris	C	.90	.76	.62	.50	.34	24,000
TEXAS—							
Amarillo	A	1.72	1.49	1.29	1.16	.42	26,000
Dallas	A	1.62	1.41	1.21	1.09	.38	26,000
El Paso	A	1.74	1.54	1.39	1.29	.43	26,000
Houston	A	1.62	1.41	1.21	1.09	.38	26,000
Laredo	A	1.74	1.54	1.39	1.29	.43	26,000
UTAH—							
Marysvale	A	3.15	2.68	2.34	1.99	.78	30,000
Ogden	A	2.65	2.20	1.88	1.55	.55	30,000
Price	A	2.65	2.20	1.88	1.55	.55	30,000
Thompsons	A	2.65	2.20	1.88	1.55	.55	30,000
Tooele	A	2.99	2.49	2.12	1.75	.80	30,000
VERMONT—							
Middlebury	B	1.04	.91	.71	.51	.41	24,000
Newport	B	1.04	.91	.71	.51	.41	24,000
Rutland	B	1.04	.91	.71	.51	.41	24,000
VIRGINIA—							
Chatham	C	1.09	.91	.71	.61	.35	34,000
Lexington	B	.94	.82	.63	.44	.35	24,000
Luray	B	.94	.82	.63	.44	.35	24,000
Richmond	B	.94	.82	.63	.44	.35	24,000
Wise	B	1.16	1.02	.81	.61	.46	24,000
WASHINGTON—							
Bellingham	A	3.00	2.60	2.20	1.90	.85	24,000
Ellensburg	A	3.25	2.81	2.35	1.95	.86	24,000
Seattle	A	3.00	2.60	2.20	1.90	.85	30,000
South Bend	A	3.00	2.60	2.20	1.90	.85	30,000
Spokane	A	3.00	2.59	2.16	1.79	.86	24,000
W. VIRGINIA—							
Charleston	B	.69	.61	.48	.34	.26	24,000
Clarksburg	B	.74	.65	.51	.36	.28	24,000
Marlinton	B	.94	.82	.63	.44	.35	24,000
Martinsburg	B	.94	.82	.63	.44	.35	24,000
Welch	B	1.16	.92	.71	.51	.41	24,000
WISCONSIN—							
Ashland	A	.65	.55	.44	.28	.17	Rule 2
La Crosse	A	.50	.42	.33	.23	.11	Rule 2
Madison	E	.47	.38	.29	.22	.09	Rule 2
Milwaukee	E	.47	.38	.29	.22	.09	Rule 2
Wausau	A	.58	.48	.34	.25	.17	Rule 2
WYOMING—							
Cheyenne	A	1.85	1.45	1.15	.92	.37	Rule 2
Douglas	A	2.41	1.97	1.62	1.32	.54	Rule 2
Green River	A	2.65	2.20	1.88	1.55	.62	Rule 2
Lander	A	2.76	2.40	2.11	1.70	.62	Rule 2
Sheridan	A	2.32	1.93	1.64	1.35	.55	Rule 2

SEARS, ROEBUCK AND CO. CHICAGO